GREAT
JOHN MACLEAN

JOHN MACLEAN

GREAT JOHN MACLEAN

Has Come Home to the Clyde

The Life and Times of Scotland's Greatest Socialist

DONALD ROBERTSON

ecosocialist, feminist and internationalist publishers

Published 2025 by Resistance Books, London.

© **Donald Robertson 2025**

All rights reserved.

The moral right of Donald Robertson to be identified as the author of this work has been asserted.

No part of this book may be used or reproduced in any manner whatsoever without prior written permission from the publisher and author, except in the case of brief quotations embodied in critical articles or reviews. Requests and inquiries concerning reproduction should be addressed to the publisher.

'The John Maclean March', by Hamish Henderson. Copyright the Estate of Hamish Henderson. Reproduced by kind permission of the Estate.

'An Cuilithionn' by Somhairle MhacGill-Eain/ Sorley MacLean; from *An Cuilithionn 1939 & unpublished poems*. Reprinted by permission of Carcanet Press.

'On John Maclean' by Edwin Morgan; from *Collected Poems*. Reprinted by permission of Carcanet Press.

'John Maclean Tortured in a Capitalist Prison', by Dora Montefiore, from the *Call*, 14th November 1918.

Every reasonable effort has been made to trace copyright holders of material reproduced in this book, but if any have been inadvertently overlooked the publishers would be glad to hear from them.

ISBN paperback: 978-1-872242-39-2

ISBN hardback: 978-1-872242-40-8

ISBN e-book: 978-1-872242-41-5

Resistance Books

Resistance books.org

info@resistancebooks.org

Type used in this book: Crimson Pro and Bebas Nue.

Cover and text design by Luke Harris, Working Type Studio.

Front cover image: Mounted on a lorry and accompanied by supporters, John Maclean waves the red flag as he travels down Renfield Street on his homecoming to the Clyde on 3 December 1918. (*Daily Record and Mail*.)

Front and back cover background: Detail from John Bartholomew, *Plan of the City of Glasgow Shewing Parks, Gardens and Recreation Grounds belonging to the Corporation of Glasgow* (1900). (Reproduced with the permission of the National Library of Scotland.)

Back cover image: John Maclean's grave, Eastwood New Cemetery, Glasgow, August 2015. (Photo by Donald Robertson.)

This book is dedicated to Di and Calum,

for love and support over the journey.

CONTENTS

I:	**THE RED CLYDE**	**1**
1	Making socialists	3
2	Second city of the Empire	15
3	Lord Kitchener wants you	23
4	Munitions of war	31
5	'We are not paying increased rent'	41
6	'A scandalous act of tyranny and a gross injustice'	45
7	Fighting the Prussians of Partick	50
8	'A person who holds advanced political views'	54
9	A question of school discipline	57
10	A great victory for the rent strikers	60
11	Peter Petroff	64
12	Conscription	78
13	Lloyd George comes to Glasgow	88
14	Suppression of *Forward* and the *Vanguard*	103
15	Defence of the Realm	109
16	The Scottish Labour College	112
17	Dilution on the Clyde	115
II	**POLITICAL PRISONER**	**129**
18	German gold, and German alarm clocks	131
19	The *Worker* trial	141
20	Peterhead	151
21	European superstar	157
22	I shall be released	164
23	A quiet life	175
24	Give peace a chance	184
25	Arthur Henderson goes to Russia	189

26	Stockholm	196
27	Russia turns red	203
28	Consolidating Bolshevik power	214
29	The release of Chicherin and Petroff	218
30	The return of the shop stewards' movement	222
31	Brest-Litovsk: the armistice	226
32	Man power	231
33	Soviet consul	242
34	Brest-Litovsk: the treaty	252
35	Accuser of capitalism	260
36	Peterhead again	270
III	**THE BELL THAT NEVER RANG**	**281**
37	Thanksgiving	283
38	The khaki election	292
39	Back to the miners	302
40	The 40-hour strike	306
41	The battle of George Square	316
42	The miners mobilise	324
43	Hands off Russia	329
44	The Coal Commission	335
45	The Third International	342
46	Soviets in Britain?	346
47	Nationalisation	351
48	The moment passes	358
49	Britain's war against Russia	364
50	Break-ups	374

IV	**THE FIRE WITHIN**	**383**
51	Alba and Erin	385
52	The Comintern lays down the law	394
53	The communism of the clans	403
54	Poland	412
55	A Scottish Communist Party	418
56	The unemployed	427
57	Decontrol	432
58	Black Friday	440
59	A state of emergency	445
60	More porridge	454
61	The Tramp Trust dissolves	463
62	The Clydesiders triumphant	467
63	Oot and aboot	476
64	The Clydesiders in London	483
65	Uproar in the House	494
66	Reconciliation	500
67	The final countdown	507
68	Tributes	516
69	Aftermath	521

Acknowledgements	524
Abbreviations	525
Bibliography	527
Endnotes	536
Index	558

LIST OF ILLUSTRATIONS

Frontispiece: John Maclean. (Reproduced with the permission of the National Library of Scotland.)

Pages vi-vii: Detail from John Bartholomew & Co. Ltd, *New Parliamentary Divisions 1918. New Plan of Glasgow with Suburbs, from Ordnance and Actual Surveys.* (Reproduced with the permission of the National Library of Scotland.).

Page 69: Peter Petroff. (Reproduced with the permission of the National Library of Scotland.)

Page: 101: Lloyd George, minister of munitions, and the platform party at a meeting with the Clyde Workers' Committee at St Andrew's Halls, Glasgow, on Christmas Day 1915. (Reproduced with the permission of the National Library of Scotland.)

Page 319: Willie Gallacher. (Reproduced with the permission of the National Library of Scotland.)

Page 389: The Tramp Trust Unlimited. (Reproduced with the permission of the National Library of Scotland.)

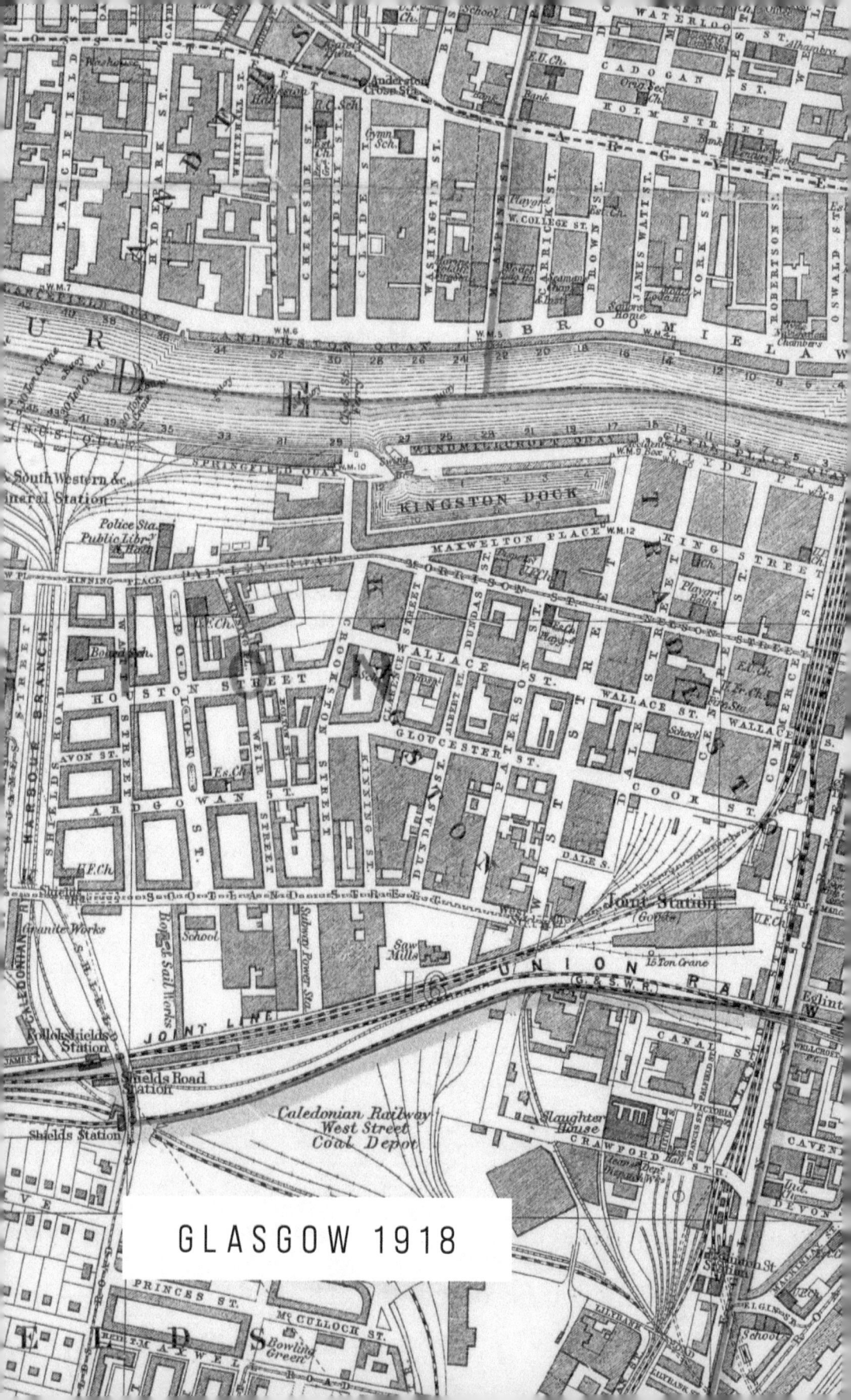

I
THE RED CLYDE

Chuala mi gum facas bristeadh
agus clisgeadh air an fhàire
gum facas ròs dearg, ùrail
thar saoghal brùite, màbte:
chuala mi mu abhainn Chluaidh
a blith air tuar na càrnaid
chula mi mu MhacGill-Eain
bhith dèanamh ceangal neo-bhàsmhor
air gach cridhe agus eanchainn
le meanmnachd thar cràdhlot.

                Somhairle MhacGill-Eain, from 'An Cuilithionn' (1939)

English version (translation by the poet):

I heard that a breaking was seen
and a startling on the horizon,
that there was seen a fresh, red rose
over an oppressed, maimed world.
I heard about the River Clyde
Being of the hue of scarlet;
I heard about Maclean
Making an undying knot
Of every brain and heart
With spirit over agony.

                Sorley MacLean, from 'The Cuillin' (1939)

1
MAKING SOCIALISTS

I'm standing at the grave of John Maclean with my newfound cousin Roddy. We're in the Eastwood New Cemetery on the southern outskirts of Glasgow. It's a clear, dry afternoon in August 2015, and the sunlight filters through the trees and dapples the green, green grass underfoot. It's quiet and very peaceful. A moment for reflection. Who was this man – and why have I come half way around the world to learn more about him?

~

As with many things in my life, it started with a song.

It was 1979. I was living in a share house in Adelaide. Donna had a record by Scottish folk singer Dick Gaughan. *No More Forever* it was called. A good record, but there was one song that stopped me in my tracks the first time I heard it. And the second. And every time since. 'The John Maclean March.'

> Hey, Mac, did ye see him as he cam' doun by Gorgie,
> Awa owre the Lammerlaw or north o' the Tay?
> Yon man is comin' and the haill toun is turnin' oot:
> We're a' shair he'll win back tae Glasgie the day.
> The jiners and hauders-on are marchin' fae Clydebank;
> Come on noo an hear him, he'll be owre thrang tae bide.
> Turn oot Jock an Jimmie: leave yer crans and your muckle gantries, -
> Great John Maclean's comin' back tae the Clyde!

In English:

> Hey, Mac, did you see him as he came down by Gorgie
> Away over the Lammerlaw or north of the Tay?
> That man is coming, and the whole town is turning out,
> We're all sure he'll return to Glasgow today.

The carpenters and rivet-holders are marching from Clydebank,
Come on now and listen to him – he'll be too busy to stay long
Come along, Jock and Jimmie, leave your cranes and your large gantries,
Great John Maclean is coming back to the Clyde.

Now I am a proud Scot. From the working class. My dad was a steelworker. He moved the family from Scotland to work at Stewart and Lloyds in Corby, Northamptonshire; and then across the seas, to BHP in Whyalla, South Australia. His father worked in an aluminium smelter in the Highlands. Both staunch union men and Labour voters. I shared my dad's taste for Scottish history – Glencoe 1692, Culloden 1745, Wembley 1967. My mother's maiden name and my middle name are also Maclean. So, I asked myself, 'How come I have never heard of this man?'

This was before the Internet, before Google, and so, many years passed before I picked up the trail again. It was the eighties. I had moved to Sydney. Browsing in a second-hand bookshop in King Street, Newtown, I came across a biography of John Maclean. It was by his daughter Nan Milton. And there it was – the whole story.

Milton told how a working-class boy became a school teacher; found socialism; started teaching Marxism to factory and shipyard workers on the Clyde; preached the new gospel on the street and in halls all over Scotland; then when most other socialists abandoned their internationalist stance at the beginning of the Great War, became the most prominent anti-war activist in Scotland.

How he was tried for sedition; imprisoned; became a socialist cult hero across Europe; and on his early release was appointed Soviet consul in Scotland. How he was arrested again for speaking out against the war; gave a defiant speech from the dock; saw prison again; went on hunger strike; and after the British War Cabinet – fearful of creating a martyr – granted him early release at the end of the war, how he returned to Glasgow to the hero's welcome described in the song written by Hamish Henderson and sung by Dick Gaughan. And after the war, the slow disintegration of his political career and his early death in 1923 at the age of 44.

My god, I thought again – how come I have never heard of this man? And the seed of a thought was planted. That this was still a dangerous man. And that his story had been excised from history.

One verse from the song haunted me:

Forward tae Glasgie Green we'll march in good order:
Wull grips his banner weel (that boy isna blate).
Ay, there, man, that's Johnnie noo, that's him there, the bonnie fechter,
Lenin's his fiere, lad, an' Liebknecht's his mate.
Tak tent when he's speakin', for they'll mind what he said here
In Glasgie, oor city – an' the haill warld beside.

In English:

Forward to Glasgow Green, we'll march in good order,
Will holds his banner well, that boy isn't shy!
Yes, there, man, there's Johnnie now, that's him there, the valiant fighter,
Lenin is his friend, and Liebknecht is his mate.
Pay attention when he's speaking, as people will remember what he said here,
In Glasgow, our city, and the whole world as well.

'Tak tent when he's speakin', for they'll mind what he said here.' What DID he say there?

What did he say in any of his thousands of speeches? He was a renowned public speaker, capable of holding an audience in thrall for hours. While many of his writings survive, there are no audio or video recordings of him speaking. His words, so potent at the time, had blown away in the wind.

~

John Maclean was born in 1879 in Pollokshaws, at that time a village just south west of Glasgow. His parents were Highlanders: his father Daniel from the Isle of Mull; his mother, Anne McPhee, from Corpach in Lochaber. With their parents, they were cleared off the land in the middle of the century. Daniel Maclean was a potter and died aged just 43 from silicosis, or 'potter's lung' as it was called.

John, the sixth of seven children (of whom only four survived), was raised by his mother, a weaver before her marriage, and with the help of his two sisters, Elizabeth and Margaret, pursued his education. His older brother Daniel had become a pupil teacher before his father's death, but no sooner had he begun his teaching career than he was diagnosed with tuberculosis. The only hope for sufferers in those days was removal to a kinder climate, so Daniel emigrated to South Africa, where he taught until his early death.

Mrs Maclean was determined that John should also have the chance of an education, so he too attended high school (Queen's Park School), then had a year as a pupil teacher at Polmadie School. He studied for two years at the Free Church Training College, from which he emerged as a certificated teacher.

John was determined to avoid his brother's fate and maintained a strong belief in the benefits of regular open-air exercise. Solidly built, he walked the four miles to teachers' college every morning during his two years of study and during his holidays worked as farm labourer and a postman. A life-long teetotaller and non-smoker, in adult life he was a veritable dynamo possessed of extraordinary energy and strength.[1]

Maclean's parents were members of the Original Secessionist Church, a Scottish Presbyterian sect that believed in the absolute authority of scripture and emphasised the importance of preaching, teaching, and prayer. The church also subscribed to the Calvinist belief of predestination - that people have no control over events because these things are controlled by God or by fate. As young John grew older, it became apparent to him that while many of the pious grandees of the church paid lip service to the gospels on a Sunday, as factory owners, landlords and business men during the rest of the week they were among the worst exploiters of the working class. Their justification was that God had given everyone their place in the world, rich or poor.

A voracious reader and keen debater, during his teacher training years Maclean became completely secularist in outlook and remained an atheist for the rest of his life. By the beginning of 1901 he was an avowed socialist. While he left the church, a belief in the importance of active preaching was a defining characteristic of his life.

Maclean obtained his first post as an assistant master at Strathbungo School in 1900, and continued taking morning and evening classes at the University of Glasgow for a Master of Arts. In a rare achievement for a man from the working classes, he eventually obtained his degree in 1904.[2]

James Burnett met Maclean shortly after the young teacher completed his university education and the two were close friends and colleagues for a decade until Burnett emigrated to Australia. Writing in Brisbane's *Daily Standard* after Maclean's death, Burnett recounted the powerful impact university had on the working class student.

> His bitter hatred of the capitalist class was a sentiment driven into the innermost fibres of his being by the experiences he underwent in

his associations with his capitalist-class fellow students when he was graduating at Glasgow University. He was of the working class and was treated accordingly by the capitalist class prigs with whom he had to associate, and to his sensitive nature this was torture unspeakable. Then, as a cultured member of the working class, he was shocked into red-hot indignation at the conditions under which so many of his class have to exist in a city like Glasgow. He, therefore, gave full vent to the fires of resentment that were thus kindled within him.[3]

~

In a lecture in 1913, John Maclean said, 'I was not brought to socialism by Marx. I am a convert of Robert Blatchford. He has given us the first elementary introduction to socialism I know of. *Merrie England* is the primary school of socialism, but *Das Kapital* is the university.'[4]

Robert Blatchford is generally acknowledged as by far the most successful proponent of socialism in Britain. Blatchford was a former *Sunday Chronicle* journalist who started the *Clarion*, a weekly socialist newspaper, in Manchester in 1891. *Merrie England,* a best-selling collection of essays making the case for socialism, was first published in 1893 and a penny edition published in 1894 had sold 750,000 copies by the end of the year. Total sales are estimated at over two million. Never a Marxist, according to Philip Snowden (chancellor of the exchequer in the first Labour government), 'He preached Socialism as a system of industrial co-operation for the common good.'

A sample of *Merrie England* gives the flavour:

> Now I assert that if the labour of the British people were properly organised and wisely applied, this country would, in return for very little toil, yield abundance for all.
>
> I assert that the labour of the British people is not properly organised, nor wisely applied; and I undertake to show how it might and should be organised and applied, and what would be the results if it were organised and applied in accordance with my suggestions.[5]

The *Manchester Guardian* summed up its influence: 'For every convert made by *Das Kapital*, there were a hundred made by *Merrie England*.'

In the closing decades of the 19th century, journals and newspapers were seen as critical in the task of educating and informing the working class. The Social Democratic Federation, which formed in 1884, had *Justice*, under the firm control of founder Henry Hyndman; the breakaway Socialist League had *Commonweal*, with artisan William Morris as editor; and other smaller journals circulated. But the *Clarion* was by far the most popular. Its circulation reached 80,000 by 1910 and it was the centrepiece of a web of initiatives and activities.

The *Clarion's* efforts to create the building blocks of an alternative socialist society saw the formation of numerous socialist choirs, socialist scouts and glee clubs. Most influential however were the Clarion Cycle Clubs, groups of young and not-so-young people who would cycle to locations outside the cities, where they would hold meetings and distribute literature to promote the ideas of socialism. By 1896, there were 120 clubs and over seven thousand members. On their longer trips to the country, some would stay in Clarion Youth Houses, forerunner to today's youth hostels.

Blatchford believed changing society was all a matter of 'making socialists' – winning people to the cause – hence the *Clarion* vans that made propaganda tours up and down the country. If enough socialists were 'made', he seemed to believe, politics would look after itself. Perhaps the best summary of this approach comes from Tom Groom in a piece in the *Clarion* in October 1914.

> The objective of the movement was to create the desire. When that desire is great enough the professional politician will supply the goods, whether he calls himself Liberal, Tory or Labour Man. Our work is to create that desire.
>
> And meanwhile, why wait for the arrival of Utopia? Why not start living the sort of egalitarian, democratic and sociable life you'd like to NOW! Hence not only the cycling clubs but also the vocal unions, choirs, camera clubs, rambling clubs, swimming clubs, dramatic societies and the always convivial Clarion Fellowship. Hence also the Cinderella Clubs that organised enjoyable trips and parties for underprivileged children.[6]

~

Harry McShane, who worked closely with John Maclean after the First World War, says the socialist movement in Scotland during the Edwardian Age (1900-12) had a romantic tinge.

> Glasgow had several socialist choirs. In the main they were under the auspices of the Clarion Scouts, but the ILP [Independent Labour Party] also had some organised by Tom Mann. Music and the arts were important to both the ILP and the Clarion Scouts, both having been greatly influenced by

William Morris's dream of socialism. There was a sort of romance about their socialism, and a looking back into the past (you've got to look back if you want to see anything romantic at all) ... Before the war this romantic type of socialism almost became a religion in itself. A large number of socialist Sunday schools were set up to educate children in the ethics of socialism.[7]

Consistent with the broader socialist movement, socialist Sunday schools came in a range of styles; from Christian Socialist, to the mysticism of Archie McArthur's Glasgow Central Socialist Sunday School, and the Marxist approach of Tom Anderson's South Side Socialist Sunday School.

The schools brought brightness and comradeship into the lives of thousands of young people and adults in the drab towns and cities. Besides their Sunday meetings, schools ran festivals of music and dancing. They took children for rambles and camping expeditions in the countryside. The highlight of their year was May Day, when they joined the rest of the Labour movement in mammoth processions for peace and workers international solidarity.

Tom Bell, a prominent member of the Socialist Labour Party and after the war, one of the founders of the Communist Party of Great Britain, also recalled those pre-war times fondly.

> The period is one of intense propaganda for labour representation and the ideals of socialism. A veritable crusade was led throughout Scotland in those years with all the fervour and fanaticism of a new holy religion. In Glasgow and other towns street corner meetings, hitherto unknown and regarded with suspicion for a long time by the more reserved and cautious workers, became more and more numerous. The villages in the countryside were visited by a corps of young men and women, missionaries of the new faith and colporteurs of its literature. (These were) the Clarion Scouts, with its 'Flying Squad' of young cyclists and ramblers who combined their week-end outings in the countryside with the distribution of all kinds of labour and socialist literature and the holding of public meetings. ... It was a period of confidence, of high optimism and enthusiastic conviction on the part of the militants in the certainty of victory, and of a new socialist society.[8]

~

In the middle of the nineteenth century, any working class hopes of progressive social reform were pinned on the Liberal Party. The party had formed in the late 1850s from a coming together of the Radicals – whose primary tenet was universal suffrage – and the Whigs – who represented the interests of religious dissenters, industrialists and others who sought electoral, parliamentary, and philanthropic reform.

Led by the charismatic William Gladstone, the Liberals won four elections between 1868 and 1892 with a policy platform of balanced budgets, low taxes and *laissez-faire* that was tailor-made for an expanding capitalist society. Dogged by the contentious question of Irish Home Rule, little was achieved in the area of social reforms, although the Third Reform Act of 1884 did extend the franchise to householders outside the cities and towns, bringing those eligible to vote to 56 per cent of the adult male population. In an attempt to equalise representation across the UK, the Redistribution of Seats Act the following year also introduced the concept of equally populated constituencies.

Radicals' disaffection with the Liberals built through the 1870s and led to many new Radical clubs being formed. In 1881, these came together as the Democratic Federation under the chairmanship of wealthy Cambridge graduate Henry Hyndman, a former cricketer and journalist who had converted to socialism after reading a French translation of *Capital* and befriending Karl Marx. The London-based federation adopted an explicitly socialist program in 1883 and changed its name to the Social Democratic Federation (SDF) in 1884. The Scottish Land and Labour League, an alliance of Lowland industrial workers and radical crofters campaigning for land reform in the wake of the Highland Clearances, quickly constituted itself the Scottish section of the SDF.

'Socialism was in the air in the 1880s,' according to Phillip Henderson. 'London was full of political refugees. Marx was being widely read. The various socialist sects were legion and were quarrelling bitterly among themselves and sometimes appeared to hate each other more than the common enemy, the capitalist ruling class.'[9] This sort of disputation would dog the socialist cause for the next 50 years and more.

It wasn't long before Hyndman's high-handed and autocratic manner created a schism in his own party and a majority of the SDF executive, including William Morris and Marx's daughter Eleanor, resigned and formed their own party, the Socialist League. The Scottish Land and Labour League disaffiliated from the SDF and followed the breakaway party.

All the socialist groups were focussed on a revolutionary path to socialism. They thought that it was only necessary to put the principles of socialism clearly before the numerically superior working class for it to rise up in a body and overthrow the state.

Given the desperate conditions endured by much of the working class at the time, Philip Henderson wondered how any reasonable person could fail to be moved:

> Faced with the misery and squalor of the industrial towns and the spectacle of whole areas of London given over to brothels, into which children of the poor were quite openly herded for the perverted pleasures of the rich, juvenile prostitution being a prevalent Victorian vice, it may seem now that it must have been very difficult for a person of ordinary decent feeling not to be a socialist. But as the starving armies of the unemployed demonstrated ever more angrily in the West End of London during the 1880s and the spectre of revolution raised its head, the more comfortable classes began to fear for their own position and what sympathy they had for the 'deserving poor' evaporated.[10]

~

While the Clarion movement got on with the business of 'making socialists', relatively free from ideological baggage, the socialist and labour movement that Maclean decided to become involved with was wracked with disputes.

Tom Bell identified three currents open to Maclean as he pondered the landscape. 'There was the labour representation movement, which retained elements of liberalism in its policy and membership. There was the Independent Labour Party, which was opposed to all ideas of the class struggle and Marxism. And finally, there was the Social Democratic Federation, proclaiming as its faith revolutionary socialism and giving its adherence to Marxism, albeit academically, dogmatically.'[11]

In early 1903, Maclean opted to join the SDF, but walked straight into an organisational crisis.

While the SDF had become avowedly socialist in 1883, at the turn of the century years of hard work and sacrifice had achieved practically nothing. Inevitably, the lack of success and isolation left its scars on the SDF: it tended to become dogmatic and sectarian. At the same time as it antagonised workers, it failed to satisfy serious Marxists. This was because the federation's leaders faced the ever-present pressure to take an illusory short cut to socialism by discarding some of their principles for short-term gain.

When the middle-aged and middle-class SDF leaders began to woo anti-socialist trade union leaders and seek electoral alliances with moderate anti-Marxist groups like the emerging Independent Labour Party, the Scottish wing of the party demurred and tried to swing it back to a purer socialist course.

In this the Scottish wing was supported by James Connolly, the Edinburgh-born Irish revolutionary who was later to be prominent in the 1916 Easter Uprising in Dublin. Connolly came over from Dublin in 1901 and 1902 and mounted successful speaking tours to denounce the 'class collaboration' of the SDF old guard. When the Scottish wing's policy initiatives – including significantly, the establishment of socialist trade unions – were thwarted by Hyndman and his colleagues at the SDF annual conference of Easter 1903, it split and formed a new party, the Socialist Labour Party.

The departure of most of the Scottish SDF presented an opportunity for Maclean, who stayed with the original party and threw himself heart and soul into a range of activities.

With his teaching background, he quickly became an accomplished soapbox orator, preaching the sermon of socialism in his summer holidays, not just in Glasgow, but also across the length and breadth of Scotland and even into northern England.

On a trip to Hawick in the summer of 1904, he lodged with a local Christian Socialist whose niece Agnes was keeping house for him. Agnes and John struck up a friendship and after she moved to Glasgow in 1906 to train as a nurse, she and John began courting. They were married in 1909.

~

John Maclean was passionate about the importance of workers' education and in 1906, was appointed lecturer in economics by the Glasgow branch of the SDF. For nearly ten years he held a Sunday afternoon class in Glasgow. Willie Gallacher, James Maxton, and many of the other key figures in the Scottish socialist movement passed through the class. Harry McShane remembered it fondly:

> Several hundreds attended each week – they became even bigger during the war. All the best elements of the working-class movement, particularly the younger people, went to them enthusiastically; countless workers were indebted to them. John packed a lot of advanced material into his lectures but at the same time he never missed what had happened yesterday or the

day before. He issued notes of the lectures at a halfpenny a time, and you could buy the whole lot for sixpence. His work seemed to grow in leaps and bounds. He lectured all over Lanarkshire and Fife as well as in Glasgow, and he was tireless. He loved every aspect of socialist work: education, agitation, meetings.[12]

As McShane says, the mining districts of Lanarkshire and Fife provided receptive audiences for Maclean's messages. Maclean and his close colleague James Macdougall took classes in Lanarkshire from 1908 on and at least one class a week in Fife from 1910.

In the summer of 1911, Maclean also made an important connection with the miners of South Wales. During his summer holidays, Maclean visited the Rhondda, where some months previously 12,000 miners had downed tools in support of 800 of their fellow workers who had been locked out by their employers. The affected miners had refused to accept terms for working in abnormally bad conditions. While that strike failed, a rank and file movement emerged that pressured the national union, the Miners' Federation of Great Britain into taking a ballot on the issue of a minimum wage for all miners. The colliery owners refused the demand and in February 1912 a million miners came out on strike.

While in South Wales, Maclean had been welcomed by the leaders of the rank and file movement: Noah Ablett, AJ Cook and Will Mainwaring. The group of which they were a part adopted the name the Unofficial Reform Committee in late 1911, and the following year issued an influential pamphlet, *The Miners Next Step*. This proposed a radical reorganisation of the South Wales Miners' Federation, making workmen the 'bosses' and 'leaders' the servants. Ditching the old conciliation approach, it envisaged 'a united industrial organisation, which, recognising the war of interest between workers and employers, is constructed on fighting lines, allowing for a rapid and simultaneous stoppage of wheels throughout the mining industry'. Acknowledging its policy was 'extremely drastic and militant', its stated objective was 'to build up an organisation that will ultimately take over the mining industry and carry it on in the interests of the workers'.[13]

This was of course music to Maclean's ears, and he did not hesitate to carry the word to the mining areas closer to home. The 1912 strike ended shortly before Easter, but there was continuing dissatisfaction among many miners. The *Coal Mines (Minimum Wage) Act 1912*, passed as the price of peace, conceded the principle for which the miners' federation had fought, although in insisting on district settlements, the owners successfully qualified the victory.[14]

Some years later, James Macdougall wrote about the aftermath of the strike in Scotland.

> The majority of Scottish miners were against the calling off of the strike and received the leaders in a very hostile fashion when they appeared at mass meetings to explain the beauties of the Minimum Wage Act ... Several popular Socialist propagandists began to criticise the action of the men's leaders, and although not themselves miners, they were acclaimed at huge gatherings of miners in Fife and Lanarkshire as the true voice of rank-and-file opinion ... The propaganda of John Maclean, J.D. Macdougall and the speakers of the Socialist Labour Party and the Industrial Workers of the World – exponents of Daniel de Leon's theory of industrial unionism – cultivated an intransigent psychology, suspicious of Labour parliamentarism and favourable to direct action ...[15]

It would not be the last time John Maclean would be out and about fanning the flames of miners' discontent.

2
SECOND CITY OF THE EMPIRE

At the beginning of the twentieth century, the Glasgow Maclean lived in had become the epicentre of a vast industrial complex, and had earned the title of 'second city of the Empire'.

It was a city transformed by the Industrial Revolution. At the end of the long Napoleonic wars (1815), textiles were the dominant industry in the west of Scotland, with the bulk of production coming from self-sufficient craft workers using home-based handlooms. But by 1830, steam-powered looms in factories had pretty much wiped out the traditional way of weaving. The weavers celebrated in the poems of Robert Burns moved from pastoral villages to factory towns.

Then, after the defeat of the Confederacy in the American Civil War of the 1860s cut the supply of cheap cotton from the slave-economy of the American South, the preeminent position of the textile industry in the west of Scotland was gradually lost to heavy industry.

Heavy industry was more profitable because of the presence of coal, railways, iron and steelmaking, shipbuilding, and engineering in a concentrated geographic area. The railways carried coal from the coalfields of Lanarkshire and Ayrshire to the furnaces of Motherwell and Parkhead and helped create demand for the iron and steel produced.

Eric Hobsbawm calls the mid-nineteenth century the age of smoke and steam, characterised by the huge growth in steam power and the associated products of coal and iron. And Britain dominated the world, producing around half the global of output of both coal and iron.[1]

The shipbuilders on the Clyde turned from wood to iron, and then to steel-hulled ships. Steam engines and propellers replaced sails. Engineering underwent a great expansion and became a great industry in itself, producing locomotives, girders, bridges, rails, machinery, and tools. Capital flowed into Clyde-based heavy industries; big companies formed and exported these products to the rest of the world; and the owners grew more and more prosperous.

The first years of the twentieth century marked the zenith of power and influence for the owners of Scotland's capital. They controlled the biggest concentration of heavy industry in Britain and dominated world shipbuilding. Their wealth and the existence of a separate Scottish banking system enabled them to command their own vehicles for international investment. From Glasgow, Edinburgh, and Dundee a network of control spread across the globe, covering shipping lines, railway companies, mining, and farmland in North and South America, Australasia and South Africa.[2]

Scottish capital also wielded significant political influence. When World War I began, both Prime Minister Herbert Asquith, and the leader of the opposition, Andrew Bonar Law, sat in Scottish seats. Asquith was married into the Tennant family, the owners of Scotland's biggest chemical firm. Tennants were partners in the combine which held patent rights for dynamite in the British Empire. Bonar Law was a director of the Clydesdale Bank and partner in a family steel-broking business in Glasgow. The firm's principal business was the import of the steel plate used for the armoured battleships built on the Clyde. For an economy that comprised only 10 per cent of Britain's GDP, the Scots appear to have excised disproportionate influence at Westminster. It was at least in part because they had to. Scotland's exports depended on Britain's foreign and colonial policies. And it was the British state that consumed the most critical part of Scotland's domestic produce: materials of war.[3]

In *The New Penguin History of Scotland*, John Foster asked 'Was Scotland's heavy industry inherently unstable?' He noted that firstly, it depended on a narrow range of products and the market for these products - ships, engines, and locomotives - was highly cyclical and tied to fluctuations in export demand. In the minds of the owners this created a fear of over-capacity and over investment. Secondly, labour. Unskilled labour was cheap and plentiful, so owners were tempted to rely on labour-intensive methods rather than spend on innovation. Third, control over how and where to invest the often very high profits. Scotland's heavy industry was tightly controlled by two to three dozen families, who were tightly interlinked with the Scottish banks and financial sector. This coupled with their political links meant they had lucrative opportunities for investing abroad rather than at home. They took them. The peculiarly Scottish institution of the investment trust used monies largely disinvested from industry and commerce in central and eastern Scotland.[4]

~

The companies that dominated Scotland's heavy industries may have prospered, but the development of factories, furnaces, and shipyards, and the expansion of collieries, meant the reverse was true for most workers and their families. As rural industries waned, people moved to where the work was, in the larger towns and cities. As a result, crowding increased and slums multiplied. Conditions were little better in industrial villages.

As detailed in Thomas Johnston's remarkable *The History of the Working Classes in Scotland*:

> ... with the growth of large towns at the beginning of the nineteenth century and with factory and steam-power production, the sudden herding of the proletariat into the odd corners in the unclean and undrained towns, a capitalism unregulated by law or by sentiment, and with long hours of ill-paid toil in death-traps, there began a massacre of human life besides which the casualties of the medieval battlefields and plagues were as farthing dips in the noon-day sun.[5]

The growing Scottish working class mainly lived in large crowded tenements, near workplaces in large cities. Illness was rife and life expectancy short. Johnston quotes Dr Gavin, the reporter in Glasgow to the Board of Health, who said in 1848 the city workman had an average life expectancy of 48 years 8 months, being 12½ years shorter than the rural workman. Little wonder, he says when:

> Damp earthen muddy floors, walls saturated with moisture ... small closed windows admitting of no perflation of air, crowded apartments thatched roofs saturated like a sponge with water, an undrained soil and ash refuse cellars, within ten feet of inhabited rooms are the general characteristics.[6]

The steady increase in typhus deaths in Glasgow – 427 in 1860, 451 in 1861 and 516 in 1862 – caused at last a real 'sanitary panic among the upper class'. It was the inability of the rich to quarantine themselves from the diseases stemming from poor housing and sanitation that led to considerable publicity and attention being paid to the revelations of such reformers as the Rev. Dr. Begg. Johnston again:

The Census Returns of 1861 shewed that one-third of the population of Scotland lived in single-room houses, and 7964 of these had no window. In Glasgow, 100,000 people lived in one-room houses; of these one-room houses 1253 housed 7 persons each, 596 had 8 persons, 229 had 9 persons, 84 had 10 persons, 30 had 11 persons, 11 had 12 persons, 5 had 13 persons, 3 had 14 persons and 2 had 15 persons. Edinburgh was as bad, 2000 dying annually from fever; but Greenock was worst of all.

Chadwick, the sanitary reformer, declared [in 1862] that the Glasgow wynds were the worst he ever saw; in some of them off the High Street the apartments were 9 or 10 feet square and 7 or 8 feet high and housed two families in each; no ventilation – 'not the slightest,' no light. 'Of course, there was no drainage … In Glasgow, 50 per cent of children born die under five years of age … also the highest proportion of still-born children in the kingdom; the ratio is one to every 12 births.'[7]

Flats were relatively cheap to rent, but there was always a large number of the homeless because income levels in the poorer sections of the population were inadequate to pay for even the most rudimentary housing. The social security safety net as we know it today in most Western economies barely existed, so for these people – men, women, and children – often the only option was the workhouse or the poorhouse. Neither of which were good options. Johnston once more:

> For those who escaped from the slums to the poorhouses, death was even more certain. In the Scots poorhouses in 1862 there were 7843 inmates of whom 23 per cent died. The wonder indeed is that so many survived in these middle-class bastilles; their daily food allowance was valued at 3½d, the sexes were separated; 'aged couples were ruthlessly parted'; the only exercise allowed was 'in narrow yards enclosed by high walls' … Prison fare was twice the size of poorhouse fare and no prison approached the poorhouses in mortality.[8]

Some seventy years previously, Robert Burns started one of his most famous poems with the lines, 'Is there for honest poverty/That hangs his head and all that?'

By the 1860s, it was obvious that poverty was the worst possible crime of all.

~

As industry flourished and profits soared, the battles between Scottish labour and capital in the nineteenth century were invariably won by capital.

Often, this was as a result of the owners' mounting their own version of the strike – the lock-out.

Although the right of collective bargaining was expressly established in 1825 by an Act of Parliament and trade unions for skilled workers proliferated in the decades that followed, wages and hours of work ebbed and flowed with the ups and downs of trading conditions.

And then there was child labour.

> In the early days of the factory system, child labour was universally employed; it was cheap, could be got for bare food; poorhouse (or hospitals as they were then called) governors were only too glad to be rid of the orphan brats whom the foreign wars and the home poverty had left parentless on their hands.[9]

Despite successive Factory Acts to regulate the hours a child might be forced to work, by 1862 there were still 100,000 British children outside the protection of the Act. In Scotland, a child under 13 in a print works might be employed from 6 am to 10 pm all the week. At the lace works, there still were children five years old working from 8 am to 8 pm. Johnston rages:

> For three quarters of a century, the factory capitalists of Scotland exploited, maimed and murdered the worker's child; for it no sunlight, no childish games and laughter and joy; it toiled and starved and died for a master's profit.[10]

District Trades Councils (which were akin to workers' parliaments for discussion and action on industrial and social issues) evolved in the 1860s, but the only really effective weapon in the workers' armoury was the strike.

As James Mackinnon notes, 'It was difficult for the working class to effect changes in its circumstances through Parliament, in which it had no representation, or through the courts of justice, which were subject to the prevailing political and class influences. Lawlessness was deemed a monopoly of the working class and a bitter sense of grievance was the result.'[11] This sense of grievance simmered through the rest of the century.

~

With the passage of the Third Reform Act however, many in the labour movement started seriously considering the prospect of independent labour representation. In 1888, Scottish miners' leader James Keir Hardie, who had been preaching a form of Christian Socialism, stood as an independent labour candidate in a by-election in Mid Lanarkshire. Although he was not elected, three months later the Scottish Parliamentary Labour Party was formed with Keir Hardie as its organiser.

Five years later, the Scottish Labour Party was subsumed into the Independent Labour Party (ILP). The formation of the ILP was a historic step towards the establishment of a British labour party, based primarily on workers' interests and with a socialist objective. The one missing but vital factor was that in the 1890s, it still did not enjoy majority trade union support. Even less could it claim to enjoy the support of a substantial section of the working class, except in very limited areas. At the founding conference of the ILP at Bradford in 1893, not a single national trade union responded to the invitation to be represented. It would take a further seven years, to the formation of the Labour Representative Committee – the forerunner to today's British Labour Party – for the trade unions to back independent labour representation. The Labour Representation Committee was a federal body to which was affiliated the ILP, the Social Democratic Federation, the Fabian Society, and a number of major trade unions. It changed its name to the Labour Party for the general election of 1906.

Why was the socialist movement in the late 19th century so ineffectual in gathering adherents from the working class? Raymond Challinor explained it thus:

> The underlying reason was the immense might of British capitalism, seemingly invincible and unassailable, which appeared to make any talk of socialism futile nonsense. Britain had an empire on which the sun never set. Britannia ruled the waves with the biggest navy in the world. Although other countries had made rapid industrial advances, Britain remained one of the foremost industrial nations, renowned for the high quality of its engineering products. Also, Britain was the world's leading trading country, while London had become the most important banking and financial centre of the world. All told, these achievements gave considerable confidence and assurance to the ruling class. The rest of society, enjoying generally rising standards of living, remained inclined to echo the paeans of praise for capitalism, the system from which it appeared all blessings flowed.[12]

~

A recognition of the futility of the ongoing bickering and wrangling between the various socialist groups eventually led to key figures organising a conference to discuss the formation of a united socialist party. Held in

Manchester in October 1911, it was attended by delegates from the Social Democratic Federation (which had renamed itself the Social Democratic Party in 1908), the Independent Labour Party, Clarion clubs and groups and other socialist organisations. After much discussion, it was agreed to form a new party, the British Socialist Party (BSP). The Social Democratic Party merged into the new body and its members comprised the bulk of the party membership.

The constitution of the new party included a specific reference to the co-operative movement: 'The object of the BSP is the establishment of the Co-operative Commonwealth – that is to say, the transformation of capitalist competitive society into socialist or communist society.'

The new party was just as fractious as the situation that had spawned it, however. The issue that split it into two camps was the prospect of war. The congress of the Second International[13] at Basel in 1912 had resolved that socialist and social democratic parties would not support a war. The position of Henry Hyndman, chairman of the BSP, who had been advocating a build-up of the Royal Navy since 1910, became increasingly untenable. He resigned as chairman in 1913, but his supporters retained control of the party's journal *Justice*.

~

John Maclean had witnessed his mother's short-lived attempt to run a small corner shop after the death of his father. Perhaps informed by her experience, in 1906 he decided to join the local Pollokshaws Co-operative Society.

Maclean devoted considerable energy and interest to the co-operative movement. In it, he recognised a microcosm of how a socialist society might feed, clothe, and provide other necessities of life.

The co-operative movement in food production and distribution was a direct result of the rise of capitalist industrialism. As Tom Johnston explains:

> The industrial capitalist gathered his workers round his factory and mine and opened a store where he sold food, clothes etc. at ruinously high prices. The employee, who was usually paid his wages monthly, of course was compelled to get his goods from his master's store on credit, and for this credit the employer exacted a heavy interest over and above the high price he charged.[14]

These outlets were called Truck Stores and it was not until their abolition by the Truck Acts (1831-1896) that co-operative trading – workers combining to purchase in bulk and retail amongst themselves – really began to flourish. This was distributive co-operation and usually took the form of a co-operative society running a shop or shops in a local area.

The next step, productive co-operation, had been attempted on a local basis in various fields of endeavour – usually as a result of a strike or lock-out. Most efforts failed however and productive co-operation only became sustainable in 1868 when the various distributive co-operative societies grew strong enough to form a Scottish wholesale society to purchase their products. As Johnston notes, productive societies were simply wage-paying societies, albeit paying better wages and providing better conditions than capitalist enterprises. But looking at the big picture, productive factories were:

> ... run on hygienic and best-equipped lines, the goods free from adulteration, the employees paid at the highest rates of wages, thousands upon thousands of working men and women trained as administrators on management boards and committees, a continuous educational propaganda on the benefits of co-operation, at least a partial check upon the rapacity of trusts and other capitalist combinations, a guarantee to workers against a food boycott, a buttress to his wage struggles, the bank of the common people, providing for the working-class a *status* and a security – who can estimate the value of all that on the health, prosperity, education and social self-reliance of the working class?'[15]

Maclean took an active and energetic part in his local society and did his utmost to position the co-operative movement as part of the socialist movement. He regarded co-operation as a significant part of the foundations of any future socialist society.

By 1914, John Maclean was a family man, with a house and a mortgage, but his program of classes both in and outside Glasgow, his party meetings, his involvement with the co-operative movement, his relentless campaigning, his contributions to *Justice* and other journals, coupled with his schoolmaster duties, meant the roles of keeping that house and raising his two young daughters, Jean (born in 1911) and Nan (1913) fell almost completely on his wife Agnes.

Then war was declared, and things got even crazier.

3

LORD KITCHENER WANTS YOU

In August 1914, the regular British Army numbered almost a quarter of a million men. A third of these were in India, and altogether more than half were stationed overseas, in the Empire. There were also fourteen divisions in the Territorials, an auxiliary home defence force of part-time volunteers. A reserve of about 300,000 was divided into two classes; a special reserve designed to fill up the regular army in the first few weeks of fighting, and the national reserve, which would provide replacements for the Territorials.

The six home-based infantry divisions, each containing around 18,000 men, together with five cavalry brigades comprised the initial British Expeditionary Force, which was deployed to France in the opening months of the war.

Lord Kitchener, who had joined the Cabinet as secretary for war, regarded the deployment of the BEF with deep misgivings. With 70 French divisions lined up against 70 German, he did not feel the British contribution would make any significant difference on the Western Front. Moreover, he foresaw a long war. 'We must be prepared,' he told a stunned and incredulous Cabinet in August, 'to put armies of millions in the field and maintain them for several years.' To fight and win a European war, Britain must have an army of 70 divisions and that army would not reach full strength until the third years of war, he calculated. The regular army, with its professional officers and especially its NCOs, would be indispensable in training up the larger army.[1]

Hopes of a quick war, 'over by Christmas', proved fanciful and by December 1914 – after the battles of Mons, Le Cateau, the Aisne and Ypres – the old regular British Army had suffered massive casualties and lost most of its fighting strength. Overseas units were recalled and sent on to France, their imperial posts being filled by the Territorials.

Military conscription was not a feature of the British armed forces, which still abided by the Duke of Wellington's maxim that recruits for foreign service 'must be volunteers'. An enlistment campaign was organised, with Kitchener as its figurehead. Posters appeared throughout the country featuring an image of Lord Kitchener pointing at the viewer above the words 'WANTS YOU'.

The first call, made on 11 August, was for 100,000 volunteers, followed by another 100,000 on 28 August. Remarkably, almost 40 per cent of volunteers were rejected for medical reasons. Malnutrition was widespread in British society; working class 15-year-olds had an average height of only 5 feet 2 inches (157 cm) while those of the upper class averaged 5 feet 6 inches (168 cm).[2] Even so, by 12 September, almost half a million men had enlisted. The enthusiasm brought in more men than the existing military machine could handle.[3]

The patriotic fervour was particularly strong in Scotland. In autumn 1914, 'no part of the country was more eager than the Clyde Valley to join the Colours, to accelerate the output of armaments or to participate in the manifold activities called out by the war.'[4]

~

When the troop trains started rolling, the left wing parties in the belligerent states wasted no time in tearing up the commitments to peace they had trumpeted two years previously at the International Socialist Conference in Basel.

The social democrats in Germany and Russia and the Labour Party in Belgium immediately rallied to their national colours. In Britain, the Trades Union Congress, the co-operative movement, and the Labour Party all pledged their support to the government, while the leading lights of the British Socialist Party - Henry Hyndman, Robert Blatchford and HW Lee (editor of *Justice*) - cheered the outbreak of hostilities and the party journal was transformed into a jingoistic propaganda sheet.

Conversely, John Maclean in Scotland, James Connolly in Ireland and Sylvia Pankhurst in England joined Karl Liebknecht and Rosa Luxemburg in Germany, Friedrich Adler in Austria and Russian exiles Lenin and Trotsky in opposing the conflict. Jean Jaurès, the renowned French socialist leader, was also staunchly anti-war, but after his assassination by a right-wing patriot on 31 July 1914, the majority of French socialists promptly changed their tune from 'The Internationale' to 'La Marseillaise'.

Maclean started a regular Sunday night meeting on the corner of Bath and Renfield streets in Glasgow in late 1914. They were supposed to be general socialist propaganda meetings, but according to Harry McShane, 'Maclean always brought them round to discussing the war and they became big and stormy.' At the beginning they attracted a crowd of a couple of hundred; then supporters of the war started disrupting them and the entire socialist movement rallied to defend the Bath Street meeting.[5]

James Macdougall described it thus:

> At the foot of the street across on the opposite side of Renfield Street stood the Tramway Office, brilliantly lit, plastered with poster appeals to men to join the army.
>
> Up the street, standing on a table in the midst of a dense crowd of the proletariat, stood John Maclean exhorting men in explicit terms under no circumstances to join the army! The war, he told them, was not an accident. It was the continuation of the peace competition for trade and for markets already carried on between the powers before hostilities broke out ... The men they were being asked to shoot were their brothers, with the same difficulty on Saturdays to find a rent for their miserable dwellings, who had to suffer the same insults and impertinence from their gaffers and foremen ...
>
> Who that ever saw can forget the tense, drawn face of the orator, his broad features, high prominent cheekbones, his heavy bushy eyebrows, firm, cleanshaven mouth, his glowing eyes, and the stream of natural eloquence that fell from his lips? As he drove on, his prematurely grey hair shone in the reflected light of the streetlamps, and his forehead became covered in sweat. The soul of the man leapt out of his eyes and took possession of that vast audience ... They knew that all the organised power of the British state was against him, ready to crush him whenever the ruling parties in London might say it would further their cause.[6]

Maclean's rhetoric was against the war, but initially at least the authorities adopted an attitude of forbearance.

~

On the industrial front, the peace promised by the Trades Union Congress in August 1914 proved brittle. Before the war, engineers on the Clyde had been negotiating for a pay increase of tuppence an hour. In an environment of rising food prices, notice of rent increases and rumours of fortunes being made from food and war materials by traders and manufacturers, a formal notice of their claim was provided to the Scottish Engineering Employers' Association on 7 December 1914.

The employers did not respond for three weeks and when they did, they said as the claim was abnormal the men should reconsider it. A meeting between the Greenock District Committee and the Employers' Association was eventually held on 19 January 1915. An employers' offer of a halfpenny an hour was rejected by the men's delegates. A counter offer of a penny halfpenny an hour in two stages of three farthings an hour was refused by the employers. Given the impasse, the matter was referred to a conference of the Engineering Employers' Federation and the Amalgamated Society of Engineers, the Steam Engine Makers' Society, the United Machine Workers' Association, and the Amalgamated Society of Toolmakers. After discussion it was agreed by all parties to recommend that the employers should grant and the workmen should accept an advance of three farthings an hour on time rates and seven and a half per cent on piece rates for the duration of the war.

But before the ballot on this recommendation could be taken, the storm burst.[7]

~

RJ Morris identifies the notion of 'craft conservatism' as central to understanding the skilled workers of the period.[8] The concept is often associated with that of the 'labour aristocracy'.

By the mid-19th century, a distinct cohort could be observed in many industries. It consisted of men with better pay, more regular earnings, and some control over the pace and organisation of their work. Engineers, printers, and stonemasons were central to this group, while other older occupations shared many of its features.

The 'labour aristocracy' had their own network of organisations; friendly societies, craft unions, perhaps a temperance society or a literary club. Their values were fierce independence, sobriety, saving, and rigid family morality. They were neat in home and dress.

Often mistaken for the middle class, their critical point of difference was the aggressive collective defence of craft custom. The right to control the pace of work, which was often essential to a man's health, was a cornerstone of these customs. One reason for strikes against the employment of non-union labour was that such men worked too fast, thus reducing the overall demand for labour.

In politics, these men were Gladstonian Liberal, democratic, anti-landlord, anti-despot, fiercely moralistic, and often internationalist in outlook. They had a pride in their independence and their ability to earn good money against all the pressures of capitalism.

By the turn of the century, things were changing, especially for the engineer. New, semiautomatic machinery threatened their ability to control the labour process. New methods of management, speed-ups, and increased subdivision of labour were equally threatening. Employers used every chance they could to change the frontier of control.

Socialists had increased their influence in the Amalgamated Society of Engineers by putting themselves in the forefront of an aggressive industrial movement to resist technical and organisational change. Confrontation with the employers followed, in the form of a lock-out in 1897-98, which ended in total defeat for the union. This did nothing to resolve the underlying tension, in fact resistance to technical change became sharper than before.[9]

Crucially for what happened during the First World War on Clydeside, it is estimated that 70 per cent of the male labour force could have been in skilled occupations.[10] The attempts by employers and the government to increase the production of munitions by introducing unskilled labour to engineering workshops in unprecedented volumes ran into a labour aristocracy that had been fighting against exactly that notion for many, many years.

~

Against this background, the action of William Weir in importing American engineers to work at Messrs. G & J Weir's engineering works in Cathcart – and paying them six shillings a week more than the locals – proved incendiary.

Brothers George and James Weir had founded the company in 1871 and moved from Liverpool to Glasgow in 1874. Younger brother James had a flair for innovative design and the firm developed a range of ground breaking pumping equipment. The Clyde was the centre of the shipbuilding universe and the company's proximity to the powerhouse of shipping fuelled its early success.

William Weir, the eldest son of James, became managing director in 1902. A contemporary described him as small and neat in appearance and quiet in manner; a lively talker and an excellent listener; a man of energy, originality, and force.[11]

The firm had a factory in New York State producing pumps for its American market. Weir had helped to organise the plant on the latest principles of scientific management. This became known as Taylorism, a system developed to increase efficiency by evaluating every step in a manufacturing process and breaking down production into specialised repetitive tasks.

For years struggles had taken place between Weir and the firm's workforce in Glasgow over the introduction of Taylorism. A compromise was eventually hammered out, with the unions conceding on some issues but retaining some restrictions. As a result of the long-running contest over working conditions, the shop stewards at Weir's were a hard-headed and tight-knit bunch.

In his memoirs, Tom Bell gave an outline of the role of the shop stewards at the time:

> The shop steward was an integral part of the trade union machinery, especially the engineers, before the war. Most unions had their delegate on the job or in the shop, for the collection of contributions, checking up on defaulting members or on non-union workers; for reporting changes in the conditions of work, and as a link between the union branch and the works.
>
> The functions of the stewards, of course, varied in the workshops, depending on the numbers employed, the nature of the work, and the degree of militancy of the members. With the advance of the industrial system, of industry on a large scale, with its departmental divisions, the coming together of several stewards in the carrying out of their duties was inevitable. It was not long before they became an organised force in the shop to deal with general questions as well as the narrower business of the trade union.[12]

When war broke out, there were no factories on the Clyde producing shells. Weir was quickly into action and by the middle of October was 'awaiting forgings for machines to make shells',[13] had taken on 'considerable shell contracts for Sheffield friends',[14] and was advising the Admiralty that 'all his heavy tools were occupied on shell work'.[15]

Frustrated with the drawn-out wage negotiations with the engineers and angered by the ban they had imposed on overtime; Weir issued a pamphlet on 30 January 1915 titled 'Responsibility and Duty'. Distributed throughout the factory and beyond, in it he called on his workmen to give up restrictive practices because, 'every hour lost by a workman which COULD HAVE been worked, HAS been worked by a German workman, who in that time has produced, say, an additional shell ... to kill the British workman's brother-in-arms or perhaps a bomb to be dropped on his wife and children.'[16] His clumsy attempt to resolve the industrial situation went over like a lead balloon.

In December 1914 Weir had written to the TCN Company in Harrison, New Jersey seeking 'a dozen good turners who would be able to come over for six months'.[17] When the Americans began work at Weir's in February, earning six shillings a week more than the existing workers, the local engineers downed tools. Although unofficial, the strike quickly spread to other workplaces on the Clyde and a committee, the Clyde Labour Withholding Committee, was formed to conduct the action. Two of its leaders, chairman Willie Gallacher and secretary James Messer, were both socialists who had studied with Maclean. Without strike pay, the stoppage only lasted two weeks and the engineers went back to work after accepting an increased pay offer.

But as Harry McShane recalled, the event had far-reaching consequences. 'It started the organisation of workshop committees in factories which had never had them. Most of the old shop stewards ... disappeared. Many of the younger ones who led the struggle during the war were socialists from the British Socialist Party, the Independent Labour Party, and the Socialist Labour Party.'[18]

On the employers' side, Weir was not only furious about the strike, but also with the reporting of it. The *Times* was unsparing in its denunciation of both sides of the quarrel. Of the men, it said, 'Either they do not realise the war and their share in it, or they are on the enemy's side.' Of the alleged profits being made by employers, it said:

> We do not ignore the men's side in this and other disputes. We have urged the favourable consideration of their claims on employers, and we understand very well their feelings about the rise in prices and the alleged profits made out of the needs of the public. ... The Clyde engineers must not suppose that 'profiteering' at this time is excused any more than striking, though there is this difference between them. The former may rob the public, but it does not interfere with the operations of war or jeopardise the lives of the men who are fighting. Morally however it is despicable, and any man to whom it was brought home would be placed in the pillory, a mark for public scorn.[19]

Weir wrote to the paper's proprietor Lord Northcliffe about its reporting on 18 March, telling him he had 'a very keen resentment at the reproaches contained therein', citing in particular the leader of 1 March which 'charges Clyde engineering employers with being profiteers and therefore guilty of despicable conduct'.[20]

The stoppage may have kick-started the Clydeside shop stewards' movement that would be a thorn in the side of the employers and the government for the following twelve months; but it also galvanised the man who would help to crush it. That man was William Weir.

4
MUNITIONS OF WAR

By the end of 1914, the German and combined British and French forces on the Western Front had reached a stalemate that led to a new form of conflict – trench warfare. With the defensive positions of both sides so strong, the focus swung to munitions as the key to any advance.

As early as October 1914, Prime Minister Herbert Asquith had expressed concern about the supply of ammunition to the army. Chancellor of the Exchequer David Lloyd George was also concerned about the evident lack of forethought about munitions supply. A Cabinet committee was appointed to investigate the issue, but was stymied by the opposition of Lord Kitchener to a civilian body having any say on the matter.[1]

The drain of working men to the army was also having a serious impact on industry. Although these losses could be offset to some extent by the recruitment of new hands, it was not possible to easily replace skilled men. And in the manufacturing of munitions, skill was essential. The precision required for the making of tools, jigs, and gauges; the manufacture of new machinery, and the adaption of old; all required experience and high accuracy.

The solution, the government thought, was the reorganisation of workplaces such that the skilled worker concentrated on work that only he could perform, and all other tasks devolved to unskilled labour. This process came to be known as dilution. Controversially, it would require the suspension of the rules, customs and practices designed to protect workers' rights that had been achieved by trade unions through long years of struggle with employers.

Surveying the state of British munitions production and the continuing series of disruptions and stoppages, in March 1915 the government introduced a Bill to outlaw strikes and lock-outs and force compulsory arbitration of disputes. However, Lloyd George thought that he could persuade the trade union leaders to accept the proposals without the need for legislation.

On 19 March 1915, following two days of meetings at the Treasury, what became known as the Treasury Agreement was signed by representatives of the government and the unions. The agreement suspended (for the duration of the war) trade union regulations that hampered munitions production. It also allowed bodies of skilled labour to be diluted by semi-skilled and unskilled labour, on the condition that these workers were paid the same wages as skilled labour. The agreement also sought to replace strikes with arbitration and limit the private profits of manufacturers. Notably, the country's biggest union, the Miners' Federation of Great Britain, refused to be bound by the agreement.

The trade union leaders agreed to recommend their members accept these changes for the duration of the war. While the leaders may have acquiesced, among the rank and file in the major munitions manufacturing areas, particularly on the Clyde, there was deep disquiet at the prospect. And those anticipating the opportunity for cheaper labour were not shy in expressing their view. An article in the *Scottish Law Courts Record* crowed, 'This is work that could and should be done by women and boys and girls, who could readily be taught, and whose pay would be less than that of men.'[2]

Implementation of the agreement was dependent on employers agreeing to the profit-limiting scheme proposed by the government. When the employers refused this, the agreement was a dead letter. In the end the government did have to legislate, and most of the provisions of the agreement were incorporated into the Munitions of War Act later in the year.

~

Throughout March 1915, Lloyd George continued to agitate for the establishment of a Cabinet shell committee and after Prime Minister Asquith faced down a threat from Lord Kitchener to resign, the committee was announced on 15 April with Lloyd George as chair.

On the Western Front, the deficiencies in the supply of ammunition had started to become apparent. At the first of the Allied spring offensives, the battle of Neuve Chapelle that started on 10 March, a meticulously organised battle plan resulted in initial gains in territory by the British forces that were not followed up. At first, the British Commander-in-Chief Lord French called the action a 'triumphant victory', but the truth that it was a 'horrible costly failure' gradually percolated out. There were a few factors at play, including the breakdown of communications between units, but the defence advanced by Lord French for breaking off the engagement just as it was about to succeed was that his gun ammunition had run out.[3]

The second battle of Ypres (from 22 April well into May) and the attack on Aubers Ridge (which began on 9 May) clearly revealed the deficiencies in ammunition supply. On 14 May, the *Times* published a dispatch from its military correspondent in northern France about the British attacks. It led with the sentence: 'The want of an unlimited supply of high explosive was a fatal bar to our success.'[4]

While this was not news to members of the government or the opposition, Lloyd George 'grasped at once that if the general public was told with sufficient vehemence that we were failing in France for lack of gun ammunition he would be powerfully aided in forcing his own munitions policy on the reluctant soldiers'.[5]

That very day, events occurred that led to the rapid demise of the Liberal government. After a prolonged and fundamental disagreement over naval strategy between, in the government corner, First Lord of the Admiralty, Winston Churchill; and in the navy corner, First Sea Lord, Admiral Lord 'Jackie' Fisher; Fisher suddenly tendered his resignation. The Unionist opposition,[6] which had promised loyal support to the government on the outbreak of war, could just about tolerate Churchill (who had defected from the Unionists to the Liberals in 1904) so long as the head of the navy was a strong man who could keep him in check. Although Churchill did not appreciate it, if Fisher was allowed to go, the truce between the government and the opposition would be over.

When Fisher informed Andrew Bonar Law, the leader of the Unionists, of his resignation, Bonar Law immediately sought out Lloyd George. 'Fisher was the darling of the Tory party, Churchill had become its bugbear,' wrote Lord Beaverbrook. 'Was the first to go and the second to stay? The rank and file of the Opposition would not tolerate it.' Lloyd George saw the position in a moment – it was either rupture or coalition. 'Of course, we must have a coalition for the alternative is impossible,' he said, and immediately took Bonar Law to meet Prime Minister Asquith. It was quickly agreed; a coalition War Cabinet would be formed.[7]

When the new ministry was announced on 19 May, Lloyd George was appointed minister of munitions. Lord Northcliffe needed very little encouragement to trumpet Lloyd George's message that fundamental changes were urgently required on the industrial front to increase the output of war material for the military. The 'shell scandal' filled newspaper column inches for weeks.

~

On the same day Lord Fisher resigned and set in train the precipitous fall of the Liberal government, William Weir put his case for reorganisation of munitions production in a letter to the Glasgow and West of Scotland Armaments Committee.[8] At the suggestion of Winston Churchill, Glasgow Lord Provost Thomas Dunlop had established the committee on 30 April. Constituted along similar lines to a body in the north-east of England, it contained representatives of employers and workers in munitions manufacture, along with officials from the Home Office, the War Office, and the Admiralty.

The tone of Weir's proposals can be gleaned from a letter he sent to Commander Emden of HMS Achilles the previous day. He wrote, 'Frankly I am of the opinion that nothing other than martial law in munitions districts will solve our troubles and difficulties.'[9]

On 20 May, Weir sent copies of his proposals to a long list of politicians, government officials and fellow employers. Details were also published in the *Glasgow Herald*.[10]

To Unionist Party leader Andrew Bonar Law, he wrote, 'The constructive scheme embodied in the letter does not represent the first thoughts of a worried employer of labour but the considered essentials demonstrated by 8 months of trying experience of the futility of individual attempt to control labour during war time when labour and discipline by any form of war time legislation is uncontrollable.'[11]

Weir asked the Liberal whip, John Gullard, to provide copies to Asquith and Lloyd George, writing in his cover note, 'Articles in the *Times* over the last few days show the labour situation especially as regards the engineering section on Clydeside is in an extremely unsatisfactory condition. As a matter of absolute fact, the output of government work in the future entirely dependent on immediate government action.'[12]

Weir managed to briefly discuss his proposals with Lloyd George in Liverpool on 7 June. After touring the country giving speeches about the situation and much discussion behind closed doors with unions and employers, Lloyd George introduced his Munitions of War Bill into parliament on 23 June. In summary it decreed trade union regulations must be suspended; workers were forbidden to strike or change jobs for the duration of the war;

employers' profits must be limited, skilled men must fight, if not in the trenches, in the factories; man-power must be economised by the dilution of labour and the employment of women; private factories must pass under the control of the state, and new national factories be set up.[13]

On 2 July, the day the Bill passed into law, Weir wrote to Lloyd George.

> Even with the new Industrial Army, there will be a shortage of skilled men. Many employers at present are content to be satisfied with pre-war output, some from indolence, many from fear of consequences. Many skilled men are now utilised on government work of a nature that unskilled men could perform perfectly efficiently and thereby relieve the skilled men for the urgent and difficult work for which their skill qualifies them.
>
> Accordingly, now that the Trade Unions have agreed to waive all questions of demarcation, it is necessary that the Ministry should insist on employers making full use of the advantage secured for them and not simply content themselves with the same methods they have hitherto employed. The shortage of men can be largely met by a definite policy of the Ministry in this regard and accordingly I suggest the issue of the following instructions.
>
> 1) On and after this date, any employer regularly utilising the services of a skilled man to do work which can be done by unskilled men will be considered to be acting against the best interests of the State and Trade Union officials are requested to bring to the attention of the Local Area Committees all occurrences of this nature so that skilled labour, as the most valuable asset of the country at this crisis may be conserved to the best advantage.
>
> 2) Further, the Ministry recommend that all employers should carefully review their shop methods with the definite object of releasing as many skilled men as possible by the increased use of unskilled men – for example by using one skilled man to teach and supervise, say six unskilled men, and to suitably remunerate him for such work.
>
> A definite instruction of this nature will in my opinion, do more to help the skilled labour shortage than anything else I know.[14]

Lloyd George obviously liked the cut of Weir's jib. On 31 July, it was announced that Weir had accepted his invitation to be the chief representative of the Ministry of Munitions in Scotland.[15]

~

The *Munitions of War Act* extended the provisions of the Treasury Agreement and profoundly changed the relations between employers and workmen. In an unprecedented move, it gave the newly created Ministry of Munitions the power to declare factories that were making munitions 'controlled establishments'. The first tranche of these, on 12 July 1915, numbered 134. By the beginning of 1916, there were 2422.

The provisions that applied to controlled establishments were designed to promote industrial discipline and to minimise interruptions to the production of war material. The major provisions were five-fold. These were firstly, a prohibition on strikes and lock-outs and the substitution of compulsory arbitration in their place; secondly, a system of statutory wage regulation; thirdly a system of factory discipline, the details of which were contained in the accompanying Ordering of Work Regulations; fourthly, a suspension of workplace practices that would tend to restrict output or employment; and finally, a requirement to obtain a leaving certificate from an employer before changing jobs.

The last rule caused widespread problems. Employers could be fined £50 if they employed a workman who did not have a leaving certificate from his previous employer or a munitions tribunal. The stiff penalty naturally dissuaded employers from employing anyone who could not produce a certificate. Many workmen did not discover this until they had left their work and were looking for a new job. They then lost time applying to their previous employer for a certificate, which he often refused to issue as he was under no obligation to do so. While the workman could apply to a tribunal to issue a certificate, he would lose at least five days' work and wages. There was no penalty for the unreasonable refusal of a certificate, and if a workman could not establish a case in front of a tribunal, he would have to walk the streets for six weeks.[16]

Much more serious was the consequence of giving unregulated power to the management. Some managers and foremen became more autocratic and dictatorial, and with the right to strike suspended, some enforced changes that would have only previously been possible by negotiation.

For the unions themselves, the new arrangements threatened their very existence. Some workers argued that since the unions could no longer protect its members at work, there was no reason to keep paying union dues.

~

The machine tool trade was the first branch of engineering for which definite proposals for dilution were developed. Messrs. J Lang & Sons of

Johnstone was one of the principal firms in the country making shell lathes and became a test case for dilution in the west of Scotland. The company gave notice of its plan to introduce female labour and asked the engineers' union for its reaction. On 27 August, the firm met with its shop stewards and local and national representatives of the union. The union's position was unequivocal. It would oppose strenuously the introduction of female labour into any workshops where engineering or toolmaking was carried on, apart from the production of shells and fuses. The local committee decided, 'That no woman shall be put to work a lathe, and if this was done, the men would know how to protect their rights.'[17]

When other employers saw the engineers at Lang's defy the government with impunity, they decided not to risk trouble by proposing dilution schemes in their own works. The apparent inaction of the Ministry of Munitions also emboldened those who opposed the Munitions of War Act completely.

The government went back to the trade union leaders to formulate a policy of dilution that would be acceptable to them. At a conference of trade union executives on 16 and 17 September 1915, support was expressed for the creation of a Central Munitions Supply Committee, which would develop the policy. The committee, which was appointed on 20 September, included union, employer and government representatives and was chaired by the leader of the Parliamentary Labour Party, Arthur Henderson.[18] Its brief was to 'advise and assist the Ministry of Munitions in regards to the transference of skilled labour and the introduction of semi-skilled and unskilled for munitions work, so as to secure the most productive use of all available labour supplies in the manufacture of the munitions of war.'

The committee drafted a letter to controlled establishments setting out the principles of dilution and called for returns showing the number of skilled men that would be set free by their adoption. It was sent under Lloyd George's signature on 1 October, but the returns were so patchy that it was resolved that implementation of dilution could only be carried out through local investigation by expert engineers and driven by a strong executive department.

The committee felt it was necessary that the dilution policy needed to be explained authoritatively in the principal centres of industry and the objections of the workmen met by argument and persuasion. On 22 October, Arthur Henderson wrote to Lloyd George, urging him to visit Sheffield, Newcastle, and Glasgow to meet with employers and shop stewards, inspect the factories and familiarise himself with their operations. Due to other commitments, Lloyd George was unable to organise these visits until the end of the year.

~

In the October issue of the *Vanguard*, James Macdougall penned an overview of the industrial scene inside workplaces on the Clyde. He wrote:

> The need for solidarity is breaking down the old craft jealousies, the spread of Socialism is showing to workers their essential unity as a class, in spite of all superficial differences of occupation. In many shops on the Clyde vigilance committees, composed of delegates from each of the trades in the shop, have been formed, and have already many times demonstrated their usefulness. It should be the duty of militant Socialists and unionists in shops where such committees do not exist, or where they have been only partially formed, as in Beardmore's, Clydebank, to see that a complete organisation is set up. Then the vigilance committees are linked together in a central committee, which contains the most trusted men of the labour movement in Glasgow.[19]

That central committee was the unofficial Labour Withholding Committee, which had continued to meet regularly after the settlement of the 'tuppence an hour' engineers' strike in March.

A sense of grievance in the various workshops on the Clyde had been simmering since the application of the Munitions of War Act. In late August, despite the ban on strikes contained in the Act, a dispute broke out at Fairfield's shipyards in Govan over what was seen as the unfair dismissal of two shipwrights, and 400 men stopped work. On 3 September, seventeen of the ringleaders were tried at a Munitions Tribunal and were each fined £10, or thirty-days imprisonment.

On 14 September, Harry Hopkins, secretary of the Govan and District United Trades Council, wrote to Lloyd George advising him the men had declared 'their intention of going to prison before they will submit to the wrong of a money penalty out of all proportion to the offence'.[20]

The matter was taken up by the shop stewards and when three of the men refused to pay and were jailed on 6 October, the union officials also got involved. But as Willie Gallacher recalled, instead of immediately calling for strike action, the union officials 'made statements to the press, sent deputations here and there and had interviews with all sorts of important people'.[21]

The officials called a conference of the district committees of the 23 trade unions engaged in engineering and shipbuilding on the Clyde. The resolution put to the meeting was addressed to the prime minister, meekly appealing to him to secure the liberation of the shipwrights. An alternative resolution hastily put together by Gallacher calling for Fairfield's to stop work and for the other workplaces to support the stoppage was not accepted by the chair and the meeting broke up in disorder.[22]

A meeting at Fairfield's on 13 October was expected to call for a strike, but the government moved quickly and announced an inquiry into the problems being experienced by munitions workers on the Clyde, with the shipwrights' case the first matter to be examined. The inquiry was conducted by Lord Balfour and Lynden Macassey and the official unions managed to persuade the men to stay at work pending the outcome. On 21 October, the commissioners released an interim report, recommending changes to the operation of clearance certificates under the Munitions Act. But they stated they had no power to re-try the imprisoned shipwrights, or even to make recommendations concerning them.

This was a devastating outcome for the union officials, who had virtually pledged themselves to secure the release of the imprisoned men. They informed the commissioners they refused to take any further part in the inquiry, and convened a conference of the district committees. The conference passed a resolution, which was sent to the government on 23 October, expressing profound alarm at the commission's statement, urging the remission of the balance of the men's sentences, and demanding an answer within three days.

A deputation from Glasgow was summoned to London to meet with the Minister of Munitions, Lloyd George, and the Secretary for Scotland, McKinnon Wood. On 26 October Lloyd George told the deputation the prerogative of mercy could not be exercised under the pressure of such a threat and said nothing further could be done until the resolution was publicly repudiated. The deputation retired to consider their position and met again with Lloyd George the following morning. They said they could not repudiate the resolution without going back to the men who had voted for it. Lloyd George said there was another course. The deputation might take steps to see the fines were paid. As these were now only two and a half guineas a head, that seemed a reasonable suggestion. The representatives of the trade unions took the advice and the fines were paid.[23]

The Labour Withholding Committee realised that the government was going to be completely ruthless in crushing strikes. It also realised the official unions were not going to be organising any militant action on behalf of their members. To broaden its base, it decided to dissolve and reconstitute itself with unofficial representatives from all allied trades in the engineering and shipbuilding trades. Railwaymen and miners were also admitted. And even a teacher – John Maclean.

This was the genesis of the Clyde Workers' Committee, a loosely organised body of shop stewards and delegates from across the Clyde area, numbering several hundred. Above the signatures of Willie Gallacher, president, and James Messer, secretary, it introduced itself in a leaflet addressed to all Clyde Workers.

> Since the outbreak of the European War, many changes have been brought about of vital interest to the workers. Foremost amongst these has been the **scrapping** [original emphasis] of Trade Union Rules, and the consequent undermining of the whole Trade Union Movement. To the intelligent workers it has been increasingly clear that the officials have failed to grasp the significance of these changes, and as a result have been unable to formulate a policy that would adequately protect the interests of those workers whom they are supposed to represent.
>
> **The support given to the Munitions Act by the Officials was an act of Treachery to the Working Class.** Those of us who refused to be **Sold** have organised the above Committee, representative of All Trades in the Clyde area, determined to retain what liberties we have, and to take the first opportunity of forcing the repeal of the pernicious legislation that has been imposed upon us ...
>
> Our purpose must not be misconstrued, we are out for unity and closer organisation of all trades in the industry, one Union being the ultimate aim. We will support the officials just so long as they rightly represent the workers, but we will act independently they misrepresent them. Being composed of Delegates from every shop, and untrammelled by obsolete rule or law, we claim to represent the true feelings of the workers. We can act immediately according to the merits of the case and the desire of the rank and file.[24]

The battle between the Clyde Workers' Committee and the government over dilution of the workforce and control of the workshops would rage over the following six months.

5

'WE ARE NOT PAYING INCREASED RENT'

After the war began, a shortage of accommodation in the Clyde Valley, apparent from 1912 onwards, was aggravated by a tremendous influx of munitions workers. By early 1915, the region was saturated and landlords, acting through their factors,[1] seemed determined to exploit the situation. 'They started to raise the rents and to apply for eviction orders against the old tenants who couldn't pay,' recalled Harry McShane. 'The hardest hit were the unemployed and the elderly, and the soldiers' wives, but it even became difficult for the employed workers, despite increased wages, to meet the demands of the house-factors.'[2]

Several bodies had formed in the years leading up to the war to campaign against increased rents. In 1913, the Glasgow Labour Party formed a housing committee that included representatives from the Glasgow Trades Council, the Labour Party, and the Town Council Labour Group. Its convenor was councillor Andrew McBride, and its flagship policy, drawn up by fellow councillor John Wheatley, was subsidised housing for workers from revenues derived from the takeover of the tramways by the town council.

Also in 1913, the British Socialist Party organised the Scottish Federation of Tenants Associations to fight against rent increases and to ask for state provision of housing.[3] In the pages of the BSP journal *Justice*, John Maclean kept up a running commentary on the issue throughout 1913 and 1914.

But the most important organisation in the field was the Glasgow Women's Housing Association. It was formed in 1914 by the Independent Labour Party and the Women's Labour League, a group that promoted the political representation of women in parliament and local bodies. The Women's Labour League promoted the formation of housing associations in each ward of the city and encouraged them to affiliate to the umbrella body. Mary Burns Laird, president of the Partick branch of the Women's Labour League, was the first president of the Glasgow Women's Housing Association and chaired its first meeting, on 16 February 1915 in Morris Hall, Govan.

Following the establishment of the South Govan Women's Housing Association, Govan quickly became the centre of the protest movement about increasing rents. Mary Barbour, an active member of the Kinning Park Co-operative Guild, and a member of the Independent Labour Party, was instrumental in setting up the local body. Other key figures were suffragette Helen Crawfurd and Mary Jeff, whose husband Andrew was chair of the South Govan Tenants Committee.

∼

After its representations to Westminster about housing on the Clyde fell on deaf ears, the Glasgow Labour Party Housing Committee decided to advocate direct action. In March 1915, at a hall in Partick, Andrew McBride advised the audience to refuse to pay rent increases.[4]

Fearful of the consequences, few tenants in Partick stepped forward, but in April Andrew Jeff wrote to McBride and invited him to address a meeting of tenants in South Govan. On 23 April, Messrs Neilson, house factors, had announced increases in the rents of their extensive Govan properties – the fourth since Govan had been incorporated into Glasgow in 1912, and the second since the start of the war.

The South Govan Women's Housing Association convened a public meeting in mid-May which was addressed by McBride. 'As a result,' he wrote, 'it was decided to fight the House-owners.'[5] Of the 250 houses involved, a majority of tenants signed a petition of protest against the rent rise and 120 tenants started a rent strike, whereby they would continue to pay the old rent, but not the increase.[6]

All manner of peaceful activities were used to prevent evictions. There were constant meetings to keep one step ahead of the sheriff's officers, and all kinds of signals were employed to raise the alert when one was spotted. Whistles, drums, rattles, and bells would sound and women would come rushing from the tenements and closes to block any attempt to serve an eviction order. Amid a chorus of angry denunciations, it was not uncommon for a sheriff's officer to be also pelted with flour and pease meal to drive them away.

Govan was a trade union stronghold. All the rent strikers were trade unionists and more than half were involved on government work. The Govan Tenants Defence Committee, dominated by newly active women, at once began a series of open-air demonstrations outside the shipyards. A mere seven days after the campaign began, the Glasgow Labour Party was 'pleased to announce that the Factor, beaten to his knees, has accepted the rents at the old figure'.[7]

The issue really came to wide attention through coverage of the case of the McHugh family, who lived in Glasgow's East End. The family of nine was behind on their rent and the father, Michael McHugh, was summonsed to appear in court on Tuesday, 8 June 1915 for eviction proceedings. One problem. Michael McHugh was a wounded soldier lying in hospital in Rouen, France. One of his sons was at home in Shettleston, also recovering from a war wound, and another was in army training in preparation for the trenches. Two of the remaining five children were seriously ill, one with pneumonia and the other with whooping cough.

Mrs McHugh attended in her husband's stead. Despite the family circumstances, and the fact the local branch of the miners' union (of which McHugh was a member) was arranging to clear off the arrears, the matter was dealt with summarily and Mrs McHugh was given 48 hours to vacate. Councillor John Wheatley attended the hearing and wrote in *Forward*:

> Mrs McHugh and her five children will not leave without a struggle. A protest meeting has been arranged, and if I know the spirit of Shettleston, violent measures will accompany any attempt to execute this warrant. I shall publicly advise the people what to do in this case and they will do it. Michael McHugh is defending the country against foreign invasion. Shettleston must defend his family against the Huns at home.[8]

Shettleston did not let the family down. On Thursday, the day of eviction, the order was not carried out. The *Glasgow Herald* reported:

> Demonstrations by people of the district, whose sympathies are strongly on the side of the tenant, were made yesterday, beginning early in the afternoon and continuing until a late hour of night. These demonstrations were, for the most part, directed against the factor for the house, and a rather violent

disturbance occurred in front of his residence, resulting in the smashing of several windows and necessitating the intervention of an augmented force of police.[9]

The events in Govan and Shettleston inspired others. Tenants in three streets in Richmond Park, west of Govan on the south side of the Clyde, adopted Govan's 'we are not paying the increase' position. A street in Partick, on the north bank of the Clyde followed suit. But appeals by Andrew McBride to Glasgow Town Council and the War Office to take some action were ineffectual, and in late July the landlords met and decided to raise rents yet again.

The supply of housing finance had been severely impacted by the government's war loans. When the government issued the Second War Loan with a return of 4 and a half per cent, many bondholders transferred their funds into the more lucrative war loan and the prospect of widespread foreclosures seemed imminent. To maintain their profit margins, the landlords needed to increase the rents on their properties.[10]

The factor in Govan turned to the courts, while fear of eviction led to the collapse of the Partick strike. By the end of August it looked like the movement had been defeated. But the beginning of autumn would see a big turnaround. And John Maclean would be right in the thick of it.

6

'A SCANDALOUS ACT OF TYRANNY AND A GROSS INJUSTICE'

While the ructions over rent had been rumbling around him, John Maclean had been engaged in a battle of his own. At the end of 1914, a dispute had arisen between him and Hugh Fulton, his headmaster at Lambhill Street School, Kinning Park. Maclean wrote detailed accounts of the twists and turns of the case, which ultimately cost him his job. The following is taken from a handwritten note, dated 15 June 1915.

> On 18 December [1914], Fulton made a speech at a presentation ceremony on the occasion of a lady member of staff leaving to get married. Instead of making the usual speech, he turned around and insulted the staff on whose behalf he was supposed to be speaking. He accused them of speaking in cars and on the subway about him. The conduct of the infant mistress afterwards clearly shows that he meant that teachers were speaking about the relationship between himself and her. For years, board members, teachers, school children and the people in the neighbourhood have been discussing the two. A frequent question is – why does he not marry her?
>
> The day after the cowardly speech – so planned so that no one would wish to injure the recipient of the present by creating a scene – the supplementary teachers met at 11 am to fix a time when all the staff might meet to discuss what to do. Just as the whistle blew, the headmaster rushed in like a 'Hun' and ordered the staff to their duties. All in surprise stood still. He repeated the insulting command a second time. John Maclean, the chairman of the meeting refused to be bullied although no class was waiting on him. Illegally he was suspended but was reinstated the next day.[1]

Maclean wrote to the Govan Parish School Board, forwarding on behalf of 22 members of staff, a 'document addressed to the headmaster in which strong exception was taken to certain actions of the headmaster and an apology was asked for'. At the board's January meeting, the convenor said he had seen Maclean and the headmaster and had instructed Maclean to return to work until the matter was dealt with. A subcommittee was appointed to investigate the issue. In February, three of the board members were directed to meet with the headmaster and the complaining staff and tell them the board 'expected them to cultivate more harmonious relations with each other'.[2]

At its March meeting, the board had before it letters from the 22 complaining teachers requesting a reinvestigation of their grievances; a letter from John Maclean protesting about his suspension; and letters from the teachers and the headmaster about the unsuccessful attempts to arrange a meeting 'with a view to an amicable settlement'.

The dispute simmered through the spring and Maclean wrote the following about the next flare-up.

> He [Fulton] seized his chance or rather he made his chance. This lady [Jennie Smith] usually had a class of boys. On Weds 28 April, she had another class to teach in the afternoon, a class of girls in the Supplementary school. She saw her class of girls in. A male teacher was responsible for her class of boys. The head kept the boys waiting in the Elementary School Hall and sent over for the lady to see them to their room, while the male teacher was kept waiting for them. This male teacher had to pass through the boys' playground to get to the room and so naturally it was his duty to see them up. But anything for a catch. The head ordered the lady to see him in his room. Mr Maclean promised her he would watch to see what was going on. She was so brutally insulted that she had to leave school for the afternoon.
>
> Maclean couldn't sleep. Next day arrived just after nine. That morning Maclean went straight to her room to see if she was present. Immediately after him came the headmaster and from the door ordered him to his class. The children heard and nudged each other. Mr Maclean only went out at the request of the lady. He had a word or two with the headmaster. The latter reported both for insubordination.[3]

At the board meeting on 10 May, a letter was read from the headmaster that Miss Jennie Smith and Maclean were disregarding his orders. A special meeting of the board was convened for 19 May at which the headmaster,

Maclean and Smith were interviewed. After a motion that the headmaster be transferred to another school was defeated, the board decided that Maclean would be transferred to Lorne Street School on 24 May and arrangements would be made to transfer Jennie Smith 'on the earliest possible date'.[4]

If the board thought that would settle the matter, they had not counted on the resolve of Maclean. He proved to be someone who did not back down from a fight.

At the monthly board meeting of 16 June, there were three items of correspondence to consider. The first was from the Maclean Defence Committee, 'asking to be heard by deputation in support of a resolution passed at a public meeting on the 6th instant, calling for the transference of the headmaster at Lambhill Street School and the reinstatement of Mr John Maclean as third master in Lambhill St'. Board member Harry Hopkins [secretary of the Govan Trades Council, and member of the Independent Labour Party] moved that the deputation be heard but the motion was not seconded. The board agreed not to hear the deputation because the matters referred to had been disposed of.

The second letter was from the South Western District Branch of the Amalgamated Society of Engineers, 'protesting against the transference of Mr John Maclean from Lambhill Street School to Lorne Street and asking the Board to reinstate Mr Maclean in Lambhill Street'. It was agreed to pass from this letter.

The third letter was from Maclean himself, protesting about his transference which he considered a 'scandalous act of tyranny and a gross injustice'. The letter proceeded to say, 'the one who should be removed from Lambhill Street is Mr Hugh Fulton for his brutal insolence and bullying'. Ominously, by eight votes to six, the board approved a motion that Maclean should be asked to withdraw his letter. Schools were about to break for the summer holidays, so Maclean's response would not be considered until the board's next meeting in September. Plenty could happen before then. And it did.

~

On 2 September, the day that schools went back, Maclean was arrested while speaking at an outdoor meeting in Shawlands. He later described the incident in an article for *Vanguard*.

A bit of a breeze arose in Glasgow as the result of a slip on the part of two policemen who foolishly interfered with me whilst I was addressing a crowd at the Fountain beside Langside Hall.

On Thursday 2 September, I started off to speak at the spot referred to above, intending to show the economic cause of modern wars and the importance of the economic side of the present war with the specific purpose of booming our usual winter classes in Economic and Industrial History.

I had not gone far when I incidentally referred to the war as 'this murder business'. Unfortunately, in the crowd that was gradually assembling happened to be a soldier obviously under the influence of John Barleycorn. He at once shouted out and wished to know if I called him a murderer. ... I tried to turn the interrupter off, but he was determined to hang on, and even went to the length of brandishing his fist. However, he soon settled down to a wordy warfare with a few around him ...

As it began to approach 9 pm, when the public houses had to close, some of the inspired petty Junkers (or Tories) of the district, who long ago had tried every dodge to get us away from the spot, approached the meeting. When they heard me refer to a lecture I had given in 1910 showing that late King Edward was not entitled to be called 'The Peacemaker' they got upset a bit, so they made a few interjections and told two policemen, who had just arrived, that I ought to be stopped.

These two brawny men asked me to desist as my language was likely to cause a breach of the peace but I refused. Last year, the same trick was tried, but was defeated when I put the matter to the crowd ... The crowd favoured proceeding so I went on. This time no such chance was afforded, and I was marched down to the Queen's Park Police station. There I was charged with using language likely cause a breach of the peace ...[5]

Maclean was not held in custody and three days later related the incident to the audience at his regular Sunday night meeting at Bath St. A Free Speech Committee was quickly organised and on 9 September, one week after Maclean's arrest, a demonstration back at Langside Halls attracted over two thousand people – the largest crowd ever to assemble at that location.

~

Maclean's dispute with headmaster Fulton was back before the Govan Parish School Board at its monthly board meeting on 21 September. The clerk reported that he had written to Maclean informing him the board disapproved of the terms of his letter of 20 May and requesting him to withdraw it, but had no reply. The board passed a motion that Maclean be asked to attend its next meeting, on 19 October.

At that meeting, a letter from Maclean was read stating that he was prepared to withdraw his letter on 20 May when the board exercised its powers to see that Fulton withdrew his insulting remarks and when the board reinstated him in Lambhill Street.

Maclean, who was in attendance, stated in reply to the chairman that he adhered to the decision communicated in that letter and was not prepared to withdraw unconditionally his letter of 20 May.

Thereupon, board member Mr McFie gave notice he would move a motion at the next monthly meeting, on Tuesday 16 November, 'That the Board hereby resolve to terminate the engagement as a teacher under the Board of Mr John Maclean, M.A., third-master, Lorne Street Public School.'[6]

A couple of days later, Maclean received a summons under the Defence of the Realm Act, to answer charges of 'making statements likely to prejudice recruiting'. The indictment listed not only the incident at Langside Halls, but also a speech at Bath St on 28 August, during which he was alleged to have said, 'I have enlisted in the Socialist army for fifteen years. God damn all other armies.'[7]

On 27 October, Maclean appeared in court and pleaded not guilty. The trial was set for 10 November and while the sheriff granted bail, he sought an undertaking from Maclean that he would refrain from making similar comments in the meantime. When Maclean asked if the prohibition extended to speeches he might make on the rent question, the sheriff replied, 'You had better be careful what you say.'[8]

7
FIGHTING THE PRUSSIANS OF PARTICK

Agitation over rent increases appeared to have died down as the summer drew to a close. But it was the calm before the storm. Matters flared up again in Partick, where around 130 to 140 tenants 'of the respectable working class', occupying houses 'of a very good class', decided to pay the old rent minus the increase. When the house-factor, Daniel Nicholson, came to return their remittances, 'he was followed by a very large and hostile crowd, who booed and hissed him and he was liberally splattered with pease meal'.[1]

Coordinated by local housing associations, rent strikes started popping up all over the city, including in Dennistoun, Ibrox, Bellahouston and Parkhead. The Parkhead outbreak was of particular significance. On 25 August, 300 tenants united to fight the house-factor and their action struck a responsive chord at Beardmore's Parkhead Forge, the massive steelworks that dominated the area.

David Kirkwood was the leading shop steward at Parkhead Forge. At the beginning of the war he had been a member of the Socialist Labour Party, but under the influence of John Wheatley, moved over to the more moderate Independent Labour Party. Willie Gallacher described him as 'a big, generous, clean-living fellow'.[2] Kirkwood was a typical nineteenth century radical trade unionist, and never a revolutionary by conviction, according to Tom Bell. 'As a trade union engineer,' he wrote, 'he had all the characteristics of an aristocrat of labour.'[3]

Kirkwood wrote to the town clerk on 3 October, saying he had been instructed by the shop stewards of the ordnance department, and by a general meeting of the workers of that department, to draw his attention to the housing situation in the East End.

> During the past few years, housing accommodation for the working class became steadily scarcer month by month, until, at the outbreak of war, an empty house of a healthy type was a very rare commodity. Matters have now reached a crisis. The national demands on Parkhead Forge have added thousands to the number of workers with a consequent increase in domestic overcrowding, and houses and lodgings cannot be obtained even by persons offering premium. And during the next few months the state of affairs will become immeasurably worse. New works are being constructed for which additional thousands of men will be required. Where are they to be housed?
>
> Property owners, taking advantage of the difficulties thus created, have been increasing rents, and the tenants have no way of preventing this unless by organised refusal to pay the increase. As this course might lead to the eviction of one or more families, the men here wish to make it perfectly clear that they would regard this as an attack on the working class, which called for the most vigorous and extreme reply, and one which might have the most disastrous consequences. We sincerely hope the Corporation will take steps that will prevent its happening.[4]

On 8 October 1915, amid reports of German attacks in Champagne, a combined Austro-Germany invasion of Serbia, the withdrawal of Britain and France's ally Greece from hostilities and the news that a month's fighting at Suvla Bay had resulted in an Allied advance of a mere 300 yards, the *Glasgow Herald* described an unprecedented demonstration in the streets of the city the previous day.[5]

At noon, rent strikers from South Govan, Denistoun, Parkhead, Cathcart and Partick had assembled in St Enoch's Square. The Herald estimated the number as over a thousand, nearly all of whom were 'women and children of the respectable working class'. A notable feature of the demonstration, the Herald remarked, was 'the largeness of the gathering, the tidy, well-dressed appearance of the women, and their quiet demeanour throughout the proceedings'.

Once assembled, the demonstrators marched to the Municipal Buildings in George Square, causing quite a stir as they passed along Buchanan Street and St Vincent Street. The Partick contingent held high a banner that read: 'Our husbands, sons and brothers are fighting the Prussians of Germany; we are fighting the Prussians of Partick: only alternative – municipal housing.' One of the boys from Denistoun carried a placard that said: 'While my father is a prisoner in Germany, the landlord is attacking my home'; while another read, 'My father is fighting in France, we are fighting Huns at home.'

The town council, which was meeting that day, received a deputation from the demonstration and the town clerk also read out the letter from David Kirkwood of Parkhead Forge. The council listened to the deputation but declined to discuss the issue immediately and voted to consider both matters at its next meeting.

After waiting in George Square for half an hour, the strikers were joined by the deputation and the procession moved to Royal Exchange Square where a resolution was passed, calling on the government to take steps to restrain the houseowners of Glasgow from increasing rents; and insisting that all such increases imposed since the beginning of the war should be refunded to the tenants.

The Herald went on to note that five of the rent strikers in the Partick area had been summonsed the previous day to appear in the Small Debts Court, where their factor would apply for ejectment notices.

While the demonstration seemed to have little impact on the majority of town councillors, it created a big splash in the press, notably in the national papers. 'The extension to housing of the moral opprobrium associated with profiteering had become a critical feature of the campaign,' notes David Englander. 'The projection of the campaign as a parallel of the military struggle captured popular imagination in a way in which all the tedious tales of mean streets and the turgid details of housing schemes, however meritorious, had never been able to do.'[6]

The threat to munitions work certainly caught the attention of the government, and on 11 October, the Secretary for Scotland, Thomas McKinnon Wood, and the Lord Advocate, Robert Munro,[7] caught the train to Glasgow for a secret meeting with councillors James Stewart and Andrew McBride about the rent agitation. Following the meeting, McKinnon Wood established a committee to inquire into the issue, and Lloyd George told the House of Commons that he was aware 'that the unpatriotic course adopted by certain landlords in taking advantage of the national need to extort increased rents in munitions areas is aggravating labour unrest in certain districts' and indicated government intervention was a real possibility.[8]

Within two weeks of Lloyd George's statement, the strike had spread to

Govan Central, Craigton, Govanhill, Kinning Park, Possilpark, Polmadie, Maryhill, Woodside, The Garngad, Anderston and Overnewton.

McKinnon Wood appointed Lord Hunter to chair his committee of inquiry, which provided an interim report after two weeks, finding an average rent increase of 6 per cent since the start of the war. The highest increases were in Govan and Partick, and it was in the latter that matters came to a head.

Having failed in his efforts to evict defiant tenants, the Partick housefactor Daniel Nicholson applied to the Small Debts Court for the arrestment of wages of 18 tenants, including Andrew Hood, the chairman of the Partick Tenants' Defence Association.[9] The association was largely composed of munitions workers, and all but two of those summonsed were shipyard workers. It was the rampant profiteering, Hood said, to which they took exception: 'so far as Partick is concerned, it is largely a fight on principle'.[10] The court showdown was set for 17 November, and the mood that percolated through the shipyards and factories was, bring it on.

8
'A PERSON WHO HOLDS ADVANCED POLITICAL VIEWS'

John Maclean appeared at the Glasgow Sheriff Court on 10 November 1915 to answer the charges brought under the Defence of the Realm Act of making a statement likely to prejudice recruiting for His Majesty's forces. Maclean's defence was organised by the Free Speech Committee, a body linked with various unions, the Glasgow Trades Council, the Govan Trades Council, the Independent Labour Party, the British Socialist Party, and the Socialist Labour Party. Solicitor John Cassells appeared for Maclean, and immediately challenged the relevancy of the complaints.

On the first count, he contended there was nothing in Maclean's comments at the Bath St meeting in August that specifically referred to His Majesty's Army. On the incident at Langside Halls, he said the charge, which included the phrase 'or words to that effect', was too vague. Sheriff Lee rejected the objections, saying they could be used in defence, but until the evidence had been heard, he could not rule on what was meant by the comments.

At that point, Maclean pleaded not guilty and a large crowd of Maclean's supporters was admitted to the public gallery, causing a lengthy interruption to the proceedings.

Both *Forward* and the *Vanguard* carried extensive accounts of the proceedings.[1] The prosecution called a squad of policemen, who attempted to recall what had been said at Bath Street. They admitted that none of them had made notes at the time. Then a parade of soldiers, including the one who had threatened to 'punch Maclean down' for calling him a murderer, gave various accounts of the events at Langside Halls. The defence called only two witnesses, James Macdougall and Maclean himself.

Macdougall had been at the Bath St meeting and confirmed that when asked by someone in the crowd why he did not enlist, Maclean replied that he had already enlisted in the Socialist Army, and then said; 'God damn all armies.' But Macdougall was quite positive he was not referring specially to the British Army, because it would have been entirely contrary to the policy of the Socialist Party. 'We believe in international action,' Macdougall said, 'consequently we are opposed to the singling out of any one country for attack.'

After Macdougall came Maclean. He commenced his statement by saying that the words he used at Bath St were 'I have enlisted in the Socialist Army fifteen years ago; the only army worth fighting for, God damn all other armies,' and added, 'take out of that what meaning you like.' He pointed out that in his speech at the Langside meeting he did not desire to injure the feelings of any soldier. 'The major portion of the army is drawn from the working class, and I certainly did not say that soldiers were murderers. And the soldiers belonging to the working class are those who will not get any benefit from this war. I say here and now that the soldiers themselves are not murderers, but those who sent them and are sending them to the war are murderers.'

John Cassells began the closing speech for the defence by noting that when the Defence of the Realm Act was introduced into the House of Commons, various government ministers piously declared it was not designed to curb freedom of speech. As he began to make the point that the accounts of the police witnesses differed materially one from the other, Sheriff Lee interrupted him. 'Suppose we strike out all the evidence for the prosecution,' he said. 'There is nothing in the evidence of the prosecution that has not been repeated in the defence.'

Sheriff Lee delivered his judgement, in what *Forward* described as 'a quiet conversational tone'. Referring to the Defence of the Realm Act he said: 'We certainly are dealing here with a very exceptional piece of legislation. This is not the ordinary law of the land, and in some ways it is in opposition to the ordinary law of the land ...

'Of course, this particular legislation is an interference with the liberty of the subject, but there is no question, I think, at all that in these times of war, the liberty of the subject has been interfered with over and over again, and in many different ways. Only the other day it was said that the result of the war had been to destroy, for the time being in the country, the liberty of conduct, the liberty of speech, and even the liberty of thought. All, however, that we have to deal with in this case is the liberty of speech ...'

Regarding the words spoken at Bath St, the sheriff said there was no doubt as to what they meant. There could be no doubt, he said, that the vast majority of people who heard them actually supposed they meant the King's army. That was all that was necessary under the charge. 'Could anything be more likely to prejudice recruiting?' he concluded.

As to the second charge, Sheriff Lee said there was no doubt the crowd took the expression to be something about every soldier who killed another being a murderer. He did not think that charge nearly so serious. However, it was not a proper thing to say in the streets of Glasgow and it was not likely to benefit recruiting: it certainly was a thing to prejudice it, and in those circumstances, he had no option but to convict.

'I wish however, to say this because I think it is important,' Lee continued. 'I asked a selection of the witnesses what the general impression of the audience was, and I asked questions to try and find out what the general line of the accused's speeches was. Now the accused makes no bones about this, that he is a person who holds very advanced political views and opinions. Holding these views, it will be difficult for him to so choose his words and so express himself as not to give offence. He has been making speeches over a long period, and so far as I can gather, we have only got these two offences libelled against him. Only on these two occasions has he allowed himself to slip. I think on one of the occasions there was a certain amount of provocation in respect that a person interfered with the meeting in what many might consider an irrelevant and impertinent way. On neither occasion did the accused seek to prosecute or elaborate upon what he had probably said on the spur of the moment.'

In his summing up, Sheriff Lee said these circumstances allowed him to take a much less serious view of the penalty and announced a sentence of £5, or five-days imprisonment.

The surprisingly light sentence was greeted with delight by Maclean's supporters. 'Three cheers for Maclean! Three cheers for the Revolution!' someone called out; and hundreds of people in the court, in the galleries and in the corridors, vigorously responded. The officials and police were horrified to hear the strains of the 'The Red Flag' rising in the sacred precincts of the court.

Outside, a large crowd of men and women, unable to obtain admission, had been waiting patiently to hear the result of the trial. When those who had been inside came out with the result, cheers were given, and Maclean, on his appearance, received a tremendous ovation.

9
A QUESTION OF SCHOOL DISCIPLINE

Six days after his trial, the Govan Parish School Board met to consider the motion to dismiss John Maclean from his employment as a teacher. Word had spread about Maclean's peril and a boisterous crowd of his supporters gathered outside the board's offices at 151 Bath St to protest about the proceedings. While they waited for the meeting to begin, they were addressed by several speakers and the socialist song 'The Red Flag' was sung. When the meeting opened there was a rush for the available seating, which was quickly filled, leaving a substantial crowd outside, estimated at over 300.[1]

Maclean had two supporters on the board, Harry Hopkins from the Independent Labour Party and Robert Stewart, a co-operative member. The board had previously decided to hear Maclean's motion in private, but at the start of the meeting Hopkins moved that it should be heard in public. When the crowd cheered, the acting chairman, Reverend James Wallace, ordered the room to be cleared. The crowd laughed and one wag interjected, 'You'll have a job.'

Stewart seconded Hopkins' motion, but when the rest of the board voted it down, the crowd erupted and it was impossible to continue. The board members adjourned to an ante-room, and after some time, Harry Hopkins managed to persuade the crowd to leave. No sooner had they exited than a second crowd rushed in, A shop steward from Beardmore's made a strong speech to the applause of his fellow workers and a brawny riveter from Fairfield's shipyards occupied the vacant chair.[2]

When Hopkins promised the crowd he would convey the board's decision to them, the crowd departed, singing 'The Red Flag' as they went, and the board members resumed their places. The clerk then submitted letters from a dozen bodies asking the board not to dismiss Maclean. They were:

1. The South Side Socialist Sunday School.
2. The Clyde Workers' Committee (representing 15 trades in the Clyde area).
3. The 27th (Plantation) Ward Committee
4. The Pollokshaws Branch of the British Socialist Party.
5. The Govanhill Socialist Sunday School.
6. The Amalgamated Society of Engineers – Govan East Branch no. 643.
7. The Glasgow and West of Scotland District Council of the National Union of Railwaymen.
8. The Clydebank Branch of the Independent Labour Party.
9. The Govan and District United Trades Council
10. The Southern District of the Associated Ironmoulders' Union
11. The Amalgamated Society of Carpenters and Joiners – Glasgow 9th Branch
12. The South Side Branch of the British Socialist Party.[3]

The pleas fell on deaf ears and the motion to dismiss Maclean was carried 10-2 (with Hopkins and Stewart dissenting). It was agreed Maclean's services would cease forthwith and that his salary would be paid up till 15 February 1916.

The board was at pains to stress that its decision was unrelated to Maclean's recent conviction under the Defence of the Realm Act, stating it 'was based on a question of school discipline with which the board had been dealing with for a considerable time.'[4]

Whatever the board said, there were few on the labour side who believed Maclean's anti-war stance and conviction had no influence on the decision.

Nan Milton noted a 'characteristic resolution' was received shortly afterwards from the shop stewards at Weirs.

> That we immediately get in touch with all Convenors of Shop Stewards or representatives of the Kindred Trades with a view to levying ourselves 1d [a penny] or 2d [tuppence] or such a sum as would be sufficient to employ our victimised fellow-worker John Maclean, as an independent organiser, at a salary equivalent to what he was in receipt of from the Govan School Board. Furthermore, that we henceforth labour unceasingly until Comrade Maclean is reinstated in his former position.[5]

That was not the end of it. At the board meeting of 21 December 1915, a deputation from the Govan Trades Council and the Govan Labour Representation Committee attended in connection with Maclean's case. The members of the deputation were admitted to the boardroom just before the conclusion of the public business. The chairman informed them that the communications they had sent would be considered by the board, and an answer would be sent.[6]

Whatever that answer was, it did not get Maclean his job back.

10
A GREAT VICTORY FOR THE RENT STRIKERS

In the days leading up to the appearance of 18 rent strikers in the Small Debts Court, preparations were being made by local housing associations and unofficial vigilance committees for a large demonstration. Meantime, behind the scenes the government was making frantic efforts to head off any stoppage by munitions workers. On the day before the scheduled hearing, the Munitions Board informed the vigilance committees that the proposed strike had been rendered superfluous, as the factor had given an undertaking 'to make a statement in court which he hopes will settle the matter'. The factor advised the tenants that evening that, in deference to the wishes of the authorities, he would adjourn the matter for three weeks, on condition they continued to pay the old rents.[1]

The tenants rejected the offer.

On the morning of 17 November, all across the Clyde women and children assembled again to protest about increases in rent. But this time they had reinforcements from the workshops and shipyards. From far away Dalmuir to the west, from Parkhead in the east, from Cathcart in the south, and Hydepark in the north, the workmen came. Willie Gallacher described the scenes on the north bank of the Clyde.

> At the Albion [Motor Works, Scotstoun] we formed up at breakfast-time and were joined by Yarrow's and Meachan's. In the main road we awaited the contingents from Dalmuir and Clydebank. Then on we went, leaving the factories empty and deserted, shouting and singing.[2]

On the south side, the workers from Fairfield's and the other yards in Govan called in at Lorne Street School, where John Maclean was in attendance, although under notice of dismissal. The workmen called him out and carried him shoulder-high through the streets until they reached the court. It was Maclean's last day as a school teacher.[3]

The different groups met in the city centre and formed a procession that was led through the November fog to the Sheriff's Court by a ragged band playing whistles, hooters, and a big drum. The proceedings were due to start at 10 am, and by then an estimated crowd of 10,000 had gathered outside the court, where they were entertained by a number of speakers. In Hutcheson Street, right in front of the court entrance, Maclean held forth against the rapacious landlords and factors while perched on an improvised platform of a newsagent's poster board held on the shoulders of six well-matched workmen. In other nearby streets, Andrew McBride, Willie Gallacher, James Macdougall and Helen Crawfurd spoke to the assembled demonstrators. A resolution was passed condemning the action by the Govan School Board in dismissing Maclean. A further resolution passed was:

> That this meeting of Clyde munitions workers requests the government to definitely state, not later than Saturday first, that it forbids any increases during the period of the war; and that this failing, a general strike will be declared on Monday, 22 November.[4]

John Maclean was sent into the building to ask the city officials to forward the resolution to Prime Minister Asquith.

Inside the court the start of proceedings was delayed while Sheriff Lee (fresh from Maclean's sedition case a week previously) met with the factor Mr Nicholson and his lawyer Mr Gardner in chambers in an attempt to get them to drop the case. After two hours and with the gallery becoming restive, Councillor Izett approached the bar and asked who was in charge. In the name of the workers present, he protested about the delay. The protest evoked a loud outburst of cheering, which brought the sheriff from his chambers into the court. He rebuked the demonstrators and threated to clear the court if there was a repeat of the outburst.

On the sheriff taking his seat on the bench, one of the tenants came forward and asked if he would hear from a deputation. The sheriff pointed out his position was purely a legal one and he could not involve himself in any political questions. Given the exceptional circumstances however, he was prepared to take the risk of hearing from the deputation. Four of the tenants spoke with the sheriff in chambers.

~

The parties had previously agreed that a test case would be heard, that of William Reid, secretary of the Tenants' Defence Committee and the result would apply to all the other cases. When Sheriff Lee returned to the bench, Mr Gardner advised the court that after Reid refused to pay the increased rent, he was given notice to leave his house by 28 September. Reid and the other tenants involved remained in their houses. Negotiations were entered into to forego any increase until 28 November, if Reid and the others were prepared to abide by the decision of the commission of inquiry currently underway, or by any legislation that might follow. However, these negotiations had fallen through.

Gardner then advised the court of a request received from the minister of munitions the previous day, asking the factor to drop the cases or continuing them to allow the legislation that was promised to come into force. He said a letter was sent to the defender in common with the other defenders to the effect, in deference to a special request from the Munitions Board, the rent case against him could be continued.

Sheriff Lee pulled him up immediately. 'You had no right to say it would be continued,' he said.

'With consent, of course,' Gardner spluttered.

'But there won't be a consent, I am afraid,' the sheriff said.

William Reid told the sheriff the tenants' committee had decided they must have a decision one way or another. Munitions workers were involved in 15 of the cases, and they did not want to stay off work to come here and discuss the question of rent. They had a bigger battle to fight in the workshops, and they wanted to fight loyally there.

The sheriff said he could quite understand the position of the men. They were liable for a fine or imprisonment for being away from their work. The petitioner seemed confident there was going to be legislation. Could he not see his way to adopt the other alternative and drop the cases? The sacrifice might be considerable: the public usefulness of the action would be very much more considerable.

After some further discussion, Mr Gardner said he was instructed on consideration of the situation and in deference to the request of the

Munitions Board, as well as in the public interest, to agree to the sheriff's suggestion and drop the cases.

The concession was greeted with loud cheering in the court.[5]

~

The government's inquiry recommended that rents be restricted for the duration of the war, and on 25 November, a Bill was introduced to give effect to its recommendations. The *Increase of Rent and Mortgage Interest (War Restrictions) Act 1915* received royal assent on 23 December 1915. It rewound rents to their August 1914 level for the duration of the war.

It was a great victory for the rent strikers, and Maclean was exultant, writing in the *Vanguard*:

> It should be noted that the rent strike on the Clyde is the first step towards the Political Strike, so frequently resorted to on the Continent in times past. We rest assured that our comrades in the various works will incessantly urge this aspect on their shop-mates, and to prepare the ground for the next great counter-move of our class in the raging class warfare – raging more than ever during the Great Unrest period of three or four years ago.[6]

On 19 November, having decided he would not pay a fine, Maclean entered Duke Street Prison to serve the five-day sentence imposed for his breaches of the Defence of the Realm Act. On the morning of his release, forty miners from South Lanarkshire, wearing their pit clothes and miners' lamps, arrived at Central Station and marched to the prison to greet Maclean. Fearing such a demonstration, the authorities had released Maclean early, so the group proceeded to Maclean's house to wish him well.

From there, they headed to Fairfield's in Govan, where a dinner meeting at the shipyard passed resolutions against the government, the Govan Parish School Board, the Munitions Act, and conscription. Then home they went, carrying greetings from the shipyard workers to the miners of Lanarkshire.[7]

11

PETER PETROFF

When John Maclean was summonsed in late October 1915 for his speeches at Langside Halls and Bath Street, he realised he might be facing at least six month's imprisonment. To maintain the wide range of activities in which he was engaged, he decided reinforcements were required. With the approval of the Glasgow District Committee of the British Socialist Party (BSP), Maclean sent a telegram to Russian émigré Peter Petroff in London, asking if Petroff and his wife Irma could come to Glasgow. The invitation was for Petroff to take up lecturing in Maclean's economics classes and to join the editorial board of the *Vanguard*.

Maclean had first met Petroff on the Clyde in 1908. Both were members of the BSP and had combined to advocate changes to the BSP's policies at its Easter 1914 annual conference. The duo wanted to see a common platform laid down for candidates and for the BSP journal *Justice* to be controlled by the party through a system of elected trustees and an elected editor, rather than simply being a mouthpiece for Henry Hyndman. While both moves failed, the collaborative effort strengthened the bond between the two men.[1]

When war was declared later that year, like virtually every British left-wing organisation, the BSP was split on the issue. While Maclean, Petroff and the bulk of the party membership were anti-war, most of the key office-holders and party veterans, including Hyndman, argued that the war should be supported. Across Europe, those in favour of their country's war efforts were variously called 'social patriots' or 'defencists'. Those opposed to the war called themselves 'internationalists' and adhered to the principle that working-class people of all countries must unite across national boundaries and actively oppose nationalism and war in order to overthrow capitalism.

It was out of frustration with the pro-war line run by *Justice* that Maclean successfully persuaded the Glasgow District Committee of the party to launch a revolutionary anti-war paper, the *Vanguard*. The first issue appeared in September 1915.

~

Peter Petroff was one of the many exiled Russian socialists and revolutionaries who arrived in London in the years following the failed 1905 Russian revolution. Petroff had joined the Russian Social Democratic Labour Party (RSDLP) in Odessa in 1901 and had been politically active leading up to and during the revolution; and for those activities he had spent time in prison and internal exile. In 1907, he managed to escape from Russia, initially spending time in Geneva, then coming to London to attend the 1907 congress of the RSDLP.

The British tradition of granting political asylum had given it a long-standing reputation as a safe haven for refugees. In the last two decades of the 19th century, the number of foreigners in the UK doubled, with many having fled increasing antisemitism in Eastern Europe and the repressive tsarist regime in Russia. A large proportion of these immigrants found work in the sweated tailoring trade in East London, and given the police and racial persecution they had experienced, it was no surprise that many of them were socialists and anarchists. Other refugee clusters were to be found in Leeds, Newcastle, Glasgow, and Edinburgh.[2]

One of the first Russians to play an important role in British social democracy was Theodore Rothstein. He arrived in England in 1891 and joined the Social Democratic Federation (SDF) four years later. From 1901 until 1906, he was a member of the party's National Executive, and continued to play an active role in its affairs until his return to Russia in 1920. In the post-war period, he was a key player in the establishment of the Communist Party of Great Britain. He was also a key reason John Maclean did not join that party.

In its turn, Britain played a significant role in the development of Russian social democracy. In 1902, Vladimir Lenin and his wife Nadezhda Krupskaya arrived in London from Munich where with Julius Martov and others he had founded the first all-Russian socialist newspaper *Iskra* (*The Spark*). In the 18 months he spent in Munich, Lenin also wrote the hugely influential pamphlet *What is to be done?*

Iskra was produced in secret and smuggled into Russia, where it was distributed by an underground network. When the printer in Munich judged the risk of printing was becoming too great, Lenin decided to move the base of operations to London, where the SDF placed the facilities of the Twentieth Century Press at his disposal. Copies of the newspaper continued to be sent to Russia and distributed by clandestine means.

Lenin left London for Geneva in spring 1903, but returned for the second congress of the Russian Social Democratic Labour Party in July–August 1903. The congress began in Brussels but moved to London after the Belgian police forced the delegates to leave the country. The gathering was dominated by the argument about who should be allowed to be a member of the party. Lenin argued party membership should be limited to 'professional revolutionaries'. The counter view propounded by Julius Martov favoured the establishment of a mass party on the west European model. In the final vote the majority (bolshevik in Russian) favoured Lenin over the minority (menshevik). Henceforth, the two factions adopted those respective names.

London also was the venue for the fourth congress of the party in 1907. It was the last one before the Russian revolutions of 1917 and more than three hundred delegates attended, including Lenin, Martov, Leon Trotsky, Josef Stalin, Rosa Luxemburg, Georgy Plekhanov, Grigory Zinoviev, Pavel Alexrod and Maxim Litvinov. The SDF played a supportive role, with Theodore Rothstein heavily involved, and the British body hosted a massive welcoming demonstration for delegates at Holborn Hall on 24 May.

The SDF journal *Justice* wrote that 'the Russian comrades – strike one as scholars, mainly young men, slender, with clever, intellectual looking faces. It did not need a physiognomist to tell us that here were the most vital elements of modern Russia ... One felt that here one was in the presence of some of the noblest men and women that the world has ever produced.'[3]

In their account of how wealthy American soap manufacturer Joseph Fels stepped in with funding to save the congress from a premature end, historians Arthur Dudden and Theodore von Laue paint a vivid picture of the impact the delegates made in the streets of London.

> To the unsophisticated Londoners they seemed a wild and motley crowd. Their appearances in the streets ignited instant sensations. The Russian, Polish, Lettish [Latvian], and Jewish delegates for the most part wore black cloaks, black flowing ties, wide-awake hats, and dark beards, representing the very essence of conspiracy and intrigue. Still more exciting, however, were the delegates from the Caucasus, whose bizarre appearance was

accentuated by their sheepskin *shappkas*, together with the handful of Tartars and Siberians who brought with them the exotic flavour of remote steppes. While the party leaders met almost incessantly to complete arrangements for the sessions which were about to begin, some of the delegates loitered about the scantily furnished rooms of the Socialist Club eating thick slices of buttered bread and drinking coffee, examining maps of London, and conversing volubly in groups or in pairs. The *Morning Post* reporter was impressed by their appearance of 'deep study and thought,' and pronounced them the 'pick of Russia's intellectual workmen.'[4]

The congress, held at the Brotherhood Church in Hackney and opened by Labour MP and future prime minister James Ramsay MacDonald, was a stormy one. Running for 35 sessions between 13 May and 1 June, Dudden and von Laue explain its significance as follows: 'The future of the RSDLP was at stake, and in retrospect the fate of the entire revolutionary movement and all of Russia as well. The congress itself was composed of an unusually brilliant galaxy of revolutionary theorists and practitioners, and its sessions claimed their full attention. At the base of the debates, which were alternately superficial and profound, there simmered the unresolved conflict over the fundamental nature of the party and its tactics for revolution. Fundamentally the trouble was that the differences between the moderates and the extremists were already of long standing, being divisively rooted in differing conceptions of the nature of the Russian revolutionary process.'[5]

Peter Petroff witnessed the rival conceptions of the party expounded by Martov and Lenin at first hand. He wrote:

> Both men were perfectly sincere ... but they differed widely in their methods, habits, and notions. While Martov was an absolute European, a typical Bohemian, a brilliant publicist, witty in his speeches (though no great orator) distaining demagogy, always taking a wide view, fair and honest towards friend and foe – Lenin on the contrary, was a typical Russian, pedantic in his personal habits, convincing by his iron logic in his powerful speeches and in his brilliant writings which were effective though of a peculiarly heavy style, an iron character heading straight for a fixed goal, at times not over-scrupulous in the choice of his means, inscrutable for friend and foe.[6]

~

After the 1907 congress, Petroff was approached to carry out political work with the 400 Russian sailors stationed with the *Rurik*, a new Russian flagship being built at Barrow-in-Furness. When the ship and crew moved to the Clyde, Petroff went with them and established contact with the local branch of the Social Democratic Federation there. John Maclean was among the SDF members who harboured and fed him 'with a regard for the rules of conspiracy'.[7]

After an interlude in Paris, Petroff settled back in London, finding a home in the pulsating cultural life of the East End, surrounded by Russian émigrés, other foreign socialists, and radical Jewish groups. He joined the Kentish Town branch of the Social Democratic Party (the new name of the SDF), one of the party's largest, liveliest, and most radical branches. Petroff was a member for ten years, and wrote in his memoir:

> The Branch was not satisfied with registering its decisions; it wanted to attain some results and would therefore send its resolutions to the Executive, to other organisations, government departments, municipal authorities, members of Parliament, as the case might be. It was therefore not an easy job to be secretary of the Kentish Town Branch; not merely clerical skill was wanted for this; considerable political education was required as well as a great capacity for work since there was no remuneration of any kind and the secretary had not even a typewriter at his disposal.[8]

Petroff met his German-born wife Irma Gellrich at a socialist Sunday school in 1911 and they considered themselves married, although they did not undergo a legal process.[9]

Sylvia Pankhurst described Petroff as 'a brown-face Russian, whose whimsical smiles had drawn crow's-feet from the corners of his eyes, a revolutionary of revolutionaries...' Irma she described as 'a serious intellectual young woman'.[10]

Irma became a London correspondent for the German social democratic press while Petroff made his living from journalism and translations, writing for *Justice*, Lucien Wolf's anti-tsarist *Darkest Russia* and St Petersburg weeklies *Nasha Zarya* and *Luch*. He was a delegate to the SDP national conference in 1910, and after the SDP merged with other groups to form the British Socialist Party in 1911, he was a delegate to each BSP national conference between 1912 and 1915.

~

11 Peter Petroff

Peter Petroff: '... a brown-face Russian, whose whimsical smiles had drawn crow's-feet from the corners of his eyes, a revolutionary of revolutionaries...'

With the Russian ambassador spurring the Home Office to crack down and harass Russian revolutionaries and their organisations, life in wartime London for the Petroffs was proving a struggle. When, in October 1915, they received Maclean's invitation to join him on the Clyde, they did not hesitate. Locking their London flat and giving the keys to a colleague, Petroff and Irma boarded a train for Glasgow. On arrival, the couple moved into the Maclean household at Auldhouse Road, Newlands, which Petroff described as 'kind of a centre for the movement and headquarters of a manifold activity'.[11]

The BSP appointed Petroff second organiser for the Glasgow district and paid him £2 a week. This enabled him to devote his whole time to the movement. He described the goings-on in his memoir.

> A wide field of activity lay open to me. The masses were in a state of unrest, both the membership and the influence of our Party were rapidly increasing; it was essential to create an organisation strong and elastic enough to cope with the demands of the time and steadfastly to withstand all persecutions. Furthermore, I had to represent the Party in various other organisations, including the Free Speech Committee which had been established in September and to which almost every labour organisation was affiliated.
>
> Together with Maclean I went for some time almost daily, during the breakfast interval to one or other of the large works to hold short meetings at the works gate. These workgate meetings enabled us to get in direct touch with the working masses and to explain to them our point of view. Here we were advocating the ideas of our Party, propagating the 'Labour College for Scotland' planned by John Maclean, and called the workers to our demonstrations and Sunday meetings.
>
> In addition, we found time for a big campaign in favour of the Co-operative Societies which were then threatened by a system of coupons which certain capitalist concerns were introducing. Our school and all our wide net of fighting organisations were brought into action and developed a strong propaganda for the idea of co-operation. Later on, when government pressure deprived us of our halls, the co-operatives came to our rescue, placing at our disposal their hall for a big conference that was attended by about four hundred delegates, Maclean acting as chairman.[12]

Although Maclean's active partnership with Petroff lasted less than three months, it was significant in several ways. Brian Ripley and John McHugh observe:

It brought Maclean into a fuller realisation that his developing opposition to the war was shared by other European socialists. It thus reaffirmed his belief in, and commitment to Internationalism. The connection with Petroff also saw *The Vanguard* adopting a more assertive and forthright critique of the BSP Executive than before. Maclean had made no secret of his differences with the Executive but now those differences were confronted head on.[13]

Discussions with Petroff sharpened the general tone of Maclean's political propaganda. This was demonstrated in their challenge to the Clyde Workers' Committee to adopt a definite anti-war stance and to channel industrial discontent in that direction. While many of the shop stewards in the CWC were socialists and anti-war, as a rule they submerged their politics in workshop struggles inside the factories.

On this issue, Maclean was particularly critical of CWC chairman and fellow-BSP member Willie Gallacher. Harry McShane recalls that at the beginning of the war Gallacher had spoken at an anti-war meeting in Govan organised by the BSP and the Independent Labour Party. But when he came to speak at a Bath St meeting towards the end of 1915, he did not mention the war at all. The following Sunday, Maclean laid into him. 'How could any man calling himself a socialist come to speak at a meeting at this time and not refer to the war that is raging in Europe?'[14]

Normally only shop stewards were present at CWC meetings, but Maclean and his colleague James Macdougall were welcome to attend, and allowed full right to participate in all discussions.[15]

The different positions on the war exploded in spectacular fashion one Saturday afternoon when Macdougall brought Peter Petroff to the weekly CWC delegate meeting. Willie Gallacher was in the chair, James Messer (Independent Labour Party) was the secretary and there were around 250 to 300 shop stewards present.

At the meeting Johnny Muir gave a lengthy report on the campaign the CWC was preparing on the issue of dilution of labour. Muir, recognised as the 'intellectual' of the committee, was a member of the Socialist Labour Party (SLP) and took the position that they should accept the war as a fact and work for what they could get in the circumstances. While most other members of the SLP were anti-war, they did not oppose Muir on the CWC; and neither did the BSP members.[16]

Petroff stood up and criticised the speech, saying Muir had spoken only on industrial questions and had neglected the most important issue, that of the war itself. Petroff wrote:

> Muir gave a long report, expressing himself on the one hand against 'dilution of labour', while on the other hand trotting out the lame hobby horse of the SLP, the formation of one big union with the assistance of the all-embracing Clyde Workers' Committee. In the discussion, I emphasised the contradiction between the two contentions of the speaker and developed our Socialist point of view: 'Dilution of labour will come because it must come,' I explained, 'the rationalisation of production cannot be prevented, least of all in time of war. Such an attempt would be a fight against windmills like the struggle of the Luddites who wanted to break the machines. We are opposed to the war and wish to see it ended, but that can be attained only by international action, not by an attempt to keep back the wheel of industrial development and to hamper the increase of production. You are talking constantly about 'workers' control' – we are still waiting to hear what you mean by that. It seems every one of you means something different. Your 'control' is just an empty phrase. And while on the one hand you are defending the privileges of a labour aristocracy, you are on the other hand talking about 'one big union'. How does this tally?'[17]

There are differing accounts of what happened next, but all agree that Petroff's comments caused an uproar. Petroff said Gallacher seemed not to understand the argument, 'but felt that I had stepped on the corns of his hero, Muir, and went into hysterics'. In *Revolt on the Clyde*, Gallacher wrote:

> I called Petrov to order and after some difficulty got him to resume his seat. I then said that in view of what had been going on for some time, we could not view such an outrageous attack as he had made on Johnny Muir other than as a deliberate attempt to disrupt the committee; therefore I would take a proposal from the meeting that Petroff not be allowed to attend any further meetings. At this Macdougall jumped up in a passion and declared that I was taking advantage of a foreigner. 'It's an example of race hatred,' he shouted.
> 'All right,' I replied, 'just to show there isn't anything racial about it I'll ask the delegates to add your name to the proposal.'[18]

The motion was put, and except for the small group of BSP members around Macdougall and Petroff, was passed overwhelmingly.

~

The scope of Petroff's activities widened and began to take in talks to miners in Lanarkshire, and then Fife, where Maclean had given Marxist classes at least one night a week since 1910.

Petroff's first Fife visit was to Bowhill, a modern up-to-date village with a new colliery that employed 1800 men. He gave a lecture on the economic situation during the war and the perspectives after the war. Afterwards the miners expressed a desire to hear Petroff speak about Russia and a second meeting was arranged. Bowhill was deemed a 'prohibited area', a district where enemy aliens were not permitted and friendly aliens had to register before entering and leaving. Petroff therefore attended the police station at nearby Lochgelly on his way in and on his way out again to complete the formalities.[19]

When he returned for his second lecture on 22 December, Petroff got off at Lochgelly to register, but the policeman who was dealing with registration 'happened to be absent'. Petroff left a note notifying his arrival and asking to be advised by telephone when he could come for formal registration. At Bowhill, he had tea with his mining friends, then on his way to the meeting was arrested, 'by order from London' it was first stated. Afterwards, this was conveniently forgotten and he was charged with having failed to register.

Petroff's arrest sparked indignation at the miners' meeting and the workers went on strike, demanding his immediate release. The following morning the strike was spreading and the authorities quickly took Petroff to the court in Dunfermline, where he pleaded not guilty, was fined £3, and then released.

~

The London leadership of the British Socialist Party failed to acknowledge the implications of the collapse of European social democracy when war broke out in 1914. It kept faith with the Second International, even though that body had split into three factions: the pro-war social democratic parties in the Central Powers, the pro-war parties of the Allies,[20] and the various anti-war parties. The BSP regarded the International Socialist Bureau as the force that would pull the working class back from Armageddon, overlooking the fact that its chairman Emile Vandervelde (a member of the Belgian Cabinet) had made it clear he had no intention of calling a meeting of the International while a single German soldier remained on Belgian soil.[21]

With his contacts among European socialists, including Leon Trotsky in Paris, Petroff had a direct channel for news from the continent. When anti-militarist socialist parties convened an international conference in Zimmerwald, Switzerland from 5-8 September 1915, Petroff provided a report from London for the October issue of the *Vanguard*. He wrote:

> In spite of the British Government's prevention of British Socialists attending a gathering of representative Socialists in Switzerland by the refusal of passports, a most successful conference took place ...
>
> The conference was attended by seven delegates from the anti-war section of the German Democratic Party, two from the French trade unions (the French Socialist Party being hopeless), three from the Italian Socialist Party, and others representing Bulgaria and the other Balkan States, Norway, Switzerland, and Russia. 'Socialist patriots' were excluded.[22]

Never one to miss an opportunity to attack *Justice* and 'the bourgeois members of the Central Branch of the BSP', he concluded the piece with the following.

> We draw attention to the fact that Hyndman's paper, 'Justice,' which boasts its international information, was totally innocent of the International conference. At least, it said so. 'None so blind,' etc. From what we have seen in Britain, we must put down the bell on those who are constantly whining, 'Trust your leaders.' Faithful Social Democrats here have been led a sorry dance by the bourgeois members of the Central Branch of the B.S.P. Our business is to trust ourselves and our cause and line up with our world comrades as quickly as we can.
>
> We assure our comrades that we in Glasgow are internationalists first, last, and all the time.

Petroff followed up with an article in the November issue which started, 'Whichever State will emerge victorious from this world war – one thing is perfectly clear: the working class of all the belligerent countries has suffered the most disastrous defeat'; and finished by saying, 'The war has revealed all that was bad in the Labour and Socialist movement. The progress of the war, with all that is accompanying it, is strengthening those elements who will build a new International on a more sound basis.'[23]

The attitude of the executive committee of the BSP to the Zimmerwald movement was initially equivocal, but by December 1915 had hardened to the point where it said it was 'not in favour of any move to form a new international organisation apart from or in opposition to the International Socialist Bureau'. Raymond Challinor notes that since the ISB did not function, this meant doing nothing.[24]

In his final article on Zimmerwald in the December *Vanguard*, Petroff took the opposite position.

> ... it is natural that signs should begin to appear, in all the countries, of a desire for the reconstruction of the International organisation of the proletariat. Those sections of the working class who maintained the honour of the International, are growing in numbers and influence. Resolute attempts are being made by them to cleanse the Augean stables of jingoism in the working class movement, and to prepare for serious national and international action against the war ...
>
> The prolongation of the war with all that that means will revolutionise the masses of the people and make drastic action not only possible, but imperative. And the step taken at Zimmerwald, we hope, will prove to be the commencement of a steady progress towards the realisation of our objects.
>
> We must, therefore, purify our parties and immediately proceed to gather our forces, participate in all the chance encounters between the workers and the capitalists, sharpen the class struggle and make ourselves ready for drastic, revolutionary action.
>
> We call upon our comrades in the various branches to affiliate with the Committee of the Zimmerwald Conference. The E.C. of the British Socialist Party adopted a resolution expressing pious approval of the Conference, and then, almost in the same breath, announced that the Belgian Minister of State, Vandervelde, required money, which will undoubtedly be used by him for the further demoralisation of the International. We would suggest to those members of. the E.C., who pose as the opposition in the B.S.P. to sit down fast on one of the two stools between which they are wavering. It is clearly impossible to support the manifesto of the Zimmerwald Conference and at the same time Vandervelde, Hyndman and company. The majority of the E.C. are so international that they did not even reprint and circulate the very mild manifesto issued by the Conference. Yet they are appealing for £200 for the 'reconstruction' of the International with Vandervelde sitting at its head.[25]

Petroff's criticisms eventually prompted a vicious response in the 23 December issue of *Justice*. In an anonymous paragraph, the journal advised workers on Clydeside to question the motives behind Petroff's presence in the area.

> Many of us have known of Peter Petroff for some years, though we have known little about him save that he has usually acted as a disintegrating nuisance. That he places a high value on his knowledge of and services to the Socialist movement we readily admit. He has now been for some weeks on the Clyde. What he is doing there, and what may be his object is best known to himself. It is for the representatives of the Glasgow workers to determine what is his status on the Clyde Workers' Committee, and to make whatever inquiries concerning him they may deem necessary. His recent scurrilous attacks on Emile Vandervelde, however, may enable some to judge of the manner of man he is. The International Socialist Bureau naturally requires money to function as well as it can under the present most difficult circumstances. To say that such money is going to be used by Vandervelde 'for the further demoralisation of the International' is a gross slander. We will leave the Executive committee of the B.S.P. to deal with his 'criticism' of their actions![26]

The article prompted strong condemnation from Georgy Chicherin, on behalf of the London branch of the Russian Social Democratic Labour Party, and from John Maclean whose scathing letter of 30 December to *Justice* pointed out that neither he nor his associates were dictated to by Petroff, but that he was working under their direction.[27]

On 17 January 1916 from Maclean's house in Newlands, Petroff himself wrote to *Justice* about the character assassination.

> It was a disgraceful, low, and stupid attack on me with the object both of injuring my political reputation and of assisting the British and Russian authorities in the action they have taken against me.
>
> This paragraph appeared on the same day I was arrested in Fife, where I was to speak at two meetings of miners. At the same time raids were made upon the offices of the Russian Seamen's Union and the Central Bureau of the Foreign Committee of the Russian Social-Democratic Labour Party. Thus the action of those responsible for 'Justice' curiously coincided with the action of the authorities.[28]

It was obvious that Petroff was squarely in the sights of the powers that be. In the week after Christmas, he was summonsed to appear in court on 3 January charged with failing to register as an alien in Glasgow on his return from Bowhill. The absurd contention was that as Petroff had registered in Lochgelly, a prohibited area, on Saturday 4 December and after giving his lecture, stayed over the weekend in Bowhill (having been unable to return to Glasgow the same night) he was deemed to have resided in a prohibited area and was required to register in Glasgow on his return on Monday.

In his autobiography, Petroff wrote that he was clearly aware what was happening. 'It was just a pretext – and a very stupid pretext – for a political persecution.' At the court hearing Petroff refuted the indictment point by point, but the sheriff was unmoved, found the Russian guilty, and sentenced him to two months imprisonment. Petroff protested the sentence and asked the sheriff to state a case for appeal to the High Court of Justiciary. He spent a week at Duke Street prison, but was released pending a decision on whether his appeal would be granted.

12
CONSCRIPTION

The continuing carnage on the Western Front and the failure of the British and Commonwealth campaign on the Gallipoli peninsula meant that by the end of summer 1915 the volunteer scheme promoted by Lord Kitchener was falling short in providing the number of troops required for the army. Compounding this problem were the schemes for limiting recruitment.

On the domestic front, the necessity of retaining workers in key industries, particularly in those involved in the manufacture of munitions, had become apparent by the end of 1914. The great armament firms complained that the drain of skilled workmen to the forces was affecting their output. This led to first the Admiralty, and then the War Office, drawing up lists of trades and firms whose workers were barred from enlisting. Partly to offset accusations of shirking and the distribution of white feathers, a system of War Service badges and certificates was instituted.[1]

When the Ministry of Munitions was created in July 1915, it was estimated that one-fifth of the men employed in essential munitions industries had enlisted.[2] The ministry took over the issuing of badges and checked the recruitment of skilled workers. It also refined the process of precisely identifying the industries, firms and occupations which needed protection from recruitment.

Realising they needed a stocktake of the country's resources, in July 1915 the government introduced the *National Registration Act 1915*. All men and women between the ages of 15 and 65 were required to provide details of their personal circumstances, their skills, employment, and whether they were undertaking government work. While Prime Minister Asquith said in answer to a question in the House of Commons that no scheme of forced labour or conscription was contemplated, it was immediately obvious that the Bill provided the basis for compulsion.

While the register was being compiled, in August 1915 a committee of Cabinet was appointed to consider the duties and requirements of the country and develop a policy to meet them. Looking to the campaign of 1916, the War Office considered it was the duty of the country to maintain 70 divisions in the field. A larger number could not be formed before the spring of 1916, even if conscription was introduced. The deficit in the production of munitions and the lack of efficient officers were among the key limiting factors.

To maintain 70 divisions in the field throughout 1916 would require 1,500,000 recruits over the following 12 months. Voluntary recruiting was producing 20,000 a month instead of the required 30,000. If the register revealed a pool of men available for the army who had not yet volunteered, the arguments for compulsion would be strengthened.[3]

The Treasury drew attention to another aspect of the situation. The economic and financial liabilities undertaken by the country were already straining its resources to the utmost. Expansion of the army would mean increased expenditure and diminished production; greater difficulty in financing the purchase in America of munitions, materials, and food essential to Britain and its allies; and increasing the risk of inflation, with its effects on the cost of living and wages.[4]

The report of the War Policy Committee to the government dated 7 September included a supplementary memorandum from the supporters of compulsion. It declared it was still within the power of the country to meet its obligations and maintain 70 divisions in the field, 'but we can only do this if all our resources in wealth and man power are employed without reserve with the most thorough and far-sighted efficiency'.[5] Lloyd George agreed. His point of view was dominated by the magnitude of Russian losses on the Eastern Front in 1915 and the implications for the Western Front;[6] the shortage of skilled labour due to recruitment; and the restriction of output by sectors of the workforce in munitions establishments.

The opponents of compulsion in the government included the First Lord of the Admiralty (and former Liberal prime minister) Arthur Balfour, who said that compulsion would be more likely to be generally accepted if it could be proved that the voluntary system could not meet the need for men. He argued any attempt to introduce compulsion before the military necessity for it was demonstrated would split the nation into bitterly opposed factions.[7]

Balfour's view was supported by the only Labour member of the Cabinet, Arthur Henderson, who also provided a supplementary memorandum to the committee's report. Henderson said there was great feeling in the country against conscription. He advised he had received more than 300 resolutions against it, from nearly all the important industries.

The main arguments Henderson put forward were that the working man did not believe he had an equal and legitimate share in government. Thousands of working men would deny the competence of the parliament elected under the current franchise and registration system to bind them on an issue affecting life and death. As a volunteer, the working man felt that the rich man fighting beside him had, like himself, made great sacrifices. As a conscript, he would feel that he had been placed in the trenches by the votes of rich men who were not there themselves.

If conscription was introduced in a passion of class feeling, Henderson argued, class feeling would attend the conscript army in the field. If the pay and conditions of the conscript were to be less than the volunteer, the dissatisfaction would be dangerous in its intensity. The working man believed that conscription was a capitalist weapon for interfering with the rights of the workman.

Only by exhausting the possibility of volunteering being able to meet the army's man power needs and proving the necessity of compulsion would disruption be avoided. And if compulsion was to be introduced, Henderson stressed there needed to be some guarantees. The inequalities in the electoral system should be removed by establishing universal suffrage. Taxation should be spread over all classes according to ability to pay, and should be aimed primarily at luxuries, unearned incomes, and war profits; and secondly at rents and profits in general. Conscription should not be continued after the war, special arrangements should be made to resettle soldiers into industry, and conscription should not be used to make any changes to existing industrial arrangements.[8]

The policy recommended by Messrs Balfour and Henderson was adopted.

~

As the government considered the conscription issue, the urgent need for more men to feed the European killing machine was highlighted by the Battle of Loos. Raging just north of Lens in northern France from 25 September to 8 October, it was the biggest offensive of the British Army during 1915. German defensive proficiency continued to prove superior, however, and the outcome was a British defeat. The total of 59,247 losses was more than 20 per cent of the total British casualties on the Western Front in 1915. The defeat, which many in command blamed on the lack of artillery shells, led to the replacement of Sir John French by Douglas Haig as commander-in-chief of the British Expeditionary Force in December 1915. Robert Graves' classic autobiography *Goodbye to All That* includes a detailed description of his experience at the Battle of Loos as a junior officer in the Royal Welch Fusiliers.

~

In his speeches and articles at this time, John Maclean was a fierce critic of conscription. In the *Vanguard*, he wrote:

> So far as mere trade unionists are concerned, we warn them that conscription means the bringing together of all young men under the control of the military authorities, whether they be in the field of battle or in the factory and workshop. Every controlled factor comes directly under military discipline as well, and thus the old as well as the young will be bound hand and foot to Mr William Weir and his capitalist friends. Military conscription implies industrial conscription, the most abject form of slavery the world has ever known.[9]

When James Macdougall went into print, he was equally scathing of what he saw as the ulterior motives of conscription's proponents. He also mounted a vehement defence of Maclean and the attempts being made to muzzle his comrade's voice.

> The parrot cries of the conscription gang are merely meant for the deception of the people. They know perfectly well that [should] any large proportion of the eligible workers still to be found in Britain be sent abroad then military, industrial and financial ruin will descend upon this country and her friends.
>
> Why do they want conscription? They desire it in order to destroy the liberties of the working class. Let the workers first be mobilised and, says the Simpleton, 'sent to the front'! No, you fool! Sent back into the workshop **under military law** [original emphasis]. Then indeed, we may say farewell to trade unionism. To-day it has reached the point of being almost completely shorn of its influence; under military law it will entirely disappear. Nothing will be left for the workers but illegal organisations and secret plotting in

cellars. Let it be repeated, again and again, these repressive measures are not merely for the 'duration of the war', but will be maintained so long as they serve capitalist interests.

This is the reason why the attacks of the capitalist press upon those who oppose resolutely industrial and military conscription have become so savage. In this way is explained the action of the Government in attempting to put out of the way such a vigorous and courageous fighter as John Maclean. They know well that in assailing Maclean for speeches in favour of peace, in defence of the interests of the working class, against all forms of conscription, they not only destroy the elementary political rights of the people, but pave the way for their reactionary plots against the people. Maclean stands in the way of conscription in Glasgow, of repressive legislation against the working class; he leads the fight against the house factors and all oppressors. Therefore – he must be eliminated, he must be deprived of his means of livelihood. While the Government uses its judicial machinery in order to gag him, the Govan School Board comes forward with a proposal to dismiss him – to separate him from the children of the people. They, however, are mistaken. Maclean will triumph together with the cause of the people.

Arouse yourselves, workers! Soon it will be too late. Do not rest content with congresses and resolutions. The war has placed power in your hands. Resort to action! Use your force wisely now and prevent conscription with its countless evil consequences from being imposed upon your class.[10]

~

Willie McGill, the Glasgow convenor of the Herald League,[11] had organised a public meeting in late November to protest against conscription, and to celebrate the release of Maclean after his five-day prison sentence. McGill asked the Free Speech Committee initiated by Maclean to co-operate and *Daily Herald* publisher George Lansbury and renowned suffragette and socialist Sylvia Pankhurst were invited to join Maclean on the platform. The City Hall was booked for Monday 29 November, a deposit was paid and tickets and posters issued.

Lansbury and Pankhurst travelled up from London together on the Sunday beforehand, but as soon as they reached Glasgow, they learned the lord provost, with the backing of the town council, had cancelled the booking and prohibited any meetings on the grounds they would be prejudicial to recruiting.

Sunday evening meetings for the London visitors were hastily organised by the British Socialist Party, the Independent Labour Party, the Govan

Trades Council, and the Clarion Scouts. Peter Petroff wrote, 'The two speakers whom the lord provost had desired to silence made a tour of those meetings, addressing a few words of encouragement to the workers at our Panoptican meeting, as well as at the Metropole, in the Pavilion and at Govan, being enthusiastically cheered at each meeting.'[12]

For Maclean the cancellation was like a red rag to a bull. The Free Speech Committee issued an urgent appeal to the workers titled 'The Town Council Scandal' in which they declared the doors must be opened on Monday and the demonstration proceed. Lansbury later wrote, 'John MacLean proclaimed far and wide that he would bring the lads from the Clydeside shipyards and docks armed with crowbars, hammers and spanners to break down any opposition which the authorities might organise to prevent us holding the meeting.'[13]

Peter Petroff recalled sitting cheerfully with Sylvia Pankhurst at Maclean's house having tea on the Monday when George Lansbury appeared in a panic.

> 'Comrades, the Chief Constable has warned me there will be bloodshed,' he [Lansbury] cried. 'Would it not be better to cancel the meeting?' This was met by great merriment.
>
> 'Sit down and have tea,' said Maclean, 'you can stay here if you are afraid. No police will prevent us from holding that meeting.'
>
> Seeing that his untimely peace mission fell on deaf ears, Lansbury became brave. 'Well comrades, if that is your decision I will come with you.'[14]

Pankhurst and Lansbury were taken by Bailie Stewart to see the lord provost, but he could not be found at the municipal offices. 'We saw the Town Clerk,' Pankhurst wrote, 'but he told us he had no power to revoke the lord provost's decision to refuse the hall. On being informed that the munitions workers were coming from the Clyde to attend the meeting, and since it was hinted by Lansbury and the others that they might prove riotous if flouted, the Town Clerk and the Chief Constable agreed that an open-air meeting might be held in Albion Street, a narrow throughfare near, but not too near, the City Hall. To hold the meeting in the big square in front of the Town Hall, would seem like 'defiance' of the lord provost's orders. The meeting in Albion Street was agreed to by Lansbury and the local men.'[15]

On the Monday evening, a crowd of over 3,000 munitions workers and others stood for two hours in the rain listening to vigorous speeches. 'The night proved so wet it was a marvel to get any audience at all,' Pankhurst wrote. 'Yet in the almost pitch-darkness of war-time nights, thousands of men and women stood in the drenching rain and puddles ankle-deep, to cheer defiant words.'

Peter Petroff quotes from an article in the *Herald* by a special correspondent who had been sent to cover the event.

> Glasgow in these days is wonderful. It is a place of many meetings, a place rumbling with revolt. I would recommend any pessimistic progressive to spend a week in Glasgow. Yes, Glasgow is a tonic, a holiday and a pick-me-up all in one ... If the Labour Party is weak; if the rest of civilisation is on the road to decay, we have still got Glasgow. The movement in Glasgow ought to float itself as a Limited Liability Company to supply backbone to the rest of the United Kingdom.[16]

From the experience, and her other interactions with him, Pankhurst provided the following pen sketch of John Maclean.

> Maclean was then widely regarded as the most revolutionary propagandist in Glasgow. Thick-set and swarthy as a Neapolitan, he recalled to me irresistibly the thought of a great brown bear. His small eyes, dark and twinkling, his mouth, opening unusually wide, seemed to show, as he talked, his entire set of gleaming white teeth, like a dog, at times playfully opening his mouth in a game, at others drawing his lips back with a snarl. Both expressions were common in him. A kindly fellow, gentle and probably incapable of belligerent action, his mind leapt ever to theoretical extremes. His economics class, inaugurated ten years before, was spoken of as a dynamic focus of discontent in Glasgow, and he with bated breath as a 'wild man' ...
>
> Yet he had caused many young men to think and read for themselves, and many spoke of him with gratitude, almost with reverence. The iconoclast of iconoclasts, I have heard him in his hoarse voice, with delighted smiles, expound to his class the Marxian theory of Labour values, and repeating the parable of the three coats, as though the very hearing of it were the universal cure-all, the true wine of life.[17]

Pankhurst was also intrigued by the Clyde Workers' Committee, writing: 'Having a similar conception of the co-operative social order which would some day replace this sad era of conflict, I was eager to come in contact with the pioneers who were leading this workshop movement.' She gave these impressions of Kirkwood:

Kirkwood ... was in those days a fair, well-knit man, in appearance more like an Army officer than a factory worker. An I.L.P.er and later a Labour Member of Parliament, he was singularly unlike the typical members of the Left Wing industrial movement, with which, as it proved, his connection was brief. He knew little, if anything, of the doctrines of Marx and De Leon; his opinions were often utterly illogical and inconsistent; but he was the sort of good-natured, impulsive, emotional person who can rise to the occasion when indignation and enthusiasm need a leader and a spice of daring is required to take the lead.[18]

Of Willie Gallacher, she wrote:

Gallacher was a jolly and volatile fellow, more Irish than Scotch in blood and temperament. He had a fund of genuine kindliness, was ready to help any work-mate in trouble. Genial and brotherly, almost paternal in manner, though he had barely reached his forties, he seemed impelled by a readiness not to climb out of the workshop on the back of his mates, but to struggle for the betterment of his class. This trait endeared him to men who were smarting under the desertion of their Trade Union officials.

In his lighter moments, Gallacher prided himself as a rhymester; his particular *penchant* was for humorous songs. [Arthur] McManus poured scorn on such efforts and once, as Gallacher told me plaintively, had even destroyed the manuscript of some of his most cherished jingles. In the view of McManus, it was Gallacher's duty not to act the irresponsible comedian but to add dignity and popularity to the Clyde Workers' Committee.[19]

~

On Sunday 12 December, which was the final day for recruits to volunteer under the Derby scheme (see below) large 'No Conscription' and 'Free Speech' meetings were held in Glasgow. Many of the leading lights of the socialist movement spoke and were booked by the police for obstructing North Hanover and North Frederick Streets. Those who subsequently went to trial at the Central Police Court on 29 December included John Maclean, Willie Gallacher, James Maxton, Emmanuel Shinwell, Arthur MacManus, Harry Hopkins, and Councillor P J Dollan.[20]

For the meeting chaired by Shinwell the charge was 'That on the 12th day of December 1915, occasion an obstruction in North Hanover Street, by causing to place thereon a horse and a lorry and respectively delivering speeches from said lorry causing a crowd of persons to assemble on said street, and preventing the free passage along or through the same.' The trial lasted six hours and although the charge was proved 'on technical grounds', no convictions were recorded or punishments imposed.[21]

~

The last effort of voluntary recruiting was led by Lord Derby. His object was to canvass and if possible, enlist every man of military age and fitness who was not required for munitions work or other indispensable services at home. Those who wished to join up at once would be allowed to. The rest would be divided into groups who could be called up as they were needed.

The announcement of the scheme caused an initial rise in recruitment, as some men preferred to go to the recruiting office rather than wait for the inevitable. The process began with each eligible man's registry card, from the August 1915 National Registry, being copied onto another card which was sent to his local constituency's parliamentary recruiting committee. This committee appointed 'canvassers' who they considered 'tactful and influential men', and not themselves liable for service, to visit the men in their homes. Many canvassers were experienced in politics, though discharged veterans and the fathers of serving soldiers proved the most effective, while some just used threats to persuade. Although women were not allowed to canvas, they did contribute by tracking men who had moved address.

Every man would be given a copy of a letter from the Earl of Derby, explaining the program and stating that they were in 'a country fighting, as ours is, for its very existence' and had to state whether or not he was willing to attest to enlist.

Those who did agree to attest had to promise to present themselves at their recruiting office within 48 hours, while some were accompanied there immediately.

The scheme was undertaken during November–December 1915 and Lord Derby's report, dated 20 December 1915, was made public on 4 January 1916. The scheme obtained 318,553 medically fit single men, but the report showed that over a million single men had not offered themselves for service, of whom just over 650,000 were not exempted by reason of their occupation. The following day, Prime Minister Asquith introduced the first Military Service Bill, which for the first time in Britain's history provided for compulsory conscription.[22]

Every unmarried man and childless widower between 18 and 41 was offered three choices: enlist at once; attest at once under Derby's system; or on 2 March 1916 be automatically deemed to have enlisted.

The Bill became law on 27 January 1916.

13
LLOYD GEORGE COMES TO GLASGOW

To address issues that had arisen from the operation of the Munitions of War Act, in September 1915 a decision was made to draft an amending Bill. The principal reason was legal advice that government factories could not be declared controlled establishments, because the Crown could not be bound by the regulations and penalties that applied to such workplaces. An amending Bill also provided an opportunity to deal with the unforeseen consequences of requiring munitions workers to obtain a leaving certificate from their employers when changing jobs. Evidence taken by the Balfour-Macassey Commission into the grievances of the Clyde munitions workers was considered in framing the Bill, and one of the new rules required employers to give leaving certificates to workmen on dismissal or discharge, and to prohibit the entry of any mark or observation on the certificate.

The Bill affected the Ministry of Munitions in two important aspects. It gave the ministry the power to grant certificates of exemption from military service and it made certain provisions to prevent industrial conscription.

In the debate on industrial compulsion several fears were raised. The most obvious was that unscrupulous employers might use the liability of their workmen to military service on dismissal to counter claims for better wages and conditions. Another possibility was that the state might coerce a workman by threatening to send him to the trenches if he refused to work where, how or for whom he was told. And thirdly, there was the scenario that enlisted men subject to military law might be employed in large numbers in munitions work to break strikes, lower wages, and diminish conditions.

After considering comments from the unions and employers, an Amendment Bill was introduced to parliament on 9 December. It was read for the second time on 15 December and considered in committee on 17

December. The plan was to take the Bill to report stage on 22 December, but after appeals from various MPs, Prime Minister Asquith agreed to postpone further consideration of the Bill until the first sitting of the new year.

~

Punishing incitement to strike was one of the original motives of the amending Bill. When a clause about this was felt to be a 'violently contentious measure' and might hold up the whole Bill, it was removed and instead given effect by Order in Council on 30 November which amended Regulation 42 of the Defence of the Realm Act. The new version, [addition in italics] would prove to be of major consequence to the life and work of John Maclean. It ran:

> If any person attempts to cause mutiny, sedition or disaffection among any of His Majesty's Forces or among the civilian population, *or to impede, delay or restrict the production, repair or transport of war material or any other work necessary for the successful prosecution of the war,* he shall be guilty of an offence against these Regulations.[1]

The drastic power of the Regulation was raised on 4 January 1916 by Walter Roch, the Liberal MP for Pembrokeshire, in the debate about abolishing imprisonment for munitions offences. Roch noted the Regulation enabled the penalty of penal servitude for life. He was reassured by Lloyd George that no person guilty of an offence under the Munitions Act could possibly be dealt with under the Regulation. 'The workman who turns up late, or breaks Regulations, or commits a breach of discipline is dealt with under the Munitions Act, but the cases referred to under the Order in Council are those in which there is incitement to mutiny to prevent workmen from doing their best to assist in the output of munitions,' Lloyd George stated.

William Anderson, Labour MP for Sheffield Attercliffe, also had concerns about the revised Regulation 42. 'The words used in Council are very wide and very vague,' he said, before going on to seek reassurance they could not include offences under the Munitions Act. Lloyd George said he would take counsel's advice on the words. But Anderson had made a very good point. The 'wide and vague' words in Regulation 42 were a very broad brush with which to go after those whom the government wanted out of the way.[2]

~

On Monday 20 December 1915, Lloyd George gave a major speech to the House of Commons reviewing the work of the Ministry of Munitions since its formation in July. He concluded the speech with an appeal to labour.

> We have appealed to the employers, and they say they have not got the labour, and it is true. They have not got the skilled labour. There are many of these operations that can be effectively enough discharged by unskilled men and women. We have done everything to supply skilled labour and to increase its efficiency. We have done our best to secure good conditions of labour and to get munitions volunteers to fill up the gaps. We have tried to get men from the colours. It was almost like cutting barbed wire entanglements without guns. There were entrenchments behind entrenchments. Everyone fought to prevent the men coming away.
>
> We have been able to get a considerable number of men, but nothing like enough and it all depends on organised Labour. Unless they allow us to place unskilled men and women in work which hitherto has been the monopoly of skilled workmen you cannot do it. The leaders of the trade unions in Parliament agreed, but we found exactly the same difficulties as we found in the release of men from the colours. There is an action to be fought in every area, every district, every town, every workshop, every lodge – they all fight against it.
>
> The weakness is this. Our bargain was that we should restrict the profits of the employer to a certain extent, and the fact we have kept our bargain has been against us. A few employers have done their very best to dilute the labour, and they have been met with unquestionable resistance. The rest of the employers know this and say at any rate – 'We have no personal interest in the matter. If we increase the output by means of night shifts it does not increase our profits.' The personal interest has been completely eliminated and when men are working hard, superintending anxious work, and suffering from overstrain, they really do not feel like embarking on a conflict with their own men to increase the output.
>
> There is only one appeal to employer and employed. It is the appeal to patriotism. The employer must take steps. He is loath to do it. It is a sort of inertia which comes to tired and overstrained men, as they all are. They must really face the local trade unions, and put forward the demand, because until they do the State cannot come in. We have had an Act of Parliament, but the law must be put into operation by somebody, and unless the employer begins by putting on unskilled men and women to the lathes, we cannot enforce that Act of Parliament. The first step therefore is that the employer

must challenge a decision on the matter, and he is not doing so because of the trouble which a few firms have had. But let us do it.³

~

The schedule for Lloyd George's long-planned visits to Newcastle and Glasgow to plead the case for dilution had originally included a day in each city. He travelled to Newcastle on Wednesday 22 December, arriving in the afternoon and holding a meeting in the evening with shop stewards and union officials. While in Newcastle, a statement was issued that Lloyd George had decided to extend his visit to Glasgow and had arranged to spend three days on the Clyde, visiting various workplaces before meeting with the shop stewards and union officials. In addition, a meeting that had been arranged by officials of the Federation of Engineering and Shipbuilding Trades for the evening of Thursday 23 December, at St Andrew's Halls in Granville Street, was cancelled and arrangements were made for a new meeting at the same venue on Saturday 25 December.

Lloyd George and his entourage, which included Arthur Henderson, chairman of the Parliamentary Labour Party, arrived at Glasgow's Queen Street Station on Thursday afternoon. Prominent among the greeting party were Lord Murray of Eubank, director-general of Munitions Workers Recruiting and William Weir, director of munitions for Scotland.

First port of call for Lloyd George and his party was Parkhead Forge, where they were met by the works' owner Sir William Beardmore and Admiral Adair, manager of the ordnance factory. After visiting the 18-pounder field gun shop and the heavy gun shop, where they witnessed the forging of an ingot for a heavy naval gun, they returned to the main offices where they met the shop stewards.

The Clyde Workers' Committee had originally decided to boycott Lloyd George altogether, but not for the last time, Parkhead's convenor of stewards David Kirkwood broke ranks. As Ian McLean observed:

> Any revolutionary egalitarianism that David Kirkwood might have possessed was tempered by a large dose of snobbery, or (to put it more generously) pardonable self-interest at the way in which he was accustomed to deal on equal terms with Sir William Beardmore. He was clearly so delighted at receiving a telegraphed summons from Lloyd George addressed to David Kirkwood, Parkhead Forge, Glasgow and asking the Parkhead shop stewards to meet Lloyd George that he agreed with relish ...⁴

Kirkwood was invited to chair the meeting; a role he accepted on condition he would be free to put questions and discuss what was said.

'This is Mr Lloyd George,' Kirkwood began. 'He has come specially to speak with you, and no doubt you will give him a patient hearing. I can assure him that every word he says will be carefully weighed. We regard him with suspicion because every act with which his name is associated has the taint of slavery about it.' He would find that as Scotsmen they resented this, and if he desired to get the best out of them, he must treat them with justice and respect.[5]

Somewhat taken aback, Lloyd George gathered himself and launched into his pitch, urging the need for guns and shells, and the necessity of using unskilled labour for work on which skilled men were currently employed.

When he had finished, Kirkwood asked him if he was prepared to give the workers a share in the management of the works. As socialists, he said, they welcomed dilution of labour, which they regarded as the natural development in industrial relations. But this scheme of dilution must be carried out under the control of the workers. Otherwise, cheap labour would be introduced. Unless their demand was granted, he said, they would fight the scheme to the death.

When Lloyd George responded by saying that the workers were not capable of managing the workshops, Kirkwood cut him off.

'These men, for whom I ask a say in the management, carry the confidence of the workers and have confidence in themselves,' he said angrily. 'They brought out the men of the Clyde in February in defiance of you, in defiance of the government, in defiance of the army, and in defiance of the trade union leaders. They led them out and they led them back victorious. They let it be known that if their demands were not met, masters might force them back to the workshops but could not make them work.'

Kirkwood was on a roll. Who ran the workshops now? Men drawn from the ranks of the working class. The only change would be responsibility to the workers rather than the present employers. If production was to be improved the benefit must go to the workers.

Lloyd George replied that this was a revolutionary proposal, and the present was not a time for revolutions, when the country was engaged in a life and death struggle with a foreign foe. (Given the revolution the Munitions of War Act had already wrought on industry, this was a moot point.)

There followed a discussion on the Munitions of War Act, during which Kirkwood remarked that it bound the workers at Beardmore's as effectively as if they had a capital B branded on their foreheads.

Lloyd George said he was not responsible for the Munitions Act. It emanated from their leaders, indicating Arthur Henderson and James Brownlie (secretary of the Amalgamated Society of Engineers), who were in attendance. Kirkwood turned towards Henderson and retorted: 'We repudiate this man. He is no leader of ours. Brownlie had been told the same to his face. And if you, Mr Lloyd George, want to know the mind of the workers, don't go to these men. If you wish to do away with discontent in the workshops, do away with the cause.'[6]

With Kirkwood's robust declarations ringing in his ears, Lloyd George and his party moved on to the Cathcart works of Messrs G & J Weir, former fiefdom of his Scottish appointee William Weir. The minister's party inspected the new Flanders factory for producing heavy shells and the aircraft factory, where they were shown the latest designs in British war planes. But if Weir thought he had tamed his factory's shop stewards after their February strike, he was sadly mistaken. Lloyd George met the management board of the Glasgow and West of Scotland munitions area in the firm's offices, but the shop stewards refused to meet with him. 'If Lloyd George wants to discuss conditions on the Clyde,' said Jack Smith, the convenor of shop stewards, 'tell him he'll have to discuss them with the Clyde Workers' Committee.'[7]

~

Lloyd George's last-minute change in meeting arrangements was not appreciated by the workmen. A meeting of union delegates to the Federation of Engineering and Shipbuilding Trades, which had organised the initial conference, was held at the Amalgamated Society of Engineers Hall in Carlton Place on Thursday evening. Willie Gallacher gave an account of the meeting in *Revolt on the Clyde*:

> Sharp, Lorimer and Bunting[8] were at the table at the end of the hall, sorting out bundles of tickets. When they had the tickets sorted out to their liking, Sharp reported on the visit to Newcastle. He told us that the Minister had asked them to arrange a meeting of the shop stewards for Saturday, the twenty-fifth, in St. Andrew's Hall, the tickets for which he had supplied, and these were now before us, so many for each union. The Minister had agreed

to pay each shop steward 7s 6d for expenses, so they would have to be careful in distributing tickets, as each one represented that amount.

As soon as he had finished, Harry Hill, of the Shipwrights, walked up to the table, got his tickets, and turned to leave the hall. I jumped to my feet and said, 'Brother Chairman, before Brother Hill leaves with those tickets, we've got to discuss and decide whether we're going to have anything to do with the meeting.' There was quite a commotion following this, in the midst of which Hill went stamping out of the hall. But he was scarcely out when the door burst open and he was back in.

'There's your tickets,' he shouted. 'To hell wi' them, and to hell wi' you. By Christ, I never met your equal for making trouble!' He slammed the tickets down and went banging out again. We all had a laugh at this, after which I addressed the meeting.[9]

Gallacher argued against participating in the meeting, asking, 'Are we to be at the beck and call of this avowed enemy of the trade union movement?' and when it was put to a vote, 60 of the delegates voted against participating with only 5 in favour.

When Sam Bunton saw how the vote was going, he slipped out of the meeting and got on the phone to the Central Station Hotel, where Lloyd George's party were staying. On his return, he told the delegates that Arthur Henderson had asked him if he could come over and have the opportunity of saying a few words to the meeting. It being past 10 pm, Gallacher said, half-jokingly, 'Tell him we'll wait if he'll provide us with taxis when the meeting's over.' Bunton left the hall briefly and when he came back, he said, 'Mr Henderson thanks you very much and he has instructed his secretary to order a fleet of taxis.'

Henderson duly arrived and made his appeal for the workmen to assist Lloyd George in the great fight he was making to win the war. Gallacher then produced a speech Lloyd George had recently given in Manchester in which he attacked the trade unions. As a trade unionist, Gallacher asked Henderson, would he repudiate Lloyd George's statement? When Henderson refused to do so, Gallacher appealed to the meeting.

'Isn't it clear that Henderson isn't here as a free agent? He is permitted to come and speak to us as the servant of one of our worst enemies. How is it that a man can fall so low? Fellow members, let us send him back with a message to his master that the Clyde trade unionists are not the lackeys of the workers' enemies.'[10]

The vote was taken again, with the same result as before.

~

The next morning, Gallacher was at work when he received a message from Lord Murray requesting his attendance at a meeting at the Central Station Hotel. On arrival he found a group of union officials from the previous night's meeting. Lloyd George was absent so Lord Murray chaired the meeting. He told the officials what a wonderful man Lloyd George was, how much he sympathised with the workers; how under normal circumstances he would do anything for the workers, but now his one thought was victory in the war. Would they help him?

When he had finished, everyone in the room looked at Gallacher. 'None of us here are prepared to accept the statement that Lloyd George is, or ever was, a friend of the workers,' Gallacher countered. 'If he's so keen on winning the war, let him tackle the employers, stop their profits. They're piling up profits at our expense. However, that's our war, the war against the employers. We don't mind him being with them. It's what we expect, but when he asks us to assist him in carrying through their plans, that's treating us cheap, to say the least of it.'

Bailie Whitehead jumped to his feet to interject. 'My Lord Murray,' he said. 'This man is out for bloody revolution. He is not here representing trade unionists. He is here representing a group of irresponsible revolutionaries like himself and they don't care if the war is won or not.'

Once the hubbub that followed had died down, Sam Bunton rose slowly to his feet. 'My Lord,' he said, pointing at Gallacher. 'This man has been repudiated by his own people.'

'What do you mean?' asked Lord Murray.

'My Lord,' replied Bunton, 'while he was at our meeting last night getting us to turn down the Lloyd George meeting, his own committee [the Clyde Workers' Committee] met at the Central Hall and decided to carry on with it. A group of them came round to our hall this morning and took away the tickets.'

Lord Murray looked at him in consternation. He immediately realised what Bunton had failed to grasp.

When Gallacher confirmed that the Clyde Workers' Committee had indeed scooped up the tickets for the Christmas Day meeting, Lord Murray left the room to consult with Lloyd George who had just returned to the hotel. Shortly afterwards, the two men returned and Lord Murray abruptly declared the meeting over. As the union officials filed out in some confusion, he asked Gallacher to stay.

When everyone else had gone, Lloyd George asked Gallacher if he could arrange for the Clyde Workers' Committee to meet with him that evening. Certainly, Gallacher replied, we'll meet you here at seven o'clock.

~

At the appointed time, Gallacher, together with Johnny Muir, David Kirkwood, Arthur MacManus, James Messer, Tommy Clark, and others, including two women workers who had been added to the committee, returned to the Central Hotel where Lloyd George and his colleagues awaited.

Lloyd George gave the CWC his standard speech about the ravages of war, how munitions were the key to victory, how thousands of new workers were needed and concluded by saying he recognised 'that strong spirit of independence that would never tolerate the military domination of Germany' and he knew they were 'the very men to rely on in a crisis'.

Gallacher then called on Johnny Muir 'one of the best comrades in the movement for presenting and arguing a case' to respond.[11]

The CWC's position on dilution had obviously evolved because Muir said the committee had no objection to the principle of dilution. He explained:

> We regard it as progressive from the point of view that it simplifies the labour process, makes labour more mobile, and tends to increase output. In short, it is a step in the direct line of industrial evolution. But – and this is where the present difficulties arise – its progressive character is lost to the community unless it is accompanied by a corresponding step in social evolution.[12]

Muir said dilution had been going on tardily for some months, not with the goodwill and co-operation of the skilled men, but against their sullen and barely concealed opposition. Instinctively the mass of the workers felt that their future was menaced.

The concern was that large scale dilution would be used by the employers to introduce cheap labour. The employers would gain; but the standard of the whole working class would be lowered.

So long as real safeguards were absent, he continued, there would be no hearty co-operation between the skilled men and the newcomers.

Trouble could be averted only by making the scheme of dilution conform to three conditions. Its benefits should not accrue to any one class in the community; it should not react detrimentally on any grade of labour; and organised labour must have a share in controlling it.

The CWC position was that these conditions could only be fulfilled if the government took over the factories, right out of the hands of the employers, and that organised labour took on the role, directly and equally with the present managers, of the management and administration of the workplaces.[13]

While Muir was speaking, Gallacher noticed Lloyd George's attention starting to wander. 'I have never in all my life seen such a pitiful example of uncontrollable conceit,' Gallacher wrote in *Revolt on the Clyde*.

> He brushed at his moustache, he pawed at his hair, looking around to see if he was the centre of attention. His 'yes-men' played up to him. They had their eyes on him, not on Johnny Muir. Then to crown it all, he turned to [Arthur] Henderson on his right, and started whispering. This meant he was half-turned away from Johnny Muir.
>
> I suddenly said, 'That'll do Johnny. Stop!'
>
> Johnny stopped. They all sat up with a start. Addressing Lloyd George, I remarked, 'Excuse me, Mr Lloyd George. If you don't want to hear us, we'll go. We're not here to waste our time.'
>
> 'But I've been listening,' he hurriedly exclaimed. 'I've heard every word.'
>
> 'You haven't been listening,' I said. 'All the boys here know you haven't. As for you, Henderson, you ought to be ashamed of yourself. You, a trade unionist, lending yourself to such indifference when a fellow trade unionist is stating a difficult case. Either you give Johnny attention or we go.'
>
> 'Please go on, Mr Muir,' Lloyd George begged. 'It's very interesting.'[14]

Muir finished his address with everyone's full attention. David Kirkwood, Arthur MacManus and the two women on the committee also spoke, then Lloyd George responded.

Rarely had it been his pleasure to hear a case so clearly and ably put, he said, but the proposals were impossible; he could not consider them.

'Why not?' Gallacher interjected.

'Because,' Lloyd George said, 'it would mean a revolution, and you can't carry through a revolution in the midst of a war.'

Discussion then moved on to the arrangements for the 'conference' the following day. Lloyd George proposed that Arthur Henderson, as chairman, would speak for about 20 minutes, then Lloyd George for 60 minutes, and then he would answer a few written questions.

In response, the CWC proposed Henderson speak for two minutes, Lloyd George for 30 minutes, then Johnny Muir with a statement about the committee's views, followed by a discussion on the floor.

Lloyd George rejected the counter offer.

The meeting broke up, and the members of the CWC left the room. As they were donning their hats and coats, one of Lloyd George's secretaries came running out. 'Oh, Mr Gallacher,' he said. 'Mr Lloyd George would like a word with you.'

Gallacher asked the rest of the committee whether he should go back in. They said, yes, let's see what he has to say.

Putting his arm around Gallacher's shoulders in a familiar manner, Lloyd George said he was very anxious that the meeting would be a success and since it was obvious that Gallacher had the confidence of his colleagues, he wanted to make a personal appeal for Gallacher's support. Would Gallacher come on the platform with him?

Gallacher replied that he would, on one condition. That Lloyd George had half an hour, then Johnny Muir, then an open discussion.

'Conditions, conditions, conditions,' an exasperated Lloyd George responded. 'You know I can't accept such conditions.'

'Well,' said Gallacher, 'you can't get our support and believe me, you won't get anywhere without it.'

'I can't talk to you – you're impossible,' Lloyd George barked, and went barging out of the room.[15]

Gallacher rejoined his comrades and they had a good laugh. The scene was set for a Christmas Day showdown.

~

Peter Petroff gave an account of the St Andrew's Halls' meeting in his memoir. 'The British Socialist Party had in connection with this meeting issued a leaflet printed on red paper; this we distributed in front of the hall,' he wrote. 'A strong police force protected the entrance to the hall, also inside the hall there were many police. Maclean and I had been supplied with tickets by the workers, but when I approached the entrance just about to produce my ticket, a group of workers from Weir's works came up, took me in their midst and said to the scrutinising police inspector: 'he needs no card, he belongs to us.'"[16]

There had been considerable anxiety at the Ministry of Munitions about how Lloyd George would be received by workers on the Clyde, and how his visit might be reported. Accordingly, the ministry instructed the Press Bureau to issue a D notice (D335) on 24 December, which stated, in part:

> Mr Lloyd George will address a meeting in Glasgow tomorrow and it is particularly requested that no report other than the authorised version of his speech should be published. Should any disturbance occur at or in the neighbourhood of the meeting the Press are earnestly requested to refrain from publishing any reference to it.[17]

The major newspapers, including the *Glasgow Herald* and the *Times*, duly published the authorised version on Monday 27 December. The report was prepared by a Press Association reporter and circulated to the papers which subscribed to that association. In a signal to its readers, the *Glasgow Herald* prefaced its account with the words, 'We are authorised to publish the following report: – ...'

The Glasgow socialist journal *Forward*, which was neither on the Press Bureau circulation list nor a member of the Press Association, published its own account of the meeting, based on the shorthand notes of one of its own reporters. Its report, generally acknowledged as a more accurate account of the stormy reception Lloyd George received, not only landed *Forward* in a whole lot of trouble, as will be detailed shortly, but also had ramifications for other Clydeside-based journals and the people who published and wrote for them.

Introducing *Forward*'s report, editor Tom Johnston, wrote:

> We have no desire to touch on the military or 'preparedness' side of the speech, but the purely political side must not go unrepresented. It is simply stupid to go about deluding people that only an insignificant minority, and not the vast overwhelming majority of the meeting was angry ...

The meeting began with a storm of hissing and booing, *Forward* reported, and the chairman (Arthur Henderson) suffered a running fire of interruption. On rising to speak, Lloyd George was received with loud and continued booing and hissing. There was some cheering and a score of hats were waved in the area, but the meeting was violently hostile. Two verses of 'The Red Flag' were sung before the minister could utter a word. Owing to the incessant interruption and the numerous altercations going on throughout the hall, it was quite impossible to catch every word of Lloyd George's speech.

After some minutes of the cacophony, David Kirkwood stood up and appealed to the meeting to hear the speaker. Some semblance of order was restored and Lloyd George's closing remarks were able to be heard. He said:

> Mr Kirkwood did not restrain himself from telling me what he thought about the Munitions Act and about me; but at any rate, he knows the value of free speech, and I am very thankful to him for his assistance in obtaining order ... I have but one more word to say. I want to talk to you in all sincerity as a man brought up in a worker's home. I know as much about the life of a worker as any man here. The responsibility of a Minister of the Crown in a great war is not an enviable one. ('The money's good,' and laughter.) I can assure you it is no laughing matter.
>
> ... There will be unheard of changes in every country in Europe; changes that go to the root of our social system. You Socialists watch them. It is a convulsion of nature; not a merely a cyclone that sweeps away the ornamental plants of modern society and wrecks the flimsy trestle-tables of modern civilisation – it is more. It is an earthquake that upheaves the very rocks of European life.
>
> And to go on chaffering about a regulation here, and the suppression of a custom there, under these conditions, why it is just haggling with an earthquake. Workmen, may I make one appeal to you? (Interruption.) Lift up your eyes above the mist of suspicion and distrust. Rise to the heights of the great opportunity now before you. If you do, you will emerge after this War is over into a future which has been the dream of many a great leader. (Cheers; loud hissing and booing.)[18]

At the close of his address, Lloyd George proceeded to answer the written questions that had been handed up from the body of the hall. He promised to reply to them all if he possibly could, but he had an appointment at 12 o'clock, and he said if he failed to get through them, the remaining answers would be published.

At this point, the BSP leaflets handed out before the meeting had an effect. 'We were aware that Ministers had acquired a peculiar habit of bringing harmless questions with them prepared by their secretaries,' wrote Peter Petroff. 'We had therefore advised those near us to write their

13 Lloyd George comes to Glasgow

Minister of Munitions David Lloyd George (front row, third from left) and the platform party at the meeting with the Clyde Workers' Committee, at St Andrew's Halls on Christmas Day 1915.

questions on the back of our red leaflets. This advice had been followed by a number of them. When Lloyd George got up to reply holding in his hand a pack of only white papers those who had sent up questions written on coloured paper got very angry and shouted: "Answer our questions! These are not our questions." Unaware of the reason for their anger, Lloyd George repeated: "But I am answering".' An uproar followed.[19]

Amid the furore, Johnny Muir of the Clyde Workers' Committee got up on his seat and demanded an opportunity of stating the case for the workers. This, he said, had been promised, and he was not going to wait any longer. Both Lloyd George and Arthur Henderson appealed to him to resume his seat; but Muir was determined not to be put off. As it was impossible to hear either the minister or Muir, the chairman closed the proceedings and the meeting broke up in disorder.[20]

14

SUPPRESSION OF *FORWARD* AND THE *VANGUARD*

The Ministry of Munitions was deeply interested in Clydeside and the effects of socialism in the west of Scotland on the munitions drive. It had been collating information from various sources for some time to balance the appropriate mix of concessions and coercion to deliver dilution of labour. The attempt to manage press coverage of Lloyd George's visit through the issuing of a D notice on 24 December illustrates the sensitivity it felt. The fact that *Forward*, a well-read journal in the region that was highly likely to report on the visit, did not receive the notice has led some to speculate that the oversight was deliberate.[1]

On the afternoon of 31 December 1915, the January issue of *Forward* went on sale. As soon as Glasgow officials of the ministry obtained a copy, they contacted London. Their message was that the issue contained an account of the meeting at St Andrew's Halls that deviated from the official version, and included details of the interruptions and injections that had disrupted the meeting. Publication of the article, 'was likely to have an extremely unfortunate effect on the feeling of the men on the Clyde, to throw obstacles in the way of carrying out the dilution of labour, and to impede seriously the production of munitions'.[2]

That evening at a meeting attended by Lloyd George, his Parliamentary Secretary Dr Christopher Addison and three senior civil servants (Sir Hubert Llewelyn Smith, W.H. Beveridge, and Charles Rey), it was provisionally decided to suppress the issue and seize all the copies.[3]

Rey took the train to Edinburgh, and on 2 January, met with the Lord Advocate, Robert Munro and the Commander-in-Chief, Scottish Command, General Sir Spencer Ewart. It was decided to proceed with the seizure.

Instructions were issued to the police to seize all copies of the issue, and the machinery of the Civic Press where it had been printed, under Regulations 2, 18, 27 and 51 of the Defence of the Realm Regulations.

The following day, a contingent of police and soldiers raided and occupied the *Forward* office and the adjacent Civic Press. All copies of the 1 January issue were seized and over subsequent days newsagents and even subscribers' houses were visited to track down copies that had been distributed.

At the Civic Press, the proofs of the January issue of the *Vanguard* were also discovered. The paper included an article about the St Andrew's Halls meeting by John Maclean. It said that the men:

> ... laughed cynically and irreverently that a Cabinet Minister, a member of the Government, ultimately responsible for the campaign against political liberty, pleaded for a fair hearing ... Seldom has a leading representative of the governing class been treated with so little respect by a meeting of workers.[4]

The proofs were seized and on 8 January the *Vanguard* was suppressed by the police on military authority under the Defence of the Realm Regulations.

~

On 4 January, questions were asked in the House of Commons about the actions of the authorities. William Anderson, Labour MP for Sheffield Attercliffe, asked the Lord Advocate, Robert Munro, upon whose authority and by whose orders *Forward* had been seized and on what grounds? William Pringle, Liberal MP for North West Lanarkshire, asked whether the newspaper had been suppressed, if so, under what Regulation or Order in Council this had been done, and whether the editor would be brought to trial and proceedings conducted in public? And Robert Outhwaite, Liberal MP for Hanley, Staffordshire asked whether the paper had been seized because of a report of a recent meeting held by the minister of munitions showing he received a hostile reception from organised labour on the Clyde?[5]

Lloyd George said that if he had been given notice about the questions, he could have shown that *Forward* had been deliberately inciting the workers not to carry out an Act of Parliament designed to promote the output of munitions. Under pressure from MPs, the prime minister agreed to consider listing the matter for discussion at a future date.

When the matter was fully debated on the evening of Monday 10 January,[6] William Pringle led off. He noted that the Press Bureau had issued a notice to forbid the publication of any but the official version of Lloyd George's speech. But the notice had not been sent to the editor of *Forward*, despite it being well known to be one of the most widely circulated weekly newspapers in the area. The expectation would have been that the Press Bureau would have sent out a report. But it did not. What was sent out was a report by the Press Association,[7] passed by the Press Bureau. If you were not a member of the Press Association (which *Forward* was not) you did not receive a copy of the report.

Pringle then gave an account of Lloyd George's Clyde meetings, with details provided to him by those who had attended. He said he understood that the minister should desire an official report issued, because he desires a free hand, free from press reporters, when he speaks frankly about the supplies available to the army and our allies. The minister is therefore extremely desirous that nothing that might be contrary to public interest should be published in the press. But in this case, Pringle said, the editor of the paper took the utmost pains to omit every single reference in the speech to the supplies of munitions.

Pringle went on to consider Regulation 27 of the Defence of the Realm Regulations, under which it was alleged the paper committed an offence. Reading it sentence by sentence, he asked:

> 'No person shall by word of mouth or in writing or in any newspaper periodical, book, circular or other printed publications spread false reports.'
>
> Is this a false report?
>
> 'Or make false statements, or reports or statements likely to cause disaffection to His Majesty.'
>
> Have I read anything likely to cause disaffection to His Majesty?
>
> 'Or to interfere with the success of His Majesty's Forces by land or sea or to prejudice His Majesty's relations with foreign Powers or spread reports or make statements likely to prejudice the recruiting, training, discipline, or administration of any of His Majesty's Forces, and if any person contravenes this provision he will be guilty of an offence against these Regulations.'
>
> I have gone through this number with the greatest possible care. I can find nothing whatever on any page in any column or in any paragraph which comes within Regulation 27.

Pringle deplored the fact that the action of the minister had taken away the livelihood of the editor Tom Johnston, and that Johnston might not have the possibility of a trial. 'Unless judicial proceedings are taken,' he railed, 'this can only be branded as action of the most oppressive and tyrannical character.'

He concluded his speech by accusing Lloyd George of inflaming the situation on the Clyde by his action. 'I believe that he is stimulating, increasing, accentuating the unrest that there prevails,' he said. 'He should take the offender into Court, have him tried for his offence, if indeed he has committed an offence ... and thereby he will convince these men on the Clyde that he is willing to have his action fairly tried, and if he can make out a case in regard to this he will do something to remove the unfortunate, I might almost say the disastrous, effect of such tyrannical action.'

The official history of the Ministry of Munitions concedes that *Forward*'s report of the St Andrew's Halls meeting was accurate. It then goes on to say: 'Therefore, whether or not the suppression was justified depends on the answer to the question – was the *Forward*'s presentation and criticism of the policy of dilution an attempt to restrict the production of munitions?'

The author of the official history concluded that whatever one might think about *Forward*'s doctrines or its tone, no clear case of contravention of the Defence of the Realm Regulations was made out against it. Furthermore:

> ... an impartial critic, reviewing the quarrel after the hand of time has brought the conflicting elements into their true perspective, will probably conclude that a more generous confidence in the good sense of the British public would have been a wiser policy and more consonant with the British Government.[8]

In his essay 'The Suppression of the *Forward*', Tom Brotherstone finds the official history's 'magnificent fair-mindedness not altogether convincing'. He notes the decision to suppress was not taken precipitately, nor was it rapidly rescinded. Considerable effort went into the preparation of a case against *Forward*, which had nothing to do with the immediate reason for the suppression.

> ... the facts which can be established do seem to point to an interpretation concerned to stress the tactical struggle between the government and the real 'troublemakers' on the Clyde – those who sought to defend the workers' interests against the imposition of the employers' version of dilution. In

this struggle the *Forward* was no more than a pawn. Whatever their initial intentions, the men at the Ministry of Munitions, by giving Johnston's paper an aura of martyrdom, helped to divert attention from the serious business in hand, the defeat of the Clyde Workers' Committee.[9]

~

In his response to Pringle's attack, Lloyd George said he was in no doubt 'about the gravity of any interference with a newspaper, any interference with the actual liberty of the Press, or the liberty of free speech'. He agreed that:

> Nothing but the most overwhelming reasons could possibly justify the action that has been taken by the Government upon this particular occasion, nothing but the supreme interests of the State ...[10]

He claimed the case was a cumulative one, saying the paper has 'deliberately for months been trying to stir up disaffection amongst workers in a district that is more important to the equipping of the Army and the Navy than any other district in the United Kingdom'.

Then he pivoted, to John Maclean's *Vanguard*.

'There are two newspapers,' he said. 'They are both turned out by the same press, and they were both seized. One is the *Forward*, which is the more moderate of the two. (HON MEMBERS: 'What is the other paper?') It is the *Vanguard*, which is edited by a person who was fined because at a street corner he made a speech during the war damning the army and denouncing every soldier who shoots a German as a murderer. Both took the same line of action.' (HON MEMBERS: 'No, No!')

The briefing note for Lloyd George had been prepared by ministry official William Beveridge. Beveridge felt *Forward*'s report about Lloyd George's Christmas meeting did not lend itself to the citation of specific passages, but there was no question of its 'directly mischievous tendency', and that it was exactly the sort of article that Regulation 27 was designed to stop.

In his memoir, Beveridge recalled the *Vanguard*'s existence as a fortunate coincidence and wrote, 'Lloyd George made great play with the *Vanguard* ... the impression he left on my memory was of defending the suppression of one paper by attacking a different paper.'[11]

So, when Lloyd George got going in the House, not only did he deny that the report of his visit was central to the case against the *Forward*, he introduced a second newspaper (the *Vanguard*) to confuse the issue; he blithely ignored a major flaw in the government's case (the Press Bureau's oversight); and to top things off, introduced a second Regulation that had not been previously mentioned, Regulation 42.[12]

Most of his quotations were aimed at showing that Regulation 42 had been contravened. *Forward* editor Tom Johnston was indignant – it had not been mentioned when his paper was suppressed.

Brotherstone's assessment of Lloyd George's speech is withering.

> By a dexterous combination of evasion, innuendo, quotation out of context, and the lie direct, Lloyd George proceeded to 'prove' his point.[13]

Beveridge was in the public gallery, after having been called away from the Drury Lane pantomime to carry out the urgent task of preparing a defence of the suppression that made no mention of the events on Clydeside over Christmas. He described Lloyd George's performance as: '... a more than liberal occasion ... It was a Parliamentary triumph exceeding in dexterity the trick cycling which I had just seen at Drury Lane.'[14]

15

DEFENCE OF THE REALM

Things changed after Lloyd George's visit to the Clyde. His failure to persuade the hard heads of the Clyde Workers' Committee to get on board with the plans for dilution meant the tougher approaches previously urged by ministry officials and others were not long in coming.

In a letter to the Secretary of the Ministry of Munitions, Sir Hubert Llewellyn Smith, dated 17 January 1916, the Ministry of Munitions' Chief Labour Officer for the West of Scotland, Mr J Paterson, gave his frank and undiluted opinion about the men whose removal from the Clyde 'would go a long way towards helping production'.

First on the list was David Kirkwood, who Paterson said 'has a much greater influence over the workmen in the district than any half-dozen trades union officials who could be named'. Then came Willie Gallacher and JM Messer, chairman and secretary of the Clyde Workers' Committee, 'a body that is causing the greater part of the trouble in the Clyde district'. Third was listed JW Muir, 'a prominent member of the Clyde Workers' Committee who adopted a most uncompromising syndicalist[1] attitude at one of the Minister's meetings the other week'. And rounding out the representatives of the CWC, Paterson also nominated Arthur MacManus and Tommy Clark.

Paterson then nominated A McLean [sic], 'an ex-schoolmaster recently dismissed by Govan School Board, who is spending his time holding meetings and in other ways doing his best to poison the minds of the workmen men [sic]' and Peter Petroff. He described Petroff as, 'a Russian Socialist of a very dangerous type. The easiest thing to do with Petroff is to have him repatriated, when, from all I am told, he will be shot within 24 hours of landing in Russia.'

Paterson concluded, 'I am afraid that the removal of any one of these men (with possibly the exception of McLean and Petroff, who are not working men or officials of societies here) would at once cause a big strike.'²

Petroff had been waiting to hear whether his case for appeal against his conviction under the Alien Restriction Act would be heard by the High Court of Justiciary. Two weeks after Paterson's memo, that waiting period ended abruptly. On Monday 31 January, two plain clothes policemen arrived at the Maclean residence at breakfast time with a warrant for his arrest.

The previous Friday, the Secretary for Scotland, Thomas McKinnon Wood, had authorised an internment order under the Defence of the Realm Act because Petroff's 'activities and associations were regarded as hostile to this country'.³

Petroff was whisked off to Edinburgh Castle and placed in the hands of the military authorities.

~

Lloyd George's mention of John Maclean as the editor of the *Vanguard*, and the minister's invocation of Regulation 42 of the Defence of the Realm Regulations in the Commons on 10 January, was a big hint that surveillance of Maclean was being stepped up. And so it proved.

On 6 February, Maclean was arrested after speaking at his regular Sunday night meeting in Bath Street. He was held overnight at Glasgow's Central Police Station, before being transferred to Edinburgh Castle the following day. Writing to his wife Agnes from the castle, he said he was being held as a 'prisoner of war' until his trial. 'I can be tried by the High Court of Justiciary or by Court Martial,' he said. 'Naturally I'll choose the High Court. I have been well treated so far, so need not feel anxious.'⁴

On 17 February, there were questions in the House of Commons about Maclean's situation from George Barnes, Labour MP for Glasgow Blackfriars and Hutchesontown, and James Hogge, Liberal MP for Edinburgh East. In response, the Lord Advocate, Robert Munro, advised that Maclean had been arrested for an offence against Regulations 27 and 42 of the Defence of the Realm Regulations. He had been detained in military custody in Edinburgh Castle until he opted to be tried by the High Court of Justiciary. He was then handed over to the civil authorities. On application being made for bail, he was released on 14 February on bail of £100.⁵

When an indictment was eventually served on Maclean, on 25 March, it cited six speeches he had given in January. They were on 9 January at the

Morris Hall, Govan; on 16 January, at Brunswick St, Glasgow; on 17 January outside G & J Weir, Cathcart; on 19 January outside Beardmore's at Parkhead; and on 20 and 30 January at the Nelson Monument, Glasgow Green. His trial was set for 11 April.

~

The third leg of the government's attack on free speech swung into action on 7 February, the day after Maclean's arrest. When *Forward* and the *Vanguard* were suppressed, the Clyde Workers' Committee decided to launch its own weekly paper, the *Worker*. The first issue was published on 8 January.

The first three editions did not fall foul of the law, but the fourth, published on 29 January, contained an anonymous article titled 'Should the Workers Arm? A Desperate Situation'. Although a reading of the article showed that the author answered the question in the negative, the title alone was enough to prompt the Ministry of Munitions to suggest to the War Office on 1 February that the journal should be suppressed, under Regulation 51 of the Defence of the Realm Regulations. This was done by the relevant military authority.

What action was to be taken against the persons responsible for the publication of the article was not decided upon until some days later. There were three options open to the authorities: deportation; to proceed summarily (a trial by a judge); or by way of indictment (trial by jury). The ministry initially favoured deportation, but the Lord Advocate, Robert Munro, decided to indict, reasoning a conviction in a jury trial would have a bigger impact.

On 7 February, Johnny Muir, editor of the *Worker*; Willie Gallacher, chairman of the Clyde Workers' Committee; and Walter Bell, business manager of the Civic Press; were arrested and charged with attempting to cause sedition and disaffection amongst the civilian population and to impede and restrict the production of munitions.[6]

The arrests prompted an immediate strike of over 2000 men at Messrs. John Brown; G & J Weir; Albion Motor Works; W Beardmore, Dalmuir; Barr & Stroud; and Coventry Ordnance Works. The strike petered out when the three men were released on bail.

Their trial was set for 14 April in Edinburgh.

16

THE SCOTTISH LABOUR COLLEGE

John Maclean was, in essence, an educator. When he was dismissed from his job as a school teacher, it was no surprise that he turned his focus to his work as an educator of working class adults. Maclean had been a keen observer of efforts to provide adult education for the working class for over a decade. He had been involved in that work since 1906, almost as long as his employment as a teacher. He decided the time was right to activate his long held plan for a Scottish Labour College. He wrote in *Justice*: 'The authorities thought a collapse would come with my dismissal. We gained as a consequence, and we are making straight for a Labour College.'[1]

An early effort in the field of adult education for workers had been Ruskin Hall (later, Ruskin College) in Oxford, a free university offering evening and correspondence courses. It was founded in 1899 by two Americans who had studied at Oxford University and decided that the same level of education should be available to everyone, not just the elite.

In 1908 some of the young trade unionists who studied there rebelled against the class content of the education they were receiving. Leading them was South Wales miner Noah Ablett, who recalled how they 'found the specious lies of the professors in contrast to their workaday experiences; how impossible to them seemed the mutual understanding between employer and employee there advocated'.[2]

Ablett began organising classes in Marxian economics and history as an alternative to the traditional liberal curriculum. A group of Ruskin students then founded the Plebs League to promote the principles of independent working class education. They reasoned that just as it was necessary for workers to organise independently in industry and politics, through trade unions and the Labour Party, so it was in the educational field.

In November 1908, Oxford University announced that it was going to take over Ruskin College. The chancellor of the university was George

Curzon, the former Unionist MP, and Viceroy of India. His reactionary views were well-known and he was the leader of the campaign to prevent women having the vote.

In January 1909, Ablett managed to turn several branches of the Independent Labour Party in the Rhondda into de facto branches of the Plebs League. The Rhondda Plebs would form the core of the South Wales Unofficial Reform Movement, the rank and file organisation that produced the influential pamphlet *The Miners Next Step* in 1912.

In early 1909, Ablett organised a strike of the student members of the Plebs League at Ruskin to protest the sacking of Denis Hird, the college principal who was sympathetic to their views.

After the college was closed for a fortnight, the students returned, but in August, 1909, Ablett and fellow student George Sims organised a conference to discuss the formation of a new institution. The meeting was attended by 200 trade union representatives. Sims explained that the 'last link which bound Ruskin College to the Labour Movement had been broken, the majority of the students had taken the bold step of trying to found a new college owned and controlled by the organised Labour Movement'. Ablett moved the resolution: 'That this Conference of workers declares that the time has now arrived when the working class should enter the educational world to work out its own problems for itself.'[3]

The conference agreed to form the Central Labour College (CLC), with Hird invited to be principal. The college was initially based in two houses in Oxford, then in 1911 moved to London, where it was financially supported by the South Wales Miners' Federation and the National Union of Railwaymen.

Nan Milton says that from that time on, 'Maclean's educational work was aimed towards the formation of a Labour College in Scotland after the style of the CLC.'[4]

~

On 25 December 1915 an article by Maclean appeared in *Forward*. It began:

> For some years an Economics and Industrial History class has been conducted in Glasgow during the winter ... Out of the class has been formed a committee to promote a Labour College for Glasgow. It is intended to call a conference of delegates from all working class organisations early in 1916 to discuss the question of establishing a representative provisional committee for the realisation of a Labour College.[5]

The proposal met with an enthusiastic response and the conference at the Co-operative Hall in Clarence Street on 12 February attracted 496 delegates. The organisations represented numbered 348 and included trade unions, trades councils, socialist bodies, co-operative societies, and women's guilds.[6]

Robert Smillie, president of the Miners' Federation of Great Britain, was to have presided over the meeting, but had contracted a cold and could not attend. George Shanks, the president of the Glasgow Trades Council, took his place. Another absentee was Maclean himself, who had been arrested six days previously and was not released on bail until 14 February.

James Maxton, chairman of the Independent Labour Party in Scotland, moved a resolution about Maclean's arrest in the following terms: 'That the conference protests against the arrest of John Maclean without warrant, and without any charge being made, and demands that the arrest be set aside as unconstitutional and that he be immediately released.'

Councillor PJ Dollan seconded, saying the arrest of Maclean and the three members of the Clyde Workers' Committee had proved the strength of the rebel movement on the Clyde. Fifteen thousand men from twelve workshops had come out in protest. Had that not happened, the three men of the *Worker* would still have been in prison and John Maclean would not have had the option of a civil trial as opposed to a trial by the military. The authorities could not have chosen a more effective way of fanning the dying discontent of the Clyde workers than the arrest of these men.

The resolution was passed unanimously.[7]

Maclean had been due to give an address on the proposed college, but had not managed to finish the speech before his arrest. The speech was completed and read by James Macdougall. The first part dealt with the necessity of Marxian economics being the basis of the college's curriculum and the second part, by Macdougall, dealt with the teaching of industrial history, his speciality, and other parts of the proposed curriculum.

It was agreed to establish a provisional committee and 32 members were elected. As well as the original class committee, they included Robert Smillie, James Maxton, Helen Crawfurd (Women's International League) and James McClure (Plebs League).

17

DILUTION ON THE CLYDE

Immediately following the rowdy Christmas Day meeting at St Andrew's Halls, Lloyd George met with a deputation from the Amalgamated Society of Engineers, who promised they would try to reach an agreement with the employers about the introduction of dilution.

It was not just labour that was dragging its heels on dilution. The unwillingness of certain employers to avail themselves of munition workers trained at the behest of the Ministry of Munitions was called 'pig-headedness' by a senior official of the ministry's Labour Supply Department. 'On the one hand we have cases of the most renowned firms accepting this class of worker freely and making magnificent use of his services,' he complained. 'On the other hand, too many employers are so conservative and prejudiced against any form of men trained in a technical institution that they have refused to accept them.'[1]

At this point, faced with the widespread intransigence of employers, official labour, and unofficial labour, William Weir sat down and drafted a memorandum to Lloyd George setting out his scheme for a dilution program.[2]

The scheme envisaged, first, a statement by the prime minister (of which Weir helpfully provided a draft); and secondly a statement by Lloyd George commanding the trade unions' support. Then thirdly, the appointment of a commissioner, who would visit selected large plants. Weir laid out detailed instructions for these visits. When the commissioner saw the shop stewards, he would tell them: 'A shorthand writer will be in attendance and any expression of open resistance or obstruction on the part of any individual should be carefully noted with the name of the man concerned.'

If a strike started, Weir suggested a flurry of strong action: an immediate summons under the Act; the arrest of any striking shop steward who had attended the dilution meeting; and a careful watch by detectives on the actions of members of the Clyde Workers' Committee and others specified on a private list.

If this was ineffective and the strike spread, Weir suggested, among other things, the suspension of the Trade Disputes Act, military guards at works, and the proclamation of martial law where rioting broke out.

Ian McLean observed: 'Arguably a programme as draconic as Weir's would have been the only thing that **could** [original emphasis] have produced revolution on Clydeside in 1916.'[3]

The ministry prepared a summary of the program, with modifications, on 20 January.[4] The modifications cut out Weir's excesses, which sprang from his undying hostility to craft unionism. The ministry's plan, although still firm, did not have the elaborate detail of Weir's scheme, which would certainly have provoked strikes.[5]

~

On 21 January 1916, as recommended by Weir, Prime Minister Asquith was asked in the House of Commons whether the government was experiencing any difficulty in introducing dilution. Lamenting that what had been accomplished fell short of what was required, Asquith said that steps would be taken to implement dilution without further delay. Instructions would be issued to controlled establishments that had not yet introduced the policy and special representatives would be sent to districts to assist in its implementation.

That same day, the meeting between the employers and the Amalgamated Society of Engineers promised to Lloyd George at Christmas finally took place. It was a complete failure, according to Sam Bunton of the ASE. He wrote to Lloyd George pointing out that employers and the government were introducing dilution schemes without the sanction of the men and their officials and if this was to continue, 'so long will dissention exist'.[6]

The following day, the government appointed a three man commission to oversee the introduction of dilution on the Clyde. Their procedure was as follows. First, they required the employer to prepare a draft scheme to their satisfaction. They then invited a deputation of shop stewards and union officials to a meeting where they explained the scheme, stressing that the object was to increase output not profits; that all alternative sources of skilled labour were exhausted; and that reversion to pre-dilution conditions was assured by an Act of Parliament.

Copies of the scheme were supplied to the men and a second meeting was arranged two days later to discuss any issues. If the employer was able to commence, the scheme was fixed and came into operation three days later.[7]

In most instances, the procedure worked well. However, at Messrs Lang in Johnstone a dispute blew up at the first meeting over whether women could perform part of the work hitherto done by a skilled man and receive the full skilled rate. The issue was referred to the ministry, which confirmed the woman was not entitled to the full skilled rate. On 31 January, the dilution commissioners instructed Messrs Lang to proceed with their scheme, and issued similar instructions to Beardmore's and Weir's.

The following day, the Paisley committee of the Amalgamated Society of Engineers informed the ministry that they refused to accept the interpretation, and 400 men at Lang's went on strike.

The ministry contacted the executive council of the ASE and asked them to call on the men to resume work. The ASE replied on 2 February, complaining they had not been consulted about the setting up of the Dilution Commission and expressing surprise about the minister's interpretation of the issue. The minister reluctantly agreed to meet the ASE to discuss the matter once work had been resumed and the ASE instructed the men at Lang's to immediately resume work, which they did on 7 February.

The meeting between Lloyd George and the ASE took place on 24 February and was a stormy one. Lloyd George complained that he could never get a firm bargain with the society. They only used the concessions he made as an opportunity for raising new obstacles to the introduction of dilution. And all the time contracts vital to the army and the nation were being held up. After dealing with questions of women's wages and making guidelines mandatory, the ASE was satisfied and felt it could fulfil the promise they had made to the government.[8]

~

The Clyde dilution commissioners approached their task in a painstaking manner, consulting with the workmen and working out individual schemes tailored to each workplace. Women were introduced at the bottom of the industrial ladder, leading to the upgrading of the semi-skilled men higher up the ladder and the squeezing out of the skilled men at the top. The skilled men would take on some supervisory duties and form the nucleus of a night shift which would be fleshed out as women and semi-skilled men were upgraded.

By the end of February, the commissioners could report that schemes of dilution were in place at 10 establishments, which provided for the release of 740 men and apprentices for more skilled work and the introduction of 1333 new workers, the bulk of whom were women. A further 30 schemes were in train and these would release 853 men to be replaced by an equivalent amount of low skilled labour.

~

The policy of the Clyde Workers' Committee was that the workers should attempt to control the conditions under which dilution took place. The CWC was opposed to the dilution schemes proposed by the dilution commissioners, viewing them as entrenching the powers of employers and limiting the powers of the stewards. It published a statement attacking the proposals. Then a delegate meeting decided that no factory committee would have anything to do with the commissioners. Instead, any approach should be referred to the CWC, which would meet them and discuss the Clyde as a whole.[9]

So, as dilution schemes began to be introduced, the fight began to be about the rights of shop stewards. During the process of the introduction of new labour – women, unskilled men, and soldiers – the stewards insisted it was important for them to have the right to call meetings and unionise the new workers, and to be able to move freely around the factories.[10]

A week after Johnny Muir, Willie Gallacher and Walter Bell were released on bail following their arrest on sedition charges, the CWC met and was 'utterly staggered' to learn that Parkhead Forge had broken the policy and signed a separate agreement with the dilution commissioners. They queried David Kirkwood, the convenor of shop stewards, who confirmed the news. When the CWC pointed out the Parkhead agreement contained no provision for a shop committee to regulate conditions or transfers in the various departments, merely a committee to meet with management when a dispute arose on wages, Kirkwood was unrepentant. He declared he was concerned with Parkhead alone and as the agreement safeguarded the Parkhead workers, he was satisfied. When the news that Kirkwood had broken ranks with the CWC circulated across the Clyde, it caused 'incalculable harm' according to Gallacher.

The dilution commissioners made progress at several other factories, but when they came to Gallacher's workplace, Albion Motor Works, it was a different story.

> ... our factory committee persuaded the management to dispense with the services of the Commission, claiming that we and they, the management, were quite capable of deciding what had to be done in such matters. The Commission were invited, very courteously of course, to leave the premises, after which the factory committee and the management worked out an agreement on the conditions under which the dilution would take place. This was a model agreement in the circumstances. All 'Dilutees', women and men, would start at 30s. per week and in three equal monthly increases would draw the full rate, with all bonuses, at the end of three months. Full inspection of conditions to be allowed to the factory committee with no interference or limitation in the ordinary functions of the committee.[11]

Immediately the agreement was signed, Gallacher took a copy to Johnny Muir at Barr and Stroud's and Muir was successful in getting the same agreement in place there.

But then things blew up at Parkhead Forge.

~

Unlike many other establishments where the whole works was under one roof, Parkhead Forge covered more than 90 acres and was broken up into several buildings separated by different main gates. It had been the custom for the convenor of shop stewards, or the chairman of the factory committee, to be able to go to any department where there was trouble, or for a representative of that department to visit the convenor. But the agreement Kirkwood signed prohibited him from leaving his own department, and prevented anyone from another department reporting an issue to him.

Kirkwood described the events that followed in his autobiography, *My life of revolt*.

> I was told that Sir William [Beardmore] had given orders that I was not to be allowed to move about the works as I had always done. It was useless being chief shop steward, responsible for the settling of many misunderstandings and disputes inevitable in a large workshop, unless I had the run of the place. I therefore resigned my position as chief shop steward and returned to my bench.[12]

The situation was the talk of the works for the next fortnight. Every effort was made to persuade the management to resume the former system. They refused.

A demand that the convenor of shop stewards should have the right to leave his work and go to any other department to investigate how dilution was being carried out was placed before the management on 15 March. They said they could not grant the demand, but were prepared to offer the convenor of shop stewards all reasonable facilities to ascertain what was being done if he asked permission to go into the different departments. Two days later the men presented an ultimatum to the firm. When it was rejected, at noon 1000 men engaged in the manufacture of heavy howitzers and naval ordnance went on strike at Parkhead Forge.

Kirkwood later wrote:

> At midday the works were empty. I left my bench, and, on reaching the yard gate, I found thousands of men, our own day-shift-men, and all the night-shift workers from other yards on the Clyde. I was acclaimed as their leader, and having made a speech, I said I would stand in with them.[13]

A deputation met with the owner Sir William Beardmore that afternoon. Beardmore said the matter was out of his hands as he had referred it to the dilution commissioners. He read out to them the clause in the Munitions of War Act prohibiting the stoppage of work, to which Kirkwood responded, 'We do not recognise that Act; we look upon that as a scrap of paper – it means nothing to us.' When Beardmore asked why they had not brought in the local officials of the Amalgamated Society of Engineers, Kirkwood was dismissive. 'We do not recognise them, and in any case, they are our paid servants and have to do what we tell them; but we do not recognise them and we have taken this matter into our own hands ourselves.'[14]

Once again, as he had done with the visit of Lloyd George in December 1915, Kirkwood placed what Ian McLean terms 'the paternalistic master and servant pattern' that existed between himself and Beardmore over everything else. 'This excluded not only the trade union officials ... but also of management.' But ultimately, for Beardmore the harmony of the works depended on a proper management structure rather than one individual workman, so Kirkwood had to be cut loose.[15]

Over the next few days workers in other establishments struck in sympathy. On 21 March, staff at the North British Diesel Works went out on strike. The men in the gun department at Beardmore's in Dalmuir indicated they would not proceed with the scheme of dilution agreed with, and indicated they would go on strike on 23 March.

~

With the munitions required for the 1916 campaign imperilled, it was quickly decided strong action was required. But the authorities needed to be circumspect. The last thing they wanted was to inflame the situation and cause the disturbances to widen. Some of the advisors to the Ministry of Munitions suggested declaring martial law on the Clyde. Others thought the Clyde Workers' Committee, which was felt to be orchestrating the actions, should be supressed. To prevent picketing, some argued the Trade Disputes Act should be suspended.

On 24 March, the dilution commissioners delivered a report to Lloyd George about the situation. The commissioners suggested the Amalgamated Society of Engineers should be asked to repudiate the strikes and entreat the men to return to work. While they believed the Clyde Workers' Committee was behind the strikes, they did not consider they had sufficient evidence to mount a prosecution of the ringleaders in the courts. However, action to destroy the influence of the prominent leaders who had taken part in the stoppage was required. Accordingly, the commissioners recommended these men should be removed from Glasgow, under Regulation 14 of the Defence of the Realm Regulations. The military authorities advised they stood ready to deport the strike leaders on receipt of requests from the minister and the War Office.[16]

That evening, William Weir sent a telegram to Lloyd George marked 'Urgent and Important'. It ran:

> Just returned here after four days absence (Stop) Find that Beardmore's men are still on strike also others (Stop) This started seven days ago and is delaying seriously output of guns and howitzers of special importance (Stop) I cannot find that any prompt and decisive action has yet been taken to secure necessary cleavage between loyal men and others (Stop) Also find that no instructions have been issued to Amalgamated Society of Engineers' Executive in London to publicly repudiate the action of their members and call back the loyal men to work (Stop) No note yet struck by the Government as regards strong support and vigorous protection of those willing to resume work (Stop) Also suggest necessity for publicity and education of public

opinion (Stop) Continued delay in acting on the procedure already laid down and agreed on with you at time of inception of Dilution Scheme is making the position daily more difficult and dangerous (Stop) Would recall to you policy and means consistently advised for avoiding situation now developed (Stop) Kindly wire and let me know if I can advise or act or if I am to leave the present policy to be pursued.[17]

After considering the commissioners' report and Weir's telegram at a meeting later that night, Lloyd George decided the men should be deported. A telegram was sent to the procurator fiscal asking him to advise the military authorities to proceed with the deportation action, 'if there is reasonable evidence to your and the commissioners' satisfaction that the men have incited to strike. "Reasonable evidence" is only such as shows a *prima facie* case under Regulation 14.'[18]

The military acted with alacrity. At around three o'clock in the morning on 25 March they arrested David Kirkwood and two other shop stewards from Parkhead Forge (Sam Shields and James Haggerty). Two shop stewards from Messrs. G & J Weir, James Messer and Arthur MacManus, were also arrested. All were members of the Amalgamated Society of Engineers. The men were taken to Glasgow's Central Police Station, brought before the military chief for the district, and given a choice of going to Edinburgh or Hawick. They chose Edinburgh. Two days later another Parkhead Forge employee Robert Wainwright was arrested and deported.

Under the banner headline BANISHED! *Forward's* report seethed with anger at the injustice.

> No charge! No bail! No trial! Men whose families have lived four generations in the same district, men whose personal character is unblemished, men who have the respect, the esteem and the confidence of their fellows, simply whipped off – as if we did not live in a free country. Nothing since the war began has aroused greater indignation in Glasgow ...[19]

~

On Sunday 26 March, a large demonstration at Glasgow Green braved heavy showers of snow, hail, and sleet to protest about decisions of the Military Services Tribunals regarding conscientious objectors, and to demand the repeal of the Military Services Act. It had been established that conscientious objectors were entitled to absolute exemptions and the Glasgow tribunals had been wrong to hold that they could only be exempted from combat service. The demonstration was a fiery affair and James Maxton, James Macdougall and Jack Smith, a shop steward from Weirs, all gave speeches advocating strike action to prevent the implementation of the Act.

Both Maxton and Macdougall were conscientious objectors and were refusing to go into the army. At the time, conscientious objectors got a terrible time in prison and Harry McShane claimed that John Maclean advised both men to get arrested on a political charge instead.[20]

The three speakers were detained on 29 March and charged with sedition. The indictment stated Maxton told the demonstration it was now for the workers to take action, and that action was to strike and down tools. 'In case there are any plain-clothes policemen present I will repeat that for their benefit – "strike and down tools!".' Macdougall followed and said: 'Strike, strike, strike, down tools and to hell with them.'[21] Smith was charged over comments he made advocating strike action at a street meeting on 27 March. They were held in Glasgow's Duke Street Prison without bail until their trial.

Further arrests and deportations were carried out over the next few days.

On 27 March, men engaged on howitzer parts and auxiliary machinery for warships at Weir's in Cathcart went on strike. That same day, workers engaged on naval gun mountings at the Coventry Ordnance Works also came out. On 28 March, men went on strike at Messrs. Duncan Stewart and Co. and Messrs. Mavor & Coulson, both sub-contractors of Beardmore's, and the following day, were joined by men at Albion Motor Car Co.

William Weir shot off another agitated telegram to Lloyd George on 27 March.

> Limited deportation action insufficient as Beardmore's men and others still on strike and two hundred and ninety at Weir's gone out this forenoon (Stop) Procedure ineffective unless strongly continued (Stop) All shop stewards who are on strike should be arrested this afternoon under Defence Realm Act for impeding production their action being specially harmful owning to their official position (Stop) Much disappointed no clear public statement published this morning shewing wicked nature of strike and effect on national needs and to secure cleavage between good and bad followed by publicity campaign shewing disloyal character of those remaining out (Stop) More necessary than ever obtain today public unqualified repudiation by Amalgamated Society of Engineers' Council of strikers and their guarantee

to punish offenders (Stop) Unless resolute action taken immediately and followed up strongly position will become much more serious (Stop)[22]

On 28 March, at a meeting in Bonar Law's room in the House of Commons, it was decided to deport the shop stewards at Weirs if there was sufficient evidence against them. Accordingly, H. Glass, G Kennedy and RA Bridges were arrested the following day and deported to Aberdeen.[23]

~

On 28 March, in answer to a question from Alexander MacCallum Scott, Liberal MP for Bridgeton, Glasgow, Dr Christopher Addison, parliamentary secretary for the minister of munitions, gave a statement in the House of Commons about the deportations. Addison reminded the House that in January, Lloyd George had appointed three dilution commissioners on the Clyde and to date, their efforts had been conspicuously successful. He continued, 'In the course of the past week, however, a number of strikes had been organised in some of the most important munition works in the Clyde district, and energetic attempts to extend them are being made at this moment.'[24]

Addison laid the blame squarely on the Clyde Workers' Committee, which he said 'decided about a fortnight ago to embark on a policy of holding up production of the most important munitions of war in the Clyde district with the object, I am informed, of compelling the government to repeal the Military Services Act and the Munitions of War Act and to withdraw all limitations of questions of wages and of strikes and all forms of government control.'

Addison's statement prompted a response from Liberal MP William Pringle. Pringle said Addison had made a very grave statement. 'I am authorised to say on behalf of the Clyde Workers' Committee, against whom certain charges were made, that they repudiate entirely the construction which has been placed upon their action by the Ministry of Munitions. Whilst I make that repudiation, I do not desire to enter into a discussion at the present moment, because I believe under present conditions such a discussion would not be beneficial to the public interest.'

The following day, the Clyde Workers' Committee issued a statement rebutting Addison's accusations. The statement noted the restrictions placed by management on Kirkwood's movements at Parkhead Forge; his resignation as convenor of shop stewards; the decision of management not to reinstate the long-held custom of access by the convenor; and the subsequent decision of the men to stop work.

The committee refuted the serious accusation that there was a deliberate ploy to stop work on a type of gun vitally needed for the army. Parkhead Forge was finishing a gun, it stated, the rough work which had been carried out by a sub-contractor. When the men at the sub-contractor were asked to do the finishing work, they refused on the grounds it would be 'black work'. And the workers at Beardmore's Dalmuir, who for some months had been in a state of unrest over a grievance of their own, decided of their own accord to strike in sympathy.[25]

~

That night, Willie Gallacher and Johnny Muir travelled to London, where Labour MP Ramsay MacDonald had arranged for them to meet with Dr Addison. Gallacher and Muir wanted to put the proposition that the agreements they had negotiated with the Albion Motor Works and Barr & Stroud should be made applicable all round, and the deportation orders withdrawn. This was considered more possible, Gallacher later wrote, because Lloyd George was in France and Addison was in charge at the Ministry for Munitions.[26] Addison was initially reluctant to include William Pringle in the meeting but Gallacher pressed the point and Addison relented.

With the assistance of MacDonald and Pringle, Gallacher believed he and Muir almost had Addison at the point of agreeing to rescind the deportation orders, and a meeting had been fixed for the following morning to decide on a formula. But overnight Lloyd George returned from France and when he found out what had been happening behind his back, he ordered Addison to break off the negotiations.[27]

Heated discussion about the situation continued in the House of Commons on Thursday 30 March. In answer to a question from Alexander MacCallum Scott during Question Time, Lloyd George said there was no foundation for the statement issued the previous day by the Clyde Workers' Committee. He claimed the demand by the men at Parkhead Forge was 'a great extension of the privileges previously enjoyed by the convenor', and that under the terms of the recently signed dilution agreement any dispute was to be referred to the dilution commissioners. 'The men had declined to accept any arbitration on the subject and went out on strike immediately,' he said.

William Pringle then asked Lloyd George if he was aware of any attempt to reach a settlement whereby the men would return to work. Lloyd George replied that every possible attempt had been made, not merely for days, but for weeks and months, but every bargain that had been made had been broken.

Pringle followed up by asking if Lloyd George was aware that negotiations, started on Tuesday night, were broken off by the Ministry of Munitions at a time when prospects of settlement were extremely favourable?

'I was not here on Tuesday night,' Lloyd George responded, 'but I have been making considerable inquiry. I understand there is not a syllable of truth in it.'

'I was a party to those negotiations,' Pringle interjected.

'There was an attempt made, that is perfectly true,' admitted Lloyd George, 'but my colleague quite properly refused to have anything to do with men who at that moment were absolutely defying the law.'[28]

Which law Gallacher and Muir – both of whom were parties to dilution agreements and neither of whom were on strike at the time – were defying is unclear.

~

Concerned with leaving the impression their heavy-handed action in deporting men may have been unwarranted, and that they had then turned up the chance at a resolution of the dispute, Lloyd George and Addison arranged for the matter to be raised again that evening in the House. A lengthy back and forth discussion then ensued.

Addison started off with a complaint about the public outing of what he called 'a private meeting' with Gallacher and Muir. In response, Pringle denied any breach of confidence and said he understood the details of what occurred were confidential but the fact a meeting had taken place was fairly common knowledge.

Pringle told the House that in the previous day's debate on Addison's statement, he had originally planned to say that 'as negotiations were going on, a discussion would not be beneficial'. At Addison's request, he had amended that to 'under present conditions', as Addison did not desire it to go out that negotiations were going on.

Pringle said he regarded the statement about the strikes on the Clyde made by Addison on Tuesday as most unfortunate and believed it was an inaccurate account of the situation. It was also deplorable that there should go out a statement from a responsible minister that there was a treasonable conspiracy going on in the country. To suggest the Clyde Workers' Committee were organising strikes for the purpose of obtaining the repeal of two Acts of Parliament was completely untrue.

Lloyd George then stood up and indulged in a semantic shell game, saying that while Gallacher and Muir had made 'certain suggestions in the course of conversation', that these did not amount to 'negotiations'.[29]

Gallacher and Muir were in the public gallery when this was going on and Gallacher perked up when Lloyd George drew attention to the fact that the men involved were coming up for trial shortly and as the case was *sub judice* he would not say anything to influence it. Gallacher later wrote, 'His touching impartiality almost brought tears to our eyes.'[30]

~

On Friday 31 March, a large public meeting on Glasgow Green protested about the deportation of the workmen. Despite the Amalgamated Society of Engineers instructing its members not to leave work to attend, a crowd estimated by the *Glasgow Herald* of 5,000-10,000 munitions workers were present.

The meeting had been organised ten days previously by the Clyde District Committee of the Federation of Engineering and Shipbuilding Trades[31] to demand an increase in wages to compensate workers for the increase in the cost of living. In light of the partial strikes and deportations that had occurred in the interim, supporters of the deported men took advantage of the occasion to protest the government's actions. After the meeting, many of the attendees marched from the Green to the city. The *Glasgow Herald* was less than impressed. In its leader, it wrote:

> Is it true that we are only supposed to be at war? Is it a lie that many hundreds of thousands of our fellow-countrymen are fighting in France and Flanders and in Mesopotamia today, and that thousands upon thousands have already died? Spectators of the humiliating scenes could be excused from thinking the hardest things. Throngs of cynical and callous demonstrators marched defiantly. They demanded more wages some of them, more wages because food is costing more, and the Government was warned that if compensation is not given 'they will take their own way'. Others clamoured for the return of deported ringleaders. 'Bring our brothers back' was the motto of their

inspiring banner. And sympathisers here and there along the route were pleased to lift their hats graciously as their humble 'comrades' in the ranks threw out a recognising cheer. Wasn't it a brave show?[32]

On Gallacher and Muir's return to Glasgow after their Westminster adventures, they found that while Parkhead was still out, only Dalmuir, Albion's and Meecham were supporting them. With the benefit of hindsight Gallacher thought that if he had gone to see several other factory committees instead of going to London, the strikes might have spread. But there was no chance now of getting others to act.[33]

On 3 April, shop meetings at the striking workshops were held. At each meeting the workmen were told that the Central Board Committee (otherwise, the strike committee) had placed the dispute wholly in the hands of the Glasgow District Committee of the Amalgamated Society of Engineers. The strike committee recommended a return to work so that the district committee could open negotiations with the dilution commissioners to have the men's complaints considered. All meetings voted to return to work immediately.

The strikes were over. It was time for the trials.

II
POLITICAL PRISONER

Comrade right valiant with heart and with head
Comrade who always the Vanguard has led
Comrade your sufferings shall not be in vain!
Thousands are greeting you: 'Hail, John Maclean!'

Full well we know what you've done, what you've dared.
How all your actions with conscience are squared;
Now that we've heard of your torture and pain
Thousands will stand by you; 'Hail, John Maclean!'

Hark, through your prison bars thunders the call
'To hell with the torturers! Down with them all!'
Capital's power's at last on the wane!
Millions are helping you; 'Hail, John Maclean!'

Men such as Liebknecht and you are our need.
The People are rising; they ask for your lead;
They seek out the men of staunch heart and good brain.
They honour you . . . follow you . . . 'Hail, John Maclean!'

    Dora Montefiore, 'To John Maclean Tortured in a Capitalist Prison' (1918)

18

GERMAN GOLD, AND GERMAN ALARM CLOCKS

On Saturday 25 March 1916, some seven weeks after their arrests, indictments were served on John Maclean, Willie Gallacher, Johnny Muir, and Walter Bell. All were charged with contravening the Defence of the Realm Act.

Maclean was charged with six counts of making public statements 'likely to prejudice recruiting, and calculated to cause mutiny, sedition and disaffection among the civilian population'.

Gallacher, Muir and Bell were charged with the publication of an article in the *Worker* titled 'Should the workers arm? A desperate situation', which it was alleged 'contained statements calculated and intended to cause sedition and disaffection among the civil population and to impede, delay and restrict the production, repair and transport of war material and other work necessary for the successful prosecution of the war'.[1]

At a pleading diet[2] in Glasgow on 1 April, each pleaded not guilty and all were remitted for trial by the High Court of Justiciary in Edinburgh. The trials were set for 11 April, and they were released until that date.

The British Socialist Party announced that it would make provision for the Maclean family (John's wife Agnes and their two daughters), while *Forward* made an appeal for funds to support the dependents of Gallacher, Muir and Bell.

Maclean kept up his furious round of lectures, meetings and commitments in the days leading up to the trial, and a steady stream of well-wishers visited his house at Auldhouse Road.

On the morning of 11 April, a large party boarded the train to Edinburgh. Accompanying John and Agnes were John's sister Lizzie, and a crowd of young engineers and miners, who had taken the day off work to offer their support. 'Every now and then the strains of a violin rose above the chug-chug of the train,' wrote Nan Milton, 'and fervent young voices joined to sing "The Red Flag". Those who were there found it difficult to forget the expression in Maclean's eyes as he sang the last verse, "Come dungeons dark or gallows grim" – those words, so often sung lightly and thoughtlessly, had become full of painful meaning.'[3]

The weather in Edinburgh was dry and sunny, although cool, with the temperature reaching 10C later in the day. After alighting from the train, Maclean's entourage made their way to the High Court on the Royal Mile. Inside the court, the mood was decidedly frosty.

> The court was full and many hundreds had been turned away, for the trial had aroused tremendous interest and excitement. The audience, representative of aristocratic and conservative Edinburgh, was bitterly opposed to the man in the dock and the hostile atmosphere was sufficient to daunt all but the most forceful of personalities. However, his [Maclean's] keen consciousness of the symbolic part he was playing rendered him quite unaffected by the enmity surrounding him.[4]

The temper of the city had not been improved by a Zeppelin raid the previous week. On the night of 2 April, two German airships snuck up the east coast and reached Edinburgh before midnight. They flew over the city for about 40 minutes, dropping an estimated 24 bombs in less than an hour. Thirteen people were killed and 24 injured in Edinburgh and Leith.[5]

~

The Lord Justice General,[6] Lord Strathclyde was the presiding judge.[7] Leading the prosecution was the Lord Advocate, Robert Munro, KC, assisted by Advocate-Depute Mr MP Fraser. Defending Maclean were advocates Messrs MacRobert and Duffes.[8]

The charge against Maclean was read out. It was alleged that on the dates and at the places detailed below, in each case to an audience forming part of the civil population, he made the following statements:

> 1. On 9 January at the Morris Hall, 63 Shaw Street, Govan, in presence amongst others, of police officers, he stated that conscription was not required in this war, that there were plenty of soldiers and plenty of munitions, but conscription would be used after this war to get cheaper labour, and if any

of the workers went on strike they would be called up as conscripts and sent back to their work as soldiers, as was the case in the French railway strike some years ago. That if the government were to enforce the Military Service and Munitions Acts, the Clyde workers should down tools, but do it discreetly. That if the British soldiers in all parts would lay down their arms, he (the accused) was certain that the Germans and the soldiers of all other nations who were fighting would also lay down their arms, as they were all tired of the war long ago.

2. On 16 January, in Brunswick Street, Glasgow, he stated that the best weapon the workers could use against conscription just now is the strike; that his hearers should endeavour to get men to leave their work and attend a meeting to be held on 19 January 1916.

3. On 17 January, in Newlands Road, Cathcart, Glasgow, opposite the main entrance to the works of G & J Weir Limited, engineers, he stated that his hearers should down tools and fight against conscription; that men sent to the war were only sent there to slaughter and be slaughtered; that Lloyd George had brought German gold to Weir's works, and it was that gold that Weir's men were being paid with now.

4. On 19 January, in East Wellington Street, Parkhead, he stated that if conscription became law, the workmen would become conscripts to industrial labour as well as to the army, and the government were more anxious to pass the Bill for that purpose than to get men for the Army; that the workers were being made slaves of to suit the bloody English capitalists, which was pure Kaiserism and Prussianism.

5. On 20 January, at Nelson's Monument, Glasgow Green, Glasgow, he stated that the Clyde workers should strike at once, and that his hearers should not go back to work, and those that had guns should use them.

6. On 30 January, at Nelson's Monument, he stated that he did not advise his hearers to strike, but that they should sell or pledge their alarm clocks and sleep in in the morning and not go to their work.

Which statements, continued the indictment, were likely to prejudice the recruiting, training, discipline, and administration of His Majesty's Forces, and by which statements the accused did further attempt to cause mutiny, sedition and disaffection among the civilian population, and to impede, delay and restrict the production, repairs, and transport of war material and other work necessary for the successful prosecution of the war, contrary to the Defence of the Realm Act and Regulations.

Maclean pleaded not guilty and a jury was impanelled.[9]

~

The pattern of the trial was set early. On each count, the prosecution would call several police witnesses who had attended the meetings at which Maclean had spoken. Almost none of them had retained any notes they may have made at the time, but recited parrot-like the phrases Maclean was alleged to have uttered.

When it was the turn of the defence, they called numerous civilian witnesses who had also attended the meetings. In every case, these workmen denied that Maclean had said what was detailed in the indictment.

Emmanuel Shinwell, Glasgow branch secretary of the British Seafarer's Union and chairman of the Glasgow Trades Council, said he presided at the meeting on 20 January. He said the meeting was perfectly constitutional, and the remarks of all the speakers were equally constitutional. No suggestion was made that the workers should go on strike, and that those who had guns should use them. He would not have permitted such a statement to be made at a meeting of that sort. Most emphatically nothing was said by Maclean about guns. If Maclean had advised his hearers to strike, he [Shinwell] could never have forgotten it.

Detective-Inspector McLennan, Glasgow, said he was present at the meeting of 30 January and heard Maclean use the words about alarm clocks. He said there was laughter after the statement.

'Did you laugh?' asked Maclean's counsel.

'I smiled,' said McLennan, to laughter in the court.

'You did not treat it seriously?'

'I did not.'

A civilian witness, Joseph Bremner, blacksmith, explained that Maclean was referring to the attacks in the papers on the lack of patriotism of the Clyde workers. Maclean said if they carried patriotism to the extreme and pawned or sold their German-made alarm clocks they would not be able to turn out in the morning. It was a joke. Some of the speeches on 30 January were much stronger than Maclean's, he said.

The final Crown witness was Chief Detective-Inspector McGimpsey, who said he had arrested Maclean on an order from the military. During the month of January there was an anxious situation on the Clyde, he said. There was a good deal of unrest.

Mr MacRobert said, 'I think there was a good deal of unrest at Westminster also in regard to the Conscription Bill?'

'I believe so,' said McGimpsey, to laughter in the court.

~

Maclean entered the witness box on the morning of the second day of the trial. He did not take the oath in its usual form, but affirmed he would tell the truth.

He was 36 years of age, he said, a socialist and a member of the British Socialist Party, although he held no office in that party. He had been 17 years a socialist and lived all his life in Glasgow. He was closely associated with the efforts being made for the better housing of the workers. He was secretary of the National Housing Association, but there was no honorarium yet attached to the office. He was a school teacher by profession. He was dismissed by the Govan School Board with three months' salary in lieu of notice. He had been devoting his time to the most important thing in the world – the establishment of a labour college. He had been speaking lately almost every day on the labour college. He had spoken on conscription, and had addressed meetings of munitions workers at Beardmore's and Weir's.

Maclean was cross-examined by Robert Munro. 'I suggest it was your purpose to get the workers to strike and endeavour to get the government to withdraw the Military Service Bill,' said Munro.

'No. It was my object to explain the dangers of conscription,' Maclean replied.

'Are you against strikes or in favour of strikes to achieve particular objects?'

'I am in favour of strikes.'

'Even at this particular juncture of the nation's affairs?'

'That depends.'

'Are you in favour of striking at this particular juncture of the nation's affairs in order that workmen might achieve a particular aim?'

'I have never considered that matter.'

'Consider it now and give me an answer.'

'I am against it so far as munitions workers are concerned.'

'You never thought of that before?'

'No. It was quite legal for other workers to strike.'

'May I take it from you that you have never on any occasion advised munitions workers to strike?'

'I did.'

'Where and when was that?'

Maclean explained that when the workers at a meeting passed a resolution giving the government a week to make up their minds on the question of rent, he went round advising the workers to stand by the men who passed the resolution. He went to the work gates on 17, 18 and 19 November and told the men to stand by the resolution. That was the form his advice to strike took. Since then, he had not done that. The Regulation prohibiting incitement of strikes came into force on 30 November.[10]

Coming to the indictment, Munro asked, 'Is your view that the case against you is a conspiracy on the part of the police?'

'Conspiracy is a strong word,' said Maclean. 'I don't suggest that.'

'How otherwise do you explain the offence to which I have referred?'

'I am puzzled to know.'

'In other words, there is no explanation that suggests itself to your mind other than the one I have mentioned?'

'I have not thought about whether it is a conspiracy or not.'

Regarding the first charge, Maclean insisted he had not said that workers should put down their tools discreetly. He said nothing like that. As to the workers coming out in a body, he never said anything of the kind; it was rubbish. In the middle of his address, he said he believed the soldiers were tired of war.

On the second charge, Maclean said he knew two constables were present from the beginning. He never said that the best weapon the workers could use against conscription was the strike. He did not advise his hearers to endeavour to get men to leave their work and attend a meeting to be held on 19 January. He was aware of the Regulations which made any such advice unlawful. He was not going to run his head against a wall.

When the constables made a charge against him [outside Weir's] he did not deny it. He did not think it was necessary. It was constantly said that anything that was said would be used against a prisoner. He had been told that when he went to Weir's gates the clerks telephoned for the police.

'Is it your suggestion,' Munro asked, 'that having said nothing about downing tools, two policemen came up and charged you with something you did not say?'

'Yes,' said Maclean.

'In what way do you suggest resistance to conscription?' Munro queried.

'By demonstration – that was my method,' replied Maclean.

Maclean described the fifth charge as false and containing not a word of truth, and the sixth as chaff. He quite admitted at any moment he would say Lloyd George was a liar (laughter in the court). They had proof of it.

Maclean admitted he had never made a speech in favour of recruiting. He had made none against it – let every man choose for himself.

~

After the conclusion of his cross-examination of Maclean, Munro addressed the jury. The charges had been proved up to the hilt, he contended. Section 27 of the Defence of the Realm Regulations prohibited any person from making statements intended or likely to prejudice recruiting, and Section 42 prohibited any person from attempting to cause mutiny, sedition or disaffection or impede the production of material of war.

Infringement of these Regulations was a very grave offence, said Munro. It was a felony punishable by penal servitude for life, and in certain circumstances by death. Any man who at this juncture of affairs interfered with the procuring of men for the army or with the production of munitions of war was a traitor to his country.

The charges were proved on the evidence of 18 members of the police force, and the jury could return a verdict for the accused only on the view that the police witnesses had perjured themselves, and had engaged in a gigantic conspiracy to defeat the ends of justice, to deceive the jury, and to ruin the prisoner.

Maclean's counsel Mr MacRobert, in his concluding address, said the question for the jury was not whether they approved of Maclean's political or social views, but whether he had committed a crime. The indictment was an extraordinary document, he said. From information supplied by the police, the Crown had taken sentences here and there out of Maclean's speeches and had founded the charges upon those isolated sentences.

It was not necessary for him to assert that the police had invented a conspiracy, said MacRobert. What he did say was that the police had misinterpreted what was said by Maclean. On the other hand, he asked the jury to accept the testimony of the witnesses for the defence. Some of them had not known the accused, and there was no doubt they spoke truthfully when they said the material language quoted in the indictment was not used by Maclean.

~

In charging the jury, the Lord Justice General said that in normal times, the expressions alleged to have been used by the accused would not have come under the cognisance of the criminal law of Scotland. But they were not living in normal times, because the nation was engaged in a life and death struggle for existence. Accordingly, the legislature thought fit to pass an Act of Parliament empowering the King in Council to issue Regulations to secure public safety and the defence of the realm. It was these Regulations, which had the force of statute, that the prisoner was charged with having violated.

The case was undoubtedly a difficult one, he said. A breach of these Regulations by the use of words was likely to prejudice recruiting; to cause sedition among the civilian population; and to impede the production of munitions. It was common ground that the words which the accused was said to have used were susceptible of bearing that meaning, but it was for the jury to say whether they did bear that meaning or whether they did not.

The more serious question was whether the accused used the words or not. That was entirely a question for the jury. It was no part of their duty any more than of his to consider the questions of the advisability of strikes or conscription or of the increase of munitions. These were questions outside their purview. All they had to consider was whether or not the prisoner used the words which were said to have been spoken by him at these meetings, and if he did so, whether they bore the meaning which was placed on them in the indictment.

Lord Strathclyde went over the charges and said undoubtedly there was a conflict of evidence, but there was evidence for the Crown to support the charges libelled. He pointed out that a verdict against the Crown would involve a charge of conspiracy against the police. There was no doubt that the charges against the prisoner were of the very gravest description. If an offence were committed against these Regulations, then he must regard it as a felony, and a punishment for a felony might be penal servitude for life.

Of course there were many degrees of guilt, and nobody, he thought, would suggest that this was a case so grave as to warrant punishment so severe. Unquestionably these charges under the present circumstances – in the grave crisis through which the country was now passing – were not to be regarded with a light hand, and merited careful and anxious consideration.

The jury retired at 3.15 pm.

~

An hour later, the jury returned. Through their foreman they advised they found Maclean guilty on the first four charges, the fifth charge not proven and on the sixth charge, not guilty. The finding was unanimous.

Lord Strathclyde, in passing sentence said, 'John Maclean, after a patient and prolonged consideration and investigation of your case, you have been found guilty, not for the first time, of contravening the Regulations of the Defence of the Realm Act. On a former occasion a very light sentence was passed upon you, with the intention, no doubt, of being a warning and acting as a deterrent. It seems to have failed. To a man so intelligent and highly educated as you appear to be, it would be idle of me to dwell on the gravity of the offence of which a jury of your fellow countrymen have found you guilty of today. It is thoroughly well known to you, as it is to the whole community. The sentence of the court is that you be sent to penal servitude for a period of three years.'

Maclean took the sentence quietly and as he was led from the dock, someone in the gallery cried out, 'Cheer up, John.' Maclean responded with a wave of his hat and some of his friends in the gallery shouted 'Good old John,' and immediately a large number of sympathisers started to sing 'The Red Flag'. An order was given to clear the court, but Maclean's supporters continued to sing as they filed out of the gallery. They then gave three cheers for Maclean.

~

Four men were arrested in connection with the disturbance and appeared in court before Lord Strathclyde the following morning. They were Thomas Connelly and William Meek, both miners of Blackburn, by Bathgate; Matthew Robertson, engineer, of Busby; and Thomas Halliday, bricklayer, of Edinburgh.

The clerk of the court said the men had been arrested and detained overnight for unseemly behaviour and shouting and singing in the court the previous day.

Their advocate Mr Duffes said the men now realised the extreme gravity of the offence they had committed and offered their humble apology for that offence. He was asked to assure his Lordship that there was no intention to express any opinion as to the justice of the sentence, or to show any disrespect of any sort to his Lordship.

Lord Strathclyde said he was profoundly grateful that the men had thought fit to tender an apology to the court for the very disgraceful exhibition in which they had participated. Had the apology not been tendered, he would have inflicted a term of imprisonment on each of them of considerable duration, for the offence was a very grave one.

Courts of justice in the country were open to all citizens, he said, but they were only open to them so long as they observed an orderly demeanour, and there could be nothing worse for the administration of justice in the country than that exhibitions such as they saw the previous day should be for a moment tolerated and he was determined it should not occur in that court while he presided there.

He felt it his duty to impose the very moderate sentence on each of them – keeping in view the apology which had been tendered in such judicious terms by their counsel – of a fine of £2, with the alternative of 14 days imprisonment.[11]

19

THE *WORKER* TRIAL

On Thursday 13 April, the second sedition trial began in the High Court of Justiciary, again before the Lord Justice General, Lord Strathclyde. The accused were Walter Bell, business manager of the Socialist Labour Press, which printed the *Worker*, organ of the Clyde Workers' Committee; Willie Gallacher, chairman of the Clyde Workers' Committee; and John Muir, editor of the newspaper.[1]

The charge was that between 22 January and 7 February 1916, they produced printed, published and circulated among the civil population, and particularly among the workers in and in the vicinity of Glasgow engaged in the production, repair, and transport of material and other work necessary for the successful prosecution of the war, issue no. 4 of the *Worker*, dated 29 January, containing an article bearing the heading 'Should the Workers Arm? A Desperate Situation', which contained statements calculated and intended to cause sedition and disaffection among the civilian population, and to impede, delay and restrict the production, repair, and transport of war material, and thereby they contravened the Defence of the Realm Consolidation Act and Regulations.

In the article it was stated that:

> The workers are being attacked. A savage and persistent offensive is being launched against their rights and liberties. They are being forcibly legally deprived of their health, strength, leisure, and money. The attack assumes a fresh and more cunning form almost every week. The workers must fight. They must fight to win. And in fighting to win they must make careful choice of the methods and weapons they will employ.
>
> When a ruffian begins to fasten a chain upon your neck, so that you may not move, and a gag in your mouth, so that you may not cry out, and then proceeds to starve you into a state of feebleness before going through

your pockets, you want to shoot that man. The workers are at present being shackled, gagged, and robbed. Are they going to shoot?

Who is the enemy? The enemy consists of that small, cunning, treacherous, dirty, well-organised and highly respectable section of the community who, by means of the money power, compel the worker to sweat in order that their bellies may be full and their fine ladies gowned in gorgeous raiment. They are the owning class. They own Britain, and all the wealth in Britain, and all the people in Britain. In order to keep the people obedient and pliable they employ many and divers agents – gaffers, managers, editors, preachers, law-makers, and, let it be confessed with a lump in the throat, sometimes Trade Union leaders.

In order that we might not reproach them with disorderly conduct they commit all their outrages in a scrupulously legal manner. Ruffianism can be quite lawful when the ruffians are in power. ... So before launching an attack on the people they pass an Act of Parliament which transforms their contemplated atrocity into a virtue.

They pass a Munitions Act to chain the worker to his master. They 'dilute labour' to call into being an invisible army which can be mobilised at short notice to defeat the struggles of striking artisans. They place a gate before our lips and call it a Defence of the Realm Act. They clap agitators into jail, and suppress popular newspapers for speaking the truth at inconvenient moments. They multiply their plunder by raising food prices, at the same time preventing the workers from taking suitable steps to increase their wages proportionately. Finally, they pass a conscription law to compel reluctant men to fight and bleed in defence of 'their' country. ...

The attack of the masters must be resisted. The workers must fight. What shall the weapon be? Trade Unionism, all honour to it, seems powerless in the present whirlwind onslaught. Trade Unionism, as we have hitherto known it, seems a suitable weapon for gaining laborious concessions at so many farthings an hour. But the present crisis finds it unequal to the attack: Sending Labour MPs to Parliament seems even less successful. The chloroforming influence of that assembly has ruined many an honest man.

There is a fascinating attraction in the idea of meeting force with force, violence with violence. It is undeniable that many of the more thoughtful among the toilers would consider that their lives had not been spent in vain if they could organise their comrades to drilled and armed rebellion. Their minds turn pleasurably in the direction of rifles, bombs, and dynamite.

If the internal clash of armed forces can be avoided in this country it should be avoided. There is another method which, if conducted on a thorough scale, should prove completely successful. A worker's labour-power is his only wealth. It is also his strongest weapon. The irritated cart horse that snorts and kicks in impotent rage makes no impression on its master so long as it continues to drag its load along the way. But when it sticks its hoofs into the macadam and refuses to budge, then the driver is up against a tough proposition. But the workers need not think of using this weapon so long as they are split and divided into sects, and groups, and crafts. To be effective they must organise as workers. An organisation that would include all the workers, skilled and unskilled, throughout the entire Clyde area, would prove irresistible.[2]

The Lord Advocate, Robert Munro, KC, and Advocate-Depute Mr MP Fraser, conducted the prosecution. The prisoners, who pleaded not guilty, were defended by advocates Messrs Paton and Duffes.

The first witness for the Crown, Superintendent Dugald McPhater, Glasgow Police, said on instructions from the chief constable of Glasgow he went to the premises of the Socialist Labour Press at 50 Renfrew Street, Glasgow about 10 pm on Wednesday 2 February 1916. He was accompanied by Detective-Inspector Campbell, Detective-Inspector Forbes, and several other policemen. The police were acting on the instructions of the military, a warrant having been issued. His purpose was to examine the premises and take possession of documents found there.

McPhater found there four men and two women. One of the men was the accused, Walter Bell. He asked Bell what connection the premises had with the *Worker*. Bell replied the paper was printed at the premises, but not composed there. McPhater took possession of a large number of documents. Certain leaflets were headed 'Clyde Workers' Committee' and they were signed on behalf of the committee by William Gallacher, president.

Chief Detective-Inspector Allan Campbell, who accompanied McPhater on his initial visit, said he returned to the Socialist Labour Press on 7 February with a warrant and arrested Walter Bell. Campbell and another officer proceeded to Paisley to arrest Willie Gallacher. Gallacher said he had been expecting the police, and asked them not to read the warrant as his wife was unwell. He said they could search his house but that they wouldn't find anything.

Chief Detective-Inspector Duncan Weir, Central Division, stated that on the evening of 7 February he arrested John Muir at his house. In answer to a question, Muir said he was editor of the *Worker*. Weir took possession of certain documents in the house.

~

The defence team, which included solicitor Rosslyn Mitchell, John Wheatley and the two advocates, Messrs Paton and Duffes, had advised the three accused not to take the witness box, arguing that the prosecution had no direct evidence of responsibility, which they would try to get if anyone went into the box. Despite all their efforts, they were unable to dissuade Willie Gallacher.[3]

His appearance did not go well.

Examined by Mr Paton, Gallacher said he was chairman of the Clyde Workers' Committee, which was formed in September 1915. Two or three of them had kept in touch with one another since the trouble in February, and there were so many reports of grievances and squabbles that it was decided to call a meeting of shop stewards from the different shops to consider the forming of such a committee with a view to building up an organisation of a better kind than was in existence. The opinion was very general that the trade union movement was to all intents done for. One general body was wanted to supersede all the separate bodies.

It was laid down at the beginning that the committee could not and should not call a strike. He always made it his business to rule out of order any proposal to strike. As chairman of the committee, he set himself against strikes in any shape or form. During his whole working life, he had never been out on strike until February of the previous year, when the whole organisation was out. He was not in favour of impeding the output of munitions. He had been working on munitions all the time. He had been able to get organisation in his shop. There had been no trouble there, or in Muir's shop.

When they met the minister of munitions on Christmas Eve, Muir laid it down that they recognised the absolute necessity of the government getting the maximum output, and they were prepared to do all in their power to assist them. There was a strike in Johnstone, and he used his influence to prevent the trouble spreading. Any time 'down tools' was mentioned at a meeting; Muir could always be depended on to oppose it.

Robert Munro cross-examined.

'The Clyde Workers' Committee was the Labour Withholding Committee under another name?'

'No,' said Gallacher.
'Did you know about the Labour Withholding Committee?'
'Yes.'
'Do you approve of its policy?'
'Yes.'
'Do you know that it carried through what is termed in a leaflet signed by you one of the best organised strikes in the annals of Clyde history?'
'But the Labour Withholding Committee had nothing to do with causing that strike. It came into existence after the strike to keep the men together.'
'I put two questions to you. This pamphlet says the Labour Withholding Committee was set up to organise the strike. Is the leaflet correct? And do you approve of their doing so?'
'I say no the first part of the question.'
'The leaflet is signed by Mr Gallacher?'
'Quite so, but it was not written by me.'
'Who wrote it?'
'A small committee drew it up.'
The judge intervened. 'Did you read it before signing it?' he asked.
'Yes,' said Gallacher.
'Did it appear to you to be correct?'
'We were not very critical, my Lord, in the reading of it.'
Munro wryly observed, 'Well, the jury and the judge will try to put a critical interpretation on it.' He then resumed his questions.
'Do you approve of the conduct of the Labour Withholding Committee? Do you approve of the strike?'
'No-one approves of the strike, just as no-one approves of war, but they may become inevitable. I regarded it as inevitable.'
'Do you approve of the article in the *Worker* complained of?'
'Had I been editor, I feel I would have put the article in.'
The judge asked, 'Suppose you had seen this article in manuscript before it was printed, would you have used such influence as you have to prevent it appearing or would you have passed it?'
'Probably I would have passed it,' answered Gallacher. 'I am not very critical.'
Re-examined by his counsel, Gallacher said he did not think the article would cause trouble. He was desirous of putting forward the idea of industrial organisation. He would not have published the article if he had

thought it would do anything as had been suggested since it was published. The writer of the article seemed to answer the question 'Should the workers arm?' in the negative. He would answer it in the negative, and the Clyde workers would answer it that way also.

In further reply to Robert Munro, Gallacher said he disagreed with the writer of the article on the matter of force. He would have put a note to the article that thoughtful men did not allow their minds to turn pleasurably to rifles, bombs, and dynamite, but there was a small section on the Clyde and other places that did believe in force.

In his memoir, Gallacher glumly recalled that 'the questions and answers went on until it was obvious we were well sunk.'[4]

~

Walter Bell also took to the witness box, where he gave evidence on his own behalf. He had been manager at the Socialist Labour Press for two years. He was not a member of the Clyde Workers' Committee. In January 1916 they published four issues of the *Worker*. He was entirely against the use of force in labour disputes. Knowing Muir's opinions, he would not have thought Muir would have sanctioned an article advocating force.

Under cross-examination, Bell said all the copy for the paper came from Muir. He said he had now read the article and forming an opinion on the article as a whole, he thought the writer of the article was asking himself a question and answering it in the negative. Taking the article as a whole, he would have published it.

~

In addressing the jury, Mr Munro said the case was characterised by two features – gravity and simplicity. It was grave because it was a felony and it was simple because there was no dispute the article was published. They did not know who the writer of the article was. Why did not the writer come forward like a man and take the responsibility? Why, like a coward, did he skulk somewhere behind and not come forward to take the verdict of the jury? It was because he dared not. The article advocated a policy of force and was a breach of the Regulations, and manifestly the responsibility for the article rested upon the accused.

Mr Paton, for the defence, said he had endeavoured to show that there was nothing in the men's previous history to suggest any intention to attempt to impede the production of munitions. The article was no doubt couched in lurid language, but it was metaphorical from beginning to end. The publication of the article may have been indiscreet, but if the accused had imagined that the article was capable of a sinister meaning they would not have published it. As had been proved, the accused were not advocates of the policy of force and had no intention of creating disaffection. The idea in the article was industrial union, which would put an end to strikes and lock-outs and carry out the policy of mutual conciliation which was at present in force in two works in Glasgow.

~

In charging the jury Lord Strathclyde said the sole question was whether the article in question on a fair reading was calculated to stir up sedition and impede the production of munitions. The jury should not leave out of view that when the issue containing the article was published it was a time of unrest and a critical situation and the paper was circulated among 15,000 workers.

The scheme of the article was to show in lurid language that the workers were attacked with so much violence they must fight and the writer asked, 'Are they going to shoot?' That was not the language of jest, said the judge. According to the article the enemy were the capitalists, and their weapons were not open violence but legal means and constitutional methods; in fact, Acts of Parliament such as the Munitions and Military Service Acts, and by dilution of labour. Trade unionism and Labour representation were, in the author's view, failures and the author said workers were turning their eyes to physical force and violence. 'Their minds,' he said, 'turned pleasurably in the direction of rifles, bombs, and dynamite.'

The writer did not advise workers to adopt these means, but it was for the jury to say whether the statement was not calculated to unsettle the minds of the workers and constitute an attempt to stir up civil disaffection. In the last paragraph, the writer said that if physical violence could be avoided it should be avoided and other methods adopted. The accused said they meant industrial unionism, but the Crown suggested they meant a strike. The jury were the judges and the three accused sailed in the same boat and were responsible if the article bore the meaning attributed to it by the Crown.

The jury retired at five minutes past six o'clock and returned just twenty-five minutes later. The foreman said the jury unanimously found the three accused guilty as libelled.

Mr Paton pleaded for leniency. The article having been found to have a sinister meaning, the accused, he said, humbly apologised for it and they were willing to give any undertaking not to issue during the war any such articles. Muir and Gallacher were both expert munitions workers and his Lordship might consider the adoption of a course which would not withdraw the men from their employment.

The Lord Justice General said he would pronounce sentence in the morning.

~

When the three accused were brought up the next morning, Lord Strathclyde said he had considered their case with the greatest anxiety. He had not found it easy, for a jury of their fellow countrymen, after patient and careful investigation had unanimously concluded, apparently without difficulty, that they had been guilty of publishing an article intended to stir up sedition, and to hinder the production of munitions of war. That was at the present juncture, as they very well knew, one of the most serious charges that could be preferred against citizens of the country.

He had great difficulty in believing that they did not realise the gravity of the offence they had committed. He had great difficulty in seeing that they could possibly believe – being sensible and intelligent men – that the article was merely calculated to induce the workers of the country to form themselves into a larger and more powerful organisation to protect themselves, after the war had come to a conclusion, against the attack, real or imaginary, of the people who were referred to in the article.

On the contrary the article seemed to him in very plain and simple language to tell the workers that physical force and violence was their last and only resort if the method of a universal strike failed to protect the workers against the supposed attack made upon them through the Munitions Act, the Military Service Act, and the dilution of labour. It was not easy to believe they were not cognisant of that.

On the other hand, they had, through the mouth of their counsel, expressed their regret for the publication of that article. He was sorry that the regret was not expressed at an earlier stage of the case, not expressed before the jury had come to consider their case, but was tendered only after the jury, having fully considered the whole of the evidence, had concluded that they had committed that offence.

He said he had also in view that the evidence disclosed quite satisfactorily to his mind that in recent times at all events William Gallacher and John Muir both exerted influence, very considerable influence apparently, for good among their fellow-workers and against the application of physical force or a universal strike for the purpose of righting their wrongs, real or imaginary, and that their character had been impeachable – indeed, it was not impeached by the Crown – and that they were good workmen, and would never commit an offence of that kind again.

Accordingly, he was not disposed to inflict what he otherwise undoubtedly would have done, having regard to the extreme gravity of the offence committed – namely the punishment of penal servitude; but the punishment could not be light for an offence of that kind. The sentence of the court was that Gallacher and Muir be imprisoned for a period of twelve months, and that Bell be imprisoned for a period of three months.

~

On 11 May, James Maxton and James Macdougall came up before Lord Strathclyde in the last of the sedition trials. They were charged under the same section of the Defence of the Realm Act and Regulations as Gallacher, Muir and Bell for their exhortations, at a Glasgow Green meeting on 26 March, for workers to strike.

Jack Smith, an English anarchist living in Glasgow was also charged. At a meeting of munitions workers at Balmoral Street, Glasgow on 27 March, it was alleged he urged his hearers to support war workers on the Clyde who were on strike and put before the meeting a resolution favouring a strike among munitions workers.

At the last minute, all three of the accused changed their pleas from not guilty to guilty. In the case of Maxton and Macdougall, their advocate Mr Duffes said they regretted their quite inexcusable action and he pleaded with the judge for leniency. Saying he was very willing to believe their expression of contrition was genuine, Lord Strathclyde sentenced Maxton and Macdougall to twelve months imprisonment. Smith received eighteen months.[5]

~

Willie Gallacher deeply regretted how his trial and the subsequent trial of Maxton, Macdougall and Smith had been conducted. 'If Maclean held high the banner of revolutionary struggle, we dragged it, or allowed it to be dragged in the mire,' he wrote. 'Even now it is hard to think of it without a feeling of shame.'

It was another example of the lack of experience and leadership capable of a policy that would cover such a situation and provide those involved with the necessary guidance in carrying through a working-class fight. 'The conduct of both cases, following the stirring example of Maclean, was a disgrace,' he concluded.[6]

On the other hand, the leader writer in the *Glasgow Herald* was grimly satisfied.

> The minorities through whose sinister activities Glasgow has been defamed will in their turn be discredited. Either they will realise that the obligations of citizenship, for which men are dying bravely every day, are precious things that at least we can conserve by the subordination of self to the common interest. Or they will be taught that there is a 'must' behind the tolerance of our Constitution – an iron hand within the velvet glove. But if folly and fanaticism demand drastic medicine, let them have it.[7]

20

PETERHEAD

Fishing off the east coast of Scotland has been hazardous throughout recorded history. The unpredictable weather, the strong tidal streams on many parts of the coast and the complex underwater geography means many fishing vessels have met an untimely end, and hundreds of fishermen have lost their lives there.[1]

In the 19th century, one of the plans to improve safety was to build safe harbours or 'harbours of refuge', where sail-driven fishing boats operating in the North Sea could find shelter in bad weather.

In 1852, a Royal Commission recommended a National Harbour of Refuge be built at Peterhead, a busy fishing and whaling port with ambitions to expand. Lying midway between the Firths of Forth and Cromarty, Peterhead Bay also had the natural advantage of a sand-free rocky coastline. However, because of the massive costs, of which two-thirds would be sought from the local harbour board, the project did not proceed.

South of the border in England, major public works were being undertaken at the time using convict labour, and because Scotland did not have a convict prison, this labour force included 600 Scots. When the Prison Commission (Scotland) was created in 1877, its first appointed commissioner, John Hill Burton, proposed a prison be built at Peterhead. It was estimated that the prison would provide 500 convicts to work on the harbour scheme.[2]

In 1885, the government passed the Peterhead (Harbour of Refuge) Act, which gave the Admiralty power to construct massive breakwaters across Peterhead Bay. The Act also authorised the Prison Commissioners for Scotland to build a convict prison south of Peterhead to provide convict labour for the project. The prison was opened on 8 August 1888. And on 9 May 1916 welcomed its latest resident, John Maclean.

~

The first month of John Maclean's sentence was spent in Edinburgh's Calton Jail. James Macdougall, who served his twelve-month stretch there, described it as 'a gloomy, tomb-like building run under the rigorous "separate and silent" system'.[3]

Extracts from a letter written by Agnes Maclean to Mary Bridges Adams, a journalist and fervent supporter of Maclean and his educational work, were published in Lancashire's *Cotton Factory Times* on 12 May. Agnes wrote:

> If John had decent treatment as a political prisoner it would mean so much to him. When I saw him in Edinburgh two weeks ago, through a sort of grating (we were not even allowed to shake hands!) he said the treatment was most degrading and injurious to the health. The feeding is very poor, about one hour is allowed for exercise daily, and the rest of his time is filled up in doing prison work picking oakum. He is allowed to read some, but no newspapers, no contact with the outside world at all. I do not know how he will stand that for so long. He is not allowed to write or see me for another seven months. When he wrote saying I was to be allowed to see him, he said I could bring one or both of the children. Naturally I took both, thinking it would please him to have them beside him for a short time. You can imagine his feelings when they were not allowed near him at all.[4]

While Calton's physical hardships were manifold – poor food, hard bunks, and pitiless warders – it was the prohibition on communication that had the direst effects. No speech, no social intercourse, no reading – it drove many a man round the bend.

For Maclean, Peterhead was a change for the better, at least initially. The hard labour of the penal prison meant the convicts worked in gangs, and although silence was decreed, a certain amount of furtive communication took place.

Each day the inmates were ferried the three miles to and from Stirling Hill quarry on a small railway, the only state-owned passenger railway in the UK at the time. The railway was built to high standards, with its own fleet of locomotives, coaches, and wagons. The coaches were specially-built vehicles with small barred windows. The prisoners were shackled in transit.[5]

Once at the quarry, the men used hammers to crush red granite, which the railway carried to the Harbour of Refuge Works, just south of the prison. There it was mixed with concrete and cast in great blocks to construct the southern breakwater. The project began in 1889 and was not completed until 1956, by which time the demise of sail meant the herring fleet no longer needed a harbour of refuge, and weather forecasts had made its initial purpose obsolete.[6]

Initially, Maclean adapted reasonably well to prison life. Working outside, he appreciated the fresh air and exercise. And while the cells were cramped and the amenities spartan, he conceded, 'The general condition of food, clothing and bedding are superior to those of multitudes outside prison, and the hours of labour are short and not over-straining'.[7] As the weather turned cold however, he suffered a sore throat and then worked inside.

∼

Outside the prison, the storm of agitation about the removal of the Clyde's most militant leaders that Maclean had expected failed to materialise.

Mary Bridges Adams made an early impassioned call to action, appealing to trade unions to render all the assistance they could 'in resisting this very serious attack on liberty in Britain'.[8] She also railed at the lack of critical comment in the labour press about Maclean's trial and the 'brutal severity of the sentence'. She wrote, 'I would urge that the attitude of the Press should be studied, and some reason sought for the amazing silence of such papers as the "Nation", "New Statesman", "Railway Review" and also the organ of the movement which claims to be the present day expression of the ideals of Robert Owen.' The latter was a reference to the British Socialist Party journal *Justice*. Bridges Adams also lamented the indifference of the *Co-operative News*.[9]

It was hoped that the British Socialist Party would take a strong stand about the incarceration of one of its prominent members, but coverage of its Easter conference in Salford (on Sunday 23 and Monday 24 April) was dominated by the walkout by Henry Hyndman and the rest of the 'pro-Allies' delegates on the opening day.

The issue that split the conference was whether proceedings should be held in camera to allow a frank discussion of positions on the war. The pacifist bloc proposed a closed session, and when the vote went in their favour, Hyndman took his bat and ball and retreated to the Deansgate Hotel in Manchester, where an alternative conference was hastily arranged. Those proceedings received fulsome coverage by the members of the press denied entry to the official meeting at Caxton Hall.

The majority body did eventually get round to addressing the issues on the Clyde on Monday afternoon, passing protests at the suppression of workers' newspapers; the suppression of free speech; and the internment of Peter Petroff. Regarding the Clyde deportations, arrests and imprisonments, the conference unanimously demanded the immediate release of Messrs Maclean, Bell, Muir, Gallacher, Maxton and Macdougall; and the abrogation of the restrictions on the deported trade union leaders. In a further show of support, Maclean was elected as a member of the BSP National Executive.[10]

The following Saturday, 29 April, the Scottish Trades Union Congress meeting in Glasgow passed a resolution protesting at 'the vindictive sentence passed upon Mr John Maclean', and urged that he should be treated as a political prisoner until his release. The congress also passed a resolution protesting the action of the authorities in deporting trade unionists and munition workers from Glasgow without trial or specific charges, and calling for their immediate return.[11]

~

Under the guidance of his trial solicitor John Cassells, the Glasgow District Council of the British Socialist Party began organising a petition for Maclean's release. However they discovered that for it to be effective, it had to either contain an appeal for leniency, or an appeal for the quashing of the sentence on the grounds of the contradictions between the evidence of the police and that of the defence witnesses.[12]

Maclean had made it very clear at his trial that he would not permit a plea for leniency, so it was felt he should be consulted before going ahead. Agnes Maclean was not due a visit to see her husband until November, but considering the circumstances managed to bring it forward to July. As expected, Maclean would not entertain the idea of a begging petition. His attitude was that he was not sorry, he had nothing to apologise for, and what he said he would say again. Instead, he suggested that his case could be used for a general agitation for the introduction of political rights for political prisoners in Scotland. While these were granted in England, and even in Germany and Russia, they were not part of the penal system in Scotland.

In the last week of June, a paragraph ran in George Lansbury's *Herald* announcing that 'our Scotch comrades have decided not to petition for the release of John Maclean until after the war'. The news dismayed Mary Bridges Adams, who queried Lansbury about its source. He told her the news had been conveyed to him by Willie McGill, the Glasgow convenor of the Herald League. McGill had been advised of the decision by the Glasgow branch of the British Socialist Party. Bridges Adams wrote:

> It is unfortunate that this should have appeared just at this moment. For ever since the trial of Maclean numerous workers – rank and file workers, needless to say – have been doing much by correspondence, by discussion in branch meetings of trade unions, and also by contributions to the press, to draw the attention of the organised workers to the great value of John Maclean's educational work for the workers and also later pointing out the brutal severity of the sentence of three years' penal servitude on Maclean as compared with the sentence of three months on Captain White, who was charged with making statements of a highly seditious nature. As a result of this agitation there is a possibility of the matter coming before the House of Commons, for letters have been written to a large number of MPs, some of whom are taking the trouble to acquaint themselves with the facts of the case.[13]

In July, Agnes Maclean wrote to Albert Inkpin, secretary of the British Socialist Party, expressing Maclean's disappointment that no demonstrations or physical protests had been launched on his behalf. In reply, Inkpin said that since they were expressly forbidden by Maclean to submit any claim for clemency that would involve an admission of guilt, there was little the BSP could do, apart from passing resolutions and getting sympathetic MPs and other public figures to take up the case. In fact, the Scottish Office was deluged with resolutions about Maclean from socialist and labour organisations from all over the country[14]

Maclean's case was eventually raised in the House of Commons, on 16 August 1916, by Philip Snowden, Labour MP for Blackburn. He asked the Secretary for Scotland, Harold Tennant:

> ... if he will take into favourable consideration the remission of the sentence of three years' penal servitude now being served by John Maclean, in Peterhead prison, for alleged seditious political utterances, in view of the severity of the sentence and the much lighter sentences which have been passed for similar and more serious offences in England and Wales, and in view of the character of the police evidence on which Maclean's conviction was secured?[15]

Tennant dismissed the request, saying, 'I cannot undertake to give any promise of remission on either of the grounds stated, and I must enter a protest against the suggestion implied in the concluding portion of the question.'

But while Maclean's case struggled against headwinds in Britain, it was quite a different matter on the continent.

21
EUROPEAN SUPERSTAR

When German troops marched into France in August 1914, the wave of nationalism and patriotism which swept up most French socialists also carried with it many of the Russian socialist émigrés living in Paris. By September however, some of the Russians had begun to take a second look at the conflict, and a new Russian-language newspaper, *Golos*, emerged in Paris as a rallying point for internationalists opposed to the war. French military authorities banned the newspaper in January 1915, but in its stead the daily broadsheet *Nashe Slovo* ('Our Word'), quickly appeared to carry on the struggle.

The paper's editorial policy was to accept contributions from all quarters, with the aim of bringing together internationalists of all organisational origins. Constantly under attack from French and Russian authorities as a vehicle of pro-German propaganda, and ever faced by financial disaster, *Nashe Slovo* nevertheless maintained its precarious existence until autumn 1916.[1]

After leaving Vienna on the outbreak of war to avoid arrest as a Russian émigré, Leon Trotsky arrived in Paris, via Switzerland, in November 1914. He was there as the war correspondent for the Ukrainian newspaper *Kievskaya mysl*, but contributed to *Golos* and when *Nashe Slovo* was launched, he asked to join its editorial board. The request was not without controversy; the editors knew his domineering personality and there was a worry he might disturb the working atmosphere. But it was recognised he had unmatched literary flair and was committed to working with every anti-war Marxist, from Martov, leader of the Mensheviks, to Lenin of the Bolsheviks. His request was accepted.[2]

Nashe Slovo had an editorial line which reflected the changing balance of opinions on its editorial board. Even so, it consistently printed views from all shades of socialist thought. This helped it to attract contributors from across Europe. Through its correspondents it attempted to keep its readership acquainted with events in all the belligerent countries, so that even those who disagreed with its editorials eagerly sought out *Nashe Slovo* to keep abreast of the latest developments. Of particular interest was news of any action by the workers which could be interpreted as taking an anti-war, pro-socialist direction. It is in this context that events in Glasgow during the First World War achieved a special prominence in *Nashe Slovo*, the more so as events there included collaboration between Scots and Slavs.[3]

~

Twenty articles about Scotland appeared in *Nashe Slovo*; the first in April 1915, and the bulk between January and July 1916. The arrest and subsequent internment of Peter Petroff received extensive coverage in February 1916, as did the arrest and trial of Gallacher, Muir and Bell for publishing a seditious article in the *Worker*.

An article on 'British socialism and the war' by Theodore Rothstein, printed in the issue of 7 December 1915, prompted a response by fellow London-based Russian émigré Georgy Chicherin.

On coming into an inheritance in 1904, Chicherin had renounced title to his estates, abandoned a career in the tsarist diplomatic service, and joined the Russian Social Democratic Labour Party (RSDLP). Fleeing Russia after the 1905 revolution, he initially settled in Germany, but was then compelled to seek asylum in France. He was active in the German, French and Belgian socialist parties, and as secretary of the RSDLP Foreign Central Bureau helped to organise the party's 1907 London conference. In the Bolshevik/Menshevik split that followed, he gravitated to the Menshevik side led by Plekhanov, Martov and Dan. When the German armies rolled into Belgium in 1914, he left the continent and arrived in London.

Initially favouring the cause of Britain and France, his belief in the progressive nature of their bourgeois democracies rapidly dissipated and he abandoned his 'defencist' views and joined Peter Petroff and others in the anti-war internationalist camp.

Chicherin became an active member of the Kentish Town branch of the British Socialist Party, where Petroff was already a member.[4] In spring 1915, he formed the advocacy group Russian Political Prisoners and Exiles Relief Committee. In establishing contacts with the British left to raise funds for this cause, he was immeasurably aided by Mary Bridges Adams, a founding member of the Central Labour College and a passionate and long-time campaigner for workers' education. Collection of funds was only a part of the committee's activities; equally important was its political work and propaganda activities, which amounted to 'systematic agitation against tsarism'.[5]

While both Chicherin and Rothstein favoured the internationalist position, they had different views of how to improve that position within the British Socialist Party. The BSP journal *Justice* was firmly in the control of the party elders, who were social patriots, but in his *Nashe Slovo* article Rothstein said the internationalist viewpoint was favoured by a large proportion of the party membership and a majority of the central committee. Rothstein suggested the internationalists were gradually wresting control of the party and a point would be reached when they would effect a smooth takeover.

Chicherin disputed Rothstein's analysis. He said Rothstein overestimated the internationalist forces in the BSP, and in fact its only active internationalist section was in Scotland, which had an almost completely independent existence. In contrast to Rothstein's recommended 'committee manoeuvres', Chicherin called on internationalists to found a fighting publication like Glasgow's *Vanguard* and appeal to the masses.

In response, Rothstein agreed that the internationalists did not always pursue their cause with sufficient vigour, but cautioned against them splitting from the party, arguing that would leave it in the hands of the social patriots at the forthcoming party congress. He also noted that while the mass of workers was concerned about the erosion of their workplace rights and the introduction of forced conscription, they remained in favour of the war and the production of munitions.

Despite the reasonableness of Rothstein's argument (and the success of the 'committee manoeuvres' at the BSP Easter 1916 conference, which saw the social patriots resign *en masse* from the party), *Nashe Slovo* turned to Chicherin. His five-part survey titled 'The Scottish labour movement and the reaction in England' was published in May-June 1916.

The first article, in the 18 May issue, set out 'to introduce, at last, the internationalists outside England to this most remarkable phenomenon in today's labour life'. Chicherin attributed the source of Marxist radicalism and its broad influence across the west of Scotland to the economics classes of John Maclean. He wrote:

> An exceptionally important role, as yet unparalleled on the Continent in this area, is played in the recent Scottish movement by the network of

educational establishments created over many years by a large number of dedicated activists who had devoted themselves to this cause, of whom the most exceptionally talented, knowledgeable, energetic, enthusiastic, and revolutionary-minded man is Comrade Maclean ...[6]

The elements that congregated around these classes, Chicherin said, belonged to the most advanced and class-conscious vanguard of the movement. The model of a socialist intellectual providing the necessary precondition, education in Marxism, would have been familiar in Russian social democratic circles. Indeed, the formation of workers' education circles was an important part of the history of Russian social democracy.[7]

During his time on the Clyde, Peter Petroff had kept up a correspondence with Chicherin. In a January 1916 letter, Petroff accused the central committee of the British Socialist Party of being unrepresentative; and depicted the Scottish movement as 'clearly Marxist in character'; and 'in close contact with the working class in its educational work and factory meetings'.[8]

In his article, Chicherin amplified the point:

> The progressive elements of the Scottish movement are also the organisers of ongoing, continuous meetings and rallies at the gates of factories and plants, near mines, in the vast city and town halls, in town and village streets. It was these factory, mining and street rallies that nourished, expanded and strengthened that vigorous movement that had made the rulers of the British Empire tremble and caused them to try to smother it with harsh sentences.[9]

Chicherin told the readers of *Nashe Slovo* how the last months of 1915 in Scotland had been a 'period of intense work, daily meetings, publications, lectures, travels between places, endless production of leaflets and proclamations, all in the heightened, intense atmosphere of a fast-growing mass-movement'. He remarked on John Maclean's 'special rapport' with the Scottish coal miners; the strong ties forged with the miners of South Wales; and the formation of the Clyde Workers' Committee, which had been 'created to protect the economic interests of the working class, in view of the entirely unsatisfactory behaviour of the trade union leaders'.

The second article, 'Lloyd George and the Scottish Labour Movement' appeared two days later. In it Chicherin recapped some of the key events of 1915: the February strike; the passing of the Munitions Act, commonly known as the 'worker slavery act'; the battle over the mixing of skilled and unskilled workers (dilution of labour); Maclean's first trial and conviction over comments at public meetings; and his dismissal as a teacher. Of the rent strike, he wrote approvingly: 'Revolutionary elements of the Scottish movement do not turn away from the current tasks of everyday struggle: on the contrary, they use the everyday tasks to involve the masses in the movement and revolutionise them.'

The article concluded with a blow-by-blow description of Lloyd George's visit to the Clyde at Christmas 1915, and the minister's disastrous attempt to sell his dilution policy to a mass meeting of workers. Chicherin did not spare any punches:

> Rising on a wave of superficial demagoguery and ostentatious reformism, this political scoundrel, this would-be dictator supported by the yellow press, stumbled against conscious workers' resistance. His reputation as a wonder-worker able to tame the violent masses vanished into thin air. Revenge was to be expected. His career was on the cards; he had to retaliate with repressions.[10]

~

The last three pieces of the series detailed the decline in fortunes of the anti-war internationalists, as the government set out to crush the movement. Firstly, Chicherin recapped the persecutions of his colleague Peter Petroff and his wife Irma, both of whom were arrested in Scotland before being interned without trial in England.

He then recounted the ratcheting up of the government's measures: the suppression of *Forward*, the *Vanguard* and the *Worker*; the arrests of Maclean, Gallacher, Muir, Bell, Maxton and Macdougall; and the deportation of prominent shop stewards.

The fight against the government's plans for conscription had brought together moderate and revolutionary elements, he explained. When those advocating a strike against conscription ran up against the Independent Labour Party's campaign of rallies ('rituals without action', in Chicherin's withering description) and a trade union bureaucracy that did not even want that, the mass fight against conscription was thwarted. The Military Service Act was passed, 'the tide had turned; the Scottish working masses were in the grip of despondency'.[11]

In his conclusion however, Chicherin struck a note of optimism:

In this nightmarish atmosphere, all the forces of violence, deceit and half-heartedness are deployed against the Scottish labour movement. The entire coercive state machine, the economic pressure, the bourgeois press are all against it; the chauvinist renegades like [Robert] Blatchford who wrote that 'the people are tired of Syndicalist sluggards' are against it; [Henry] Hyndman and his agents are against it; moreover calming down the revolutionary mass movement is the policy of the opportunistic circles ruling the Independent Labour Party which are filled with Anglican and Dissenter priests, Quakers, sentimental moralists and saturated by bourgeois political buffoonery which detests the revolutionary mass movement.

But this movement has now penetrated too deep and nothing will be able to stop it. It may have been stripped of its brave leaders and experienced chiefs; the time has come for the masses who have already undergone the initial education to learn to rely on their own strength, and elements of this are in evidence.[12]

~

There is little doubt that these articles by Chicherin, and *Nashe Slovo*'s treatment of John Maclean in general, helped to give the Scottish educator and agitator a reputation as a socialist hero across Europe. 'The Parisian newspaper's devotion to Maclean amounted to a minor cult,' according to historian Ian Thatcher, who observed:

> No other workers' leader, from Scotland or elsewhere, had his photograph printed at the top of an issue's front page. No other workers' leader's writings achieved such authority and attention. Although the careers of Maclean's colleagues earned mentions, no leader's achievements and tribulations were covered in as much detail as Maclean's.[13]

The appreciation was shared by other Russian revolutionaries, such as Lenin's close collaborator Grigory Zinoviev, who wrote in July 1916:

> Unity between socialists and servants of the bourgeoisie is impossible. Muranov and Petrovsky in Russia, Liebknecht in Germany, Höglund and Heden in Sweden, MacLean in Britain - all of these are our comrades, sent to prison by the governments of their 'homeland'. Here are the true carriers of the idea of a new workers' international. For the Third International![14]

And Lenin himself was also impressed, writing in December 1916:

> Two Internationals already exist. One is the International of

Sembat-Südekum-Hyndman-Plekhanov and Co. The other is the International of Karl Liebknecht, MacLean (the Scottish school-master whom the English bourgeoisie sentenced to hard labour for supporting the workers' class struggle), Höglund (the Swedish M. P. and one of the founders of the Zimmerwald Left sentenced to hard labour for his revolutionary propaganda against the war), the five Duma members exiled to Siberia for life for their propaganda against the war, etc. On the one hand, there is the International of those who are helping their own governments wage the imperialist war, and on the other, the International of those who are waging a revolutionary fight against the imperialist war. Neither parliamentary eloquence nor the 'diplomacy' of socialist 'statesmen' can unite these two Internationals. The Second International has outlived itself. The Third International has already been born.[15]

The reputation acquired of a committed revolutionary loved by the people, led to the many honours bestowed on Maclean by the Bolsheviks following the 1917 Russian revolution. But the hand that gives can also take away; and it was Moscow's machinations after the war that led to his excision from the socialist mainstream in Britain, and contributed to his early demise.

22

I SHALL BE RELEASED

In November 1916, John and Anges Maclean were allowed to write to each other for the first time since John's trial. Agnes informed John that the Glasgow Trades Council and others were urging the Labour Party to get something done for political prisoners, and that his cause was more alive than ever. She told him about a John Maclean Sale of Work at Glasgow's Central Halls on 14 October that had been organised by the Women's Guild. The event had raised £180, and Agnes said they could have raised double the money if the hall had been bigger. 'Crowds of people could not get near the stalls at all,' she wrote. 'It would have done your heart good to have had a peep in that day. The enthusiasm was great.'

In his reply, John told Agnes not to worry about him. His throat was much better; he had regained the weight he had lost in summer; and he was sleeping well. He said, 'I have never been ill yet, not even indigestion. I can get out more than ever, the air's so bracing …'

After that, things went seriously downhill. He later wrote:

> After one settles down, the day, the weeks, the months and the years slip in very quickly if one is a reader. As a matter of fact, one could enjoy twenty years in Peterhead better than ten in a coal mine, say were all I have described the only side of Peterhead life. I enjoyed my first stay in Peterhead – until the 'fun' began, and then it was an intractable hell through the drugging of the food.[1]

In the winter of 1916-17 Maclean fell ill and was convinced it was because his food was being drugged. While it was entirely possible his illness was due to the appalling diet that prisoners endured – a diet that was poor to start with and deteriorated as food shortages in Britain started to bite – it was sufficiently serious in February 1917 for him to be transferred to the prison hospital in Perth, where he spent the next three months.

On 13 February, Willie Gallacher and Johnny Muir were released from prison. James Maxton and James Macdougall had been released ten days earlier, and all four were guests of honour at a welcome home meeting at St Mungo's Halls on Friday 16 February. In his speech Gallacher mentioned 'one missing that night, John Maclean'.[2]

Gallacher later recalled the enthusiasm of the evening:

> ... when I and the subsequent speakers declared for all our forces being brought into the fight to release John Maclean, the roof was nearly lifted off the building. 'All in favour of the fight to release Maclean?' A sea of hands. 'Good! Now into the factories with the agitation and rouse the workers as they've never been roused before. Maclean must be released!'[3]

On 21 February, in the House of Commons, Charles Duncan, general secretary of the Workers' Union and Labour MP for Barrow-in-Furness, asked the Lord Advocate, Robert Munro:

> ... whether he is aware that there are persons in Scotland convicted of political offences who are being treated like ordinary criminals and are compelled to do routine work usually allocated to prisoners of the most degraded type; and whether he will consider the advisability of introducing legislation to secure that persons convicted in Scotland of political offences may be punished in a manner commensurate with the offence and not be placed in the same category as ordinary criminals, and thus bring Scottish law into conformity with that prevailing in England?

Munro batted the question away:

> I am not aware how precisely my hon. friend would define a political offence, but it is the case that no special treatment has in Scotland been accorded to offenders against the Defence of the Realm Regulations. In England a court may, in the exercise of their discretion, allocate offenders to the first or second division. This system has not been applied to Scotland, and I am not prepared, under existing conditions, to introduce legislation for the special benefit of this class of offenders.[4]

Later that day, Labour MP Philip Snowden asked Munro if he would take into favourable consideration the question of releasing Maclean. In response, Munro said the offence of which Maclean was convicted was a serious one. He had, moreover, been convicted of a similar offence. 'In these circumstances I am not prepared, at a time when he has served ten months only of a three years' sentence, to advise any remission.'⁵

Over the next few weeks, however, circumstances changed. A revolution in Russia galvanised the British socialist movement, and the campaign to release Maclean gathered unstoppable momentum.

~

It had been a turbulent time at Westminster while John Maclean had been locked up in Peterhead. In June 1916, Lord Kitchener drowned when the ship he was on hit a German mine west of the Orkney Islands and sank. He had been on his way to Russia on a secret mission to discuss munition shortages and military strategy with the Imperial government. Lloyd George replaced him as minister for war.

Lloyd George took office on 4 July, three days after the British and French armies launched the offensive that became known as the battle of the Somme. Thirteen British divisions went 'over the top' in regular waves. According to historian AJP Taylor, the attack was a total failure. 'The slaughter was prolonged for weeks, then for months,' he wrote. 'Kitchener's army found its graveyard on the Somme. Not only men perished. There perished also the zest and idealism with which nearly three million Englishmen [sic] had marched forth to war.'⁶

Events at sea were even graver. Attacks on merchant ships by German U-boats led to shortages of food and other supplies. By November 1916, Lloyd George had become increasingly critical of Prime Minister Asquith's failure to wrest control of defence strategy from his military commanders, and his failure to adapt the machinery of government to the needs of war. He decided that responsibility for the day to day running of the war should be taken away from the Cabinet and given to a newly created three-man War Cabinet, which he himself would chair. The Unionist leader, Bonar Law and Ulster Unionist chief, Edward Carson would make up the numbers.⁷

After reluctantly accepting Lloyd George's proposal, Asquith then rejected it, prompting Lloyd George to resign. Bonar Law threatened to follow, whereupon Asquith himself resigned, and the coalition government fell. The King invited Bonar Law to form a new government. When he declined, the invitation was extended to Lloyd George, who accepted with alacrity.

Faced with a choice between a negotiated peace or war socialism,

Lloyd George chose the latter. Setting his face against the Liberal Party's foundational tenet of *laissez-faire*, he promptly set up five new departments: shipping, labour, food, national service, and food production. The new controls took time to work, however, and in the meantime food and fuel ran short, trains were slow and crowded, and the queue became a characteristic British institution. Nineteen-seventeen was for civilians the worst year of the war and economic discontent fuelled political protest.[8]

And the war was dragging on. On the Western Front, the Germans had spent the winter of 1916-17 building the heavily-fortified Hindenburg Line, 25 miles behind the Somme frontline. The Allied offensive of spring 1917 involved the British attacking in the north of the line at Arras, with the major push coming from the French on the Aisne. The British made some early gains, but then ran up against the Hindenburg Line. The French assault was a complete failure. When the battle of Arras was over, the British and Empire forces had suffered twice as many casualties as the Germans. The French Army was near mutiny and incapable of any further offensives that year.

~

Massive strikes by workers, civilian protests about food rationing, and mutiny by sections of the army in Petrograd in February 1917 (Old Style),[9] led to the fall of the Russian government and the abdication of Tsar Nicholas II. The revolution saw the establishment of a provisional government, which had the task of organising elections for a new constituent assembly. But it also saw the emergence of a rival power group, the Petrograd Soviet of Workers' and Soldiers' Deputies. Holding to the socialist belief that the revolution would move through stages and the bourgeoisie must take power first, the soviet offered its conditional support to the provisional government.[10] Meantime, in Zurich, Lenin began enunciating his political position and investigating options to return to Russia.

On 9 April (27 March OS) 1917, the Russian provisional government published a statement of war aims largely based on a peace policy developed by the Petrograd Soviet. The policy came to be called revolutionary defencism and comprised two main elements. As well as pressing for a general peace without annexations, it called on the Russian people to defend the homeland and the revolution against foreign invaders.

Under pressure from the Petrograd Soviet, the provisional government formally cabled the statement of war aims to the British and French governments. When this was ignored by Britain and France, it was easy to allege that the war was dragging on because of French designs on Alsace-Lorraine, and the anticipated spoils from the Ottoman Empire in the Near East and Germany's colonies in Africa.

The Russian announcement rekindled hopes among European socialists that peace might be achievable. On 22 April, the Dutch section of the International Socialist Bureau advised they were going to convene a special meeting of affiliated European socialist parties. The date was tentatively set for 15 May, in Stockholm.

~

The Easter conferences of the Independent Labour Party and the British Socialist Party throbbed with excitement about the events in Russia. A meeting of the ILP on the eve of the conference decided to send a telegram to the people of Russia: 'Great mass meeting in Leeds sends greetings and congratulations to the Russian people. Success to International Socialism!'[11]

The message from the BSP was equally enthusiastic: 'In the name of the International Socialists in Britain we send our greetings to the revolutionary Russian working class and express our unity with them in their struggle for international labour solidarity.'[12] The BSP conference also passed a resolution from the Anderston branch protesting against the continued imprisonment of Maclean.[13]

The surge continued at Glasgow's biggest May Day celebration ever, with an estimated seventy to eighty thousand people marching in the procession and around a quarter of a million lining the streets. The procession wound its way to Glasgow Green, where from sixteen platforms resolutions were passed condemning capitalism; expressing solidarity with Russian workers; and clamouring for the release of John Maclean.[14]

The following Sunday, 13 May, a mass meeting to celebrate the Russian revolution was held at St Andrew's Halls. Guest of honour George Lansbury made an eloquent plea for Maclean's liberation, and a John Maclean release committee was formed with Harry Hopkins as secretary.

~

The British Left's celebrations of the revolution culminated with a major gathering in Leeds on Sunday 3 June. It was organised by the United Socialist Council, a body established in 1913 at the behest of the International Socialist Bureau. It contained representatives of the British Socialist Party, the Independent Labour Party and the Fabian Society, and its mission was forging unity among the reformist and revolutionary sections of the British Left.[15]

The Conference of Labour, Socialist, and Democratic organisations of Great Britain (the Leeds Conference) was attended by 1150 delegates: beside the BSP and ILP, organisations represented included trades councils, local Labour parties, trade unions, other socialist societies, women's organisations, co-operative societies, adult schools, peace societies and May Day committees.

A message was read out at the start of proceedings from the Executive of the Soldiers' and Workmen's Deputies in Petrograd. The executive sent fraternal greetings and hoped to meet representatives of the Leeds Conference between 15 and 30 July, in Stockholm.

The meeting was chaired by Robert Smillie, president of the Miners' Federation of Great Britain, and it considered four resolutions.

The first, moved by Ramsay MacDonald (ILP) and seconded by Dora Montefiore (BSP), hailed the Russian revolution. It was carried unanimously. The second was moved by Philip Snowden (ILP) and seconded by EC Fairchild (BSP) It hailed the foreign policy and war aims of the Russian provisional government and declared:

> ... we pledge ourselves to work for an agreement with the international democracies for the re-establishment of a general peace which shall not tend towards either domination by or over any nation, or the seizure of their national possessions, or the violent usurpation of their territories – a peace without annexations or indemnities and based on the rights of nations to decide their own affairs; and as a first step towards this aim we call upon the British Government immediately to announce its agreement with the declared foreign policy and war aims of the democratic Government of Russia.[16]

The resolution was carried, 'with two or three dissentients'.

Charles Ammon, chairman of the Postal Clerks Union, moved the third resolution relating to civil liberties. It called on the government to 'carry into immediate effect a charter of liberties establishing complete political rights for all men and women, unrestricted freedom of the Press, freedom of speech, a general amnesty for all political and religious prisoners, full rights of political and industrial association, and the release of labour from all forms of compulsion and restraint'.

Ammon opened his address with a reference to the man in Peterhead:

> I think it would be well if we refreshed our memories as to what exactly the Russian charter of freedom does and so realise what we have lost. It establishes an immediate amnesty for all political and religious offences; it establishes freedom of speech, the Press, Labour organisation and the right to strike. Unless we can take them in defiance of the present Administration, do we enjoy any of these liberties? Many of the best public-spirited men are lying in prison – men like John Maclean, who is now entering upon his second year of imprisonment. Will you let him go through a third year? ('No.')[17]

The fourth resolution, calling for the establishment of workers' and soldiers' councils, or to give them their Russian name, soviets, was the most contentious. It began:

> This conference calls upon the constituent bodies at once to establish in every town, urban and rural district, Councils of Workmen and Soldier's Delegates for initiating and co-ordinating working-class activity in support of the policy set out in the foregoing resolution, and to work strenuously for a peace made by the peoples of the various countries, and for the complete political and economic emancipation of international labour. And, further, that the conveners of this Conference be appointed a Provisional Committee, whose duty shall be to assist the formation of local Workmen's and Soldiers' Councils and generally to give effect to the policy determined by this Conference.[18]

The resolution was moved by MP William Anderson (ILP). He said:

> I gather from Press reports that this fourth resolution is regarded as the ugly duckling among the resolutions, and therefore I claim for it on that ground your special solicitude and support. ('Hear, hear.') I saw a paragraph the other day in that dear old mid-Victorian journal the *Morning Post* – (*laughter*) – which states that the fourth resolution is the one that really matters, being more than mere rhetoric. 'This resolution is clearly,' it says, 'a violation of the law as inciting to the subversion of Army discipline and military authorities.' ('Hear, hear.') 'Those who move such a resolution and those who act on it are liable to severe penalties.' (*Laughter.*) 'It is therefore unthinkable that the Government will wittingly permit such action.' Well, I move the resolution without any apology of any kind, and if they want criminals (the speaker made a sweep of his arm towards the packed hall), there is a pretty haul of them in this hall. (*Cheers.*) But I wish

to say emphatically that the resolution was not intended to be subversive of military responsibilities. What we do say is that soldiers and workmen alike are men and have the rights of men, and we ask the newspapers to howl until they are black in the face if they so desire. (*Cheers.*) We shall go on with the work to which we have laid our hands. (*Cheers.*) If we are going to have justice for the soldiers, for the wives and the widows and the children of the soldiers, and if we are going to have industrial freedom for the workmen, the workman and the soldier must join hands. (*Cheers.*) Ah, they say, this is revolution. If a revolution be the conquest of political power by a hitherto disinherited class, if revolution be that we are not going to put up in the future with what we have put up with in the past, we are not going to have the shams and the poverty of the past, then the sooner we have revolution in this country the better. (*Cheers.*)[19]

After further speeches from Robert Williams (secretary of the National Transport Workers' Federation), Mrs Philip Snowden, Sylvia Pankhurst, Fred Shaw, Willie Gallacher and Noah Ablett, among others, the resolution was put to the meeting, and carried, 'amid enthusiasm with only two or three dissentients'.

It was agreed that the following reply should be sent to the Russian Workmen's and Soldiers' Council:

The largest and greatest Convention of Labour, Socialist and democratic bodies held in Great Britain during this generation has to-day endorsed Russia's declaration of foreign policy and war aims, and has pledged itself to work through its newly constituted Workmen's and Soldiers' Council for an immediate democratic peace. The Convention received your telegram of congratulation with gratitude and enthusiasm.

The conference decided that the country should be divided into thirteen districts, each of which would add a representative to the provisional committee.[20]

~

The grand plan fizzled out. Part of the reason was a fundamental difference of views between the pacifists and the revolutionaries. In the latter camp was Tom Quelch of the BSP, who was appointed secretary of the national committee. He saw the hallmark of a revolutionary peace movement as the attempt 'to organise the masses for a definite resistance to the war on the basis of a general strike in munitions factories and kindred industries'.[21] Quelch was keenly aware of the importance of linking anti-war activity with the shop stewards' movement, a sentiment shared by Glasgow delegates Willie Gallacher, Tom Bell and Arthur MacManus.

In his speech Gallacher banged the revolutionary drum. 'This conference seems to be agreed that the Russian Revolution is definitely settled, but is it? No. The Russian Workers' and Soldiers' Delegates have the biggest fight on, not against the capitalists of Russia, but against the capitalists of other countries who have determined that the socialists of Russia have to be beaten back. Give your own capitalist class in this country so much to do that it will not have time to attend to it.'[22]

However the revolutionary tendency was heavily outnumbered by the pacifist bloc, which viewed the conference more as an end in itself, a national demonstration of opinion in favour of an early democratic peace.[23]

As philosopher and pacifist Bertrand Russell commented, 'it was a wonderful occasion, but a little disappointing from the point of view of practical outcomes. Snowden and MacDonald and Anderson are not the right men – they have not the sense for swift dramatic action.'[24]

'It was the first breath in England of the Bolshevik wind,' observed AJP Taylor.[25] It was also an early example of the British Left's propensity to adopt a Russian model that did not fit British conditions.

Once the dust had cleared, the government clamped down. Tom Quelch was conscripted into the army, and the district conferences that the Leeds Conference called for found venues cancelled and meetings banned. When they did occur, they were subject to attacks by mobs of 'patriots' while the authorities stood by (see following chapter).

~

In this febrile environment, when the Glasgow Town Council invited Lloyd George north to receive the freedom of the city, there was a storm of protest on Clydeside. Perhaps mindful of the torrid reception the prime minister had received on his previous visit as minister of munitions, steps were taken to lower the temperature. On 4 June, the day after the Leeds Conference, the deportation orders applying to David Kirkwood, Tommy Clark, James Messer and Arthur MacManus were withdrawn, meaning the men could return to their families on the Clyde.

Protests about Maclean's continued incarceration grew louder. On 7 June a leading article in the British Socialist Party journal the *Call* included the following:

> The brutality of Maclean's sentence was undoubtedly occasioned by the terror with which the master class was seized by the seething unrest that at the time existed on the Clyde ... The rapid advance which Socialism has made in Glasgow is a tribute to Maclean's wonderful energy and keen interest ... It is to be feared that prison life will have a serious effect on his mental and physical health. He has already suffered a serious breakdown which has necessitated his removal to the prison hospital at Perth. If his incarceration is continued there is a serious danger that the consequences will be irreparable. This must not happen. It will be a standing disgrace and shame on the workers with whom he has been so long associated and on whose behalf he has devoted his life's work, if the ruling class is permitted to wreak its vengeance on John Maclean and remove him permanently from its path.[26]

On 12 June, George Lansbury wrote to Lloyd George pleading for clemency for Maclean on humanitarian grounds. He noted that Maclean had many of the radical characteristics that Lloyd George would recognise in himself, and urged him to secure Maclean's release. According to Lansbury, Maclean was suffering from delusions and becoming mentally unbalanced. 'His wife dreads his going mad,' he wrote. If Maclean was released, Lansbury undertook to take him to the south coast of England where he could recuperate with his family in peace.[27]

On 19 June in the House of Commons, Joseph King, Liberal MP for North Somerset, asked the Secretary for Scotland, Robert Munro: 'whether John Maclean is still in prison at Perth; whether his health is showing serious signs of deterioration; and whether any requests and, if so, how many have been received urging his release?'

Munro responded: 'The answer to the first part of the question is in the affirmative and to the second part in the negative. The most recent reports which I have received point to an improvement in Maclean's general health. I have received a number of resolutions in favour of his release.'[28]

The effect of the agitation was bringing things to a conclusion. On 25 June, again in the Commons, Henry Watt, Liberal MP for Glasgow College, asked Munro, 'whether he will now consider the advisability of liberating from gaol John Maclean, a graduate of Glasgow and a school teacher by profession, who has been imprisoned for more than a year under the Defence of the Realm Act for making speeches of an inflammatory character, in view of the fact that prisoners of other nationalities are being released wholesale by order of the Government?'

Munro replied: 'John Maclean has now served more than half of the normal term for which he would be under detention. I have come to the conclusion, having regard to all the circumstances, and in particular to the possible effect of continued imprisonment upon his health, that I am justified in sanctioning his early release on license, and I propose to issue instructions to that effect.'[29]

~

Lloyd George came to Glasgow on Friday 29 June to receive the freedom of the city. Large numbers of workmen ceased work to give the prime minister a 'reception'. They had not forgotten that 15 months previously he had pulled out all the stops to crush the workers' movement on the Clyde. But, Willie Gallacher recalled, it was impossible to get anywhere near him.

> When he drove in an open carriage to St Andrew's Hall, the spectacle was a sight for the gods. Ordinary police, mounted police, special police and military units lined up in front and behind, not only holding the 'Welcoming' masses back, but also completely hiding the little fellow from view. He was receiving the 'Freedom of the City' with the whole police force, supplemented by the military, detailed to protect him.[30]

After the ceremony, Lloyd George was hurried away to a hotel, but the workers were not finished with him. Gallacher wrote:

> All around the centre of the city the workers were gathering and shouting for the release of Maclean. Given a start there was no saying what might have happened. The workers were in a mood to tear up Glasgow by the roots. Police officials were running here and there, whispering and consulting. Then we were approached by police officials who told us that the order for the release of Maclean had been signed and he would be out in the morning.[31]

It was true. Maclean had been transferred from the hospital at Perth Prison to the Duke Street Prison in Glasgow. He was released on Saturday 30 June, on licence from the secretary of Scotland. But he would be back inside in less than a year.

23

A QUIET LIFE

In the week after his release, a reporter from the *Call* came to interview Maclean and was shocked by what he found. Expecting to find a shattered individual, instead: 'What struck me most was the fierce intensity of his devotion to the cause of socialism. He is big and strong, energetic and capable looking.'[1]

Naturally, his Glasgow comrades wanted to give him a public 'welcome back'. The gathering on Tuesday 10 July at St Mungo's Halls 'far exceeded anything of this character we had ever had before', according to Willie Gallacher,[2] with thousands unable to get into the building and an overflow meeting held outside. *Forward* editor Tom Johnston was in the chair and commented that on the platform 'were all the men most fit to welcome home a "convict", for they were all men who had been in prison, men who would probably be in prison and some who ought to be in prison!'[3]

Maclean spoke of his prison ordeal, and urged agitation for the release of conscientious objectors and other political prisoners. He went on to criticise the Allies' war aims and declare his support for a workers' Russia as the only free Russia. To great acclaim, he called on all the forces of the workers' movement to be thrown into the fight against the war and the overthrow of capitalism.[4]

The following day, according to Willie Gallacher, 'the message of this great demonstration was carried into every factory and supplied the drive for meal-hour meetings and discussions all over the Clyde'.[5]

~

As arranged by George Lansbury, John and Agnes and their two daughters went to Hastings for a holiday by the seaside. On the way, Maclean called in to the London offices of the British Socialist Party and dropped off a letter to readers of the *Call*. He thanked everyone for the work they had done to secure his release, and for the money gathered to support his family and help with his legal expenses. He went on:

> In my lone cell I resolved that, on my return to civil life, I would appeal to the workers to demand the release of conscientious objectors, especially those detained in ordinary prisons, on the grounds of the harsh treatment meted out to them. ...
>
> At the same time I particularly appeal to everyone on behalf of Comrade Peter Petroff and his wife. These good comrades came to serve the cause in Glasgow at my suggestion. I consequently assume all responsibility. They did nothing here that they were not entitled to; at any rate, to put it mildly, they did nothing to justify their internment. The British Government has no case against them, and thus has no grounds for their continued detention. Unless they are immediately released, I ask our Russian comrades (who, by the way, along with the Irish rebels, were largely responsible for my own liberation) to cease negotiations with the British Government until both are set free. Meantime, let us get on the move.[6]

Maclean indicated he would be on holiday until the start of his economics class, back in Glasgow on the first Sunday of October. But that was much too ambitious a resolution. There was too much going on.

~

James Macdougall was a conscientious objector. On his release from prison in February 1917, as an alternative to military service, he had gone to do work 'of national importance'[7] at Blantyre in the Lanarkshire coalfields. He had not been idle.

The miners' reform movement that flourished in South Wales before the war had lapsed into inaction there, but Macdougall felt conditions were ripe for its revival in Scotland. By August 1917, the cost of living had soared 80 per cent above the pre-war level while the wages of Scottish miners had only increased by 43 per cent. There were serious shortages of basic foodstuffs; there was rampant profiteering by merchants and shipping companies; and in Lanarkshire – whose concentration of iron, steel, engineering and mining enterprises made it one of the important munitions-producing areas of the country – the influx of workers had led to serious overcrowding, with a quarter of the population living in one-room dwellings. However, as most of the agents and officials of the miners' organisations had embraced a patriotic truce with the owners and government, these wartime grievances saw little redress through official union channels.[8]

Macdougall organised a conference of unofficial delegates from across Lanarkshire at Hamilton in July 1917. The Lanarkshire Miners' Reform Committee was formed at the meeting and the heads of a manifesto were agreed upon. Fifty thousand copies were printed and distributed at the pits. Macdougall described the manifesto in the following terms:

> It presented a reasoned argument along Marxian lines pointing to the inevitable concentration of capital which is the outcome of competition, and showing the miners the impossibility of grappling with the united forces of capitalism unless by the amalgamation of all the county associations into a genuine British Miners' Industrial Union, with pooled resources, centralised direction and a wide enough scope to embrace every worker of whatever craft in the industry. The ultimate aim of the organisation must be: 'The common ownership of the mines and the direct control of production by the workers in the mining industry.'[9]

In Blantyre, the militants persuaded the local district committee to call a one-day strike, an 'idle day', to protest about inadequate food rations and call for peace by negotiations. Twelve pits and 2000 men were involved. A member of the Blantyre group successfully proposed a resolution to the Lanarkshire Miners' Union for a county-wide strike over the same demands. On 2 August 1917, 50,000 miners struck with thirteen separate demonstrations calling on the government to put an end to profiteering.[10]

John Maclean was exultant, writing in the *Call*:

> Last Thursday the whole of the miners in Lanarkshire, with the exception of Harthill, where a holiday was held on Friday, did not dig coal, but made a hefty dig at the paunch of the profiteers and their flunkey Government. More than fifty thousand were engaged in this most healthy exercise. After processing, they assembled at thirteen places of meeting to call on the Government immediately to reduce prices. Smillie himself hinted to the whole working class that, if the Government did not take the hint, they ought to 'take action'.
>
> This event is certainly the most important in the whole history of the working class in Scotland. It easily transcends the spontaneous strike on the Clyde, that forced the Government to give us the House Letting Act. At the time those of us who did our bit in getting that Act realised that for the

first time the workers of Scotland (perhaps Britain) struck for a political object of a class nature. In this case the object is also political, but it is a larger object - the whole cost of living. More significant still is the fact that the strike has been organised by the executive committee of the Lanarkshire Miners and loyally supported by the rank and file; for in the Clyde strikes the Buntons of the A.S.E. and the Sharps of the Boilermakers were in reality helping the masters against the men, and as a result have now obtained jobs from the capitalist class. The greatness and grandeur of Bob Smillie (the mightiest fighter the workers of Scotland have ever had) is seen in his refusal to accept the Food Controller's job thrown at him by the Government, and the powerful lead he is giving to our class to force the Government's hands on the food question. The organised miners have now raised themselves to the highest level; that is, as champions of the whole working class, and not merely of miners as miners. That is the beginning of the end of capitalism if other organised workers follow suit. I am confident, at any rate, that my comrades in the engineering and shipbuilding industries of the Clyde will fully appreciate the significance of Thursday's great event in Lanarkshire.[11]

~

Regional conferences to establish the district councils in England and Wales proposed by the Leeds Conference were scheduled for 28 July. However, there were strong forces in the country opposed to the notion of workers' and soldiers' councils, and they organised to make their point by word, and by deed. In many places, the police persuaded the owners of the public halls where the conferences were to happen to cancel their bookings at short notice.

The speakers at the London meeting were to be John Maclean, Joe Fineberg, secretary of the Stepney branch of the British Socialist Party, and Ethel Snowden, wife of Labour MP Philip Snowden. At the last moment the meeting was switched to the Brotherhood Church, in Southgate Road, Hackney, after the original booking at the Memorial Hall in Farringdon Road was cancelled. The church was the centre of a range of radical and socialist activities; notably, the Russian Social Democratic Labour Party had used the building in 1907 for its fifth Congress.[12]

There had been some attempt to keep the location of the meeting private, but the authorities were well prepared.

Sir Basil Thompson, head of the Special Branch, arranged for a reception party to meet the delegates. Leaflets announcing that a pro-German meeting was taking place were issued, and they urged East Enders to 'Remember the last air raid and roll up.'

The police seemed to have gained the co-operation of the Army, which sent along loyally patriotic soldiers. Gleefully, Sir Basil wrote in his diary on 27 July: 'They will have a rude awakening tomorrow, as I have arranged with the *Daily Express* to publish the place of their meeting and a strong opposition may be expected.'[13]

Thompson's expectations were more than fulfilled. Long before the meeting was due to start, a mob had started to gather. It was estimated that it eventually numbered around 8,000, with many in uniform.

By 3 pm the church was surrounded and by quarter past the front door had been smashed in by a sledgehammer. The delegates who had already arrived, estimated at 500 by the meeting's chairman, William Anderson MP, retreated to the small hall at the rear and closed the doors as securely as they could. The mob proceeded to smash up the main hall; windows and fanlights were broken and frames ripped out, the furniture was almost completely destroyed, water pipes were pulled out of the walls, and the hall was partially flooded.[14]

Philosopher Bertrand Russell, who was one of the delegates, described his experience:

> The mob burst in led by a few officers; all except the officers were more or less drunk. The fiercest were viragos who used wooden boards full of rusty nails. An attempt was made by the officers to induce the women among us to retire first so they might deal as they thought fit with the pacifist men, whom they supposed to be all cowards. Mrs Snowden behaved on this occasion in a very admirable manner. She refused point blank to leave the hall unless the men were allowed to leave at the same time. The other women present agreed with her. This rather upset the officers in charge of the roughs, as they did not particularly wish to assault women. But by this time the mob had its blood up, and pandemonium broke loose. Everyone had to escape as best they could while the police looked on calmly. Two of the drunken women began to attack me with their boards full of nails. While I was wondering how one defended oneself against this type of attack, one of the ladies among us went up to the police and suggested they should defend me. The police merely shrugged their shoulders. 'But he is an eminent philosopher,' said the lady, and the police still shrugged. 'But he is famous all over the world as a man of learning,' she continued. The police remained unmoved. 'But

he is the brother of an Earl' she finally cried. At this the police rushed to my assistance. They were, however, too late to be of any service, and I owe my life to a young woman whom I did not know, who interposed herself between me and the viragos long enough for me to make my escape. But quite a number of people, including several women, had their clothes torn off their backs as they left the building.[15]

When John Maclean arrived at the church all he saw was 'a howling mob of male and female dervishes' skirmishing around the place and the meeting was completely broken up.[16]

There were similar scenes at the Newcastle meeting, where 'a number of persons hostile to the meeting rushed the hall, and there were free fights, at which some soldiers and sailors took part', and at Swansea, where:

> The patriotic citizens of Swansea prevented the holding of a peace delegates meeting in the Elysium Hall yesterday afternoon, and after chasing the delegates from the building into a cul-de-sac compelled them to surrender their sticks and umbrellas, which they had been using freely against attackers.[17]

Meetings at Bristol, Leicester, Manchester and Norwich on the same day passed without violence, although in the case of Norwich that was probably because the gathering was held in a 'secluded place' and thus escaped the attention of any possible assailants.[18]

~

The Glasgow convention of the workers' and soldiers' councils was scheduled for Saturday 11 August. The organisers had booked St Mungo's Halls, which was the property of the Scottish Co-operative Wholesale Society.

On 8 August, the War Cabinet authorised the secretary of Scotland to prohibit the proposed meeting. To inhibit alternative arrangements being made, the announcement was not to be made until after 4 pm on the Friday before. It also called on the secretary of state for war to make an announcement in parliament, but not until after the secretary of Scotland's announcement, that the Cabinet regarded the objects of such meetings as illegal, and would not permit them to be held.[19]

The *Glasgow Herald* reported:

At the request of the Magistrates of the City of Glasgow the Secretary of Scotland has, in terms of the Defence of the Realm Regulations, authorised the Lord Provost and Chief Constable of Glasgow to issue an order prohibiting the meeting in Glasgow called for tomorrow by the Provisional Committee of the Workers & Soldiers Council.[20]

The ban did not deter the organisers, who spread the word that there would be a demonstration outside the hall at the same time as the original meeting had been scheduled. This aroused the opponents of the convention to a frenzy. Labour MP Ramsay MacDonald had been nominated to be the principal speaker and was subjected to a torrent of abuse and insult in the press. Amid the ferment, the organisers made their preparations. Willie Gallacher recalled:

> We organised a great muster of shop stewards to protect the demonstration in the event of an attack by our enemies. We lined them up four deep in the streets adjacent to the place of the demonstration, and then, when the delegates and others participating were gathered around the platform, the shop stewards marched around and completely encircled the demonstration with an unbreakable barrier of resolute workers. When this manoeuvre was completed, MacDonald was brought along in a taxi and led through an already prepared human channel to the platform.[21]

Despite the attempts of the press to whip up a protest, the patriots failed to appear and the gathering was a great success.

Why did the workers' and soldiers' councils prompt such visceral antipathy from the authorities and the establishment? Harry McShane offered an insight in his memoir.

> For the Glasgow socialist movement the new Soviet system was a revelation. … We had realised that they were workers' and soldiers' councils, a new kind of rank-and-file organisation, and everybody had welcomed the Leeds conference in June. But what some there had not understood was that this organisation was the form of government of the future. When Lenin called for 'All power to the Soviets' it meant that they had discovered a system of working-class self-government through which the old crowd could be completely destroyed. We had only known working class revolt: now we could talk about working-class power.[22]

~

In the period immediately following the patriotic riot at the Brotherhood Church, John Maclean spent some time in East London and met with Georgy Chicherin. According to Ripley and McHugh, Maclean and Chicherin 'had a long talk, a few days before the latter's internment'. Chicherin had been warned by the police of his impending arrest on 10 August and a few days later was in Brixton Jail.[23]

As 1917 dawned, Chicherin had been despondent, believing that imperialism had triumphed because it had 'succeeded in splitting the forces of the proletariat, in winning the "labour-bureaucracies" to its side and in using them to fight its battles among the lower classes'.[24]

He wrote in the *Call*, '... the proletariat's task – its present historical mission – the international struggle against war, against the very foundations of the capitalist system, must be carried on without taking the least notice of the interests of the military defence of the respective countries'.[25]

While delighted by the news of the February revolution, Chicherin was quick to attack the 'insidious' attempt by the Allies to represent the Russian revolutionary movement as bent on pursuing the war to total victory over the Central Powers. He contested the notion that the Russian revolution was patriotically rather than internationally inclined and missed no chance to attack those in favour of Russia's continued participation in the war.[26]

It was the latter that lead to his arrest. The official complaint read, in part, 'That having regard to his anti-ally and pro-German activities and sentiments, he is a danger to the public safety and the defence of the Realm.'[27]

Chicherin's colleague Mary Bridges Adams bombarded the labour press with demands for his release and was bitterly critical of the 'inaction of the leadership'.[28] But the centre of gravity of the campaign to release Chicherin, as well as Peter and Irma Petroff and other Russian internees, gradually shifted to Glasgow, where Maclean and Russian émigré Louis Shammes established the Russian Political Refugees Defence Committee and began to ramp up their advocacy. The committee won the support of the Glasgow Trades Council, and the Foreign Office was bombarded with protests from more than twenty Scottish trade union branches, plus a number of branches of the British Socialist Party.[29]

After their London meeting, Maclean wrote to Chicherin, expressing the view that Marxism was 'growing rapidly and with it, the interest in and importance of all connected with Russia, yourself included'.[30]

The letter was deliberately withheld from the Russian, but Maclean's words were prophetic. The interest in, and importance of, Russia was about to explode.

24
GIVE PEACE A CHANCE

In the immediate aftermath of February's Russian revolution, the governments of both the Allies and the Central Powers reached out to the new Russia, but for diametrically opposed reasons. The Allies wanted to be reassured that the new regime would stay the course with the war; while the Central Powers were keen to explore the possibility of a settlement on the Eastern Front and the withdrawal of Russia from hostilities. Both sides used men of the left for these interactions, believing that they were more likely to have influence in Petrograd.

As early as 27 March (14 March OS) the Petrograd Soviet had issued a manifesto, drafted with the help of noted writer Maxim Gorky, that called for a just peace, without annexations or indemnities. The manifesto was well received in the war-weary country but was at variance with the views of Pavel Milyukov, foreign minister in the provisional government. When Milyukov gave a press interview on 5 April (23 March OS) detailing Russia's desire to acquire the Ukrainian elements of the Austro-Hungarian Empire plus Constantinople and the Dardanelles Straits, the soviet was outraged. Under pressure, the provisional government issued a statement of war aims on 9 April (27 March OS) that was firmly rooted in the soviet's manifesto.

Lenin returned to Petrograd from Switzerland on 16 April 1917 (3 April OS). His immediate call for 'All power to the soviets' and an end to the dual power arrangement between the provisional government and the Petrograd Soviet initially caused consternation, not just with members of the government, but also with the Bolsheviks, Mensheviks and the All-Russian Conference of Soviets. But as more Bolshevik exiles returned to their homeland in the weeks that followed, they proved to be more radical than those who had remained. In an environment where the economic hardships of the country were worsening; the inadequacies of the provisional government were growing clearer; and the brief honeymoon of cross-class collaboration was souring; Lenin's position began to attract increasing support.[1]

Milyukov did not back down on the issue of war aims, telling the *Manchester Guardian* that the provisional government's statement did nothing to change Russia's commitments to its allies. In response, the Petrograd Soviet insisted the statement be forwarded to the Allies as a 'diplomatic note'. Urged on by Milyukov's rival Alexander Kerensky, on 1 May (18 April OS) the provisional government eventually complied with the request. But Milyukov still was not done. He appended a note to the cable stressing that it did not mean that Russia was planning to leave the war, and it remained determined to fight on for the 'high ideals' of the Allies.[2]

When the Petrograd Soviet learned of the Milyukov note it was incensed, and when the note was published it prompted furious protest demonstrations by workers and soldiers, many of whom urged the soviet to assert its power and arrest the provisional government. Not confident of its capacity to rule, the soviet rejected the calls and insisted it must help the government regain its authority. The Bolsheviks condemned the note and reaffirmed its view that the end of the war would only become possible when the soviet took power – but did not call for the workers and soldiers to come out.[3]

In early May, the provisional government acknowledged it was not in control in Russia and sought a coalition with the Petrograd Soviet. There were strong forces in favour of the move, and their position was supported by visitors from socialist parties in the Allied countries.

After initially rejecting the overture, the soviet opened negotiations and decided to accept the proposal, albeit with conditions. The second provisional, or first coalition government was formed on 18 May (5 May OS), with six socialist ministers, including the Menshevik Kerensky as minister for war. The Petrograd Soviet voted to support the coalition, although the 100 Bolshevik members cast their ballots against the move.

After the vote, a comrade newly returned from exile in Europe, via the USA and Canada, was invited to speak. Leon Trotsky was warmly welcomed and began by praising the revolution. But then, to a room growing more and more quiet, he condemned the entry of socialists into the government. What was needed, what he called for, was not a dual power, but a single power. That of workers' and soldiers' deputies. 'Our next move,' he said, 'will be to transfer the whole power into the hands of the soviets.' The formula could have been Lenin's.[4]

Leading Menshevik Julius Martov, Trotsky's colleague from the Paris days of *Nashe Slovo*, also arrived back in Russia in May. He declared he was appalled by his party's 'ultimate stupidity' of joining the government without extracting a commitment to end the war.

~

The idea of a peace conference at Stockholm, involving socialists of both the Allies and Central Powers, as well as neutral countries, bounced around Europe for the rest of 1917, without ever quite managing to land.

The Petrograd Soviet viewed it positively; both 'social patriot' and 'pacifist' socialists of all countries were generally in favour; and the British and German governments at times entertained the idea. However, the Bolsheviks were resolutely opposed; as were the governments of France, Italy and the United States.

After the war began, the International Socialist Bureau had moved from occupied Belgium to The Hague. Once established in neutral Holland, it added three local socialists to the executive committee to demonstrate its neutrality to the socialists of the Central Powers. Camille Huysmans, the Belgian secretary of the bureau, first discussed the idea of an international socialist conference with the Dutch socialists on 15 April (2 April OS). At that meeting, they decided to go to Stockholm and form an ad hoc committee with the Scandinavian socialist parties to prepare for an all-party conference.

Huysmans wanted to secure the collaboration of the Russian socialists before announcing the project, reasoning it would put pressure on the British and French to participate. However, the Dutch wanted to move more quickly and their view prevailed. On 22 April (9 April OS) the Dutch-Scandinavian Committee issued an invitation to an international socialist conference to take place on 15 May (2 May OS) in Stockholm. But as will be seen, the date moved forward several times during the rest of the year, until finally it disappeared completely.

The initial reactions to the proposed conference were not encouraging. On 9 May (26 April OS) the British Labour Party Executive declined the invitation; and the next day the French majority socialists did likewise. Then on 12 May (29 April OS) the German Spartacists wrote to the Petrograd Soviet refusing to attend any conference at which the German Social Democratic Party (SPD) was present.[5]

Three weeks before the Dutch-Scandinavian Committee issued its invitation, the Social-Democratic Party in neutral Denmark had put the International Socialist Bureau on notice, telling it that if it did not organise a conference, one would be arranged without its assistance.

Danish socialist Frederik Borgbjerg set off for Petrograd on 7 April (25 March OS) carrying not only an invitation to a conference but also details of the peace terms the German Social Democrats would find acceptable. Two days after he delivered his request, a representative of the Petrograd Soviet is reported to have told him, 'Your mission has succeeded. The Workers' and Soldiers' Council has decided – as has been announced in the Press – to issue invitations to a conference. It will be easier for the English and French to take part. A clashing with the other conference is then out of the question.'

The 'other conference' was the Stockholm conference, for by this time, the invitation from the Dutch-Scandinavian Committee had reached Petrograd. The German and Danish Socialists, on Borgbjerg's return, decided to support the Petrograd Soviet's initiative.[6]

For his troubles, Bjorgberg was denounced as a German agent by Lenin and the Bolsheviks. On 8 May (25 April OS), Lenin told the Bolshevik Party congress, 'We must not forget the real issue, the motives underlying this whole affair. I shall show you that behind this comedy of a so-called socialist congress we shall find the very real political manoeuvres of German imperialism. The German capitalists, through the medium of the German social-chauvinists, are inviting the social-chauvinists of all countries to the conference. Why do they do it through the socialists? Because they want to fool the working masses.'[7] The Bolsheviks also declared their opposition to the Stockholm conference proposed by the Dutch-Scandinavian Committee.

~

Despite the minority Bolshevik opposition, enthusiasm within the Petrograd Soviet for a socialist peace conference remained strong. Therefore, when members of the soviet joined the first Russian coalition government on 18 May, the possibility of some form of conference convening at Stockholm rose. The prospect prompted alarm in London. The fear was that in the absence of Allied representation the Germans 'would impress on the Russians that the British Empire and France were alone standing in the way of peace'.[8] The nightmare scenario of Russia signing a peace deal with Germany and Austria-Hungary that closed down the Eastern Front would totally change the balance of the war. Not only would it release German troops to be transferred to the Western Front, but also Austrian armies would be freed to threaten Allied forces in Italy and the Balkans.

On 21 May, the British War Cabinet considered the question of sending British representatives to attend the socialist conference at Stockholm. The acting Secretary of State for Foreign Affairs, Lord Robert Cecil, urged that a strong deputation of the British Labour Party, headed perhaps by Arthur Henderson, the party secretary and a member of the War Cabinet, should be sent to Stockholm. He also suggested Henderson 'might with advantage be sent on a special mission to Petrograd'. The mission would correspond to that of Albert Thomas, a senior French socialist who was already in Petrograd.

Henderson pointed out the difficulty of now sending British representatives to Stockholm given that less than two weeks earlier, 'in accordance with the wishes of the War Cabinet', he had used his influence with the executive committee of the Labour Party not to take part in the proposed Stockholm conference. Instead, he had suggested calling a conference of Allied socialists in London.

During the War Cabinet discussion, it emerged that what was taking place at Stockholm were separate and successive conversations between the Dutch-Scandinavian Committee and representatives of the various socialist parties of the belligerent nations. The Belgian socialist Vandervelde had already taken part in such a conversation, and Russian and German delegations were expected there shortly.

It was generally agreed that if a conference should take place, British representatives should attend. Otherwise, the Russian and German socialists would fraternise without any counteracting influence, probably with the worst results to the cause of the Allies. It was realised that a British refusal to participate would have a very serious effect in Russia and would strengthen the German anti-British propaganda there.[9]

The War Cabinet met again two days later and decided that the British ambassador in Petrograd, Sir George Buchanan, was no longer the ideal British representative, considering his close association with the tsarist regime. The Cabinet invited Henderson to 'make a personal sacrifice' and go to Petrograd on a similar footing to Albert Thomas, who had taken over as French ambassador there. Henderson decided to accept the invitation and left for Petrograd the following day.

25
ARTHUR HENDERSON GOES TO RUSSIA

Arthur Henderson arrived in Petrograd on 1 June (19 May OS). That very day, the executive committee of the Petrograd Soviet again endorsed the Stockholm project, declaring the purpose of such a conference would be to 'liquidate the policy of "national unity" with the imperialist governments and classes which make a struggle for peace impossible.'[1]

The soviet set a date, 8 July (25 June OS), for the conference to meet. However, it was not until a month later that a Russian delegation reached Stockholm, and the formation of the Russian-Dutch-Scandinavian Committee that was to organise the conference did not happen until 11 July (29 June OS).[2]

The unexpected announcement by the soviet led to Henderson's first encounter with the moderate socialists Alexander Kerensky and Irakli Tsereteli, who were members of both the provisional government and the Petrograd Soviet. At a meeting on 3 June (21 May OS), Henderson joined with the leaders of the French and Belgian socialist delegations (Thomas and Vandervelde) in 'castigating the Russians for their unwarranted action'.[3] The following day, the Allied socialists drafted an open letter to the soviet in which they declared their 'complete agreement' with the idea that socialists should rupture their agreements with 'governments whose war aims are tainted with imperialism', but that a 'national union against aggressive imperialism' was a duty incumbent on all classes.[4] This was an argument for excluding from an international conference those socialists who supported the 'aggressive imperialists' of the Central Powers.

Disagreements between the Russian and Allied socialists were an inevitable consequence of their different perceptions of the war. For the Russians it was a classic confrontation between imperialist powers, while for the Allies it was a legitimate defence against unprovoked aggression. Despite their differences, each side needed the other: the Allied socialists needed to persuade the Russians to stay militarily committed, while the Russians needed the Allied socialists to bring pressure on their governments to seek a negotiated peace.⁵

While Henderson was in Russia, a third version of a peace conference was proposed. On 13 June (31 May OS), Mikhail Tereshchenko, who had replaced Milyukov as foreign minister on 18 May (5 May OS), suggested inviting Allied governments to discuss possible modifications to their war aims. This was acceptable to the majority of socialists in the soviet, as the intent was to bring Allied governments into line with their non-annexationist peace formula. The Allied governments themselves were reluctant, but were pressed by their representatives in Petrograd to 'at least give the appearance of compliance with Tereshchenko's request for fear of undermining the government's fragile stability'.⁶

~

After a month of coalition, the mood in Russia was hardening. Unrest in the countryside, the cities and at the front was growing; shortages were getting worse and people were hungry. After an anti-government demonstration proposed for 23 June (10 June OS) was deemed premature and cancelled at the last minute, Kerensky persuaded the All-Russian Congress of Soviets, against the opposition of the Bolsheviks and other internationalists, to resolve that 'the Russian revolutionary democracy is obliged to keep its army in a condition to take either the offensive or the defensive'. Thus the doctrine of 'defencism', to maintain the gains of the revolution, slid back into the mode of traditional war-making.⁷

With the pro-war forces in the ascendent, Kerensky reimposed traditional military discipline and visited the troops at the front to bolster morale ahead of an anticipated new Russian offensive. The threat of transfer to the front provoked anger amongst the troops stationed in revolutionary Petrograd. Bolshevik influence was increasing among this cohort and the hard-left Bolshevik Military Organisation started considering plans for an armed demonstration against Kerensky's plans.

On 1 July (18 June OS), the new Russian offensive began in Galicia. The same day, a demonstration was organised by the Petrograd Soviet to support the ideas of a democratic republic, general peace and a constituent assembly. On taking to the platform at the conclusion of the march, the organisers were horrified to see the bulk of the 400,000 on the streets were Bolshevik supporters carrying banners denouncing the non-socialist ministers in the government, protesting the army offensive, and calling for 'Peace! Land! Bread!' The newspaper *Novaya zhizn* wrote: 'Sunday's demonstration revealed the complete triumph of Bolshevism among the Petrograd Proletariat.'[8]

After two or three days of successes, the Kerensky offensive stalled, and when German forces counterattacked, the Russians began retreating and then deserting in vast numbers. Officially 170,000 soldiers ran away during the offensive, but the real number was undoubtedly very much higher.[9]

'The mass desertions,' said Trotsky, 'are ceasing in the present conditions to be the result of depraved individual wills and are becoming an expression of the complete incapacity of the government to weld the revolutionary army with inward unity of purpose.'[10]

The unequivocal Bolshevik position of 'Down with the war and immediate peace at any price', conveyed throughout the country by a well organised network of cadres, was easily understood and gained more and more support.

~

Six weeks in Russia was sufficient for Henderson to realise that if the provisional government could not extricate Russia from the war, there were others, as Lenin had made clear on his arrival in April, who would undoubtedly sue for a separate peace at the first opportunity.

Before he left Petrograd for Stockholm on 16 July (3 July OS), Henderson completed a report on his mission, which was presented to the War Cabinet on his return. The report covered in some depth his impressions of the industrial scene, the military position, and the volatile political situation in Russia. His conclusion was sombre:

> ... on the facts within my knowledge, my judgement is that while, in the interests of Russia, our own good name, and the peace of the world, we are bound to stand by her faithfully and generously till the end, we should be wiser, if the war is to last beyond the coming autumn, not to reckon on her being able to give us sustained and effective support.[11]

On the proposed Stockholm conference, Henderson wrote that towards the end of his stay he had an interview with Irakli Tsereteli, the minister for posts and telegraphs, and according to Henderson, 'the chief exponent of the Menshevik idea'. Tsereteli showed little appetite for Henderson's idea of an Allied socialist conference in London. He was much more interested in having a Stockholm conference of socialists ahead of a meeting of the Allied governments, 'in order to take some of the edge off the differences that separate the belligerents'.[12]

A few days before his departure from Petrograd, Henderson told a Reuter's representative that he was more than ever convinced that the Russian socialists were determined to have a peace conference, with or without British and French representatives. He said he was personally in favour of such a conference, provided that it was organised under proper conditions and preceded by a conference of Allied Socialist and Labour parties.[13]

In Stockholm on 17 July (4 July OS) Henderson had a long meeting with Hjalmar Branting and Camille Huysmans, the two key figures in what was by then the Russian-Dutch-Scandinavian organising committee. Huysmans had brought the Dutch to the project, while Branting was the leader of the Swedish Social Democratic Party and was widely regarded as staunchly pro-Allies in his views.

With the governments of France, Italy and the United States having banned their citizens from attending, and the separate conversations with the socialist parties of the belligerents finding little common ground, prospects for the conference were not looking good. But flushed with the success of reaching agreement with the Russian delegation the previous week, Branting and Huysmans believed that if they could persuade Henderson to get on board, and could get his party to follow suit, the situation would be totally turned around.

There is no record of the conversation, but in an interview later that day with the *Times* (published on 24 July, the day after he returned to England), Henderson declared himself 'fully convinced of the desirability that such a conference [Stockholm] should be held and wishes the Labour and Socialist parties of all Entente countries, including America, to be fully represented in the persons of their most prominent leaders'. Henderson pronounced himself at one with Emile Vandervelde and his optimistic vision of a Stockholm conference being the beginning of rebuilding the Socialist International from the bottom up.[14]

This was exactly one of the major reasons Lenin was against the whole idea. He recognised that if Stockholm succeeded, the 'floating' centre of socialist opinion, neither 'patriotic' nor 'revolutionary', which had previously supported the Zimmerwald internationalist movement, would return to the Socialist International, and that Huysmans would succeed in keeping the International together. He realised that in a revived International he and his supporters would again become an impotent minority, a small 'ginger group' and that the opportunity given to him by the revolution and his return to Petrograd would be lost, at least in international affairs and possibly also in Russia itself. In the hope of forestalling such a development and retaining the initiative, he worked consistently against Stockholm and sought the establishment of a Third International, led by the Bolsheviks.[15]

~

In the two days after Henderson left Petrograd, things that had been simmering came to the boil in the Russian capital. The First Machine Gun Regiment had been formulating plans for an armed uprising. The Bolshevik Military Organisation learned of the plans and told the party's central committee that a movement of the soldiers was inevitable – the question was, how should the party relate to it? The leadership felt the time was not yet right for insurrection, and urged restraint. The message went unheeded.

The demonstration that started on 16 July (3 July OS) was violent from the start, with marchers overturning trams and machine gunners setting up posts on bridges. The left and the hard right forces clashed, punches were thrown, shots were fired, wounded demonstrators staggered away from the fighting. The militant crowd made its way to where the Petrograd Soviet was in session and a delegation burst in. They were disturbed to hear that the soviet was considering entering a new coalition government. That, they said, was something they could not allow.[16]

The following day saw half a million people on the streets of Petrograd. They were joined by thousands of sailors from Kronstadt, who arrived in a makeshift flotilla. At the Bolshevik headquarters, Lenin reluctantly addressed the sailors, who were armed and ready for battle. They were taken aback by his appeal for self-restraint and the necessity for a peaceful demonstration.

The marchers made their way to the Tauride Palace, where the leaders of the soviet were bunkered down. 'All power to the soviets!' they chanted. After a hasty discussion, the leader of the Social Revolutionaries Viktor Chernov was sent out as an emissary to calm the mob. His attempt at oration failed dismally however, and as the mood turned ugly a big worker pushed his way through the crowd and shook his fist right in Chernov's face.

In one of the most famous phrases of 1917, he bellowed 'Take power, you son of a bitch, when it's given to you!'

Realising the danger their colleague was in, other members of the soviet rushed out to help. Chernov had been bundled into a car, and first to reach him was Trotsky. A trumpet sounded, the crowd quietened, and Trotsky demanded the crowd listen as he climbed onto the bonnet.

'Comrade Kronstadters,' he shouted. 'Pride and glory of the revolution! You've come to declare your will and show the soviet that the working class no longer wants the bourgeoisie in power. But why hurt your own cause by petty acts of violence against casual individuals? Individuals are not worthy of your attention.'

Trotsky faced down the furious heckling that followed, and then called on those who were in favour of violence to raise their hands. When no-one in the crowd did, he opened the car door and said, 'Citizen Chernov, you are free to go.'

Bruised and humiliated, Chernov scurried back inside the palace.[17]

With the crowd still clamouring outside, and sporadic firefights between patriotic Cossacks and workers breaking out across the city, the soviet debated what to do. The Bolsheviks, the Left Social Revolutionaries and the Menshevik Internationalists insisted the current arrangements could not continue. The mainstream Social Revolutionaries and Mensheviks countered that at the country's current state of development, a government without non-socialists would be a disaster, and a coalition was essential.

When a vote was taken, the right bloc prevailed and the decision was to support the provisional government until the Soviet Executive Committee could meet. Shortly afterwards, regiments of soldiers arrived to defend the soviet and the militants melted away.

~

The following day, stories spread that Lenin was a German spy. The claims were fanciful at best, but had a devastating effect. The public mood swung strongly to the right, with Cossacks and other loyalists meting out punishment to anyone suspected of taking part in the previous day's demonstration.

The Bolsheviks, wielding what influence they could, called on their supporters to disperse, while most of the leadership decided to go into hiding. The soviet accepted these measures and declared no further punitive actions would be taken and demonstrators not accused of specific crimes would be released.

The provisional government was not so forgiving, and a strong force was dispatched to round up the remnants of the insurrectionists. Arrest warrants were issued for the 'organisers' of the troubles, with Lenin top of the list. Deciding discretion was the better part of valour, the Bolshevik leader went into hiding, from where he resolutely protested his innocence of the charges levelled against him

The Bolsheviks were in disarray, but the provisional government was in little better shape, and on 21 July (8 July OS) Prime Minister Prince Lvov resigned, citing an unbridgeable gulf between himself and the Cabinet socialists. He invited Kerensky, the man with a foot in both the government and the soviet, to replace him. The offer was immediately accepted, and Kerensky started the process of putting together a new unity government.

On his first day in his new position, Kerensky made the fateful appointment of General Kornilov as the commander of the south-western front, where the Russian army's disintegration was most severe. Kornilov immediately demanded the authority to execute fleeing soldiers, and the government granted his wish within a matter of days.

On 29 July (16 July OS) Kerensky met with the Russian High Command, and was shaken by the vitriol of the generals towards the revolution and its measures relating to the army, which they said had undermined military authority and led to the army's collapse. He decided that the gravity of the situation meant Kornilov should be appointed commander-in-chief.

Shortly after Kornilov was confirmed in the position, an anonymous note from a 'true friend and comrade' was delivered to the executive committee of the Petrograd Soviet. It read: 'Comrades. Please drive out that fucking son of a bitch General Kornilov, or else he's going to take his machine guns and drive you out.'[18]

26

STOCKHOLM

Accompanying Arthur Henderson on his return journey from Stockholm were four delegates from the Petrograd Soviet. Their mission was to discuss with British and French socialists the proposed Allied socialist conference scheduled for 8 and 9 August in London, and the international socialist conference proposed for Stockholm the following week.

Henderson's journey was delayed by three or four days by the inability of the British government to send a warship to bring him back from Norway. When he finally arrived on Monday 23 July, awaiting him was an urgent invitation from the French socialists, addressed to both the Russian socialists and the British Labour Party, to proceed at once to Paris to discuss the two conferences.

On Wednesday 25 July, before he had a chance to meet with the War Cabinet, Henderson had to attend a scheduled meeting of the Labour Party's National Executive Committee. In the presence of the four delegates from Petrograd, he gave a report on his trip to Russia. Then, after discussion, a vote was taken to convene a special party conference on 10 August, at which the committee would recommend the party being represented at the Stockholm conference. It was also decided to accept the French socialists' invitation, with Henderson, the party's treasurer Ramsay MacDonald, and the committee chair, George Wardle being chosen as the party's representatives.

Immediately the decision to accept the French invitation was reached, Henderson cabled Prime Minister Lloyd George, who was in Paris attending an Allied war conference. He also arranged naval transport, as that was the only way the British and Russian representatives could cross the channel to France. The following day, Thursday 26 July, he attended a meeting of the War Cabinet and 'frankly discussed' the trip to Paris with his colleagues. At this point there were some crossed wires, as the National Executive Committee was under the impression that the trip had been sanctioned by the government, while the War Cabinet understood it had been approved by the prime minister.

On 19 July, the German Reichstag had passed a resolution for a 'peace of understanding' whose terms were no annexations, no indemnities, freedom of the seas, and international arbitration. On the same day that Henderson attended the War Cabinet, Ramsay MacDonald stood up in the House of Commons and, in light of the Reichstag resolution, called on the government, in conjunction with the Allies, to restate their peace terms accordingly. The suggestion was strongly opposed by Asquith and Bonar Law, overwhelmingly rejected by the House, and roundly criticised in the press.

When it emerged the following week that the Royal Navy had taken the 'notorious' pacifist MacDonald to France, in company with a member of the War Cabinet, for meetings about a socialist peace conference at Stockholm, members of parliament were outraged and the press had a field day.

The meetings in Paris proved disappointing for Henderson. While he managed to move the dates of the conferences forward – the Allied socialist gathering to 28 August and Stockholm to 9 September – he could not persuade the French and Russians on the issues of representation, or whether conference resolutions would be binding or non-binding. The French were firm in their view that where parties affiliated to the pre-war International had split, the separate fractions should retain their rights of representation. The Russians hoped that binding resolutions would force the belligerent socialists into greater efforts for peace; the French that a binding resolution on the return of Alsace-Lorraine to France would put the Germans in a quandary.[1]

~

On his return from Paris on 1 August, Henderson was summoned to a meeting with Lloyd George to explain his actions. This was followed by a War Cabinet meeting later that afternoon, at which Henderson was left cooling his heels outside for an hour while his colleagues discussed the situation. When he eventually was invited in, he outlined his view of what had occurred.

Henderson first pointed out that when he had left London for Petrograd in May, the War Cabinet had agreed that if a peace conference was held at Stockholm, it would be advisable for British representatives to be present. While circumstances may have changed, until he met his colleagues, he had no information that their attitude had changed. While in Russia, the

Russian foreign secretary had impressed on him the great importance of Stockholm in clearing away Russian suspicions of British imperialist designs. He had accepted the invitation to go to Paris, as he believed it was important to be there with the Russian socialists. As to the selection of Ramsay MacDonald, he believed it was important that those who held different views to himself should be represented.

Wary of forcing the issue and risking a split with Labour, the War Cabinet accepted Henderson's explanation and talk turned to how he might address the issue in the House of Commons. It was agreed that Henderson would point out the advantages of his dual role as a member of the War Cabinet and secretary of the executive committee of the Labour Party. In the first role he could keep the government abreast of the attitudes of labour towards the prosecution of the war; in the second, he could represent British views at conferences of Allied socialists.[2]

On the evening of 1 August, Henderson addressed the House, his value to the government was endorsed by Lloyd George, and while parliament and the press were not entirely satisfied, the manoeuvre took most of the heat out of the issue. On Stockholm, Lloyd George told the House the government was by no means committed to British attendance, but would continue to discuss the matter before stating its final position.

In fact, opposition to Stockholm was hardening within the War Cabinet, with Bonar Law telling the House of Commons on 2 August that permission to attend would not be given without 'the most careful consideration' and 'probably not at all'.[3]

The War Cabinet meeting of 8 August, which Henderson attended, discussed two points: whether the government should allow British delegates to proceed to Stockholm; and whether its decision should be announced to parliament.

On the first point, the Cabinet was provided beforehand with legal advice from the Attorney-General. That advice drew on the principle of common law, 'that in time of war, intercourse between subjects of this country and enemy subjects is forbidden'. The meaning of 'intercourse' had been broadened during 1915 to include 'not merely commercial intercourse, but all intercourse with an alien enemy'. The Attorney-General concluded that to 'take part in a Peace Conference with enemy subjects would ... clearly constitute "intercourse"'.[4]

It was agreed that since May, there had been decisive changes to the situation in Russia, that the influence of the Petrograd Soviet was declining, and that attendance of British delegates was less important that formerly. However, it was felt that it would be more conductive to the maintenance of good relations with the Russian government and the Labour Party, that the Labour Party should refuse to attend rather that the government dictate to it.

The Cabinet decided that attendance at the conference by British delegates would be illegal; and that such a conference could not be attended without the permission of the government. It was also decided to postpone any announcement until after the Labour Party conference on 10 August. It was noted that the conference might cast a vote in favour of Stockholm, which would place the government in a difficult position.[5]

No dissent to any of these decisions is recorded in the War Cabinet minutes. But on the other hand, neither during the meeting, nor at any time in the two days before he spoke at the Labour conference, did Henderson indicate he had changed his publicly stated support for Stockholm.

So, despite the unambiguous opposition of the War Cabinet, and in the full knowledge that it would precipitate his resignation, at the Labour Party conference on 10 August Henderson spoke in favour of participating in Stockholm. Since the Petrograd Soviet had no intention of renouncing the conference, British representatives should attend, he said, as long as its resolutions were not binding on the participants. 'The reason is simple. In my opinion, our case has never been properly stated and is certainly not properly understood to this day in Russia, and to have point blank refused to consider the question would have done incalculable harm,' he told the gathering.[6]

Paul Kellogg and Arthur Gleason provided the following illuminating pen portrait of Henderson at this time:

Henderson is one of the most deceptive men we have met. Like Ulysses, when he is seated you would take him for nobody in particular. In conversation he is a little verbose, impersonal and oratorical. But when the herd cries of a thousand strong men (representing two and a half million men) pierce through to the layers of his stored vitality, hidden under a commonplace exterior, something awakens and he puts on power and rays it out on the mass till they obey him. Unlike some men who compromise differences, he doesn't do it by soft soap and gentle conciliation. He uses a cast-iron voice and a bull vitality to pound in the sensible central interpretation of a plain man, and he does it with all the energy and noise of an exhorter of the extreme left.[7]

After all the speeches had been made, the meeting adjourned for the miners to reach a decision, which was 547-184 in favour. The miners also agreed that the British delegation should be limited to twenty-four: eight from the Trade Unions Congress, eight from the Labour Party and eight from a special conference. They wanted no separate delegations from the smaller socialist parties. When the conference re-assembled, it voted for Stockholm by an overwhelming margin (1,846,000-550,000) and adjourned until 21 August, when it was to decide on delegates and consider the memorandum on war aims drafted by Sidney Webb of the Fabian Society.[8]

The outcome was savaged by the jingoistic press, which had been working itself into a lather over the prospect of British representatives sitting down with their German counterparts while brave Tommies were being butchered by the hated Huns. Lloyd George claimed the War Cabinet was taken 'completely by surprise' by Henderson's support, and asked for his resignation. Henderson obliged and was replaced in the War Cabinet by the Minister for Pensions, Labour MP George Barnes.

The Cabinet again discussed Stockholm on 11 August and decided that delegates should not be allowed to go; a statement to that effect was prepared for the House of Commons. The debate on 13 August in the House was a watershed in several ways. For Stockholm, whether British Labour would be allowed to attend was crucial, since, if they could not, certainly French, Italian, and American Labour would not be allowed to go either. Bonar Law stated that passports would be refused; Henderson spoke on Stockholm and his resignation; and a general debate followed. But more than putting an end to the chance that Stockholm could provide an unofficial sounding-board for a negotiated peace, the debate also foreshadowed the beginning of a new policy, led by British Labour under Henderson, no longer of 'civil peace', but of independent international labour and socialist action.[9]

~

The Inter-Allied Socialist Conference in London, agreed upon in Paris at the end of July, was held on 28-29 August. Coming on top of the confusion and cross purposes over Stockholm, it is hardly surprising that it was a fiasco. British delegates predominated, but there were representatives from Belgium, France, Portugal, Greece and South Africa, as well as the four

Russians who had come from Petrograd the previous month. John Maclean was one of the eight delegates from the British Socialist Party who attended.

On the first day of the conference two committees were appointed; one to consider the questions of representation at Stockholm; the other the two memoranda on war aims submitted by the British Labour Party and the British Socialist Party, plus a note on the Labour Party's memorandum submitted by the Independent Labour Party.

The BSP had released its own statement of war aims on the eve of the conference. It called on the working class to intervene to bring the war to a speedy end, and utilise the economic and political situation to hasten the transition from capitalism to a co-operative form of society. 'Unless immediate bold and drastic action is taken by the whole organised working class movement, the return of peace will plunge the wage-earning population into all the miseries of an intensified capitalism,' it said.[10]

The note from the Independent Labour Party on the Labour Party memorandum was laid before the conference on the opening day. It accepted the Labour Party memorandum as a basis for discussion, and while agreeing with many of the proposals, differed in matters of detail.

The conference committee on Stockholm broke down into two camps; the first supporting going to Stockholm and the other against going if enemy representatives were present. Topping that in the disunity stakes, the committee on war aims split three ways. The Russians, the Portuguese and the British Labour Party (together with the annotations by the ILP) agreed on one statement; the French and Belgians made a separate statement; and the British Socialist Party stuck by their memorandum.

The only thing the conference could agree on was a unanimous vote of congratulation to the Russian revolution.[11]

The failure of the Inter-Allied Conference, the impasse over Stockholm, and Henderson's departure from the government led British Labour to work out a new three-part international socialist policy based on Sidney Webb's memorandum on war aims. The new program was initiated by the Trades Union Congress at its annual gathering at Blackpool, on 3-4 September 1917. It called for agreement on war aims within the British movement before proceeding to get inter-Allied, and finally inter-belligerent, agreement. It shifted interest away from Stockholm and towards London, away from peace proposals and towards war aims, away from the efforts of the Russians and an international outlook and towards home affairs and the winning of the war. It meant that the failure of the Stockholm movement was generally accepted as a fait accompli and that the efforts to resurrect the old Second International had broken down.[12]

While no longer in the War Cabinet, Henderson remained Labour leader and had learned his lesson. Never again, he declared, would he join a government in which Labour did not predominate. Under Henderson's guidance, Labour set out to be a national party instead of an interest group, aiming at an independent majority and running candidates everywhere in the country. This saw a change in membership rules that allowed individuals to join the party; a new platform written by Sidney Webb that called for 'common ownership of the means of production'; and the adoption of the Union for Democratic Control's principles of openness and parliamentary control of foreign policy, and a just peace settlement. In practical terms, this meant the return of Ramsay MacDonald as Henderson's partner in the project.[13]

Thus, while as it turned out the Stockholm Conference never actually took place, the episode helped to lay the foundations for the modern British Labour Party.

27
RUSSIA TURNS RED

After the tumult of the July days, the leading Bolsheviks in Russia were either in hiding or in jail, while counter-revolutionary forces began to coalesce around the newly appointed Commander-in-Chief, General Kornilov. Believing the provisional government led by Kerensky was under threat from the left, Kornilov organised troops to march on Petrograd, and planned to impose martial law, curfews and a ban on meetings and strikes. Perceiving this as an attempted right-wing coup, on 9 September (27 August OS), Kerensky persuaded the Cabinet to grant him unlimited authority to counter the move. After approving the creation of a five-man Directorate under Kerensky, the whole Cabinet resigned, bringing the second coalition government to an end. The Petrograd Soviet also agreed with the change, although the Bolshevik members voted against it.

On the ground in Petrograd, soldiers and workers mobilised and prepared for the defence of the city. Over 40,000 workers were provided with arms; the beginning of what came to be known as the Red Guards. The Petrograd Soviet established the Committee for Struggle against the Counterrevolution, and although the Bolsheviks were in the minority in that body, they wielded control. Railway lines were ripped up to prevent Kornilov's troops from entering the city; groups of soldiers and workmen intercepted the loyalist troops, explaining the situation and entreating them to stand down. When both sides realised they had mobilised in defence of the provisional government, they relaxed and began to fraternise. There had been no actual fighting and by 12 September (30 August OS), the 'revolt' was over, and Kornilov was arrested.

The tense confrontation shook up the already unstable relations between the various centres of power and control. On 14 September (1 September OS), the Petrograd Soviet voted in favour of a national government of representatives of the working class and peasantry only. Later that day, the

All-Russian Executive Committee of Soviets repudiated the decision and came down on the side of Kerensky's Council of Five instead.[1]

Trotsky was granted bail and released from prison on 17 September (4 September OS). He immediately assumed de facto leadership of the Bolsheviks, even though Stalin coveted the position, and as editor of the main Bolshevik newspaper, appeared to be in a stronger position at the time. Lenin was still hiding out in Finland, but was writing furiously and sending his missives to Petrograd.

On 28 September (15 September OS), the Bolshevik leadership was at a conference discussing a socialist coalition with the Social Revolutionaries and Mensheviks, when a letter from Lenin arrived. Sniffing the political wind, Lenin had sensed that the centre was collapsing and opinion was moving to the extremes; either to the hard right or to the hard left. Rejecting any notion of collaboration, he wrote: 'The Bolsheviks, having obtained a majority in the soviets of workers' and soldiers' deputies in both capitals [Petrograd and Moscow], can and *must* take state power into their own hands.'[2] The party leaders were flummoxed, and with no idea about how this might happen, ignored the directive.

On 8 October (25 September OS), Kerensky managed to cobble together a new government, the third coalition government, and while technically it contained a majority of socialists, they were all moderates, and none held a key post. The same day, a new presidium of the Petrograd Soviet was elected. It comprised one Social Revolutionary, two Mensheviks, and four Bolsheviks, including Trotsky. Trotsky immediately proposed a resolution that the soviet would not work with the new, weak, reviled government. It passed overwhelmingly.[3]

~

In case anyone had forgotten about the war, on 11 October (28 September OS) the German Army landed on Saaremaa, a large island in the northwest corner of the Gulf of Riga. It was the launch of Operation Albion, to gain control of the West Estonian archipelago and open a route on the Northern Front to attack Petrograd. By 16 October (3 October OS) the Russians had abandoned Reval (now Tallinin), the last bastion before Petrograd, and the government sought advice on moving the executive and key industries to Moscow. But not the soviet. When the news seeped out, it deepened the fear that the government would abandon Red Petrograd, and rid itself of the thorn in its side.

Lenin again called for the Bolsheviks to seize power, and this time the message filtered through. But while some Bolsheviks agreed, others did not, and debate raged. Then on 19 October (6 October OS) the Petrograd military commander instructed the city's troops to prepare to move to the front. This sparked a general mutiny in the Petrograd garrison. Trotsky explained:

> The right to control bodies of armed men is a fundamental right of the state power. The first Provisional Government, wished upon the people by the Executive Committee [of the Petrograd Soviet], gave an obligation not to disarm and not to remove from Petrograd those military units which had taken part in the February overturn. This was the formal beginning of a military dualism inseparable in essence from the double sovereignty. The major political disturbances of the succeeding months – the April demonstration, the July days, the preparation of the Kornilov insurrection and its liquidation – each one inevitably ran into the question of the subordination of the Petrograd garrison. But conflicts between the government and the Compromisers [the Mensheviks and Social Revolutionaries] upon this theme were, after all, a family matter, and ended amicably. With the Bolshevisation of the garrison things took a different turn. The soldiers themselves now began to recall that obligation given by the government to the Executive Committee in March and treacherously broken by them.[4]

Three days later, the mass anger the instruction from the military commander provoked in the Petrograd garrison spilled into the soviet. The Mensheviks called for a new committee of struggle, whose task would be to take part in the defence of the capital with the active co-operation of the workers. To their surprise, the suggestion was supported by the Bolsheviks.

It was an important step, Trotsky wrote, as it put the soviet in a position to turn the decision about removing the troops this way or that, according to circumstances. The Bolsheviks had already been talking about the necessity of creating an authoritative soviet committee to lead the coming insurrection; and the party's military organisation had even drawn up plans for such a body. The one conundrum they had not yet resolved was that of reconciling an instrument of insurrection with an elective and openly functioning soviet. The proposal of the Mensheviks, therefore, came up just in time to assist in the creation of a revolutionary headquarters – a body soon to be renamed the Military Revolutionary Committee (MRC).[5]

Frustrated by the lack of action, but still under threat of arrest, Lenin returned to Petrograd in disguise on 23 October (10 October OS) to attend a clandestine meeting of the central committee of the Bolshevik Party. Addressing his comrades, Lenin was impassioned. The time had come for insurrection, he insisted. The debate went back and forth into the early hours of the morning. Finally, by 10 votes to 2, the committee decided armed insurrection was the order of the day. But differences remained about the timing of an uprising.

A second meeting of the committee six days later confirmed the original resolution. Lenin wanted immediate action; but still there was hesitation and delay.

~

On 3 November (20 October OS), the Military Revolutionary Committee began operations. Nominally its staff included representatives from the presidiums of the soviet and of the soldiers' section, representatives of the fleet, of the regional committee of Finland, of the railroad unions, of the factory committees, the trade unions, the party military organisations, and the Red Guard. However it hardly ever met in that form and its activities were directed by its bureau, which was made up of two Social Revolutionaries and three Bolsheviks, including Trotsky. Although it had the appearance of a soviet organisation, it was in truth a Bolshevik body, with the SR members as 'camouflage'. It was to become the chief lever of the revolution.[6] On 4 November (21 October OS), the MRC proclaimed itself the ruling authority of the Petrograd garrison and advised the district headquarters, 'Orders not signed by us are invalid.'

Holed up in the Winter Palace, Kerensky appeared oblivious to his deteriorating position. He even began praying that the Bolsheviks would make a move, boasting, 'I have greater forces than necessary. They will be utterly crushed.'[7]

With expectations of an uprising reaching fever pitch, the Petrograd Soviet had designated Sunday 5 November (22 October OS) as a day for a peaceful review of its forces. For the third time in five days, the patriotic press announced in its morning edition the authorities' expectation of a 'coming-out'.

Petrograd Soviet Day saw Bolshevik orators whipping up crowds. Trotsky warned that Petrograd remained at imminent risk from the bourgeoise, and it was up to workers and soldiers to defend the city. Playing for time, while awaiting reinforcements from outside the city, the head of the Petrograd military district invited the MRC for talks. Kerensky, increasingly impotent, ordered the MRC to be liquidated by force. The instruction was ignored.

On 6 November (23 October OS) the soldiers at the Peter and Paul Fortress debated and decided to switch allegiance from the existing chain of command to the MRC. The imposing fortress, which sat on an island that hugged the north bank of the Neva River, contained most of Petrograd's weapons stores. And some of its cannon pointed over the river at the Winter Palace.

As Orlando Figes observed: 'The Provisional Government had lost effective military control of the capital a full two days before the armed uprising began. By 25 October [OS] the most important task of any revolution – the capture of the garrison in the capital – had already been completed; the Provisional Government was defenceless; and it only remained for the Bolsheviks to walk into the Winter Palace and arrest the ministers.'[8]

But then, another setback. The executive committee of the soviet threatened to break off relations with the MRC unless it withdrew its declaration about orders not signed by it being invalid. Fearful of losing its legitimacy, the MRC complied.

The MRC had blinked; and Kerensky stuck. He ordered an assault on the Bolsheviks. In the early morning of 7 November (24 October OS) troops were sent to break up the Bolshevik's Trud Press. As cover for the move, several other presses were also attacked. However, the disruption was only temporary. The Red Guards retook the Trud Press and an issue of *Pravda* was issued calling on the Congress of Soviets to replace Kerensky's regime. Trotsky explained how the move backfired on the government.

> An attempt to suppress the papers, a resolution to prosecute the Military Revolutionary Committee, an order removing commissars, the cutting-out of Smolny's telephones – these pin-pricks were just sufficient to convict the government of preparing a counter-revolutionary *coup d'état*. Although an insurrection can win on the offensive, it develops better, the more it looks like self-defence. A piece of official sealing-wax on the door of the Bolshevik editorial-rooms – as a military measure that is not much. But what a superb signal for battle! Telephonograms to all districts and units of the garrison announced the event: 'The enemy of the people took the offensive during the night. The Military Revolutionary Committee is leading the resistance to the

assault of the conspirators.' The conspirators – these were the institutions of the official government. From the pen of revolutionary conspirators this term came as a surprise, but it wholly corresponded to the situation and to the feelings of the masses.[9]

Trotsky called for restraint. He was waiting for the Second All-Russian Congress of Soviets of Workers' and Soldiers' Deputies, which after several postponements was due to open proceedings on 8 November (25 October OS). It seemed highly likely the Bolsheviks, who had been steadily increasing their control of soviets across the country, would have a majority of delegates and any decision the congress made would give any uprising the cloak of legitimacy. While Lenin had been advocating immediate action for some time, Trotsky's strategy of delaying any move until the congress opened prevailed.

It was difficult to stop defensive measures from spilling into the offensive however, and by the early hours of the morning Bolshevik forces had taken control of the railway stations, the post and telegraph network, the telephone system and the electricity substations. The only part of the city still under government control was the area around the Winter Palace.

~

Mindful of how hesitation had cost them the initiative in July Days, on the night of 7 November (24 October OS) Lenin decided to break cover and made his way to the Smolny Institute where the Bolshevik caucus was meeting. The Winter Palace must be taken and the provisional government arrested; he declaimed. Eventually the central committee agreed and gave the order for the insurrection to begin. A map was produced and the Bolshevik leaders began assigning military tasks.[10]

At 3.30 am, as their plans were being finalised, a dark shape made its way up the Neva River and moored beside the Nikolaevsky Bridge, a mere two kilometres downstream from the Winter Palace. Summoned by the MRC, it was the 7600 ton armoured Baltic cruiser *Aurora*, bristling with menacing guns. The previous afternoon, the army had ordered the bridge, as well as the other three key Petrograd bridges, to be raised, to prevent people from the workers' districts congregating in the central area. When the loyalist guards saw the *Aurora* arrive, they beat a hasty retreat and the sailors lowered the bridge.

An increasingly desperate Kerensky called on the Cossacks to save the government, but they politely declined to be 'live targets'. At points throughout the city, Red Guards disarmed loyalist troops and advised them to go home. The MRC got word to Kronstadt, and 1,500 Baltic sailors armed to the teeth boarded five destroyers and a patrol boat, unfurled revolutionary banners, and set sail for the capital.

A wire from the War Ministry to headquarters that morning gave an assessment of the situation: 'The troops of the Petrograd garrison ... have gone over to the Bolsheviks. The sailors and a light-armed cruiser have come from Kronstadt. They have lowered the raised bridges. The whole town is covered with sentry guards from the garrison. But there has been no coming-out. The Telephone Exchange is in the hands of the garrison. The troops in the Winter Palace are defending it only in a formal sense, since they have decided not to come out actively. The general impression is that the provisional government finds itself in the capital of a hostile state which has finished mobilisation but not yet begun active operations.'[11]

At 10 am Lenin drafted a proclamation in the name of the Revolutionary Military Committee, announcing the formation of a Soviet government. Wanting to present a *fait accompli* to the All-Russian Congress when it opened later in the day, he wrote:

> The Provisional Government has been deposed. State power has passed into the hands of the organ of the Petrograd Soviet of Workers' and Soldiers' Deputies - the Revolutionary Military Committee, which heads the Petrograd proletariat and the garrison.
>
> The cause for which the people have fought, namely, the immediate offer of a democratic peace, the abolition of landed proprietorship, workers' control over production, and the establishment of Soviet power - this cause has been secured.
>
> Long live the revolution of workers, soldiers and peasants![12]

The proclamation was quickly printed and posters were plastered up across the city. Although it was still more aspiration than fact, the outcome Lenin anticipated appeared inevitable.

~

At 11 am, Kerensky left the Winter Palace in one of two commandeered cars and headed north out of the city in search of the troops he had summoned to defend the government. His departure left the rest of the ministers shaken. They began making plans for the defence of the palace, but as none of them had any experience in military matters, the exercise was poorly executed. There was no plan of the building with the result that a side-door was left unguarded and Bolshevik spies were able to enter it freely.[13]

That afternoon, Trotsky opened an emergency session of the Petrograd Soviet. To wild cheers, he announced, 'On behalf of the Military Revolutionary Committee, I declare the Provisional Government no longer exists.' Key institutions were in the hands of the MRC, and the Winter Palace would fall momentarily, he assured the delegates. Lenin entered the room to another burst of cheering. In his first public appearance since July, he only spoke briefly but concluded with the exhortation: 'Long live the world socialist revolution!'

There were 3000 troops protecting the Winter Palace, but their morale was collapsing. They were vastly outnumbered, there was no ammunition store in the palace and there was not enough food to feed them. As the evening wore on, more and more hungry soldiers slipped away, until only 300 remained.[14]

At 6.50 pm, the MRC delivered an ultimatum to the Winter Palace, demanding the surrender of the provisional government. Initially, the communication was ignored, with the ministers believing that the Bolsheviks would be widely condemned if they resorted to force. But then at 9.40, the *Aurora* fired a blank shell, which made a huge noise, much louder than a live round. All the ministers dived for cover.

At 10.40 pm the real bombardment began. Cannons were fired at the palace from the Peter and Paul Fortress (although most of the shells landed in the river) and machine-guns opened up from the Palace Square.

At the same time, in the great hall of the Smolny Institute, the Congress of Soviets finally opened. Of the 670 delegates, 300 were Bolsheviks, 193 were Social Revolutionaries (of whom more than half were of the party's left), and there were 68 Mensheviks and 14 Menshevik-Internationals. The congress voted in a new central executive committee, comprising 14 Bolsheviks (including Trotsky) and 7 Social Revolutionaries. The Mensheviks declined to accept their three seats and Martov's Menshevik-Internationals also declined, but reserved the right to change their mind.

As the noise of the attack on the Winter Palace five kilometres to the west washed over the gathering, Martov proposed the formation of a united democratic government based on all the parties in the soviet. This was the only way to avoid a civil war, he said. The proposal was greeted by a torrent of applause – even from many of the Bolsheviks – and was passed unanimously. But then, a series of Mensheviks and Social Revolutionaries denounced the violent assault on the provisional government and declared they would have nothing to do with this 'criminal venture'. They walked out of the congress to the jeers and boos of the Bolsheviks.

Martov tried once more to argue for a grand coalition of socialist parties, but the walk-out of the right-wing Mensheviks and Social Revolutionaries had branded them as counter-revolutionaries.

Trotsky rose to speak:

> What has taken place is an insurrection, not a conspiracy. An insurrection of the popular masses needs no justification. We have tempered and hardened the revolutionary energy of the Petrograd workers and soldiers. We have openly forged the will of the masses to insurrection, and not conspiracy … Our insurrection has conquered, and now you propose to us: Renounce your victory: make a compromise. With whom? I ask: With whom ought we to make a compromise? With that pitiful handful who just went out? … Haven't we seen them through and through? There is no longer anybody in Russia who is for them. Are the millions of workers and peasants represented in this Congress, whom they are ready now as always to turn over for a price to the mercies of the bourgeoisie, are they to enter a compromise with these men? No, a compromise is no good here. To those who have gone out, and to all who made like proposals, we must say, 'You are pitiful isolated individuals; you are bankrupts; your role is played out. Go where you belong from now on – into the rubbish-can of history!'¹⁵

Angrily, Martov shouted, 'Then we'll leave!' and walked out in silence. Trotsky proposed a resolution condemning the Mensheviks and Social Revolutionaries for their 'treacherous' attempt to undermine soviet power, which was easily passed. The mass of delegates was ready to follow Lenin's uncompromising path.

~

Over at the Winter Palace, the end-game was playing out. Loyalist forces had virtually abandoned the building and Bolshevik troops could enter at will. The ministers were placed under arrest, and marched to the Peter and Paul Fortress where they were locked up.

The arrests were announced to the Congress of Soviets, to resounding cheers. Then, at 5.17 am, word came from the Northern Front of the formation of a military revolutionary committee. 'Delegations from the echelons moved against Petrograd have one after another announced to the Military Revolutionary Committee their solidarity with the Petrograd garrison. Attempts of the government to get armed help have broken against the resistance of the army.'[16] Delegates wept with relief.

A proclamation written by Lenin and addressed to the workers, soldiers and peasants was read out. 'By its mere exposition of what had happened and what was proposed,' Trotsky wrote, 'this hastily written document laid down the foundations of a new state structure.'

> The authority of the ... Central Executive Committee is at an end. The Provisional Government is deposed. The Congress assumes the power ... The Soviet Government proposes immediate peace. It will transfer the land to the peasants, democratise the army, establish control over production, promptly summon the Constituent Assembly, guarantee the right of the nations of Russia to self-determination. 'The Congress resolves: That all power in the localities goes over to the soviets.'[17]

The day that followed, 9 November (26 October OS), saw wild pronouncements, repudiations, accusations and (false) reports of bloody Bolshevik massacres. The Congress of Soviets met again in the evening. After a report about the work done during the day – abolition of capital punishment in the army; restoration of the free right of propaganda; release of officers and soldiers imprisoned for political crimes; all the commissars of the provisional government removed from office; orders given to arrest Kerensky and Kornilov – Lenin was given the floor for a report on peace. American journalist John Reed described the historic moment thus:

> ... Now Lenin, gripping the edges of the reading-stand, letting his little winking eyes travel over the crowd as he stood there waiting, apparently oblivious to the long-rolling ovation, which lasted several minutes. When it finished, he said simply, 'We shall now proceed to construct the socialist order.'[18]

He then read a declaration, 'The decree on peace'.

> The workers' and peasants' government, created by the Revolution of October 24-25 and basing itself on the Soviet of Workers', Soldiers' and Peasants' Deputies, calls upon all the belligerent peoples and their governments to start immediate negotiations for a just, democratic peace.

By a just or democratic peace, for which the overwhelming majority of the working class and other working people of all the belligerent countries, exhausted, tormented and racked by the war, are craving – a peace that has been most definitely and insistently demanded by the Russian workers and peasants ever since the overthrow of the tsarist monarchy – by such a peace the government means an immediate peace without annexations (i.e., without the seizure of foreign lands, without the forcible incorporation of foreign nations) and without indemnities.

The government of Russia proposes that this kind of peace be immediately concluded by all the belligerent nations, and expresses its readiness to take all the resolute measures now, without the least delay, pending the final ratification of all the terms of such a peace by authoritative assemblies of the people's representatives of all countries and all nations.[19]

It was unlikely, however, that any of the other belligerent governments would heed the call. Russia dropping out of the war would give the Central Powers the opportunity to redeploy troops from the east and increase pressure on the Western Front. The entry of the United States into the war in April 1917 meant Britain and France believed they could meet this challenge.

Having encouraged the revolutionary destruction of the Russian Army, it was essential for the Bolsheviks to quickly conclude a separate peace with the Central Powers. This would give them breathing space to consolidate their grip on power, reinvigorate the economy and rebuild their military strength.

Crucially, Lenin's declaration was addressed to two audiences, governments and the people. The Bolsheviks were pinning their hopes on the spread of revolution to the west. They believed that the war between nations would be transformed into a series of civil wars, in which workers would rise up and overthrow their rulers.

In essence, the decree on peace was a summons to world revolution.

28
CONSOLIDATING BOLSHEVIK POWER

After their initial seizure of power, few gave the Bolsheviks much hope of consolidating their success. 'Caliphs for an hour,' was the verdict of much of the Russian press. Others gave them 'no more than a few days', or two or three weeks.[1]

It was not just the opposition of the civil service, which immediately went on strike, but the Bolsheviks had no means of feeding the cities or halting the collapse of the economy. They were also isolated from the peasants, who were almost certain to vote against them in the upcoming election for the constituent assembly.

Nonetheless, by the time the assembly met in January 1918, the Bolsheviks had created the one-party state and soviets had spread throughout the country. The body, upon which the democratic opposition had pinned all its hopes, had been rendered powerless.

The lack of military opposition was a significant factor. The likely leaders of a counterinsurgency were so convinced the new regime was going to self-destruct that they did not bother to organise against it.

But the key to the Bolshevik success was a twin process of state-building and destruction. At the highest level of the state, they sought to centralise all power in the hands of the party, and crush any opposition. At the local level, they encouraged the destruction of existing governance structures and their replacement by decentralised bodies such as soviets, factory organisations and soldiers' committees. The creation of independent states in the former ethnic borderlands of the Russian Empire, which the Bolsheviks encouraged, also helped to break down the old order. By January 1918, Finland, Lithuania, Latvia and the Ukraine had all pronounced themselves independent.[2]

The Military Revolutionary Committee continued to function as the effective government until mid-November when enough of the people's commissars, the Bolshevik's new name for Cabinet ministers, had gained control of their respective ministries to enable the Council of People's Commissars to assume executive authority. Unusually, there was no clear division between the party and the government. The council, commonly known as Sovnarkom, discussed party and government matters interchangeably; resolutions of the Bolshevik's Central Committee were implemented as Soviet decrees.[3]

Just as the party began to overshadow Sovnarkom, so Sovnarkom started to overshadow the work of the Soviet Executive. Although the seizure of power had been executed in the name of the Congress of Soviets, Lenin had no interest in ruling through the congress or its executive. The executive acted as a brake on Sovnarkom in the first weeks after the revolution, but that changed on 28 November (15 November OS) when the left wing leaders of the Peasant Soviet were added. These 108 peasant deputies were joined by a further 150 from trade unions and revolutionary organisations in the army and navy. The result, a bloated membership of 330, rendered the executive too cumbersome to function as an efficient body.[4]

Sovnarkom decreed itself the right to pass urgent legislation without the approval of the Soviet. The Soviet Executive narrowly approved the change. Then, Sovnarkom presented the executive with a 'constitutional instruction' that stated while Sovnarkom was still responsible to the Soviet, and had to present all legislation to it for approval, it did not specify when this had to be done. The effect was that Sovnarkom could publish a legally binding decree without the prior approval of the Soviet. Which was exactly what happened.

~

Voting for the constituent assembly began on 25 November (12 November OS) and lasted for two weeks. The results were a setback for the Bolsheviks, who won just 24 per cent of the vote, most of them cast by the soldiers and workers of the industrial north. The Social Revolutionaries (SRs), who had their base in the peasantry, received the highest number of votes, 38 per cent, but there was confusion about the significance of this. After the ballot papers were printed, the party had split into the Left SRs, who supported the Bolsheviks, and the Right SRs who did not. The remaining votes were split between the Mensheviks (3 per cent), the right-wing Kadets (5 per cent) and the Ukrainian SRs (12 per cent).

Sovnarkom set out immediately to undermine the outcome, postponing the opening of the assembly and issuing a decree that electors could recall their deputies from all representative bodies, including the assembly, if the move was supported by more than half the electorate in a constituency.

Trotsky defended the move as a 'painless alternative' to the outright closure of the assembly in the event of it being opposed to the principle of soviet power. When the opposition parties organised a demonstration to protest the undermining of the assembly, it was branded as a 'counter-revolutionary' act organised by the Kadets. The Kadet Party was outlawed and denounced as 'enemies of the people', and dozens of its leaders were arrested. Lenin called the Kadet Central Committee the 'political staff of the bourgeoisie'. The arrests did not end with the Kadets, and a number of Social Revolutionary and Menshevik leaders were also detained.[5]

The Left SRs joined Sovnarkom on 25 December 1917 (12 December OS). On the same day Lenin set out his thoughts on the assembly. He wrote:

1. The demand for the convocation of a Constituent Assembly was a perfectly legitimate part of the programme of revolutionary Social-Democracy, because in a bourgeois republic the Constituent Assembly represents the highest form of democracy and because, in setting up a Pre-parliament, the imperialist republic headed by Kerensky was preparing to rig the elections and violate democracy in a number of ways.
2. While demanding the convocation of a Constituent Assembly, revolutionary Social-Democracy has ever since the beginning of the Revolution of 1917 repeatedly emphasised that a republic of soviets is a higher form of democracy than the usual bourgeois republic with a Constituent Assembly.
3. For the transition from the bourgeois to the socialist system, for the dictatorship of the proletariat, the Republic of Soviets (of Workers', Soldiers' and Peasants' Deputies) is not only a higher type of democratic institution (as compared with the usual bourgeois republic crowned by a Constituent Assembly), but is the only form capable of securing the most painless transition to socialism.
4. The convocation of the Constituent Assembly in our revolution on the basis of lists submitted in the middle of October 1917 is taking place under conditions which preclude the possibility of the elections to this constituent assembly faithfully expressing the will of the people in general and of the working people in particular.[6]

The class struggle and the defeat of the counter-revolution demanded the consolidation of soviet power and unless the assembly was ready to acknowledge this, it was doomed to extinction, Lenin argued. Ten days later at a meeting of the Soviet Executive, the Bolsheviks and the Left SRs combined to demand the closure of the constituent assembly unless it subordinated itself to the soviets at its opening session at the Tauride Palace on 18 January 1918 (5 January OS).

Lenin drew up a 'Declaration of the Rights of the Working People' to be put before the opening session of the assembly. It proclaimed Russia a Republic of Soviets, and endorsed all the decrees of Sovnarkom, including the abolition of private landed property, the nationalisation of the banks and the introduction of universal labour conscription.[7]

When Lenin's declaration was put before the opening session of the assembly, it was defeated by 237 votes to 146. The Bolsheviks declared the assembly to be in the hands of counter-revolutionaries and walked out. The Bolsheviks and Left SRs met and agreed to dissolve the assembly. Delegates continued to introduce decrees and make speeches until the early hours of the following day, at which point they filed out and the Red Guards locked up the palace.

Two days later, on 21 January (8 January OS), the Third All-Russian Congress of Soviets of Workers', Soldiers' and Peasants' Deputies convened. Nine out of ten delegates came from the Bolsheviks and Left SRs and the congress passed everything presented to it by the government. That included the 'Declaration of the Rights of the Working People', which served as the first constitution of the Soviet state.

29

THE RELEASE OF CHICHERIN AND PETROFF

Refreshed after his summer holiday in England, John Maclean returned to Glasgow in early autumn 1917 and immediately started planning an ambitious Marxist educational program. The Labour College Committee was resuscitated; James Macdougall began holding classes for miners in Lanarkshire; and other classes were started in Greenock, Johnstone, Paisley, Kirkintilloch, Leven, Cowdenbeath, Bowhill and Kirkcaldy. Besides Maclean and Macdougall, lecturers included JF Armour, HB Guthrie, R Nicol and Neil Maclean.[1]

The centrepiece was Maclean's Central Economics class in Bath Street, Glasgow which resumed on 7 October. By early November, the class had five hundred students every Sunday; a class in Govan attracted a further hundred.

'I run eight classes every week in Scotland, with a membership of over a thousand students,' Maclean wrote in the *Cotton Factory Times*. 'Macdougall conducts another five with about three hundred students. In all there are between thirty and forty classes in Scotland, with a total of over three thousand students. This excludes the host of circles and classes held at meal-times inside shipyards, engineering shops, and factories.'[2]

In the same article, Maclean wrote about the growing interest on the Clyde of the 'eloquent articles' flowing from the pen of his 'revered friend' Mrs Bridges Adams. He went on:

'Specially inspired by her brave and brilliant article on the arrest of our brave comrade George Chicherin, I had a talk with some of the Russians resident in Glasgow and as a sequel, Mr L Shammes took in hand the formation of a committee representative of the Jewish and Lithuanian political and industrial organisations having headquarters in Glasgow.

Delegates from five bodies have come together and have formed the Russian Political Refugees Defence Committee, with the object of agitating for the release of George Chicherin, Peter Petroff, Mrs P Petroff, and all other Russians wrongly interned. The secretary is Mr L Shammes ... and the writer was invited to act as chairman, a function he was only too pleased to perform.'[3]

Maclean went on to outline the circumstances leading to the arrest and internment of Peter Petroff. He described how while on his break in Hastings after his release from prison he applied to visit Petroff but his request was denied. The only person allowed to visit Petroff at the time was an Italian comrade named D'Aprano. It was also D'Aprano that took Maclean to visit Chicherin in London a few days before the police warned the Russian of his impending arrest.

'Our committee has already organised a most successful lecture to realise funds to proceed with our work,' Maclean continued. 'We have consequently been able to issue a circular to over 1000 working class organisations in Scotland, asking that an enclosed resolution demanding the release of the above mentioned be forwarded to Lloyd George, Cave [home secretary], Munro [secretary for Scotland] and Arthur Henderson [secretary of the Labour Party]. Seeing that no London organisation is taking similar steps so far, I would appeal to readers to bring the matter before the notice of the organised Lancashire workers, and have resolutions passed and forwarded in the usual way. Our Glasgow committee will soon start proceedings in England and Ireland.'[4]

Peter Petroff was aware of, and appreciative of, the committee's efforts, writing to his wife Irma, who was in detention at Aylesbury:

> The London Trades Council inserted in their agenda for 8th Nov. a resolution demanding our release and sugg. the appointment of a deputation of five to wait upon the Under Sec. of State and urge also for permission for me to visit you; in Scotland a very important and representative committee for the defence of Russian pol. Refugees was formed a number of meetings in connection with this matter ... took place and resolutions to this effect are being sent to the Gov. by hundreds of British Labour Organisations.[5]

~

In Glasgow, it was very unclear what was happening in Russia in the weeks after the Bolshevik uprising, because all foreign news, telegrams and cables were government controlled and censored.

After initial reports that forces loyal to Kerensky had foiled the insurrection, by 16 November the *Glasgow Herald* confessed: 'The news, very meagre in character and incapable of verification, which is arriving here is in almost every detail of a contradictory character. Some of the reports are to the effect that M. Kerensky is master of the situation, while others declare he has definitely lost the game.'[6]

The next day, the headlines were 'Kerensky reported to be defeated', and 'Kerensky's troops retire'; two days later the paper reported 'Kerensky's staff has been arrested and Kerensky has fled'; and by 20 November it was becoming clear the Bolsheviks had consolidated power. Then on 21 November, the clincher, 'Russia for peace: expected to withdraw from the war.'

Details of the new Russian revolution might have been still sketchy, but what news there was caused great excitement among socialists on the Clyde. Nan Milton describes a meeting of the Russian Political Refugees Defence Committee, held on the afternoon of Sunday 18 November at the Central Halls on Bath St, that was addressed by the leading lights of the movement; Maclean, Arthur MacManus, James Maxton, Helen Crawfurd and Davy Kirkwood.

'The meeting was doubly significant,' she wrote. 'It testified to the growing support for the revolutionary elements of the movement, and it testified to the fact that a large part of the Glasgow workers could interpret the events in Russia in their own way. When Maclean referred to Russia and to the supreme efforts of Lenin and Trotsky in the cause of socialism, the hall thundered with fervent applause.'[7]

~

Trotsky weighed in on the issue of the Russian detainees, sending a note on 26 November to the British ambassador in Petrograd, Sir George Buchanan, demanding the release of Chicherin and Petroff. Trotsky warned Buchanan that 'The revolutionary democracy cannot accept the position that worthy heroes languish in concentration camps in England while counter-revolutionary British citizens suffer no restraint on the territory of the Russian Republic.'[8]

When the British War Cabinet decided not to take any notice of the demands, Trotsky upped the ante. On 30 November, he issued an order forbidding British subjects to leave Russia, pending the release of Chicherin and Petroff.

The news was conveyed to Buchanan, who recalled: 'He [Trotsky] added that Chicherin was a personal friend of his, and he was particularly anxious to secure his release as he proposed appointing him his diplomatic representative in one of the Allied capitals. In the event of our Government refusing to release him he threatened to arrest certain British subjects whom he knew to be counter-revolutionaries.'[9]

On 10 December, the War Cabinet reconsidered the issue. They were impressed by the fact that by continuing to intern Chicherin and Petroff, the lives of thousands of British subjects were being endangered, and that the case for internment was not a strong one. On the other hand, they believed the dangers of traffic with the Bolshevik government were very real. Without making any changes to their general policy towards Russia, they authorised the Secretary of State for Foreign Affairs, Arthur Balfour, to deal with Chicherin and Petroff 'in the best way he could'.[10]

Balfour and Buchanan both agreed Chicherin and Petroff should be released, and once arrangements were made in Petrograd for their return, on 14 December Trotsky rescinded the ban on British subjects leaving Russia.

On 2 January 1918, Chicherin was told he was to be released and was also paid a visit by Arthur Henderson, secretary of the Labour Party. Henderson urged Chicherin to do what he could to persuade Lenin to delay signing a separate peace with the Central Powers. If Russia could remain in the war for another two months, Henderson said, he believed the Allies would agree to a general peace conference.[11]

The following day, Chicherin was released from Brixton Prison and together with the Petroffs embarked on an Admiralty steamer bound for Norway, from whence they journeyed on to Russia.

With their contacts and understanding of British and Western European affairs, on their return to Petrograd Chicherin and Petroff were immediately drafted into senior government roles. On 8 January, Chicherin was appointed a companion of the People's Commissar for Foreign Affairs. Petroff became president of the Soviet Foreign Relations Committee.

30

THE RETURN OF THE SHOP STEWARDS' MOVEMENT

In spring 1917, factories throughout Britain were seething with discontent. Following a wave of strikes in May 1917, a government commission of inquiry identified the leading cause of industrial unrest as high food prices in relation to wages. The inquiry found the cost of living had increased disproportionately to the advance in wages, the distribution of food supplies was unequal, and there was a feeling that sections of the community were profiting by the increased prices. There was also resentment about the restriction of personal freedom, and particularly the effects of the Munitions of War Acts.

'Workmen have been tied up to particular factories and have been unable to obtain wages in relation to their skill. In many cases the skilled man's wage is less than the wage of the unskilled,' the commission reported.[1]

The conditions were ripe for a resurgence of the shop stewards' movement. Arthur MacManus was one of the shop stewards deported out of Glasgow in the authorities' crushing of the Clyde Workers' Committee in spring 1916. MacManus initially went to Edinburgh, then moved over the border and based himself in Liverpool. Over the following 12 months, he met with shop stewards 'for conversations and organisation' in factories and workshops across the north of England and the Midlands. Gradually a loose network of committees was drawn together.[2]

When the government attempted to amend the Munitions of War Act in May 1917, to remove the trade card scheme that exempted craft union members from military service, the network sprang into action.

Starting in Manchester, unofficial strikes protesting at the proposed removal of the scheme spread across the engineering sector, involving

200,000 workers in 48 towns. One hundred shop steward delegates from 34 districts met in permanent session for three days, laying the ground for a national movement.

On 17 May warrants were issued for the arrest of MacManus and the other strike leaders. The shop stewards approached the officials of the Amalgamated Society of Engineers for help. Accompanied by ASE secretary James Brownlie, they met with the minister of munitions on 19 May and reached a back-to-work agreement with the government. The strike leaders were released and a condition of the agreement was that none of the strikers were to be victimised.

To secure the passage of amendments to the Munitions of War Bill the following month, the government made several concessions to the unions. These included the abolition of the hated leaving certificate and the restoration of customs and rights suspended under the Treasury Agreement.[3]

~

On 4 June, the deportation orders applying to MacManus and the other shop stewards removed from the Clyde – including David Kirkwood, Tommy Clark and James Messer – were withdrawn, meaning the men could return to their families.

On Saturday 23 June, a reception was organised at St Mungo's Halls to welcome back the deportees. MacManus spoke and told the assembled crowd of the need for carrying the fight into the factories, and for developing the political character of their work. 'The response it evoked showed how eager all were to get the movement back to its full strength,' Willie Gallacher recalled.[4]

Building on MacManus's work in England, a broadly representative conference of shop stewards' organisations assembled in Manchester in August 1917. A National Administrative Council was elected, with MacManus as chair and Gallacher a member.

Gallacher had secured a job at Beardmore's munitions works at Dalmuir though his contacts with the shop stewards there, and was soon active in 'a well-functioning factory committee'.[5] A number of other factories on the Clyde had also established workshop committees, and on 9 September, almost four hundred shop stewards and factory delegates answered the call to attend a conference to discuss better coordination.

Addressing the gathering, Gallacher argued that where a strong factory committee existed, wages and conditions were protected and union membership was enforced. A small group of industrial unionists who wanted to work outside the unions attended the meeting, but withdrew when their proposal to work outside the existing unions was defeated. Thus was the Clyde Workers' Committee reconstituted, with Gallacher elected as chairman and James Messer as secretary.

~

The CWC leadership was powerfully reinforced by the emergence of an allied independent rank and file movement among foundry workers. During 1917, Jock McBain, Tom Bell and James Gardner had been leading a movement for workshop organisation in Scottish foundries. McBain had been a member of the original CWC, and had helped keep a skeleton version of the group going in 1916-17, to raise funds to support the families of the Clyde deportees.

In August 1917, McBain and Bell called a mass meeting of moulders to discuss action against an unsatisfactory wage demand. On 13 September foundry workers throughout Scotland came out on strike for three weeks. The CWC gave considerable support to the strike and according to Gallacher, 'was ready, and if the need arose and the request was made, to bring other workers into the struggle'.[6]

McBain and Bell went to London to plead their wages case, and although Winston Churchill, the recently appointed minister of munitions, refused to meet the duo, he offered them a hearing with his assistant, McCallum Scott. Two days after the moulders returned to work, the War Cabinet awarded a bonus of 12 and a half per cent to all skilled engineering workers, including foundry workers.[7]

After the Scottish moulders strike, the next action to attract the interest of the CWC was a strike at Beardmore's East Hope shell factory. Four women had been dismissed as a result of a go-slow in November 1917 and the bulk of women came out on strike for their reinstatement. The CWC provided funds to the strikers and organised a mass meeting at Glasgow Green on 25 November to show its support. Beardmore's offered to reinstate the women, pending arbitration, and the workers went back. But fearing victimisation would resume, shop stewards from all the Beardmore works met to discuss joint action and on 30 December the CWC called 'a general meeting of convenors, shop stewards and representatives of all classes of workers in the Clyde area' to demand the reinstatement of the women. Failing this, they threatened to organise a general strike throughout Scotland, and if possible, England.

~

The order granting the 12 and a half per cent bonus issued on 13 October 1917 was the outcome of Churchill's attempt to address the grievance of skilled workers who were paid an hourly rate. The wages of this class of workers had fallen behind those of 'piece-workers', who tended to be unskilled, worked on repetitive tasks and who were paid by output.

Fears that it would be difficult to restrict the bonus within its original scope were quickly justified and the order at once excited unrest among excluded workers. On 25 October, representatives of 47 unions attending a hearing of an engineering claim expressed profound dissatisfaction with the order and anticipated a general strike. Encouraged by shop stewards, mass meetings of unskilled workers in Sheffield also demanded the bonus.[8]

With the whole of industry in a ferment, attempts to contain the bonus to the original class of workers crumbled and it was extended in turn to semi-skilled and unskilled workers, to shipyards and eventually to piece-workers, by which time it had lost its original purpose and become a general advance. However, the delays inevitable in the piece-meal handling of the advance, and the fact the bonus was made payable from different dates, caused much jealousy and unrest.[9]

The winter of 1917-18 saw militancy spread from the Clyde to other parts of the country, notably to Sheffield where the rank-and-file movement embraced almost all the factory workers. The unrest over the distribution of the 12 and a half per cent bonus broke down barriers between skilled and unskilled workers and the movement had a national leadership. In mid-December the Ministry of Munitions anticipated that 'the early months of 1918 may reveal industrial action with a view to the achievement of political ends in the termination of war conditions'.[10]

31
BREST-LITOVSK: THE ARMISTICE

Russian moves for a general peace had begun on 26 November 1917 (13 November OS) when Trotsky, people's commissar for foreign relations in the new Bolshevik government, had contacted the German High Command to suggest an armistice. The Germans agreed to open negotiations on all fronts, with the object of concluding a democratic peace. Trotsky asked the diplomatic representatives of the Allies in Russia to indicate whether they desired to participate in the negotiations, which were scheduled to open on 2 December. The Americans communicated an 'energetic protest' against the conclusion by Russia of a separate armistice; the French and British advised they did not recognise the authority of the new Russian government.[1]

The Bolsheviks had not endeared themselves to the Allies by their decision to publish the secret treaties entered into by the tsar's government. These included the 1914 Treaty of London, by which Great Britain, France and Russia agreed not to make a separate peace. That decision prompted a furious outburst from one British military correspondent: 'Our duty is surely to differentiate between honest men and those who are proving themselves traitors by revealing secret treaties and endeavouring to break the really sacred and fundamental Agreement of September 1914, by which solemn Act the Allies agreed to make peace in common, and not separately.'[2]

The armistice negotiations took place at the German High Command Headquarters East in the fortress of Brest-Litovsk, situated in the war-ravaged Polish town deep behind German lines. The German terms were based on the desire to end the war on one front, with hostilities to cease and each side to retain the position they held. With the possibility that public pressure might push Allied governments to attend, the Russians' opening position was for a six-month armistice. The Russians also proposed that no German troops should be transferred from the Eastern Front to other fronts, or even to be withdrawn behind the lines. The Germans had no difficulties with this, because before the negotiations had begun, orders had already been given to send the bulk of the Eastern Army to the Western Front.[3]

On the third day of negotiations, 5 December, the Russian delegation declared they were 'treating for an armistice on all fronts with the view to the conclusion of a general peace on the basis already established by the All-Russian Congress of Soviets'.[4]

The Germans politely enquired whether they had the authority of their allies to make such a proposal. They were prepared to negotiate on a general peace, or a separate peace with Russia, but as the Allies had chosen not to participate, should they proceed to arrange a separate armistice with Russia?

This was a question beyond the power of Adolf Joffe, the head of the Russian delegation, to answer. The Germans agreed to the face-saving formula proposed by Joffe that all belligerents should be invited to take part in the negotiations, which would resume on 12 December. This allowed Joffe to return to Petrograd for instructions. As it was still possible the Allies would join any peace talks that might follow an armistice, he was told to return to Brest-Litovsk and pursue the conversations.

Trotsky informed the Allied governments of the progress of the talks and of the opportunity to participate. He asked them 'to express their willingness or their refusal to take part in the negotiations for an armistice and peace'. The deadline for a response was 12 December, and if they refused the invitation, Trotsky said 'they must declare clearly and definitely, before all mankind, the aims for which the peoples of Europe may have to lose their blood during the fourth year of the war'.[5]

No response having been received by 12 December, Trotsky issued a further declaration, 'throwing the responsibility for Russia concluding a separate armistice on the governments which refuse the present conditions for an armistice and peace'.[6]

The armistice was signed on 15 December. Its duration was until 14 January 1918, with automatic renewal unless seven days' notice was given.

~

On 20 December, five delegations assembled at Brest-Litovsk to begin negotiations on a peace settlement. On one side were the representatives of the Quadruple Alliance (Germany, Austria-Hungary, Bulgaria and the Ottoman Empire); on the other, Russia.

Foreign Minister Count Czernin headed the Austrian contingent, while the German delegation was led by the urbane Foreign Minister, Baron Richard von Kuhlmann, with the military represented by Chief of the General Staff of the Commander-in-Chief of the East, Major-General Max Hoffmann. Hoffmann was a man 'composed of equal parts of steel and whalebone', within whose great shaven skull reposed the most brilliant brain of the German General Staff.[7]

At the first plenary session on 22 December, the head of the Russian delegation, Adolf Joffe, formally presented the details of the Russian 'no annexations or indemnities' peace program. On Christmas Day, on behalf of the Quadruple Alliance, Count Czernin replied that the Soviet proposals formed a discussable basis for an immediate general peace, without forcible acquisitions of territory and without war indemnities.

Initially the Russians thought the response meant that not only would troops be withdrawn from all occupied Russian territory, but the return of these territories to Russia was up for discussion. But it quickly emerged that they had fundamentally misunderstood the German and Austrian position. This was made clear on 28 December when Hoffmann informed Joffe that the attitude of the Central Powers was that it was no forcible annexation if portions of the former Russian Empire chose an independent existence or a protected status within the German Empire. This was the Germans' understanding of the right of self-determination for Poland, Lithuania, Courland and portions of Estonia and Livonia. Furthermore, the Central Powers reserved the right to reach direct understandings with these states, to the exclusion of Russia. The shock was severe. 'How can you talk of peace without annexation,' Joffe protested, 'when nearly eighteen provinces are torn from Russia?'[8]

The negotiations were adjourned until 9 January 1918, with the Entente nations given until 4 January to accept the opportunity of participating. Despite the deepening threat of a separate peace between Russia and the Central Powers, the members of the Entente made no direct reply. On New Year's Eve, in Paris, the French Foreign Minister, M. Pichon, told the Chamber of Deputies, 'Russia may treat for a separate peace with our enemies or not. It either case, for us the war continues. An ally has failed us ... but another ally has come from the other end of the world.'[9]

~

That ally, the United States of America, indeed was coming. President Woodrow Wilson had come to believe that the United States alone could shape an effective peace settlement because the combatants were politically and morally bankrupt. Wilson felt that American intervention in 1917 would ensure that the United States would play a decisive role and dominate the postwar peace conference.[10]

Before American troops arrived in any significant number, and mindful of the talks at Brest-Litovsk, 'to which the attention of all the belligerents had been invited', Wilson was at pains to clarify America's war aims. On 8 January 1918, the president addressed a joint sitting of Congress and outlined his peace proposals, in what became known as the 'Fourteen Points'.

Wilson began his speech by praising the Russian position. 'Russian representatives presented not only a perfectly definite statement of the principles upon which they would be willing to conclude peace, but also an equally definite program of concrete application of those principles.'[11]

He contrasted this with the attitude of the Central Powers, noting that while they had opened the discussions with the outline of a settlement that seemed open to liberal interpretation, the addition of their practical terms proposed no concessions at all. He accurately conjectured that the initial principles had come from the statesmen of Germany and Austria, while the concrete terms came from the military leaders.

After again praising the Russians for insisting 'very justly, very wisely, and in the true spirit of modern democracy' that the talks should be open, he asked himself, with whom are the Russian representatives dealing? Is it the statesmen, or the military? Or, he wondered, 'are we listening in fact to both, unreconciled and in open and hopeless contradiction?'

But whatever the results of the discussions at Brest-Litovsk, Wilson said, the Central Powers had attempted to acquaint the world with their objects in the war and challenged their adversaries to do the same. Noting that within the past week Lloyd George had spoken with admirable candour for the people of Great Britain, he said there was no good reason why that challenge should not be responded to.

'There was no confusion of counsel among the adversaries of the Central Powers,' he said, 'no uncertainty of principle, no vagueness of details. The only failure to make a definite statement of the objects of the war lies with Germany and her allies.'[12]

In his speech, Wilson directly addressed what he perceived as the causes for the world war by calling for the abolition of secret treaties, freedom of the seas, reduction of international economic barriers, arms reduction, an adjustment in colonial claims in the interests of both native peoples and colonists, various territorial and border settlements, including the reestablishment of an independent Poland, and most importantly, the establishment of a league of nations to work for peace and collective security among countries large and small.[13]

The response to the Fourteen Points was electrifying, with translations in pamphlets and books broadcast around the world. In Petrograd, the text was placarded on the walls. It was printed on a hundred thousand Russian posters and three hundred thousand Russian handbills. The American YMCA, with Bolshevik aid, distributed a million copies throughout the Russian lines and another million, in German, within the German lines on the Eastern Front.[14]

Publicly, the Allies welcomed Wilson's announcement; they did not want the Bolsheviks to have the monopoly on a peace formula, and it gave them some cover over their refusal to enter into peace negotiations. In private, the governments of Britain and France were less enthusiastic, realising a Wilsonian just peace would interfere with their vengeful desires to punish Germany.

French Prime Minister Georges Clemenceau sarcastically observed, 'Mr. Wilson bores me with his Fourteen Points; why, God Almighty has only Ten!'[15]

32

MAN POWER

On the continent, the Western Front had been in deadlock since the winter of 1915-16, and had developed into a war of attrition. Still, the British Commander-in-Chief, General Douglas Haig, believed that a frontal assault in the right place at the right time would cause a German collapse. For the third battle of Ypres (from July to November 1917), commonly known as Passchendaele, Haig assembled a force of nearly a million men. The Germans moved a similar number into place to defend their positions. The resulting battle was a slaughterhouse. Military historians disagree on the exact figures, but most estimates suggest each side suffered more than a quarter of a million casualties in the mud of Passchendaele.

'Failure was obvious by the end of the first day, to everyone except Haig and his immediate circle,' wrote AJP Taylor. 'The greatest advance was less than half a mile. The main German line was nowhere reached. Rain fell heavily. The ground churned up by shellfire turned to mud. Men struggling to advance sank up to their waists. Guns disappeared in the mud. Haig sent in tanks. These also disappeared in the mud.'[1]

It was a dismal conclusion to the British offensives of 1917.

In the closing months of the year, the British War Cabinet began to consider how it was going to obtain more men for the army before the anticipated resumption of active fighting in the spring of 1918. It decided the way to proceed was to 'comb-out' young skilled men from the munitions works and replace them by dilutees and women. A major impediment to this move was the agreement negotiated with the Amalgamated Society of Engineers and other unions in May 1917.

On 20 December, Lloyd George flagged that the conditions under which those arrangements had been made had materially changed, and it was necessary for the government to take action that would enable the call up of men currently protected.

The government began consulting unions about its proposed Man Power Bill on 3 January 1918. The ASE attended the first conference, but then decided it wanted to be consulted separately to the other engineering unions. This the government declined to do, taking the position that as the ASE had agreed to participate in consultations as part of an engineering group, it was bound to that undertaking. This stance would have ramifications.

At the last of the conferences with the unions on 5 January, Prime Minister Lloyd George surprised everyone by using the occasion to, for the first time, outline the government's war aims. It also came as a surprise to many government MPs that the aims bore a close resemblance to those adopted by a joint conference of the Labour Party and the Trades Union Congress on 28 December 1917.

Following the failure of the Inter-Allied Socialist Conference in August 1917, these war aims had been revised by ILP leader Ramsay MacDonald and the Fabian Sidney Webb, and were to be presented to an Allied Labour and Socialist Conference scheduled to meet in February 1918.[2]

Labour's statement proclaimed that the war was being fought so that 'the world may henceforth be made safe for democracy'. It called for 'the complete democratisation of all countries'; for 'the frank abandonment of every form of imperialism'; for 'the suppression of secret diplomacy'; for 'the universal abolition of compulsory military service in all countries'; and for 'the entire abolition of profit-making armaments firms'.

Lloyd George began his speech to the unions by conceding that when the government sought the assistance of organised labour to maintain the army in the field, its representatives were entitled to be clear about the government's purpose. 'When men by the millions are being called on to suffer and die, and vast populations are subjected to the sufferings and privations of war on a scale unprecedented in the history of the world, they are entitled to know for what cause or causes they are making the sacrifice,' he said.[3]

After emphasising that Britain was not seeking the destruction of Germany, Austria-Hungary or Turkey, Lloyd George dismissed as inadequate both the war aims floated by Germany the previous summer and those outlined by Austria-Hungary at Brest-Litovsk on 25 December 1917. His government's requirements for a peace settlement were, he said, in the first place, the complete restoration of the independence of Belgium, and reparations for the damage inflicted on its towns and provinces. Next, the restoration of Serbia, Montenegro and the occupied parts of France,

Italy and Romania. And thirdly, the restoration to France of the provinces of Alsace and Lorraine, which had been annexed by Germany in the war of 1871.

On Russia, the prime minister wrung his hands, saying that Russia was in separate negotiations with their common enemy and, 'Britain cannot be held accountable for decisions taken in her absence, and concerning which she had not been consulted or her aid invoked.'

Lloyd George concluded his speech to the union delegates by stating that Britain was fighting for a just and lasting peace, and before peace could be hoped for, three conditions must be fulfilled: 'Firstly, the sanctity of treaties must be re-established; secondly a territorial settlement must be secured based on the right of self-determination or the consent of the governed; and lastly, we must seek by the creation of some international organisation to limit the burden of armaments and diminish the probability of war.'[4]

~

On the same weekend Lloyd George was addressing representatives of the official unions, the national conference of the shop stewards met at Manchester. There were two main topics on the agenda: food and man power.

On man power, the conference heard reports on the opening day about the feeling in the large industrial centres of Sheffield, London, Woolwich, Chatham, the Tyne district, Barrow, Isle of Wight, Invergordon, Halifax, Coventry, Leeds, Manchester, Liverpool and the Clyde district. The essence of all the reports submitted was to resist any further taking away of men to the army.[5]

On the food issue, the shop stewards put their weight behind the National Vigilance Committee which had been established the previous month. At a conference in London the following weekend, the vigilance committee threatened to call a national strike and seize food supplies and distribute them through workers' committees. In the end, the threat was contained by the introduction of rationing schemes, but the threat helped to give revolutionary potential to the other conflicts that came to a head in January 1918.[6]

Most of Sunday was spent in discussion on the man power issue and the conference report attempted to capture the different trends of thought on the subject in the following resolution:

I. That this national Conference of Shop Stewards, directly representing the organised workers in the Engineering and Shipbuilding Industry, informs the Government that we refuse to accept any agreement on the Man Power proposals that may be arrived at as between the Trade Union Officials and the Government.

II. That this Conference is resolved to actively resist the Man Power proposals of the Government, and demands that the Government shall at once accept the Invitation of the Russian Government to discuss peace terms.

III. That this Conference further demands the immediate conscription of wealth, and that adequate provision shall be made as a national right for all victims of the war.

IV. That this Conference recommends that national action shall be taken to enforce these demands, and delegates are instructed to at once ascertain from the workers in their districts what form this action shall take and inform the N.A.C.[7]

The Man Power Bill did what the government's dilution program of two years earlier had failed to do: it united industrial unrest with anti-war agitation. As James Hinton observed: 'Inspired by the Bolshevik Revolution, and in particular the Bolshevik peace terms and Trotsky's call for peace, the leaders of the rank-and-file movement were poised for revolutionary action against the war.'[8]

The sentiment expressed in Manchester was promptly echoed on the Clyde. On 13 January 1918, the Clyde District Committee of the Federation of Engineering and Shipbuilding Trades passed the following resolution:

> That we intimate to the parent bodies and the Government that if the Government does not withdraw the Man-Power Bill before the end of January, we will advise our fellow workers on the Clyde to down tools, and we ask the Government to call an International Peace Conference to discuss peace terms at once.[9]

Undeterred by these declarations of dissent, on Monday 14 January the Minister for National Service, Sir Auckland Geddes, introduced a Bill into the House of Commons 'to repeal Sub-section (3) of Section 3 of the Military Service Act, 1916, and to provide for the cancellation of certificates of exemption from military service granted on occupational grounds'.

In his speech, he said:

> The man-power problem is the central problem of the War. It means everything – ships, armies, munitions, food, light, heat, coal – everything.

No dramatic stroke less than a divine miracle would simultaneously solve all the problems which are loosely called one problem and labelled Man-Power.

The problems change from day to day. Now we have to swing our manpower in this direction, now in that. At one time the provision of men for the shipyards may be the most urgent need, at another the provision of men for the Army, at still another it may be men for the land. These problems are being met every day and successfully dealt with on a scale of which few outside the central ring of administrative officials have any conception. It is my hope that before I sit down I shall have been able to show this House something of the gigantic work that goes on from day to day. At the moment our most anxious problems are not those concerning the supply of men for the Army. What we seek to do is to take steps now against the time when they will be the most anxious – a time which I believe I can see coming at no very distant date.[10]

To maintain the army through 1918, Geddes said, man power demands could be made from two sources: reserves at home and abroad; and men remaining in civil life. Even after readjusting home armies to enable the greatest proportion to be sent abroad, it would still be necessary to raise 450,000 men from civil life. The government, he said, was determined to make a very large number of youths engaged in essential industries available for military purposes, replacing them with women and ex-soldiers.

Alone among the unions directed affected, the Amalgamated Society of Engineers had indicated it would have nothing to do with the government's plans. Its position was that the government had agreed with them in May 1917 that dilutees would be taken before skilled men, irrespective of age or family ties, and insisted that they were entitled because of that agreement to be consulted apart from the other unions involved.

After expressing his appreciation to the leaders of organised labour with whom he had discussed his proposals, Geddes then bared his teeth to his opponents.

> Efforts are now being made by pacifists to stir up strife in the munition factories; but I hesitate to believe that in this, the last phase of this great struggle, any of the young men engaged in the vital industries will claim for themselves privileges, exemption, and immunity opposed to the urgent needs of the nation and not accorded to their fellows of the trade unions of the less vital industries, or, indeed, to any other section of the community – an immunity only to be purchased at the price of the men who have fought and been wounded, at the price of sending

their fathers to the trenches, and of limiting, if not stopping, the leave of the soldiers from the front. That is what their claim for immunity amounts to. These young men are now threatening to take what they call drastic action; in plain language, they are threatening to hold up the output of ships and aeroplanes in order to force the Government to send out the wounded men again and again, to force the Government to drag out their fathers, and to force the Government to stop the leave of the men at the front. [HON. MEMBERS: 'Traitors!'] I believe that if they do, they will meet such a blast of hatred and contempt that will surprise them. Think of the monstrosity of the claim of these young men – that we should send out the wounded again and again to fight for them while they draw high wages, that we should take their fathers and send them out while they stay at home and draw high wages, and that we should stop the leave of men from the front while they stay at home and draw high wages.[11]

~

While the Man Power Bill was still winding its way through parliament, Geddes travelled north to sell it to the workers. Things did not go well. On 27 January Geddes was in Liverpool, where he addressed a large and lively meeting of the Mersey District Federation of Engineering and Shipbuilding Trades. The meeting lasted four hours and at its conclusion a resolution was passed 'to resist by all possible means further calls upon the man-power of the nation unless the Government adopted the war aims of the Labour Party, promised an international workers' conference and agreed to a conscription of wealth'.[12]

If Liverpool was bad, Glasgow was worse. Much worse.

The meeting on Monday 28 January at Glasgow's City Hall was organised by the Clyde District Federation of Engineering and Shipbuilding Trades. Attending were the district secretaries of the trade unions, members of the district committees of different trades, and the accredited shop stewards in the Glasgow district. At a meeting the evening before, the leaders of the Clyde Workers' Committee had decided Willie Gallacher should obtain control of the meeting and make arrangements for a resolution against the Bill and in favour of an immediate armistice.[13]

The Monday meeting began promptly at 7.30 pm, and as the platform party took the stage, the audience of 3000 stood and sang 'The Red Flag'. William Lawson of the Amalgamated Society of Carpenters and Joiners was in the chair, but as soon as he rose to speak, the noise was such that not a word could be heard. When, after a whispered consultation with Lawson, Auckland Geddes then tried to speak, the racket was even louder.

Gallacher takes up the story:

> Will Fyffe then walked up to the front of the platform and said to Lawson, 'Willie Gallacher's here. If you invite him up, things will quieten down.'
>
> 'We don't want Willie Gallacher,' said Lawson, 'we know what that means.'
>
> 'All right,' said Fyffe, 'I just thought I'd mention it.'
>
> Two or three of the other trade union officials tried to speak, without avail. Then after another whispered consultation with Geddes, Lawson beckoned to Will Fyffe to come over. 'Ask Willie to come up,' he said.[14]

When Gallacher took to the stage, the din changed to roars of greeting. Gallacher proposed that the meeting would give Geddes half an hour to speak, then there would be questions, after which Arthur MacManus would move a resolution.

The crowd quietened and Geddes briefly explained the provisions of the Man Power Bill, pointing out it was only proposed to take young and fit men from industry where these could be spared without injury to the interests of the country. At the same time, he said, an effort was being made to bring back into the shipyards skilled workers who had enlisted at the beginning of the war, and it was estimated that within the next few days the first of a total of 20,000 would be in the yards on the Mersey, Tyne and Clyde.

The speech, the questions that followed and Geddes' replies 'were all subjected to many interruptions, and at times scores of speakers were trying to make themselves heard simultaneously'.[15]

When Gallacher felt the questions had gone on long enough, he called on MacManus to speak. MacManus moved the following resolution:

1. That having heard the case for the Government, as stated by Sir Auckland Geddes, the meeting pledges itself to oppose the Government to the utmost in its call for more men.
2. That we insist on, and we bind ourselves to take action to enforce the declaration of an immediate armistice on all fronts.
3. And that the expressed opinion of the workers of Glasgow from now on, so far as this business is concerned, is that our attitude should be to do

nothing, all the time and every time, in support of carrying on the war, but to bring the war to a conclusion.[16]

Gallacher wrote, 'Then in a brilliant speech he [MacManus] riddled the case for the continuance of the war, ending up with, 'Not another man for the criminal war for trade and territory! An immediate end to it. This is our challenge to the Government. For this we are fighting and will go on fighting!'[17]

James Maxton seconded the resolution, appealing on humanitarian grounds for a stoppage of the war. A direct negative was moved and seconded, principally on the grounds there had not been sufficient time for consideration of the subject. Less than half a dozen of those present voted for the amendment and the motion was declared carried practically unanimously. The meeting concluded with another rendition of 'The Red Flag'.[18]

The leader in the following day's *Glasgow Herald* was titled 'A British Soviet'.

> The two meetings which Sir Auckland Geddes had addressed in the interests of reconciliation – that at Liverpool and at Glasgow last evening – have had the effect of disclosing the real inwardness of the Engineers movement. As the public understood it in its earlier manifestations it was an industrial protest, backed by a protected organisation, against the Man-Power Bill of the Government. As now revealed, it is a political movement directed against the Government, the country and the Empire. Hostility to the Government Bill was mere camouflage. The technical objections urged against the combing-out proposals of the measure were a sham. The real point of attack was and is the national cause – the cause to which Great Britain and the Empire are solemnly pledged, to which France and Italy and the United States are irrevocably committed, and which Russia alone has deserted and betrayed. The resolution carried last night, still more eloquently than that approved by the Liverpool workers, declares the intransigent spirit which is now in ferment. It pledged the meeting which Sir Auckland Geddes had addressed to oppose to the very uttermost the call for more men, it insisted on an immediate armistice, and it audaciously claimed that the expressed opinion of the workers of Glasgow was to do nothing in the carrying on of the war. There is only one word that can pertinently be applied to this defiant announcement – Rebellion.[19]

~

The Geddes meeting in Glasgow prompted an unprecedented flood of 'loyal' resolutions from workshops and shipyards on the Clyde. These were organised by a body called the War Aims Committee, and were designed to counter the agitation of the militants and lower the temperature among the workforce.[20]

The Minister of Munitions, Winston Churchill, told the War Cabinet on 5 February, 'It should be possible to obtain from the great munitions' areas a stream of resolutions in favour of the vigorous prosecution of the war. Such resolutions should appear in increasing numbers day by day in the newspapers for at least a fortnight. They would have a marked effect on the disaffected.'[21]

The *Herald* explained how these resolutions were obtained. 'There had been an influx of war-aims experts into workshops and factories to explain to the workers why peace without further loss of life would be akin to defeat. Every facility had been given by the profiteers for their employees to attend these meetings inside the bosses' fence – and after the orations have proved that peace and treason are twins, a motion pledging those present to continue their support of the war is moved and passed "unanimously". The boss usually presides at these meetings.'[22]

Even before these propaganda measures started to have their effect, among the various workers' groups the recently forged link between pressuring the government to enter into peace negotiations and the skilled men's defence of their privileges in relation to conscription began to break.

On 25 January, the national committee of the shop stewards met to consider the responses from its member groups to its recommendation for national action. The outcomes were decidedly mixed. The delegates from London and the Clyde were keen to press ahead, with 100,000 workers in London reportedly ready to strike against the war. In Sheffield a meeting of the trades council on the 15th saw skilled and unskilled men vote for a democratic peace.

But a meeting of the Sheffield District Committee of the ASE that same week failed to even consider the question of the war. Manchester was outright against strike action against the war, while other areas had not even bothered to organise a ballot. James Hinton concluded: 'Once again the unreliability of the craftsmen as a militant vanguard was demonstrated: faced with the prospect of leading an all-out struggle against the war itself, their confidence crumbled at the eleventh hour.'[23]

The national committee faced a dilemma. To call a strike in an attempt to force the government into peace negotiations could, it seemed, be easily side-tracked into a struggle by the skilled men in defence of their privileges in relation to conscription. To call a strike merely on the issue of privileges would be to invite a break by representatives of the unskilled workers. The committee solved its dilemma by abdicating, saying it was not the body to deal with technical workplace grievances, and referring the issue back to the official unions.[24]

On the Clyde, the District Committee of the Federation of Engineering and Shipbuilding Trades met on 30 January. Two weeks previously they had threatened strike action unless the man power proposals were withdrawn by the end of January. Now, they merely expressed their 'grave concern' about the government's insistence on passing the Man Power Bill and were 'strongly of the opinion' that the government should immediately open up negotiations with the enemy countries, and provide facilities for Labour and socialist parties to meet with their allied and enemy counterparts. They warned the government that if they failed to give satisfactory guarantees, 'we will down tools'. A response was sought by 8 February.[25]

The backdown sent a message to the ASE that if they wanted to fight over the man power issue, they were fighting on their own. It also postponed the crisis, giving the government breathing space to find a way out of its difficulty.[26]

Deprived of leadership from the shop stewards national committee, the unofficial elements in the ASE were slow to organise. But the engineers were fuming. The results of the official union postal ballot were released on 12 February and showed nearly half the members had responded – a record number – with an overwhelmingly majority in favour of strike action. The government agreed to meet the ASE executive separately, but made no other concessions. It was concerned that if a strike did break out, as a result of, for example, one or two shop stewards from the Clyde or Sheffield being called up, it would be hard to contain.[27]

On 21 March, Lloyd George received a deputation from the Miners' Federation of Great Britain. Federation chairman Robert Smillie placed before the prime minister the results of a ballot on the question of supplying 50,000 men from the mines for military service. On returns of almost half a million, the result was a majority against of 29,750. In reply, Lloyd George expressed his disappointment, then went on:

'Just let me tell you about the telegram that has just come into my hands. Do you know what has happened today? Early this morning the German armies have attacked us on a front of 100,000 yards, that is 57 miles. They have attacked us with overwhelming forces. Where have they come from? They have come from the country [Russia] where democracy has failed to do its duty because each group there began to decide for itself whether it would defend its native land. Therefore have these masses been able to fall upon us. Under those conditions to discuss whether the miners and engineers are going to make their contribution to defend their native land – I am amazed it is debatable!'[28]

The executive committee of the MFGB met the following day and passed the following resolution: 'That in view of the ballot not showing a two-thirds majority, we advise the conference to advise the men not to resist the taking of 50,000 men for the Army.'

Also on 21 March, the ASE militants finally managed to get together a conference of district committee representatives to plan how to implement the union members' strike decision. The gathering in Manchester passed a resolution protesting at the putting into operation of the Man Power Bill, and 'on account of our young skilled engineers being taken into the Army whilst dilutees liable and fit for military service are retained in the workshops, we will as a protest cease work on 6 April 1918'. The conference asked that the resolution be sent to all district committees to be submitted to members and results returned before a further conference on 4 April.[29]

But in the charged atmosphere of renewed military threat, the strike movement fell away.

33

SOVIET CONSUL

On the day after the Bolsheviks seized power in Petrograd, the Council of People's Commissars appointed Maxim Litvinov its plenipotentiary in Britain. Litvinov had been in London for nearly a decade, for the greater part of which he headed the émigré Bolshevik group and represented his party at the International Socialist Bureau.[1]

The return of Georgy Chicherin and the Petroffs to Russia in early January 1918 appeared to open the way for improved Anglo-Soviet relations. From the British side there was a desire to establish relations but to avoid any formal recognition of the Bolshevik regime. To that end, on 12 January the Foreign Office, through an intermediary, contacted Litvinov and Theodore Rothstein in London. Litvinov was subsequently granted a form of unofficial recognition by the British government.[2] However, that did not mean the government was relaxed about attempts to spread the Bolshevik revolutionary message.

On 17 January, six days before the upcoming Labour Party conference was due to open in Nottingham, the offices of the British Socialist Party in London were raided by police officers from Scotland Yard. Acting under the Defence of the Realm Act Regulations, they took possession of the premises and confiscated copies of a leaflet containing a message to British workers by Litvinov and a manifesto entitled 'Russia's appeal - will British workers remain silent?', intended for circulation to the delegates of the conference. Several thousand copies of the *Call*, which contained the manifesto, as well as copies of the previous week's issue containing Litvinov's message were also seized. The party protested vehemently.

> The action of the authorities in this matter raises a question of grave concern to the organised working class movement. As an affiliated organisation of the Labour Party, the BSP sought to communicate its views to the other

affiliated societies on a matter of urgent importance that was bound to arise at the Labour Party conference. But the government intervenes and, by its arbitrary seizure of the manifestos, prohibits the BSP representatives placing their opinions before their fellow delegates, and prevents the latter from considering them. It means, in effect, that at the gravest moment in the history of the working class movement an organisation is forcibly restrained from communicating its views regarding Labour policy and Labour tactics to other organisations with which it is in political association, because those views do not meet with the approval of the government.

It is not only a further and deadly blow at the free expression of opinion. It is an undisguised attack on the liberty of political association; and it betrays the fear of our ruling class that, inspired by Russia's appeal, the working people of this country will rally, not only to impose Russia's peace terms upon the government, but to sweep away the whole capitalist system, which is responsible for the horrors, miseries and sufferings of the last three years.[3]

On the evening before the formal opening of the Labour conference, delegates from other countries were invited to address the attendees. Litvinov introduced himself as a refugee in the unusual role of representative of his government. The *Glasgow Herald* reported:

He asked his audience to disabuse themselves of the notion circulated by the capitalist press that the Bolsheviks had secured power like a band of robbers. That was false. They had carried through the Revolution in the most approved style. (Laughter and cheers) It might be asked if this remarkable experiment had justified itself. He answered the question by declaring that in the little fortress town of Brest-Litovsk more dramatic history had been made in three weeks than in three and a half years of war. 'Even if success did not result from the negotiations a revolution in Germany – and let me hope somewhere else – (cheers) may come within the range of immediate possibilities.' They had placed before the German people in Brest an alternative – Either to accept the Russian democratic formula or to continue the war for territorial conquest. Would the German people continue to shed their blood, suffer hunger and privation for junkers and capitalists? ('No.') He thought there could be only one answer. (Cheers.)[4]

Sir George Buchanan, the former British ambassador in Petrograd, was deeply unimpressed.

Litvinoff had, in a speech at Nottingham, openly preached revolution. To allow an unofficial diplomatic agent to carry on an active revolutionary propaganda in our midst seemed to me inadmissible; yet were we to take disciplinary measures against him Trotsky would retaliate with reprisals against members of our embassy. We had therefore to choose between coming to terms with the Bolsheviks, on the basis of complete reciprocity in all things, or to break with them altogether and to withdraw our embassy. I was strongly in favour of the latter course, more especially as there now seemed some prospect of the Allies affording material assistance to the loyal elements in South Russia, who had not yet submitted either to the Bolsheviks or the Germans.[5]

~

On 21 January (8 January OS), the Third All-Russian Congress of Soviets of Workers', Soldiers' and Peasants' Deputies convened in Petrograd. With an eye for the hoped-for revolutions in the west, several comrades were recognised at the congress as representatives of the revolutionary movements in their countries. So, along with the Russians (Lenin, Trotsky and the Left SR leader Maria Spiridonova), Karl Liebknecht, from Germany; Friedrich Adler from Austria; and John Maclean from Britain were elected honorary vice-presidents of the congress. The *Call* commented:

> Revolutionaries throughout the country will not fail to appreciate the honour that has been conferred on them by the appointment of Comrade John Maclean as one of the distinguished Honorary Presidents of the Russian Soviet Congress. The workers on the Clyde particularly are proud of the distinction and recognise in the action of the Russian workers in electing Maclean an invisible but nonetheless real connection between Petrograd and Glasgow.[6]

From Trotsky's point of view, preoccupied as he was with the Brest-Litovsk negotiations, Georgy Chicherin had arrived back in Russia, 'at the most opportune moment, and with a sigh of relief I handed the diplomatic helm over to him. I was not appearing at the ministry at all then.'[7]

Chicherin was well aware of Maclean's revolutionary credentials, not to mention the sterling efforts Maclean had made to secure the release of himself and the Petroffs. From his new position in the Commissariat for Foreign Affairs, he decided to offer Maclean the position of Soviet consul in Glasgow. The offer was most likely made by Litvinov and accepted by Maclean on the sidelines at the Labour Party conference in Nottingham.

Ironically, the telegram concerning Maclean's appointment was initially received by Sir Donald Maclean, a leading Liberal politician. He contacted Ramsay MacDonald, who passed the telegram on to the 'real' Maclean.[8]

Maclean's appointment was officially announced on 26 January when the following message was sent out through the wireless stations of the Russian government:

> The Department of the Occident of the Commission for Foreign Affairs announces that the Consul-General at New York, Ustinoff is dismissed and John Reed is appointed in his place. John Maclin [Maclean] is appointed Consul at Glasgow, Scotland.[9]

On the same day, it was reported that Litvinov had received letters of credentials signed by Trotsky appointing him *charge d'affairs* in Britain, and that he proposed to present them to the British government at the earliest possible opportunity.[10]

~

John Maclean was busy over the winter of 1917-18. His contemporary Tom Bell wrote: 'In connection with the Man Power Bill, the Clyde workers made a strong stand. Demonstrations and meetings against conscription were held all over the Clyde Valley. In this agitation, the irrepressible John Maclean worked like a Trojan ...'[11]

Willie Gallacher was even more effusive.

> While the movement in the factories was thus advancing, Maclean was organising a whole network of Marxist classes in the main industrial centres of Glasgow.
>
> He had worked out a whole series of studies and trained a splendid group of assistant tutors. With these in full operation the basis was laid and the plans prepared for the establishment of the Scottish Labour College. The work done by Maclean during this winter of 1917-18 has never been equalled by anyone. His educational work would have been sufficient for half a dozen ordinary men, but on top of this he was carrying on a truly terrific propaganda and agitational campaign. Every minute of his time was devoted to the revolutionary struggle, every ounce of his extraordinary energy was thrown into the fight.[12]

Revolutionary agitation in Glasgow and Clydeside, including Maclean's propaganda campaign, was being closely monitored by the authorities. The

Lord Advocate, James Avon Clyde prepared a memo for the War Cabinet meeting of 12 March 1918 that outlined how the situation had developed.[13]

Clyde recounted that during the autumn of 1917 and the winter of 1917-18, he had received reports of speeches delivered in Glasgow and Clydeside, and more recently in the mining districts of Lanarkshire and Fife, that contained possible matter for prosecution under the Defence of the Realm Regulations.

He identified the source as a small but active group of extreme revolutionary socialists in Glasgow. 'It is anti-national, anti-militarist, anti-conscriptionist,' he reported. 'It preaches class war, and tells the wage-earing proletariat that it is the tool and the dupe of a capitalistic and employing bourgeoise in every international conflict (including the present war) in which this country engages.'

The line that divided socialist propaganda of the revolutionary kind and breaches of the law was a thin one, he noted, and the group was not without skill in playing close to the line without definitely crossing it. However, the speeches being given by MacManus, Gallacher, Maclean, Macdougall and others about the government's man power proposals and the disputes over the 12 and a half per cent increase in wages dispensed with that caution. Clyde concluded these speeches contained suggestions for extreme and even forcible action, and began to consider prosecution under the Regulations.

It was at that point in late January that Sir Auckland Geddes visited Glasgow to speak about the man power proposals. At the meeting addressed by Geddes, 'two of the worst offenders (MacManus and Gallacher) moved, seconded and carried a resolution against the minister's proposals', wrote Clyde. The speeches were menacing in tone and although not themselves prosecutable, echoed features in other speeches made around the same time that, in Clyde's opinion, did amount to breaches.

Geddes' humiliation at the hands of the shop stewards led Clyde to decide the time was not right for action. 'I considered that this incident made any attempt to make these speeches the subject of prosecution inexpedient for the time being,' he wrote.

A new factor emerged shortly after, in the form of threatened food shortages. It was seized on as fresh material for agitation and some speeches were made, especially by Maclean, which Clyde considered were breaches of the Regulations. However, Maclean had been made Bolshevik consul in Glasgow, which put a new complication in the way of immediate action against him.

At the same War Cabinet meeting of 12 March, the Secretary for Scotland, Robert Munro provided an update, and sought the approval of his colleagues to take action against Maclean.[14]

After release from prison on licence (ticket-of leave), Maclean was quiet for some time, Munro wrote, 'but has recently been making speeches of a character which, in the opinion of the lord advocate and Sir Spencer Ewart [commander-in-chief, Scottish Command] would, apart from considerations which may possibly arise out of the present labour and international situation, justify the taking of criminal proceedings against him'.

Maclean had recently written to Munro advising him that in view of his new appointment he now refused to meet his parole requirement of reporting weekly to police. Maclean wrote: 'I now write to you to notify the police that the reporting shall cease. I might point out that it is meaningless in view of my public position as Russian Consul in Glasgow and is derogatory to the Great Russian Republic.'

Munro noted that Maclean had appointed as his consular assistant a Russian called Shammes. He went on: 'Arrangements were being made by the Home Office for the repatriation of various undesirable Russians, and that it should be possible to get rid of Shammes in this way.'

Maclean had recently been extending his operations from Glasgow and Lanarkshire to Fife. The chief constable of Fife considered that 'his [Maclean's] propaganda amongst the Fife miners was mischievous, and should be taken seriously'.

There was no doubt, in Munro's view, that Maclean's immunity tended to bring the law into contempt. 'That a man out on licence, after serving part of a sentence for breach of the Defence of the Realm Regulations, should openly and without challenge, be repeating such breaches must have mischievous results,' he wrote.

The War Cabinet authorised proceedings to be taken 'in any case where the Lord Advocate was of the opinion that conviction would be probable'.[15]

~

Writing from the Russian Peoples' Embassy and Consulate General in London, Litvinov advised Maclean that he was writing to the Russian consul in Glasgow informing him of Maclean's appointment and ordering him to hand over to him the consulate. Litvinov included a warning that: 'Your position may be difficult somehow, but you will have my full support.'[16]

The warning was well-advised. The existing Russian Consul Alex Debham refused to recognise Maclean or hand over the consulate at 17 Blythswood Square to him. In February, Maclean opened his own consulate on the south side of the Clyde at 12 South Portland Street, with Russian émigré Louis Shammes as secretary. However, the British government also refused to recognise Maclean, advising Litvinov, 'HM Government cannot admit the right of the present authorities at Petrograd to appoint Consuls.' A consequence was that correspondence sent by mail to Maclean by Litvinov and others was returned, marked 'Consul not recognised by HM Government.'[17]

It did not take long for the authorities to move from obstruction to more active measures. On 22 March, police raided the consulate and arrested Shammes. He was taken to Southern Police Station where an order from the Home Secretary, Sir George Cave for his deportation to Russia was read out.

In his brief period as consul, Maclean's main task was petitioning the authorities on behalf of the dependents of men who had been deported to Russia the previous autumn to serve in the Russian Army. There had been significant cohorts of Russian and Lithuanian miners working in the Lanarkshire coal mines, and their removal had left hundreds of women and children virtually destitute.

Maclean's educational work continued as well. On 16 March, the Labour College Committee held a conference attended by 417 delegates representing 271 organisations. A constitution and curriculum were agreed on, an executive committee and officials were elected, and Maclean and J Thomson of the Socialist Labour Party were appointed tutors.

~

In addition to his consular and educational work, Maclean had decided to challenge Labour MP George Barnes for pre-selection. Barnes was a former general secretary of the Amalgamated Society of Engineers who had taken the Glasgow constituency of Blackfriars and Hutchesontown from the future Unionist prime minister Andrew Bonar Law in the 1906 general election. He was one of the first two Labour MP to be elected in Scotland.

Barnes was a prominent member of the Labour Party. He had led the party for an 11 month period in 1910 and 1911 and in December 1916, was appointed the first minister for pensions in Lloyd George's coalition government. He joined the War Cabinet as minister without portfolio in August 1917.

As part of the major redistribution of the Scottish electoral map in February 1918, Barnes' seat had been split. South of the Clyde, Hutchesontown became part of the new seat of Glasgow Gorbals, while north of the river, Blackfriars was absorbed into Glasgow Central.

At a meeting of the Scottish Advisory Council of the Labour Party on 22 September 1917, a resolution had been passed by an overwhelming majority demanding an immediate peace, with no annexations and no indemnities. A further decision was to demand the withdrawal of the Labour Party from the coalition government.[18] The resolutions had no effect on Barnes.

In the week before the Labour Party conference at Nottingham in January, Barnes had criticised the 'obsession' of the ship workers and engineers with obtaining a 12 and a half per cent bonus. Such men, he said, were as bad as profiteers. It was not the poorest who were always striking, but highly paid workmen. Each strike increased the distress of the poor, including the families of soldiers.[19]

At a meeting of the Glasgow Trades Council a few days later, one of its members stated Barnes 'had proved himself to be a traitor to the Labour movement'.[20]

On the second day of the Nottingham conference, the Manchester and Salford branch moved a resolution that it was contrary to the interests of the working classes for Labour Party MPs to remain members of the coalition government. In discussion on the resolution, the *Glasgow Herald* reported 'Mr Maclean declared that Mr Barnes was "the supreme traitor".'[21]

It was the opening salvo of a clash between the two men that would run for the rest of the year. And the next round went to Maclean, when on 19 March, he was adopted ahead of Barnes as the Labour candidate for the Glasgow Gorbals constituency by the local Labour Representation Committee.[22]

~

Despite Maclean being an endorsed Labour candidate, at the British Socialist Party annual conference in Leeds over the Easter weekend he argued in favour of a proposal for the party to cease its affiliation with the Labour Party. The proposal was opposed by party chairman EC Fairchild and others and eventually an amendment was passed that a referendum of all members would be taken on the issue.

There was no doubt that there was a widening gulf between the BSP and the Labour Party on the issue of Russia. On the weekend of 26-27 January, the executive committee of the BSP had declared its wholehearted support for the Bolshevik revolution, and in February the *Call* published appeals from Petrograd for British workers to join the revolutionary fight.[23] Meanwhile, as news dribbled out from Brest-Litovsk that Russia was preparing to sign a separate peace with Germany, the bulk of the Labour leadership abandoned the Bolsheviks.

The discussions about relations with the Labour Party also underlined a fundamental difference between the two camps inside the BSP. The revolutionary group, led by Maclean, saw the BSP as the 'storm troop of the revolution encouraging the masses into action'.[24] Indeed, Maclean was actively campaigning at factory meetings, at street corners and at indoor lectures on the note that revolution was imminent and that the workers should be preparing to take power into their own hands.

'What was wanted,' Maclean declared, 'was not pious resolutions in support of our Russian comrades, but to use every action of the British Government to advance our own cause. We should get our comrades to talk and think revolution, to seize the chance when our enemy at home was weak, as a result of a wave of disgust over the war, to sweep the capitalist class out of the way and bring peace. We were in the rapids of revolution ... we should go forward ... to arouse class consciousness and revolutionary feeling amongst the workers. Let us march forward, the leaders of the working class here, as our Bolshevik comrades had been in Russia.'[25]

The reformist group, which included Fairchild and most of the other party leaders, were in favour of a negotiated peace and an end to the war. They were not in favour of unilateral action by the British working class that might hinder the war effort and contribute to a German victory. Fairchild saw only 'a long period of education and preparation before the workers could be fit to consider taking power for themselves'.[26]

However, Maclean and Fairchild were united in their criticism of the Labour Party efforts to exclude the BSP and the Independent Labour Party from the proposed international socialist conference. Maclean maintained that there could be no adequate representation of British opinion on internationalist questions if the socialist organisations were excluded. Fairchild supported the protest, remarking that when the British section met Huysmans, the secretary of the International Socialist Bureau, at Nottingham in January, Huysmans contended that the British Labour Party had no power to decide the basis of representation at the International, that the socialist bodies should send their delegates, and that the International Conference as a whole would then decide the question of admission.[27]

After the BSP conference, Maclean spent a week in Durham, where he helped the Plebs League and the Central Labour College organise classes for the miners of the district. He also gave a series of stirring anti-war public speeches at various locations in the county.

All of this was his last flourish for a while, however. Events in Eastern Europe, and their ramifications for the war on the Western Front, meant the time was opportune for the authorities to make their move. On 15 April, shortly after Maclean's return to Glasgow from England, two detectives arrived at the consulate in South Portland Street to arrest him on charges of sedition.

34

BREST-LITOVSK: THE TREATY

As the new year dawned, Lenin had begun to realise that the world revolution so earnestly hoped for, may in fact be some time off. The Russian revolution was in being, but was under threat both from within its own ranks and the organised forces of anti-Bolshevism. To improve the chances of a world upheaval, and secure a breathing space for the revolution at home, Lenin decided a policy of delay was necessary at Brest-Litovsk. He also realised that to achieve this end, someone of heavy calibre was required to take charge of the discussions. So, when the delegations returned in the second week of January, Trotsky had replaced Joffe as head of the Russian delegation.

In his book about the treaty, John Wheeler-Bennett penned a vivid word portrait of Trotsky.

> Broad-chested, his huge forehead surrounded by great masses of black waving hair; his eyes strong and fierce, yet with traces of much human suffering about them; heavy protruding lips, with their little beard and moustache, Trotsky was the very incarnation of the revolutionary in caricature. Dynamic and tireless, he was consumed with the flame of his ardour, uncompromising and bitter in opposition, fearful and scornful in defeat. Versatile, cultivated and eloquent, he could be charming in his rare occasions of good-humour, but in his more usual attitude of contemptuous anger, he was a freezing fire.[1]

When talks resumed on 9 January, the Central Powers opened with a barrage. Kuhlmann immediately announced that as the Entente Powers had failed to take up the offer of participation, the declarations made by the Central Powers on 25 and 28 December were null and void. Czernin followed, declaring that the Russians must now confine themselves to the question of a separate peace, and demanding the immediate setting up of the commissions to conduct the referendums on independence in the occupied territories. Hoffmann then weighed in with a protest about the volume of propaganda and incitement to mutiny being distributed by the Soviet government.

Trotsky sought an adjournment, and the following day responded in remarks dripping with bitter contempt. Hoffmann's objections he dismissed, saying there was nothing in the terms of the armistice or the peace negotiations that limited freedom of speech. To Kuhlmann, he said Russia refused to accept the German view of self-determination, 'by which the will of the people was replaced by the will of a privileged group acting under the control of the authorities administering the territories'.[2] He confirmed the intention of the Soviet government to continue negotiations for a separate peace, but lamented the refusal of the Central Powers to accept his suggestion to move the talks to neutral Stockholm.[3]

Both sides had set out their positions clearly and it was obvious from the start that there existed an unbridgeable chasm between them. But Trotsky and Kuhlmann proceeded to circle each other for the following four weeks, debating 'the ethics, forms, and principles of self-determination and its application to the border states'. Trotsky demanded full referendums taken without the presence of foreign military forces. Kuhlmann refused to consider the evacuation of German troops, and claimed the occupied territories had already declared their will through the bodies set up under German administration. To this Trotsky replied, 'We would prefer to talk about annexations, rather than to replace their real name with a pseudonym.'[4]

These prolonged discussions, while engrossing to the participants, were infuriating to the Austrians and the German military. The Austrians need for the food supplies sitting tantalisingly close in the Ukraine was becoming more and more desperate, with their principal cities facing actual famine. Hoffmann, who had been opposed to these tactics from the start, urged Kuhlmann to cut to the chase and issue the Russians with an ultimatum.

Hoffmann had his chance to intervene on 12 January. For the Russians, Lev Kamenev had proposed a series of evacuations of the occupied territories to be followed by plebiscites and called on the governments of Germany and Austria-Hungary to renounce any claims to annex the territories of the former Russian Empire.

Hoffmann replied firmly that as the Bolsheviks, in violation of the armistice agreement, had continued to interfere in the internal affairs of the Central Powers by the dissemination of propaganda, the German High

Command considered it necessary to prevent any attempt to interfere in the affairs of the occupied territories. Also, for reasons of a technical and administrative nature, the German High Command refused to evacuate Courland, Lithuania, Riga and the Islands of the Gulf of Riga.[5]

~

Far from setting the talks on a speedy course, the only concrete effect of Hoffmann's brutally frank statement was to provoke a chorus of indignation in the German and Austro-Hungarian press from those who still believed in a peace of understanding and the principles of the Reichstag Peace Resolution of July 1917. 'The Central Powers now stood self-convicted before their opponents and before the world. The Master Voice of Germany had spoken – Hoffmann had proclaimed the fact that he represented not the German government but the Supreme Command [established in September 1916 to exert command over all the armed forces of the Central Powers] and no further doubts could be entertained either to its power or its intentions.'[6]

Kuhlmann was willing, for the time being, to continue discussions with Trotsky, so Hoffmann turned his attention to the three young men of the Ukrainian delegation who had arrived when the talks had resumed on 9 January. The delegation represented the Rada, the Ukrainian revolutionary parliament formed in April 1917. Unlike many other councils in the Russian Republic, Bolshevisation of the Rada had failed completely, prompting the Ukrainian Bolsheviks to form a rival government based in Kharkov.

On their arrival, the youthful Ukrainians had asserted their independence from the Soviet regime at Petrograd and declared their willingness to negotiate a separate peace with the Central Powers. Hoffmann now probed for more details. The Ukrainians' opening gambit was for border adjustments in their favour; namely the Polish district around Cholm, and parts of Austrian Galicia and Burkovina. Hoffmann promised support for the Polish claim, but called the Austrian claims 'impudent' and indicated they would not be considered.

Trotsky realised the negotiations with the Ukrainians seriously weakened his position. The prospect of a separate treaty between the Central Powers and Ukraine, which would undoubtedly be followed by the occupation of Ukraine by German and Austrian troops, threatened food supplies as well as significantly raising the military risk to Russia.

Eventually tiring of the drawn out discussions, on 18 January Kuhlmann decided to force the issue. He restated the Central Powers' position, that the population in the occupied territories was not sufficiently experienced politically for referenda to be held, and that the institutions already in existence must be developed for this purpose. But above all, the spread of revolution to the territories they currently occupied must be prevented. Trotsky sarcastically enquired as to the exact area to be embraced by the German principle of self-determination. In response, Hoffmann spread a map on the table and indicated with his thumb a blue line that ran north from Brest and separated from the former Russian Empire most of Poland, all of Lithuania, western Latvia, the city of Riga and the Moon Sound Islands.[7]

Trotsky asked about the occupied areas south of Brest, to which Hoffman replied that issue would be discussed with the Ukrainian delegation. Trotsky then made a general statement to the conference, declaring Germany and Austria had made it clear they wished to retain their military reign over the occupied territories, not just until peace with Russia was achieved, but after the conclusion of a general peace. Given the Central Powers were unwilling to give details of the timing or conditions of an evacuation of these territories, 'the governments of Germany and Austria had taken into their hands the destiny of these nations'.[8]

Facing this new situation, Trotsky sought and obtained an adjournment to enable him to return to Russia for discussions. He left on 18 January, arriving in Petrograd the day after the Bolsheviks successfully closed down the constituent assembly.

~

The Central Powers were relieved at the dissolution of the assembly, having feared it might have proved a rallying-point for an alliance between the Soviet government and the patriotic forces to continue the war. The reaction in the countries of the Entente was the complete opposite. Those who had hoped the assembly would see a coming together of all the revolutionary elements of Russia received a rude awakening. Furthermore, the brutal exercise of Soviet power fatally undermined the high moral stance on self-determination in the occupied territories that Trotsky had been espousing at Brest-Litovsk.

Trotsky was convinced that before peace was agreed, the proletariat of Europe should be given a signal of the enmity that existed between Soviet Russia and Germany. He had written to Lenin, saying: 'It is impossible to sign their peace, Vladimir Ilych ... My plan is this: We announce the termination of the war and demobilisation without signing any peace. We declare we cannot participate in the brigands' peace of the Central Powers nor can we sign a brigands' peace.'[9]

Trotsky's reasoning was that it was necessary to test whether or not the Germans were prepared to send troops against Russia. If they were not, it would be a great victory for the Soviets. If they did, it would be possible to make it clear to everyone the Soviets were capitulating at the point of a bayonet.

The party leaders were split on whether to accept the German terms. Lenin argued that without an army willing to fight, Russia had to accept the proposed annexation peace. There was no point in putting the whole of the revolution at risk on the chance that a German revolution might break out, he said. But the majority of the committee, led by Bukharin, favoured fighting a revolutionary war against Germany, believing this was the most likely way of precipitating an uprising in the West. As a compromise, Trotsky put forward his slogan 'Neither war nor peace'.

On 22 January, the issue was taken to the Soviet Executive Committee, where the proposal for a revolutionary war was defeated, Lenin's motion to drag out the negotiations was passed, and then Trotsky's suggestion was narrowly agreed to. On 26 January Trotsky left for Brest-Litovsk with a free hand to spin out the talks and, when he judged the moment to be appropriate, drop the 'No War – No Peace' formula.[10]

Scarcely had Trotsky departed Petrograd than it seemed, miraculously, the hoped-for uprisings in Germany and Austria might be happening. There was a wave of strikes and outbreaks. Soviets were formed in Berlin and Vienna. 'All power to the soviets,' was heard in the streets of Berlin, where half a million workers downed tools. Hamburg, Bremen, Leipzig, Essen and Munich took up the cry. In the forefront of the demands were the speedy conclusion of peace, without annexations or indemnities, based on the self-determination of peoples, in line with the Russian peace proposals tabled at Brest-Litovsk.[11]

Though partly of revolutionary origin, the strike movement owed more to the exhaustion of the German working class, straining under the German High Command's imposition of ever-increasing burdens and privations. The authorities came down hard in response: the labour press was banned; strike meetings were broken up by the police; a state of siege was proclaimed in the cities; and seven major industrial concerns in Berlin were placed under military control. By 3 February the movement had collapsed, but the authorities were shaken and arranged for troops to be ready to act against the civilian population in the event of further trouble.[12]

~

When talks resumed in Brest-Litovsk, the situation in the Ukraine had changed in Trotsky's favour. The Bolshevik forces had won military victories over the Rada, and Trotsky added three members of the executive committee of the Soviet Ukrainian Republic to the Russian delegation, claiming only they were qualified to speak for the Ukrainian people. On 1 February, Kuhlmann and Czernin staged a three-way contest between the two sets of Ukrainian representatives and the Russian delegation. After the three groups tore strips off each other in a succession of fierce and vitriolic speeches, Czernin declared the Central Powers recognised 'immediately the Ukrainian People's Republic [the Rada] as an independent, free and sovereign state, which is able to enter into international agreements independently'.[13]

Although the outcome was a success for the Central Powers, the prolonged manoeuvre had taken three precious days, and with an important two-day conference on Austro-German affairs scheduled to begin in Berlin on 4 February, Kuhlmann abruptly adjourned the conference until 7 February.

In Berlin, after a round of discussions between the diplomats and the military, the Supreme War Command made it clear it could brook not a week's further delay on the Eastern Front. Troops must be transferred to the west. Trotsky must be confronted by an ultimatum. Either he must accept the peace terms or hostilities must be resumed. Kuhlmann reluctantly agreed, but Czernin gave notice that after the signing of the Ukrainian peace, he would make one final attempt to achieve a compromise between the German and Russian points of view.

When the parties reconvened in Brest-Litovsk, the Austrians had in the interim managed to sort out the technical details of a treaty with the Ukrainian Rada delegates. With this in hand, Czernin approached Trotsky. It was suggested that a treaty with the Soviets could remain silent on whether the territorial changes were because of annexation or self-determination. This was deemed acceptable by Trotsky, who also suggested some amendments to the proposed borders, with Russia retaining Riga and the Islands of the Moon and an adjustment in the Lithuanian frontier.

When this was presented to Hoffmann however, he flatly refused to even consider the frontier changes and demanded the immediate signing of the Ukrainian treaty to clear the way for an ultimatum to the Russians. All hopes of an agreement were therefore destroyed by the insistence of the Supreme Command on advancing into Russia and compelling unconditional surrender by the Soviet government. On the other side, Trotsky made it clear he would not accept a treaty signed with representatives of the Rada, which had been driven out of Kiev by the Bolsheviks on 5 February, and which in his view had ceased to exist.[14]

The Treaty of Peace between Ukraine and the Central Powers was signed the following day, 9 February. It ceded Cholm to Ukraine, while the Ukrainian-speaking parts of Galicia and the Bukovina were to become a separate Ukrainian province within the Austrian-Hungarian monarchy. In return, the Ukrainians undertook to place its surplus of foodstuffs, estimated to be at least a million tons, at the disposal of the Central Powers. In theory, Ukraine was now a neutral state in the world; in effect, it was now a granary and store-house for the Central Powers.[15]

Any lingering hope that Kuhlmann may have had for an agreement with Trotsky were dashed when German military operators intercepted radio-telegrams from Russia inciting German troops to mutiny, to murder the Kaiser, the generals of the High Command and their own regimental officers and conclude an independent peace with the Bolsheviks.

Furious at the news, the Kaiser ordered the German peace terms to be presented to the Russians as an ultimatum: if they were not accepted by the following day, the German and Austrian armies would be ordered to advance.[16]

The move forced Trotsky to reveal his hand, and he announced to the astounded conference that Russia was leaving the war, but refused to sign the German peace treaty. Despite the simmering threat of a revolution in Berlin, the German High Command decided to call Trotsky's bluff, and with the armistice at an end, resumed military operations on 18 February. In the face of the German advance, the Russian Army fell apart completely and the Germans advanced 240 km in five days.

On 23 February, the Germans delivered their final terms for peace. Berlin demanded all the territory its troops had occupied to date, including the Ukraine and most of the Baltic territories. With no real alternative, the Russians accepted. Trotsky resigned as foreign minister and was replaced by Georgy Chicherin. On 24 February, Chicherin headed the Soviet delegation at peace talks with Germany, and on 3 March, he participated in the signing of the Brest-Litovsk peace treaty with Germany, Austria-Hungary and their allies.

Under the treaty, Russia lost Poland, Courland in western Latvia, Finland, Estonia and Lithuania, which were all granted nominal independence under German protection. In addition, all Soviet troops were to be evacuated from Ukraine. It is estimated that the Soviet Republic lost 34 per cent of its population (55 million people); 32 per cent of its agricultural lands; 54 per cent of its industrial enterprises; and 89 per cent of its coalmines.[17]

But the Bolsheviks, led by the uncompromising Lenin, had retained power.

35

ACCUSER OF CAPITALISM

After his arrest on 15 April 1918, John Maclean was held without bail at Glasgow's Duke Street Prison. Two weeks later, he was remitted for trial at the High Court of Justiciary on charges under the Defence of the Realm Act and Regulations. The trial date was set was Thursday 9 May and on 2 May he was transferred to Edinburgh's cheerless Calton Jail.

The charges against Maclean were that on 11 occasions between 20 January and 4 April, he addressed audiences at various places in Glasgow, Lanarkshire and Fife, consisting in part of munitions workers, and made statements that were likely to prejudice recruitment to His Majesty's Forces, and to cause mutiny, sedition, and disaffection among the civilian population, thereby impeding the production, repair, and transport of war material and other work necessary for the successful prosecution of war.

Given the experience of his 1916 trial, where all the evidence of the defence witnesses was discounted in favour of that of the police, Maclean had no doubt that he would be convicted again. He therefore resolved to use the occasion as a platform to deliver a speech. Conscious that his trial was likely to be of great public interest, he understood his audience would not just be the jury and others in the court, but the working class of Scotland, Great Britain and the world beyond.

Some thirty of Maclean's supporters set out on the Wednesday night before the trial to march from Glasgow to Edinburgh, the march being intended as a demonstration against the prosecution. The *Call* reported:

> One of the most interesting sidelights of the trial was the overnight march to Edinburgh. On the Wednesday evening preceding the trial a party of about thirty Socialists assembled at the International Hall, Stockwell Street, Glasgow. For a distance of about five or six miles out of the town they were accompanied by about 1,500, and the procession created something of a

sensation in the city. The capitalist Press, as usual, of course, tried to belittle and ridicule the little band of thirty enthusiasts who covered the 44 miles and got to Edinburgh in time for the trial.[1]

They were not far off the mark. The *Scotsman* said 'As the march proceeded, the number taking part gradually diminished, and having got so far those that remained were glad to finish their journey by motor bus. Half an hour before the proceedings commenced the Court was crowded and many people who sought admission had to be turned away by the police.'[2]

The Lord Advocate, James Avon Clyde, KC, Mr Blackburn, KC, and Mr CH Brown appeared for the Crown. Maclean conducted his own defence and on being asked by the Lord Justice General, Lord Strathclyde, whether he pleaded guilty or not guilty, replied 'I refuse to plead.'

'Very well,' said Strathclyde, 'that is equivalent to a plea of not guilty.'

The jury was then balloted, and informed of his right to object to any of the men selected, Maclean raised a laugh when he replied, 'I object to the whole of them!'

The prosecution called 28 witnesses: 15 policemen; 8 special constables; 2 shorthand writers employed by the police; one newspaper reporter; one mining inspector; and one slater.

Their evidence was, in the main, a jumble of inflammatory phrases plucked from memory and devoid of context. They included: 'down tools'; 'create revolution'; 'burn farms'; 'take control of the City Chambers and take hostages'; take control of the Post Office and the banks'; 'destroy the police offices and disorganise the police'; 'replace the House of Commons with a soviet'; and 'munition workers should restrict their output'.

In his cross-examination, Maclean protested at this, saying, 'The consequences of any man's speech are always based on what goes before. The main parts of my speech, in which my themes are developed, are omitted.'[3]

The exchanges between Maclean and two of the witnesses about a meeting at the Fife mining village of Crossgates received wide coverage in reports of the trial. John Ford, a mining inspector from the Fife Coal Company, said he considered Maclean's speech there a dangerous one, and prepared a report for his employers. He took no notes.

Maclean asked him if he was aware that in the past the land had been seized violently from the people, and did he not object to the present owners holding the land when they had obtained it violently?

'I might object to that,' Ford said, 'but it is a question of how you take it from them. For instance, in answer to a question as to how these things could be got, the question being "Could we get these things by peaceful action?" you said, "I am here to develop a revolution".'

'Do you infer that a revolution means violence?' Maclean asked.

'You could not have put any other construction on your words after you said that revolution here was to be on the same lines as Russia,' said Ford. 'I understand that the Russian Revolution was a violent revolution.'

'It is the most peaceful revolution the world has ever seen and the biggest,' Maclean countered. 'Don't you know that this war is the most bloody that had ever taken place, and that revolution and bloodshed do not go together?'

'No,' was Ford's response.

George Stewart, a slater, also gave evidence about the Crossgates meeting. He said the speech was a bit strong on revolution and was likely to unsettle the audience.

'A canny place, Fife?' Maclean asked him.

'Yes.'

'I should say the last place in which a revolution would take place would be in Fife?' posed Maclean.

'It will take some working up for you,' Stewart agreed.

'Don't you think the war also has unsettled the people, that it has had an unsettling influence?' asked Maclean pointedly.[4]

~

At the conclusion of the prosecution's evidence, Maclean said that as he had been locked up, he could not call any witnesses to give evidence, and indicated he did not intend to go into the witness box himself.

Clyde, in addressing the jury, said they had heard during the evidence a good many references to socialism, social revolution; and the like. In its report of his speech, the *Scotsman* included the following:

> However inappropriate these subjects might be to the moment, there was nothing in this country or in its law, even as that law had to be framed to meet the emergency with which they were faced, to prevent any man if he pleased, from talking about politics or about Socialism. If the prisoner had been content to expound what he knew, or what he thought he knew, about socialistic theories, if he had been content to try to persuade other people of the soundness and expediency of the plans of socialistic reconstruction in which

he believed, nobody could have laid a finger on him. But there came a point at which discussion of socialistic questions or discussion of any question changed its character. At that point there came the deliberate and persistent attempt to plant seeds of disunion, disloyalty, sedition and mutiny among the people. They could not afford at the present time to have the people incited to active violence and rebellion while the enemy was at their gates.'[5]

And the *Glasgow Herald* had this:

Not one of them could see into the dark recesses of the human heart, and none of them would ever know what tempted a man at home to destroy the liberty and freedom which were being defended abroad. But just because they did not know what the motive was, they must judge the man by what he did and what the prisoner had done his best to do was to create sedition and disaffection among the civilian population. It became the duty of the State to protect the brave young working men from such insidious teaching, although, for himself, he did not believe influences of this kind were likely to smirch the honesty and integrity of their young men.'[6]

Clyde submitted that the case against Maclean was absolutely and completely proved.

~

Before delivering his prepared remarks, Maclean attacked Clyde for impugning his motives.[7] 'He (the lord advocate) accused me of my motives,' said Maclean. 'My motives are clean. My motives are genuine. If my motives were not clean and genuine, would I have made my statements while these shorthand reporters were present? I am out for the benefit of society, not for any individual human being, but I realise this, that justice and freedom can only be obtained when society is placed on a sound economic basis.'

In his opening comments, Maclean set out his political philosophy and beliefs.

For the full period of my active life, I have been a teacher of economics to the working classes, and my contention has always been that capitalism is rotten to its foundations, and must give place to a new society. I had a lecture, the principal heading of which was 'Thou shalt not steal; thou shalt not kill', and I pointed out that as a consequence of the robbery that goes on in all civilised countries today, our respective countries have had to keep armies, and that inevitably our armies must clash together. On that and on other grounds, I consider capitalism the most infamous, bloody and evil system that mankind has ever witnessed.

I know quite well that in the reconstruction of society, the class interests of those who are on top will resist the change, and the only factor in society that can make for a clean sweep in society is the working class. Hence the class war. The whole history of society has proved that society moves forward as a consequence of an under-class overcoming the resistance of a class on top of them. So much for that.

I wish no harm to any human being, but I, as one man, am going to exercise my freedom of speech. No human being on the face of the earth, no government is going to take from me my right to speak, my right to protest against wrong, my right to do everything that is for the benefit of mankind. I am not here, then, as the accused; I am here as the accuser of capitalism dripping with blood from head to foot.

Moving on to address the charges against him, Maclean disagreed that he had told the workers to 'down tools'. He noted the official engineers' committee had met and determined to down tools against the introduction of the government's Man Power Bill. Furthermore, at the Glasgow meeting addressed by Sir Auckland Geddes in January, the workers present had passed a resolution that if the Man Power Bill was put into operation, the Clyde district workers would 'down tools'. Based on those decisions, he had said, 'Now that you are determined to "down tools" it is of no use standing idle; you must do something for yourselves.'

On food and farms, Maclean said he pointed out to the workers that if they stopped work, it would be necessary to get food. He knew that there was plenty of food in stores in Glasgow, and that the farmers, who had used the war to make huge profits for themselves, had food stored up in their farms. He therefore said that if the workers went to the farmers and did not get the food stored up in the farms, they should burn the farms. 'We as socialists have no interest in destroying any property,' he stated. 'We want property to be kept because we want that property to be used for housing accommodation or other reasons, but I specially emphasised about the farmers for the purpose of drawing attention to this particular point.'

When it came to the question of seizing the press, Maclean agreed that he said that when the *Daily Record* was seized, the plant should be broken up, but clarified 'not that it is a good thing to break up printing plant, but in order to draw attention to the Harmsworth family and to the Rothermeres and their vile press, and in order to emphasise the disgust of the organised workers with regard to that particular family of newspapers.'

The reason the government was responsible for the murder of women and children was perfectly obvious, Maclean said. The government got hold of the food supplies immediately prior to and immediately after the New Year, and created a shortage. The government was therefore responsible for the queues. Women were standing in queues in the cold, and women had died of what they had contracted during their standing in the queues. The women had died therefore in consequence of the action of the government.

Not only that, but in his role as Russian consul, Maclean said he had received deputations from the partners of Russian men sent back to Russia to fight. They told him sorrowful tales of depression, disease and death resulting from the meagre amount of support they received from the British government. 'There is not a Lithuanian family in the West of Scotland but has trouble today as a consequence of the starving of these people,' he declared.

Maclean made it clear he did not resile for a moment from the charge that he posed a threat to the state. 'The lord advocate pointed out here that I probably was a more dangerous enemy that you had got to face than in the Germans,' he said. 'The working class, when they rise for their own, are more dangerous to capitalists than even the German enemies at your gates. That has been repeatedly indicated in the press, and I have stated it as well. I am glad that you have made this statement at this, the most historic trial that has ever been held in Scotland, when the working class and the capitalist class meet face to face.'

In full flow, he proceeded to give his take on recent events in Russia, and their significance for Britain.

> The Bolsheviks got into power in October, and the people wished peace, and they were doing their best to get peace. The Bolsheviks wished peace throughout the world. They wished the war to cease in order that they might settle down to the real business of life, the economic reorganisation of the whole of Russia. They therefore got into negotiation with the Germans, and they and the Germans met at Brest-Litovsk.
>
> Towards the end of December there was a pause in the negotiations for ten days, in order to allow the British and their allies to go to Brest-Litovsk. Ten days were given. The last day was 4 January of this year. Great Britain paid no attention to this opportunity, but on 5 January Lloyd George, in one of his insidious speeches, seemed to climb down as it were. He was followed by Mr

Woodrow Wilson. But a speech by Mr Lloyd George on the 5th was of no use. It was mere talk. It was mere camouflage, or, a better word still, bluff, pure bluff. Why did the government not accept the opportunity and go to Brest-Litovsk? If conditions absolutely favourable to Germany were proposed, then Britain would have stopped the negotiations and plunged once more into the war, and I am confident of this, if Germany had not toed the line and come up square so far as peace negotiations were concerned, that the Russian workers would have taken the side of Britain, and I am confident of this, that the socialists in all the allied countries would have backed up their governments in order to absolutely crush Germany, and we would at the same time have appealed to the socialists of Germany to overthrow their government.

Great Britain did not do so. On the other hand, they came on with their Man Power Bill, and also with their factor of short food. All these things must be considered in their ensemble, before you can understand the position taken up by myself. When this universal peace meeting was held at Brest-Litovsk, then Trotsky played a very, very bold game. He knew the risks he ran. He and the Bolsheviks spread millions of leaflets amongst the workers of Germany in the trenches - the German soldiers - urging them to stop fighting and to overthrow the Kaiser, the Junkers, and the capitalist classes of Germany. They made a bold bid by trying to get the German workers on to their side. Great Britain has been doing the very same thing since the commencement of the war. Great Britain has been trying to bring about, and hoping and urging for a revolution in Germany, in the hope that the working class would overthrow the autocratic class there and give us peace.

From a British point of view, revolution inside Germany is good; revolution inside Britain is bad. So says this learned gentleman. He can square it if he can. I cannot square it. The conditions of Germany economically are the conditions of Britain, and there is only a very slight difference between the political structure of Germany and that of this country at the best. And so far as we workers are concerned, we are not concerned with the political superstructure; we are concerned with the economic foundation of society, and that determines our point of view in politics and industrial action. Our Russian comrades, therefore, did the very same as the British have been doing; they appealed to the German soldiers and workers to overthrow their government.

Maclean declared he was no traitor to his country; he stood loyal to his country because he stood loyal to his class.

It was not the workers who instigated the war. The workers have no economic interest to serve as a consequence of the war, and because of that, it is my appeal to my class that makes me a patriot so far as my class is concerned, and when I stand true to my class, the working class, in which I was born, it is because my people were swept out of the Highlands, and it was only because of my own ability that I remained. I have remained true to my class, the working class, and whatever I do I think I am doing in the interest of my class and my country. I am no traitor to my country. I stand loyal to my country because I stand loyal to the class which creates the wealth throughout the whole of the world.

We are out for life and all that life can give us. I therefore took what action I did in the light of what was transpiring inside Russia, inside Austria and inside Germany. You have got to bear that in mind when you wish to understand my remarks. I therefore urged the workers of this country that if they were going to strike, mere striking was useless, because they would be starved back into work again, and that if they were going to be against the Man Power Bill, it meant that they were out for peace. And as there was no sign on either side of coming to an amicable constitutional conclusion, then it was the business of the workers to take the whole matter in hand themselves.

He then lamented that the government had thrown aside constitutional methods and deliberately and consciously suppressed freedom of speech because of the war.

War was declared! No matter the motive, no matter the cause, all constitution and order was thrown aside, and in the prosecution of the war the British Government found it necessary to throw aside every law in this country and to bring in the Defence of the Realm Act, which means the negation of all law in the country. I have repeatedly pointed out that if the government wishes to get a grip of any individual, they do so under the Defence of the Realm Act. The government have power to do anything they desire. That may be right, or it may be wrong, but the position is this, that the bringing in of the Defence of the Realm Act has thrown aside all law and order as we know it during normal periods.

In the plunge into the war we have the abolition of constitutional methods, and therefore I contended, and I contend today, that if it is right and proper on the part of the government to throw aside law and order – constitutional methods – and to adopt methods that mankind has never seen before, then it is equally right that the members of the working class, if the war is not going to cease in a reasonable time, should bring about a reasonable settlement to the workers in no victory to either side.

After an exposition on markets and the rush for empire, which included his prediction that in fifteen years' time 'we may have the first great war bursting out in the Pacific - America v. Japan ... another war, far greater and far more serious in its consequences than the present war', Maclean ended his oration defiantly, stating, 'I have nothing to retract. I have nothing to be ashamed of.'

> In view of the fact that the great powers are not prepared to stop the war until the one side or the other is broken down, it is our business as members of the working class to see that this war ceases today, not only to save the lives of the young men of the present, but also to stave off the next great war. That has been my attitude and justifies my conduct in recent times. I am out for an absolute reconstruction of society, on a cooperative basis, throughout all the world; when we stop the need for armies and navies, we stop the need for wars.
>
> I have taken up unconstitutional action at this time because of the abnormal circumstances and because precedent has been given by the British government. I am a socialist, and have been fighting and will fight for an absolute reconstruction of society for the benefit of all. I am proud of my conduct. I have squared my conduct with my intellect, and if everyone had done so this war would not have taken place. I act square and clean for my principles. I have nothing to retract. I have nothing to be ashamed of. Your class position is against my class position. There are two classes of morality. There is the working class morality and there is the capitalist class morality. There is this antagonism as there is the antagonism between Germany and Britain. A victory for Germany is a defeat for Britain; a victory for Britain is a defeat for Germany. And it is exactly the same so far as our classes are concerned. What is moral for the one class is absolutely immoral for the other, and vice-versa. No matter what your accusations against me may be, no matter what reservations you keep at the back of your head, my appeal is to the working class. I appeal exclusively to them because they and they only can bring about the time when the whole world will be in one brotherhood, on a sound economic foundation. That, and that alone, can be the means of bringing about a re-organisation of society. That can only be obtained when the people of the world get the world, and retain the world.

~

Lord Strathclyde said a question of simple fact was submitted to the jury - whether on the eleven different occasions mentioned in the indictment the accused made the statements alleged. No attempt had been made by the defence to deny that the statements were made.

The jury without retiring, found Maclean guilty of all the charges.

Strathclyde asked Maclean if he had anything to say.

'No, I think I have said enough for one day,' Maclean replied.

'John Maclean,' Strathclyde said, 'it would be idle of me to dwell on the gravity of the offence of which you have been found guilty by a jury of your countrymen after a very patient trial, and after the clearest possible evidence and because you are obviously a highly educated and intelligent man and realise the thorough seriousness of the offence you have committed. This is not the first time you have been convicted of an offence against the Defence of the Realm Act and in pronouncing sentence today I have taken into account the fact that you have still, as far as I can judge, over a year to serve of your former sentence. Today the sentence of the court is that you be sent to penal servitude for a period of five years.'[8]

Maclean seemed somewhat taken aback by the severity of the sentence, but as he was led away to the cells he recovered sufficiently to call out to his friends in the gallery, 'Keep it going boys, keep it going!'

36

PETERHEAD AGAIN

The establishment press was unperturbed about the severity of Maclean's sentence. The *Scotsman* wrote: 'The evidence for the Crown ... was conclusive; the accused who conducted his own case, made no attempt to question it, preferring, instead, to deliver what was a political harangue rather than a defence, and sentence was passed on him of five years' penal servitude. In the circumstances of the time the punishment is not one that any fair minded person will regard as excessive, neither does it take undue note of the fact that the present is not the first occasion upon which Maclean has been convicted under the Defence of the Realm Act.'[1]

On the other side, the *Call* unsurprisingly labelled the sentence 'brutal and savage in the extreme', and went on to say: 'It is a measure of the hatred which the master class feel for those who endeavour to enlighten the workers to the real causes of the exploitation, war and misery that exist today.'[2]

A Clyde District Defence Committee was formed in the immediate aftermath of the trial to campaign for Maclean's release. Marches were held in Glasgow, public demonstrations took place in London, and there was support from socialist and libertarian organisations in Europe and Russia, as well as the chairman of the Russian Council of People's Commissars. Speaking to the Fourth Conference of Trade Unions and Factory Committees of Moscow on 28 June, Lenin said:

> Perhaps you have read that in Britain recently the Scottish schoolteacher and trade unionist Maclean was sentenced for a second time, to five years' imprisonment – the first time he was sentenced to eighteen months – for exposing the real objects of the war and speaking about the criminal nature of British imperialism. When he was released, there was already a representative of the Soviet Government in Britain, Litvinov, who immediately appointed Maclean Consul, a representative of the Soviet

Russian Federative Republic in Britain, and the Scottish workers greeted this appointment with enthusiasm. The British Government has again started persecuting Maclean and this time not only as a Scottish schoolteacher, but also as Consul of the Federative Soviet Republic.

Maclean is in prison because he acted openly as the representative of our government; we have never seen this man, he is the beloved leader of the Scottish workers, he has never belonged to our Party, but we joined with him; the Russian and Scottish workers united against the British Government in spite of the fact that the latter buys Czechoslovaks and is manoeuvring frantically to drag the Russian Republic into the war. This is proof that in all countries, irrespective of their position in the war – in Germany which is fighting against us, in Britain which is trying to grab Baghdad and strangle Turkey – the workers are uniting with the Russian Bolsheviks, with the Russian Bolshevik revolution.[3]

The second of Glasgow's demonstrations for Maclean's release took place on Sunday 8 July. A large crowd assembled in George Square and set out to march to Glasgow Green. In the face of a large police presence, instead of forming up four-deep in the usual manner, a small section set off led by a band playing 'The Red Flag'. The rest of the crowd followed *en masse*, filling the whole breadth of the street, so the police could hardly interfere. The demonstration then proceeded to the entrance of Glasgow Green at Jail Square, at the foot of the Saltmarket.[4]

According to the account in the *Glasgow Herald*:

> ... the procession was stopped by the police, who acting under a by-law which requires that the permission of the Magistrates must be obtained for band performances in the street, requested the names and addresses of the men composing the band. This procedure was resented and a scuffle with police ensued. The latter, who were in strong force, ultimately took as many of the bandsmen as could be secured to the police barracks in Clyde Street, where after the names and addresses of about a dozen had been taken, the men were allowed to go. ... Considerable excitement was occasioned by the occurrence, which was however of short duration. Two men who were in the crowd were detained by police.[5]

Nan Milton provided more details of the 'considerable excitement'. When the demonstration reached Jail Square, she wrote, 'it was surrounded by hundreds of policemen. Without any reason whatever, they drew their batons and a scene wilder than any witnessed in Glasgow for many years was enacted. Hundreds of unarmed men and women were struck down violently. This brutality served only to fan the flames of anger, and thousands broke through the police barriers and crowded around the platforms on the Green.'[6]

The Herald concluded its report by saying, 'The procession proceeded to the Green, where speeches of protest were made against the imprisonment of Maclean.' Just another pleasant Sunday in Glasgow, in other words.

~

The adoption of a new constitution at the Labour Party conference in February 1918 had given Arthur Henderson the first part of what he sought after resigning from the party leadership in 1917 – an instrument which could be used for the building of an effective election machine all over the country. The second part was achieved at the party conference in June 1918, when the policy document drafted by Sidney Webb, *Labour and the New Social Order* was formally adopted.

The program unequivocally committed the Labour Party to socialist objectives, although these were couched in evolutionary terms, rather than the revolutionary socialism preached by John Maclean and the British Socialist Party. The policy aimed to assure every citizen a minimum standard of civilised life; the general enforcement of a living wage; full employment; public ownership under the control of a democratic parliament; progressive taxation; a comprehensive system of social services; and equality of opportunity for all, by means of a generous system of education, fuller provision for scientific and social research and the development of a civilisation based on the co-operative efforts of common men and women.[7]

The moderate, evolutionary, social-reform socialism of Webb and the Fabian Society appealed to most of the trade union leaders, and while a good many of the socialists in the party would have preferred stronger stuff, the BSP was too weak to fight it, and the Independent Labour Party was split into reformists and revolutionaries.

Before the policy was considered, the first day of the conference was wracked by a heated discussion on ending the electoral truce, and the party resuming its freedom to fight by-elections against government candidates of other parties. The miners' leader Robert Smillie declared his hope that they would not only end the truce but end their connection with the government completely.

George Barnes, the Labour Party's representative on the War Cabinet, argued strenuously against the motion. 'Mr Henderson asked us to remain in the government, and asked you at the same time to vote for a resolution which says you can run candidates against that government,' he told the delegates. 'I say that is an unfair and illogical position in which to put your nominees. I am for this war, whether in the government or out of the government. I believe this resolution will weaken the national effort because it will dissipate energy that ought to be devoted against the common enemy.'[8]

Despite the protests of Barnes and the other Labour members of the government, the resolution passed by a large majority. But despite Smillie's hope, the Labour members remained in the government.

Henderson advised the conference that the Labour Party already had more than 300 candidates fixed to constituencies, and with a constitution and program in place, 'he believed there was sufficient enthusiasm in the movement to place Labour in the British Parliament in a position second to none in the world'.[9]

One of those Labour candidates was of course John Maclean, who had been selected by the local Labour Party in Glasgow Gorbals. There was a further hurdle to clear however. All candidates selected by constituency bodies would have to be approved by the Labour Party National Executive.

When Kerensky, the former Russian prime minister and leader of the deposed provisional government was introduced to the conference by Arthur Henderson, the rapturous reception he received was an indication of how far sympathy for the Bolsheviks had plummeted. Approval of Maclean's candidacy therefore could not be taken for granted, particularly as firstly, he was in prison, and secondly, George Barnes decided he was going to fight for the Gorbals nomination.

Ever since Maclean's trial and sentence, Barnes had been lobbied forcefully to seek Maclean's release. And he had personal experience of the strength of feeling in Glasgow. With preparations for a general election on foot, Barnes visited the city in August to give several speeches. The local Labour branch had approached Willie Gallacher to act as Maclean's 'deputy candidate', and Gallacher told Barnes that neither he, not any other member of the government, would be allowed to speak in Glasgow until Maclean was released.[10]

At a meeting of constituents in St Mungo's Hall on 19 August, Barnes was forced to abandon the platform after a sustained volley of abuse and interjections from the floor made speaking impossible. As well as Maclean's supporters, the hostile element in the audience included members of the Federation of Discharged Sailors and Soldiers, who were angry at Barnes for his reception of a deputation of discharged men at the House of Commons, and for the part he had played in putting income tax on soldiers' pensions.[11]

When one interjector raised the issue of Maclean's imprisonment. Barnes responded that he would take back to London a report that the majority of the meeting was in favour of Maclean's release. Many in the crowd cried out 'Glasgow'. Barnes retorted that he did not accept that that voiced the opinion of the constituents or the workers of Glasgow.[12]

During the meeting a collection was taken up of behalf of Maclean. 'The hat was sent round the platform party, and when Mr Barnes allowed it to pass without contributing, his action was greeted with a demonstration of disapproval.'[13]

~

In his speech to the jury in May, Maclean had repeated the accusation of being given drugged food in prison and declared whatever was done to him, he would 'take no food inside your prisons, absolutely no food; because of the treatment that was meted out to me. If food is forced upon me, and if I am forcibly fed ... I am not responsible for the consequences but the British government.'[14]

At the start of his second stint in Peterhead, Maclean was allowed the unprecedented privilege of having his food prepared by friends outside the prison. Attempts by his wife Agnes to organise this in Peterhead during May 1918 proved fruitless however, and a request from Ramsay MacDonald to the Secretary of Scotland, Robert Munro, that Maclean be moved to a Glasgow prison where food could be supplied was refused. Maclean then went on hunger strike and from 1 July was forcibly fed twice a day by stomach tube.

When Agnes was allowed her first visit to Peterhead on 22 October she was shocked by her husband's appearance. She described her visit in a letter to the British Socialist Party.

> He (John) told me he tried to resist the forcible feeding by mouth tube, but two warders held him down, and that these men never left him thereafter, night or day, till he was forced to give in. I was shocked beyond measure by these statements (made to me in the presence of the prison doctor and two warders) and by the evidence of their truth supplied by his aged and

haggard appearance. They contradict entirely the assurances given to me by the authorities that he was in good health

One thing is clear – that he cannot much longer endure the torture of body and mind to which he is daily being subjected. The only alternatives in the conflict between the authorities and himself – either his death in prison, or his immediate release from prison.[15]

The letter was published in all the socialist papers and the calls for Maclean's release grew even louder and more insistent.

In retrospect, Maclean himself seemed quite sanguine. 'There is nothing wrong with forcible feeding if you get milk, switched eggs, margarine and Bovril. One could live for years thus fed and yet be perfectly healthy. I felt very well all the time, getting out twice a day for exercise and sitting the rest of the day reading or looking out of the hospital cell window (large and plain glass) into Peterhead harbour,' he wrote.[16]

~

On the continent, the war ground on, although the withdrawal of Russia from the conflict meant Germany was finally free to fight on one front. On 21 March 1918, bolstered by an additional 52 divisions from the east, German forces opened a general offensive on the Western Front with the object of smashing the Anglo-French armies and forcing a decision in Europe before the Americans arrived in force.

But the German Supreme Command, led by Field Marshal Paul von Hindenburg and his second-in-command and directing mind, General Erich Ludendorff, overestimated the strength of the German armies and the offensive failed. The German Army made far greater advances and gains than previously, but were still beaten decisively. By allowing the Germans to advance, the new Allied Commander-in-Chief, Marshal Foch, restored the war of movement. The Germans had started the year in high spirits, but were worn down by their own offensives, just as the French and British had been worn down before them. The Allied armies grew in confidence with each blow that was beaten off.[17]

On 8 August 1918, the Allied armies began a succession of attacks that over the following four weeks pushed the German Army back. The German line did not break (in fact it was still intact at the end of the war) but the psychological effect was shattering. It crushed the faith in victory that had carried the German Army forward. The soldiers no longer wanted to win – they just wanted the war to end.[18]

On 29 September, Ludendorff insisted there must be an immediate armistice. Partly this was because of fears the Allies would break through on the Western Front; but more so because of news from the distant and forgotten Macedonian Front, where a coalition of Allied forces (British, French, Serbian, Italian and Greek) had been locked in a stalemate for three years with Germany's ally Bulgaria. On 15 September, the French attacked, the Bulgarians collapsed, and on 29 September sought an armistice. With Austria-Hungary and Turkey also wobbling, Southern Europe was suddenly wide open to the Allies.[19]

On 1 October Hindenburg and Ludendorff disclosed their despondency about the deteriorating military situation to a meeting of the leaders of all the national political parties, thus undermining the German home front by a sudden revelation of facts long hidden from the public and its civilian leaders.[20]

The Supreme Command envisaged an armistice as a means by which Germany could withdraw from conquered territory and stand on strong defensive positions in the homeland. Germany would thereby avoid defeat and emerge from the war undiminished. To counter the fear that the Allies would impose harsh conditions on a 'militaristic' Germany, the Supreme Command proposed that Germany would become a democratic country. Problem solved.

Prince Max of Baden was appointed chancellor, the Social Democrats joined the government, press restrictions were lifted and passionate political discussion broke out. On 3 October, Hindenburg wrote to the new chancellor demanding an immediate armistice – the last order from the military to be obeyed by the government.

Prince Max decided to address the note to US President Wilson, rather than the Allied Commander-in-Chief, Foch. The note agreed to Wilson's Fourteen Points as a basis for peace negotiations; an adroit move as it put the Germans ahead of the Allies, who had never accepted them.[21]

Wilson responded on 8 October, asking if Germany accepted his further requirements for making the world safe for democracy and become a democratic country? He added that Germany must evacuate all occupied territory before he would promote an armistice on their behalf. The Allies were alarmed. It seemed they were about to be cheated of the fruits of victory at the last moment.

Prince Max replied to Wilson on 12 October, confirming Germany accepted the Fourteen Points, and asking pointedly whether the Allies did the same. On the same day, a German submarine sank the *Leinster*, a ship running between England and Ireland, with the loss of 450 passengers. Wilson was offended and on 16 October, adopted a sterner tone. Germany must stop submarine warfare at once, the armistice would be settled by military commanders, and Germany must provide more evidence she had become a democratic state. Prince Max realised he had not been quite so clever after all; the Fourteen Points really meant something.[22]

On 17 October, the German ministers and military met to debate their next move. Ludendorff had recovered from his fright of 29 September; he was now for fighting on. But the dismal first impression he and Hindenburg had provided at the start of the month had now spread throughout German political circles and the public. When the hope of achieving victory on the Western Front collapsed in October 1918, many, and perhaps even most, Germans wished only that the war would end, though it might mean their nation would have to accept unfavourable peace terms.

A third German note to Wilson, sent on 20 October, agreed to the conditions for the armistice and for the evacuation, in the express belief that Wilson would allow no affront to Germany's honour. The answering note of 23 October conceded Wilson's readiness to propose an armistice to the Allies, but added that the terms must be such as to make Germany incapable of renewing hostilities. Ludendorff saw this, militarily, as a demand for unconditional surrender and would have continued resistance. But the situation had passed beyond his control, and on 26 October he was made to resign by the Kaiser, on Prince Max's advice. On 27 October, Germany acknowledged the US note.

Wilson now began to persuade the Allies to agree to an armistice and negotiations according to the US-German correspondence. They agreed, with two reservations: they would not subscribe to the second of the Fourteen Points (on the freedom of the seas); and they wanted compensation for damage caused to civilians and their property in Allied countries. On 8 November 1918, a German delegation arrived at Rethondes, in the Oise department of northern France, where they met face to face with Foch and his party and were informed of the Allies' peace terms.[23]

~

Three days after the armistice with Germany was signed on 11 November 1918, Andrew Bonar Law, leader of the Unionist Party, told the House of Commons that Prime Minister David Lloyd George would recommend that the King issue a proclamation summoning a new parliament on 25

November. Nominations would be due on 4 December and an election would be held on 14 December.

On the same day, a special emergency conference of the Labour Party was held at the Central Hall, Westminster. The conference was convened to determine the party's reconstruction policy and whether to withdraw from the coalition government immediately or when a peace treaty was signed. While the votes were being tallied on a motion from the parliamentary party to remain in coalition (the motion was defeated), a young man from the gallery shouted, 'John Maclean is dying in prison. What are you going to do about it? Rascals.' Considerable noise ensued and it took some time for the chairman, John McGurk and party secretary Arthur Henderson to restore order.

Following the adoption of the reconstruction proposals, an emergency resolution was submitted demanding the release of Maclean, 'who is being tortured in prison' and all other political prisoners. In reply to shouts, the chairman said that conscientious objectors were included. The resolution was carried without discussion and amid cheering and the conference closed, the delegates singing 'The Red Flag' as they filed out.[24]

Later that day in the House of Commons, John Howard Whitehouse, the Liberal MP for the Scottish constituency of Mid-Lanark queried the Secretary for Scotland, Robert Munro, about the fate of political prisoners, conscientious objectors and Maclean in particular. Whitehouse said:

> There are certain special features in the case of Mr Maclean to which I wish to call the attention of the House. Mr Maclean is a man of high character. He has behind him a great record of honourable work. He has given a great part of his life in the service of teaching, and I do not think I shall be guilty of any great exaggeration if I say that some of the Clauses in the Scottish Education Bill were only made possible through his devoted work in the cause of education. He is a political offender. He received a sentence which I think is excessive, and if it was carried out it would be of a barbarous character and certainly alien to what I believe is the general feeling of the people in this country. Is there any reason why Mr Maclean and the other political prisoners should be kept in prison a moment longer in view of the end of the War? I am going to make an appeal to the Secretary of Scotland in the case of Mr Maclean and I do not base it on the ground that the case is the subject of general agitation. I am going to make my appeal for Mr Maclean on the ground that the War having come to an end a free and generous country has always in the days of peace shown great generosity to men whom it has

attacked and repressed during the passions and strain of war.

These men have held certain views with great sincerity. They have shown the highest courage when they have preferred to get up against the multitude on behalf of what they believe to be right. I say that these men are of the highest courage and are entitled to our respect. Let me remind the Right Hon. Gentleman the Secretary for Scotland that at the great Labour Conference today, which was so sensational in so many ways, a resolution was passed unanimously and without a single dissentient voice by delegates representing some millions of people demanding the release of Mr Maclean.[25]

Willie Gallacher and David Kirkwood were in London to attend the Labour Party conference and while there Gallacher recounted they attended the party headquarters to try to get the official endorsement of Maclean as the Labour candidate for Glasgow Gorbals. George Barnes had notified the Labour Party of his decision to leave the party a few days before the conference, but the leadership would not yield.

> 'Anyone but Maclean,' they said.
> We told them there would be no other. It was Maclean or nobody. The local Labour Party was solidly behind him; why should they withhold their endorsement?
> Maclean wasn't suitable.
> Why wasn't he suitable?
> Oh, he just wasn't suitable and beyond this we couldn't get.[26]

However Barnes' decision to fight the election under the brand of Coalition Labour left the National Executive Committee with no real alternative and it 'belatedly and reluctantly gave Maclean its endorsement'.[27]

The contest attracted national attention. The *Times* even sent a reporter to the area. With a finger and thumb pinching their nose, they wrote:

> The Gorbals Division of Glasgow, which will presently have to choose between Mr Barnes, Labour member of the War Cabinet, and John Maclean, Bolshevist ex-Consul, is wholly a working-class district. A few minutes' walk across the river from the centre of Glasgow's civic and business life brings you into the midst of a depressing, congested area of fish-shops, factories, filthy streets, and hideous crowded tenements. The slimy roads are full of unwashed urchins, some barefooted and many ill-clothed. There is an open space along the riverside, which seems to attract nobody, but beyond that, you may search the whole district in vain for a garden or even a tree.[28]

III
THE BELL THAT NEVER RANG

Hey Mac, did ye see him as ye cam' doon by Gorgie,
Awa ower the Lamerlaw or north o' the Tay?
Yon man is comin', and the haill toon is turnin' oot:
We're a' shair he'll win back tae Glesgie the day.
The jiners and hauders-on are marchin' frae Clydebank;
Come on noo an' hear him – he'll be ower thrang tae byde.
Turn oot, Jock and Jimmie: leave your crans and your muckle gantries.
Great John Maclean's comin' back tae the Clyde.

                  Hamish Henderson, 'The John Maclean March' (1948)

English version:
Hey, Mac, did you see him as he came down by Gorgie
Away over the Lammerlaw or north of the Tay?
That man is coming, and the whole town is turning out:
We're all sure he'll return to Glasgow today.
The carpenters and rivet-holders are marching from Clydebank,
Come on now and listen to him – he'll be too busy to stay long.
Come along, Jock and Jimmie: leave your cranes and your large gantries.
Great John Maclean is coming back to the Clyde.

37

THANKSGIVING

On the morning of Thursday 28 November 1918, the Imperial War Cabinet met at 10 Downing Street London. Outside the weather was wet and windy and the temperature struggled to reach 7 degrees Celsius. It was the American holiday of Thanksgiving. But the Americans were not the only ones feeling thankful.

The armistices signed by the Allies on 30 October (with Turkey); 3 November (Austria-Hungary); and 11 November (Germany) had brought hostilities in the Great War to a halt. The German Kaiser Wilhelm II had abdicated and fled to the Netherlands; the Austro-Hungarian Emperor Karl I had relinquished power; and while Sultan Mehmet VI still sat shakily on his throne in Constantinople, most of his Ottoman Empire was occupied by Allied forces. Great Britain and its Empire forces, in collaboration with the French, Italians and Americans, had won the war. Thoughts now turned to the peace.

The British King, George V and his two sons, the Prince of Wales and Prince Albert, having crossed the English Channel on HMS Broke the day before, awoke that morning in northern France, en route to Paris. It was a visit that would be 'a fitting prelude to the great Peace Conference which is shortly to focus the eyes of the world on Paris'.[1]

On the continent of Europe, the collapse of the monarchies in Germany and Austria-Hungary had emboldened socialists and social democrats to seek to construct new social orders, while the upper classes scrabbled to retain at least a share of power. In Germany a revolution resulted in the establishment of a republic on 9 November with the leader of the moderate Social Democratic Party, Friedrich Ebert as chancellor. German Austria, Hungary and Czechoslovakia also became republics during the month.

The Bolsheviks had been in government in Russia for just over twelve months. Russia had withdrawn from the war in March 1918, but civil war was raging as the Red Army grimly battled on a number of fronts against anti-Bolshevik groups. These groups, collectively known as the Whites, were being supported by British, French, American, Canadian, Italian, Serbian, Czechoslovak and Japanese troops. To eliminate a rallying point for the counter-revolutionary forces, the tsar and his family had been executed in July.

The previous evening in Moscow, Lenin had addressed a Moscow party workers meeting. 'The German revolution is developing the same way as ours, but at a faster pace,' he said. 'In any case, our job is to wage a desperate struggle against British and American imperialism. Just because it feels that Bolshevism has become a world force, it is trying to throttle us as fast as possible in the hope of dealing first with the Russian Bolsheviks, and then with its own.'[2]

Across the British Isles candidates were out on the stump for the first general election since 1910. Despite the efforts of Prime Minister Lloyd George, Unionist Party leader Bonar Law, and the Parliamentary Labour Party, the grand coalition that had prevailed in the parliament during the war had splintered. The Labour Party had decided to run an independent campaign, while the Liberal Party split into those following Lloyd George and those supporting the former prime minister, Herbert Asquith. Lloyd George and Bonar Law, having agreed to continue the coalition, endorsed a number of coalition candidates. Asquith disparagingly called their letter of endorsement, which was sent to candidates on 20 November, a 'coupon'; and the election later came to be called the coupon election.

~

On 28 November, Lloyd George was joined around the War Cabinet table by eleven British ministers plus a number of Imperial ministers and other advisors. Canada was represented by Prime Minister Sir Robert Borden and trade minister Sir GE Foster; Australia by Prime Minister Billy Hughes and navy minister Sir J Cook; and South Africa by defence minister Lieutenant-General Jan Smuts. Chief of the Imperial General Staff, General Sir HH Wilson; Deputy Chief of the Naval Staff, Rear-Admiral S Fremantle; and British High Commissioner to the United States, the Earl of Reading; were also in attendance.

After updates on the Western Front and the situation in the Baltic, the next two agenda items concerned international matters. The first was whether it was legally possible to prosecute the ex-kaiser for war crimes; in particular for the unprovoked invasion of Belgium in 1914 and the launch of submarine warfare against passenger ships. The second concerned a potential disagreement with the Americans about arrangements for the supply of food to Europe.

The final item was a domestic matter. The imprisonment of Scottish Marxist John Maclean, consul for the Russian Republic at Glasgow and a member of the executive committee of the British Socialist Party.

George Barnes, the Labour Party representative on the War Cabinet, had placed the matter of Maclean on the agenda. Two days before the meeting, he drafted a memorandum suggesting the Cabinet authorise Maclean's release, 'along with any others who might be in like plight for similar offences'. He wrote:

> The continued agitation about John Maclean constitutes a serious danger for the government. Mass meetings have been held in many places, including London, and resolutions continue to pour in demanding his release.
>
> I think that no good purpose is being served by keeping him in prison, and that a favourable opportunity presents itself for his release. I should not take any notice of the agitation but release him as a matter of amnesty in consequence of the signing of the armistice. I note that there is to be a meeting in the Albert Hall next Saturday [30 November], convened by [George] Lansbury and those with whom he is associated, and I have little doubt but that John Maclean will bulk very largely in the speeches. That will no doubt be followed by many similar meetings in the next two to three weeks, with, I think, bad results on the public mind.
>
> Mr Munro [secretary for Scotland] has said he would be willing to release Maclean if it was a matter of general amnesty. But the position is that in England and Wales there are no political prisoners convicted, as Maclean is, under D.O.R.A. [the Defence of the Realm Act]. There are only two in Scotland; the other being a tram conductor called Milne, who has served about forty out of a sentence of sixty days.
>
> I think it would be an act of grace therefore, to release both of them before the agitation assumes larger and more dangerous dimensions.[3]

~

Out of the public eye, Maclean had been informed that moves were afoot for his release. On 16 November he wrote from Peterhead Prison to his wife Agnes about his preferred arrangements. He asked her to send him the address of William Morrison of Aberdeen (a friend and a local member of the Socialist Labour Party) and the name and address of the secretary of the Peterhead Trades Council. He continued:

> Unless circumstances dictate otherwise, I would like to spend a night in A'deen with old friends. You might let the Morrisons know, so as to be prepared for me at any time. Bear in mind, however, that I don't know when I'll be released or from which prison, so therefore to prevent silly rumours that might hamper the actions of the Government say nothing about this letter to anyone at all. I am solely guided by the course of events & past history. If freed from here I'll wire you at once, & if I stay at A'deen, I'll wire you just before catching the train from A'deen, so that you may be prepared for me at home. My strongest desire is to get right home without anyone waiting for me at the station.
>
> Should the Government see fit to let you know some days before I get out, you might let me know before my release whether I should come right home or not. My own wish is to pass a night in A'deen with as many old friends as Morrison may be able to scrape together. But remember, absolutely no demonstration in Glasgow. That can be left till after. I have given assurances of that here already, so that my honour must be considered.[4]

~

Once the first four items had been dealt with, Lloyd George introduced the final matter on the War Cabinet agenda.[5]

'The next question concerns the release of a man named John Maclean, who is a Bolshevist. He has a great deal of ability, but has used the whole of this ability to prevent the manufacture of munitions. We had to prosecute him for inciting sedition, and he was sentenced to three years' penal servitude. We let him out after only thirteen months because the workmen said it would ease things. On his release he again started making seditious speeches, and he was prosecuted once more and is now in gaol. Now exactly the same agitation has started again. He is Mr Barnes' political opponent, and Mr Barnes thinks it will help him.'

'I do not base it on that ground,' Barnes countered. 'I want to say this, prime minister, that all the forces of opposition to the government are focusing on John Maclean, including not only the Bolshevists, but the Labour Party. They are threatening to do all sorts of things and I am afraid they will put their threats into execution one of these days. For instance, I have heard it whispered that there is on foot some scheme for cutting off the light on the Clyde and Mr George Lansbury has a meeting at the Albert Hall on Saturday and also on Sunday and I know that John Maclean will feature largely in the program there.'

'Demanding his release?' asked the Australian Prime Minister Billy Hughes.

'Yes,' Barnes replied. 'I am getting resolutions every day and I suppose every member of parliament is getting the same thing. Meetings are being held all over the country focusing all attention on the release of this man. As far as I remember the Irish objection was to the general release of all prisoners. It was thought at the time that there were a lot of these people, but there are not. There is not a single one in England or Wales; there are only two in Scotland, namely John Maclean and a man named Milne.'

'Do you propose to let out De Valera?' asked Hughes.

'No,' said Barnes, 'his case is quite separate from this case and from the case of conscientious objectors.'

'There is this difference in regard to the release of John Maclean,' said Lloyd George. 'John Maclean was imprisoned for using seditious language, but the Sinn Feiners were imprisoned for being engaged in active rebellion. There is no doubt that preparations were in hand for a German invasion of Ireland and the Sinn Feiners were to get rifles and guns. That is rather a different thing to using seditious language.'

'From the English point of view,' said the Home Secretary, Viscount Cave, 'I wish to point out that this man John Maclean is backed by the revolutionary party. I am told that the agitation in his favour in Scotland is rather dying down, but that he is being supported by the revolutionists in South Wales and in London. If you release him, I have no doubt he will be brought to London and South Wales to make speeches and it will be treated as a great triumph for them.'

'You are against his release?' Lloyd George asked.

'Yes,' Lord Cave replied.

Lloyd George then went around the table. The British Secretary of State for War, Viscount Milner; the Australian Minister of the Navy, Sir Joseph Cook; and the Leader of the House of Lords, Earl Curzon, were also against Maclean's release. Then he came to Billy Hughes.

'I favour his release,' said Hughes. 'This question is mixed up with politics. I have had to deal with this kind of thing in Australia over and over again and I think it would create a bad precedent in terms of Ireland for this very good reason, that Sinn Fein is now quite distinct from Bolshevism. If they got up at the Albert Hall and asked for the release of De Valera, they would lose 50 per cent of the seats they are trying to get. But this man, John Maclean, has a Scotch name and he is a trade unionist, and I say you will do well to let him out. His voice will be lost in the turmoil of the election if he is outside, but if he is inside, everyone will clamour for his release. If he is out, let him say what he has to say and you will be perfectly safe.'

The Canadian Prime Minister Sir Robert Borden agreed with Hughes. 'From the point of view of Canada, I am inclined to let him out,' he said. But his Canadian Minister of Trade and Commerce, Sir George Foster disagreed, saying 'I think he is a bad man and a condemned criminal and I would keep him there to the end.'

The Earl of Reading, Lieutenant-General Jan Smuts and the First Lord of the Admiralty, Sir Eric Geddes, came down in favour of release while the British Secretary of State for the Colonies, Walter Long, was for keeping him in.

The Chancellor of the Exchequer, Andrew Bonar Law said, 'From the point of view of Great Britain, I would let him out, but I would not do so until I knew what the effect would be in Ireland.'

The British Secretary of State for Foreign Affairs, Arthur Balfour, agreed. 'Like Mr Bonar Law, I consider myself on the hedge in regard to this question.'

'I am in favour of letting him out,' said the British Secretary of State for India, Edwin Montagu. 'You can let him out this week, but if you wait until after the meeting Mr Barnes talked about, it would be very difficult to do so. We shall probably have to do battle with the revolutionaries in this country sooner or later, but do not let us bring it about over the issue of a miserable creature of this kind.'

'We agree to let him out,' said Bonar Law, 'but we must first send a telegram to the Irish Government to see whether they regard it as dangerous.'

'I prefer to talk to the lord lieutenant on the telephone about it this afternoon,' said Walter Long. 'I know their views, but I do not believe myself that you can let him out and keep Sinn Feiners in.'

'Then the balance of opinion,' said Lloyd George, 'leaving out of account Mr Bonar Law and Mr Balfour, is in favour of letting him out.'

'As I understand the chancellor of the exchequer's hedge and my hedge,' said Balfour, 'it depends a great deal on the Irish aspect of the question. If the Irish government consider his release makes their position impossible, then I am for keeping him in; but if the Irish government raises no objection, then I do not mind.'

'It really is a different case,' said Lloyd George. 'The Sinn Feiners were imprisoned not merely for making seditious speeches, but for being concerned in an active conspiracy for a rebellion in Ireland against British authority. One man who was arrested had in his pocket a document showing the number of troops that could be brought together when the Germans landed. Then there was another document, if you remember – I think we had it from De Valera – referring to a rebellion in two months from that date. That I put in a totally different category to John Maclean.'

'The difficulty I see,' said Bonar Law, 'is that it will probably be said that we are letting this man out as an act of grace because he is a political prisoner. What will the Irish government say about these other political prisoners who have been put in prison, but not tried?'

'He has been imprisoned for making seditious speeches, for the good of the country, and the case it quite different,' said General Smuts.

Nodding in the direction of Walter Long, Lloyd George said, 'I suggest the colonial secretary, who I am sure will be quite impartial in spite of the fact he takes a strong line one way, should get through to the chief secretary in Dublin and say that the feeling in the Cabinet is that they would like to release John Maclean, but that the foreign secretary, the chancellor of the exchequer and I would like to release him if it did no harm in Ireland. I do not think it is worth having an agitation about a man who does far more harm in prison than outside.'

'Can I tell the Irish government prime minister, that whatever happens over this man, the Cabinet will support them in keeping the Sinn Feiners in order?' Long asked.

'I think you might say that we reached this decision on the grounds that there was a distinction between the two cases, and that John Maclean is not in the same category as the Sinn Feiners,' Lloyd George replied.

'Does this apply to the other man?' George Barnes queried.

'Yes,' said Lloyd George, 'he has practically served his time.'

~

There being no objection from the Irish government, the Secretary for Scotland, Robert Munro authorised the discharge of Charles Milne from custody the following day (Friday 29 November) and Maclean was released from penal servitude on ticket-of-leave on Monday 2 December. The ticket-of-leave was rescinded by means of a King's pardon later in the month.

Maclean's case was certainly a live one on the hustings. On the evening before the War Cabinet meeting, the Coalition Liberal candidate Winston Churchill addressed a meeting at the Kinnard Hall in his Dundee electorate. Lively scenes characterised the gathering, according to the *Glasgow Herald*.

> His [Churchill's] handling of the Bolshevik elements in the hall won the admiration of the vast majority of the audience. 'If this country had been full of John Macleans we would have been conquered by the Huns' – that is but one example of many sharp words addressed to the extremists by Mr. Churchill, who reminded them that the strong forces in this country which had enabled us to overcome so many difficulties were not afraid of John Maclean and all his backers.[6]

Meanwhile in Edinburgh on the evening of 28 November, the Lord Advocate, James Avon Clyde – Coalition Unionist candidate for the seat of Edinburgh North – addressed a meeting of electors in the Abbeyhill Parish Church Hall. Clyde, the prosecutor at Maclean's May 1918 trial, was asked if he believed that the introduction of British and Allied troops into Russia was not in the direct interests of British and Allied capitalists. Clyde's response, the *Glasgow Herald* reported, was that the suggestion was a gross slander.

> The idea that we had conducted either in Russia or anywhere else in this war military operations in defence of the interests of a class was a slander. There was not a word of truth in it. Asked if he was in favour of the immediate release of John Maclean, Mr Clyde answered, 'Certainly not. I should like to know why a man who did his best to incite his fellow citizens to burn houses, to abolish their institutions and to establish the rule of force in this country is entitled to special consideration? He will get none from me.' (Loud applause.)
>
> The Elector – Why were the same steps not taken with Sir Edward Carson?
>
> Mr Clyde – Because Sir Edward Carson's was not a like case. His action was purely political; the other was a direct attempt to upset the social order.[7]

The Carson case was indeed different from Maclean's, but not in the way Clyde stated.

In 1892, the prominent Dublin barrister Edward Carson was elected as an Irish Unionist member of parliament for the University of Dublin. He became leader of the Irish Unionist Alliance in 1910 and led its fight against Home Rule – the establishment of a devolved Irish Parliament in Dublin. In 1913, he formed the loyalist paramilitary organisation the Ulster Volunteer Force. When Irish Home Rule seemed inevitable in 1914, he authorised the purchase and smuggling into Ulster of 20,000 rifles and 2,000,000 rounds of ammunition for the UVF. Only the outbreak of the Great War prevented an Irish civil war in 1914.

To smuggle guns and ammunition in preparation for an armed rebellion against an Act of Parliament was obviously considered less serious by the first law officer of Scotland than speaking out about how the existing order oppressed those at the bottom of society.

38

THE KHAKI ELECTION

John Maclean was released from Peterhead Prison on Monday 2 December 1918. That evening he addressed a meeting of supporters at the Meatmarket Street Hall in Aberdeen. The following day, accompanied by his wife Agnes, he travelled by train to Glasgow. Despite Maclean's desire to 'get right home', word had quickly spread of his release and a large crowd had gathered at the station, many of whom had taken the afternoon off work.

The temperature was mild for the time of year, around 11C, with a blanket of cloud and some light showers. The train's arrival was delayed and in his memoirs Harry McShane, then a shop steward and member of the British Socialist Party, recalled Jimmy Johnstone, 'the old rigger' addressing the crowd while it waited.

'He had great style; he wasn't a deep thinker but he spoke real working-class language. Near the station were some tenement houses and Jimmy pointed to these "birdcages" and started talking to the crowd about what they should fight for. Suddenly he grabbed a child out of its mother's arms and shouted: "Will you fight for this?" It had a great emotional effect on the whole crowd.'[1]

It was already dark when the train arrived at Buchanan Street station at 4.36 pm. The *Glasgow Herald* reported Maclean looked 'fairly well enough although slightly worn in appearance'. McShane said he was 'so weak and worn out he couldn't speak'.

Among those on the crowded station platform were Willie Gallacher and his wife (Gallacher was chairman of the Clyde Workers' Committee and had been conducting the Labour Party campaign in Gorbals on Maclean's behalf); James Maxton, the Labour candidate for Bridgeton; and Neil Maclean, the party's candidate in Govan. Also present was Dora Montefiore, an English member of the British Socialist Party executive.

Montefiore had been a delegate to the annual British Socialist Party conference in March 1918 where she had been impressed with Maclean and had promised to speak for his parliamentary candidature at Gorbals.

On 26 November, Agnes Maclean wrote to Montefiore to tell her that Maclean's agent had booked her for two meetings on 4 and 5 December. She invited Montefiore to stay with them at their home in Newlands. On Sunday 1 December, Montefiore left her Sussex home for Glasgow and in the days that followed was a close witness to the events surrounding Maclean's release and its immediate aftermath. She wrote about them both in an account for the *Call* and later in her autobiography.

> ... a huge demonstration was arranged to meet John Maclean at Buchanan Street Station on the occasion of his return from prison. I was with my two comrades, (William) Gallacher and his wife, and a carriage was waiting inside the station yard for Maclean and his wife, when they left the train. Our little group on the platform was invited into the carriage with the Macleans, but before we reached the station gates, the horses had been taken out, and the crowd, which had completely blocked the traffic, drew the carriage through the main streets of Glasgow, while Maclean stood on the seat waving a huge red banner.[2]

The Herald estimated the crowd as 'several thousand' and Gallacher later wrote, 'By the time we got half way down Buchanan Street, the springs of the carriage had collapsed and the bottom was resting on the axles.'[3]

The procession inched its way south under the streetlights of Glasgow from Buchanan Street, down Renfield Street towards the Clyde. When it halted for a minute in Jamaica Street, Montefiore wrote:

> Maclean called for three hearty cheers for the German Social Revolution; and on these being given by thousands of voices, then called for three more cheers for the British Social Revolution, when the shouts that rent the air made a volume of sound that the capitalists of Clydeside will often remember in the near future, when they are troubled with bad dreams.
>
> For the best part of an hour, just when the trams were taking to their homes the daily loads of shoppers, those trams that were leaving the city had to travel, till the river was crossed, at the rate of John Maclean's triumphal red-flag procession, for his supporters, in disciplined orderly ranks, spread across one half of the street; while from the trams going towards the city peeped timidly or with scared faces those who for the first time had seen flaunted on the four winds the emblem which now waves over the public buildings of Petrograd, Moscow and Berlin.[4]

Eventually, the carriage progressed over the Glasgow Bridge to Carlton Place, where after short speeches, Gallacher 'got Maclean away and we drove out to his home in a taxi'.[5]

Caledun, the Scottish reporter for the *Call* wrote, 'It truly was a triumphant entry. Maclean was granted the freedom of the city in a far more real sense than was Lloyd George when behind a guard of bayonets, he received the burgess ticket from the Lord Provost [in June 1917].[6]

~

In its account of Maclean's return, the *Glasgow Herald* reported: 'In a brief conversation with press representatives Maclean said the revolutionary spirit was stronger than ever in him, and the fight, which was that of the workers, would go on. He was in ignorance of what had been going on in the political field, and so he was not able to make any long statement and he was hardly physically fit to conduct an election campaign.'[7]

Maclean also made some comments about George Barnes that did not come out quite as he had intended. On 5 December the Herald published a clarification:

> Mr Maclean sought to correct a statement which appeared yesterday with regard to his release. In the excitement attendant upon his release in the city on Tuesday, he says he made it appear as if he had spoken to Mr Barnes and told him he would be defeated and would run serious personal risks if he (Mr Maclean) were kept in prison. As a matter of fact he had never spoken to Mr Barnes. The remarks he made were addressed to the prison doctors and other officials, to whom he had said he would not be responsible for what might happen if he were kept in prison.[8]

After the emotional high of Glasgow's heartfelt welcome, the following days were a marked contrast. In the public arena, the Herald reported, ' ... he (Maclean) is resting at home but his cause is being pleaded by a number of prominent socialists who have arranged a full program of daily meetings – indoors, at street corners and at works gates, where the electors are being urged to "strike a blow at the parasites and profiteers". Greater production, desired by Mr Lloyd George, means, according to the views put before the electorate by Mr Maclean's lieutenants, a glut in the market sooner or later, resulting in "an army of men and women walking the streets unemployed".'[9]

But on the domestic front, things were far from comfortable. Montefiore wrote:

> When I stayed in his home after his second term of imprisonment, and witnessed the agony of his wife and the sorrow of his relatives, I realised more than ever I had done before the refined and machine-made cruelty of a prison system which takes the souls of men and of women (as the Inquisition used to take their bodies) and leaves them wrung-out rags of humanity.
>
> This was quite another John Maclean from the man, the ex-school teacher, whom the authorities some months before had cast into gaol, because, as he said at his trial, 'He had squared his actions with his conscience.' His thoughts were now disconnected, his speech was irresponsible, his mind, from solitary confinement, was absolutely self-centred. In a word, prison life had done its work on a delicately-balanced psychology, and our unfortunate comrade was now a mental wreck.[10]

It is obvious that John Maclean was in a bad way both physically and mentally immediately after his release from prison. But under the care of his wife, who was a trained nurse after all, he had recovered sufficiently to pen an article for the *Call* that was published on 12 December. And on the eve of the election, Friday 13 December, he was well enough to give extended campaign speeches to huge crowds at St Mungo's Hall in Ballater Street, Gorbals. He wrote in the *Call*:

> Greetings to all comrades and the mass of the working-class who forced the Cabinet to release me! George Barnes's claim that he got my release is a lie as base as his betrayal of our class. He and the Cabinet members were really afraid of their very lives, and rightly so; for the workers have now reached a stage in the evolution of our class when they will punish their enemies in the great class war.
>
> When leaving Peterhead, I told the governor, the head-warder, and others that if the workers made a bid for freedom along the lines of Russia and Germany, I would be in the thick of the fight, although aware that I would be the first to be captured by the real enemy, the propertied plunderers of Britain. Comrades can take it, then, that I am not 'tamed', although the prison people did their utmost to accomplish the usual. The doctors this time made the most thorough test of my mind and character to find out such weaknesses as they might play upon in future to corrupt me into the betrayal of my class. It was beautifully done, but I can assure comrades that I beat the doctors at their game. I let them know that I was obsessed about

nothing, not even life itself, and that they could burn all they thought they knew about me and have in tabulated and indexed form, as it would be of no use to them in my future fight against capitalism.

I have already received the greatest honour of my life in being appointed Scottish representative of the first Socialist Republic in the world, the Russian one; and the second, in being selected as the standard-bearer of my class by the Cabinet of the British capitalist class.

From a bread-and-butter point of view, I don't need to sell out. I can go to Russia and be secure till I peg out. But I am not going to Russia, except on working-class business or for a holiday. The place for every British Socialist is here at home until capitalism is overthrown. I stay at home, then, with the Clyde Valley as my centre.

My only appearance in Gorbals will be on Friday, December 13th, the eve of the poll, and I speak then only because my 'bosses' have dictated this course to me. Personally, I would have preferred to stay in Aberdeen enjoying my liberty amongst the 'boys of the old brigade', the Coopers, the Pithies, the Morrisons, the Gordons, the Wheelers, etc. Why? Because I was selected whilst in prison; my address was written and circulated by the workers whilst I lay in prison; everything was, and is being, done under the guidance of Willie Gallacher (my deputy), the witty, cheery, and popular chairman of the Clyde Workers' Committee. The fight is one against treachery; and the significance of the fight is that the workers are not lying down in disgusted despair but have roused themselves to the intensest activity to retain the honour of our class by crushing the traitor. The fight is not mine, therefore: hence my attitude.

In the international aspect the return of Barnes will be fraught with momentary misfortune for our class. The Government, knowing this, are doing everything to defeat me. If I am returned Britain will have to withdraw her forces from Russia, Germany, and Belgium, or she will feel the consequences at home. I trust that Lloyd George will cherish no illusions about that. If Barnes wins and the British troops try to crush our Russian and German comrades, Barnes had never better appear in Glasgow again and his committeemen had better leave Scotland for good. Let no one have any illusions.

The election in itself counts for nothing. Our BSP candidates and the readers of the *Call* know that – in spite of what I have just written. The real British crisis is coming, and coming quickly, too. Let us, then, keep our committees going, let us rush forward with meetings, sales of literature, discussions and organisation in the workshop, economic classes and conferences to promote Labour Colleges after we have polled, conscious that economic circumstances are going to arise in 1919 that will thrust the revolutionary section into power as on the Continent.

I place myself absolutely at the disposal of the movement, and trust that my services will be taken advantage of for educational conferences on Saturdays and lectures on other nights of the week. Keep it going, comrades, keep it going; our victory is fast approaching.[11]

'The election in itself counts for nothing,' Maclean wrote. This may have disappointed Gallacher and his colleagues, who had put so much time and effort into getting Maclean selected as an official Labour Party candidate and mounting a vigorous campaign in the Gorbals. So, while the *Glasgow Herald* – a paper certainly not noted for any sympathy towards socialists – reported Maclean's speech on the eve of the poll in straight terms, one can detect a mix of admiration and frustration in Gallacher and Tom Bell's later accounts. The election messages they had developed – messages that had been thundered from the platform by the array of guest speakers in the indoor, outdoor and work gates meetings during the campaign – were not the focus of Maclean's address. He was in the same church, but he was not singing from the same hymn sheet.

In the future this insistence on ignoring the party line and being his own man would be at the heart of Maclean's exclusion from the process of forming a Communist Party of Great Britain and his personal falling out with Gallacher. And it suited Gallacher and Bell to use this one very public event to portray Maclean as having suffered permanent mental damage as a result of his prison ordeal. The *Glasgow Herald*'s report on 14 December 1918, ran:

> He was welcomed in the dual character of candidate and 'political martyr' and the personal note predominated in his speech. The Chairman counselled the audience to maintain silence while Maclean spoke as he has suffered from the effects of a nervous breakdown. He, however, expressed himself with vigour. His address was a gust of discursive oratory, slightly autobiographical, merely adumbrating his political principles, and concentrating on his personal achievements. He had been arrested as the standard-bearer of the workers; he had been released through fear; if he had been held in imprisonment the life of George Barnes would not have been safe. He was occasionally vituperative, delivering fluent denunciation of legal and medical 'scoundrels'. His renewed imprisonment would be the

signal of revolution. The egotistical note was sounded throughout; a sense of humour was less apparent.[12]

Gallacher's account was decidedly more negative:

When I reached St Mungo's Hall, John was still going strong, with no sign of finishing. I whispered to the Chairman: 'Have you reminded him that he's due at the other meeting?' He shook his head; he was obviously too nervous to intervene. I waited about ten minutes, and then passed John a note saying they were waiting for him at the (other meeting). He didn't look at it, just crumpled it up and put it in his pocket. After another wait, I approached him and whispered 'John! Remember your other meeting!' He turned on me, shouting: 'For Christ's sake, Gallacher, leave me alone. I'm feeling fine and nobody needs to tell me what to do!'

And on he went. His energy, his flow of language, his grasp of politics and his wide range of ideas relating to the working class were unsurpassed by any other leader in the movement. It was a great speech, full of very good socialist electioneering, but marred by the sickness that had become firmly embedded in his mind: he kept on introducing the subject of how they had doped his food in prison and how he had got the better of them despite their dirty work. To me it was very painful, though I am sure many in the hall accepted the 'doping' story as true.[13]

And Bell echoed Gallacher's appraisal:

The fact that he would speak at the final rally was fully advertised, with amazing results. The whole suite of the St Mungo's Halls, the scenes for so many meetings for the release of Maclean, was fully booked, and on the final night, the Reception, the Assembly and the Grand Halls were crowded to overcapacity. Thousands failed to gain admission and it taxed all the available speakers to exhaustion to maintain a service indoors and outdoors. Never within living memory had there been witnessed such high enthusiasm.

Contrary to the wishes of his friends, who urged that he appear for a short time at the Grand Hall only, John insisted on speaking at all three meetings. The scenes of wild enthusiasm when he appeared passes description. His very presence was in itself a great victory for the campaign and a personal tribute to himself. And had he been in good health and able to hold the enthusiasm of these three meetings and the crowds outside, the story of his last days would have been very different.

As it was, he was unable to concentrate upon the problems of immediate importance in the election. Prison with hunger striking and forcible feeding had obviously had graver effects than was generally known. Persecution obsessions and questions irrelevant to the Election made up the subject matter of his speeches. The efforts of his friends to restrain him had not the slightest effect, except to provoke his feelings and to make matters worse. The wild enthusiasm with which he was received at teach of his meetings evaporated in murmurs of sympathetic concern, many people leaving the meeting while he was speaking, obviously disturbed by the state of their friend and comrade's mind.[14]

In his speech he said he was 'deliberately of the opinion that the ballot boxes of the Gorbals will be tampered with in the interests of Mr Barnes, and he suggested that at the close of the poll representatives of the workers should be chosen to accompany the ballot boxes to their destination, and that relays of men should attend throughout the fortnight before enumeration in order to keep watch and ward. The audience seemed impressed by the candidate's deliberate manner and on his suggestion pledged themselves to see to the payment of the watchers.'[15]

After three trials in which he knew a long line of police had perjured themselves to procure his conviction, added to the prison experience of hunger striking and forcible feeding, it was obvious any faith Maclean may once have held about fair play in the system had long gone.

~

The election was held on Saturday 14 December 1918. The extension of adult suffrage meant the electorate had almost tripled in size (from about seven to twenty-one million) since the previous general election in 1910. It included most women aged over thirty and all men over twenty-one. A special provision also lowered the voting age to nineteen for those who had served in the war. For most of the electorate, it was their first ever vote. Many British troops were still overseas and a failure to complete the registers for them meant that only 25 per cent were able to vote. Oh, and an influenza epidemic was raging. Given these factors and the rushed nature of the election, called mere days after the signing of the armistice with Germany, perhaps it was no surprise that the proportion of eligible people who voted – 57.2 per cent – was the lowest since 1868.

The Labour Party endorsed 361 candidates. The majority (163) were sponsored by trade unions, while constituency branches nominated 144.

The largest affiliated party, the Independent Labour Party, contributed a further 50. Eleven British Socialist Party members (including John Maclean), were chosen by local Labour constituencies and three more, including Maclean's long-time friend and collaborator James Macdougall in Glasgow Tradeston, ran under the British Socialist Party ticket.

It took two weeks for the votes to be tallied and the results were declared on 28 December. In Gorbals, Maclean polled 7436 votes against 14,247 for George Barnes. While Labour polled over two million votes nationally – a 14.5 per cent increase on 1910 – it won only one of the fifteen Glasgow seats – Neil MacLean of the Independent Labour Party in Govan – and a total of seven in Scotland. Across the country Labour won just 61 of the 706 seats. The Coalition candidates won 531 and even though the Unionists under Bonar Law won most of these, Lloyd George continued as prime minister.

At the Easter 1919 annual conference of the Independent Labour Party, chairman Philip Snowden was scathing in his assessment. 'The circumstances of the General Election were worthy of Mr Lloyd George and his associates,' he said. 'Never before in the political history of the country had a politician sunk to such depths of infamy to keep in office. The basest passions of people were appealed to, the grossest misrepresentations indulged in and impossible promises were lavishly made.'[16]

The new parliament was 'less representative than any parliament that ever sat in the political annals of this country,' according to the ILP's Ramsay MacDonald, who like Snowden lost his seat.[17]

In *The economic consequences of the peace*, his best-selling account of the Paris Peace Conference and the Treaty of Versailles, John Maynard Keynes echoed the criticism.

> The progress of the General Election of 1918 affords a sad, dramatic history of the essential weakness of one who draws his chief inspiration not from his own true impulses, but from the grosser effluxions of the atmosphere which momentarily surrounds him. The Prime Minister's natural instincts, as they so often are, were right and reasonable. He himself did not believe in hanging the Kaiser or in the wisdom or the possibility of a great indemnity. On the 22nd of November he and Mr. Bonar Law issued their Election Manifesto. It contains no allusion of any kind either to the one or to the other, but, speaking, rather, of Disarmament and the League of Nations, concludes that 'our first task must be to conclude a just and lasting peace, and so to

establish the foundations of a new Europe that occasion for further wars may be for ever averted.'[18]

These fine sentiments fell a little flat on the campaign trail, and government candidates began to feel themselves handicapped by the lack of an effective cry. Up stepped Coalition Labour candidate, George Barnes. On 30 November, he shouted from a platform, 'I am for hanging the Kaiser!'

On 10 December, the First Lord of the Admiralty, Sir Eric Geddes helpfully added some ginger on the issue of German indemnities. 'We will get out of her all you can squeeze out of a lemon and a bit more,' he shouted. 'I will squeeze her until you can hear the pips squeak.'

The parliamentary correspondent for the *Times* noted the reaction. 'It is the candidate who deals with the issues of today, who adopts Mr. Barnes's phrase about "hanging the Kaiser" and plumps for the payment of the cost of the war by Germany, who rouses his audience and strikes the notes to which they are most responsive.'[19]

Lloyd George never said that he himself believed that Germany could pay the whole cost of the war. But the program became in the mouths of his supporters on the hustings a great deal more than concrete. The ordinary voter was led to believe that Germany could certainly be made to pay the greater part, if not the whole cost of the war. No candidate could safely denounce this program, and none did so. Keynes wrote:

> The old Liberal Party, having nothing comparable to offer to the electorate, was swept out of existence. A new House of Commons came into being, a majority of whose members had pledged themselves to a great deal more than the Prime Minister's guarded promises. Shortly after their arrival at Westminster I asked a Conservative friend, who had known previous Houses, what he thought of them. 'They are a lot of hard-faced men,' he said, 'who look as if they had done very well out of the war.'[20]

39
BACK TO THE MINERS

John Maclean was on holiday 'doon the watter' in Rothesay with wife Agnes and Willie and Jean Gallacher when the general election results came out. A Glasgow friend and comrade Tom Anderson had given the two couples the use of his tenement flat at 41 Victoria Street (overlooking the Esplanade Gardens) to rest and recuperate from the exertions of the campaign and Maclean's imprisonment. Gallacher and Maclean hired clubs and played golf in the snow with red balls but Maclean could not relax. 'He was always on the move,' Gallacher later wrote. 'We would set out for a walk, but after a minute or two we would leave the two girls walking slowly while we covered several miles and then rejoined them at our lodgings.'[1]

There was much to discuss. The Bolshevik government in Russia was engaged in a bloody civil war that threatened to overturn the Russian revolution. The counter-revolutionary forces, the Whites, were being supported by British and other foreign troops. In Germany, the Marxist Spartacus League, headed by Karl Liebknecht and Rosa Luxemburg was part of the provisional government and was agitating for a social revolution. Maclean saw this as the class war playing out on an international basis and for him, the question was—how could Britain play its part in the world conflict?

Some elements of the British socialist movement were advocating a general strike to enforce a withdrawal of British troops from Russia. Maclean was more circumspect. 'Were the mass of the workers in Britain Revolutionary Socialists they would at once see that their material well-being depended on the peaceful development of Bolshevism in Russia,' he wrote later that month. 'But the workers are not generally of our way of thinking ... Some of us on the Clyde therefore think that we must adopt another line, and that is to save Russia by developing a revolution in Britain no later than this year.'[2]

The next question for Maclean was, how to get the mass on the move?

He foresaw the munitions industry being scaled back, the servicemen being demobbed, the streamlining in factories meaning less jobs. 'We can get the support of the unemployed if we can suggest a means whereby they can get a living,' he wrote. 'The only possible way is a drastic reduction in working hours per week. This reduction will appeal to the employed if they are assured of at least a pre-war standard of living. Here we have the economic issue that can unify the workers in the war against capitalism.'[3]

Harry McShane's experience of working hours as an engineer on Clydeside during the war was typical.

> Up to 1914, our week was 54 hours. All working people, including boys and girls, started at 6 am and finished at 5.30 pm and worked till noon on Saturdays. During the war it had been extended to a 12-hour day and Saturday and Sunday working. The six o'clock start was miserable: you had to get up at five and you couldn't go out or doing anything at night because you would tire yourself for the morning. When I worked at Dalmuir during the war I had to get out of the house before five to get the ferry to Anderston Cross and the train to Dalmuir; there were no lights on the train, nobody spoke, and the only sign of life was the spark from somebody's pipe. To get the hours reduced would be victory for us all as well as helping unemployment.[4]

In November 1918, shortly after the armistice, negotiations between the employer groups in Britain and the official unions in the engineering and shipbuilding trades resulted in an agreement to reduce working hours to 47 a week, with no loss of pay. The agreement was due to come into effect on 1 January, but its coverage remained loose, with workers paid by the hour set to see a significant reduction in wages.

Both Gallacher and Maclean supported the more radical program developed by the South Wales Miners' Reform Movement. Titled the *Miners' Charter* and first published in the *Merthyr Pioneer* in August 1918, the program was designed to seize the initiative in the face of imminent demobilisation, and prevent an employers' counter-offensive by ensuring ex-soldiers were reabsorbed into the industry on the miners' terms.

The centrepiece was a massive reduction of hours to a five-day, thirty-hour week. The charter envisaged no loss of earnings to compensate; rather it staked a claim for the abolition of piece rates, to be replaced by a pound a day wage. These demands, bold as they were, were only the means to an end. For members of the miners' reform movement the hope was that the fight for these reforms would culminate in the miners taking over the collieries and running them for themselves.[5]

Within days of the armistice, rank and file movements in several important coalfields had been putting pressure on their district and national leaders to adopt the demands encapsulated in the charter.

On 4 January the Scottish divisional conference of the Independent Labour Party joined the push, adopting a resolution calling for the government to prepare a Bill, to be introduced on demobilisation, making the maximum working week five days of six hours each, thirty hours in all, without lowering the standard of living. Among a raft of other resolutions was one protesting at 'the harsh and vindictive sentence passed on John Maclean and other political prisoners'.[6]

~

Maclean resolved to put his talents as a public speaker at the disposal of the miners' reform movement. Gallacher had already rejoined the revitalised Clyde Workers' Committee that had stood up for workers' rights during the war. Links between the unofficial engineers' and miners' movements had been forged on the Clyde during the 1918 demonstrations to free Maclean from prison and in his subsequent general election campaign.

There was a key difference between the two unofficial movements. The engineering shop stewards who formed the Clyde Workers' Committee and other stewards' organisations during the war set themselves up as an alternative to the official unions. They felt the officials of the Amalgamated Society of Engineers and the more than two hundred other unions in the engineering industry had abandoned the membership by surrendering workers' rights in the name of war patriotism.[7] As members of the workforce, the shop stewards were much better placed to gauge and influence the mood on the factory floor and involve broad numbers of the rank and file in direct action initiatives across multiple workshops.

The miners reform movements, as the name suggests, were more about exerting pressure on the nineteen district federations that made up the Miners' Federation of Great Britain. And at this point, after the disappointing election result for the Labour Party, the national leadership of the union was seriously considering adopting the major elements of the Miners Charter. The ramifications would be earth-shattering.

In 1919 roughly one in eight of the population lived in or came from a mining community. The MFGB was organising about a million men and was the biggest and most powerful union in the country.

Coal was the energy source that powered British industry. When burned, it created the steam that powered the steam engines in the factories. It powered the furnaces in the iron and steel works. It was the fuel for the steam locomotives of the railways, the primary mode of land transport. It powered the electricity stations and gasworks. It powered the steam engines of merchant ships and the ships of the Royal Navy. It was the main source of heating for homes and public buildings.

Maclean thought that a national miners' strike for shorter hours 'would have the potential to pull in millions of workers from other industries and could provide the basis for control of production through workshop committees'.[8] He estimated the most opportune timing for this would be March.

The Maclean family was subsisting on money raised during John's imprisonments to support Agnes and their daughters while John awaited a response to his application for reinstatement as a school teacher. Gallacher had resigned from his job to conduct Maclean's election campaign, so when the two men returned to Glasgow there was no impediment to getting straight back into the fray.

On Sunday 5 January, Gallacher chaired a meeting of the Clyde Workers' Committee that decided to organise action for a thirty-hour working week in the terms of the Miners' Charter. Maclean was back in action on the same day with a resumption of his economics lectures at St Mungo's Halls in the Gorbals. He spent the following week in the Lothian mining districts surrounding Edinburgh. The outcome was the establishment of a miners' reform committee to join the ones already active in the Fife and Lanarkshire coalfields.

After Gallacher returned to the Clyde, things there started moving quickly. Very quickly indeed.

40
THE 40-HOUR STRIKE

The transition from a war economy, where many major industrial sectors had been government controlled, to a peacetime one promised to be turbulent, particularly in industrial centres such as Clydeside. The resources that had been devoted to making munitions needed to be scaled back or retooled to resume their pre-war output. But things could not easily go back to the way they were. Deprived of British imports during the war years, the markets that had sustained the pre-war British industrial base had either started to develop their own industries or had turned to other suppliers, particularly the Americans. And while the industrialists – the shipyard, factory and mine owners – wanted a quick return to the pre-war status quo, the workers had a very different view.

Believing the industrialists had manipulated the system to generate massive war profits, the workers were determined to use their industrial muscle to try to maintain the full employment and relatively high wages the war had brought. They had earned those high wages by the long weekly hours they had worked during the war and felt there was certainly scope for a reduction in hours.

As far back as March 1918, the Scottish Trades Union Congress had passed a resolution calling for a 40-hour working week. This had been confirmed at three subsequent meetings.

On Clydeside, the influence of the unofficial movement penetrated most of the important trade unions. The district committees were in most cases led by militants out of harmony with the views of the official unions whose headquarters were generally outside of Scotland – some in Manchester, but most in London.

The Glasgow Trades and Labour Council had a strong nucleus of militant workers as delegates from the trade union branches. The hours question was repeatedly brought before the council despite the efforts of union officials to smother it. Conscious of the growing agitation of the Clyde District Shop Stewards Committee and the growing desire among workers for action, the council leaders, in conjunction with the Scottish Trades Union Congress, decided on a policy of joint action rather than let the movement develop outside its control.

On the afternoon of Saturday 18 January, a delegation from the council and the STUC met with the Clyde Shop Stewards Committee at the Industrial Workers of the World rooms at Anderston Cross. Also attending were delegates from all the works in the Clyde area, from Edinburgh and Leith, Rosyth, the Forth Area District Committee of the Amalgamated Society of Engineers, the Ayrshire district and Dumfries. Delegates from Sheffield and other areas of Yorkshire were also present. The meeting lasted three hours and discussed mainly the question of whether the demand should be for a 30 or 40-hour working week. While no decision was taken, a joint committee was appointed to take what action they might consider necessary.

That joint committee, chaired by Emmanuel Shinwell, secretary of the Glasgow Branch of the British Seafarers Union and chair of the Trades and Labour Council, met the same evening at the ASE rooms at Carlton Place. At the conclusion of the meeting a manifesto was issued in the form of a 'Call to Arms to the Workers'.

> The Joint Committee, consisting of representatives of the Scottish Trades Union Congress Parliamentary Committee, the Glasgow Trades and Labour Council, the District Committees of the Engineering, Shipbuilding and allied trade unions, the Clyde District Shop Stewards Committee, the Scottish Union of Dock Labourers, the Scottish Horse and Motor Men's Union, Railwaymen, the Municipal Employees Association and the Building Trades and Electricians met at the Engineers Hall, Carlton Place and considered the votes recorded by the men in the works in the Clyde area.
>
> After careful consideration it was decided to issue a manifesto to the workers throughout the country calling on them to declare a general strike on Monday 27 January for a 40 hours working week, with no corresponding reduction in wages. The 40 hours working week is to be tried as an experiment with the object of absorbing those unemployed consequent on demobilisation, and further action is contemplated in the event of the reduction of hours being insufficient for this purpose.
>
> If a 40 hours week fails to achieve the desired result a more drastic reduction in hours will be demanded. A general strike has been declared to

take place on Monday 27 January and all workers are expected to respond. By order of the joint committee representing all workers.[1]

In support of the decision, the strike committee issued the following statement:

> Thousands of men are being demobilised from the Army and Navy every day. Over a hundred thousand workers in Scotland have been dismissed from civil employment. They are now looking for jobs. There are no jobs for them.
>
> There is only one remedy. Reduce the number of hours. The time for action is now. Delay means failure. No more than 40 hours per week to be worked. No reduction in wages. No overtime to be worked. No work on Monday, 27 January. No resumption of work until demands have been conceded.[2]

It was made quite clear that the choice was acceptance of the demands or strike action. There was no scope for negotiation.

~

After waiting for the general election to be concluded, the Miners' Federation of Great Britain met during the first week of January to finalise its demands. The government had taken control of the mines in February 1917, so the demands were presented to the coal controller. While falling short of what the rank and file in South Wales had proposed the previous year, the official version of the Miners' Charter was still a dramatic and ambitious set of demands. They including a six-hour working day, 30 per cent wage increase, full rates of pay for unemployed soldier-miners and nationalisation of the mines with joint worker control. A special national conference in Southport, Lancashire from 14 to 16 January ratified the demands, although there was a heated debate about whether the wage demand should have been for an extra 50 per cent.

Seeking to strengthen their hand, the miners reached out to their partners in the Triple Alliance, the National Union of Railwaymen and the National Transport Workers' Federation (which covered dockers, seamen, tramway and road transport workers). The alliance had been formed in early 1914 following a long running period of industrial unrest, and was gearing up for a general strike in support of its members demands when war broke out. As many of the industries that employed their members were temporarily nationalised during the war, the alliance undertook no coordinated action during the conflict. But with the outbreak of peace, it made sense to revive the group.

At the conclusion of the Southport conference, the following resolution was unanimously adopted:

> That the Miners' Federation of Great Britain Executive be asked to take the necessary steps to call the Triple Alliance together to immediately formulate a policy to frustrate the efforts being made to hand back to private ownership the control of the mines, railways and shipping, believing that further private ownership in these key industries would be reactionary and against the best interests of the workers.[3]

~

John Maclean spent the whole week beginning 13 January in Lancashire, whipping up support for the miners' reform movement. He spoke to meetings of miners in Leigh on Wednesday the 15th and Warrington on Thursday the 16th. He was in Liverpool on Friday and Saturday, attending a British Socialist Party rally and an education conference, before returning to Glasgow for his Sunday class.

Maclean was thus not in Glasgow on 18 January when the call was made for a general strike to commence on Monday the 27th. He felt the call was premature and thought the Clydesiders should have waited for the government's response to the demands of the miners' federation. Confident the government would never agree to these, Maclean believed a general strike headed by the full power of the miners would precipitate the socialist revolution he so fervently desired.

Despite his misgivings, Maclean addressed meetings of Lanarkshire miners the following week and encouraged them to support the Clydeside action. He spoke at a packed Hamilton Town Hall on Monday 18th, then at Bellshill and Shotts, and wound up with a large public meeting on Friday 24 January at the Motherwell Town Hall, organised by the Lanarkshire Miners' Reform Committee (LMRC). He spoke as the official spokesman of the unofficial miners' movement, 'an appointment he was as proud of as he was of the position of Consul for Glasgow, which he received from the Bolshevik Government of Russia'.

In what the *Motherwell Times* called an 'impassioned address', Maclean explained the demands of the reform committee, saying it was not antagonistic to the official miners' union or its officials, but if any of them did stand in the way of the policy which they were fighting for, then they would have to go. 'A mere handful of men could not be permitted to hold back the aspirations of a million,' he said.

Dealing with the situation on the Clyde, Maclean said the Clyde men were coming out on strike on Monday morning.

> It would be said that the action of the men was unconstitutional, that it was in defiance of treaties entered into with the employers and the Government. He had to say this, that he would break through every regulation and every constitution on God's earth when it was a case of saving human life. Human life was at stake in the Clyde dispute, unless they had a 40 hours week, there were going to be large numbers of men without a job, and the men without a job had little claim on life. Human life must be the first consideration, and from that point of view the strike was justified. He looked to the miners of Lanarkshire to come out with the men of the Clyde and show the absolute solidarity of the working class.[4]

In areas where the Lanarkshire Miners' Reform Committee was strongest, miners struck in support of the strike that began on the Clyde on Monday 27 January. The following day, a one-day strike called by the LMRC received more widespread support. This was then extended into an indefinite strike for the reform committee's demands by means of mass meetings and pickets over the following days.[5]

~

Back in Glasgow, a mass meeting was held at St Andrew's Halls on 27 January. As the large crowd waited for the members of the platform to come down, Harry McShane recalled someone started singing 'My Ain Wee Hoose', a popular, sentimental song of the time.

> Just a wee but humble placey
> Just a wee bit but and ben
> Where there's aye a friendly facey
> And more comfort than ye ken
> In ma ain wee hoose, in my ain wee hoose
> For there's nae nae place in a' the world
> Like ma ain wee hoose
> Like ma ain wee hoose.

The whole hall gradually took it up and they sang it over and over, creating a terrific atmosphere of unity.[6]

Harry Hopkins of the Amalgamated Society of Engineers moved the resolution: 'That this mass meeting declares that no resumption of work will take place until the demand for a 40-hour week has been conceded. And further, that all negotiations for a settlement be made by or through the joint committee.'[7]

It was passed unanimously.

Following the meeting, about thirty thousand strikers marched to George Square, the site of the City Chambers, to hear more speeches. During the gathering, to the consternation of the onlooking lord provost and other council officials, the socialist Red Flag was hoisted from the municipal flagpole.

On Wednesday 29 January, another mass meeting was held at St Andrew's Halls and afterwards those assembled marched to Pinkston power station and then to George Square. A deputation led by Emmanuel Shinwell was reluctantly admitted to the City Chambers and met the Lord Provost, James Watson Stewart. Concerned about the strength of the strike, the lord provost offered to make representations to the prime minister and the minister for labour on the strikers' demands. He asked the deputation to return on Friday 31st for the government's response.

The National Union of Scottish Mine Workers dissociated itself from the 'erratic strike movement' and urged miners to continue to go to work, pending the government's response to its demands.[8]

But on the night of 29 January, a crowd of several thousand striking miners signalled their repudiation of this stance in a demonstration in front of the headquarters of the miners' union in Hamilton, Lanarkshire. They forcibly took control of the offices and from a balcony a number addressed the crowd which blocked the street and the tramcars for over an hour. Documents were scattered from the balcony; 'The Red Flag' was sung and two red banners were displayed.[9]

~

On Thursday 30 January, the War Cabinet met at 10 Downing Street, London to discuss the situation.[10] Prime Minister Lloyd George was in Paris attending the peace talks. In his absence, the meeting was chaired by the Chancellor of the Exchequer, Andrew Bonar Law.

Bonar Law opened the meeting with a summary of the situation. 'Gentlemen, a telegram has been received this morning from the lord provost of Glasgow, addressed to the prime minister. It is in relation to the labour situation in Glasgow. The lord provost met with a deputation from a large demonstration outside the City Chambers yesterday. They asked him to seek the government's intervention with the employers to secure the reduction of working hours to 40 per week without any reduction in wages, to provide for those who have been demobilised and are without employment. They advised him that up to now they have adopted constitutional methods in urging their demand, but should the government fail to consider this request, they will adopt other methods to advance their cause. They have agreed to delay taking any such action until this Friday in order to hear our reply. The lord advocate also advises that the men in the generating stations have joined the strike and only lighting and power for hospitals and infirmaries will be provided – and possibly lighting for private houses. In consultation with my colleague the minister for labour we have prepared a draft reply. We say, the question of working hours is precisely the question which is being dealt with at the present time between the employers and the duly elected representatives of the trades unions chiefly concerned. In these circumstances the government is unable to entertain requests for intervention made by local members of unions. Such action could only undermine the authority of those who have been chosen by the men to represent them, and would destroy the co-operation between employers and employed on which the hopes of industrial peace depend.'

'As I understand it,' said Sir Eric Geddes, 'the object of the reply to the lord provost is to reinforce the authority of the trades unions and I agree with that. I would like to know however whether we are quite safe on the merits of the case between employers and employed.'

The Minister for Labour, Sir Robert Thorne, responded. 'An agreement has already been arrived at between the employers and employed in the shipbuilding and engineering trades with regard to a 47-hour week, although there is some dispute about the application of the details. The present strike in Glasgow however is for a 40-hour week, and in Belfast for a 44-hour week, which is in contravention of the agreement reached by the accredited representatives of the masters and men.'

Bonar Law said, 'I think it is vital for us to be satisfied that there is a sufficient force in Glasgow to prevent disorder and to protect those who may take over the operation of the electricity generating stations and the municipal services.'

'There are two questions to be decided,' said the Secretary for Scotland, Robert Munro. 'What is our program? And if we agree on a program, who should put it into operation? As regards taking over the electricity and municipal services, I suggest the special constables – of whom there are 2000 in Glasgow – might be more reliable and suitable than soldiers. I assume persons could be found to supervise and direct them. Then there is the problem of guarding those carrying out the work. The police force in Glasgow has been much depleted during the war and it is necessary to get back the 500 men who were now in the forces. I suggest instructions to this effect should be issued at once.'

The Secretary of State for War, Winston Churchill, demurred. 'It would be impossible to pick out of the vast numbers who were being demobilised each day the 500 constables referred to by the secretary of Scotland.'

'I offer no opinion on the problem of demobilisation,' Munro replied, 'but I feel bound to lay the request made to me by the sheriff. There remains the question of who should take the initiative?'

The Commander-In-Chief Home Forces, General Sir William Robertson, spoke next. 'The military part of the question is quite simple. The civil authorities are responsible for law and order and the military cannot step in except at their requisition in accordance with King's Regulations. This does not apply however if martial law is declared. There are 19 infantry battalions in Scotland, all Scottish but one. One of these battalions is in Glasgow, another at Greenock and about 12 near Edinburgh. They consist of all sorts of men, old, young, convalescents and men with wounds. As regards the officers, they were not very efficient. I draw your attention to this in view of the purposes for which the troops might be used. It would not be legal to use soldiers for taking over and running the generating stations.'

The Permanent Secretary of the Ministry of Labour, David Shackleton, responded, 'General, during one of the big railway strikes in peace time a few soldiers were employed as engine-drivers and guards.'

'That is true,' said the Director of Personal Services, Major General Wyndham Childs. 'But at that time, we had a well-disciplined and ignorant army. Now we have an army educated and ill-disciplined.'

'We should not exaggerate the seriousness of this disturbance,' said Churchill. 'In times of peace we have had to go through strikes just as dangerous as this one. The situation is Glasgow has been brewing for a long time. The disaffected are in a minority and in my opinion there will have to be a conflict to clear the air. We should be careful to have plenty of provocation before taking strong measures. By going gently at first, we should get the support we want from the nation, and then troops could be used more effectively. The moment for their use has not yet arrived. In the meantime, the Defence of the Realm Act is still is force and some of the leaders of the revolt should be seized.'

'I do not disagree with a word you have said Winston,' said Bonar Law. 'I am only anxious that there should be some responsible person in Glasgow ready to call in the military when necessary. This person should be told the military has received orders to hold themselves in readiness. Steps should also be taken to get the Special Constabulary ready.'

'I could send Mr John Lamb, assistant under secretary of the Scottish Office, said Munro. 'I have full confidence in Mr Lamb.'

'Mr Lamb should get in touch with the lord provost of Glasgow and the sheriff,' said Bonar Law. 'The first responsibility in the whole matter should be taken by the secretary for Scotland and Mr Lamb should tell the lord provost that the government's view was that the situation should be dealt with patiently but firmly and the military only called in when asked for in order to prevent serious disorder and intimidation and to preserve the lighting arrangements of the city.'

'I would like to suggest to the secretary for Scotland that if there is any possibility of seizing the leaders during the strike we should do so,' said Sir Robert Thorne. 'These men are not representatives of the trades unions at all and most of them are well-known extremists.'

The Lord Advocate, James Avon Clyde, said, 'I shall consider that suggestion Sir Robert.'

'Before taking any action in dealing with the strikers we should wait till some glaring excess has been committed,' said Churchill. 'The moment this revolt advances over the line of a pure wage dispute and the strikers are guilty of serious breaches of the law – that is the moment to act.'

'I fear we are very near that stage now,' said Munro. 'There have been threats to wreck the newspaper offices in Glasgow.'

'The President of the Board of Trade has told me the railways might shut down on Saturday as the men are threatening to work only eight hours,' said Sir Eric Geddes. 'This would inevitably disorganise all railway traffic and might affect the movement of troops into Glasgow.'

'The War Office will take all necessary steps to deal with that eventuality and will consider arrangements for placing troops in Glasgow,' said Churchill.

As the meeting broke up, Robert Munro approached Winston Churchill. 'It's clearer than ever that it is a misnomer to call this situation in Glasgow a strike,' Munro said. 'This is a Bolshevik rising. I am reliably informed there are no more than 10,000 malcontents and I know public opinion will support the government in quelling any disorder.'

41

THE BATTLE OF GEORGE SQUARE

Early on the morning of Friday 31 January, a crowd of around five to six hundred striking miners marched through the streets of Bellshill in Lanarkshire on their way to picket the collieries of the district. The marchers proceeded from Tollcross to Blantyre where they were joined by a large contingent, and then on to Hamilton Palace Colliery. The police were on duty at the colliery and immediately came into conflict with the strikers. A free fight ensued and there was some damage to property. The marchers then proceeded by the Hamilton road to Bellshill and when near Bellshill Cross were intercepted by a strong body of police who went at them with the baton. The strikers broke up and sought safety. No further attempt was made to picket miners who disagreed with the stoppage.[1]

This was a harbinger of things to come in Glasgow, where striking workers started massing in Glasgow's George Square well before noon. While the sun was shining, rain had fallen overnight and the square was wet and muddy. The general strike was in its fifth day and this was the third time that week that a demonstration had been held in the square. The workers had come to hear the response of the government in London to their demand for a 40-hour week.

While the strike was going very well on the Clyde and in Edinburgh and Belfast, the news was not so good from England. The joint strike committee had expected Barrow-in-Furness, the North East coast and Sheffield to come out, but they hadn't moved. The national officials of the unions had told them to stay out of the fight. It put the strike leaders in a difficult position. There was no strike benefit and the government and press were pumping out propaganda against them.

That morning the authorities met in the lord provost's office in the City Chambers to discuss and confirm tactics. The Lord Provost, James Watson Stewart; Chief Constable James V. Stevenson; Sheriff Alastair Mackenzie;

and the General Manager of the Glasgow Municipal Tramways, James Dalrymple, were joined by the Assistant Under Secretary of the Scottish Office, John Lamb, who had taken the overnight train from London.

'I received a telegram from Mr Bonar Law late yesterday afternoon,' Lord Provost Stewart said, 'and we understand the War Cabinet's decision not to intervene while negotiations are still underway between the unions and employers.'

Lamb then outlined the thinking of the Cabinet. 'The War Cabinet has instructed me to advise you that the military will be in readiness to give their services if and when you request them. Six tanks and a hundred motor lorries with drivers have come north by rail last night. It is not regarded as safe to use the troops based at Maryhill barracks here in Glasgow, so troops from elsewhere are coming into the city this morning. The Cabinet is of the view that firm, but not provocative action should be taken to put down disorder and prevent intimidation.'

The lord provost asked the chief constable whether he thought he had sufficient men to control the crowd.

'Every available constable has been assigned to the square today – including my mounted constables,' Stevenson replied. 'But it's difficult to predict how the crowd will react when they're told the government is not going to intervene. It may be preferable to break up the demonstration before that news is delivered.'

'The Cabinet was of the view that we should have plenty of provocation before taking strong measures,' said Lamb.

'If the crowd reacts,' said Stewart, 'then the police will be ready to restore order. Yes, chief constable?'

'Yes, lord provost,' said Stevenson.

'If matters escalate,' Stewart continued, 'then Sheriff Mackenzie will read the Riot Act and the police will disperse the crowd. If there is organised resistance, we will call on the military. Mr Lamb, you will be able to convey that message?'

'Indeed,' said Lamb.

'Then gentlemen,' Stewart concluded, 'I think we are agreed.'

~

Outside in the square, the speakers' platform was on the plinth of the Gladstone Monument. Willie Gallacher and one or two others addressed the meeting while Emmanuel Shinwell, David Kirkwood, Neil Maclean and three others went in to see the lord provost.

Two rows of policemen were lined up in front of the Municipal Buildings. The strikers had their back to them, listening to the speakers.

A tramcar came along Cochrane Street towards the south-east end of the square. The police tried to push the crowd back with their batons to let it through. A mounted policeman tumbled his horse. This acted as a signal for the police who weighed into the densely packed crowd with batons swinging. Men, women and children fell in the resulting melee.

The crowd surged away from the police, who advanced in an arc towards the west side of the square. Some of the crowd took turf, daffodil bulbs and stones from the plots in the square and threw them at the police. Men were sprawled all around and a woman was lying on her side and on her face was the mark of a muddy boot.

The speakers jumped off the plinth and as the others went to help the injured woman, Willie Gallacher ran across the square to where the Chief Constable, James V Stephenson, was supervising the proceedings, surrounded by a guard of ten policemen.

As Gallacher approached, the police guard raised their batons, but he managed to land a powerful punch on the chief constable.

All the police guard tried to hit Gallacher at once but got in each other's way.

Gallacher got in a full power uppercut that caught a constable right on the chin, nearly lifting him off the ground, before he was battered to the ground.

Lying on his back, trying to lift himself back up with his hands pressed to the ground, he saw the constable he punched with his baton in the air, poised to smash his face in.

Suddenly a fellow striker, Neil Alexander, a quiet unassuming boilermaker, dove in and spread himself over the top of Gallacher and the policeman's baton landed on Alexander's head.

The police dragged the semi-conscious Alexander off Gallacher and pulled Gallacher to his feet.

Blood was rushing from Gallacher's head, all over his face and neck.

Gallacher and Alexander were half-dragged across the square towards the main entrance to the Municipal Buildings.

After retreating across the square, the strikers, many of whom were

Willie Gallacher: '... a jolly and volatile fellow ... He had a fund of genuine kindliness, was ready to help any work-mate in trouble.'

returned soldiers and sailors, turned about and started fighting back with their fists. The noise increased.

At that point, the strikers' deputation rushed out the door of the Municipal Buildings, Kirkwood at the front. He got to the middle of the roadway just as Gallacher was being dragged towards the doorway.

Kirkwood raised his arms in a gesture of protest when a police sergeant, approaching him from the rear, brought down his baton with terrific force on the back of his head. Kirkwood fell flat on his face, unconscious from the cowardly blow.

Neil Maclean, who was a pace behind Kirkwood, rushed forward to protest.

Kirkwood was picked up by the police and carried through the front door to the quadrangle of the Municipal Buildings along with Gallacher and Alexander. Gallacher was given a large piece of white cloth which he tied around his head to stop the bleeding. He lit his pipe, while Kirkwood lay on the ground groaning.

Jean Gallacher, Willie's wife, smartly dressed, came into the quadrangle to see how he was. She saw he was all right, smoking his pipe, looking worse that he really was.

'What was that funny story you were telling me last night?' she said. 'That Shinwell's head will go below a baton before yours does?'

Gallacher responded ruefully, 'The laugh's agin me.'[2]

~

As word spread about the bashings of Gallacher and Kirkwood, the enraged strikers drove police back across the square towards the Municipal Buildings.

Sheriff MacKenzie, Lord Provost Stewart and other officials emerged from the building and MacKenzie started to read the Riot Act from a piece of paper.

He only managed to get out the opening lines, 'Our Sovereign Lord the King chargeth and commandeth all persons, being assembled, immediately ...', when a striker burst onto the platform, ripped the paper out of his hand and fled. After a moment's pause, the sheriff completed the reading from memory.

'... to disperse themselves, and peaceably to depart to their habitations, or to their lawful business, upon the pains contained in the Act made in the first year of King George, for preventing tumults and riotous assemblies. God Save the King!'³

~

A big, heavy lorry loaded with boxes of aerated waters drove into the north side of George Square from North Hanover Street. Some of the strikers commandeered it and drove it into North Frederick Street, which rose at a steep gradient from the north east corner of the square.

Other strikers clambered on the back of the lorry and unloaded the boxes, forming a makeshift barricade, with the necks of the bottles facing out.

Foot police and mounted police tried to rush the barricade but were driven back by the thrown bottles.

In the rest of the square, the strikers were gaining the upper hand, forcing the police back towards and then into the Municipal Buildings.

Several trams were stopped in the square. Strikers clambered onto their roofs and disconnected the arms that linked them to the electric cable then bent them so they couldn't be reconnected.⁴

~

Willie Gallacher, Mrs Jean Gallacher and Neil Alexander were sitting on a bench as a steady stream of injured strikers were brought in for first aid treatment. Then the strikers stopped coming and all the injured coming in were policemen.

'It looks like things are not going all one way,' said Willie Gallacher.

The police guarding Gallacher and the others looked concerned as their injured colleagues were brought in.

Bailie James Whitehead, a member of the Glasgow Town Council, came along the corridor and asked Gallacher how he was feeling.

'Fine!' Gallacher replied.

'Could I get you a glass of whisky?' Whitehead asked.

'No, thank you Jimmy,' Gallacher said. 'You know I don't touch the stuff.'

'I know, I know,' said Whitehead, 'but it wouldn't do you any harm just now.'

As Whitehead moved away down the corridor, the policeman who tried to smash Gallacher's face in spoke.

'You should have taken it Willie and gi'ed it to me,' he said

Gallacher looked at him. He was white-faced and nervous.

'By Christ,' Gallacher said. 'I believe you could do with it.'

'I could,' the policeman said.[5]

~

The sound of the fighting outside became louder. A police sergeant came along and led Gallacher, his wife and Neil Alexander upstairs to a room, where they sat with several policemen. Jock McBain, a union official with the Foundry Workers Union, came into the room. His head was bandaged.

'Willie, how are you man?' McBain asked.

'I'm fine Jock,' Gallacher replied. 'What's happening out there?'

'The boys have got the police right up against the chambers,' said McBain. 'They're all set for a march to Glasgow Green for a protest demonstration there. But they won't leave without hearing from you.'

'All right all right,' said Gallacher.[6]

~

Gallacher and Kirkwood appeared at a window balcony of the Municipal Buildings. The section of the crowd near enough to recognise them gave a cheer. Gallacher presented a dramatic figure with the bloodstained bandage still wrapped around his head. His appeal was couched in short, abrupt sentences and his voice, although husky, carried well to the crowd below.

'Now keep order,' he said. 'This has been a very unfortunate occurrence. We appeal to you to get into order, to get on the march away from the square for your own good. We are all right. You don't have to trouble yourselves one little bit about us. You are only troubling us about you if you stay where you are. We appeal to you to march away from the square. Logan of the Discharged Soldiers and others will lead you to Glasgow Green or elsewhere where the situation can be discussed. March for God's sake. Are you going to do that much for us?'

'Yes!' chorused the crowd.

Kirkwood then spoke.

'Fellow workmen, we believe it is in your interest that you should go away from the square. We appeal for you to do that. The time is inopportune for you to do anything else. Be advised at the moment to leave the square and we will see what will happen later on.'

The crowd cheered and immediately started to move towards the south side of the square, down South Fredrick Street.[7]

~

That night, Harry McShane was at the entrance to Buchanan Street station with a dozen other strikers, watching as young English soldiers came out of the entrance and assembled into ranks to march to George Square.

McShane and the others tried to tell them what was going on, while the officers got in between the soldiers and the strikers.

'Listen,' McShane said. 'The men in George Square are just trying to get a 40-hour week. Which means you lads will be able to get a job when you're demobbed.'

A soldier in the ranks looked at McShane.

'Piss off Jock,' he said, and pointed to his rifle. 'This is better than bottles.'[8]

42

THE MINERS MOBILISE

While all eyes were focussed on the clashes on the Clyde, on 31 January the executive committee of the miners' federation attended a meeting with government representatives in London to discuss the outcome of the MFGB special conference at Southport. Attending on the government side were the Minister for Labour, Sir Robert Horne, and the Home Secretary, Edward Shortt; plus, the president of the Board of Trade and the coal controller. Horne undertook to put the MFGB claim to the Cabinet.

The MFGB executive committee met with Horne again on 10 February to receive the government's response. It wasn't what they wanted to hear. There was no discussion, with Horne reading a memo in which a modest increase in the hourly wage was offered, but all that was promised on the questions of number of working hours and nationalisation was (another) committee of inquiry. Early demobilisation of miners to bring the workforce back to pre-war levels was denied outright. Stifling his anger at the meagre offering and the condescending manner of its delivery, MFGB president Robert Smillie told Horne the government's response would be put to the next MFGB conference on 12 and 13 February.

After attending the first three weeks of the Paris Peace Conference, Prime Minister David Lloyd George arrived back in London on Sunday 10 February. The following day, 11 February, was the opening day of the new parliament. After the King's Speech was delivered, Lloyd George made an inflammatory address in the House of Commons squarely directed at the miners. 'Anyone who uses force,' he said, 'in order to drive unfair bargains with the community we will unhesitatingly fight with the whole might of the nation or we will cease to be a government.'

If his intent was to intimidate Smillie and the MFGB, the tactic backfired. On 12 February the MFGB conference rejected the government's offer and decided to take a ballot vote of the entire union membership for a national strike. The ballot papers were to be returned by 22 February.

The two other partners in the industrial Triple Alliance were also in action on 12 February. The railwaymen met the Railway Executive, the government body that had taken control of the railways at the start of the war, to discuss their demands on wages, hours and management representation. And delegates of the Transport Workers' Federation met to consider employers' proposal for a 44-hour week.

In an attempt to counter the looming confrontation, on 17 February the government announced the convening of a National Industrial Conference. The conference would give members of the government 'an opportunity of meeting representatives of the industries of the country, so that the general situation may be diagnosed and the views of the representatives of the employers and workpeople ascertained'.[1]

Three days later, the prime minister met with the MFGB executive committee and offered the miners representation on a commission that would consider all matters relating to their demands. The first phase of the inquiry would consider wages and hours and report by 30 March with a second phase to consider the question of nationalisation. The executive committee undertook to convene a miners' conference to consider the offer.

The government rushed a Bill into parliament to establish a Coal Industry Commission and after several days debate, an Act was passed that gave wide powers to the commission it established.

On 25 February the results of the miners' ballot became known. Of a total of 720,246 ballots received, more than 85 per cent were in favour of a strike. That day, the miners held a conference with their partners in the Triple Alliance. The resolution that resulted was: 'That no section of the Triple Alliance shall agree to any action or settlement until this conference has again been called.' The development indicated 'a combination of forces of a powerful nature if the demands of the three unions are not conceded'.[2]

Did the Triple Alliance have the power to bring down the government and precipitate a revolution? Many, including those in government, thought it did. Did the leaders of the Alliance want that outcome? The answer must be no. Aneurin (Nye) Bevan, long-serving Labour MP and architect of the National Health Service in the post-World War II Labour government, related Robert Smillie's account of a meeting between the leaders of the Triple Alliance and Lloyd George in 1919.

Lloyd George sent for the labour leaders and they went, so Robert told me, 'truculently determined they would not be talked over by the seductive and eloquent Welshman'. At this, Bob's eyes twinkled in his grave strong face. 'He was quite frank with us from the outset,' Bob went on. He said to us: 'Gentlemen, you have fashioned in the Triple Alliance of the unions represented by you, a most powerful instrument. I feel bound to tell you that in our opinion we are at your mercy. The Army is disaffected and cannot be relied upon. Trouble has occurred already in a number of camps. We have just emerged from a great war and the people are eager for the reward of their sacrifices and we are in no position to satisfy them. In these circumstances, if you carry out your threat and strike, then you will defeat us.

'But if you do so,' went on Mr Lloyd George, 'have you considered the consequences? The strike will be in defiance of the government of the country and by its very success will precipitate a constitutional crisis of the first importance. For if a force arises in the State that is stronger than the State itself, then it must be ready to take on the functions of the State, or withdraw and accept the authority of the State. Gentlemen,' asked the Prime Minister quietly, 'have you considered, and if you have, are you ready?'

'From that moment on,' said Robert Smillie, 'we were beaten and we knew we were.'[3]

~

On 27 February, the opening day of the National Industrial Conference, the General Secretary of the National Union of Railwaymen, JH Thomas, set out the position of the Triple Alliance.

> In the judgement of my colleagues and myself, the organised workers of Great Britain have made up their minds to procure for themselves an increasing share of the wealth which their labour has produced and produces. The workers moreover – and I speak more especially for the members of our threefold organisations – are determined to shorten materially the hours of labour in their respective industries. They are dissatisfied with a system of society which treats their labour power as a mere commodity to be bought, sold and used as though they were machine-like units in the process of wealth production and distribution, and they therefore demand that they shall become real partners in industry, jointly sharing in the determination of working conditions and management. Labour becomes increasingly alive to its sovereign power, and will shirk no responsibilities and will be denied none of its rights and privileges. Miners, railwaymen and transport workers stand unalterably for the ownership by the State of the mines, railways and

the means of inland and coastal transport. This is essentially in the interest of the general community as well as the increased efficiency of these three national industries.[4]

The previous day, a full MFGB conference had assembled to consider the government's offer of participating in the Coal Commission and whether to defer operation of strike notices from 15 March. The government promised an interim report by 20 March, with a final report as soon as possible after that. Despite the speeding up of the process, some delegates arrived with 'a firm determination not to accept any compromise'. The conference was unable to reach a decision, and discussions continued the following day.

For Robert Smillie, the key part of the commission's remit was '... any scheme that may be submitted ... for the future organisation of the coal industry ...'. It was Smillie's view, one shared by the MFGB executive, that nationalisation of mines was the main priority. If that was attained, all else, from wages to working hours, would follow.[5]

Smillie argued successfully for the union to participate in the inquiry, while holding the mandate to strike in reserve if the outcome proved unfavourable. On 2 March, the government appointed Justice John Sankey to head the commission. A High Court judge, Sankey had begun his practice as a barrister in South Wales, later specialising in workmen's compensation cases. With his Welsh background and career in compensation work, the miners were comforted by the fact that Sankey knew something about the realities of the mining industry.

The union's decision was not welcomed by John Maclean and his likeminded colleagues in the miners' reform movement. In the *Call*, he wrote:

> Government agents have also got at some of the other miners' leaders and convinced them that Bolshevists are responsible for the attitude of the miners, and their object is revolution and not merely a slight improvement in the miners' lot. These leaders will do anything to stave off a fight. This compromising Commission offers them a means of salvation.
>
> The miners' leaders will fail for fear of Revolution. It is thus all the more necessary that the unofficial movement prepare itself to carry on the fight independently – for the fight must go on. As long as British capitalism actively tries to crush the triumphant workers of Russia and the Spartacists of Germany, it is the duty of the fighting workers here to keep British capitalism busy.

Readers should stamp it into their minds that this preparation for the class war is not the exclusive business of the miners. The miners are but the vanguard of the workers, and they rightly expect that if they accept the dangerous front-rank position other workers will determinedly back them up.

Therefore, all readers of 'The Call' should force the pace inside their respective workshops and unions, and see that their fellows demand a thirty-hour week maximum, with a wage having a higher purchasing power than their wages had in 1914.

If the present pressure on the capitalists is to be effective it must not be the pressure of a million miners but of at least ten million workers; in other words, it must be a full working-class pressure. To achieve this, it is not necessary to have the machinery of industrial unionism: all that is required is the class spirit and unity of demand.[6]

43

HANDS OFF RUSSIA

A few weeks after the Bolshevik Revolution, on 23 December 1917, an Anglo-French convention had been concluded in Paris, regulating the future operations of British and French forces on Russian territory. This convention defined as a British 'zone of influence' the Cossack regions, the territory of the Caucasus, Armenia, Georgia and Kurdistan, while the French zone was to consist of Bessarabia, Ukraine and Crimea. There was a certain economic rationale for this convention; British investment predominated in the Caucasian oil-fields, while the French were more interested in the coal and iron mines of Ukraine.

The Allied Powers had been supplying Russia since the beginning of the war and after the signing of the treaty of Brest-Litovsk, they were concerned at the potential loss to Germany of the large quantities of supplies and equipment sitting in the ports of Arkhangel and Murmansk.

The first British landing in Russia was at Murmansk, the only ice-free port in Northern Russia, and came at the request of the Murmansk Soviet. Fearing an attack on the town from the White Finns, who had been backed by Germany in the Finnish Civil War, they requested that the Allies land troops for protection. The Allies readily agreed as the White Finns were believed to be in position to march north, seize Murmansk and enable the establishment of a German submarine base to harry the already hard-pressed Allied Atlantic shipping. British troops arrived on 4 March 1918, the day after the signing of the treaty between Germany and the Bolshevik government.

Over the following months the British forces were largely engaged in small battles and skirmishes with White Finns in support of the Red Army. In late June, 600 British reinforcements and 100 Americans from the cruiser *Olympia* arrived. By this time, Soviet–Allied relations had passed from distrust to open hostility and Trotsky raged, 'Between the Germans and the encroachments of armies of the "friendly" Allies we see no difference ... Those who twist this statement into an argument that we plan an alliance with the Germans against the Allies are either naturally stupid or are being paid to be stupid.'[1]

The troop build-up continued however, and by early autumn, British forces in the Murmansk region were 6,000 strong, and had been reinforced by the arrival of 1,200 Italians, as well as small Canadian and French battalions.

On 2 August 1918, backed by Allied forces, anti-Bolshevik forces staged a coup against the local Soviet government at Arkhangel. Allied warships sailed into the port from the White Sea, and after overcoming some resistance, 1500 French and British troops occupied the city.

On 5 August in the House of Commons, Liberal MP Joseph King asked Foreign Secretary Arthur Balfour about the aims of the government's action. Balfour replied with a straight bat. 'The aim of His Majesty's Government is to secure the political and economic restoration of Russia, without internal interference of any kind, and to bring about the expulsion of enemy forces from Russian soil. His Majesty's Government categorically declare that they have no intention whatever of infringing in the slightest degree the territorial integrity of Russia.'

Hastings Lees-Smith, Liberal MP for Northampton followed up, asking, 'Would the right hon. Gentleman make a statement that they do not intend to assist any of those factions in Russia who are attempting to overthrow the Soviet government?'

'Without internal interference of any kind,' repeated Balfour.[2]

The Soviet of the People's Commissars had no doubt about the intentions of the British and other Allied governments. In a pamphlet addressed to the workers of those countries, dated 1 August 1918 and signed by Lenin, Trotsky and Chicheren, they said:

> Everything that the press of your capitalists and their agents say in justification of the savage assault upon Russia is nothing but hypocrisy, intended to conceal the facts of the case. It is for other purposes that they are preparing their campaign against Russia. They have three aims in view: their first aim is the seizure of as much Russian territory as possible so that its wealth and its railways can be used to secure payment to French and English capital of the interest on loans; their second aim is the suppression of the workers' revolution for fear that it may inspire you, and show you how to throw off the yoke of capitalism. Their third aim is to create a new

eastern front so as to divert German forces from the western front to Russian territory.³

Major General Poole, the British commander at Arkhangel, obviously did not feel constrained by his government's stated policy. He declared martial law, and prepared to invade along the rail line to Vologda, 400 miles south. An armoured train was commissioned to support the advance, and a battle took place between Allied and Bolshevik armoured trains on 18 August. The Royal Air Force provided air support to the advancing Allied infantry, conducting bombing and strafing runs.

On 4 September 1918, the landing of 4500 American troops at Arkhangel brought the number of Allied forces there to 10,000 and fighting with the Red Army continued south along the River Dvina until the winter freeze.

British and Bolshevik forces also clashed in the Transcaspian region (modern Turkmenistan) before the signing of the armistice. Concerned about the Bolsheviks and German and Turkish military activity, in August 1918 the British government decided to send a small force from British India to the area. In conjunction with local anti-Bolsheviks, they were involved in a series of engagements before their withdrawal in April 1919.

Home reaction to the British intrigues was not long in coming. On 25 August, at a meeting in Edinburgh, a Russian Anti-Intervention Committee declared, 'whereas the International Capitalist class, led by Germany and Britain, terror-stricken at the establishment of an Industrial Republic in Russia, [and] fearful of its extension to their territory ... have determined to crush the Workers' Soviets in Russia ... [and] with this end in view, the British ruling class have landed armed forces at various places in Russia ... be it hereby resolved that we workers do hereby solemnly pledge ourselves to do everything in our power to maintain the Soviet Republic of the Russian workers.' The bodies represented at the meeting were the Socialist Labour Party, the Independent Labour Party, the Plebs League, the Workers' International Industrial Union and the Forth Area Workers' Committee.⁴

In September, with a small financial contribution from Moscow, Sylvia Pankhurst established the People's Russia Information Bureau (PRIB) to publish reliable and supportive information about Soviet Russia. The bureau was a broad left organisation that included affiliates from a range of labour movement organisations. Much of the information it published, mainly in the form of newsletters and pamphlets, was sourced directly from Russia.

On 11 November, the signing of the Allied-German armistice meant that the Allies' stated objective of removing enemy forces from Russia was now irrelevant. However, the British forces did not leave. From this point onwards, the sole objectives of Britain and her Allies were to restore a White government and to remove the Bolsheviks from power.

On 18 January 1919, the 'Hands off Russia' campaign to oppose British military intervention in support of the White armies' attack on Bolshevik Russia was launched. The movement brought together all the major left wing groups of the time. As well as the British Socialist Party, they included the Independent Labour Party, the Socialist Labour Party, the Workers' Socialist Federation and the South Wales Socialist Society.

~

The flurry of rallies in January 1919 that saw John Maclean addressing miners in Lanarkshire, Fife, Ayrshire, West Lothian and Cumberland, as well as meetings and conferences in Glasgow, set the tone for the next six months. And as a member of the British Socialist Party executive and the recognised spokesman for the Russian Revolution he became more of a presence in the rest of Britain, speaking at huge meetings in London, Lancashire, Yorkshire, Cumberland, Durham, South Wales and Dublin.

Maclean believed the best way to protect the Bolshevik revolution was for workers to create their own social revolution in Britain. In this he saw the prime role being played by the coal miners. A strike by the miners leading to a general strike would lay the groundwork for workers councils to take over the means of production. That was the vision anyway.

On Sunday 2 February, Maclean was the chief speaker at a large Hands off Russia rally in Manchester. The following week, he spoke at meetings in London, culminating with the top billing at the Hands off Russia demonstration in the Albert Hall on Saturday 8 February.

At this meeting, Neil Maclean, Independent Labour Party MP for Govan, moved a resolution demanding the end of intervention in Russia, the withdrawal of Allied troops, the end of the economic blockade and the complete cessation of all support accorded to the opponents of the Soviet administration by means of money and munitions. Fresh from the Battle of George Square eight days earlier, he said it should not only be a cry of 'Hands off Russia', but 'Hands off Glasgow'.[5]

Other speakers at the packed meeting included Sylvia Pankhurst, leader of the Workers' Socialist Federation, George Lansbury, editor of the *Herald*, Cathal O'Shannon from the Irish Trades Union Congress, and the Red Countess, Lady Warwick. But the star turn was John Maclean.

According to the *Call*, when EC Fairchild announced Maclean, 'round on round of applause greeted his rising, the whole vast gathering breaking into song'. The *Call* report concluded:

> In a fine peroration, he maintained that armies and navies would never cease until production was socialised, and that the only way to help Russia was to abolish our system of industry and by making the workshop the unit of industry, march towards socialism on the lines laid down by Russia.[6]

~

In early 1919, the Supreme Allied War Conference in Paris attempted to organise a peace conference to settle the Russian civil war. Woodrow Wilson sent invitations to the Bolsheviks and various anti-Bolshevik administrations to meet in February on the island of Prinkipo in the Sea of Marmara, less than 20 km from Constantinople. French Prime Minister Clemenceau and the British Secretary of State for War, Winston Churchill, both rabid anti-Bolsheviks, were opposed to the plan; the White Russians greeted the idea with dismay; the Bolsheviks were initially in favour, but refused to implement a cease-fire; so, when Wilson, whose health was failing, returned to America, the whole idea fell over.[7]

Churchill regarded the Bolshevik regime with visceral distaste. Ten years later, in the final volume of his account of the war, he described the Russia of the time as 'not a wounded Russia only, but a poisoned Russia, an infected Russia, a plague-bearing Russia, a Russia of armed hordes smiting not only with bayonet and cannon, but accompanied and preceded by typhus-bearing vermin, which slew the bodies of men, and political doctrines which destroyed the health and even the souls of nations'.[8]

On 16 February, the day after the deadline for the proposed Prinkipo peace conference expired, Churchill wrote to Lloyd George. 'I do not see that we are called upon to show our hand immediately. It will be a more prudent course to set up a Military Commission at once to take stock of the situation, to prepare out of the resources available a plan of war against the Bolsheviks.'

Lloyd George responded immediately. 'Am very alarmed at your telegram about planning war against the Bolsheviks. The Cabinet have never authorised such a proposal ... If Russia is really anti-Bolshevik than a supply of equipment would enable it to redeem itself. If Russia is pro-Bolshevik, not merely is it none of our business to interfere with its internal affairs, it would be perfectly mischievous: it would strengthen and consolidate Bolshevik opinion.'[9]

The state of neither war nor peace between the Allies and Russia would persist for the rest of the year.

44

THE COAL COMMISSION

The Coal Industry Commission (popularly known as the Sankey Commission) held its first meeting on 3 March 1919 and conducted public examinations of witnesses for the following two weeks. The evidence provided proved startling.

The make-up of the commission under the chairmanship of Justice Sankey was as follows: four members appointed by the MFGB (president Robert Smillie, general secretary Frank Hodges, vice-president Herbert Smith, and former MP and economist Sir Leo Money); three government nominees; three representatives of coal owners, and two members agreed between the government and the MFGB (economic historian Richard Tawney and economist Sidney Webb). The venue was the Kings Robing Room in the House of Lords. Robert Smillie was impressed:

> I had never seen such a place before ... it had a magnificently carved vaulted ceiling, frescoes on every wall, portraits of monarchs, the largest of which were those of Victoria and Albert, a royal-blue carpet in which you lost sight of your shoes. ... In the centre was an oak witness box and, facing that in a horseshoe shape, were the tables and chairs for the twelve of us serving as commissioners. Behind the witness box, members of the press and public were crowded, many of them standing. Hundreds have been turned away.[1]

The first witness was Arthur Dickenson, the financial advisor to the coal controller. His revelations about the profiteering in coal during the war caused an immediate revulsion of feeling against the coal owners. From the evidence of the government witnesses who followed, it became clear that the private ownership and distribution of coal had not only meant swollen profits wrung out of the low wages paid to the miners and high prices paid by the public, but had also hampered the war effort by inefficiency and wastefulness. Particularly deadly was evidence given showing how huge profits were concealed by the capitalisation of reserves or other readjustments of capital.[2]

Evidence from John Robertson, chairman of the Scottish Union of Mine Workers, about the appalling housing conditions endured by many mining communities and the sickness and infant mortality that resulted shocked many, including Justice Sankey. Sankey's interim report said, 'There are houses in some districts which are a reproach to our civilisation. No judicial language is sufficiently strong or sufficiently severe to apply to their condemnation.'[3]

At the halfway point of the hearings, Beatrice Webb summed things up:

> The ostensible business of the Commission is to examine and report on the miners' claim for a rise in wages and a reduction of hours; but owing to the superior skill of the miners' representatives it has become a state trial of the coal owners and royalty owners conducted on behalf of the producers and consumers of the product, culminating in the question 'Why not nationalise the industry?'[4]

The belligerent tone adopted by the miners' representatives had the effect of turning the proceedings into a microcosm of the class struggle. The *Daily News* wrote:

> No-one who attends the proceedings can help coming away with the impression that it is the mine-owners and not the miners whose case is on trial. So skilfully have Mr Smillie and his colleagues managed the proceedings that they have become virtually a labour tribunal. More than once, when Mr Smillie or Mr Webb has let himself go, I have been reminded of reports of proceedings of revolutionary tribunals in France or Russia.[5]

The proceedings received blanket coverage in both the mainstream and left wing press. Miners were captivated, with entire communities turning out to hear local union officials recount what was happening day by day in the House of Lords. In South Wales, the *Merthyr Pioneer* reported 'vast audiences' were 'spellbound' by accounts of the hearings.[6]

The *Labour Leader* was in raptures:

> The Revolution is evolving. Labour has already got as far as the King's Robing Room ... The rugged figure of Robert Smillie, the miners' intrepid leader, in

that gilded setting is symbolic of the day that is yet to dawn – but will dawn – when Labour shall enter its full inheritance.[7]

The hearings concluded on Monday 17 March and, it proving impossible to agree to a unanimous report, on 20 March three reports were released. The Majority Report, signed by the four MFGB representatives and the two independent commissioners, endorsed the miners' claims for a 30 per cent rise in wages, the six-hour day, and nationalisation of the mines. The conclusions were backed up by pages of evidence gained from the inquiry.

The Minority Report from the three coal-owners was confined solely to the questions of wages and hours. It recommended an additional one shilling and sixpence per day for persons over 16, ninepence for persons under 16; a seven-hour day for miners and an eight-hour day for surface workers.

The Chairman's report, signed by Justice Sankey and the three government members, recommended a seven-hour day for underground workers from July 1919, moving to a six-hour day at the end of 1920, 'subject to the economic position of the industry'. Wages to increase by 2 shillings per day for those over 16, and one shilling for under 16s. Careful consideration should be given to collecting a penny per ton to be used to improve the housing and amenities of colliery districts, the report said. But the key recommendation was on nationalisation.

> Even upon the evidence already given, the present system of ownership and working in the coal industry stands condemned, and some other system must be substituted for it, either nationalisation or a method of unification by national purchase and/or joint control.[8]

The three reports were presented to parliament on 20 March and that very evening the Leader of the Commons Andrew Bonar Law announced the government's adoption of the Chairman's report, 'in spirit and in letter'.

But he also delivered a barely-veiled warning. 'If a strike came either from the railwaymen or the miners, the Government would not hesitate to act with vigour,' the *Glasgow Herald* reported. 'He [Bonar Law] said the Government could not be expected to accept proposals for nationalisation without further examination; but Mr Justice Sankey had promised him that day that if the commission were to continue, he would be prepared to report on nationalisation on 20 May next.'[9]

Robert Smillie and the MFGB executive were buoyed by the surge in public support for their case created by the commission hearings, and were enticed by the prospect of the smooth path to nationalisation held out by Sankey's report. The day after the reports were released, an MFGB conference was convened to consider the next steps. In his speech to the conference, Smillie hardly mentioned the concessions the miners were being asked to accept, rather focussing heavily on the commission's future potential. He assured delegates that not only would nationalisation and joint control inevitably follow, but that the commission would continue to sit over the following year, issuing regular reports that would transform the mining communities.[10]

The conference authorised the executive committee to continue negotiations with the government on what Sankey had proposed. They recommended to the mining districts (whose strike notices expired on 22 March) that they continue working on day-to-day contracts until the conference reconvened.

On 26 March the conference met again. After discussion, it was decided to take a ballot of members about acceptance of the government offer. Ballots were to be returned by 14 April. James Brown, secretary of the Scottish Mine Workers and MP for South Ayrshire, captured the mood when he said in an interview, 'It would be sheer madness to vote against the settlement.'[11]

Executive members repeatedly stressed that if the miners were to strike and lose, they would forfeit everything the commission had promised them. The appeal to miners written by Robert Smillie and Frank Hodges and distributed to the coalfields in the run up to the ballot set out a stark choice:

> The Coal Industry Commission has hardly commenced its work. Its greatest and most important tasks lie before it. Nationalisation, effective control by the producers whether by hand or brain, economies in production, elimination of waste, maximum economic value of the product for the community with maximum social amenities for the men who produce the ... coal. The choice is between definite and systematic progress and the dangers of social disorder.[12]

In South Wales, where the campaign for the Miners' Charter had seem the emergence of a political group, the South Wales Socialist Society (SWSS), that encouraged direct action (i.e., strikes) to achieve its goals, there was widespread disagreement. The SWSS, which grew out of the Unofficial Reform Committee that had drafted the original charter before the war, held meetings in several districts to drum up support for a wildcat strike against the Sankey Report. On Monday 24 March collieries in the Rhondda Valley and the Pontypridd area came out on strike. After the decision of the MFGB conference on 26 March to recommend acceptance of the report, the strike – for adoption of the full Miners' Charter – spread rapidly. Two-thirds of the collieries in the Rhondda came out, and were joined by pits in Monmouthshire, Aberdare, Tredegar, Rhymney Valley, East Glamorgan, Merthyr and Ebbw Vale. At its peak, an estimated 75,000-85,000, or half the miners of South Wales, were on strike.[13]

The South Wales Miners' Federation was forced to call a conference for Saturday 29 March to reconsider the MFGB recommendation to accept the Sankey Report. The SWSS argued that the South Wales strike should continue, the ballot should be boycotted and the MFGB should call a national strike. The conference rebuffed the calls for unity from the officials and voted 168-102 that members be 'strongly recommended' to vote against the Sankey Report in the ballot. At this point, the MFGB was in danger of losing control of the most important area in the federation.[14]

The resistance was not limited to South Wales. In Derbyshire, 'conversations between miners on their way to work and railwaymen at the Chesterfield stations led to an unofficial strike of about 8,000 miners against the MFGB's decision'.[15] A strike inspired by the South Wales action also broke out in Staffordshire (around 15,000 miners) and another involving between 10,000 and 20,000 men flared up in the Sheffield area. Altogether, over 100,000 mine workers were caught up in the brief but threatening action.

Had there been a coordinating body to link up the local rank and file movements, it is possible that these strikes could have formed the basis of a concerted challenge to the acceptance of the government's offer. But as James Macdougall later wrote, there had only ever been tentative efforts to establish a national Miners' Reform Committee, and 'nothing came of it'.[16]

Throughout March, John Maclean had been continuing his campaign of gingering up the miners' unofficial movement with a week in Lanarkshire, followed by a week in Lancashire and a week in Sheffield. Then with fellow socialist William Paul, he visited South Wales to see if it was possible to link the rebels there with the rebels on the Clyde.[17]

He was scathing of what he saw as the capitulation of the Triple Alliance to Lloyd George's manoeuvres.

> Alarmed by the monstrous majority of miners for a strike and the prospect of support not only from the other members of the Triple Alliance, but also from other sections of the organised workers, the government established the Industrial Peace Conference as well as the Coal Commission.
>
> The result has been enough to gladden the heart of the very last ditchers of the capitalist class. The miners' paid officials and unpaid delegates have accepted the immediate offer of the seven-hour day and 2s a day extra, and have advised the rank and file to vote for acceptance of the offer. The NUR leaders also advise their followers to take the government compromise without even the farce of a Commission. And now Bob Williams [Robert Williams, secretary of the Transport Workers' Federation] justifies the capitulation of the Triple Alliance on the ground that it is not strong enough to successfully face the organised forces of the master class, and suggests that to gain real successes the next offensive must be made by the whole working class. With him we all agree that only by a general offensive of the working class as a whole can any effective gains be obtained, but we cannot accept this is a justification for the collapse of the Triple Alliance. It was the business of the Alliance to start the fight, and then call in all other sections of the workers to the rescue.
>
> While the Coal Commission was openly performing its part and giving us stale statistics and staler thrills of horrors about miners' slums, the Industrial Peace Conference were secretly deliberating, and let us know their principal findings the day JH Thomas accepted the compromise for the railwaymen. The principal finding was the forty-eight-hour week, one good enough for ten thousand years ago, but hardly adequate for a revolutionary working class.[18]

But should Maclean have been surprised? From the start of the year, the goal of the miners' executive had been reform of their industry, not a socialist revolution. The same was true for the heads of the rail and transport unions. The threat of a general strike was a bargaining chip to these men, not a considered plan.

Also in the minds of the union leaders must have been the likely reaction of the state to a full-blown industrial conflict. The deployment of troops in Glasgow after the police riot in George Square during the 40-hour strike was fresh in the memory. In the years before the war, then Home Secretary

Winston Churchill had called on the army to deal with strikes in South Wales and Liverpool. And, of course there was the failed 1916 Easter Rising in Dublin, which led to martial law in Ireland and the execution of 16 of its leaders, including the trade unionist and socialist James Connolly.

~

When the ballots were tallied from the coalfields on Tuesday 15 April, the results were overwhelmingly in favour of accepting the terms offered in the Sankey Report – a complete turnaround from the vote to strike 18 days earlier. Just over ninety percent of ballots (693,084 out of 770,076) supported acceptance. The MFGB special conference the following day ordered the withdrawal of the strike notices.

The Triple Alliance met that evening. While the miners, railwaymen and transport workers were not fully satisfied with the proposed settlements of their respective claims, it was nonetheless resolved to formally ratify the proposals as submitted.

The miners had accepted a compromise, but on the firm understanding and expectation of future victory. Robert Page Arnot later wrote: 'The miners, and the whole trade union movement were clear on the point, that the Government had pledged itself to the ending of private ownership of mines. The tension was loosened. The Government had weathered the crisis.'[19]

45

THE THIRD INTERNATIONAL

In January 1919, a radio message was sent out from Russia calling on representatives of socialist groups to attend a conference in March 1919 with a view to establishing a new (Third) International.

The First International had been formed in London in 1864 and aimed to unite a number of left wing (socialist, communist, anarchist and trade union) groups. After the Paris Commune of 1871, an irreconcilable difference of view developed between the anarchist faction (lead by Mikhail Bakunin) and the Marxist faction (led by Karl Marx). Bakunin characterised Marx's ideas as authoritarian and argued that if a Marxist party came to power its leaders would end up being as bad as the ruling class they had fought against. The anarchists upheld the central role of trade unions in the class struggle and called for a general strike to replace the state with a free association of producers. The Marxist faction proposed the seizure of state power by a political party.[1] The First International split into communist and anarchist wings in 1872, both of which fizzled out later in the decade.

The Second International was established in 1889 as a successor. It was made up of political parties and trade unions with properly elected leaderships, political programs and membership bases in each country. It stood for parliamentary democracy and finally, at its congress in 1896, expelled from its ranks the anarchists, who opposed it. From the start it pronounced itself staunchly anti-war, but the advent of the Great War saw many of its members drop their pacifist stance and pledge support to their national flag. The International effectively split into three factions: the pro-war social democratic parties in the Central Powers, the pro-war parties of the Allies, and the various anti-war parties, including the parties in neutral countries. These internal schisms eventually led to the collapse of the organisation in 1916.

The invitation to the March 1919 meeting included a preface that set out the situation as seen by Lenin, Trotsky and the rest of the Russian Bolshevik leadership.

> THE UNDERSIGNED parties and organisations consider it urgently necessary to convene the first congress of a new revolutionary International. During the war and the revolution, it became conclusively clear not only that the old socialist and social-democratic parties and with them the Second International, had become completely bankrupt, not only that the half-way elements of the old social-democracy (the so-called 'centre') are incapable of positive revolutionary action, but that the outlines of a really revolutionary International are already clearly defined. The gigantic pace of the world revolution, constantly presenting new problems, the danger that this revolution may be throttled by the alliance of capitalist states, which are grouping together against the revolution under the hypocritical banner of the 'League of Nations', the attempts of the parties of the social-traitors to get together and, having 'amnestied' each other, to assist their governments and their bourgeoisie to deceive the working class yet again; finally the extraordinarily rich revolutionary experience already gained and the internationalisation of the entire revolutionary movement compel us to take the initiative in placing upon the order of the day the convening of an international congress of revolutionary proletarian parties.[2]

The organisations invited to send representatives included the Spartacist League of Germany; the Communist Parties in many other European countries; the revolutionary left wing of various social democratic or socialist parties; and elements in the revolutionary workers' movement.

The British groups invited were: the left elements in the British Socialist Party *(in particular the group represented by Maclean* (emphasis added)); The Socialist Labour Party; The Industrial Workers of the World; The Industrial Workers of Great Britain; the revolutionary elements among the shop stewards (Great Britain); and the revolutionary elements in the Irish workers' organisations. It is notable that the only person mentioned by name in the British organisations was John Maclean (one of only four invitees thus singled out from the 39 organisations invited).

The first congress convened in Moscow from 2 to 6 March 1919, with 51 delegates present. Of these, there were 35 with decisive votes, representing 17 countries; and a further 16 with consultative votes, representing 16 countries. According to Arthur Ransome, a British writer visiting Moscow at the time, the congress was held in a smallish room in the old Courts of Justice and initially was shrouded in secrecy.[3] Because of the Allied blockade not all those sent invitations arrived. The only British representative present was Joseph Fineberg, a translator and former member of the British Socialist Party who had left London for Russia in July 1918.[4]

At the final session on 6 March, the International, which called itself the Communist International (Comintern), adopted a manifesto 'to the workers of the world'. It was published in the first issue of *Communist International*, the organ of the Comintern which appeared in Russian, German, French and English in May 1919. The manifesto concluded:

> If the war of 1870 dealt a blow to the First International, disclosing that there was as yet no fused mass force behind its social-revolutionary program, then the war of 1914 killed the Second International, disclosing that the mightiest organisations of the working masses were dominated by parties which had become transformed into auxiliary organs of the bourgeois state!
>
> This applies not only to the social patriots who have today clearly and openly gone over to the camp of the bourgeoisie, who have become the latter's favourite plenipotentiaries and trustees and the most reliable executioners of the working class; it also applies to the amorphous and unstable tendency of the Socialist Centre which seeks to re-establish the Second International, that is, to re-establish the narrowness, the opportunism and the revolutionary impotence of its leading summits. The Independent Party of Germany, the present majority of the Socialist Party of France, the Menshevik group of Russia, the Independent Labour Party of England and other similar groups are actually trying to fill the place which had been occupied prior to the war by the old official parties of the Second International. They come forward as hitherto with the ideas of compromise and conciliationism; with all the means at their disposal, they paralyse the energy of the proletariat, prolonging the crisis and thereby redoubling Europe's calamities. The struggle against the Socialist Centre is the indispensable premise for the successful struggle against imperialism.
>
> Sweeping aside the half-heartedness, lies and corruption of the outlived official Socialist parties, we Communists, united in the Third International, consider ourselves the direct continuators of the heroic endeavours and

martyrdom of a long line of revolutionary generations from Babeuf – to Karl Liebknecht and Rosa Luxemburg.

If the First International presaged the future course of development and indicated its paths; if the Second International gathered and organised millions of workers; then the Third International is the International of open mass action, the International of revolutionary realisation, the International of the deed.

Bourgeois world order has been sufficiently lashed by Socialist criticism. The task of the International Communist Party consists in overthrowing this order and erecting in its place the edifice of the socialist order. We summon the working men and women of all countries to unite under the Communist banner which is already the banner of the first great victories.

Workers of the World – in the struggle against imperialist barbarism, against monarchy, against the privileged estates, against the bourgeois state and bourgeois property, against all kinds and forms of class or national oppression – *Unite!*

Under the banner of Workers' Soviets, under the banner of revolutionary struggle for power and the dictatorship of the proletariat, under the banner of the Third International – *Workers of the World Unite!*[5]

In his biography Tom Bell, then a senior member of the Socialist Labour Party, writes that he managed to establish contact with his Russian comrades and from them came the suggestion of uniting all the socialists and militant workers in Great Britain favourable to the Russian revolution into a single party. Conversations began with the British Socialist Party, the Workers' Socialist Federation and others, but immediately ran into differences of opinion about whether a united Communist Party, when formed, should participate in the parliamentary process and affiliate with the Labour Party.[6]

46

SOVIETS IN BRITAIN?

The 1919 annual conference of the British Socialist Party was held in Sheffield over the Easter weekend. Resolutions on the agenda included one denouncing the government's policy of 'fastening conscription upon the workers'. Another applauded 'the revolutionary courage and insight displayed by the workers and peasants of Hungary and Bavaria in following the glorious initiative of their brothers in Russia'. And a third proposed that the conference 'should pledge itself to do all in its power to rouse the workers of Britain, not only for the protection of the New Soviet Republic, but for the overthrow of capitalism in their own country'.[1]

A difference of view had crystallised within the party about its revolutionary identity. In an article in the *Call* published in the week before the conference, Theodore Rothstein entreated members of the party to decide where they stood.

> To my mind—and I have made it up long ago—the choice is quite simple. We all, from the most moderate to the most revolutionary, are agreed that the Social Revolution, that is, the conquest of power by the working-class and the subsequent transformation of our capitalist into a Socialist society, is inevitable. If we did not believe in its coming, we should not be Socialists. But there are some who do not believe in revolutionary methods at all, and there are others who believe them to be practicable in other countries, but Utopian and unnecessary in ours.
>
> Are we 'in' for such a revolution? Is it our mission to agitate and work for it? Then our place is in the Third International. If not, then the sooner we recognise our mistake in identifying ourselves with the Russian and other Communists and in sending greetings to the revolutionary proletariats of Hungary and Bavaria the better for everybody concerned.[2]

Rothstein had been working closely with the Bolshevik ambassador Maxim

Litvinoff, and when Litvinoff was arrested and deported in September 1918, Rothstein became Russia's official agent and the dispenser of Soviet funds.³

Rothstein's revolutionary position was shared by Maclean, but was opposed by party chairman EC Fairchild, who continued to adhere to the Second International's worldview and criticised the formation of a 'Third' International by the Russian Bolsheviks.

The difference was apparent in the discussion on the executive's emergency resolution that pledged the party to 'a world revolution which in all countries would seize the reins of power, overthrow the rule of the capitalist and landlord classes parading in the shabby cloak of Parliamentarism and sham democracy, establish the direct rule of workers and peasants by means of soviets, and wind up the capitalist order of society'.⁴

Fairchild moved an amendment to delete the words 'by means of soviets' and replace them with a reference to revolution 'by superseding capitalism'.

'Mr Fairchild contended that there was a vital difference between our people and those of Eastern Europe,' the *Glasgow* Herald reported. 'The adoption of Soviets in this country would mean the abandonment of an industrial policy a century old. To ask our workers to imitate those of other countries would be a fatal mistake.'⁵

John Maclean strongly supported the original resolution, and attacked Fairchild for going over to the enemy. 'The last Clyde strike was a class strike, and a new development for the British working classes,' he said. Maclean also complained that a leaflet on the subject of 'A Soviet for Scotland' had been refused insertion in the *Call*, and said the only thing to do was to go on fighting industrially and that he was opposed to compromise.⁶

Fairchild's amendment only attracted 11 votes from the 100 delegates present, and the original resolution passed with three dissentions.

Maclean submitted an anti-conscription resolution and said the use of the police baton had done more for the workers than anything else and would develop stronger action. The motion was adopted.

On the second day of the conference, Monday 21 April, a motion was carried that steps should be taken to unite the British Socialist Party, the Independent Labour Party and the Socialist Labour Party in a United Socialist Party. A sub-committee was appointed to draft a scheme for the consideration of branches. A motion to sever ties with the Second International, and to affiliate to the Third International established at Moscow, was also referred to branches for discussion.

The conference then heard from the BSP's national organiser George Ebury, one of the twelve men charged with offences related to the Battle of George Square. An eleven-day trial at Edinburgh's High Court of Justiciary had concluded on 18 April, with eight of the accused, including Ebury, being found not guilty. Emmanuel Shinwell had been found guilty of incitement, and sentenced to five months imprisonment. Willie Gallacher had also been found guilty of incitement, but was recommended for leniency and was sent to prison for three months. Two others were convicted of rioting and sentenced to three months each.

Ebury moved a motion that the conference demand a public inquiry into the conduct of the Glasgow police on Friday 31 January, and demand the release of Gallacher and Shinwell. He said the judge on the last day of the trial practically advised the jury to acquit in all the cases, and yet the jury were so biased that they were determined that a conviction be recorded against some of the prisoners. Ebury's motion was adopted.[7]

What the *Glasgow Herald* described as an 'animated debate' took place on the issue of affiliation to the Labour Party. During a 'vigorous speech', Maclean said, 'It is entirely owning to the BSP that we have got a drift towards the revolutionary position. The [Arthur] Hendersons have to go, the [JH] Thomases have to go, and are going. The general strike will be the next stage towards getting the land and the means of production into our hands.' [Cheers].'[8]

The conference eventually voted in favour of affiliation, but the issue would bedevil attempts over the following 15 months to unite the various socialist groups in Britain into one party.

~

Maclean's attendance at the BSP conference was followed by a few days with the miners in South Wales. On his return to Scotland, he spoke at May Day gatherings at Hamilton, Kilmarnock and Paisley, before headlining an evening meeting at St Andrew's Halls with Constance Markiewicz, the heroine of the Irish Rising and now minister of labour in the Irish Republican government. He told the audience:

> ... they must not be content to have a Republic only in Ireland, but must also strike out to have a Socialist Republic all over Britain as well as Ireland, and to have in addition a Socialist Republic all over the world. ... He hoped when

the Revolution came about in this country that the Celtic fringe would play an important part in the struggle.⁹

Maclean may still have been burning with evolutionary fervour, but elsewhere the May Day message was much more soothing. Ramsay MacDonald, Philip Snowden and other leading Labour figures went to South Wales, the stronghold of direct action politics, on May Day 1919. The central theme of their speeches was that Sankey had proved the constitutional road to socialism was alive and well. There was no need for a workers' revolution as the commission would result in the old order being destroyed.¹⁰

~

While Maclean's agitational work had taken precedence in the turbulent opening months of 1919, he hadn't completely neglected his educational endeavours. Promptly after his release from prison, he had restarted his Sunday afternoon economics class and had been having regular meetings with the members of the Scottish Labour College committee. During the spring, district conferences took place at Aberdeen, Arbroath, Dundee, Fife, Edinburgh and Falkirk, and some local trade union branches agreed to levy their members to support the work of the college.

The Labour College committee also had meetings with the Plebs League, the English organisation connected with the Central Labour College in London. As a result, the two organisations agreed to unite. A joint conference on 24 May was attended by 571 delegates, and it was decided to open day classes all over the country on 1 September. In August, Maclean and William MacLaine, a leader of the English shop stewards' movement and a prominent member of the BSP, were appointed full-time tutors.

Maclean's whirlwind procession of meetings and speeches continued through the early summer. On 25 May he was at Glasgow Green protesting about the detention of US socialist Eugene Debs. In the last week of May he was in Huddersfield and in Ayrshire, campaigning with the miners. In early June he was back at Glasgow Green, protesting about the imprisonment of Willie Gallacher, then he was off again fanning the flames of discontent with the miners in Durham and West Lothian. On 3 July he spoke at the welcome home for Gallacher before accepting an invitation to visit Dublin. There he found the whole city bristling with soldiers. No declaration of war had yet been made and the Dáil of the Irish Republic had not been declared illegal, but the British Army was there in full force. Maclean was disappointed to see Scottish regiments among the troops.[11]

His visit to Ireland gave him much to think about, although it wasn't until the following year that he penned a series of articles and pamphlets that set out his views.

47

NATIONALISATION

The second set of Coal Commission reports was released on 20 June. The majority report from chairman Justice Sankey recommended nationalisation of the coal industry. His report was assented to by the six representatives of the miners, who nevertheless submitted a separate report that included some differences of emphasis. The most significant of these was that the mineral owners should not receive any compensation for the mineral rights to be acquired by the state. A third report was submitted by the government nominees and coal owners' representatives while a fourth bore the signature of Sir Arthur Duckham.

While in general the latter reports agreed that the system of individual private ownership was not the most effective, and perhaps the state had a role to play, their real position was expressed thus:

> We have carefully weighed the whole of the evidence, and have come to the conclusion that the nationalisation of the coal industry in any form would be detrimental to the development of the industry and the economic life of the country.[1]

The reports presented Lloyd George with a problem. The government had promised to adopt the interim report, nationalisation proposals and all, 'in letter and spirit'. But the coalition government Lloyd George headed was composed overwhelmingly of Unionist MPs, who were ideologically opposed to nationalisation in any form. The coal owners, who had been caught off guard during the first phase of the inquiry, regained their composure during the second round of sittings and began to make the argument that the nationalisation of the mines would be the first step towards the nationalisation of all industries.[2]

The Mining Association of Great Britain (MAGB) started to rally the support of its own members and those of other employer associations. They contacted MPs who represented business interests; and the Parliamentary Coal Committee, an organisation of coal owner MPs, circulated a memo calling for steps to be taken 'to protect our great industries against the organised, revolutionary and predatory forces of direct action, and against the nationalisation of the mines'. Three hundred and five MPs signed the memo, and it was presented to Lloyd George in mid-July.[3]

On 8 July, the Cabinet agreed on a strategy to exploit the poor state of public finances to paint the miners' demands as excessive and damaging to the national economy. It was decided to increase the price of coal by 6 shillings a ton, with the rise to come into effect on 15 July, the day before the first Sankey Award came into effect. In announcing the increase in the House of Commons on 9 July, the Minister of Reconstruction, Sir Auckland Geddes, explained, 'It is hoped that this increase will meet the increased cost due to the payment of the Sankey wage, the forthcoming reduction in hours, and the diminished output per man shift.'[4]

Evidence about the decrease in productivity had been placed before the Sankey inquiry, but there had not been time to examine its causes. However, the miners believed the deliberate under-resourcing of pits by owners faced with the prospect of nationalisation was the primary cause. The coupling of the drop in output with the increase in the price of coal was recognised by the miners as a pincer movement by the owners and the government against nationalisation.

Bonar Law applied a clever twist in a Commons debate on 14 July when he offered to delay the price rise for three months, if the miners were prepared to work with the coal controller to increase output and agree not to strike. Although the miners' MPs favoured accepting Bonar Law's offer, the MFGB annual conference which opened at Keswick on 15 July resoundingly rejected it.

There was widespread disgruntlement among miners over the practical implementation of the Sankey Award, whose provisions came into effect on 16 July. Many had interpreted the rearrangement of hours and piece rates to mean local differentials would continue and their working hours would be reduced by one hour, rather than the more literal 'that seven hours be substituted for eight'. The bigger problem, which affected all areas, was how far piece rates should be increased to guarantee the same earnings from a shorter working day. This was being worked out between miners and owners at a district level, when the coal controller, on the instructions of the Cabinet, intervened and announced there would be a 12.5 per cent ceiling on any increase. This was a bombshell for the miners, who held that 14.3 per cent, or the one-seventh increase necessary to bridge the difference between the eight and seven hour shifts, was the absolute minimum they would consider. Suddenly the Sankey Award seemed to represent a pay cut.[5]

In Yorkshire, the district miners' association and the owners had already agreed on the 14.3 per cent increase and were in discussion about the hours issue when the coal controller intervened. The owners withdrew their offer and on 16 July 200,000 Yorkshire miners began a month-long official strike. By the end of the week, another 200,000 miners were on strike on issues arising from the Sankey Award. The areas affected included Scotland, Lancashire, Nottinghamshire, Derbyshire, the Midlands, the North-East, South Wales and Kent.

Lancashire, where only 30 per cent of the workforce was engaged in mining, was not an area noted for its militancy. But at a large Hands off Russia protest in Wigan on 20 July calls for action on the government's coal policy came to dominate proceedings. The next day 1000 miners waiting for trains to take them to the pits outside the town held an impromptu meeting and decided to strike. An unofficial meeting that evening voted to spread the strike across the coalfield.

Wigan became the storm centre of the strike due to the presence of an active miners' reform committee, which had been formed with the assistance of James Macdougall.[6] By means of weekly meetings the MRC had built up a base in the latter stages of the war and had been boosted by a recent tour by John Maclean. Their audience had been greatly enlarged by the Yorkshire strike and the unwillingness of the local officials to lead similar action.[7]

Quickly the strike movement began to move beyond its original aims, and the fight became not only about the implementation of the first Sankey Report but about nationalisation. Suspicion about the government's bona fides was heightened by its apparent collusion with the owners. The MFGB's response seemed weak and insufficient.

On top of this, the government's support for the White armies in Russia strengthened the view that it was fundamentally pro-capitalist and anti-working class. Hands off Russia meetings held during the strike often turned to the issues of output and nationalisation, while strike meetings usually carried resolutions for ceasing intervention in Russia.[8]

~

More generally the public mood was dark, and there was a hard edge of bitterness in what Labour MP and miners' leader Vernon Hartshorn described as 'the profound stirring of the masses' in July and August. After the signing of the Versailles peace treaty on 28 June, the national peace celebrations that followed on the weekend of 19 and 20 July only served to deepen public discontent. As Martin Ives observed:

> For many of the poorest sections of society, the military victory had been pyrrhic. Halfway through 1919 and a land fit for heroes was nowhere to be seen. The cost of living had continued to rise, food was still scarce in some places, and of poor quality in many more, there was significant unemployment in some sectors of the economy, and nothing substantial had been achieved in the area of social reform. On top of this there was the continuation of conscription (another broken promise) and Churchill's adventures against the infant Soviet Union. Taken together these created a sense of bitterness and betrayal that was as wide as it was deep. The dry social tinder was ignited by Peace Day riots which erupted in spectacular fashion in Luton, and then spread across Britain.[9]

As well as Luton, where the Town Hall was burned down, there was serious rioting at Coventry, Edinburgh, Greenwich, Hull, Liverpool, Swindon and Wolverhampton. Aggrieved ex-servicemen were often at the root of the disturbances, which tended to flare up and quickly dissipate. But they were accompanied by a revival of industrial militancy, which heralded a mighty battle between labour and capital.

The miners' partners in the Triple Alliance were both on the move. The National Union of Railwaymen was preparing a national program for submission to the Railway Executive Committee, and the Transport Workers' Federation was demanding a 10s pay rise. The bakers were on strike in several districts, causing a shortage of bread and at the end of July even the police voted to strike, in protest at the Police Bill that outlawed trade unionism in the force.

The government was deeply worried. Sir Auckland Geddes was fearful the Yorkshire strike might result in a complete strike of all the miners, and this might be followed by the Triple Alliance coming out.[10]

He wasn't far wrong. A Triple Alliance delegate conference on 23 July decided to ballot its union members on 'direct action to compel the Government to abolish conscription, to discontinue military intervention in Russia and military intervention in trade union disputes at home'.[11]

On 21 July, Lloyd George told the War Cabinet he would like to see the mine owners, because if the government was to fight it must be on firm ground and have public opinion behind it.

> The whole of the future of the country might be at stake and if the Government were beaten and the miners won, it would result in a Soviet Government. A similar situation might result to that of the first days of the Revolution in Russia and though Parliament might remain, the real Parliament would be at the headquarters of the Miners' Federation in Russell Square.[12]

~

The only way the Yorkshire Miners' Association could realise the 14.3 per cent increase being offered was to give up its local customs and work a longer day on Saturday. To increase pressure on the government, on 19 July the district council pulled out the pumpmen and winding-enginemen, thereby opening the pits to the danger of flooding. The government responded by sending in 2500 Navy ratings to pump the mines. In announcing the decision in the House of Commons, Lloyd George said, 'The action which has been taken by the miners in that district has not only jeopardised their own means of livelihood, but also threatens with disaster everyone in the district in which they live.'[13] The establishment press was characteristically outraged, with the *Times* calling the miners' behaviour 'naked sabotage'.[14]

But the *Times* leader in the same edition also criticised the government for its failure to give the country a clear lead on nationalisation. 'Suspicion that Ministers are prone not to decide questions on their merits and on broad questions of public policy, but are mainly occupied in manoeuvring for tactical positions, lies at the root of much of the distrust with which the government is regarded,' it said. Furthermore, it observed, 'The Coal Commission reported under a time limit. And yet, after pressing the Commission to report, the Government proceed as though the definition of their own policy were not a matter of urgency.'[15]

Indeed, when questioned in the House of Commons the very next day, Sir Auckland Geddes played a very straight bat in response. 'The whole of the recommendations in the Reports are receiving the earnest consideration of the Government,' he said, 'but I am not in a position at the present time to make a statement on the subject.'[16]

Facing the escalating strike movement, with Yorkshire resolute and the unofficial movement growing in influence everywhere else, the government decided to back the authority of union executive power. On 25 July, the government conceded the MFGB's demands on piece rates passed at its Keswick conference. Following mass meetings in all districts on the weekend of 26 and 27 July, miners drifted back to work. Although not in Yorkshire.

The formula of an 11.1 per cent increase for the loss of 47 minutes only gave Yorkshire a maximum increase of 12.2 per cent, a figure that the district council regarded as completely unacceptable, and after referring the issue to the branches, it was decided to fight on.[17]

The Yorkshire strike was solid, but all attempts to widen its goals beyond local terms and conditions proved fruitless. The miners passively accepted the directions of their leaders not to interfere with the Royal Navy sailors deployed to the pumps, nor to encourage other districts to come out in support. Council delegates told their members to conduct themselves as if they were on holiday. Families flocked to the seaside and many of the younger men 'played an immense amount of cricket'.[18]

The government, having reached a national agreement with the MFGB on piece rates was loath to grant any further concessions. It played a waiting game, and as the weeks passed its only comment on nationalisation of the mines was that it was still 'under consideration'.

The stalemate continued until financial hardship and food shortages started to bite. On 12 August, delegates at a Yorkshire district council meeting voted to recommend that branches call off the strike. The branches accepted the recommendation, and two days later delegates met again and voted to approve an immediate resumption of work.

The subsidence of the unofficial strikes and the defeat of the Yorkshire action were accompanied by other defeats and retreats in the industrial world. The police strike collapsed, a rail strike in the north-east was contained, and then, on 12 August. the Triple Alliance executive voted to postpone its ballot on military conscription and military intervention in Russia.[19]

On 18 August, the last parliamentary sitting day until 22 October, Lloyd George stood up in the House of Commons and provided a review of the trade and industrial position of the country. During his address, he announced the government had decided to reject nationalisation of the mines.

Instead, he proposed the minerals were to be purchased by the state; a fund would be set up to improve housing and social conditions in mining communities; that the state would not purchase the business of the mines and certainly not run them; that unification should be promoted by a scheme of amalgamation in defined areas; and that miners would have representatives on the boards responsible for district management.

Robert Page Arnot summed it up as not even a plan for 'one national coal trust, but a dozen or so gigantic combines that would benefit neither the nation nor the consumer, nor yet the miner'.[20]

Vernon Hartshorn spoke for the miners in the House later that day. 'We did not ask for a commission. We accepted it. We gave evidence before it. Why was the commission set up? Was it a huge game of bluff? Was it never intended that if the reports favoured nationalisation we would get it? Why was the question sent at all to the commission? That is the kind of question the miners of the country will ask, and they will say, "We have been deceived, betrayed, duped".'

Robert Smillie later reflected: 'You may wonder why those words came from Vernon rather than from me. As President of the MFGB I should have been the first to respond on behalf of the miners. The simple truth was I was in no fit state to respond. Again exhausted beyond belief, every emotion torn from me, I was in despair. I do not mind admitting that, alone in my hotel bedroom that night, I wept. No doubt there was an element of self-pity in that but most of the tears were shed on behalf of the mining community. I wept for men and women who had been the victims of a heinous act of betrayal.'[21]

48

THE MOMENT PASSES

The MFGB took a measured approach to the news of the government's denial of mining nationalisation. An executive committee meeting on 2 September recommended that a full delegate conference scheduled for the following day condemn the government's decision on nationalisation, but to abstain from strike action until the Trades Union Congress considered the question. They further proposed that the TUC commit to 'fullest and most effective action'.[1]

At the full delegate meeting the next day, Robert Smillie said the executive had rejected the government's scheme because they honestly believed it was not the best method of getting the largest possible output of coal. He also stressed that while they were referring the issue to the forthcoming TUC meeting in Glasgow, they reserved their right to strike.

Vernon Hartshorn summarised the whole affair by outlining the reasons, as he saw them, why the government had gone back on its pledges to the miners.

> The coal owners practically purchased the press of the country. Look at every meeting of directors that is held in the mining industry today. What do you find? You find what had never appeared before – whole pages of the daily papers are devoted to the advertisement of speeches of directors of colliery companies, and in every speech that is being delivered they are making nationalisation their one and sole topic. They have been passing resolutions, issuing circulars, and sending them to the members of the House of Commons, practically amounting to a threat that if they wanted in the future the support of these shareholders in the mining industry they must vote against nationalisation. The prime minister was informed that he must not introduce a scheme of nationalisation. What has happened is simply this, that the prime minister and the government have surrendered to the mass of stakeholders.[2]

The executive committee's resolution on nationalisation was passed unanimously.[3]

~

On 4 September, a full delegate meeting of the Triple Alliance accepted the decision of its three unions to adjourn the ballot vote on direct action to secure the abolition of conscription and the withdrawal of British troops from Russia until after the Trades Union Congress.[4]

The Glasgow congress was scheduled to open on 9 September and was framed as a battle between supporters and opponents of 'direct action', i.e., strikes. Anticipating the debate to come, on the eve of the opening day TUC president Stuart-Bunning made his position perfectly clear. "I do not believe in industrial strikes on political matters. I do not despair of constitutional methods. There is no political reform which the working people cannot achieve by the ballot box, and direct action is a confession of failure.'[5]

The congress got under way with a paragraph by paragraph consideration of the TUC executive committee report. Back in April 1919, the committee had denied a resolution from the Triple Alliance calling for a special congress to consider conscription and British intervention in Russia. Its reasons, as set out in the report were: 'To have called a special congress to consider a strike ballot would have identified the congress with the policy of a national strike on political matters.'

Robert Smillie moved that the paragraph should be referred back to the committee – tantamount to a vote of censure. He declared that the committee had lost the confidence of the trade union movement and they must be taught that they were its servants and not its masters. He stressed the question was whether the committee was justified or not in refusing to give the movement the opportunity of expressing its feeling through a special conference. The motion was passed. It was a slap in the face to the opponents of direct action.[6]

On the morning of the third day of the congress, the issue of nationalisation of the mines was considered. By an almost unanimous vote, the congress declared its readiness 'to cooperate with the Miners' Federation of Great Britain to the fullest extent, with a view to compelling the Government to adopt the scheme of national ownership and joint control recommended by the majority of the Coal Industry Commission.'[7]

The resolution instructed the TUC parliamentary committee, in conjunction with the MFGB, to immediately interview the prime minister to insist on the government adopting the majority report. The sting in the resolution was in its tail. It read, 'In the event of the Government still refusing to accept this position, a special congress shall be convened for the purpose of deciding the form of action to be taken to compel the Government to accept the majority report of the Commission'.[8]

An attempt was made on the following day to explicitly rule out direct action. A resolution from MP Tom Shaw of the Textile Workers sought a declaration 'against the principle of industrial action in purely political action'.

Speaking in favour of his resolution Shaw said: 'In opposing direct action on purely political grounds, one has to deal not only with the words "industrial action" but with the explanations given by its apostles – I refer to Mr Robert Smillie and Mr Robert Williams [Transport Workers] (cheers). They have over and over made clear without a shadow of a doubt what their idea of industrial action. Their idea of industrial action is to create a revolution in this country, and their idea of government is the Soviet Government system of Russia.'[9]

JH Thomas from the National Union of Railwaymen pointed out the downsides of a vote either way.

> '... I should be blind to the danger if I did not say frankly that this motion, if carried, may be construed by our opponents as a lever against legitimate industrial action. On the other hand, if defeated, it will mean to our rank and file that we are in favour of direct action, which we are not. You may ask: "What are you supporting?" (Hear, hear.) My answer is that I am trying honestly to put the logic of the position before you. We have arrived at a decision this week that requires above everything else that this congress should leave Glasgow as a united congress. I am anxious also because I believe we shall have a general election and Labour in the next few months will have such a chance as it never had before. Thus I beg the congress not to give a lever to the opponents of Labour which would be ruinous to every Labour man standing in any constituency. I am not afraid of the issue of direct action in the sense in which it has been discussed. I am not concerned in arguing its application to Lenin or Trotsky: but I am concerned with letting it be the declared policy of this congress that we still believe in industrial power, we still believe in political power, and we are going to do nothing by vote or action that will weaken the possibilities of either.' (Cheers.)[10]

Shaw's assertion was roundly rejected by Frank Hodges, general secretary of the miners' federation. 'He {Shaw] said, to my surprise, that the desire of the direct action movement is to establish the Soviet system of government in this country. There is nothing more remote from the truth. I do not believe that with the characteristics of the British race, and with our traditions and institutions, a Soviet system would ever become adaptable to our country.'

Hodges called the resolution theoretical, saying if a conference be asked to give a decision on the question of direct action, let it be on a concrete fact. 'If that fact is big enough, if it is unsocial enough, if it is sufficiently in antagonism to the best interests of the working class, I have no fear that the working class will not say, "We will use to the very fullest capacity the power that we possess to rid society of a tradition and an institution which dwarfs and threatens and thwarts the working class wherever they turn." (Cheers).'[11]

No doubt acutely conscious of the divisive nature of the resolution, and even though more than a dozen delegates rose to continue the debate, the president accepted a motion for the 'previous question', that is, that the resolution be not further discussed or voted on. The previous question was put and narrowly carried, although it emerged the following day that the miners had voted against the motion to secure a straight vote.

Discussion of direct action continued the following day. JH Thomas moved the foreshadowed Triple Alliance resolution calling for the repeal of the Conscription Acts and the withdrawal of British troops from Russia, and failing compliance by the government, that a special congress should be called 'to decide what action should be taken'.

Responding to Tom Shaw's comments, Robert Smillie declared, to cheers and laughter, he was 'an evolutionary revolutionist'. He continued, 'I have for 30 years preached the necessity of an industrial revolution in this country, and I will go on preaching that as long as my life continues. Life at the present time, and in the past, has not been worth living and it is our business to advocate an industrial revolution.'

He strongly supported the resolution, saying: 'It goes the length of saying we will approach the government on the two very important questions of conscription and intervention in Russia, and if the government does not give a satisfactory reply, then it will be compulsory on the parliamentary committee [of the TUC] to convene a conference, in which I hope there will be no dodges to prevent us from getting a true issue. I hope congress will pass this resolution with such unanimity as will let the government know we are really in earnest.' (Cheers.)[12]

The resolution was carried with only two dissentient voices.

The *Times* concluded that the trade union movement no longer considered its grievances as 'sufficiently acute to justify recourse to a general strike'. Furthermore, it had decided that the methods of indirect action should be exhausted before the question of direct action is even considered.[13]

On 9 October a thirty-strong deputation from the parliamentary committee of the TUC and the executive committee of the MFGB met with Lloyd George and other Cabinet ministers at 10 Downing Street. Lloyd George listened patiently as Robert Smillie ran through the arguments for nationalisation that had been detailed in the Sankey Report. The prime minister then trotted out all the reasons the government couldn't possibly agree, including that they never pledged to implement the findings of the Coal Commission; that the commission was unbalanced (even though he appointed it); that because of the public mood after the recent railwaymen's strike, a strike against the government as employer, the moment was 'inopportune'; that it was a 'risky business' and would be an 'experiment'; and so on. Realising they were beaten, the deputation thanked Lloyd George for his time and meekly retired.[14]

Nevertheless, John Maclean was upbeat about the outcome. Writing in the *Call*, he set out the template for his revolution that never was:

> Can the miners afford to wait a month or two, until March if need be? I believe they can, if they apply the ca'-canny[15] policy and are backed up similarly by other workers.
>
> Time tells in our favour. The miners are rightly starting off on a publicity campaign. Let them perfect their organisation, and see to it that a Central Committee of Labour is at once established, whilst the unions amalgamate along the lines of industry.
>
> Let the unofficial movement also play its part in furthering the workshop committees with appropriate district and national committees. Let them also adopt a united programme around which all workers can rally.
>
> At this stage we of the BSP can play a supremely important part. We can call into being workshop committees with a right class bias; we can provide them with a programme identical with that of our South Wales comrades for the mining industry.
>
> Let us urge full socialisation of mines and other trustified industries,

full industrial control by the workers involved, though modified to permit of the use of the co-operative movement, control of the education of the workers, a thirty-hour week, fifty per cent increase in wages, communally produced houses, withdrawal of British troops and aid from all parts of the world, the abolition of the army and the navy and the establishment of a workers' defence force, and the transfer of the functions of Parliament to Labour's Central Committee.[16]

The movement for nationalisation of the mines gradually lost impetus. At the next TUC meeting in December 1919, instead of taking action as flagged at Glasgow, or even discussing it, the congress decided to take no decision for another two or three months. Instead, there was a majority in favour of a 'Mines for the nation' campaign to win public support.

Addressing the delegates, Robert Smillie accused the government of going back on its word regarding the Sankey report because of the power of the coal-owning interest. 'If the government refused to carry out the finding of their commission, then it would be the duty of the miners to leave the solution to the whole organised labour movement. Unless they nationalised the mines, action would be taken and it would be constitutional action, because the great trade union movement was perfectly entitled to use its power to force the government on a question of that kind.'[17]

The public campaign was a fizzer, and when the Trades Union Congress met again in March 1920 to consider a request from the MFGB for a general strike, the vote to strike was lost, with less than 22 per cent in favour. Nationalisation of the mines was added to the list of issues on which Labour would fight the next general election.[18]

49
BRITAIN'S WAR AGAINST RUSSIA

The Hands off Russia movement that gathered momentum in the early months of 1919 had good reason to be concerned about the fate of the Soviet government. Short of declaring outright war, the Allies were doing every in their power to throttle the infant regime before it found is feet. When Woodrow Wilson's Russian peace proposals fell over in February 1919, the Bolsheviks were under threat from all points of the compass, with Allied forces providing crucial support to the White Russian counter-revolutionaries.

In the west, a British fleet pinned the Soviet Baltic fleet in its base at Kronstadt and provided military supplies to a variety of forces fighting the Bolsheviks. In North Russia, there were around 30,000 Allied troops, mainly British, in the areas around Murmansk and Arkhangel. A further 30,000 were with the White Russian General Denikin in the Caucasus in the south. Most formidably, in the east a motley collection of foreign troops was operating in the Urals and Siberia cheek by jowl with forces led by the White Russian leader, Admiral Kolchak of the Black Sea fleet. In January, Denikin had acknowledged Kolchak as the Supreme Ruler of Russia.[1]

The situation in the Baltic was complicated. After securing its independence from Russia after the Bolshevik revolution, Finland had descended into four months of bloody civil war. The White Finn forces, led by General Mannerheim, and supported by 13,000 German troops, prevailed against the Finnish Red Guards and established a government hostile to the Bolsheviks.

In November 1918, White Russian General Nikolai Yudenich arrived in Helsinki. Calling on the 2500 Russian officers who had fled to Finland, he set about raising an army. Admiral Kolchak appointed Yudenich commander-in-chief of the Northern Corps, which included the White Russian forces in Estonia. Neither the Finns or the Estonians welcomed Yudenich, or any anti-Bolshevik Russian supremacist who refused to acknowledge their independence, but gritted their teeth. As it is said, the enemy of my enemy is my friend.

Following the signing of the Allied-German armistice, on 22 November Lenin ordered the Red Army to move into Estonia. On 1 December, Bolshevik forces also invaded Latvia and then, on 12 December, Lithuania. But in all three Baltic states there was strong resistance. In each case, the fight was for national identity and independence from Moscow.

The Estonian government appealed to Britain for military support. The War Cabinet authorised the dispatch of a naval squadron to Tallinn with rifles, Lewis guns and artillery. Two Soviet destroyers sent out from the Kronstadt naval base to investigate reports of the British arrival were captured and handed over the to the Estonians. The Estonians counterattacked on 7 January and by mid-February had forced the Red Army back over the border.

German troops were permitted to stay in the Baltic region pending the conclusion of the peace conference at Versailles. In many cases they provided the most effective barrier to Bolshevik expansion. On 16 January a combined Latvian/German/White Russian force pushed the Red Latvian Rifle Brigade back and gave the Latvian government breathing space to build up its forces. In Lithuania, Red forces had occupied two-thirds of the country by mid-January but fighting there would eventually involve Russians, Germans and Poles.[2]

In the Baltic Sea, the Royal Navy's 1st Light Cruiser Squadron dominated the eastern coastline, providing cover for the flanks of the various anti-Bolshevik forces on the shore.

~

On the Black Sea, the withdrawal of the Germans from southern Ukraine after the armistice saw French-led forces land at Odessa. Throughout December 1918 and January 1919, the Allies managed to take control of various cities in Ukraine and Crimea, including Sevastapol and Kherson. However, with troops short in number and demoralised, unwilling to risk their lives in Russia for a cause they did not understand, the French commanders saw little future for the campaign. To the north, the Red Army recaptured Kiev and Kharkov in January, then forced the French to abandon Kherson in March. On 1 April, with little more than the area around Odessa left under French control, Paris reluctantly gave the order to evacuate.[3]

~

Lloyd George had appointed Winston Churchill as secretary of state for war in January 1919. At the War Cabinet meeting of 4 March, Churchill sought a definite policy on Russia. All Lloyd George could offer was to have the matter discussed at the peace conference on his return to Paris. In the meantime, the general intention of the government was to withdraw troops from every part of Russia as soon as practicable, and then to supply Russian commanders with guns, airplanes, munitions and everything else that might be of use, except troops and money.[4]

Churchill sought the authority to take 'adequate military measures to support and reinforce the men in North Russia until they could be withdrawn'. Unless he was given the authority, he warned the consequences could be 'absolutely disastrous'. In the Caucasus, subject to a date agreed in Paris, his wish was to evacuate 30,000 troops, but to 'make it up' to General Denikin by replacing them with a military mission of 1000 NCOs. He also proposed to recall the two British battalions in Siberia and send a similar military mission to Admiral Kolchak.

In April, Lloyd George updated the House of Commons on the Paris peace talks and used the address to outline the government's policy towards Russia. Noting that some were saying 'Use force', while others said 'Make peace', he declared, 'Russia is a country which it is very easy to invade, but very difficult to conquer. It has never been conquered by a foreign foe, although it has been successfully invaded many times. It is a country which it is easy to get into, but very difficult to get out of. You have only to look at what has happened in the last few years to the Germans.'[5]

He continued, 'I should not be doing my duty as head of the Government unless I stated quite frankly to the House my earnest conviction - that to attempt military intervention in Russia would be the greatest act of stupidity that any Government could possibly commit.'[6]

He justified the government's support for Kolchak, Denikin, and the other White Russian forces by claiming, rather fancifully, they had raised their armies at the instigation of the British to stop Germany accessing Russian resources. 'It is our business, since we asked them to take this step, since we promised support to them if they took this step, and since by taking this stand they contributed largely to the triumph of the Allies, it is our business to stand by our friends. Therefore, we are not sending troops, but we are supplying goods.'[7]

While White and Red forces were in continuous conflict throughout Russia in 1918, evidence of Lloyd George's claim of White Russians fighting Germans is difficult to find.

~

Fresh from a trip to the peace conference in Paris, on 11 June Churchill reported to the War Cabinet that the British commander General Ironside proposed certain operations in North Russia. These would depart from the hitherto defensive policy and constitute 'definite aggressive action against the Bolsheviks'. Churchill said he understood the plans had been submitted to Lloyd George who had 'accorded his sanction, subject to ... the approval of the War Cabinet'.[8]

In late May and early June, when the ice had melted sufficiently, the British garrisons in North Russia had been replaced by two brigade groups of 4000 men each, and the unhappy troops who had endured the Arctic winter were evacuated. Ironside's plan was for these fresh troops to mount an assault up the River Dvina to Kotlas and there to link up with the Czechoslovak troops on the right wing of Admiral Kolchak's Siberian forces. Once the line had been established, the British would gracefully withdraw to Arkhangel and embark for home. The plan looked spiffing on paper, but the vast distances and unhospitable terrain made the scheme unrealistic.

The War Cabinet approved the operations, but almost immediately word came of serious setbacks for Kolchak. Concerned about White advances west of the Urals that threatened Kazan and opened a route to Moscow, the Bolsheviks had moved troops up from the south. On 8 June, Red forces retook Ufa, which the Whites had captured in March. This prompted a general White retreat and by the end of the month, the Czechoslovak troops to the north were also in retreat. The War Cabinet meeting of 9 July was informed that the British 'offensive-defensive operation' had been abandoned.

Ostensibly, by the end of June General Ironside had 22,000 Russian troops under his command. However, the numerous mutinies of these soldiers had a corrosive effect on the morale of Allied troops. In early July 1919, a White unit under British command killed its British officers and deserted to the Bolsheviks. Then on 20 July, 3,000 White troops in the key city of Onega mutinied and handed over the city to the Bolsheviks. The loss of the only overland route between Murmansk and Arkhangel was a significant blow.

On 11 August General Rawlinson arrived to supervise the evacuation of British forces. It was planned to mount offensives against the Bolsheviks on both the Dvina and Murmansk fronts in August and September to leave the White forces in a good position after the withdrawal.

~

In the south, the Royal Navy had the Caspian Sea well in hand, with a deployment of eight armed merchantmen, twelve coastal motorboats and seaplanes. They were supplying the Ural Cossacks at the sea's northeast shore and bottling up Red warships in the Volga estuary. When the ice in the north of the sea broke up, the Soviet fleet relocated to Alexandrovsky Fort on the eastern shore. On 21 May the British attacked, and the Reds lost nine vessels, including a destroyer, a minelayer, a floating battery and auxiliary units, while the Soviet flagship, the auxiliary cruiser *Caspian*, was damaged by two direct hits.

Over the following days the remaining ships of the Soviet fleet managed to escape back to the shallow waters of the Volga estuary below Astrakhan, where the larger British ships could not follow. On 20 July, over Churchill's protests, the British personnel were ordered to withdraw, and left via Baku and Batumi. Their ships were handed over to the naval forces of General Denikin.[9]

In June, with the assistance of the Royal Air Force, the White Army of the Caucasus took Tsaritsyn [later named Stalingrad (1925–1961), and now Volgograd]. During the attack on the city, RAF Sopwith Camels dispersed Red Army cavalry and shot down an observation balloon that would have spotted the six British tanks lining up for the assault. There was only enough fuel for one tank, but it made short work of the barbed wire defences and the first line of trenches and was enough to put the Red defenders to flight.[10]

~

In the east, the overall Allied commander was the French General Pierre Janin. Appointed by the Supreme Council in Paris, under his command were a French colonial battalion and 3000 Romanians at Irkutsk; 8500 Americans between Vladivostok and Amur; two British battalions from Hong Kong; a Canadian battalion and 1600 Italians at Vladivostok; and controlling the trans-Siberian railway, 70,000 Czech troops ostensibly on their way to Vladivostock, and thence to Prague. There was also a Japanese contingent of 12,000, not under Janin, who had landed at Vladivostok in April 1918 and rapidly spread west.[11]

Even though there seemed little hope of an early resolution to the conflict, the Allied Powers in Paris stated at the end of May that they were prepared to continue supplying Kolchak's forces with munitions, supplies and food 'provided they are satisfied that it will really help the Russian people to liberty, self-government and peace'. The conditions included the summoning of a constituent assembly, the recognition of independent states formerly part of the Russian Empire, and that foreign debts would be honoured.

On 12 June, the leaders of the Allied Powers expressed their satisfaction with Kolchak's apparent acceptance of their conditions. Churchill pushed for the British government to recognise Kolchak as the head of the Russian government, but the furthest Foreign Secretary Lord Curzon would go was to accept him as the leader of the Siberian provisional government.[12]

~

At the War Cabinet meeting of 27 June, the Permanent Secretary of the Ministry of Labour, David Shackleton, was invited to give his views on the attitude of labour towards the government's Russia policy. Shackleton, who became a cotton worker at the age of nine, had previously been a union leader, a Labour MP and the chairman of the Trades Union Congress. Before the war he had impressed Churchill, who in 1910 invited him to join the civil service. He told the cabinet that the feeling in labour circles was very strong about British intervention in Russia.

The moderate section of the Labour Party was doing its best to restrain the more ardent spirits, he said, but it was doubtful they would be able to resist them for more than the next few weeks. It appeared likely that the Triple Alliance proposed to call a general strike to compel the government to withdraw all troops from Russia and refrain in future from interfering in its affairs.

Practically all the most influential Labour newspapers declared there was a chance of establishing a successful government along Soviet lines and the main obstacle in its way was the policy adopted by the British government. He was surprised at the extent to which men of all classes were now coming round to the view that the Soviet government should be given a fair chance. A further point was that Britain had never attempted to interfere when the tsar was in power. There was no doubt that this feeling was spreading and he was afraid that the agitation might assume formidable proportions.

Shackleton warned the War Cabinet that there was bound to be trouble if in early September, in or about the meeting of the TUC, a casualty list was published of British casualties killed in Russia while fighting to suppress a Soviet government.[13]

~

At the War Cabinet meeting of 4 July, the Admiralty proposed that in the event of the peace terms being signed in Paris, the position in the Baltic should be reviewed. British naval forces there were 'safeguarding the flanks of our friends'. If the Germans succeeded in occupying the Baltic provinces, those flanks would disappear and the Germans could control the coast from East Prussia to Petrograd. The Admiralty recommended that peace not be ratified until the Germans were out of the Baltic provinces; that the blockade of Petrograd be maintained until it was 'in the possession of our friends'; and that the supply of munitions and equipment should be redoubled and hastened.

Churchill responded that the War Office was taking no responsibility for the capture of Petrograd. The threat to Petrograd from General Yudenich's Northwestern Army (formerly the Northern Corps) had the effect of drawing Red troops away from the south, but he thought the capture of the city unlikely.

The Admiralty did not want to maintain a big fleet in the Baltic, but sought a decision from the government as to whether in the event of the Bolshevik fleet attempting to come out, the navy ships were authorised to engage them. Both the Admiralty and the naval officers on the spot were in ignorance of the exact position; the question was, were we, or were we not, at war with the Bolsheviks?

In reply, Lloyd George said, actually, we were at war with the Bolsheviks but we had decided not to make war. In other words, he did not intend to put great armies into Russia to fight the Bolsheviks.

The War Cabinet decided: 'In fact, a state of war did exist between Great Britain and the Bolshevik Government of Russia' and as a consequence, 'our naval forces in Russian waters should be authorised to engage enemy forces by land and sea, when necessary.'[14]

On 5 August in the House of Commons, Liberal MP Lieutenant Commander Joseph Kenworthy asked whether war had been declared between Great Britain and the Russian Soviet Republic and if not, why a blockade was being exercised against the Russian Soviet Republic.

The Under-Secretary of State for Foreign Affairs, Cecil Harmsworth responded. 'The answer to the first part of the question is in the negative,' he said. 'No blockade has been declared or is being exercised against any part of Russia. ... Although no blockade exists either in the White, Baltic or Black Seas, the existing conditions which are the result of the aggressive measures taken by the Soviet party in Russia against those portions of the former Empire which decline to acknowledge their authority render it, I believe, physically impossible for goods to reach the interior of Russia.'

Captain William Wedgwood Benn asked, 'Are we at war with the Soviet Republic?'

Harmsworth adroitly dodged the question. 'The hon. and gallant Member knows that that subject has been discussed in this House.'[15]

Sir Donald Maclean, Liberal leader of the opposition, then asked if Churchill would state the estimated cost of British operations in Russia, and the estimated cost of munitions of war, food, or money sent in support of Russian military operations since the armistice. Churchill said he proposed to make a statement on the subject before the House rose.[16]

On 15 August, the costs of the Russian intervention, from 11 November 1918 to 31 July 1919, were published in the *Times*. The grand total was £69.28 million (equivalent to £4.57 billion in 2025 currency). The first category, British naval and military operations was broken down into three parts: occupation and withdrawal from Murmansk and Arkhangel (22 per cent of the overall total); maintaining an army in the Caucasus (4 per cent); and naval operations in the Baltic and Black Seas (7.5 per cent). The second category, assistance to the Russian armies, was also broken down into three lots: 4 per cent went to the Baltic states, including the Northwestern Army; 21 per cent to Admiral Kolchak; and 37.5 per cent to General Denikin.[17]

On 6 September, the commanding officer of the 2nd Battalion Hampshire Regiment, Lieutenant Colonel John Sherwood-Kelly, published an open letter in the *Daily Express* lambasting the North Russia campaign, stating that the volunteer British troops were being used for offensive actions (despite being told that they wouldn't be) and that the regional White puppet government 'rested on no basis of public confidence and support'. He was court-martialled for his whistle-blowing.[18]

On the morning of 27 September, the last Allied troops departed from Arkhangel, and on 12 October, Murmansk was abandoned.

~

On 14 October, General Denikin occupied Orel, 360 km south of Moscow and was threatening Tula, the munitions-manufacturing centre, only 180 km from the capital. The south demanded all the Bolsheviks' attention. Just then, the Northwestern Army launched an offensive against Petrograd. The Red defenders were thrown completely off balance, and began to roll back with hardly a show of resistance, abandoning arms and supplies as they went. By 20 October, the Whites were at Tsarkoe Selo, just 25 km from Petrograd.[19]

Trotsky rushed to Petrograd to organise the defence of the 'cradle of the revolution'. On 2 October he issued an order to the army and the navy that showed he was in no doubt British hands were still around Russia's neck.

> Red warriors! On all the fronts you meet the hostile plots of the English. The counter-revolutionary troops shoot you with English guns. In the depots of Shenkursk and Onega, on the southern and western fronts, you find supplies of English manufacture. The prisoners you have captured are dressed in uniforms made in England. The women and children of Arkhangel and Astrakhan are maimed and killed by English airmen with the aid of English explosives. English ships bomb our shores ...
>
> But, even to-day, when we are engaged in a bitter fight with Yudenich, the hireling of England, I demand that you never forget that there are two Englands. Besides the England of profits, of violence, bribery and bloodthirstiness, there is the England of labour, of spiritual power, of high ideals of international solidarity. It is the base and dishonest England of the stock-exchange manipulators that is fighting us. The England of labour and the people is with us.[20]

Suddenly, the tide turned in the Bolsheviks favour. By the end of October, Yudenich had been driven back from the outskirts of Petrograd; the Latvian Rifle Division had helped the Red Army retake Orel; and Denikin's White Army was in retreat on a front stretching from Kiev in the west to Tsaritsyn in the east. On 12 November, the Red Army captured Omsk, the administrative capital of Admiral Kolchak's Siberian government.

Addressing the Lord Mayor of London's Guildhall banquet on the evening of 9 November, Prime Minister Lloyd George was uncharacteristically downbeat about Russia. 'There will be no peace until peace is established in Russia,' he said. 'I dared to predict earlier this year that Bolshevism could not be, and its dangerous doctrines could not be, suppressed by the sword. Other measures must finally be resorted to for restoring peace and good government in that distressed land.'[21]

He concluded by saying, 'I am hopeful that when the winter gives time for all sections there to reflect and to reconsider the situation, an opportunity may offer itself to the great Powers of the world to promote peace and concord in that great country.'

The remarks were widely interpreted as signalling the withdrawal of support for the White forces and the end of the British intervention in Russia. On 17 November in the House of Commons, Sir Donald Maclean, the Leader of the Opposition, didn't mince his words.

> The policy of intervention has failed. Look where you like on the military field, the anti-Bolshevik military position in Russia is one of disaster. I read in the 'Observer' yesterday - I forget the exact words - a most emphatic sentence, that the anti-Bolshevik campaign has ended in disastrous failure. So far as I am able to observe - and I have only the opportunity to observe what one reads in the papers - that seems to me a not unfair description of the whole of the anti-Bolshevik operations in Russia. And what is the Bolshevik position? I should think it is perfectly fair to say that the Bolsheviks are in a stronger position to-day in Russia than they ever have been. Militarily they are increasingly efficient - and, from the point of view of the administration of the country - whether it is a democratic administration or not, I do not know - certainly that is also growingly efficient.[22]

50
BREAK-UPS

Since the beginning of the year, John Maclean had been dashing around the country, fanning the faltering flames of revolution wherever he could find them. When he returned to Glasgow from Dublin in early August 1919, his priority was preparing for the opening of the Scottish Labour College in September. However, this didn't prevent a quick trip down to Durham to rev up the miners, or a week in Fife on the same mission. Then because the end of the war had meant the end of the Rent Restriction Act that he had campaigned for, Maclean marched at the head of the Gorbals contingent at the big rent demonstration organised by the ILP in the middle of the month.

Maclean turned 40 on 24 August 1919. He wouldn't make 45.

~

Agnes Maclean finally got sick of it. It had been her hope that after the 1918 election campaign, John would rest and recuperate and perhaps even get a teaching job again. However, on 21 January, while John was away in Lanarkshire with the miners, the Govan School Board notified him it refused to consider his application for reinstatement as a teacher. He saw little choice but to continue in his role as 'professional revolutionary'.

According to Maclean's daughter Nan Milton, Agnes believed the most effective contribution she could make to her husband's activities was to make his home life happy and comfortable, and this she had done supremely well. 'Moreover, he made many demands on her to provide hospitality for socialist comrades, and I understand our home was often like a hotel,' Milton wrote.[1]

What Agnes saw as her husband's reckless disregard for his own health and well-being eventually led her to speak up. She entreated him to give up his political activity until he was really fit. From Maclean's point of view, the potential for real revolutionary change all hinged on the miners' campaign and he felt he had to do all within his power to assist. Absorbed in the fevered atmosphere of the times, he took the stance that those who were not with him were against him. He became suspicious that his wife had been 'got at'.

When he queried Agnes about her reasons for asking him to step back, it was the last straw for her. In autumn 1919, she left him, vowing not to return until he gave up his revolutionary activity. Eight-year-old Jean was farmed out to Agnes' brother and his wife in Maryhill, and six-year-old Nan to Maclean's younger sister Elizabeth. Agnes herself took a position as a maternity nurse, living in with each case. As winter hit, Nan suffered a bad dose of pneumonia and says it was only her mother's devoted nursing that saved her. Agnes decided it was time to leave Glasgow with its fogs and polluted air and taking both her daughters with her, went to live with her sister in Bonchester Bridge, near Hawick in the Scottish Borders.[2]

~

Things were also changing at the British Socialist Party. The split over revolution, and affiliation to the Third International, versus reform, and sticking with the Second, debated at the 1919 Easter conference had been referred to the party's branches for decision. Maclean was on the revolutionary wing, while the reformist faction was headed by party chairman EC Fairchild and treasurer HW Alexander.

In May 1919, Fairchild resigned as editor of the party journal the *Call* and debate about the issue continued in its columns until September. The ballot results were announced in the 9 October edition and were conclusive: 98 branches were in favour of affiliation to the Third International and only four voted against.

Fairchild and Alexander resigned from the party altogether, giving as their reasons, 'emphatic disagreement ... with the advocacy of forcible revolution in preference to action through Parliament, municipal bodies and trade unions'.[3]

Russian intervention in the hitherto tentative moves to form a British communist party arrived that summer in the form of a representative from the Communist International (Comintern). The emissary attended the annual conference of the Workers' Socialist Federation in London on 7 and 8 June and 'imparted much interesting information about the Third International and the methods of Russian Bolshevism. ... In reply Miss

[Sylvia] Pankhurst spoke of the honour done to the Federation in having a delegate sent to the Annual Congress direct from the Soviet Government of Russia.⁴

The Russian visitor told the British Socialist Party that it was the duty of all sincere communists to work for the unity between the revolutionary left wing organisations in Britain. As a result of the Comintern initiative, on 13 June a meeting was held in London at which members of the British Socialist Party, the Workers' Socialist Federation, the Socialist Labour Party and the South Wales Socialist Society had a lengthy discussion about the possibility of merging the four organisations into a new party.⁵

The second anniversary of the Russian Revolution was celebrated in Labour circles all over the country. Maclean was the main speaker at a large BSP event held at Kingsway Hall, London on 10 November. The resolution was:

> This meeting of London workers, assembled to celebrate the Second Anniversary of the Socialist Revolution in Russia, expresses its admiration of the boundless courage and glorious achievements of the Russian workers and peasants, who have set an example to the world by the establishment of a Socialist Republic, and have thus realised the dream of ages for the first time in history. It congratulates the Soviet Government on its resistance to the combined forces of world Capitalism, and rejoices in the continued military successes of the Red Army; it condemns the British and Allied Governments in unmeasured terms for the help given to them in men, money and munitions to the Tsarist generals and counter-revolutionary capitalists; and it calls on the organised workers of this country to enforce the raising of the starvation blockade of Russia and the establishment of diplomatic relations with the Soviet Government. This meeting further pledges itself to help forward, by all the means in its power, the world wide social revolution of which the Russian workers and peasants are the gallant pioneers.⁶

Tom Mann, secretary of the Amalgamated Society of Engineers; JF Hodgson, a member of the BSP executive; and Fred Willis, who became editor of the *Call* after EC Fairchild's resignation, spoke in favour of the resolution. The final speaker was Maclean and if the report in the *Times* is any guide, he was in full flow.

> Mr John Maclean referred to three of their comrades who were in prison – Billy Watson [arrested for sedition for a speech at a 'Hands Off Russia'

meeting at the Albert Hall and sentenced to six months' imprisonment], Jim Larkin [arrested in New York on 7 November 1919 during a series of anti-Bolshevik raids and charged with 'criminal anarchy'] and Eugene Debs [America's most famous political prisoner, serving time in a Georgia penitentiary for violating the US Espionage and Sedition Acts] - and said they must secure the freedom of those who had been fighting for the rights of the working classes. They must do their best to emulate Russia by overthrowing the tyrants at home. For two years now the red flag had waved high in Russia. German, British, American and Japanese capitalism had made their united effort to crush the working class triumphant in Russia, but it had failed and would fail. The doom of capitalism was sealed two years ago. This country was moving towards the rapids of revolution. He had been in the midst of the mining areas and had seen the spirit shown by the rank and file. The Miners' Federation had so manoeuvred as to involve the whole working class, and the day had come when there must be a general advance of the whole working class army. The greatness of the tactics of Smillie had been in his attempt to unite the workers. If they were ready for a Labour offensive in this country they could foil any attempt to break their movement on the Continent.

... Away with everything, he cried; on with the class war! They had the ball at their feet ... They were out for socialisation not nationalisation, and for full control not joint control. The class war had begun in the States; it was going to spread to Japan; it was coming here. Let them get their guns ready (cheers); if they could not get guns, then them get behind the guns of the soldiers and the sailors. The doom of capitalism was at hand; labour would be free, armies and navies would no longer be necessary, and there would be peace on earth and good will to all mankind.[7]

On Sunday 30 November, Maclean was again the headliner at a Hands off Russia demonstration at St Andrew's Hall in Glasgow. Councillor Pat Dollan appealed to the audience of over 5000 'to do all they could to help the working people of Russia in their attempt to organise a new civilisation – a civilisation based on common sense and humanity, on fraternity and co-operation.' On Wednesday, he said, the Glasgow Trades and Labour Council would consider the advisability of calling a 24-hour strike on the Clyde to bring pressure on the government to leave Russia alone.[8]

Maclean was introduced as Soviet consul in Glasgow, and when he rose to speak, 'he received a truly wonderful ovation, and his speech was one scathing attack on British imperialism throughout the world'.[9]

Maclean moved the resolution, 'That the meeting send fraternal greetings and congratulations to the workers of Russia on the magnificent stand they had made in defence of national freedom and socialism, and call on the organised labour movement of the country to use all its strength in support of the efforts being made by the Soviet Government to secure a people's peace in all parts of the world.'

Russia, Maclean said, was anxious for peace. Great Britain was not anxious for peace for Russia. Great Britain was asking for a breather until she made her next offensive. There could be no peace between capitalism and socialism. The working class, once on the go, could not stop short of Bolshevism.[10]

The resolution was seconded by Lieutenant Colonel Cecil L'Estrange Malone, Coalition Liberal MP for East Leyton. During the war, Malone had been in the Royal Navy, had captained several ships and headed a seaplane squadron. He became air attaché at the British Embassy in Paris, in which capacity he was the air representative of the Supreme War Council in Versailles in 1918. He was elected to parliament in the 1918 election.

In 1918 he was also on the executive of the virulently anti-communist Reconstruction Society, and so, it was rather strange that in September 1919 he obtained a passport to travel to Estonia, and from there made his way to Petrograd. In his account of his trip, published in 1920, he wrote: 'My ultimate object was to meet the responsible heads of the Soviet Republic as a member of the British House of Commons, and as such I wished to explore the possibility of negotiations with a view to establishing peace in the remaining fields of war.'[11]

During his visit, Malone met with the former Soviet ambassador to Britain, Maxim Litvinov and foreign minister Georgy Chicherin in Moscow. He also travelled on Trotsky's armoured train when the people's commissar for military and naval affairs went to review Red Army troops at Tula. On Malone's return to Britain he adopted a pro-Bolshevist stance, joined the British Socialist Party and was drafted into the Hands off Russia campaign as a speaker, on the initiative of Theodore Rothstein.

Maclean was deeply suspicious of Malone. Given his military background, the apparent ease by which he had managed to overcome the ban on British travel to Russia, and the 180-degree turn in his political persuasion, Maclean, not unreasonably, thought it was highly likely that Malone was a government agent, tasked with infiltrating the British socialist movement.

Maclean's concerns about the sudden elevation of Malone were just one symptom of his deeper misgivings about the direction of the BSP. Maclean had been a member of the party and its predecessors, the Social Democratic Party and the Social Democratic Federation, since 1903. He was on the executive committee and had probably the highest public profile of anyone in the party. In the *Call*, he praised the BSP, writing, 'Events this year have proved that no organisation in Britain has a greater influence than the BSP on the policy of the working class.'[12]

But after the visit by the emissary from the Comintern in summer 1919, the primary focus of the party became the unity process. As Ripley and McHugh observed, 'The unity negotiations were all-absorbing and the priority of party creation wholly appropriated whatever strategic and tactical thinking the BSP possessed.'[13]

Harry McShane, who was soon to join Maclean in a grass roots campaign, wrote, '… he [Maclean] objected to their lack of an industrial and political perspective for Britain: "hands off Russia" was the only policy they had'.[14]

~

Maclean continued to write for the *Call* until the issue of 26 February 1920. In that issue, he was advertised to be a speaker at a Hands off Russia demonstration at the Albert Hall in London two day later. Lieutenant Colonel Malone was also listed to speak. But Maclean did not appear.

At the meeting, Malone moved a long resolution 'condemning direct or indirect intervention in Russia, noting with satisfaction the continued success of the Soviet Republic, demanding the complete cessation of the blockade and the establishment of friendly relations immediately, and calling upon the working class of Great Britain to enforce the demand by the unreserved use of its political and industrial power'. The resolution was seconded by prominent Zionist author Israel Zangwill. There was no mention of John Maclean.[15]

Maclean had refused to share the platform with Malone, later writing, 'To ask me to work with Malone for Revolution is a joke. A man like that ought not to be allowed in a Revolutionary Marxian Party.'[16]

Under the previous BSP leadership of Fairchild and Alexander, Maclean had had a high degree of freedom to pursue the activities that he felt would best 'keep capitalism busy at home'. Thus, Maclean's active campaigning on the note that revolution was imminent and workers should be prepared to take power into their own hands was acknowledged and appreciated, even if it not acted on by other elements of the party.[17]

Harry McShane was secretary of the Glasgow Tradeston branch of the BSP. Maclean was also a member there, having joined on the closure of the Pollokshaws Branch.[18] After Fairchild and Alexander resigned, McShane observed that under the influence of Rothstein, and without any discussion with the membership, the BSP began to take over some of the future functions of the Communist Party. 'A lot of resentment built up,' he wrote. 'Most of it centred on the attitude of the leadership. The BSP became more and more inefficient, with no clear policy, but the people and the top were bureaucratic and authoritarian. They appointed an organiser, Ernie Cant, who came to Scotland for a while. He looked at our bookshop, took notes of this and that, but it was obvious he had no politics at all. Although we were one of the most active branches in Scotland, with forty members, we finally broke with the BSP in January 1920.'[19]

Maclean attended the BSP annual Easter conference, held at the Bethnal Green Town Hall, London on 4 and 5 April 1920, where, as he later wrote, he voiced his objections to '[Arthur] Inkpin and Co' [the BSP leadership] publicly and privately'.[20]

In 1995, Bob Pitt provided details of Maclean's intervention in a series of articles in the journal *Workers' Liberty*. Pitt quoted from a Cabinet intelligence report, 'evidently based on information supplied by a genuine spy on the BSP executive'.

> There was a curious incident during the conference. John Maclean rose and made charges against the leaders of being police spies; he further cited the money spent on young [Andrew] Rothstein's education at Balliol and hinted that he was an agent provocateur of the government. It was decided to hold a secret meeting of the executive to investigate the charges. At this meeting Maclean argued quite temperately and with some superficial logic that the money received by Theodore Rothstein and Albert Inkpin was government money; he cited incidents that could only be explained on this hypothesis, and he challenged them to produce evidence of the source of the money. In reply, Inkpin assured his hearers that every penny came directly or indirectly from the Soviet Government; that it came by secret couriers to him and that he handed it on to Theodore Rothstein.[21]

Nan Milton described Maclean's break with the BSP as 'the only mysterious part of John Maclean's life', and indeed there are differing accounts of what happened. Both Milton and Harry McShane wrote that Maclean left the party at the Easter conference.

Milton wrote, '... one of the bones of contention was Malone, who was actually elected to the executive committee of the BSP at the conference that expelled Maclean'.[22]

According to Harry McShane, Maclean left after Rothstein offered him a salary to concentrate entirely on the Hands off Russia campaign. 'They were asking him to drop all the educational and agitational work that he had done for years. John refused to do that; he and the executive of the BSP fell out, and finally he left ... I discovered that John Maclean had left the BSP on May Day, 1920.'[23]

Later, in December 1920 Maclean claimed Rothstein's approaches 'created a situation that compelled the BSP to gently slip me out'.[24]

Nan Milton suggested that wasn't the only reason.

> In addition, he didn't want to make himself dependent on Russian money, and did not like the situation developing at the BSP, which was becoming more and more dependent on Russian subsidies. He remembered the situation where Hyndman maintained his domination of the party by financial means and felt that 'The man who pays the piper calls the tune'.[25]

Curiously, Maclean seemed to consider himself still a member of the BSP in the lead up to the Communist Unity Conference, held in London in August 1920. He accused the BSP's Scottish organiser Ernie Cant of trickery, and that Cant's refusal to recognise the Tradeston Branch of the BSP, of which Maclean was a member, meant Maclean was automatically excluded from the unity convention at which the Communist Party of Great Britain was formed.[26]

Brian Ripley and John McHugh argued the way in which Maclean could be 'slipped out' with such ease has to be a reflection on his organisational abilities. 'The need for a party as provider of leadership, discipline, direction and a focus for disputed strategy or theory is entirely absent from Maclean's output,' they wrote.[27]

The assessment is echoed by Tom Bell in the conclusion to his biography of Maclean.

John Maclean had most of the higher qualities that make for political leadership. He combined a high standard of general education with a wide knowledge of Marxism. Though cautious in temperament, he was a man of action, and endowed with great moral courage. Thickset and physically strong, he was fearless in face of danger, and tenacious in purpose to the point of fanaticism. The injustices of the industrial system awoke in his sympathetic nature a burning desire to seek redress ... He remained to the last a man of socialist convictions and principle.

But for political leadership something more is needed besides personal qualities. A *party* [original emphasis] is necessary, embodying collective experience and collective criticism of mistakes and successes. The BSP to which Maclean belonged was weak in numbers and *personnel* in Scotland. During the war, as Maclean frankly acknowledged at a social gathering of his party friends, the question of party had been neglected and subordinated to mass action. And since he had no powerful trade union connections, his activities became individualistic and without collective guidance. When finally the question of a new party was raised, particularly following the Russian Revolution, he was unable to rise above personal antipathies and a limited national outlook. He came under the influence of the popular mass demonstrations. He saw the revolution coming out of spontaneous mass movements and the general strike. He did not seem to realise that a political general strike if successful would necessarily develop into insurrection, that, as Marx insisted, 'insurrection is an art quite as much as war or any other', and that for that a centralised political party was necessary.[28]

Harry McShane, Maclean's close colleague in the Tramp Trust, said, 'He had a saying when he was speaking at some of his meetings, the only bit of humour he really had. He kept saying. "The Clan Maclean have a boat of their own." It meant that he was independent, that he was doing things on his own.'[29]

However and whenever it happened, Maclean was out of the BSP and would never be a member of the Communist Party of Great Britain. On May Day 1920, he struck out on his own.

IV
THE FIRE WITHIN

'I for one will not follow
a policy dictated by Lenin until he knows
the situation more clearly.'
  Which Lenin hadn't time to,
and parties never did – the rock of nations
like the rock of ages, saw-toothed, half-submerged,
a cranky spluttering lighthouse somewhere, as often
out as lit, a wreck of ships all round,
there's the old barnacled 'Working-class Solidarity',
and 'International Brotherhood' ripped open and awash,
while you can see the sleekit 'Great-Power Chauvinism'
steaming cannily past on the horizon
as if she had never heard of *cuius regio*.
Maclean wanted neither the maimed ships
nor the paradox of not wanting them
while he painfully trimmed the lighthouse lamp
to let them know that Scotland was not Britain
and writs of captains in the Thames
would never run in grey Clyde waters.

Edwin Morgan, 'On John Maclean' (1973).

51

ALBA AND ERIN

The 1920 May Day demonstration in Glasgow was the biggest ever. Over a hundred thousand people gathered at Glasgow Green on a dry, bright afternoon to listen to speakers representing 290 different organisations. The resolution adopted at all 26 platforms was:

> That this meeting declares for the overthrow of the capitalist system of production for profit and the establishment of a Cooperative Commonwealth based on production for use, and further that this meeting of workers sends their fraternal greetings to the European Soviet Republics and the workers of the world. Also we protest against the arrest and deportation of subjects without trial. Further we urge the immediate withdrawal of the military forces from Ireland and all armies of occupation elsewhere, and declare in favour of the 1st day of May being observed as International Labour Day.[1]

When John Maclean appeared in the throng selling copies of the *Vanguard*, rather than the British Socialist Party journal the *Call*, 'it caused quite a sensation'.[2]

~

The *Vanguard* had started in September 1915 as an antidote to *Justice*, the BSP journal that had become a mouthpiece for the jingoistic Henry Hyndman. The fifth issue, dated January 1916, was seized by the police prior to publication for carrying a report of Lloyd George's attempt to cajole Clydeside workers into accepting dilution at a meeting on Christmas Day 1915. Under threat from the authorities, no printer was willing to take it on after that.

Maclean outlined his reasons for reviving the paper in the opening article.

> The skill and cuteness of the government prevented a strike of the miners, who might have received the support of the rest of the workers to the

detriment of the British proposals at the Peace Conference, to the defeat of Britain's anti-Russian policy, and to the endangerment of British capitalism itself. Whilst giving free scope to [Robert] Smillie and his colleagues at the Coal Commission - now seen to be a farce to stave off revolt - the government set itself to the task of breaking up the miners' reform movement and driving [James] Macdougall out of public life. This accomplished, it then faced up to the Miners' Federation itself, and has now succeeded in driving Smillie out of the fighting ranks, has defeated direct action for nationalisation of the mines, and has isolated the miners from the other trade unions.

At the same time it has paralysed the BSP and the SLP [Socialist Labour Party], and may do so to the ILP [Independent Labour Party] as well, so as to clear the ground for a safe and sane Labourism; safe and sane, because dominated by ideas of the reform of capitalism rather than by the determination to destroy capitalism and inaugurate the workers' republic.

Dissatisfaction with the plight of the BSP, maimed by the year's onslaught of capitalism, has compelled us to resurrect *The Vanguard* in the hope that we may concentrate the minds of the workers on the revolution to be gone through in this country as well as on the one gone through already in Russia. The main use of the Russian workers' success is the inspiration we ought to derive from it for the accomplishment of a similar feat within the bounds of Britain.[3]

Harry McShane, an engineer, a former shop steward at Weir's Works and a fellow member of the BSP's Tradeston branch, went to help Maclean sell the new paper across the Green. 'He told me he was going to do a meeting that night at his old spot at Bath Street, and asked me to take the chair for him,' McShane later wrote. 'I went that night and the subsequent Sundays; the third time, my foreman was in the audience and I got the sack from A & W Smith's. I was ready to go after another job, but John asked me to take part in a campaign with him and said the campaign would pay our wages. I agreed.'[4]

The central element of Maclean's revolutionary industrial campaign was a 'Fighting Program', based on the minimum demands of the miners' reform movement that Maclean had promoted at meetings throughout 1919. A leaflet was produced outlining the program, which comprised five immediate demands: a six-hour maximum working day; a minimum wage of £1 a day; reduction of prices to half the present level; rationing of work to absorb the unemployed; and payment of full wages to the unemployed.[5] It's interesting to note the emphasis on the unemployed. Maclean was prescient, because by autumn 1920 Britain's short post-war boom had gone into reverse. With its workforce concentrated in heavy industry, Scotland was especially badly hit.⁶

~

Maclean and McShane based themselves at the BSP branch in Morrison Street, Tradeston and campaigned around the Glasgow shipyards, before venturing to Clydebank, Dundee and the rest of Scotland. McShane described their routine thus:

'Every day we held a factory gate meeting at lunch time, handed out the leaflet, and announced our evening meeting. After lunch we chalked all the pavements for our meeting at night, which we held at the most prominent street-corner in the area. The meetings were a roaring success; we got big collections and sold a lot of literature. The collections paid our expenses and wages … We ate in restaurants and money was no problem, although it became one later.'⁷

At the end of May, a local man Sandy Ross spoke at their Dundee meeting. An ex-policeman from Glasgow, he had been a conscientious objector during the war, for which he served time in Wakefield Prison. Ross had been a member of the ILP and was a humorous public speaker. Maclean, who was always so serious on the platform, thought this was terrific and invited him to join the crew. Ross then brought in Peter Marshall, another conscientious objector who could entertain a crowd with his wit. Sometimes the quartet was augmented by Maclean's long-term colleague James Macdougall, who McShane called 'the best orator in Scotland'. Maclean labelled the team 'The Tramp Trust Unlimited' and the joke stuck.⁸

As was his custom, Maclean took the opportunity to combine his educational activities with his industrial campaigning. While he was in Dundee, local socialist EG Carr organised for him to provide a course of 19 lectures on 'Economics and the Social Revolution'. Following the success of these, a Dundee and District Committee of the Scottish Labour College was formed, with Carr as secretary. The following week, Maclean and Carr held a Labour College conference in Arbroath.⁹

The annual meeting of the Scottish Labour College was held on 29 May. It was attended by 530 delegates, who heard that district conferences had been held in Aberdeen, Dundee, East and West Fife, Edinburgh, Falkirk and Arbroath. It was also reported that both Fife and Lanarkshire miners had set aside funds for students to attend a day college if one was established in the 1920-21 session.[10]

The *Glasgow Herald* commented, 'The report of the Scottish Labour College this week probably drew attention to a movement the extent of which no doubt surprised the general public.' While critical of what it called 'the narrowness of outlook and the ill-balanced teaching', it did concede that 'much of what is called orthodox political economy is not free from the same defects'.[11]

~

In May, Maclean produced a pamphlet on the situation in Ireland, *The Irish tragedy: Scotland's disgrace*, and followed it up with an article in the June issue of the *Vanguard* titled 'The Irish fight for freedom'.

Maclean's pamphlet led off with a plea to fellow Scots.

> Let me address myself to Scots people particularly at this critical juncture in the world's history - just as critical as in August, 1914 - to save Ireland from a tragedy that is bound to come if a stop is not put to the bloody career of the present Coalition gang of unmitigated scoundrels.
>
> My plea is that Britain has no right to dominate Ireland with constabulary armed with bombs, and with an army and navy considered foreign by the Irish. We Scots have been taught to revere the names of Sir William Wallace and Robert Bruce because these doughty men of old are recorded as championing the cause of freedom when Edward I and Edward II tried to absorb Scotland as part of English territory. All Scots must therefore appreciate the plight of Ireland, which for over seven centuries has chafed under the same English yoke, and now ought to stand by Ireland in her last great effort for freedom; the last because triumph is bound to be hers very soon.
>
> Right through the war the British Government justified its prosecution of the war on the ground that it was a war of 'democracy' against Prussianism, and that the war would guarantee the rights of small nations if the Allies won ...
>
> But to let Ireland have independence is a different story. Despite Ireland's wonderful unity and solidarity on the issue of separation from Britain, the Coalition Government violently persists in keeping its hold on Erin.
>
> Nothing but loathing and disgust must animate any straight-thinking person when he or she recalls the continuously repeated cry that Britain must release German democracy from the blight of Kaiserism and Junkerism and Prussianism, and recollects the lying bleat that the Bolsheviks, in deposing

THE TRAMP TRUST UNLIMITED.
Sandy Ross   Jas. D. MacDougall
Peter Marshall   John MacLean M.A.   Harry McShane

The Tramp Trust Unlimited: 'The meetings were a roaring success; we got big collections and sold a lot of literature.'

Kerensky, had over-ridden the principle of democracy, and that, though a minority, they held the reins of power in rustic Russia. As a matter of simple fact, the alleged 'dictatorship by terrorists' was the stock argument used all last year by Winston Churchill and his press puppets to justify the spending of close on two hundred million pounds in the direct and indirect attempt to overthrow the vast Russian Communist Republic. Even yet Britain is chary about trading with Russia because of Russia's alleged repudiation of the principle of democracy.

To any right-thinking person Britain's retention of Ireland is the world's most startling instance of a 'dictatorship by terrorists', as Britain rules Ireland against Irish wishes with policemen armed with bombs and a huge army equipped with over 40 tanks and as many aeroplanes, machine guns galore, and all the other beautiful manifestations of Christian brotherhood, love, and charity.[12]

The Irish War of Independence had been bubbling along since January 1919. However, up to this point there had been a limited amount of violence, with much of the nationalist campaign involving popular mobilisation and the creation of a state within a state, in opposition to British rule.

In the 1918 general election Sinn Féin had won 73 of the 105 Irish seats, and having pledged not to sit in the UK Parliament at Westminster, set up an Irish Parliament known as the First Dáil. It met in Dublin on 21 January 1919 and adopted the 'Declaration of Irish Independence', which ratified the Proclamation of the Republic read at the start of the Easter 1916 rising. It also issued a 'Message to the Free Nations of the World', which, as can be seen below, stated that there was an 'existing state of war, between Ireland and England'.

> The Nation of Ireland having proclaimed her national independence, calls, through her elected representatives in Parliament assembled in the Irish Capital on January 21, 1919, upon every free nation to support the Irish Republic by recognising Ireland's national status and her right to its vindication at the Peace Congress.
>
> Naturally, the race, the language, the customs and traditions of Ireland are radically distinct from the English. Ireland is one of the most ancient nations in Europe, and she has preserved her national integrity, vigorous and intact, through seven centuries of foreign oppression; she has never relinquished her national rights, and throughout the long era of English usurpation she has in every generation defiantly proclaimed her inalienable right of nationhood down to her last glorious resort to arms in 1916.

Internationally, Ireland is the gateway to the Atlantic; Ireland is the last outpost of Europe towards the West; Ireland is the point upon which great trade routes between East and West converge; her independence is demanded by the Freedom of the Seas; her great harbours must be open to all nations, instead of being the monopoly of England. To-day these harbours are empty and idle solely because English policy is determined to retain Ireland as a barren bulwark for English aggrandisement, and the unique geographical position of this island, far from being a benefit and safeguard to Europe and America, is subjected to the purposes of England's policy of world domination.

Ireland to-day reasserts her historic nationhood the more confidently before the new world emerging from the war, because she believes in freedom and justice as the fundamental principles of international law; because she believes in a frank co-operation between the peoples for equal rights against the vested privileges of ancient tyrannies; because the permanent peace of Europe can never be secured by perpetuating military dominion for the profit of empire but only by establishing the control of government in every land upon the basis of the free will of a free people, and the existing state of war, between Ireland and England, can never be ended until Ireland is definitely evacuated by the armed forces of England.[13]

On the same day as the First Dáil convened, in a deliberate act to start a war, several members of the Irish Republican Army (IRA), acting on their own initiative, attacked and shot two Royal Irish Constabulary (RIC) officers. In the months that followed, the IRA adopted guerrilla tactics; volunteers without uniforms mounting fast violent raids for funds and arms, attacking British government property and targeting members of the quasi-military RIC, who were routinely armed and billeted in barracks.[14]

Since Maclean's visit to Dublin in July 1919, the British had clamped down. The Dáil Éireann was declared illegal in September 1919, and the British Cabinet settled on a policy of creating two Irish Home Rule parliaments – one in Dublin and one in Belfast – with a Council of Ireland to provide a framework for possible unity.

In trying to re-assert their control over the country, British forces resorted to arbitrary reprisals against republican activists and the civilian population. In the first 18 months of the conflict, it was estimated British forces carried out 38,720 raids on private homes, arrested 4,982 suspects, committed 1,604 armed assaults, carried out 102 indiscriminate shootings and burning in towns and villages, and killed 77 people, including women and children.[15]

Reluctant to deploy the regular army in greater numbers, the British bolstered the RIC with unemployed ex-British soldiers demobilised after World War I. Nicknamed the 'Black and Tans', they were first deployed to Ireland in March 1920, and while officially part of the RIC, in reality they were a paramilitary force. The nickname arose from the improvised uniforms the British recruits initially wore. Due to a shortage of RIC uniforms, the new recruits were issued with a mixture of dark RIC tunics and caps, and khaki army trousers. They rapidly gained a reputation for drunkenness and ill-discipline that did more harm to the British government's moral authority in Ireland than any other group.[16]

Across Britain there was almost complete ignorance of what was going on in Ireland, and according to Harry McShane, there was little effort to change the situation. 'Though it was a major struggle to deal with the Irish question in Glasgow, the Scottish Workers' Committee, which was the remnants of the old CWC [Clyde Workers' Committee] did nothing about it. Neither did anyone else, except the Tramp Trust Unlimited.'[17]

~

In the months following its publication, Maclean and his crew sold more than twenty thousand copies of *The Irish tragedy* pamphlet, and held 'great open-air meetings on Ireland' all over Scotland.

'In June 1920 we held one in Motherwell,' McShane wrote, 'which was always an Orange [Protestant] centre; the Orangemen smashed the platform, but some of the Irish came and fought them off and we were able to maintain a meeting.'[18]

Maclean wrote a lively account of 'The Battle of Motherwell' for the August edition of the *Vanguard*.

> As soon as I started the howling started in earnest. Shouts of 'traitor!', 'Peterhead', 'square-head', and even obscene language was shouted at me whilst policemen and plainclothes men were in the audience. Had Socialists used such language at a [Sir Edward] Carson demonstration ... the police would at once have arrested fifty (probably innocent) persons and had them fined heavily or imprisoned for up to six months ...
>
> When I told the crowd that the Sinn Féiners and nationalists by vote in January had captured 'Derry and that therefore 'Derry walls had surrendered,

this galling statement was too much for the hooligans who had come to enrage me. Like mad bulls amidst shouts of 'Up 'Derry!' they rushed down on me. My friends dived forward, too, to save the bag and the literature in front of the ILP platform. In the scramble, the platform collapsed.

Just at that moment, to my surprise, up rose the determined shout, 'Up Dublin!' and with that, a company of young Irish Volunteers, who had kept as quiet as Pussyfoot all through the Orange rowdiness, rushed from behind in a frontal attack on the hooligans.[19]

He ended the article with a passionate plea for the Scots to line up with the Irish.

My lecture on Ireland is meant particularly for Scotsmen in view of the fact that the government intends particularly to use Scottish regiments to do their dirty work in Ireland. My desire is to prevent Scotsmen being used to smash our sister race, the Celts of Ireland, for English capitalists who are descended from the Germans. Scotsmen have been taught to hate the Irish as a different race. They are not. The Welsh, the Scots and the Irish are all of Celtic origin, so that from a racial point of view, the Welsh and the Scots ought to line up with the Irish.[20]

The racist pillorying of the English sat strangely with the man who had in December 1915 written 'the only war worth fighting is the class war against robbery and slavery for the workers'.[21]

52

THE COMINTERN LAYS DOWN THE LAW

nfluenced by Maclean's relentless campaigning in 1919, much of it under the auspices of the Independent Labour Party,[1] the Scottish Division of the ILP voted at its annual delegate meeting on 3 January 1920 to sever its connection with the Second International and affiliate to the Third International (aka the Communist International, or Comintern) established in March 1919. Around the same time, the ILP Welsh Division passed a similar motion. This led to the setting up of an unofficial organisation, called the ILP Left Wing, at the ILP 1920 Easter conference.

At the conference, the ILP Left Wing joined with the centre to carry a vote to withdraw from the Second International. However, a motion to join the Third International was only supported by the Left Wing; the centre and right factions combined to thwart the initiative. The conference concluded without a decision on affiliation, but authorised the national committee to consult about the possibility of establishing an all-inclusive International.[2]

On 27 April, ILP chairman Dick Wallhead and national committee member Clifford Allen accompanied an official Labour Party delegation to Russia. During their visit, Wallhead and Allen made formal contact with the leaders of the Comintern and investigated at some length the desirability of the ILP joining the group.[3]

On 25 May, Wallhead and Allen submitted a list of 12 questions to the Comintern. Lenin, Radek and other leaders in Moscow met informally with the ILP delegates to discuss the questions and replied in a long letter 'to the workers organised into the Independent Labour Party'. Wallhead returned to Britain on 29 June and reported to the ILP's National Administrative Council at its meeting of 22-23 July. The NAC decided to publish both the questions and the response.[4] The Executive Committee of the Comintern sent its response to Walton Newbold of the ILP Left Wing and that group also published a version of the exchange.

The ILP delegates had asked in what respect Communism differed from other forms of socialism. In response, the Comintern provided a brief history of contemporary socialism, from its birth to the time of its crisis during the war and down to the present.

After castigating both the right-wing pro-war elements of the Second International, and centrists who protested in words against the war, but did not organise the workers against it, the Comintern identified a third group.

> The third current, represented in England by John Maclean and his friends, in France by Loriot, in Germany by Karl Liebknecht and Rosa Luxemburg, in Russia by the Bolsheviks, branded the policy of the reformist Socialists as assistance to the bourgeoisie, as treason to the working class. It branded the Pilate politics of the Centrists, politics which disintegrates the energy of the working class; it formed illegal organisations, called the workers to street demonstrations, called them to revolutionary action, called them to civil war against imperialist war. The bourgeoisie hunted down the representatives of this third, the Communist group, as traitors to the fatherland; threw them into prisons and sentenced them to penal servitude – perfectly well aware of the fact that although weak at first, this group is the deadly enemy of the bourgeoisie.[5]

In its letter, the Comintern expressed a dim view of British Labour. In England, they wrote, the right wing reformists, led by Arthur Henderson, talk of a Labour government, but deep down in their hearts, they like Churchill are convinced that the working class is unable to govern the country and wish to save English capitalism from the revolution. The centre of the Second International, in the persons of Ramsay MacDonald and Philip Snowden and the majority of the ILP, aid the right wing by persuading the workers that the socialism can only be obtained by constitutional means, it continued. It exerts itself to restrain the workers from bringing direct pressure on the capitalists, thus making itself the chief obstacle to the revolution.[6]

The Comintern was unsparing in its conclusion.

> There are no other forms, there is only Communism. Whatever else goes under the name of Socialism is either wilful deception by the lackeys of the bourgeoisie or the self-delusion of persons or groups who hesitate between life and death struggle and the role of assistants to the expiring bourgeoisie.[7]

The introductory notes of the pamphlet produced by the ILP's National Administrative Council listed the matters that British socialists needed to consider in deciding whether or not to affiliate to the Third International. They were:

> The Dictatorship of one section of the International Socialist movement over the rest, or the refusal of that section to associate with other national Socialist Parties except on terms imposed by itself.
>
> The insistence by one section upon its policy and methods for the establishment of Socialism being followed in all countries.
>
> The deliberate provocation of civil war (the disarming of the bourgeoisie and the arming of the proletariat) for the overthrow of capitalism.
>
> The morality and practicability of a minority imposing its will upon an apathetic or helpless majority by what is called the Dictatorship of the Communist Party.
>
> The morality and permanent value of suppressing the voice and influence of a minority, even during a revolutionary period.
>
> The destruction of Parliamentary institutions and the forcible imposition by a minority of new forms of government and administration.
>
> The adoption of methods of sabotage and disingenuous methods of propaganda inside existing Socialist, political, Labour and industrial organisations.
>
> Whether the free use of denunciation and misrepresentation of Socialists who differ from the Communist leaders is to be the accepted method of Socialist fellowship.[8]

In summary, the National Administrative Council said the Comintern's letter contained 'abundant evidence of the conviction of the authors that their doctrines, and policy and methods are held by them to be unimpeachable, and that Socialism cannot be found or realised except through their narrow dogmatism'.

In contrast, the foreword to the pamphlet produced by the ILP Left Wing Group included the following:

> Our Russian comrades are deeply concerned to bridge the gulf and overcome the obstacles which, for one reason or another have intervened between you and an acquaintance with and understanding of their program and policy. We submit their message without modification or abbreviation.[9]

John Maclean was delighted by the unwavering stance adopted by the Comintern, not to mention the recognition afforded him and his followers and the position they had adopted. He wrote in the *Vanguard*:

This pamphlet must play a greater part in the moulding of British thought than even Marx and Engels' *Communist Manifesto* did in the past. Out of it we who claim to be Communists must get the basis of Communist Unity in Britain ... Before the winter Scottish Communists ought to come together in conference and discuss unity on the basis of this momentous document.[10]

~

On 22 April 1920, the Executive Committee of the Communist International voted to hold a Second World Congress of its member parties. This was followed on 14 June by the formal publication of a call for a congress to be held in Moscow one month hence. Political parties pledging allegiance to the organisation were urged to send delegations at once.

Despite distancing himself from the executive of the British Socialist Party, John Maclean was still highly regarded in Moscow and historian Walter Kendall says there can be little doubt he received an invitation to attend the Second Congress.[11]

Maclean applied to the Foreign Office for a passport on 15 May, shortly before the departure to Russia of the two BSP delegates William McLaine and Tom Quelch.[12]

He received the following response. 'Lord Curzon is unable to give a reply to your request at this moment, but if you will apply to him again at the end of June, he will consider whether the necessary facilities can be granted to you or not.'[13]

Maclean wrote again on 17 June, a few days after the date of the congress had been announced, 'requesting permission to visit Russia during the months of July and August'. When that request was turned down, on 7 July he applied, via Cook's, for documents to travel to Denmark and Sweden. This request again led to nothing.[14]

There was no blanket ban, but the government was cautious about who it would permit to travel to Russia to meet with the Bolsheviks. In public statements, Maclean repeatedly made it clear he demanded the right to visit Russia openly and freely, as Labour Party, ILP and BSP delegates did with government-issued passports.

During this period Soviet Russia was subject to an armed blockade by land and sea, making travel extremely difficult. Legal passage was possible only through the Estonian port of Revel (now Tallinn). Some who were also denied passports decided to make the trip illegally. Willie Gallacher was one. 'I had travelled as a stowaway from Newcastle to Bergen,' he later wrote. 'Then as an ordinary tourist from Bergen to the North Cape [in Norway], from the North Cape to Murmansk, from Murmansk to Leningrad [still Petrograd at the time], and thence to Moscow.'[15] Sylvia Pankhurst was another who made the journey covertly.

Helen Crawfurd, a member of the ILP's Left Wing and Maclean's comrade from the wartime Glasgow rent strikes, did have a passport, but on reaching Vardoe in north-east Norway was forbidden by the police there from continuing. Undeterred, she arranged for some local fishermen to ferry her to a cargo ship bound for Alexandrovsk [now Polyarny] on the Murmansk coast, from where she made her way to Moscow. While she missed the congress, many of the key figures who attended lingered, and in the three months she spent in Moscow and Petrograd she met with Lenin, his wife Nadezhda Krupskaya, Maxim Gorky and others, and soaked up the post-revolutionary atmosphere.[16]

Crawfurd's recounted her meeting with Lenin in her unpublished autobiography. Keira Wilkins writes, 'Crawfurd also fondly describes a conversation regarding the Labour Colleges that had begun on Red Clydeside. She appears to take great pride in the fact that Lenin saw the radical potential of such a local education scheme that had been so successful in early 20th century Glasgow.'[17]

One can only image the reception John Maclean would have received, and the conversations he would have had, had he managed to make it to Russia in 1920. Tom Bell called not going one of the biggest mistakes Maclean ever made.

> It is a thousand pities that John Maclean never visited Soviet Russia to see in life, with his own eyes, that revolutionary order which he had been working all his life to establish in Scotland ... We cannot help thinking that the failure of Maclean to get there is one of the mistakes of his great life.
>
> In a world torn and ravaged by four years of war, with the 'White' terror raging in some countries, men and women were taking the lives into their own hands to get to the [Second] Congress, with no passports or documents of any kind to assist them. Maclean with others, who were not *persona grata* with Lord Curzon was invited, and what his Scottish friends were able to do to get there he certainly could have done. But instead of stooping to conquer when it was obvious there was no alternative, he preferred to carry on a forlorn wordy warfare with Lord Curzon.[18]

In Petrograd en route to Moscow, Willie Gallacher was handed a copy hot off the press of Lenin's latest book, *"Left-Wing" Communism: an infantile disorder.* Written in April 1920, it was Lenin's attempt to encapsulate the lessons the Bolshevik Party had learned from its involvement in three revolutions in twelve years, in a manner that European Communists could relate to. Lenin gave personal attention to the book's type-setting and printing schedule so that it would be published before the opening of the second congress. Each delegate received a copy.[19]

In the chapter '"Left-Wing" Communism in Great Britain', Lenin wrote that while there was no Communist Party in Great Britain yet, there was a growing movement that engendered hope. He listed the British Socialist Party, the Socialist Labour Party, the South Wales Socialist Society and the Workers' Socialist Federation as groups that were negotiating to form a Communist Party and noted an article by Sylvia Pankhurst in the *Workers' Dreadnought* that described progress of those discussions. He also noted that the greatest obstacle appeared to be the disagreement about participation in parliament and affiliation to the Labour Party.

Gallacher had outlined his opposition to these propositions in a letter to the editor in the same issue of *Workers' Dreadnought.* Reading the chapter in the Smolny Institute while waiting for his travel papers, Gallacher was taken aback by Lenin's criticisms of his position.

> The writer of the letter fully realises that only workers' Soviets, not parliament, can be the instrument enabling the proletariat to achieve its aims ... But the writer of the letter does not even ask - it does not occur to him to ask - whether it is possible to bring about the Soviets' victory over parliament without getting pro-Soviet politicians *into* parliament, without disintegrating parliamentarianism from *within*, without working within parliament for the success of the Soviets in their forthcoming task of dispersing parliament.[20]

Lenin concluded that the British Communists should unite their four parties into one, form a bloc with the Labour Party, participate in parliament, but retain complete freedom of agitation, propaganda and political activity. If Labour accepted these terms, the Communists would be the gainers, he said. Not only would they help Labour attain government sooner, they would more quickly help the masses understand their propaganda against

Labour. If Labour rejected a bloc with the Communists, it would show that the [Arthur] Hendersons and [Philip] Snowdens preferred their close relations with the capitalists to the unity of all the workers.[21]

At the thirteenth session of the congress on 6 August both Gallacher and Sylvia Pankhurst argued against affiliation to the Labour Party. Pankhurst said, 'If one were to say to the parties that they should join the Labour Party and allow themselves to be tied by a common discipline and action one would thus give the fate of the English proletarian revolution into the hands of the old trades unions.' And Gallacher pleaded, 'The position of the Scottish comrades should not be made difficult and intolerable by a decision being forced upon them which they cannot defend in their position because it contradicts everything that they have defended previously in their lives and everything that they grew up with.'[22]

Lenin was unmoved, declaring:

> Comrade Gallacher and Comrade Sylvia Pankhurst, who have both spoken here, do not as yet belong to a revolutionary Communist Party. That excellent proletarian organisation, the Shop Stewards' movement, has not yet joined a political party. If you organise politically, you will find that our tactics are based on a correct understanding of political developments in the past decades, and that a real revolutionary party can be created only when it absorbs the best elements of the revolutionary class and uses every opportunity to fight the reactionary leaders, wherever they show themselves.
>
> If the British Communist Party starts by acting in a revolutionary manner in the Labour Party, and if the Hendersons are obliged to expel this Party, that will be a great victory for the communist and revolutionary working-class movement in Britain.[23]

The motion, that 'English parties' affiliate to the Labour Party, was adopted by 58 votes to 24 with 2 abstentions. It's an interesting use of 'English', given what John Maclean was about to start arguing about Scotland's right to have its own Communist Party.

~

JT Murphy, a British delegate representing the Shop Stewards' Movement, summed up the Comintern's Second Congress in the following terms. 'The proposals of the Russian representatives were for a centralised international party with an Executive elected by the Congress and continuously sitting in Moscow and directing the work of the national sections. The national sections of this International Party were to be modelled on the Communist Party of Soviet Russia and subordinate to the Executive Committee of the Communist International, the World Communist Party.'[24]

The congress embodied its decisions in a series of theses. These defined the character of a Communist Party, including its role and its duties, in considerable detail. One set, the so-called 'Twenty-one points', set out the conditions an organisation had to fulfill to be eligible for affiliation to the Communist International.

~

While the congress had been meeting, a Communist Unity Convention held in London between 31 July and 1 August established the Communist Party of Great Britain. The discussions that had begun in June 1919 between the British Socialist Party, the Socialist Labour Party, the South Wales Socialist Society and the Workers' Socialist Federation had finally borne some fruit. The outcome was far from all-encompassing however. Sylvia Pankhurst's Workers' Socialist Federation had withdrawn from the negotiations in June 1920 and constituted itself as the Communist Party (British Section of the Third International). Neither the Socialist Labour Party nor the South Wales Socialist Society attended, so the first iteration of the CPGB was in essence a merger between the British Socialist Party and the Communist Unity Group (a splinter group from the Socialist Labour Party led by Tom Bell, Arthur MacManus and William Paul).

On the second day of the convention, by a narrow 110-85 majority, the delegates voted for a policy of affiliation to the Labour Party. Walter Kendall commented that the refusal of the two anti-affiliation parties (the Communist Party (British Section of the Third International) and the Socialist Labour Party) to attend for fear of being outvoted on the crucial issue seems 'astonishingly inept'. He concluded the participation of either group would have tipped the balance the other way.[25]

~

In Moscow, the new executive of the Comintern was chosen on 7 August and three days later met to consider the British Question and passed the following resolution.

The EC decrees: a single Communist Party must be formed in Britain in virtue of the decisions of the Second World Congress of the Communist International

For the solution of this problem, in the course of four months a general Congress of all the Communist groups and organisations of Great Britain and Ireland must be convened. In this Congress will take part: (1) The United Communist Party [the newly formed Communist Party of Great Britain], (2) the Communist Party [Communist Party (British Section of the Third International)], (3) The Shop Stewards Committees, (4) The Scotch Communist Groups, (5) The Groups of Wales (6) The Irish Communists (7) The Socialist Labour Party (SLP), (8) The Left Wingers of the ILP.

For the convocation of this conference and for the principle of unity, a general Committee of Action shall be formed of one representative from each group under the chairmanship of a representative of the E.C.

Thus, as Kendall observes, the program and policy of the Communist Party of Great Britain had already been decided in every essential detail by the Second World Congress and the subsequent progress towards unification flowed directly from the proceedings in Moscow.

Sylvia Pankhurst for the Communist Party (British Section of the Third International); Willie Gallacher for the Scots Communists and shop stewards; JT Murphy for the national shop stewards' movement; Jack Tanner and David Ramsay for the London shop stewards, and Helen Crawfurd and Walton Newbold for the ILP Left Wing all went to Moscow and each returned bringing the Comintern's imperative instructions for fusion.[26]

Before he left, Gallacher had an interview with Lenin. The Soviet leader asked him three questions: Do you admit you were wrong on the question of parliament and affiliations to the Labour Party? Will you join the Communist Party of Great Britain when you return? Will you do your best to get your Scottish comrades to join?

'To each of these questions I answered "yes",' Gallacher wrote. 'Having given this pledge freely I returned to Glasgow.'[27]

53

THE COMMUNISM OF THE CLANS

On 21 July 1920, John Maclean had a visitor at his home in Auldhouse Road, Newlands. Ruaraidh Erskine of Marr was an aristocrat, with a complicated descent through the Scottish earls of Erskine, Buchan and Mar. His father, the 5th Baron Erskine, sat in the House of Lords and as a second son Erskine held the title the Earl of Marr.

Erskine had spent the previous decade building a political and social network and was the publisher of two periodicals - the bilingual *Guth na Bliadhna* (Voice of the Year) and the pro-independence *Scottish Review* - that were successful and had an impact. His biographer Gerard Cairns claims Erskine had almost single-handedly radicalised Scottish nationalism and Gaelic activism. After the armistice, he agitated for Scotland (and Ireland) to be represented at the Paris Peace Conference. He arranged for the Scottish Home Rule Association to prepare a memorandum claiming separate representation for Scotland and presented it to US President Wilson. One of the people he asked to support this 'memorial' was John Maclean.

Maclean replied through the columns of the *Call* that he was in favour of a parliament or soviet of workers for Scotland, with headquarters in Glasgow. But it would not come through negotiations of Scotsmen with the 'quack Peace Conference', but rather through the revolutionary efforts of the Scottish working class itself.

'Were I to thank anyone for actual services rendered to the cause of Home Rule,' he wrote, 'I would certainly thank my glorious comrades Lenin and Trotsky. The only thanks they would appreciate would be the successful revolutionising of Scotland by its wage slave class. My life has been spent in making for this goal, and this year I mean to do more than ever for the ending of capitalism in Scotland – as elsewhere in the world – and the establishment of the socialist republic in which alone we can have Home Rule.'[1]

By the time the winter 1919 edition of the *Scottish Review* was published,

Maclean had joined Erskine's National Committee, whose stated purpose was to 'familiarise the continental nations and the press with the idea of Scottish independence'. The committee's other members included Robert Smillie, the leader of the miners' federation; Labour MPs Neil Maclean and John Robertson; Tom Johnston, editor of *Forward*; future Labour MPs David Kirkwood and James Maxton; and Angus MacDonald, president of the Highland Land League.[2]

As historian Patrick Witt commented, the make-up of the National Committee can be seen as the culmination of Erskine's efforts to merge Lowlands labour interests with Gaelic Highland agitation. 'A study of its dynamics allows one to note Erskine's trend of mirroring the Irish separatist example. The Easter Rising was not solely the effort of Erskine's associate, cultural nationalist Patrick Pearse. An essential component of the Rising's leadership coalition was James Connolly, the Scottish-born Belfast labour leader. Erskine's coalition with Maclean represents two components of Erskine's vision. He recognized the obvious; any revolutionary Scottish movement needed labour involvement. He also continued to be instructed in insurrection by the Irish example.'[3]

~

Born in Brighton in 1869, Erskine was raised in Edinburgh – where he claimed to have learned Gaelic from his nanny – and was educated at Uppingham School in Rutland. As a young man in the early 1890s he moved into the worlds of journalism and politics, establishing three London-based periodicals during the decade and joining the first Scottish Home Rule Association in 1891. In the second part of the decade, he became even more drawn to Scotland, studying Gaelic in earnest and adopting the name Ruadri (Gaelic for Roderick), later amending it to Ruaraidh.

After the left wing Highland Land League reformed in 1909, Erskine became a supporter and was elected vice-president of the organisation in 1917. The league had initially formed in the 1880s to protest about the abuse and exploitation of crofters in the Highlands and Islands. The evictions that characterised the Highland Clearances peaked in the 1860s and saw many Highlanders emigrate or move to the industrial belt of Central Scotland, as Maclean's parents did. The remaining populace was herded into small landholdings by aristocratic absentee landlords, who turned their former lands over to sheep grazing, deer hunting and grouse shooting.

Crofters' protests about their plight sometimes took the form of direct action, often prompting a forceful response. In one incident, a gunboat was sent to Skye in February 1882 to facilitate the arrest of three crofters in Glendale for their part in deforcing a sheriff-officer. The most famous disturbance, the 'Battle of the Braes', occurred at the foot of Ben Lee, in Skye, two months later. Historian DW Crowley described it thus:

> In protest against an attempt by Lord Macdonald, their landlord, to deprive them of some pasturage to which they claimed a right, some of the crofters were refusing to pay their rents – a measure that was becoming widespread at this period. When an attempt had been made on 7th April to serve summons of ejection upon them, they had responded by burning the summons and mildly assaulting the sheriff-officer's assistant. Then, on 17th April, a force of fifty Glasgow police, sent to the area to effect the arrests of six ring-leaders, was set upon, when making the arrest, by some hundreds of crofters with sticks and stones. It succeeded in withdrawing the prisoners, no major injuries being suffered by either side.[4]

After several Land League and Crofters' Party MPs were elected to parliament in 1885, the *Crofting Holdings (Scotland) Act* was passed. It granted security of tenure of existing crofts and established the first Crofters Commission, which had rent-fixing powers. Rents were generally reduced and outstanding arrears cancelled. The Act failed however to address the issue of severely limited access to land, and crofters soon renewed their protest actions. The Land League fragmented during the 1890s after the Liberal Party adopted many of its objectives.

The second iteration of the Highland Land League took a decidedly leftish position, declaring that Liberalism had been the deadly enemy of the Highland proletariat. Crofters and workers were to be united in a common cause and a link with the young Labour Party would last until the league's demise in the early 1920s.[5]

At the 1917 annual general meeting that elected Erskine, the Land League adopted new aims and objects. Scottish autonomy should be a foremost plank of policy. Within a year this had solidified into explicit support for Scottish independence. The Gaelic language would become central to the organisation's activities, taking its place next to the ventilation of crofters' grievances and advocacy for the return of the land to the people. It was no accident that the new aims and objects matched the trajectory of Erskine's *Scottish Review* at the time.⁶

~

The *Scottish Review* of winter 1919 that announced Maclean's membership of Erskine's National Committee also contained an article by its editor, the Aberdonian trade unionist William Diack, about the Scottish Labour College. The college was proving to be a resounding success, the article noted approvingly, with a total of 565 students attending the 13 evening classes running in Glasgow, and a further 43 classes running throughout the rest of Scotland. The student roll was over 2,000, 'a wonderfully good record for two years work', and the promoters hoped to extend their activities from Sunday and evening classes to full time study.⁷

Diack pointed out a weakness in the curriculum however: 'the absence of any definite place for the study of Scottish history from the national and democratic point of view'. After listing all the books recommended for pupils, from Marx's *Capital*, to Shakespeare's *Julius Caesar*, he pointed out the 'extraordinary omissions which must at once strike the impartial observer'.

> Not a single distinctively Scottish book in the whole selection! Not a single book bearing directly on Scottish history, on Scottish land and labour problems, or on any phase whatever of Celtic literature.
>
> ... I feel very strongly that in a Scottish Labour College, Scottish literature, Scottish land and labour problems and Scottish national history ought to be adequately represented. Scotland may be relegated to the background in our ordinary schools and colleges, but there is no reason why Scottish history – and particularly Scottish political history of the past 120 years should be omitted from the Labour College curriculum. The story of the Scottish political martyrs. The economic teachings of the early Scottish land reformers, the black story of the Highland clearances – all these things ought to receive at least as much prominence in the curriculum of a Scottish Labour College as the history of the Sassenach Co-operators.⁸

The comments struck a chord. From August 1920, Maclean's writings were peppered with references to 'the treacherous deed' of 1707 (the union of the English and Scottish parliaments), the Jacobite rebellions, the Highland Clearances and other incidents of Scottish history. And the following year, he was calling the journal *Liberty* the best paper 'from a Scots standpoint' and praising the editor, John MacArthur, for teaching 'true Scots history instead of the false and perverted variety taught in the school books'.[9]

Gerard Cairns suggests the turmoil in Maclean's life over the winter of 1919-20 had led to a process of reflection on his identity, a process that crystallised in a conception of himself as a Scottish socialist as distinct from a British one.[10] Certainly one insight Maclean gained through his visits south of the border in 1919 was that the war had caused the Scots working class to swing further to the left than their English counterparts.

~

There is no written account of the discussion between Maclean and Erskine of Marr in July 1920. But Cairns says there were outputs. 'From these outputs we can ascertain that the two learned gentlemen spoke about Scottish history, the prospects for Scottish independence, Celtic communism, Ireland, and Maclean's dispute with the leaders of the new Communist Party of Great Britain.'[11]

Maclean also responded positively to Erskine's long standing advocacy for the Gaelic language. Maclean's parents had been part of a strong Glasgow Gaelic community. The language was spoken in the house. While he was not a Gaelic speaker himself – English being the language of education and progress - it is notable that before the war he contributed to the journal *Justice* using the penname Gael. As far back as 1912, he posited a Scottish parliament as a distinct possibility that could be utilised as a machine for democracy.[12]

In the week after Maclean and Erskine met, the Highland Land League released its annual report. The report was to be submitted for approval at its annual general meeting to be held in Glasgow on 21 August. Maclean was to be a speaker, quite likely at Erskine's invitation.

The report dealt with various phases of the land question, particularly as it affected the Highlands. It said:

> The outstanding event of the year has been the land revolution in the islands. In Lewis, Skye and Raasay members of the league took forcible possession of holdings promised to them during the years of the European War; and it was not until the men entered on their promised land that it was realised that the English Government's promises were merely scraps of paper, intended for the duration of hostilities. Warrants, with the concurrence of the Government,

have been issued against our members in Back and Coll Back (Lewis) and others in Skye and Raasay have been served with prolix interdict. ... But even in its infallible and seraphic majesty, the law, has been held up; and the 'felons' who were to be dungeoned for daring to claim the right to live are still sharing in that measure of liberty permitted to our tributary country.[13]

In 1918, Lord Leverhulme had purchased the Isle of Lewis for £150,000 from the Matheson family. He envisaged that the island environment would be transformed and its inhabitants would be rescued from the poverty of centuries by the economy being driven by the exploitation of the vast fish resources in the surrounding seas. However, conflict soon arose when island seamen and servicemen returned from the war to discover a new landlord whose declared intent was to uproot their identity as independent crofters and fishermen and turn them into tenured wage-earners. The government had promised land to these returning war veterans who fought back against Leverhulme's land re-settlement plans. Ensuing confrontations resulted in riots and land seizure by the islanders.[14]

Maclean travelled to Lewis in the first week of August 1920 and after meeting with the land raiders, he addressed a public meeting in Stornoway. The *Glasgow Herald* reported:

> The land crisis in Lewis and the hardships endured in various parts of the island by ex-Service men and others who are unable to obtain land for homes and holdings were investigated this week by Mr John McLean, Govan. Among other places he visited the farms of Coll and Gress, which were seized some time ago by ex-Service men. He found that many were away at the East Coast fishing, but those at home were busy securing the hay crop. They stopped work, however, and accorded the visitor a hearty welcome. Their grievances were explained, and Mr McLean assured them their case was receiving the close attention of the trade union movement generally, and particularly on the Clyde, where so many of their fellow countrymen were employed.[15]

On Sunday 8 August, Maclean was back on the Clyde, attending a demonstration organised by the Glasgow Labour Party Housing Association. The gathering was to protest about proposed rent increases and attracted a crowd of several thousands.[16] Harry McShane recalls that Captain White from the Irish Citizen Army turned up with a regiment of men. 'He lined them up and drilled them on Glasgow Green. That created one sensation ...' The other sensation was Maclean's new pamphlet, *All hail, the Scottish Communist Republic!* in which he came out unequivocally for an independent Scotland.[17]

He wrote:

> Scotland must again have independence, but not to be ruled over by traitor chiefs and politicians. The communism of the clans must be re-established on a modern basis. (Bolshevism, to put it roughly, is but the modern expression of the communism of the *mir*.) Scotland must therefore work itself into a communism embracing the whole country as a unit. The country must have but one clan, as it were - a united people working in co-operation and co-operatively, using the wealth that is created.
>
> We can safely say, then: back to communism and forward to communism.[18]

Neil Davidson suggests that Maclean was using the supposed communist nature of the historical clans for two purposes: first, to reassure his readers that communism was not an alien form of society in Scotland, but was already present in Scottish history; second, to make the Russian communist experience more comprehensible by comparing Scottish clan society to the Russian *mir*.[19]

On the evening of Saturday 21 August, Maclean spoke at the meeting of the Highland Land League in Glasgow. 'Celtic impulsiveness' attended the meeting according to the *Glasgow Herald*, 'with a degree of animation rarely encountered in public meetings today'.[20]

The meeting, which was chaired by the league's president Angus MacDonald, saw a strong difference of opinion among the audience about the land seizures in Lewis. MacDonald's contention that there was enough land to spare for those who had fought for it was vigorously disputed.

Graham Peace, a representative of the Commonwealth League, prompted uproar when he said that it was a fact that when Lord Leverhulme bought the island, he bought the 28,000 inhabitants. 'It's an insult to Lewis, sir – a vile insult, sir!' one Islander exclaimed.

Peace reasoned:

> There was no man, woman or child on that island who could live unless they had access to the land and the things that came from it by human labour. Lord Leverhulme would have no small holdings, because he knew perfectly well that his power to exploit the labour of others lay in their being dispossessed of the

right to labour for themselves. Was he right? he asked. The responses showed a diversity of opinion.[21]

Peace then fell foul of Highland sentiment by mentioning he was speaking at a meeting in Edinburgh next day.

'On Sunday!' ejaculated a Highlander in a tone expressive of surprise and deprecation. ... 'Clear out; away with you,' shouted another interrupter. 'Off you go to your Sabbath-breaking.'[22]

Roland Muirhead, national secretary of the Scottish Home Rule Association, moved a resolution demanding the restoration of Scottish independence. John Maclean seconded, with an explanation that he was out for a Scottish Communist Republic.

> Their independent Scotland would be ruled by the men from the workshops, from the fishing boats, and from the land. Glasgow would be their capital and not Edinburgh, the English capital of Scotland.
>
> Mr Maclean, in the course of his remarks said he had recently visited Stornoway. He found that people were afraid to open their mouths. Cowardice had come to the Highlands. It was their state of dependence upon Lord Leverhulme that made them cowards. The same servile spirit that had characterised Highland gamekeepers and Highland policemen was at work in Stornoway. [Applause and dissent.][23]

A resolution was passed expressing 'full sympathy with the land raiders who have been obliged to take forcible possession of holdings' and a collection was taken in aid of the raiders.

In the *Vanguard*, Maclean had noted that the biggest part of the discussion on the Scottish estimates in the House of Commons on 4 August 1919 had been taken up with the question of the raids, and the Secretary for Scotland, Robert Munro had promised to visit Lewis.[24]

> Mr. Maclean suggested that the Land Leaguers should appoint one or two delegates to visit the raiders about the same time as the Secretary for Scotland 'to strengthen the men against any temptation that might be put in their way'.
>
> A member of the Highland opposition element expressed the opinion that the people of Lewis were quite capable of taking care of themselves without the advice of any clique from Glasgow.

> The Chairman intimated that the League would adopt Mr Maclean's suggestion.[25]

Maclean was all-in with his new pals, and when illness prevented Erskine from chairing a September event celebrating the 600th anniversary of the Declaration of Arbroath,[26] Maclean happily stepped up in his place.

Maclean's Highland fling didn't last long. By early 1921, Erskine had given up his flirtation with Bolsheviks and was headed back to the right, while Maclean wrote no more of his Celtic communism.

54

POLAND

In July 1920, the British government announced that it would send military supplies to Poland to assist the Poles in their fight against Bolshevik forces advancing on Warsaw. The Labour movement was deeply concerned, later writing: 'During the early days of August it became evident from the tone of leading articles in the press that there was every possibility of the clandestine hostility being pursued by the British Government against the Russian Government being transformed into open warfare.'[1]

The Hands Off Russia campaign had been advocating industrial action for some time. Most notably, on 10 May 1920, London dockers had paused the loading of 18-pounder guns and ammunition ordered by the Polish government onto the *SS Jolly George*. Their reason was 'that the Poles were at war with the Russian Soviet Government and that they were determined to prevent these munitions from leaving the country'. Three days later, the cargo was discharged.[2]

On 9 August the Labour Party and the Trades Union Congress formed a Council of Action. Its manifesto declared 'The war against which Labour for two years has warned the people is now upon us.' It went on:

> The misgivings and intense feeling manifested in all ranks of Labour in the present crisis are due to the failure during nearly two years to make with Russia that peace which the Soviet government, whatever its defects, has so obviously from the first desired and which the dire needs of the world demand. The workers are profoundly convinced that if now, when world war or world peace is in the balance, they consent to aid by their labour a policy which means war, then they would have their share of guilt in the crime which that act would constitute.[3]

A general conference of trade unions and Labour Party affiliates on 13

August considered a resolution to give the Council of Action the power to authorise direct action, i.e. a general strike.

The General Secretary of the National Union of Railwaymen, JH Thomas MP, was clear that what was contemplated was not a simple 'down tools' policy. 'It is nothing of the kind,' he said. 'If this resolution is to be given effect to it means a challenge to the whole constitution of the country.'[4]

It was a full-blown crisis.

~

Before the First World War, Poland had been part of the Russian Empire. During the war, German and Austrian forces overran Russia's Polish provinces and under the Treaty of Brest-Litovsk in March 1918, Russia gave up Poland and the Baltic states of Lithuania, Latvia and Estonia to Germany and Austria-Hungary, and recognized the independence of Ukraine, Georgia and Finland. After the armistice with Germany, Russia renounced the treaty, and called on the working masses of the border states to decide their own fate. The installation of Soviet-led governments, Lenin explained, would enable the Red Army to arrive as liberators.[5]

The Poles had other ideas. Poland declared its independence and Józef Pilsudski, leader of the Polish Socialist Party, arrived in Warsaw from a German prison and was declared head of state of the Second Polish Republic. Pilsudski envisaged Poland's future as a modern version of the 18th century First Polish Republic, encompassing the lands of the former Grand Duchy of Lithuania.

On 19 December 1918, Warsaw warned Moscow that it would defend 'the integrity of the territories occupied by the Polish nation', including Belarus and Lithuania.[6] Conversely the Russian government lent its fraternal support to the creation of soviet governments in Belarus and Lithuania, as obstacles in the path of any eastward move by the Poles.[7]

At the Paris Peace Conference, the Allies found it difficult to reach agreement about Poland's borders and the status of Soviet Russia. The British and Americans were inclined to accept the Bolsheviks as the de facto government. The French however were aggressively anti-Bolshevik and supported elements of the deposed Russian provisional government who were against the independence of parts of the former Russian Empire. For the Allies, Poland represented a bulwark against the spread of Bolshevism into Europe. For the Soviet government it was a bridge for exactly that purpose.

~

With the Soviet government deeply engaged in civil war throughout 1919, fighting White Russian forces at all points of the compass, Polish forces took the opportunity to expand east, capturing Vilnius in April, Lwów (Lviv) in July and Minsk in August. At that point, having gained control of Eastern Galicia, most of Belarus, and the Volhynia region of north-west Ukraine, the Polish Army paused. Churchill urged the Poles to link up with White Russian forces under General Denikin for a combined push on Moscow. Pilsudski felt the Polish Army had reached its limits however, and mindful of Denikin's reluctance to recognise Polish independence, he declined Churchill's suggestion.

When Denikin captured Kiev from the Red Army in August, the anti-communist Ukrainian leader Simon Petliura turned to the Poles for assistance. On 2 December 1919, Petliura and Pilsudski agreed to cooperate. A fortnight later, Kiev changed hands again when the Red Army displaced Denikin's forces.

On 8 December the Supreme Allied Council at Versailles finally decided on an eastern boundary for Poland. Called the Curzon Line, after British Foreign Secretary Lord Curzon, it ran from Grodno in the north, through Brest-Litovsk, to the former Austrian-Russian border in the south. It took no account of Pilsudski's aspirations, nor the territory he had occupied since the start of the year.

British Prime Minister Lloyd George was critical of the Polish moves against the Lithuanian and Belorussian Soviet Republics, which were in open defiance of the peace conference. At the end of 1919 his position was that Polish claims to territory not ethnographically Polish were 'extravagant', and he would not support them. He would send arms to Poland for defensive but not offensive purposes. He would not encourage co-operation with the Russian Whites. And he would undertake no responsibility for the consequences of a Polish campaign in Russia which got into difficulties.[8]

In the first two months of 1920, Russia concluded peace agreements with Estonia and Latvia and was negotiating with Lithuania and Poland. At the same time, the Allied Supreme Council decided it would offer military support to border states if the Red Army crossed legitimate frontiers, including the Curzon Line.[9]

Despite the Polish-Russian peace discussions, Pilsudski pursued the military option. In March, Polish troops advanced to a position that interrupted the railway connection between two Soviet armies. The Russian

Commissar of Foreign Affairs, Georgy Chicherin, accused Poland of starting an offensive war against Soviet Russia and the 'independent Ukrainian Republic'. In lobbying Western powers, Polish diplomats accused Russia of provoking war. A Soviet note of 23 April 1920 insisted to the contrary that Russia wanted peace.[10]

On 21 April, Pilsudski and Petliura agreed a swap deal whereby Ukraine would get Kiev and Poland would get Lwów. Four days later, combined Ukrainian and Polish forces crossed the Ukrainian border and made for Kiev. The city was taken on 7 May and Pilsudski returned to Warsaw in triumph, confident that Russia would fold.

It was a grave miscalculation. In fact, as Trotsky commented, 'The capture of Kiev by the Poles did us a great service ... it awakened the country.' British opposition leader Herbert Asquith concurred. 'Wantonly undertaken and connived at by the tacit acquiescence of Europe', the Polish invasion had managed 'to unite Russia and to fuse into one body that which has proved a more powerful and effective military force including men of the old as well as the new regime'.[11]

~

The Russians may have been talking peace, but they were prepared for war. Their counteroffensive began on 29 April. On 12 June, the Red Army recaptured Kiev, and as the Polish troops retreated, took control of Ukraine. To the north, the Russians took Minsk on 11 July, and over the following week added Vilnius and Gredno. By 1 August, the Red Army had captured Brest-Litovsk, 125 miles east of Warsaw.

London and Paris became increasingly alarmed. On 11 July Lord Curzon urged Moscow to call a truce, but Lenin decided to push ahead. On 21 July, Lloyd George told the House of Commons that an independent Poland was essential to the whole fabric of peace, and that the extension of the borders of triumphant Sovietland right up to the frontiers of Germany might rob the Allies of the fruits of their dearly-won victory. Therefore 'the Allies had decided that they must take such steps as were available to save Poland and stay the Bolshevik advance'.[12]

On 4 August the *Times* noted the Bolshevists were continuing hostilities as actively as ever, the invasion had passed well beyond the Curzon Line, and a Soviet government had been established in those parts of Poland occupied by the Red Army. 'So,' it wrote, 'the "Red bridge of Social Revolution" is being flung boldly across Europe, as Comrade Trotsky promised, and as Mr Lloyd George foretold, while the Allies, so far as the world knows, are doing nothing to make good their warnings, except to await the results of reports and consultations. In the meantime, Poland is being strangled. At a certain stage of the operation, assistance comes too late.'[13]

When the situation appeared to be on the verge of a massive escalation, the tide of battle suddenly turned. Much as Poland had overreached by capturing Kiev in May, so the Russians had advanced on several fronts while not consolidating their gains. On 6 August, Pilsudski identified a gap between the northern and southern Red Army groups east of Warsaw. He ordered Polish armies into the gap. The Russian forces lacked coordination and failed to appreciate the threat. On 16 August the Poles drove unimpeded through the opening in the lines and the Red forces retreated in disarray. By 21 August, Pilsudski had destroyed three Soviet armies, while another was trapped and forced over the German border into captivity. Driving on, by mid-October, the Poles had once again captured Vilnius and Minsk.

On 25 August, the Politburo in Moscow designated Wrangel's White Russian breakout from the Crimea as its primary focus and accepted Lenin's admission that the time to talk peace had come. Poland and Russia signed an armistice on 12 October 1920.[14]

The crisis passed, but in its final report, the British Council of Action stated, 'There is no doubt whatever that the action of the Labour Movement early in August prevented open war with Russia.'[15]

~

For John Maclean the British Council of Action's contemplation of direct action was the right threat, but for the wrong reason. He decided to reissue the Bolshevik pamphlet *Russia's appeal to the British workers*, originally distributed among British troops in Russia in 1918 and 1919. The pamphlet criticised the system of capitalism in Britain and contrasted it with the new Russia 'being slowly created' by the Bolsheviks.

In a new preface, dated 21 August 1920, Maclean said he had taken the step in light of the attempt by the British government to test the resistive power of British Labour against another world war. 'I wish to incite the workers to fight the real enemy – the Landlords and Capitalists at home,' he wrote.

But in a significant development of his political outlook, for the first time he called for a Scottish Communist Republic.

Lloyd George knows he could not beat Russia in the open as the Irish at home would paralyse him – and Ireland would have the support of Revolutionary Labour in the process.

Britain must first smash Ireland, and thereafter by blockade starve Russia out of Communism. If these two moves succeed, then she braces herself for the war with America.

We Communists must Prevent the Murder of the Irish Race as the first step to Save Humanity.

The Labour Council of Action will not fit the bill. There are plenty of honest men acting as leaders of Labour, but proved traitors are at the helm – the Hendersons, the Thomases, and the Clynes.

WE COMMUNISTS ARE THE ONLY ONES THAT CAN LEAD SOCIETY TO COMMUNISM. Therefore we must form a Communist Council of Action to assume the real power when the proper moment arrives.

In the process I favour a Scottish Communist Republic as a first step towards World Communism, with Glasgow as the head and centre.

We must have a Rank and File Dictatorship through delegates directly representative of the various workshops and industries.

We must start Scottish Communism round the organisation of the Scottish Co-operative Society and the distributive branches, as food supplies are the first requisite.

Let, then, at once a Central Communist Committee be formed in Glasgow, and on with the World Revolution.[16]

Maclean didn't hang around. At a meeting in Glasgow on 28 August, at which he presided, 'it was decided to form a Communist "Council of Action" representative of the Lanarkshire Miners' Communist group, the Socialist Labour Party, the Clyde Workers' Committee and the International Union of ex-Service Men. It is intended to form a Scottish Communist Party which will not be affiliated to the Labour Party, and which will oppose all Labour Party candidates in Glasgow and Lanarkshire at the next General Election.'[17]

55

A SCOTTISH COMMUNIST PARTY

The Communist Unity Convention in London at the beginning of August had been conspicuously light on Scottish representation. The British Socialist Party's refusal to recognise its Tradeston branch meant that John Maclean was excluded. Only seven Scottish branches of the BSP were represented (Central, College and Gorbals from Glasgow, plus Dumfries, Edinburgh, Greenock and Paisley). The Communist Unity Group sent one Scottish delegate, Tom Bell, as did a Glasgow branch of the ILP. There was also a delegate from the Greenock Workers' Social Committee. Out of a total of 152, there were a mere 10 Scottish delegates.[1]

The CPGB's decision at the unity convention to apply for affiliation to the Labour Party provoked immediate hostility among the Scottish Communist groups. On 14 August, the *Worker*, the journal of the Scottish Workers' Committees, called the decision an 'unpardonable mistake' adding that 'Communists in Scotland are nine-tenths anti-Labour Party' and that there was 'not the slightest prospect of the Communist party in its present form making any headway north of the border'. In the following issue, Alex Geddes, who attended the conference as the delegate from the Greenock Workers' Committee, called for 'a Scottish Communist Party'.[2]

A meeting on 11 September between Maclean's supporters, the *Worker* group and the Socialist Labour Party to discuss the formation in Glasgow of a Scottish Communist Party proved to be 'quite amicable', according to Harry McShane, and a further meeting was scheduled for 2 October.

On 27 September, Willie Gallacher returned from Moscow. Like Moses descending from the mountain with the Ten Commandments, he brought with him Lenin's directives that there was to be one British Communist Party and it must seek affiliation to the Labour Party. He immediately sought to intercede in the process of forming a Scottish party.

Maclean did not attend the 2 October meeting at City Hall, but Harry

McShane and James Macdougall were there representing the Tramp Trust. Gallacher turned up and asked to be allowed to make a statement before any decision was taken, which was eventually agreed to.

'I made a short report of the discussions at the Second Congress,' Gallacher recalled, 'and went on to explain the case that had been put by Lenin. I ended up advising the delegates not to go ahead with the formation of a party or the election of an executive but to elect a provisional committee, responsible for opening unity negotiations with the recently formed Communist Party of Great Britain.'[3]

In an attitude Walter Kendall described as either naïve or Machiavellian, Gallacher told the delegates 'We can rally our anti-Parliamentarian forces for the next meeting of the Third International and endeavour to carry the Conference in deleting this clause.'

McShane recalled Gallacher being fierier than that. 'Gallacher jumped up at the meeting and pointed out all the anti-parliamentarians and said that none of them was eligible to join the Communist [International]! It was a great shock to all of us.'[4]

The weight of Lenin's tablets told, and a resolution repudiating parliamentary tactics was defeated by forty-one votes to nine.[5]

The group called itself the Communist Labour Party and elected an executive. McShane nominated James Macdougall, but 'he didn't get on'.[6]

Maclean was scathing of Gallacher's intervention. In the November edition of the *Vanguard,* he wrote:

> Gallacher and *The Worker* have sneered openly at the idea of a 'Scottish' Communist Party, although all connected with *The Worker* have been compelled to trade under the name of the 'Scottish' Workers' Committee. There is no reason for the existence of the Communist Labour Party as its object is the very same as the Communist Party of Britain ...
>
> Such brutal wanton shattering of the hopes and spirit of the best fighting elements in Scotland becomes a base betrayal of the wage-slaves of the world and the subject peoples of the world at such a critical juncture as this ...
>
> We refuse to be bluffed by Gallacher that Lenin says we must have only one Communist party in Britain. Why does Gallacher start another Communist Party if he is so anxious about Lenin? *I for one will not follow a policy dictated by Lenin until Lenin knows the situation more clearly than he possibly can know it from an enemy of Marxian Economic Classes* [original emphasis] as Gallacher privately declared himself to me to be.[7]

The CPGB's decision to apply for affiliation to the Labour Party was a prime reason for the formation of the CLP. Application was one thing, acceptance was another. The CPGB applied on 10 August and the Labour Party refused the application on 11 September 1920. Correspondence between the two parties ensued, ending with a further Labour Party refusal on 18 November[8]

In the December *Vanguard*, John Maclean summoned all in Scotland who favoured the conditions for membership of the Third International [the so-called '21 points'] to attend a conference to form a Scottish Communist Party. Maclean wrote:

> Let attention be paid to point 17, 'Each party must change its old name to that of communist party of such and such country, section of the Third International.'
>
> William Gallacher is going the rounds ridiculing the idea of a 'Scottish' Communist Party because he has been to Russia and poses as the gramophone of Lenin. Nothing in point 17 precludes the formation of a Scottish party as Scotland is a definite country. The exercise of a little honest thinking will demonstrate that.[9]

Gallacher was not only taking aim at the idea of a Scottish party but also had begun to target Maclean himself. In his *Last Memoirs ...* (1966) he gives an account of his campaign, which amounted to nothing less than attempted character assassination of his former close comrade.

Firstly, Gallacher claimed that in the week following the 2 October meeting where he had successfully scuttled the formation of a Scottish Communist Party, he had met with Maclean. Gallacher told Maclean that Lenin had expressed a strong desire to see him. Maclean responded by saying he had certain commitments, but when they were concluded, he would make the trip to Moscow. Gallacher was happy at the outcome of the conversation and 'despite his anger at what had happened with regard to the separate party, we were on the friendliest terms'.[10]

This sits awkwardly with Maclean's previous failed attempts to obtain a passport to travel to Russia, and his determination only to travel with official papers. Aside from Gallacher's account, there is no other evidence of such a change of heart by Maclean.

Gallacher goes on to say that about a month later, he learned that Maclean had decided not to go to the Soviet Union. He sought Maclean out in the Ingram Street hall where he was using a room as the headquarters of the Tramp Trust. Sandy Ross was also there and in Gallacher's account, when pressed on his 'promise' Maclean said, 'How do I know that what you told me about Lenin is true?' Why are you so anxious to get me away from Scotland?' Gallacher professed to be astonished, and his suspicion immediately fixed on Ross, who would be out of a job if Maclean did go to Russia.

'One thing led to another,' Gallacher wrote. Indeed, they did. Gallacher says he learned that a prominent member of the Socialist Labour Party had told Maclean that he, Gallacher, was jealous of the standing Maclean had with the working class and wanted him out of Glasgow. 'I was mad, blazing mad,' Gallacher wrote.

> When I got home I made a very bad blunder, one of many of which I have been guilty on occasions. I wrote a letter. I marked it *Private and Confidential* and sent it to the secretary of the SLP, a lad named [Thomas] Mitchell, asking him to put it before his Executive. I explained what had taken place between John and myself, when he agreed to go to Moscow, and how a prominent member of the SLP had succeeded in getting John to call off the visit by telling him that I was jealous of him, a very silly statement and one that would have had no effect if John had not been a very sick man. I went on to say that this was a very serious matter; that John was suffering from hallucinations and, if he didn't receive treatment, it could mean the end of him as a working-class agitator and teacher.[11]

Mitchell gave a copy of the letter to Maclean and the following Sunday evening Maclean read it out to a packed audience at St Mungo's Halls, telling them 'Gallacher is trying to make out that I am mad. He is trying to put me in an asylum.'[12]

~

In conjunction with the SLP, Maclean organised a meeting to discuss the formation of a Scottish Communist Party. It was held at the SLP Hall in Renfrew St on Christmas Day 1920.[13]

When Gallacher and a colleague pushed their way in to the packed hall there was a 'sort of hushed gasp'. James Macdougall was in the chair and after a few seconds shouted, 'What do you want?'

'I want to make a short statement about a letter I wrote about Comrade John Maclean,' said Gallacher.

'You'll make no talk here! Get out!' Macdougall yelled.

'After I make the talk,' insisted Gallacher.

John Maclean shouted, 'Gallacher, you're a waster!'

A man in the audience, in a very clear voice, said, 'Mr Chairman, I think we should hear what Comrade Gallacher has to say.'

Amid a slowly rising muttered chorus of 'Let him speak', Macdougall slowly sat down, while Maclean continued standing, glaring at Gallacher.

'A private letter that I wrote to the executive of the Socialist Labour Party has been provided to John Maclean,' Gallacher began. 'In that letter I stated that John Maclean was suffering from hallucinations and I am here to offer proof.'

The meeting erupted. Gallacher looked around and waited until the noise abated sufficiently for him to continue.

'There is no-one in this meeting who has stood more by John Maclean than I have done. But there are men and women who are leading Maclean on to his ruin.'

There was renewed uproar and a member of the audience interjected, 'It's you that is suffering from hallucinations Wullie ...'

The noise again abated ...

'I have been told that Maclean was poisoned in prison – ' Gallacher continued.

'How would you know?' interrupted Maclean.

'I am happy to go into the whole circumstances of our differences if your friends will name a date for public discussion,' Gallacher offered smoothly.

'I don't meet with a man who writes dirty letters about me. A man who did that is no better than a government agent!' exclaimed Maclean heatedly.

'Let's have a date when this can be discussed publicly eh?' responded Gallacher.

There was hubbub in the audience. Someone called out, 'This is humiliating!' Someone else said, 'No - let's hear them out!'

Maclean left the table and advanced down the centre aisle towards Gallacher. Gallacher also advanced until the two men were just three metres apart.

'Why have you come to this conference?' demanded Maclean.

Appealing to the audience, Gallacher said, 'I assure everyone I am here in the best spirit. I just want to hear the arguments for and against.'

Pointing at Gallacher, Maclean said, 'He has come to burst up this organisation!'

Gallacher responded, 'It's a dirty lie that I am here to cause disruption of any kind. Is there no one prepared to meet me say next week to discuss our attitude towards Russia and other questions?'

Maclean said hotly, 'A man who goes behind my back and writes letters about me is a reptile and I will not meet him on any platform.'

Harry McShane later wrote, 'I never saw John involved in anything like that – Gallacher's letter had done it.'[14]

At the two glared at each other, a member of the audience called out, 'I suggest this meeting be adjourned. No good is likely to result from the present temper.'

Several other audience members voiced their agreement, 'Aye', 'Aye.'

From the chair, Macdougall said 'The business of the meeting will be done in spite of Gallacher.'

The man who had called out responded, 'Well, I may tell you, the majority of those left are disgusted with the meeting.'

At that point, a spokesman for the SLP informed the audience that the party was not prepared to fuse into a Scottish Communist Party.[15]

Maclean returned to the platform and conferred with Macdougall amid a loud hubbub throughout the hall. Eventually Maclean turned to the audience.

'I move that any unattached Socialists here join the Socialist Labour Party.'

There were hoots of derision at such a feeble resolution, and the meeting broke up.

~

On the day a further unity conference convened in Leeds to fuse the various revolutionary groups into the Communist Party of Great Britain, Maclean's 'Open letter to Lenin' was published in the *Socialist*. Having seen his own plans for a Scottish Communist Party scuppered, it was a declaration of war on everyone involved in the unification process.

Maclean led off by advising the Soviet leader to discount anything he had been told by recent British visitors.

> A conference is being held today (Sunday, 30 January) at Leeds to form a united Communist Party as the British section of the Third International. I

believe that you have too good a grasp of affairs to be very far deceived by the situation in Britain, and by the pretentions of most of the prominent ones who will be present. A various assortment of personages visited Russia last year, openly, secretly, and 'secretly' whilst the authorities were winking the other eye.

From printed reports of statements issued by them in the name of people who did not delegate them we learn that you are asked to believe that large numbers of workers are organised on a workshop basis ready for the signal of revolution, and that a well-organised and disciplined party will be got ready to head the way through the revolution.

You will recognise that it is the business of the British government to deceive you and get you to make false calculations, as it made the Kaiser form wrong estimates and lay plans for the defeat of Germany. You must therefore recognise that anybody or anything coming from Britain should be treated with the utmost caution and scepticism after Russia's treatment by Britain during the last two years and more. British capitalism is not out to recognise or trade with Russian communism, whatever temporary expedients it may resort to. It realises more clearly than any other section of capitalism that a struggle for supremacy has now commenced between capital and labour, and it is determined to crush labour by crushing the Russian republic, and to restore reaction as it is in process of restoring reaction in the defeated countries still called the 'central powers'.[16]

After outlining his view that England was gathering her forces for a coming struggle with America, Maclean warned that if America pressed hard this year while British trade was paralysed, Britain would seek an accommodation with Russia.

A sham Labour government, with our beloved friends MacDonald and Snowden (and ethereal Ethel, too) in it, will be formed, although the real work will be done by the 'old gang' under the guise of the Privy Council.

This expedient of itself would not deceive you, since you and your comrades have the exact measure of the leaders of Labour and of the ILP, and that Lloyd George well knows.

He must, therefore, make way for a Communist Party whose 'leaders' are controlled by him. Those who are coming together are a heterogeneous mixture of anarchists, sentimentalists, syndicalists, with a sprinkling of Marxists. Unity in such a camp is likely to be impossible; but should unity lead to any menace, then the 'leaders' will conduct surplus energy through 'safe' channels - safe to Lloyd George.[17]

This was conspiracy theory taken to fanciful extremes.

Maclean proceeded to denounce the likely parliamentary leader, Lieutenant Colonel Cecil Malone, MP, and the editor of *The Communist* (the official organ of the CPGB) Francis Meynell, who Maclean said was never in either the Social Democratic Federation or the British Socialist Party. 'It is only in a country such as Britain, ruled by the most unscrupulous and cunning capitalist class that has ever disgraced this earth, that totally unknown, untried, and inexperienced men could be thrust to the front,' he wrote.

Maclean then turned his attention to Willie Gallacher. He detailed Gallacher's efforts to sabotage Maclean's attempts to form a Scottish party, his slandering of Maclean, and his bursting up of James Clunie's Marxist classes in Fife. He went on:

> He [Gallacher] has led you to believe that there is a workshop movement in Scotland. That is a black lie. I have been at work gates all summer and autumn up and down the Clyde valley, and I am positive when I say that victimisation after the premature forty hours strike crushed the workshop movement. Unemployment today has struck terror into the hearts of those at work, as starvation is meant to tame the workless. No industrial movement of a radical character is possible at present outside the ranks of the miners, and that movement has been revived and is being carried on by SLPers.
>
> I am of the belief that the workshop movement in England is as dead as it is in Scotland.
>
> Do not place reliance, then, on the United Communist Party that will be formed today, and do not rely on the workshop movement either.[18]

Maclean implored Lenin to take advice about Britain from Peter Petroff, 'the only Russian who knows the working-class movement intimately in London and Glasgow'. He reminded Lenin that it was he, Maclean, who started the movement in 1917 for the release of Petroff and Chicherin, and that it was on Petroff's advice Lenin made him consul for Scotland. 'It was my fidelity to you and the cause of revolution that got me the five years' sentence in 1918,' he said.

Maclean concluded by describing his work with the unemployed and the wider implications of the industrial slump.

> As more and more are thrown idle and begin to starve for the government means them to starve you can realise that, sooner or later, a mass movement, vaster and bolder than ever before, is bound to show itself. The situation becomes all the more serious, since many wage-slaves here are Irishmen, whose country is being more and more cunningly and cruelly tortured. The rightful racial and class hatred of these men is going to make for an avalanche of opinion and feeling that are bound, sooner or later, to break through the bonds of English capitalism.[19]

It's unknown whether Lenin ever saw Maclean's letter. If it did make it to Moscow, it is likely it would have been under a covering message from the CPGB characterising it as evidence of an unbalanced mind.

In any event, Lenin had larger concerns. As Orlando Figes notes:

> Once the Whites had been defeated the peasants turned against the Bolsheviks, whose requisitionings had brought much of rural Russia to the brink of starvation. By the autumn of 1920 the whole of the country was inflamed with peasant wars.
>
> The consignment of grain to the cities had been brought to a halt within the rebel strongholds. As the urban food crisis deepened, workers went on strike.
>
> The strikes that swept across Russia during February 1921 were no less revolutionary than the peasant rebellions. Workers had been angered by the Bolsheviks' attempts to subordinate trade unions to the party-state. In 1920 a Workers' Opposition emerged within the party to defend the rights of the unions in management.
>
> A rash of workers' meetings called for an end to the Communists' privileges, the restoration of free trade and movement (allowing them to barter with the peasants), of civil liberties and the Constituent Assembly.[20]

56

THE UNEMPLOYED

A couple of hours after the Battle of George Square in 1919, a hundred of Clydeside's biggest employers met to discuss tactics. As well as firing off demands for military intervention and calling on the civic authorities to stand firm, they also discussed contingency plans. One was to set up their own paramilitary forces. It did not happen, but at that moment they were not far off what fellow employers were to initiate a few months later in Belfast, where they armed their Orange workplace loyalists - or in another type of uniform in Northern Italy.[1]

In *The New Penguin History of Scotland*, John Foster posed the question, 'Did the Red Clyde cost Scotland two decades of industrial investment?' He said there certainly were employers, e.g. Sir William Beardmore and James Lithgow, who urged immediate dismissals in 1919 to restore discipline. Their colleagues did not agree. The post-war boom was in full flow and even when the boom burst in 1920-21, many employers strove to keep their workforces together in the hope that trade would improve. It never did. The Swedish, French and American shipbuilding industries pulled ahead of Britain in terms of technology and fabrication techniques.

To find the answer, Foster said we must travel to Whitehall and the Bank of England. Once there, we would find them full of Scots. 'We would quickly meet Lord Weir, wartime air minister and later government adviser on armaments, James Lithgow, wartime controller of shipbuilding and later industrial advisor to the Governor of the Bank of England, Lords Maclay and Inverforth, wartime controllers of shipping. Allan Smith MP, leader of the Engineering Employers, Sir Andrew Duncan, wartime controller of steel and later advisor to the Bank of England, Sir Eric and Sir Auckland Geddes, directors of railway companies and tea and rubber plantations, both Cabinet Ministers and not least Bonar Law, Chancellor of the Exchequer and by 1922, Prime Minister.'[2]

These men shared a common perspective about the way forward for the British economy. In general, they wanted deflation - getting the pound back on the gold standard, squeezing inflation out of the system by hiking interest rates and drastically cutting public expenditure. They were well aware of the consequences. It would mean a recession. In their view it was going to happen anyway, so better to get it over and done with and restore the pound as the world's banking currency. That way, world trade would be re-established and Britain would take over from where it had left off in 1914. For Scots employers, so heavily dependent on export markets (and capital export), this policy made good sense. Or so they thought. It also met another concern: the degree to which the wartime economy had grossly over extended industrial capacity.[3]

The post-war boom broke abruptly in the winter of 1920-21. British manufacturers had assumed there would be an insatiable demand for goods they had been unable to export during the war. They invested in new capital and pushed up their prices. However, the world market turned out to be a phantom. Europe was in political and economic turmoil. The overseas producers of food and raw materials were in even worse straits. The wartime expansion of non-European agricultural production had led, with the recovery of European producers, to supply outstripping demand and prices plummeting. There was a glut of shipping throughout the world and British exports of coal and cotton shrank to almost nothing.[4]

Between November 1919 and April 1920, the financial markets and the Bank of England moved. The Treasury bill rate nearly doubled (from 3.5 to 6.5 per cent) and Lloyd George was forced to cut back government spending on housing and welfare. Eric Geddes drew up the program of cuts. As demand dropped, whole sections of the economy became technically insolvent. On Clydeside, shipbuilding employment fell from 60,000 to 25,000 in 18 months. The rise in unemployment began to change the balance of power in industry.[5]

~

In October 1920, John Maclean called a meeting of the unemployed on Glasgow Green. Maclean and Harry McShane marched the men up to the City Chambers, where they sent a deputation to the town council. 'We demanded food at municipal restaurants as the most urgent question of all,' Maclean wrote in the *Vanguard*. 'Then work on farm colonies at trade-union rates of pay, with representation on all committees employing the unemployed. We requested houses to shelter full families on the colonies. We urged the corporation to proceed with all available work of a new and repair character. Failing work we urged emigration to Russia, amidst the laugher of the men who do not intend to lose their slave class. Finally, we requested use of a city hall in which the unemployed might meet and comfortably discuss the situation.'[6]

Under the Scottish Poor Law, support for the poor, homeless and disabled was administered by local parish councils. However, there was no relief for people who were unemployed, and no able-bodied man could get 'outdoor relief' (in the form of money, food, clothing or goods to alleviate poverty) for his wife and children without himself going into a workhouse. Even when relief was granted, the amount was at the discretion of the parish council.

The strictures of the Poor Law were in some cases offset by unemployment insurance, which had evolved in a piecemeal fashion since the advent of the 1911 National Insurance Act. The Act introduced a contributory unemployment insurance scheme, initially limited to three trades where employment was most likely to fluctuate (building, engineering and shipbuilding). Contributions came from the insured person, the employer, and the state. The scheme applied to about three million workers; a million more were added when coverage was extended to munitions workers during the war.

The wartime government promised that after the war there would be financial help for soldiers as they looked for work. A non-contributory scheme saw out-of-work payments (or dole, because they were doled out) made to ex-servicemen in 1918, and they were soon extended to cover many civilian workers. These were means-tested payments for limited periods and meant to cover basic subsistence, including for dependents. This was only a short term arrangement – to end in 1921 – for what was expected to be a temporary problem, but it set an important precedent.

In November 1920 compulsory unemployment insurance was extended to cover 12 million out of Britain's 19 million workforce. The sole object was to provide insurance against casual short-term unemployment. But reliance on an insurance-based system immediately proved inadequate. By the time the extensions came into effect, the short post-war boom had gone into reverse.[7]

The *Worker* group, which had been steered into the new Communist

Labour Party by Willie Gallacher in October, tried to take over the unemployed movement established by Maclean and McShane. Led by Gallacher's protégé, JR Campbell, they argued that the unemployed movement should be developed by linking it with employed workers. The problem was, McShane wrote, 'workshop organisation had largely disappeared and the employed were frightened that they might be made unemployed. The Glasgow Communist Party had done no real work with the unemployed. They were just putting forward propositions to try to get popularity, and we were able to hold them off.'[8]

In *The origins of British Bolshevism*, Raymond Challinor described the obstacles facing Maclean and McShane with the unemployed movement.

> In January 1921, Maclean, backed by the Socialist Labour Party, proposed that a general strike should be held as a protest again mounting unemployment. He failed to secure a response. Similarly, on 23 February 1921, when Maclean held a conference in Glasgow to build an all-Scotland movement of the unemployed. James Clunie in the *Socialist* described the attendance as 'a very sad affair'. In most towns the unemployed remained disorganised. In the few places where organisations existed, funds were virtually non-existent, quite inadequate for sending delegates to conferences and maintaining contact with groups elsewhere. But even more important as a cause of fragmentation was that responsibility for poor relief stayed with local authorities. Initially, therefore, the struggle was seen in a parish pump, not a national, context.[9]

Accordingly, Maclean and McShane focussed their efforts at the local levels, where they did manage to have an impact. McShane recalled, 'There was so much anger about [the Poor Law] that we were able to get tremendous demonstrations and fight individual cases at the parish councils. We were particularly concerned with two parish councils, Glasgow in the north of the city and Govan in the south. Both were made up mainly of shopkeepers, with one or two trade unionists, but the worst councillor in each was a Catholic priest. Both did everything possible to prevent anyone getting anything. The Scottish parish councils were much more parsimonious than the boards of Guardians in England.'[10]

Through the winter of 1920-21 Maclean and McShane held packed meetings in the City Halls and elsewhere. 'Their efforts gave the Glasgow unemployed organisation an ideology,' observed Challinor. 'The reserve army of Labour in Central Scotland spoke with a Marxist voice.'[11] But preoccupied with the day to day struggle to survive, men who were out of work did not have the money, or the energy to help build a revolutionary party.

~

In the early months of 1921, Maclean aligned himself with the Socialist Labour Party, discontinued publication of the *Vanguard*, and began writing for the SLP journal, the *Socialist*. Probably influenced by their anti-nationalist stance, he backed away from his enthusiastic embrace of Scottish independence and focussed his campaigning on the unemployed and the Scottish Labour College.

Then the miners needed a hand, and as usual he was quick to answer the call.

57

DECONTROL

On 12 March 1920, the day after the Trades Union Congress had rejected a motion for a general strike for the nationalisation of the mines, a conference of the miners' federation immediately turned its attention to the pent-up demand for higher wages.

As early as 8 January 1920, the miners' executive had sought a meeting with Prime Minister Lloyd George to discuss the enormous increase in the price of export coal, which had resulted in enhanced profits to coal owners; the high price of industrial coal for domestic users; and the effect of the high price of home coal on the cost of living. The executive suggested there should be an immediate reduction in the price of industrial coal, followed by government action to reduce the price of commodities that largely used coal for their manufacture. Alternatively, the federation would seek an increase in wages to offset the high cost of living.[1]

The reason for this novel attitude was political. The federation was offering an alternative policy to that of the government. The government was usually in the position of protecting the consumer. However, in July 1919, it had added six shillings a ton to the price of coal, an increase the miners felt was unwarranted by the industrial position, and was designed to influence public opinion against the miners' claims for higher wages, shorter hours and nationalisation. High prices meant swollen profits, and in the miners' view, were a preparation for a speedy decontrol of the industry, for handing it back to the owners.[2]

The government refused to consider reducing the price of coal, so on 12 March the federation launched its wage claim. Discussions began again and on 29 March, Lloyd George made his 'final offer'. A miners' conference ballot vote resulted in a small majority for acceptance, and an agreement was signed on 29 April 1920.

Within a fortnight, the government suddenly raised the price of coal.

While some thought the government was again attempting to blacken the miners by linking the rise to their wage increase, historian R Page Arnot took a longer view. 'The government's intention, as was made abundantly clear by subsequent events, was to place each district and each pit on a profit-making basis. For this, no matter what swollen profits were drawn by the better pits and districts, would enable the government to meet the wishes of the coal owners and revert to a completely uncontrolled industry.'[3]

The Coal Mines Control Agreement under which the government controlled the mining industry was scheduled to expire on 31 August 1920. In March 1920, the government brought in the Coal Mines (Emergency) Act, to deal with the finances of the industry up to that date, while flagging another Bill that would deal with the regulation of the industry generally.

When that Bill, the Ministry of Mines Bill, was introduced in June 1920, it was strongly opposed by the miners' federation. The miners particularly objected to the pit committees, district committees, area boards and national board proposed in the Bill, under which they claimed it would be impossible to continue their national wage system. At the annual conference of the federation in July, Vernon Hartshorn announced that 'the executive had arrived unanimously at the conclusion that a more reactionary Bill, or a Bill more prejudicial to the best interests of the miners of the country, could not possibly have been conceived by the biggest enemy of their movement.'[4]

At the conference, federation president Robert Smillie argued strongly for the reduction of household coal prices coupled with a wage increase. After sometimes stormy debate, the conference approved the policy.[5]

The government's reply was an uncompromising negative on both counts. When a special conference of the miners met on 21 August, a vote to issue a strike ballot was carried 168 votes to 3.

The miners began discussions with their partners in the Triple Alliance, the National Union of Railwaymen and the Transport Workers' Federation. On 31 August, the alliance declared they believed the miners' claim was just, but informed the government they were willing to discuss the question. In the meantime, the miners would take their own action to deal with the case.

The miners' ballot resulted in a majority of over 70 per cent for strike action, and on 2 September a notice was issued for all members to cease work on 25 September.[6]

Discussions with the government continued, and on 16 and 17 September, the President of the Board of Trade, Sir Robert Thorne, offered to refer the miners' wage claim to an arbitration tribunal but refused to consider the question of the coal price. Thorne also raised the question of output, stating he was prepared to take a totally different view of any wage claim that was based on increased output.[7]

On Wednesday 22 September, a deputation from the Triple Alliance met with Lloyd George, Bonar Law and the President of the Board of Trade, Sir Robert Thorne. The government's position was unchanged; either a reference of the dispute to arbitration or an advance in wages conditional on higher output.[8]

At a miners' conference the following day, 23 September, Robert Smillie pleaded for the meeting to take a ballot vote on the arbitration offer. There were fierce arguments against, including from South Wales firebrands AJ Cook and Noah Ablett. When the vote was taken, Smillie's viewpoint was defeated 545-360.[9]

When the news was conveyed to the railwaymen and transport workers later that afternoon, their statements made it clear that having both accepted arbitration methods that year, they were not enthusiastic about the strike prospects.[10]

That night at a meeting of the full Triple Alliance, there was a fierce debate. JH Thomas announced that the railwaymen had decided not to come out on 25 September in support of the miners. Harry Gosling, chairman of the Transport Workers' Federation, said he supported a further effort being made to avoid a strike. These announcements angered the miners, and Vernon Hartshorn proposed the immediate dissolution of the conference. Ben Tillett for the transport workers pleaded with the meeting not to pass that resolution, but for the alliance to ask the government what they meant by a tribunal.

In the chair, Robert Smillie said, 'Mr Tillett, this full conference will not send a delegation. We have your decision. We have the best and worst of it, and the position now is that if the miners stop work, they will stop alone.'[11]

Tempers cooled and when the debate continued, Vernon Hartshorn gave the miners' argument for rejecting the offer of arbitration.

> We have already been before a tribunal – the Sankey Commission. The other side put all the brains and wealth they had at the disposal of those who

represented them before their tribunal in order to defeat us in a contest of evidence, and they got beaten. What did they do with us? They spent hundreds of thousands of pounds in a press campaign by means of which they created an atmosphere in this country against the miners. They have called in the press on this occasion, and with the same end in view. A greater campaign of villainy and perjury has never been inaugurated, even in the press, against us. If we allow the press to defeat us in this campaign, then good-bye to trade unionism.[12]

The following morning, Friday 24 September, the miners' executive went to Lloyd George to tell him in person that they were going to stop work the next day. Lloyd George expressed his deep regret, and then began to discuss the question of output. He asked whether the miners could postpone the strike notices for a week and see if they, in discussions with the mine-owners, could develop a scheme to increase output.

The executive discussed the suggestion, and putting aside their dignity, decided to advise their conference to suspend the strike notices for a week. The conference agreed and later that afternoon, the railwaymen and transport workers were advised of the decision. JH Thomas and Harry Gosling expressed their relief, but before the meeting closed, Ernest Bevin from the transport workers made a prophetic observation.

> The men in the country believe that since this Triple Alliance was formed constructive organising work has been going on to make it a workable machine, and my charge is that the six men who are at the head of affairs have not constructed an organisation that is capable of working when the test comes. It has not been capable of working during the present test. I have appealed at meeting after meeting of my own executive and others when the Triple Alliance question has come up, for that to be done. I have said it over and over: 'When the test comes, if you do not make it a real organisation it will be found to be a paper alliance. By God, it has revealed itself to be a paper alliance this week.[13]

~

Negotiations immediately resumed between the miners and the owners on the idea of a wage rise linked to increased output. Despite a week of discussions, the two sides failed to reach agreement on a formula. A ballot on the owners' offer was taken and almost 80 per cent of miners voted against acceptance.

The national strike began on 16 October. It was known as the Datum Line strike, because of the disagreement about what the datum line, or baseline, should be to calculate increased output.[14]

On 21 October, the railwaymen backed the miners, declaring 'unless the miners' claims are granted or negotiations resumed by October 23rd, which result in a settlement, we shall be compelled to take the necessary steps to instruct our members in England, Wales and Scotland to cease work'.

Lloyd George immediately reached out to the miners' executive with a proposal for further talks. The miners suggested the railwaymen postpone their threatened strike action and resumed discussions with the government. After five days of negotiations, the government offered the miners' federation an improved deal. It would continue only until the setting up of a National Wages Board, to be negotiated between miners and owners, who were bound to report on a permanent scheme by 31 March 1921.

In a further ballot, the miners narrowly rejected the offer, but as the result did not meet the required two-thirds majority for continuing the strike, the men went back to work.[15]

~

In January 1921, Sir Robert Thorne summoned the miner's executive for an 'informal discussion of certain questions affecting the coal mining industry'. He advised that considering the deteriorating price of export coal the government proposed to remove the controls relating to coal prices and distribution on 1 March. The pooling of profits would continue to a date in the future, by which time he hoped the miners and owners would have come to an agreement on wages.

The issue was discussed at a Cabinet meeting on 28 January. It was explained that control of the coal industry had been continued because of the shortage of output and the high world price of coal. The absence of control would have resulted in either a very high home price or an acute shortage at home, due to the pull of the export price.

The control of price and export necessitated the incidental control of profits, wages, and the distribution of home supplies. All powers of control were due to expire on 31 August 1921, and if the powers to control export and prices were dropped before that date, the power to control wages would lapse.[16]

Since the wage settlement concluded the previous November, there had been a substantial increase in the output of coal, the Cabinet was told, but it had been accompanied by a 'sensational' drop in export prices. The price per ton had dropped from over 80 shillings to scarcely 40, and of the latter, wages made up 25 shillings.

Owners were guaranteed quarterly payments under a profit sharing arrangement. Profits were aggregated and pooled, whereby an amount equivalent to the pre-war industry profit, plus 10 percent of excess profits (if any) was distributed amongst the owners. The balance was held in reserve and could only be distributed by legislation.

If the current conditions persisted, it was predicted that the proceeds of the industry would be insufficient to pay the owners their guaranteed profits for the March quarter and the Treasury would be called on to make up the deficit, which would run into millions of pounds.[17]

The Cabinet was presented with three options: a) an increase in the price of home coal; b) a reduction in wages; or c) decontrol of the industry.

After noting the political difficulties presented by a), and the likelihood of a prolonged miners' stoppage if b) was implemented, Sir Robert Horne, president of the Board of Trade, said the proper course was to take immediately steps to decontrol the industry.

The Cabinet decided that control over home price and export quantities of coal would be removed on 1 March 1921; and that legislation should be introduced with a view to the decontrol of profits, by means of the repeal of the Coal Mines (Emergency) Act on 31 March.

On 1 February, the Mines Department announced the lifting of controls on prices and distribution of inland coal, to come into effect on 1 March. The following day, in a speech in Glasgow, Sir Robert Horne flagged that the financial control of the coal industry would be removed 'as soon as practicable'.[18]

On 23 February, in separate meetings, Sir Robert Horne met with the owners and miners. Horne pointed out the urgency of the sides coming to an agreement, given that decontrol would mean all provisions relating to wages would expire. He also informed miners' leaders Robert Smillie and Frank Hodges 'in private conference' that the government had decided to decontrol the industry on 31 March. It was the last straw for Smillie.

> On the night of February 23rd, 1921, I sat alone in my hotel room in the Imperial Hotel and considered the wreckage of the negotiations with the Government. Could I have handled it differently? What else could I have

done that could have produced a better outcome for us? I honestly could not think of anything. That conclusion forced me to a bitter truth. Which was that a man who cannot see a way forward in a difficult situation should step aside and allow someone else to do so. On hotel stationery I wrote a letter of resignation in such clear terms as to prohibit anyone from even considering trying to dissuade me.

Next morning, I rose early, packed my bag and made my way to Russell Square [miners' federation headquarters] before other Committee members arrived. I handed in the letter, addressed to Herbert Smith, then caught the first train north. It was over.[19]

~

The government's decision came amid the collapse of the post-war boom in the winter of 1920-21. The mining industry was not immune. The predictions of an expanding world demand for coal had proved illusory and coal exports declined in both value and volume. On 1 March, the whole of the wage increase secured by the miners in the settlement of November 1920 was wiped out by the fall in coal output caused by trade depression.

At its meeting on 3 March Cabinet approved a Bill to decontrol the coal industry. The Bill was entirely concerned with the distribution of profits to the coal owners, splitting the profits pool into two periods, the first ending on 31 December 1920 and the other covering the period 1 January to 31 March 1921. In the first period, the owners received their full profits under the pre-war standard. This left a surplus of around sixteen million pounds in the reserve fund. In the second pooling period, the owners would receive nine-tenths of their standard, which would involve payment by the state of up to nineteen million pounds. The surplus in the reserve fund would be available to meet this. The owners were satisfied with the arrangement. The miners got nothing.

Commenting on how the situation developed after the introduction of the Bill, Frank Hodges wrote in the *Times*:

> The coal owners were advised that decontrol would automatically revoke the wage advances given during the period of control. The owners gave notice to the miners to terminate contracts on 31 March. They also sought to impose new district wage agreements, involving tremendous reductions in the miners' earnings. These developments, quite unexpected by the miners, brought to an abrupt end the national negotiations for a joint agreement on the wage question which were proceeding on the anticipation that proposals

for the future regulation of wages and profits in the industry would be formulated in ample time to come into operation when control ended.

The new district wage proposals put forward by the owners had then to be considered by the miners with notices running out. These wage proposals could not possibly be accepted. To have entered into such contracts on such a basis would have placed the miners in many districts actually in a worse position than they were in during the war.[20]

The vexed question of national wage agreements was thus at the centre of the coal crisis in 1921. The miners refused to abandon the sanctity of national agreements; the owners argued that pits in the less profitable regions could not afford existing wage rates.

The miners tried to resolve this problem by proposing the idea of a national pool. Under this scheme a levy would be fixed on every ton of coal raised and so assist the poorest collieries by providing a national fund on which they could draw to cover any losses and meet wage bills. If it really was impossible for a very large number of companies to pay a living wage, as the owners suggested, then the only alternative to closing pits down or cutting wages savagely was to accept the national pool.

The owners opposed the pool because they believed in the merits of competition and higher profits for the more competitive pits, even if this meant the less profitable pits would have to close and thousands of colliers be thrown out of work.[21]

So, the owners rejected the miners' demand for a national pool to equalise wages; the miners rejected the owners' new terms; and the owners posted lock-out notices at many pits. These notices informed miners that if they did not accept proposed wage reductions, they would be locked out of the mines. They would be barred from working and would not receive pay, essentially forcing them to strike against their will. On 30 March the miners' federation bit the bullet and sent notices to the mining districts instructing their members to cease work at midnight on 31 March.

On Friday 1 April, a million men were locked out of the mines.

58

BLACK FRIDAY

After a three hour meeting of the Triple Alliance on Thursday 7 April, a statement was issued by JH Thomas of the National Union of Railwaymen. He said unless negotiations were reopened between the miners' federation, the mine owners and the government, the full strike power of the Triple Alliance would be put into operation at midnight on the following Tuesday, 12 April.[1] The next day in the House of Commons, Lloyd George read out a Proclamation from the King mobilising naval and military reserves for active service.

Rank-and-file rail and transport workers enthusiastically prepared for the strike, setting up local committees and public events, stepping up their financial collections, and organising picketing.

Discussions between the miners' executive and the owners resumed on Monday 11 April, but barely passed the preliminary stage of each side stating its case before being adjourned to the following day. That evening, the Triple Alliance released a manifesto, declaring, 'Unless an offer is made to the miners which their colleagues in the Triple Alliance can feel justified in recommending them to accept, a stoppage of railwaymen and transport workers will begin.' It continued:

> The lock-out of the miners is a crisis in the history of the Labour movement. The issues involved in it are of vital importance in every section of the working classes. Organised Labour, as it has repeatedly informed both employers and the Government, will allow no encroachment on the standard of life of the people and will resist to the uttermost every attack upon the trade union organisation by which that standard is defended. The proposal that the mine owners, with the support of the government, are seeking to enforce are a menace to both.[2]

After condemning the owners' proposed wage reductions as 'monstrous', the manifesto strongly endorsed the principle of national wage agreements and cautioned that unless resisted, the conditions being sought would be imposed on other workers. It then criticised the government for its hasty and ill-judged action in abolishing control of the mines ahead of schedule, and ignoring warnings that its move would provoke a dispute - and that the dispute would spread. It went on:

> We have begged it [the government] to consider the economic consequences of a prolonged conflict at the present moment, and have pointed out that the financial loss entailed by its continuance is far greater than the amount of any temporary subsidy required by the coal industry. It has replied by calling out the reserves and seeking to enrol volunteers to defeat their fellow-workers.
>
> We are driven reluctantly, but irresistibly, to the conclusion that the present Government is not an impartial arbitrator in industrial negotiations, but an active, if secret, partisan, and that while it speaks of peace it behaves in a manner calculated to encourage war.[3]

As evidence, the manifesto cited not only the government's conduct in the current dispute, but its record since January 1919 – notably its refusal to implement the recommendations of the Coal Commission and its provocation of the railways strike in September-October 1919 by attempting an arbitrary cut in wages.

On Tuesday 12 April, a coal conference broke down after proposals advanced by the government were rejected by the miners. The government offered financial assistance for a short period to bolster wages in the districts most affected by the proposed wage cuts, but would not countenance the national wage rates and national profits pool sought by the miners.

In the evening, the Triple Alliance met to consider the miners' report and after an hour, JH Thomas emerged to announce 'No strike tonight'. The message sent to all railwaymen and transport workers was, 'Continue to work until further instructions are issued.'[4]

On Wednesday morning, the full conference of the executives of the Triple Alliance met at 11 and after three-quarters of an hour JH Thomas made the announcement: 'The transport workers and railwaymen have unanimously decided to declare a strike at 10 o'clock on Friday night.' Other unions promptly sent in applications to join in the strike, including the Electrical Trades Union and Associated Society of Locomotive Engineers and Firemen.[5]

On Thursday evening, the political wing of the Labour movement swung behind the strike. A meeting of the Parliamentary Committee of the Trades Union Congress, the National Executive Committee of the Labour Party and the Parliamentary Labour Party declared itself convinced of the justice of the claims put forward, and pledged its support to the miners, railwaymen and transport workers, and appealed to all sections of the Labour movement to stand solidly against the attack on the workers' position. It also condemned the government's actions, particularly the military preparations made in the previous week, as 'calculated to provoke public feeling and so create disorder'.[6]

~

Then, at the eleventh hour, there were dramatic developments. The House of Commons, deprived of the opportunity of debating the matter, took matters into its own hands. A large body of members, drawn mainly from coalition ranks, invited the coal owners to a meeting in one of the committee rooms upstairs. The owners' representatives explained in detail the actual schedule of wages that would apply under their scheme. Many of the members were plainly disappointed with the case made by the owners, with some commenting that the wages proposed for some districts were too low.

A call was made for a similar meeting with the miners' leaders. The miners' secretary Frank Hodges was contacted and a meeting was arranged for 9.30 pm. By this time many other members were aware of the initiative and hundreds of members trooped up to Committee Room 14, the largest committee room in the Houses of Parliament, to hear the miners' case. Hodges laid stress on the demand for a national settlement backed by a national pool and temporary aid from the government, impressing many with his general argument, and then dealt faultlessly with a barrage of questions until about 11.30 pm.

Then, responding to a question from Captain Colin Coote, Liberal MP for the Isle of Ely, Hodges said:

> If between now and tomorrow the owners are willing to withdraw their proposed scheduled wages, any competent authority that puts forward a scheme which offers a chance of fair wages being acceptable, and permits of some hope for a permanent basis of agreement to be subsequently arrived at, would cause the miners to agree at once to reopen negotiations and the strike to be deferred.[7]

Hodges was asked if the Triple Alliance supported the view he had just expressed and whether, if the House of Commons or some other authority could get negotiations going again, they would call off the strike.

Sensing an opportunity, JH Thomas rose and said he better reply. He could only speak as an individual, he said, but he felt he could express the views of the Triple Alliance. He stood behind Hodges in all he had said, and that if Hodges' proposal bore fruit, the Triple Alliance would have no cause to take action.[8]

As soon as the meeting concluded, two private cars and half a dozen taxis carrying a dozen members drove to 10 Downing Street where the deputation had a prolonged meeting with the prime minister.[9]

Sitting in pyjamas and dressing gown, and shaking the sleep from his head, Lloyd George quickly got his shrewd tactical brain to work and dictated a letter to the miners' executive which would exploit this new split in the labour ranks under the camouflage of offering to re-open negotiations immediately.[10]

The miners' executive had a meeting very early the following morning. The executive was evenly split between those of 'advanced' and those of 'moderate' opinion, and the former indicated that Hodges had gone beyond his brief. Hodges offered to resign, but was not called on to do so.

While the meeting was in progress, the invitation came from the prime minister to discuss the possibility of further negotiations, on the lines apparently suggested by Hodges. A similar invitation was sent to the mine owners. The owners and government representatives assembled at the appointed hour, but the miners did not appear.

The miners had joined their partners in the Triple Alliance at the railwaymen's headquarters, Unity House. By mid-afternoon the various discussions that ensued had made a mockery of the venue's name. The transport workers' representatives led an attack on the miners' position which swept the resistance of some of the railwaymen out of the way. Controversy centred on Hodges' offer, which had been repudiated by more than half his executive. The *Times* wrote:

> Extremists of all sections tried hard to keep the battle flag unfurled, and Mr CT Cramp, industrial general secretary of the railwaymen, led an attempt to secure postponement of the strike rather than cancellation. Recriminations were mutual, and while the transport workers in particular were accused

of not desiring to give full support to the miners, the transport workers retorted by reference to weak-kneed action which had led to the matter being raised at this juncture at all.[11]

Eventually the miners left and went back to their office at Russell Square. About 1 pm a deputation came from the railwaymen and transport workers and stayed about 40 minutes. Both meetings resumed in the afternoon, the miners at Russell Square and the railwaymen and transport workers at Unity House, with communications passing between the two gatherings.

Just before 4 pm, JH Thomas emerged from the conference room at Unity House and made an announcement. 'The communication from the three organisations – the National Union of Railwaymen, the Associated Society of Locomotive Engineers and Firemen, and the Transport Workers' Federation – to their members is that the strike announced for tonight is cancelled.'[12]

What came to be called Black Friday was to all intents and purposes, the end of the Triple Alliance.

~

In his pamphlet, 'The Lesson of Black Friday', Gerald Gould points out that the Triple Alliance knew it was to be called on to act in conjunction with the miners, and the rest of the Labour movement knew it would have to either support the action taken or repudiate it.

It was perfectly well known for months ahead, he says, that the trade slump and the growth of unemployment would be used by the employers to force down wages. 'For weeks before the coal owners posted their lock-out notices, it was known and announced in the press that the lock-out was coming, and that it was going to be followed by similar actions in other industries.'[13]

The key organisations of the Labour movement – the Parliamentary Committee of the Trades Union Congress, the Labour Party Executive and the Parliamentary Labour Party – declared the demands of the miners were just and were on board with the proposed action.

Echoing the observation that Ernest Bevin made during the Triple Alliance discussions in September 1920, Gould says there was no organisation to make that view effective. There was no mechanism by which their opinion could be circulated among the rank and file and a response obtained. If it had emerged that the mass of workers was against a general strike, a compromise settlement could have been negotiated and a damaging episode avoided.

59
A STATE OF EMERGENCY

In March 1920, the British Home Office was asked to compile a list of powers that would be necessary to deal with a 'grave emergency' after the Defence of the Realm Act expired. In a memo dated 14 May, Home Secretary Edward Shortt set out a course that could be taken to provide for the possibility that 'an emergency may arise as great or greater than the Railway Strike of September 1919'.[1]

Shortt suggested preparing a Bill to enable parliament to be assembled within three days, and to include in the Bill a power to make Regulations for the public safety on lines similar to the Defence of the Realm Regulations. The Regulations would have to be confirmed by parliament within a week.

A draft Emergency Powers Bill was submitted to the Cabinet meeting of 4 August and a decision sought as to whether it was desirable or practicable to pass the legislation before parliament's autumn recess.

The Cabinet decided to hold the proposed Bill in abeyance, reasoning that a peace treaty with Turkey was unlikely to be ratified for some time and therefore the Defence of the Realm Regulations would still be in operation. It also felt such a Bill could be passed far more easily in an actual emergency.[2]

Thus, on 22 October, in the middle of the miners' Datum Line strike, the government introduced its Bill and rushed it through parliament within a week. The Emergency Powers Act introduced drastic powers of suppression and arrest to ministers and the police that had never been known in time of peace.

~

On Thursday 31 March 1921, the day before the miners' lock-out, the King issued a Proclamation of emergency under the Emergency Powers Act, and by orders-in-council made Regulations 'deemed necessary to secure the essentials of life to the nation'.

The far-reaching Regulations enabled any government department to take possession of land, buildings, or works (including those supplying gas, electricity and water) and property (including plant, machinery, equipment and stores). The minister for transport could regulate and restrict transport on road, tramways, light railways and canals. Any department could take possession of food or forage. The Board of Trade could close any port or harbour, requisition any ship and specify where cargo could be loaded and unloaded, and where passengers could embark or disembark. It could also prohibit the shipment of any goods for export. The same department could take possession of all coal mines, collieries and colliery buildings and control the production, distribution and price of coal. But not content with seizing control of the economic infrastructure of the country, the Regulations also sought to impose rules on what people could say and do about the situation.[3]

On 5 April, Sir Robert Horne, appointed chancellor of the exchequer four days previously, moved in the House of Commons that the Regulations made under the Act continue in force for one month after their proclamation. In protesting, Labour and Liberal members focussed their attack on the Regulations that impacted freedom of speech and assembly. These included Regulation 19, which stated that 'any person attempting or doing anything likely to cause disaffection among the civilian population was to be deemed guilty of an offence against the Regulations'; Regulation 20, which empowered the authorities to prohibit any meeting which they thought likely to give rise to disorder; and Regulation 27, which gave the police power to arrest without warrant any person known or suspected to be guilty of an offence against the Regulations.[4]

When the debate continued into the following day, Colonel Josiah Wedgwood, Labour MP for Newcastle-under-Lyme, moved to strike out Regulations 6, 16, 19, 20, 22, 23, 27, 28 and 29. He said:

> I cannot help thinking when one looks at these Regulations giving power to the Government to commandeer land, mines, railways, and canals and giving the Executive an absolute right of dictatorship, that they must have been brought to the notice of the British Government by M. Krassin or some of the other advocates of Bolshevism in Russia. This indeed is a dictatorship. One could say a good deal about it, but we have to realise of course that in time of war dictatorship does become very nearly necessary. When the Great War began we passed DORA [the Defence of the Realm Act], which was very like these Regulations, though not so strict in some parts and more

extensive in others. Now the Government tell us that we are face to face with such a crisis that they have to treat it as though it were a case of civil war or prospective civil war and enact all these Regulations which amount to autocracy.[5]

The Regulations to which Labour particularly objected were those dealing with the liberty of the subject and Colonel Wedgwood proceeded to go through them one by one. He said:

When we get to Regulation 19 the really important steps are taken to interfere with the legitimate freedom of the subject. Under 19, if any person does any act likely to cause disaffection among the civilian population, or to delay any measure taken for the supply of necessities for maintaining the means of transit, he shall be guilty of an offence against the Regulations. That seems to me to be throwing your net a little too wide, even in the dangerous situation imagined by His Majesty's Government. Is it really supposed that anybody who can be supposed to be stirring up disaffection - it does not state against whom, but I presume against the Government—is committing a crime. ...

Regulation 20 is even more interesting. That gives the police power to prohibit any meetings or any processions. Where there appears to be reason to apprehend that the assembly of any persons ... will cause undue demand to be made upon the police, any such meeting can be prohibited. ...

The next Regulation, No. 23, deals with the wicked person who obstructs or withholds information. According to it, any persons who withholds any information which he may reasonably be required to furnish by any officer or other person who is carrying out the orders of any Government Department is guilty of a crime. It is not enough not to do anything - silence is to be a crime under these Regulations. That goes far beyond anything we had under DORA. I do not think even a state of civil war in this country or the alarming prospect in front of us would authorise you to treat as a criminal a man who merely remained silent. ...

Regulation 27 re-enacts the old DORA provision as to arrest without warrant. Any police constable may arrest without warrant any person suspected of being guilty of an offence against these Regulations. Good Heavens! Any person in the country may be suspected of getting in the way, or saying nothing, or harbouring somebody who has taken part in a prohibited meeting, or any of the other hundred and one ways in which you are now enabled to commit crime by doing nothing! We have during these years of war come to disregard the liberty of the subject pretty completely, but I do protest against this being re-enacted one moment before it is necessary.

Then comes the Regulation dealing with attempts to commit offences, No. 28. Under it any person who endeavours to persuade another person to commit any act prohibited by the Regulations, or who harbours any person whom he knows to have acted in contravention of the Regulations, is guilty of an offence. If you allow your son to come home late at night from a meeting and sleep in the house you may be making yourself a criminal. How any body of citizens can make it a crime to harbour a man who, after all, whether guilty or not, may surely out of Christian charity be given a meal and a bed, I cannot imagine.[6]

Wedgwood's amendment was defeated 285-69, and after the government conceded Regulation 29, which dealt with the closure of premises, the other Regulations were approved, by 270 votes to 60.

~

The repressive wave was well under way before the new Regulations came into effect, with three prominent socialists, Sylvia Pankhurst, Cecil Malone and Willie Gallacher, already behind bars.

Pankhurst was charged under Regulation 42 of the Defence of the Realm Regulations with publishing a series of articles likely to cause disaffection to the navy and the civil population. The articles, which appeared in the *Workers' Dreadnought*, were 'Discontent on the lower deck', 'How to get a Labour government', 'The datum line' and 'The yellow peril and the dockers'. On 28 October 1920, Pankhurst was sentenced to six months imprisonment. She appealed, but on 6 January 1921, the conviction and sentence were confirmed.[7]

Malone, John Maclean's nemesis in the British Socialist Party, was arrested after a fiery address to a Hands off Russia demonstration in the Albert Hall on 7 November 1920. In his speech he said he hoped the day was not far distant when they would meet in the Albert Hall to bless the British revolution. The *Times* reported what came next:

> They were out to change the resent constitution, he declared, and if it was necessary to save bloodshed and atrocities, they would have to use the lamp-posts or the walls.
>
> What were a few Churchills [British minister for war] or Curzons [British foreign secretary] on lamp-posts compared with the massacres of thousands of Indians at Amritsar, or compared with the condemning of harmless Egyptians, or the reprisals on hundreds of Irishmen in Ireland? What were

the punishments of those world criminals compared with the misery they were causing to thousands of men, women and children in Russia?[8]

Malone was arrested in Dublin on 10 November and charged with sedition under Regulation 42 of the Defence of the Realm Regulations. He was convicted and sentenced to six months imprisonment. He also appealed, but like Pankhurst, was unsuccessful.[9]

Willie Gallacher was arrested in Liverpool on 11 February 1921, and charged, again under the Defence of the Realm Regulations, with having attempted to cause sedition among the civilian population. The charge related to a meeting of the National Shop Stewards and Workshop Committee Movement on 27 January in Birmingham. Gallacher claimed that while the police could find nothing untoward with his own speech, the speaker who followed, 'an old comrade from Glasgow', let rip with a vengeance. The prosecution argued that Gallacher's speech had to be considered in light of what followed, and despite Gallacher's protests, the judge agreed and Gallacher got three months.[10]

~

Aware of the increasingly repressive atmosphere, John Maclean wrote in the *Socialist* that the government was being provocative, 'anxious to incite the revolutionary elements, associate the communists with Sinn Fein and to give us a taste of Paris at the end of the Commune'.[11]

That didn't mean Maclean was sitting at home waiting for the knock on the door. Under a headline of 'Bolshie propagandists busy in Lanarkshire', Glasgow's *Daily Record* reported that Maclean, Sandy Ross, James Macdougall and the organiser of the Irish Citizen Army, Captain Jack White addressed a meeting of miners at Blantyre on Saturday 9 April. Maclean counselled the miners to follow the example of Russia, while 'Captain White characterised the present crisis as an arranged blow on Trades Unionism, and said if the capitalists organised their White Guards, he and his confederates would organise Red Guards.'[12] Throughout April the Tramp Trust went all round Lanarkshire rallying support for the miners.

In the first week of the lock-out, there were disturbances in several Scottish mining areas. In most cases they involved strikers clashing with volunteers engaged to pump water from the mines. On 5 April, police reinforcements were drafted into the Lanarkshire villages of Holytown, Carfin, West Benhar and Harthill after a near riot at the Benhar Colliery.

The same night there were similar confrontations at Cowdenbeath and the Leven Colliery in Fife.[13] The following day in Lanarkshire, police were stoned and hayricks set alight in Shotts, the pithead frames at the Hallon Rigg Colliery at Bellshill were seriously damaged and there was a demonstration of 3000 strikers at the Hamilton Palace Colliery.[14] Matters quietened down after the decision was taken to withdraw pumpmen from the pits.

After Black Friday, the threat of a general strike receded, but suppression and arrests increased. On 4 May, there was a police raid on the premises of the Scottish Labour College, however nothing incriminating was found. On 5 May, Tom Mitchell, secretary of the Socialist Labour Party and editor of the *Socialist* was arrested. On 7 May, police raided the head office of the Communist Party in London and arrested the secretary, Albert Inkpin. The charge was that he had procured the National Labour Press to print and publish matter called the 'Theses of the Communist International', an act likely to cause sedition and disaffection among the civilian population. On Monday 9 May, Robert Stewart, general organiser of the Communist Party was also arrested.

Then on 13 May, John Maclean and Sandy Ross were arrested by Glasgow police. They were driven to Airdrie where they were charged on eleven counts of making seditious speeches and statements in Airdrie on 26 April.

Maclean and Ross were tried at Airdrie Sheriff Court on 17 May. A large contingent of their supporters marched there from Glasgow and a large crowd waited outside, although the court only held a few hundred so many were disappointed.[15]

Chief Constable Christine and Sergeants Ross and Turner gave evidence. In their somewhat garbled accounts, they said that Maclean urged the people to give their money to revolutionary agitation rather than bookmakers, thereby getting a better return; that when the miners were locked out the government brought lorries guarded by soldiers to carry food to the upper and middle classes; that the government had called out all the machinery of war to force the people to accept lower wages and to support the capitalists who were robbing them; that they were to see that the fight did not stop short of world revolution, and that he was not going to risk a revolution until he had a body of men and all the accoutrements of war.[16]

Maclean cross-examined the chief constable for more than two hours. Then he began to reel, and Sandy Ross explained the had taken no food that day and was preparing to go on hunger strike if sent to prison. Ross continued with the cross-examination while Maclean took a glass of water and recovered.

During his evidence Maclean gave an outline of the speech in question, which he pointed out was the same as he had given in many other places. Harry McShane summarised it in the *Socialist*:

> He [Maclean] said that the revolution he advocated was the coming to power of the working class. He did not believe in exhorting men to violence when they had not the accoutrements of war. He had consistently warned the workers not to run their heads below batons, nor their stomachs against bayonets. The object of the meeting was to encourage the miners and this was clearly stated by the Chairman ...
>
> The [Procurator] Fiscal, cross-examining, questioned Maclean about what he meant by revolution. Maclean held out two hands, one above the other; he said they represented the two classes in society, the top one being the capitalist class. He then swung his hands around to the reverse position, and said that was revolution.[17]

Maclean and Ross were both found guilty. Maclean was sentenced to three months imprisonment, while Ross received three months, plus a 20 pounds fine. Failure to pay the fine would mean a further three months.

On 3 June in the House of Commons, Sir William Raeburn, Coalition Unionist MP for Dumbartonshire, asked the secretary for Scotland 'if his attention has been drawn to a statement in the Press that John Maclean and Sandy Ross, convicted of sedition and sentenced to three months' imprisonment, and who announced when sentence was passed that they would hunger strike, are receiving special privileges, such as food sent in from outside, newspapers, clothes, beds, etc.; and, if this be so, what are the reasons for treating these prisoners in an exceptional way from ordinary prison rules?'

Robert Munro replied:

> Maclean and Ross were convicted of a contravention of No. 19 of the Emergency Regulations, 1921, namely, causing sedition or disaffection. Following the practice in previous cases of this nature, they have been accorded the treatment prescribed in the rules which apply in Scotland to prisoners convicted of sedition. These rules, which have Parliamentary authority, and which, so far as the privileges conferred upon such prisoners are concerned, are substantially the same as in England, have been in

existence for many years. The privileges allowed under them to prisoners convicted of sedition are substantially those set out in the questions. I may add that the treatment accorded to these prisoners has nothing whatever to do with any statements or threats made by them or either of them, before their term or imprisonment began.[18]

The previous day, parliament voted through a month's extension of the Emergency Powers Regulations made by the King on 27 May. At the start of the debate, Neil Maclean, Labour MP for Glasgow Govan, moved an amendment, to insert the words 'except Regulation 19'.

> My purpose in asking that this Regulation shall be deleted is to be found in the conditions that prevail today in the Courts up and down the country. We find as the result of the dispute in the mining industry, which was really the cause of these Regulations having been introduced and passed in such a hurried manner, many working men, not only miners, but engineers and men engaged in various industries, who are arrested and brought to trial for what is called sedition. Even the magistrates and the judges who are trying those cases differ very materially as to what they believe sedition amounts to. We find in one part of the country men being sentenced for circulating a certain leaflet and in another part of the country men being dismissed when charged with circulating the same leaflet, the judge in this instance saying that the contents of the leaflet cannot be included in any charge of sedition as made by the police. Then we have newspaper offices being raided, not only in Ireland but in this country, we have editors being called to answer charges of sedition, we have printing establishments brought before the Courts for printing these papers and leaflets, and we have even the homes of the employees in the offices belonging to these parties raided and searched, with the object no doubt of finding out if they have been taking home with them any of the literature that is being printed or published which the Crown authorities may consider of an incriminating character. In the attitude that has been adopted by the Government and the persecution - because one can call it by no other name - of working men such as we have at present, the Government is really fanning the flame that they imagine is burning, and they themselves, by the attitude they have taken up and by the manner in which their servants are carrying out what are undoubtedly the instructions of the Crown, are doing more than any agitator has done to cause disaffection among the people.[19]

Under the headline 'Fight for freedom of speech' the *Daily Herald* saluted the Labour Party's 'brave but vain attack', noting that it had been stated during the debate that there had been 60 prosecutions under Regulation 19. 'This is the regulation which the government has used in its notorious attempt to stamp out freedom of speech and the Press,' it protested.[20]

~

On 21 June, Peter Lavin, the secretary of the Scottish Labour College, wrote to John Maclean's wife Agnes, telling her he had visited John in Barlinnie Prison and that he was in good health. Harry McShane was visiting him every week, and taking one of the college students with him. On financial matters however, things were not so good. Maclean had arranged for half his college salary to be sent to Agnes in the event he was imprisoned. The other half was to go to whoever replaced him. Given the miners' lock-out and the general industrial slump, money had only been coming in slowly, and he apologised that nothing had been forwarded to Agnes before now.[21]

The Scottish Labour College held its annual general meeting in June. Lavin reported that there were two full-time tutors in Glasgow, Maclean and one other, and one full-time tutor in each of Aberdeen, Dundee, Fife, Edinburgh, Stirling and Renfrew. These were supplemented by several voluntary tutors. A total of 1800 students had enrolled during the session, 800 of them in Glasgow.

In opening the discussion James Macdougall noted the scarcity of money in the mining districts, with the Lanarkshire miners, 50,000 strong, only being able to send three full time students. He hoped they would be able to send twelve for the next session. The income of the college had dropped by 50 per cent, a sure reflection of the perilous plight of the miners at the time.[22]

60

MORE PORRIDGE

John Maclean and Sandy Ross were due to be released from Barlinnie Prison on 2 August 1921, and it had been arranged that they would address a meeting of the unemployed at Glasgow Green in the afternoon. However, that morning it was only Sandy Ross who emerged. He had received a remission for good conduct, whereas Maclean had declined work and refused to conform to prison tasks and served his full sentence.[1]

Maclean was released on 17 August. Within hours, he was at the Central Police Court appearing, along with Ross, as a witness for Harry McShane, who had been charged with contravening the by-laws by selling socialist literature on Glasgow Green. Maclean told the court he had been speaking and selling socialist literature on the Green for more than twenty years, often with more than ten detectives present, and had never been stopped. McShane was fined five shillings.[2]

Shortly afterwards, Sandy Ross was arrested for his speech at Glasgow Green. Bail was refused and he was imprisoned pending trial.[3]

Maclean was straight back into his agitation on behalf of the unemployed. On the afternoon of Monday 5 September, a fifty-strong delegation representing the unemployed was received by the Trades Union Congress in Cardiff. Maclean was one of three speakers who addressed the congress, which welcomed ex-miners' federation president Robert Smillie back to public and trade union work after ill health had forced his retirement. With Smillie on the platform were the leaders of the other two members of the shattered Triple Alliance, JH Thomas and Harry Gosling, representing the railwaymen and transport workers respectively.

The first speaker for the delegation was Jack Holt, chairman of the National Unemployed Workers' Movement, a federation of unemployed committees from across the UK. He said their demands were work, or full maintenance. In London they were determined that they would pester the guardians and make them realise their responsibility. The guardians in turn would have to make the government realise its responsibility and the Trades Union Congress could assist in that task. The business of the congress was to take action and put gunpowder behind the government – not merely to pass resolutions.

The second speaker, E Pitt, declared that if action were not taken the unemployed would have to take the problem in their own hands. Next winter was going to be hell for the unemployed unless something was done for them. The bosses were setting hard faces against them and did not trouble the least bit about their problem.

John Maclean then gave what the *Daily Telegraph* called 'a most violent speech'. He told the congress that unemployed Welsh miners had that broiling day walked 20 miles on empty stomachs to back their comrades. He said he represented not only Scotland but also Sheffield, where 3,000 unemployed had elected him their delegate on the previous night. Unless a full wage was going to be paid to the unemployed the tendency would be for them to 'scab' and reduce the wages of the employed. The position in Scotland where there were no guardians was desperate. The *Glasgow Herald*'s report continued:

> 'We are going to watch you,' Maclean shouted, 'and unless you are going to act I am going to tell the workers in Scotland to allow not one of you to speak in public.' (Dissent and uproar.) 'The boss class,' he added, 'tried to smash the miners' federation. The turn of the railwaymen is coming, and JH Thomas will get his share.' (More dissent and interruption).[4]

There were cries of 'Chuck him out', to which someone responded 'Chuck Thomas out!' The chairman, EL Poulton said, 'We have decided to give them half an hour. They may use it wisely or unwisely. That is for them.'

Continuing, Maclean said that for twelve months workers' wages would continue to fall stage by stage unless they were all, employed and unemployed, united. A general strike was their only effective weapon.

The delegates applauded sympathetically, and before the deputation withdrew, the chairman assured them that when the congress dealt with this question, they would draw up a resolution which would aim at not only giving relief but also of abolishing such an inhuman system as present existed (Cheers).[5]

~

The area where Maclean and the Tramp Trust was best known was Govan. It was also where their agitation on behalf of the unemployed had had the biggest impact; they had wrung a lot of concessions from the Govan Parish Council, which covered the whole of the south side of the Clyde. In an extension of their agitational struggle, Maclean and Harry McShane decided to stand as Glasgow unemployed committee candidates for Kinning Park and Kingston in the municipal elections of November 1921. Their election address, drafted by Maclean, was more of a revolutionary statement than a policy on unemployment, but McShane said they waged a great campaign.[6]

As part of that campaign, on 12, 15 and 19 September, Maclean addressed meetings at Stanley Street, Kinning Park. Then, on Tuesday 20 September, he addressed a large meeting of the unemployed at South Portland Street, Gorbals. At the close of the meeting Maclean was arrested and taken to the Southern Police Office. On the way, according to the *Glasgow Herald* report, the crowd who followed the constables assumed a threatening attitude. 'Shouts of "Rush the police" were raised, and several constables were assaulted. A man and a woman were detained in connection with a charge of assaulting the police.'[7]

At the Southern Court the following day, Maclean was charged with committing sedition by stating, 'I stand with Sandy Ross, and as long as I am a free man, I will say "move", that is if you cannot get food in a constitutional way, I say take it.' The magistrate refused bail, and Maclean was reported to be refusing food in prison.[8]

On the night Maclean was arrested, a crowd of 2000 gathered at Govan Cross to protest. 'We were using the pillar box as a platform,' McShane recalled. 'Jimmy Macdougall stepped up to speak, and I warned him to be careful, because I didn't want him to go to jail again.'[9]

Macdougall disregarded the advice and told the crowd that a half brick thrown at the windows of certain factory would do a lot of damage. He went on, 'There are also a number of plate glass windows along the street there with plenty of food behind them. If you are hungry, don't starve, take the food, but take it in a way that they can't take you.' He was arrested the following day as he was about to address a meeting of the unemployed in Tradeston.[10]

A movement to raise funds for the defence of the Tramp Trust Trio was quickly organised. An advertisement appeared in the *Daily Herald* on 19 September. 'Help! Help!! Help!!! John Maclean, Sandy Ross and James D. Macdougall,' it ran.

These men have been sent to Prison for Fighting the Fight of the Workers. Do you want to retain Freedom of Speech? If so you must get these Men released. Get Resolutions of Protest passed everywhere. In order to fight the Enemy, Money is urgently required for the Defence and the Maintenance of these men's dependents. All donations will be thankfully received ...[11]

Macdougall was convicted on a charge of sedition and sentenced to sixty days' imprisonment. Maclean was enraged and went on hunger strike in protest. He became so ill he was moved to the observation ward of Duke Street Prison. On 11 October the *Daily Herald* reported that he had been forcibly fed after being on hunger strike for 16 days. The prison authorities had decided to feed him, and it was alleged that Maclean did not resist. It was explained that he refused to take food on principle, but did not object to having it thrust upon him. Meanwhile, Maclean's application for bail had been referred to the High Court in Edinburgh for a decision. On 7 October, bail was refused.[12]

~

Maclean's sixth and final sedition trial took place on 25 October 1921 in the Summary Court, County Buildings, Glasgow.[13] The trial, before Sheriff Boyd and a jury, lasted nearly 11 hours. Maclean defended himself and was cheered as he entered the dock. He immediately said he wished to make a protest at being held in prison for five weeks without a trial. The sheriff dismissed the protest. Asked if he pleaded guilty or not guilty, Maclean laid a counter charge against Glasgow's lord provost for being responsible for the starvation of thousands of good and true citizens. The sheriff said that was equivalent to a plea of not guilty. The jury was then empanelled and Maclean said he had had no opportunity of protesting about the jury. This was a political case, he claimed and he ought to be tried by a jury of unemployed wage-earners.

The charge against Maclean referred to the speeches in Stanley Street, Kinning Park, during which he was alleged to have said to the hungry to take food if they could not get it in the ordinary way, and to have described the lord provost as a murderer for allowing the unemployed to starve on the streets.

Detective William Patterson of Govan Division testified that at one of the meetings Maclean told the audience they [the Tramp Trust] were having processions daily and that they had tried to get the cathedral, churches and

Tent Hall in the Saltmarket as shelters for the homeless. After saying Sandy Ross had been put in prison for telling the hungry to take food, Maclean said, 'I say here and now, if you are hungry, there is plenty of food around. Take it! Take it, I say.'

Patterson said Maclean then went on to speak about the municipal election, saying that in the event of him being returned to the town council, he would continue raising hell until Ross was released. Maclean told the audience that unless they meant to support him heart and soul, they could keep their votes as it was a revolution he was out for and nothing less would satisfy him.

At a further meeting Maclean said they were out to fight the capitalist class, and in fighting that class they were up against a great organisation which had the army and navy at their disposal and would use them. He told the audience that that they must have unity. They must do as the Irish had done; they must vote them out of it. They must stick together and, if necessary, he hoped they would be as brave as the Irish and fight together. They must not fear imprisonment, punishment, or even worse, but must fight on until they had established a republic in Scotland. He told the people that while they were marching in procession, they were to be orderly, because the police were itching for the chance of a riot.

Further police evidence was led with regards to Maclean's speeches and subsequent arrest and all the witnesses were subjected to cross-examination at considerable length by Maclean. When the last prosecution witness had been examined, Maclean said his first witness was Harry McShane.

The procurator fiscal stood up and said that the list of witnesses had not been placed in his hands at the proper time and therefore Maclean had no legal right to lead evidence. Maclean rose and exclaimed excitedly that he had been detained in prison and had not had a proper opportunity of obtaining witnesses. He went on to say he had gone on hunger strike for 18 days until he was forcibly fed. The sheriff said that did not prevent him from giving the names of his witnesses to the prosecution. In reply to the sheriff, the fiscal said he did not object to witnesses being called for the defence.

Harry McShane told the court he had been associated with Maclean for 18 months and had never heard him advocate violence. Maclean had said that 'if there was any rioting, he would drop the reins'. McShane admitted that their advice was that individuals who were on the verge of starvation should take food rather than die, but they were not to go in crowds nor use violence.

Fifteen witnesses for the defence were examined and then Maclean took the stand and spoke on his own behalf. His contention was that starving people should take food rather than die of starvation. That was his principle and he would hold on to it so long as he lived. He had said to the people that he didn't want their vote under false pretences. He wanted them to vote for him as a revolutionist. But revolution did not mean bloodshed or violence.

A sudden burst of cheering greeting this pronouncement and the sheriff ordered the court to be cleared, to the accompaniment of angry protests from the public.

During his evidence Maclean was in constant conflict with the sheriff on the question of relevancy. After numerous patient protests, the sheriff eventually refused to allow Maclean to continue in the rambling manner he had been doing, whereupon Maclean left the witness box.

The fiscal asked for a conviction and the jury retired, returning after an absence of several minutes with a verdict that the words libelled were used, and that they were calculated to excite popular disaffection, commotion and resistance to lawful authority, but it was not the primary intention of the accused to incite violence.

The sheriff, addressing Maclean, said that he was a man of education and had used his influence in an attempt to lead people into courses which would certainly have brought them into trouble. He passed sentence of 12 months imprisonment. Maclean attempted to address the court, but was hurried away.

~

The next day, Sandy Ross appeared in front of Sheriff Harvey and a jury on a charge of sedition arising from his speech at Glasgow Green on 2 August. The prosecution alleged the speech used language intended and calculated to excite popular disaffection, commotion and violence and resistance to lawful authority.

Several policemen testified that Ross uttered the words complained of in the indictment, although they admitted no notes were taken during the speech itself.

Harry McShane was the opening witness for the defence. He stated that Ross's speech was a criticism of his trial and sentence at Airdrie on a charge of sedition. He denied that Ross had used the words specified in the charge. Other defence witnesses gave similar evidence.

In the witness-box, Ross declared that some of the remarks in the indictment were interjections from the crowd and were not remarks by himself. In cross-examination he said he was far from agreeing with all of John Maclean's views. He did not agree with Maclean on the necessity for a Scottish republic or Soviet rule.

He denied he had advocated revolution. He was not a member of the Socialist Labour Party and could not agree with the statement that he was Maclean's right-hand supporter and assistant. He admitted that at one time he had received five pounds a week from Maclean, but he had been a lecturer on social subjects for a long time. He had never advised people to take food forcibly if they could get it otherwise.

After an absence of about ten minutes the jury returned a verdict of guilty. The sheriff said he had formed the impression that Ross was a misguided man, but honest in his opinions and enthusiasms. But what he had to consider was whether it was fair to the people that the accused had addressed that he should incite them to disaffection, violence and contempt for the law.

The sheriff said he would take into account the fact that Ross had already been in prison for nearly sixty days and would limit the sentence to one of four months' imprisonment.[14]

~

As well continuing the organisation of the unemployed and attempting to raise money for Maclean's defence, Harry McShane had been keeping the municipal campaign going. 'I visited him [Maclean] in prison every week and discussed our campaign with him,' he recalled. 'We worked with the Socialist Labour Party but we weren't members and it wasn't their election campaign. Our team were not SLPers; some were ex-British Socialist Party members; others were just sympathisers. We worked until five o'clock every morning. We covered the area with posters on all the hoardings. In those days we struck up proper sized bills, large ones in separate pieces like cinema posters; to do it you needed a team with a ladder, and the bills, and paste.'[15]

The election was held on 1 November. Running as a Communist, Maclean came second to a Moderate in Kinning Park, but beat the official Labour candidate by 2421 votes to 1885. McShane, also running as a Communist, came third in Kingston, behind a Moderate and Labour, but still polled a respectable 1107 votes. The two other Communist candidates in the election didn't do quite as well. Helen Crawfurd ran third in Govan with 634 votes, while Dominic Kennedy also ran third in Cowlairs with 178 votes. Overall, the Labour Party went backwards, losing five seats in the 113 member council.[16]

In its edition of 12 November, the *Worker* lashed out at Maclean's savage sentence.

> Twelve months! Was ever such a monstrous sentence passed on any man for such a trivial offence? A week or two ago, there was a protest right throughout the press of the country because a London magistrate had sentenced a man to six weeks for selling a pamphlet with blank pages. Six weeks, and the Home Secretary was forced to step in and squash the sentence. But John Maclean, who has done no wrong, who has always tried to fight the battles of his class, who has ever put education in the forefront of his propaganda, is condemned to fifty-two weeks, and the press of this country is silent. Why? Surely the reason in plain ... Maclean is in prison because he is a threat to the privileged class who hold power in society today. If the workers can be crushed and demoralised through their active leaders being imprisoned then the boss class will see to it that the necessary imprisonment takes place ... The attack on Maclean is an attack on the whole working class he represents ... That class should take up the challenge and never cease fighting till Maclean is free again ...[17]

The *Daily Herald* also protested about the treatment meted out to Maclean and others of his ilk. In an article criticising the British justice system, it wrote:

> John Maclean is in prison in circumstances which, for a man of his enfeebled health after a long hunger-strike, are only too likely to involve death. His crime is to have made speeches which, *even if they were what the prosecution alleged* [original emphasis] would be no worse than the activities of the Ulster leaders in 1914. No worse, did we say? Why at the worst, John Maclean made a speech! But Galloper Smith [Frederick Smith, Lord Birkenhead] who is now Lord Chancellor and Carson, who is now a Law Lord, organised an army to fight against the British constitution.
>
> It was admitted by the judge at the trial that Maclean did not desire violence. Yet the sentence inflicted upon him was as savage and vindictive as if he had been guilty of a serious crime ...

The brutality of these sentences is a disgrace to the country and nothing can remove the disgrace except the organised power of Labour.[18]

Despite the British government's release of Sinn Fein prisoners after the signing of the Anglo-Irish Treaty in December 1921, and the American government's release of Eugene Debs and other socialists in the same month, the *Daily Herald's* ongoing campaign for freedom of speech and the release of all British political prisoners, including Maclean and Ross, fell on deaf ears.[19]

61

THE TRAMP TRUST DISSOLVES

In prison, John Maclean was again accorded the privileges of a political prisoner, and it fell to Harry McShane to provide him with the support he requested. Maclean had the right to wear his own clothes and have his meals brought in from outside. McShane organised changes of underclothing and the cooking of his food. 'We got a different woman to prepare his meals every week; we paid them for it, although they would have been proud to do it for nothing,' he recalled.[1]

Maclean had arranged for his friend William Montgomery, a member of the Socialist Labour Party who lived in Pollokshaws, to live in his house at Auldhouse Road while Maclean was in prison. On 7 November, Maclean wrote to Montgomery requesting some reading matter. 'You might bring Cohen's *Organic Chemistry* ... Otto's *German Grammar* ought to be among the loose books. Also fish out Marshall's *Principles of Economics*, and another of similar size Cunningham's *Industrial History* ... Gibson's *Introduction to the Calculus* ... Also Thomson's *Zoology* and Haliburton's *Physiology*.'[2]

He was a prolific letter writer, many to his good friend James Clunie who was one of the first full time tutors at the Scottish Labour College and had taken over the editorship of the *Socialist* after the jailing of Tom Mitchell.

On 16 December, Maclean wrote to Clunie, telling him, 'I've made arrangements for you to visit me next Thursday along with Harry McShane ... Thanks for the money which I wish you to hand over to Harry as he is looking after all financial matters relative to my private as well as public affairs. All you need to do is explain to him the use he has to put the money to and he'll carry out your wishes ... At present, I'm wading through Marshall's *Principles* once more. How weak, how insipid next to Marx's *Capital*. Still, I enjoy it, because I oppose Marshall at every turn. It's like reading the leaders in the *Glasgow Herald*.'[3]

While Maclean was ranging far and wide in his intellectual pursuits, his personal life was strictly off limits. In June 1922 he had a visit from his old friend James McNabb, who had been best man at his wedding. Some months later McNabb wrote to Agnes about the visit.

> I hope you are in happier frame of mind than when you last wrote. After all we have all got to meet with disappointments and we have got to get through them for the sake of everyone we love especially for the young. I saw John about 2 months ago at Barlinnie. He was in good form and looking very well indeed. He was filling much of his time reading books on Electricity, Physiology and other sciences as well as on Economics. He did not mention family affairs, nor did I. On a former occasion John asked if you had written to Mrs McNabb and I said yes. He seemed to think it was wrong for you to write to her on family matters as if you had been trying to turn his friends against him. I know very well that you are as well disposed to him as ever you were. He seemed so unreasonable on this point that I let the subject drop and never talked of his family affairs again.[4]

Maclean wrote to James Clunie in July, and said he was looking forward to his release three months hence. 'I've been wondering how you've been pulling along these dull industrial days, your contact with miners, whose plight must be deplorable, your struggle to arose enthusiasm for next winter's class work and your propaganda work.'[5]

In August he received a sympathetic letter from his old friend and comrade Tom Mann. 'The movement generally, is flat,' Mann wrote, 'the economic depression is so serious the number of unemployed and the reduced standard of those employed, all operating naturally, brings about a lack of vigorous activity ... The products of the Labour Colleges should be making themselves felt now, but I wish more young fellows were coming out fully equipped.'[6]

The Reverend William Fulton was assistant chaplain at Barlinnie Prison at the time and shared his reminiscences of Maclean with author John Broom.

> We in Glasgow had all heard of John Maclean. Two of my sisters were teachers who were associated with him and regarded him as a 'bonny fechter'[7] in matters affecting his profession ... As a political prisoner he had certain privileges. He wore his civilian clothing and had his hour's exercise alone between nine and ten each forenoon. This was the chaplain's quiet hour, so relieving a warder on my days on duty, I was allowed to walk around

the exercise yard with John. He proved the best of company, could talk freely on any subject, or about the books he was then reading. I should say he had around fifty books in his cell, but at that time he was intent on psychology. This had, he said, been neglected in his earlier education. I remember telling him he had nothing to learn about 'mass psychology', which greatly amused him ... He was of course fully informed about Russian affairs, names of Russian leaders literally tripping off his tongue ... Lenin, John particularly admired, Lloyd George he abhorred – any mention of his name rousing him to a fury ... John's creed was somewhat distant from extreme Socialism.

At his request, I was allowed by the governor to visit his wife ... I was very much taken with her, a nice quiet homely woman who accepted her lot uncomplainingly. ... I had a warm welcome and was able to report to John, as I know his home was constantly in his thoughts.[8]

~

Harry McShane recounted that the Tramp Trust fell apart when Maclean was in prison. 'Sandy Ross had gone back to Dundee, and later went to India. Jimmy Macdougall was completely unreliable after he came out [of prison]. He only did one or two meetings and at one of them he argued that there was no chance of a revolution in the next ten years and all we could do was return a Labour government to power. ... Peter Marshall was teaching a Scottish Labour College class at Falkirk, but never came to any of the big propaganda meetings we were holding in Glasgow.'[9]

McShane was arrested in May 1922 in connection with an eviction protest and with two others was charged with taking possession of a house without permission of the owner. In addition, McShane was charged with making two seditious speeches.

All those arrested were refused bail and a big agitation, led by the Communist Party, developed about the case. McShane's fellow accused were bailed after three weeks, but he languished in jail for seven weeks before coming to trial. Expecting a prison sentence of one to two years, he arranged for someone else to see to John Maclean's prison meals. Maclean didn't like the person, so McShane got James Maxton to do it. Maxton dropped the ball, and after six weeks Maclean went back on prison food.

McShane was fortunate that his case was heard by Sheriff Lee, who in 1915 had given John Maclean a lenient sentence in Maclean's first sedition case. Lee had also presided in the dramatic rent strike case that year which saw the withdrawal of eviction notices and a victory for the rent strikers.

When it emerged during the eviction protest hearing that the eviction notice had been served on the wrong person, the charges were dismissed. When the sheriff deemed evidence relating to that case to be irrelevant to McShane's sedition trial, and refused to allow it to be led, the case against McShane fell apart and the jury returned a majority verdict of 'not proven'.

The seven weeks in jail gave McShane time to ponder his situation. He was feeling overwhelmed with all the responsibilities involved with carrying on the propaganda of the Tramp Trust, plus the unemployed agitation, and looking after Maclean. And on top of that, trying to get by on just fifteen shillings a week was leading to troubles in his marriage.[10]

> In reality the Tramp Trust had dissolved. For two years we had done hundreds of factory-gate meetings and other meetings, and organised countless demonstrations. But although we had conducted the best propaganda and agitation in the West of Scotland, we had left no organisation behind us. When I was arrested there was no-one to carry on the work except the Communist Party or the Labour Party. Realising this, I thought I must make a choice about what I was going to do. I decided to join the Communist Party.
>
> I came to the decision with difficulty. It was I who had held the communists at bay on the Glasgow Unemployed Committee. When we met on that committee, I had often exploded at them. I felt a great deal of loyalty to John Maclean and I resented their attitude to him. But, conscious that I was isolated, I knew I had to join an organisation. The Communist Party's work on the unemployed committee after my arrest convinced me that their aspirations for the movement were the same as mine, and that they were serious. I joined the Communist Party in July 1922 and did not regret my decision.[11]

McShane's decision meant a complete break with John Maclean, and the two didn't speak again until McShane's own eviction fight in May 1923.

62

THE CLYDESIDERS TRIUMPHANT

Maclean was raring to get back into the fight, and in the period leading up to his release from prison on 25 October 1922 he accepted an invitation from the Unemployed Committee to run in the Glasgow municipal council election. There was a hiccup when they went to nominate him for the Kinning Park Ward and it was discovered that his name had been deleted from the electoral roll. The error was rectified however and the town clerk accepted a nomination paper on his behalf.

While four Communist candidates had campaigned in the previous council election, Maclean was the only one who ran as a Communist this time. His opponent was the Moderate incumbent, James Macfarlane, an accountant who was president of the Clan Macfarlane Society, a director of the Angus and Mearns Benevolent Society, and a governor of the West of Scotland Commercial College.[1]

In the election, Labour increased its representation by one seat overall, but the Moderates retained control of the council 74 to 39. Macfarlane came out on top in Kinning Park, with 5840 votes to Maclean's 4287. Given the circumstances, Maclean was not unhappy with his showing. He wrote to his daughters, '...altho' I lost I got a great vote. I'm now busy in the Gorbals and expect by Wednesday, the election day, to have lost my voice.'[2]

Maclean was busy in the Gorbals because suddenly the whole country was going to the polls.

~

For most of the year dissatisfaction with Lloyd George had been growing among the Unionist backbenchers who comprised the bulk of the coalition government's members of parliament. However, the party's leading figures in Cabinet continued to support the prime minister.

On Thursday 19 October, Unionist Party leader Austen Chamberlain called a meeting in which he hoped to browbeat the rebels into continuing the coalition. Instead, the Unionists voted to fight the next election as an independent party. With the coalition effectively broken, Lloyd George resigned as prime minister that afternoon. On Monday 23 October, Andrew Bonar Law, who had stepped down as leader of the Unionist Party in March 1921 due to ill-health, was re-elected leader at a party meeting and was appointed prime minister later the same day. He immediately called a general election, to be held on 15 November.

The Labour Party had been preparing for an election for some time, and its success in by-elections in 1921 and 1922, where it had taken nine seats from the government, was an indication of its increasing popularity. Nowhere was this more apparent that on Clydeside, where on all the crucial issues, including housing, unemployment and pensions, Labour, in the form of the Independent Labour Party, was the dominant force.[3]

As soon as he was released, and despite already having committed to run for the town council and being 'without committee, money or anything',[4] Maclean decided to throw his hat in the ring again for the parliamentary seat of Glasgow Gorbals.

James Downes was secretary of both the local unemployed committee and the central council. He introduced himself to Maclean at Kinning Park Town Hall where Maclean was holding a big meeting and asked if Maclean would like to speak at a meeting for the local unemployed the next night. To Downes' surprise, Maclean jumped at the offer and said that would be the start of his Gorbals campaign. Downes was nominated as Maclean's election agent, an election committee was appointed and they started work. An anecdote from Downes gives a flavour of the campaign.

> He was really a very hard man to work with. One instance where we had booked a picture house for a meeting, a women only, and the night before we were all in this little election room, it was just a wee bit of a shop, there wasnae a decent light in fact. We had eighteen helpers all addressing envelopes and it was a beautiful night. So I decided, given it was a good night, to gie them a breather, and we went out chalking this meeting for the following day. We took the whole lot out and we spread out all round the walls chalking up the meeting for women only. Just about eight o'clock in the morning the rain came on. Oh, it poured. Washed it all out. Well, the next best thing to do was, we made two sandwich boards, and had two men parade round about ... When the time for the meeting came there was about

three or four women turned up. Maclean was raging: 'I've been stabbed in the back" – being stabbed in the back after the big effort we 'd put in ... It was things like that you know. You had to be able to take them ...⁵

Maclean's election address was an uncompromising statement of his principles and policy.

ELECTORS AND FELLOW MEMBERS OF THE WAGE-SLAVE CLASS

I stand in the Gorbals and before the world as a Bolshevik, alias a Communist, alias a Revolutionist, alias a Marxian. My symbol is the Red Flag, and it I shall always keep floating on high. For twenty-five years I have been a Socialist and have devoted the best part of my energy to convert workers to Socialism and to teach Marx's writings on wealth production and his interpretation of the course and meaning of historical development in that period ...⁶

Maclean explained that in 1919 he had started a campaign for a united effort to overthrow British capitalism by a general strike. He then launched into a tirade against his perceived enemies that was steeped in conspiracy theories.

The government's reply was the break-up of my family, the blocking of my every move through traitors inside the Socialist movement, the attempted ruin of my reputation and loss of my tutorship in the Scottish Labour College ... through the dirty work of that Communist clown, Wm. Gallacher.

While I was carrying on the exhausting work with the unemployed, William Gallacher, Communist candidate for Dundee, did his utmost to break up my work and the unemployed movement, as he had tried to break up the Scottish Labour College and have me dismissed therefrom, so that I might be starved to death like better men before me. That, and other things, throw light on my reference to him as a Communist clown.⁷

Maclean concluded his pitch with his wish for a Scottish Workers' Republic, and promised that if elected, he would not go to Westminster but stay in Scotland helping the unemployed, standing by those at work, educating in the Scottish Labour College and carrying his revolutionary propaganda all over Scotland, and in to England too. Finally, he said 'If you cannot vote for me, then vote for George Buchanan, the representative of the Labour Party. On no account vote for anyone else.'⁸

George Buchanan had been a town councillor for four years and his supporters were feeling confident given he had been returned by a large majority in the recent municipal election. Interviewed by the *Glasgow Herald*, he nominated unemployment as the most urgent question of the day. 'The government must give work or full maintenance,' he said. He called for a stop to rent increases, no income test on old age pensions and adequate pensions for soldiers. Ireland's freedom must be protected and Scotland should have self-government, he declared.[9]

~

In Glasgow, the official program issued by the Labour Party was largely ignored and the general election was fought on a series of leaflets and manifestoes drafted mainly by John Wheatley of the Independent Labour Party (ILP). According to Robert Middlemas, the actual machinery of electioneering was organised by ILP Councillor Pat Dollan. 'At the work of organising, canvassing, meetings, impromptu speeches, rallies, and handling pressure groups, Dollan was a master,' he wrote.[10]

Election night in Glasgow was enlivened by a screen erected by the *Glasgow Herald* in Buchanan Street to show the results as they came in. The newspaper described the scene thus.

> Election results are matters of climax and crises. Figures are the essence of mundanity, and those that seek them must come boldly; expecting only fulfillment or disillusionment – certainly not the solace of a compromise. It takes then a certain courage to stand for an indefinite period on a raw November night, warmed only by one's zeal and buoyed only by one's hope to hear ultimately, perhaps, the worst. Glasgow is apparently a city of stout-hearted Brobdignags, judging by the aspect of Buchanan Street last night – and this morning. Like the scriptural deluge, a small crowd of folk which had by seven o'clock gathered in the vicinity of 'The Glasgow Herald' screen, on which the results were to be shown, increased with alarming rapidity until, by eight o'clock, St Enoch Square and St Vincent Street were joined by caps.[11]

Topical pictures and caricatures were displayed as the crowd waited, and Labour propagandists moved slowly through the crowd holding placards of candidates whose fate had already been decided. Including Maclean.

> One procession, composed of men and women fearsomely garbed and heralded by bells and whistles, did all that flags and voices could do on behalf of John Maclean, and aroused in its vicinity the first sparks of badinage and strife.[12]

The crowd's excitement grew as the results tumbled out; three Labour gains in succession, including Ramsay MacDonald's win in Aberavon, whipped them into a frenzy. But there were also periods of quiet, when tiredness and cold seeped into the crowd.

'Then, arose a melodian player,' the *Glasgow Herald* reported, 'who deserves to go down to immortality along with the pied piper. Led by him, the great multitude broke into song, and for hours there was music – raucous and untuned perhaps, but a great stimulus to a weary waiter.'[13]

The local results started flowing after midnight. Neil Maclean was returned in Govan, with an increased majority; and James Maxton in Bridgeton was Labour's first gain. Another Labour gain was St Rollox, where former Bailie James Stewart was successful. When Shettleston went over to John Wheatley by a large majority, followed by Springburn falling to George Hardie by an even bigger margin, the *Glasgow Herald* commented, 'Labour's series of successes were not far short of astounding.'[14]

The excitement was not over. Thomas Henderson took Tradeston for Labour; the prime minister's seat of Glasgow Central went to a recount (Bonar Law eventually pipping Labour's Rosslyn Mitchell by around 2500 votes); and in a final flourish, Labour's Campbell Stephen took Camlachie from the Unionists, and John Muir repeated the feat in Maryhill.

There is no doubt, John Broom wrote, that the virulence of Maclean's comments during the election campaign, and particularly the slurring of Gallacher, had an impact on his vote. George Buchanan won Gorbals easily, polling 16,427 votes. The National Liberal candidate, J Erskine Harper, came second with 8278; and Maclean was third with 4027, almost 3000 votes fewer than he received in the 1918 election.

Maclean's adoption of the Sinn Fein tactic of boycotting Westminster, if elected, caused much surprise. According to Tom Bell, it derived from a fundamental misreading of the similarities between the two Celtic nations.

> The Irish Republican movement ... had a great influence on Maclean. He would adopt the same methods for Scotland. What he failed to see, or take into sufficient consideration, was the peculiar features and background of the Irish Republican movement, in particular that the Irish movement was the culmination of years of political repression; of trial and experience in the British parliamentary system. Preceding the boycott of the British House of Commons a whole movement had been going on for years in the spirit of nationalism, including the revival of the Irish language, literature, drama,

and the preparation of physical resistance to the rule of the alien English. To adopt the methods of the Irish Republicans, to call upon the Scottish Labour members to boycott Westminster and to set up a Scottish council or parliament was unreal in the circumstances when no such traditions or condition existed: the more so since none of the Labour members ever subscribed to revolutionary action.[15]

~

The Unionists won the 1922 election convincingly, taking 345 seats, but Labour was second with 142, and for the first time became the official opposition party. Lloyd George's National Liberals won 59 seats and the Asquith Liberals 57.

Across the UK, the ILP and local Labour parties won 56 of Labour's 142 seats, which meant the Parliamentary Labour Party was almost a different party. In the previous parliament, almost all its members had been union nominees and all had been working-class. Now the trade unionists comprised little more than half, and middle-class and even upper class men sat on the Labour benches for the first time.[16]

The electoral map in Scotland was completely redrawn. In the new order, Labour was the largest party, with 29 seats (a gain of 23). The Asquith Liberals were second with 15 (down 7); the Unionists 13 (down 17); and Lloyd George's National Liberals had 12 (down 13). Two seats went to minor parties: John Walton Newbold took Motherwell for the Communist Party; and in Dundee's two-seat constituency, Edwin Scrymgeour of the Scottish Prohibition Party took one seat and Labour's ED Morel the other, deposing Winston Churchill in the process. A sitting member there since 1908, Churchill could only manage fourth place, coming in behind the other National Liberal candidate. Willie Gallacher, running on the Communist Party ticket, came sixth and last with just under 6000 votes.

The performance of the Scottish Independent Labour Party was spectacular. It won 23 of Labour 's 29 Scottish seats. In addition to ED Morel's victory in Dundee and the successes in Glasgow, where it captured 10 of the 15 constituencies, there were triumphs all across the west of Scotland. David Kirkwood took Dumbarton; Emmanuel Shinwell won in Linlithgow; John Robertson, James Welsh and Duncan Graham took seats in Lanarkshire; Robert Nichol and Robert Murray in Renfrewshire; and Lauchlan MacNeill Weir and Tom Johnston in Stirlingshire.

~

On Sunday 19 November, the Clydesiders left for Westminster on the evening train. Their departure was preceded by a full day of enthusiastic demonstrations and celebrations. In the afternoon, the MPs attended services of dedication in St Andrew's Hall and the City Hall, Glasgow. Eight thousand people crammed in to hear their new members take a pledge suffused with visionary hopes.

> The Labour Members of Parliament for the city of Glasgow and the West of Scotland, inspired by zeal for the welfare of humanity and the prosperity of all peoples, and strengthened by the trust reposed in them by their fellow-citizens, have resolved to dedicate themselves to the reconciliation and unity of the nations of the world and the development and happiness of the people of these islands.
>
> They record their infinite gratitude to the pioneer minds who have opened up the path for the freedom of the people.
>
> They send to all peoples a message of goodwill and to the sister nations of the British Commonwealth fraternal greetings.
>
> They will not forget those who suffered in the war and will see that the widows and the orphans will be cherished by the nation.
>
> They will urge without ceasing the need for houses suitable to enshrine the spirit of home.
>
> They will bear in their hearts the sorrows of the aged, the widowed mother, and the poor, that their lives shall not be without comfort.
>
> They will endeavour to purge industry of the curse of unhealthy workshops, restore wages to the level of adequate maintenance, and eradicate the corrupting effects of monopoly and avarice.
>
> They will press for the provision of useful employment or reasonable maintenance.
>
> They will have regard for the weak and those stricken by disease, for those who have fallen in the struggle of life and those who are in prison.
>
> To this end they will endeavour to adjust the finances of the nation that the burden of public debt may be relieved and the maintenance of national administration be borne by those best able to bear it.
>
> In all things they will abjure vanity and self-aggrandisement, recognising that they are the servants of the people, and that their only righteous purpose is to promote the welfare of their fellow citizens and the wellbeing of mankind.[17]

Neil Maclean said they accepted in the spirit and the letter the words of the dedication. The words showed that the work of the Labour movement was only beginning. He also spoke about Scottish Home Rule: 'Home Rule did not mean a palace at one end of the glen and a ruined crofter's cottage at the other. It would mean civilisation in Scotland, plenty and security for the Scottish people in the land of their birth.'

The new MP for Tradeston, Thomas Henderson, went a step further. He said he wished his colleagues had taken his advice not to go to London that night, but to go to Edinburgh on Monday morning and take over the old House of Parliament and set up a government in Scotland.[18]

The rejoicing continued in the evening, with a great crowd assembling in the Metropole Theatre in Stockwell Street to celebrate the achievements of the ILP and give the newly minted MPs a worthy send-off. The main speaker was the former miners' leader, Robert Smillie, who was given 'a magnificent reception', with numerous tributes being paid to his pioneering work in the ILP with the late Keir Hardie.

Before Smillie spoke, several of the successful candidates addressed the audience. James Maxton said the new members from Scotland would make the House of Commons different from anything they had had before. 'People talked of the atmosphere getting the better of the Labour men. They would see the atmosphere of the Clyde getting the better of the House of Commons. All the Labour members were personal friends. They were not leaving Glasgow as so many individuals, but as a team working towards a goal, and that goal was the abolition of poverty.'

Robert Smillie said he was glad to have lived to see the glorious victory. He did not glory so much in the defeat of their ordinary political opponents, but he was glad they had defeated so many of the leaders of their opponents. One who had been defeated was largely responsible for the cry that Labour was unfit to govern. Winston Churchill said Labour had not reached the level of mental development that made them fit to take the reins of government. He [Smillie] was convinced that all the other political parties combined could not pick from their number as many men so well equipped as the 150 Labour members.

Smillie concluded on a nationalist note. 'He wanted the Labour members not to forget the needs of Scotland and not to forget that ever since the union of the Scottish and English parliaments, the predominant partner has shamefully ill-treated Scotland and the Scottish people. Their ordinary

Scottish Liberal and Tory members put up with that kind of thing. The Labour members, while working in season and out of season with their comrades south of the border, would not be prepared to sit in the House of Commons and have Scotland ill-treated in the future, as she had been in the past. (Applause).'[19]

That night John Maclean held back-to-back packed meetings at St Mungo's Halls in the Gorbals, then led his audience across the Clyde to the station in a torchlight procession. Additional processions reached the city centre from Govan, Springburn, Bridgeton and other districts; some were headed by brass bands and there was much singing of 'The Red Flag'.[20]

Most of the Labour MPs who attended the Metropole were entertained afterwards with a supper at the Kenilworth Hotel in Queen Street hosted by the ILP executive. There were remarkable scenes in the area around St Enoch's station, where the train to London was due to leave at 10.45 pm. Fully two hours before, a crowd estimated at 50,000 packed St Enoch's Square and surrounding streets hoping to catch a glimpse of the new members. The crowd around the station was so dense that some members and their friends had difficulty squeezing their way through. James Maxton told the crowd they were absolutely delighted with the friendship they had been shown. It had been more difficult to get into St Enoch's station that night than it had been for most of them to get into the House of Commons, he said, but just as they had managed one, they had managed the other. He finished by shouting – 'Rely on us; we rely on you!'

Two hundred people were admitted to the platform, including officials of the ILP and the Trades and Labour Council. Shortly before the train steamed out of the station 'The Red Flag' was sung and hearty cheers raised.[21]

The Clydesiders had a red-hot send-off; they would experience a much cooler reception south of the border.

63

OOT AND ABOOT

When the general election was over, John Maclean's situation seemed grim.

He was back in his own house, but his family were away in the Borders. His paying tutorship at the Scottish Labour College was no more. The college had fallen into financial difficulties while he had been in prison and was unable to pay any tutors. His application to the Glasgow Education Authority for reinstatement as a teacher was unsuccessful. His working relationship with the Socialist Labour Party had evaporated. The Tramp Trust had dissolved and there were outstanding bills from the printer for the literature and leaflets it used to sell. The unemployed movement he had helped to found had, with the assistance of Harry McShane, largely fallen under the influence of the Communist Party.

Maclean's fight against the war, against capitalism, and for the socialist revolution, had been conducted on a national, and even an international stage. Now his sphere of influence had shrunk to Glasgow, or to be more precise, the south side of the Clyde. If he wanted to rebuild his influence, he had to do it from scratch. And while hitherto his struggles had been with the authorities and the government, he now was now also engaged in hand to hand combat with fellow socialists and other would-be educators of the working class.

While Maclean had ended his association with the Socialist Labour Party, he continued to contribute to its journal, the *Socialist*. Despite his quarrels and misunderstandings with its printing works, the Socialist Labour Press, in a letter of 24 November he told James Clunie the press 'must be saved for Marxism, if possible. ... I see in the press a mighty engine for the development of Scotland'.[1]

He thought there was no use reviving the *Vanguard*, till the workers had money and he had the machinery to sell it. 'As a matter of fact,' he told

Clunie, 'it will take me all my time to wipe out the debts incurred while I was in B. [Barlinnie] and to clear myself of the balances of my municipal and parliamentary contests. You can see it would be folly for me to risk a venture that might land me deeper in debt. I have great plans for the summer, and so wish to be quite ready.'[2]

During his Gorbals campaign he had staggered the people by saying he wouldn't go to the House of Commons if elected but would stay in Scotland. 'I urged a Scottish Workers' Republic,' he wrote. 'My business is now to create a keen desire for it and so lay the basis for a Scottish Communist Party or a Scottish Workers' Party. The [Communist Party] is going "rocky" and as it fades the ground will be cleared for a real fighting party independent of outside dictation and finance.'[3]

Maclean was looking ahead, but still seemed troubled by dark thoughts. 'A real mass movement is simmering in Glasgow, despite every mode of repression and treachery'.[4]

It wasn't all trouble and strife, however. In his Christmas letter to his daughters Jean (now 11) and Nan (now 9) in Bonchester, near Hawick, he wrote about happier pursuits.

> On the eve of Xmas with plenty of snowflakes and frost, about the only thing there is plenty of round Bonchester way.
>
> Fancy your father at a dance on Thursday night, going to another this Thursday and one on 2nd Jan. As Shakespeare should have said – 'All the world's a whirl and all the men and women merely dancers.'
>
> I've been so busy going to unemployed meetings and classes at night that I've had no time to read, let alone write, and dancing has left me so tired that I think I'll go off to Robinson Crusoe's island and sleep for twenty years ...
>
> If I'm not getting a turkey to eat, at least I'll be as fat as a turkey, for I'm going to Mr Ross's for my Xmas dinner and then to the football match as we did long years before you chicks (beg pardon, big young ladies!) were born at all ...[5]

At the football match, John's team Queen's Park beat Stenhousemuir 4-1 at Hampden Park to maintain their four point lead at the top of Scottish Division Two. In that 1922-23 season they would go on to win the league and gain promotion back to the top division.[6]

~

One of Maclean's first actions when he was released was to restart his

Sunday afternoon economics class in Glasgow. On 8 November, the day after the council election, he also started a class in Greenock. Under the Scottish Labour College banner, Maclean added to his classes with a series of Thursday evening lectures on economics and industrial history at the Cooperative Library in Wishaw, Lanarkshire, beginning on 4 January 1923.[7]

As Maclean began his final 12 month prison sentence in October 1921, the Scottish Labour College had joined with other colleges in the National Council of Labour Colleges. Based at London's Central Labour College, its role was to act as a co-ordinating body for the movement. While Maclean was in prison attempts to make the Scottish college more 'respectable' academically had persisted. Such ideas had involved fusion with the Plebs League, various associations with the Workers' Education Association, and even arrangements with universities.[8] All these suggestions were anathema to Maclean, who saw the independence of the college as the only way to maintain its uncompromising agitational attitude. But not only were there outside influences that threatened to dilute his cherished project, internally there was an attempt by the Communist Party to wrest control of the organisation.

A meeting of the central committee of the Scottish Labour College was called for 27 January in Edinburgh, and Maclean was invited to draft a constitution for the college. Unbeknown to Maclean, JCP Millar, the secretary of the SLC Edinburgh district council was given the same task. The two men clashed at the meeting, Maclean afterwards writing to James Clunie:

> Peter [Marshall] and I were at Edinburgh on Saturday. Millar's chance whilst I was in Barlinnie came, and he seemingly took it. His bent seemingly is to kill our day college ideal and make Scotland an adjunct to the London College ... Now, Millar must be fought.[9]

~

Maclean's advocacy on behalf of the unemployed continued apace. A Sunday night propaganda meeting at St Mungo's Halls in the Gorbals was arranged. The booking only lasted until the end of the year, as although he was packing the hall, the contributions from the impecunious audience were insufficient to cover the rent. The Sunday night meeting moved to the cheaper Hippodrome picture house in Oatlands.

On Sunday 6 January, along with several Labour MPs, he was a speaker at an unemployed demonstration at Glasgow Green. Heavy rain kept the numbers down, but around a thousand marched from Blythswood Square to the Green where a resolution was carried demanding the immediate reassembling of parliament to deal with the question of unemployment.[10]

Maclean's new political party, the Scottish Workers' Republican Party was built up around those parts of the unemployment movement that had not been commandeered by the Communist Party. Its first showing was at a council election in February 1923, when Maclean stood as a candidate in the 30th Ward. His election address set out the party policy.

> I come before you this election at the request of many members of your ward as a COMMUNIST or RED LABOUR candidate. Pink Labourism is of no use to the workers, never will be.
>
> As unemployment is a weapon to cow the workers into accepting lower wages and a longer week, it must be clear that the main problem before the workers of Glasgow is unemployment. That was my attitude in October 1920 when I started the present unemployment movement in Glasgow; that is my attitude today. I propose, if returned, to place before the Corporation a scheme that would absorb all the unemployed of Glasgow. The gist of my proposal is to reclaim all the moorland lying around Glasgow, and establish a system of co-operative or collective farming on scientific lines. Out of this vast experiment would arise experience enough to modernise Scottish agriculture ...
>
> I am in favour of municipalising every industry suitable for local control, as a brief intermediate system leading on to social control, i.e., ownership free from interest payment.
>
> I wish to see the city extended so as to control the whole of the Clyde Valley; in other words its conversion into a Provincial Council so as to enable the workers more adequately to control all the industries in this clearly defined area.
>
> The limits imposed by Parliament on the Corporation necessitate a Scottish Parliament. I wish and am striving for one independent of England altogether, for reasons beyond those of Glasgow's immediate interests. I wish a Scottish Workers' Republic, within which the workers in control can evolve present-day capitalist property into working-class property as a stage on the road to communal use of all the wealth produced.[11]

After this election, at which again he was unsuccessful, Maclean no longer referred to himself as a communist, as he did not want to be associated with Willie Gallacher, Tom Bell and the others in the Communist Party who he felt were betraying the working class.[12]

Never one to sit still for long, Maclean wrote to James Clunie on 20 April, telling him he had been busy canvassing for the anti-war pledge (protesting the French occupation of the Ruhr); going to conferences on the issue of industrial unity; and getting his Scottish Workers' Republican Party (SWRP) underway.[13]

But the issue that had really occupied him at this time was a boycott of the Govan Cross Picture Palace in Helen Street, Govan. Maclean had been holding large meetings of the unemployed in the cinema on Sunday evenings. The manager, James Hamilton, was dismissed for allowing this, so Maclean and friends began organising meetings outside and advising people not to attend. Maclean told Clunie that this had been going on for a month and involved leaving his house at 5 pm and getting back often after midnight.

The manager got his job back but Maclean and Tom Macgregor, a fellow member of the SWRP, were arrested. They were charged 'with having between 3 and 7 April used words and behaviour with intent to provoke a breach of the peace'. The *Worker*, which was now opposed to Maclean nevertheless commented:

> The opinion is deeply-rooted in this city that Maclean has been continually victimised by the police on account of his Socialist activities, and all sections of the movement, whether they agree with Maclean or not, will resent and oppose any attempt to send him to prison.[14]

Both Maclean and Macgregor were found guilty and fined. Both refused to pay, and when policeman arrived to arrest Maclean some months later, Maclean told him he was off to Dublin that day, and was allowed to depart. The fine was never collected.

~

Maclean had decided to use council by-elections as a means of gaining publicity and members for the SWRP. There was certainly little chance of him getting elected. The franchise for council elections was more limited than it was for parliamentary elections. The key difference was that young men living in furnished rooms, a cohort that was highly likely to favour left wing candidates, were excluded. Probably more importantly, liberals and conservatives had formed an unofficial electoral pact and ran candidates under the label 'Moderates', with the singular purpose of keeping Labour, and other socialist parties, out of office. While Labour had won a majority of Glasgow's parliamentary seats in 1922, it would not be until 1933 that it took control of the council.[15]

Maclean fought a three-cornered by-election in Kingston on 29 May against Labour's Peter Campbell and a Moderate candidate. On 23 May he wrote to James Clunie enclosing two leaflets. 'My address is every time bringing out sharper and sharper the difference between the pinks and reds – the dialectic process in the political process, or rather political part of the process. You can show both around amongst comrades as signs of the titanic struggle for supremacy in Glasgow, and then in Scotland. We are stirring Glasgow despite the wintry weather, not only in Kingston, but elsewhere as well. We'll pull Glasgow our way by autumn. At least, that's the aim.'[16]

He described the climax of the campaign in his next letter to Clunie.

> On Sunday prior to the election we had a big march from W. Regent St to West St (Kingston) and there held a meeting. This had a powerful effect. On the Monday we had another march with a flute band thro' the ward. We had a grand following, with meetings at intervals. On the Tuesday we had out a bugle, bells and boards – round the streets and courts. So we enjoyed ourselves.[17]

In the election Maclean was delighted to beat the official Labour candidate, Peter Campbell into third place. The Moderate, Armstrong, took the seat with 3169 votes, but Maclean's 2008 topped Campbell's 1865. The result was achieved despite the Labour Party, the Independent Labour Party, the Co-operative Party, the Trades and Labour Council, and the Communist Party campaigning for Campbell. Maclean was particularly unhappy that Harry McShane, who had run for Kingston on a joint ticket with Maclean 18 months previously, campaigned against him. It was obvious to everyone that if Maclean hadn't split the left wing vote, Labour would have won easily.

Maclean told Clunie that the result 'has created a profound impression in working-class circles in Glasgow as all now realise that a deadly fight has started between the 'Pinks' and the 'Reds'.'[18]

The day after the Kingston by-election, Harry McShane was evicted from his house in Thistle Street, Gorbals. That evening, Maclean had been debating Councillor Ratcliffe at Anderston over the Helen Street cinema boycott and when the news about McShane became known, Maclean led a vast march to McShane's house. 'A simultaneous march by the CPGB added to the stir-up,' Maclean told Clunie.

We had the preponderance of the crowd, and there we announced Norman McNeil as our Red candidate in Gorbals ward in November. We also challenged the Pink MPs to come home and fight evictions here. I've sent the letter to them in the Commons and also to those in the Town Council. So we're getting down to grips. We had a collection for Thos. Hitman (CPGB) lying in Duke St awaiting High Court trial on June 13. Thereafter, we had a march to Mrs Hitman's house in Norfolk Court (Gorbals) and gave her over £2. That night's work created a profound impression in view of McShane's hostility in Kingston.[19]

It was his ambition to fight every working-class ward in the November council election, Maclean told Clunie on 13 June. 'The fight between the Pinks and the Reds is getting really hot as a result of these by-elections,' he wrote.

64

THE CLYDESIDERS IN LONDON

Following their arrival at Westminster, the public attitude of the Clydeside MPs started to win them the approval of the Communist Party, and this tended to distance them from the rest of the Labour Party. Ranjani Palme Dutt, a founding member of the Communist Party of Great Britain and the editor of *Labour Monthly*, wrote: 'The new Glasgow group are Socialists. That is the whole innovation. They hold a definite political position, and they regard the capitalist class as their enemies. That is all, but it is a great thing. For from that everything can follow. In the conventional press they are spoken of as extremists. This is of course ridiculous. They are very far from being extremists. On the contrary it would be much easier to question their Socialism.'[1]

In its assessment of the Labour contingent from the Clyde, the *Times* singled out James Maxton as providing the House with its most picturesque figure. 'Swarthy as Mr Saklatvala [the Indian-born Labour member for Battersea North], with long, lean features, deep-set eyes, and a great sweep of jet-black hair that reaches almost to his shoulders, Mr Maxton has driven the sketch writers back to the days of the French Revolution for an appropriate parallel.' Maxton observed there had been a lot of talk about his hair. 'It is shorter than Mr Lloyd George's,' he quipped, 'and in my opinion it has more to protect.'[2]

The first issue to really galvanise the group was the government's response to an unexpected decision by the Law Lords on rents. Rent controls had been in place since the rent strikes of 1915, while the housing shortage due to the war had resulted in significant increases in house prices. Once the war was over, the pressure from property owners to increase rents was considerable. This was naturally resisted by the working classes, but they were not alone. Middle class tenants whose homes were not covered by rent control faced two options; 'purchase or quit' as their leases came to an end, or pay greatly increased rent. Pressure built up for an extension of rent control.

In 1920 the Salisbury Committee examined the issue and, in its report, recommended the continuation of rent control for the time being. It suggested an increase of rents upon a graduated scale, spread over three years, leading to a maximum increase of 40 per cent over pre-war rates, but no increase of rent to be permitted if the house was not maintained in proper repair.

The *Increase of Rent and Mortgage Interest (Restrictions) Act 1920* gave effect to the committee's recommendations. It extended the duration of rent control and raised rateable value limits such that almost all dwellings came within its scope.[3]

The rent increases were paid in most parts of the country, but they were opposed on the Clyde and by December 1922 at least 20,000 householders in Glasgow and tens of thousands more in the west of Scotland were deliberately withholding rent; most only the new increases, some hundreds the total rent due.[4]

The situation hinged on ambiguities in the Act concerning the formal means by which owners or their agents were to inform tenants of increases. The Clyde tenants fought a prolonged and skilful legal battle in the courts contesting the legality of the orders in Scotland, culminating in a narrow but favourable verdict in the House of Lords in November 1922. In effect the judgment invalidated all increases up to that date - a considerable victory for the tenants.[5]

The tenants pinned their faith in the decision of the Law Lords; the landlords had equal faith in the ability of the Cabinet and parliament to set aside the judgment. John Wheatley, MP for Shettleston and President of the Scottish Labour Housing Association told the *Times* in December that for the government to set aside the decision of the House of Lords would be a prostitution of parliament. 'We are prepared to negotiate with the landlords,' Wheatley said, 'about the manner in which the illegal increases may be repaid, but it must be negotiation within the four walls of the decision.'[6]

In February 1923, the government introduced a Rents Restriction Bill that sought to circumvent the decision of House of Lords. It retrospectively provided that notices of rent increase issued from 1 December 1922 should hold good, even though they were not accompanied or preceded by the required notices to quit. Landlords could not recover arrears uncollected before that date, but arrears kept back since then would be recoverable.

The Labour Party immediately moved the Bill be rejected. John Robertson, MP for North Lanarkshire said the government seemed to be very anxious about the rights of landlords, but they were not so anxious about the rights of tenants. The Bill might create a suspicion that the government was acting as the tool of the property-owners, instead of upholding the decisions of the highest court of the country and protecting the poor.

The rejection was seconded by John Wheatley who protested about the retrospective character of the Bill, and said that if the public were led to understand that if any decision which was unacceptable to the party in power in parliament might be overturned by retrospective legislation, then all respect for courts of justice would have gone forever and the authority of parliament itself would be undermined.[7]

The Bill was vigorously opposed by Labour MPs, both in the House of Commons and in committee. The third reading debate on 8 May 1923 was their last chance to rail against its injustice, and they made the most of the opportunity.

Ramsay MacDonald led off.

> It [the Bill] is a very conspicuous example of class legislation. It is an attempt to do for what is called property that which the last Parliament declined to do, and which is only done because property has got the ear of the Government to an inordinate and an unjust extent. What is the cause of this Bill? Houseowners after the War made claims to be allowed to increase rents. They were well organised; they sent deputations to this House; they saw responsible Ministers; and Parliament, in its wisdom or otherwise, decided that they should be allowed to increase their rents, but it imposed conditions, and one of the conditions was that if a landlord increased his rent he had, first of all, to put himself in the position of an owner who is virtually in possession of his house. I suppose the Attorney-General will take the point that the houseowners have been taking, especially since the case was decided in the House of Lords, that the law was not clear and that the intention of the House of Commons was never plain. The contention is absurd. The law was perfectly clear, and the intention of the House of Commons was quite plain.[8]

John Wheatley took up the cudgel.

> Parliament to-day is engaged upon a very dirty job. ... I do not think it could be more aptly described than to say that it is a piece of sordid and

unromantic robbery. It is the robbery of the poor by the rich. It is the robbery of the weak by the strong. I do not think that the right hon. Gentleman or any of his friends on the other side of the House questions the legal right of the tenants to increases which were improperly imposed. ... Their legal right to those increases at the moment is as strong as the right of any hon. Gentleman opposite to his capital, or to any hon. Gentleman opposite to his land. When the right to have those increases returned cannot be questioned, the Attorney-General and his friends turn the question on to another point, and in fact the right hon. Gentleman says, 'We do not question their right to the increases, but we want to know how that right was acquired,' and they turn the question on to how the right to these increases was acquired. Is that a test only to be applied to the poor, or is it to be applied generally? In future are we to be at liberty to say that the mere possession of a thing is not sufficient justification for its retention?

It is not enough to prove that you have the right to that property at the moment. We are entitled to ask how you acquired the right, and if you acquired the right to your capital in a way that does not suit our wishes, or in a way that we do not approve of, we are entitled, according to the precedent you are setting up to-day, to ask you to hand over that capital because you never had any moral justification for its possession.[9]

George Buchanan gave notice of his intent to resist.

What will be the effect if you pass this law? I have heard of poor landlords and of the effects on certain people. May I remind the House that there always has been a good law – 'the greatest good of the greatest number.' That has not been a bad thing in the main. How many landlords will lose any food or clothing if this Bill be rejected? How many landlords in Scotland or England will not sleep to-night because of evil thoughts of lack of nourishment to-morrow if the Bill be rejected? Not one landlord will go foodless, houseless or clotheless because of the evil effects if this Act be not passed. In my constituency, five children die for every one that dies in Hillhead, not because the parents are less moral, not because of lack of virtue, but because of the horrible social and housing conditions that this generous, decent crowd have imposed on my people for centuries. When you have these conditions causing the death of these children, do you not think that you have a duty to them, and not towards the people who kill the children? Frankly, I admit that you will carry your Bill to-night, but remember that movements have arisen out of less things than this in the past.

For my part, I do not care for your law because it is neither right nor just.

The moment law ceases to be right and just it is oppressive, and it is not worthy of respect by the masses of the people. I will defy your law in my place, and I will urge my people to resist, no matter what the consequences may be. You have no right to impose this law. These people have been out of work in many cases, and, with the nine months' rent which you say they will have to refund, they have bought boots for little Johnny who is at school; they have bought food for themselves, and now you are going to enrich an already rich class, and these people will have to deny themselves food for the next nine months in order to make them richer. I am not having it.[10]

And David Kirkwood said this.

I want the Attorney-General to keep this fact in his mind, that he is dealing with a people who have hammered this question inside out for over seven months. It is not a matter of a moment; it is a matter that has been hammered out by a thoughtful race and not a flippant people who can be turned by any wind that happens to blow. They believe that, unless you make some further concession, they are being seriously wronged - particularly, as I pointed out in Committee, the people who did not take our advice. It is not the people who have acted as I have acted - because I have not paid any rent in order to eat up the increases which were paid illegally according to the decision of the highest Court of my native land - but the people who rested their confidence in you, who believed you would do justice no matter what it cost, who believed that justice would be done should the heavens fall and who believed that there was a sense of honour in the English speaking people - the people who did not listen to the voice of Labour warning them - these are the people whom you are turning down.[11]

All the fine words were to no avail. The Bill was read the third time, and passed. After ping-ponging between the House of Commons and the House of Lords, the Bill eventually received Royal Assent on 31 July 1923.

~

The ongoing unemployment crisis was creating social and financial difficulties for the government and authorities. The situation in Scotland, where under the Poor Law of 1845, relief of the able-bodied poor was not recognised, was particularly acute. In November 1921, the government decided to extend the Scottish Poor Law to enable relief to be given to the able-bodied, as it had been in England for centuries. The *Poor Law Emergency Provisions (Scotland) Act 1921* authorised parish councils to borrow funds to provide relief to able-bodied persons who were 'destitute and unable to obtain employment'. The Act was envisaged to be a temporary measure, but with unemployment still high in May 1922, it was extended for a further year.

In March 1923, the new secretary for Scotland was Ronald Munro Ferguson. He had been governor-general of Australia between 1914 and 1920, and on his return, home was raised to the peerage as Viscount Novar. When the coalition government collapsed in October 1922, Bonar Law brought him into the Cabinet as secretary for Scotland.

In early March Novar was lobbied from two separate quarters on the issues of local taxation and unemployment relief. First up was a deputation from the Parish Councils Association of Scotland. They made the case that the Emergency Provisions Act should be extended for a further year; that responsibility for the relief of necessitous children should remain with the education authorities instead of being transferred to the poor law authorities; and that the government should bear at least some of the cost of providing parish relief. They got little joy from Novar. He told them they could hardly expect the taxpayer in England to maintain the able-bodied in Scotland while the able-bodied in England were maintained out of the rates. As regards the feeding and clothing of school children, he said his opinion was, let education be education and let health be health.[12]

A deputation of Scottish Labour MPs fared little better at the Scottish Office a fortnight later. They also wanted to discuss unemployment and the burden of local taxation in Scotland. Novar said the government had spent four hundred million pounds on unemployment relief, and while he acknowledged the burden borne by local authorities in Scotland, the government had done much to aid them. He was not surprised at the demand made for a national scheme of relief, but repeated the conundrum of the long-standing differences between England and Scotland. He also repeated his previously expressed view that parish councils should be responsible for health matters and education authorities for education, saying one of his reasons was that 'the education rate in many districts presses with great severity, and it is inexpedient to charge to education rate anything more than education'. He concluded by saying that in Scotland, where farms ran to the edge of new streets, much might be done to add to the variety of the life and the increase of the income of the town-dwellers.

The parliamentary deputation was unimpressed with Novar's platitudes. John Robertson said it was difficult to get land in Scotland. Joseph Sullivan expressed 'bitter disappointment' at Novar's remarks about unemployment relief, saying the Scottish parish councils had paid out over two million pounds in relief and the government should make good their claim for reimbursement. James Stewart said the situation was acute and growing worse, with Glasgow alone having to bear a burden of a million pounds over five years, with the rates meantime increasing. John Robertson said the parish councils might go on strike and leave the government to deal with the difficult itself.

James Maxton, a former teacher himself, raised the matter of the feeding of school children. He thought that a matter affecting the health of thousands of children would lend itself to agreement without any heat. But Novar had said he would like to see the educational burden quite distinct from the parish burden, because he was so anxious for the progress of education that he did not want it to carry social works like feeding on its back. They would accept this as a sound view if they did not know that the Scottish Office had cut down on the social side of educational services, had crowded the classes, depleted the teaching staff and prevented the proper development of secondary education. The secretary did not want the education rate to appear swollen, but ratepayers did not look at the details of their tax paper but at the total, and poor law relief and education were totted up together. He had in fact passed over this urgent problem of the deterioration of our children with general phrases.

When Novar attempted to argue that provision was being made for the children, Maxton was having none of it. The secretary only had to apply to the School Medical Inspection Department to find out the physical deterioration that was taking place, said Maxton. An alarming report had just been issued about the condition of children in the East End of Glasgow. They wanted the children fed. They did not want decrepit Scotsmen in the future. The secretary had not given the matter the close consideration it deserved, and he asked him to do so, recollecting the feelings of the people of Scotland in the matter. When he [Maxton] went home last weekend, he was met at the station by children selling flags to feed the school children.

George Buchanan said the teachers' time was more taken up with providing food than with teaching. One had only to walk through the streets of his constituency to see what this matter meant. It was not that the children's parents were drunk or foolish. They simply had not the wherewithal to live. He had, he declared heatedly, never heard a statement from a man that angered him more than the callous statement which the secretary had made that day. He had come from Glasgow, where he saw children starving, to listen to remarks like that.

Finally, Campbell Stephen urged the withdrawal of Scottish Office Circular 51, which sought to take away the powers of education authorities in dealing with the feeding of school children. After Lord Novar said he would have to give the matter his deep consideration, the deputation withdrew.[13]

~

The latest in a long line of measures to crack down on the inconvenient exercise of freedom of speech was introduced in the House of Commons on 27 March. Sir John Butcher, Conservative MP for York, sought leave to introduce a Bill to prevent the teaching of seditious doctrines to the young. The Bill was squarely aimed at the hundred or so communist Sunday schools in England. 'Communist Sunday schools advocated the destruction of the existing constitution, by force if necessary, the setting up in its place of revolution on the Russian model, and for this purpose class hatred, the rebel spirit, disaffection to the King and constitution were taught, loyalty and patriotism denounced and private property owners were held up to execration,' Butcher fulminated. 'Advantage was taken of their tender years to inculcate pernicious doctrines into the minds of young people. If we took measures to protect the bodies of the young, why should we not also take steps to protect their souls and morals from contamination in their early years?'[14]

In the debate on the Consolidated Fund Bill that followed, the government boosted its solution to the unemployment problem – emigration. Thomas MacNamara, Conservative MP for Camberwell North West and a former minister for labour in the coalition government, told the House that the permanent unemployment problem was going to be quite different to the position before the war. Quite a large number of the unemployed would be young and vigorous men, he said, and the thing to do was to use the Empire Settlement Act to give the young men a chance overseas.

Eight days previously, at a lunch at the Savoy Hotel, the Premier of New South Wales, Sir George Fuller, declared that following the passage of the Empire Settlement Act, he had come to the Mother Country with a clear cut program of co-operation in emigration with Britain. 'The men sent out from this country had become good Australians, but had not ceased to be good Englishmen,' he said. 'Those present must realise the danger which existed in the isolation of the spare population of the Australian continent, surrounded as it was by teeming millions of yellow races. They could not hope to hold that great fertile rich continent unless they filled up, in the very near future, the empty spaces in their land. At least ninety-eight per cent of their people today were of British stock and the great object they had in view was a white Australia – not only to keep the land for the white races of the world, but as a land in which the surplus population of Great Britain could come and make their homes amongst them.'[15]

Joseph Westwood, Labour MP for Peebles, criticised MacNamara for suggesting emigration when there was over a million acres of land in Scotland that could be used for afforestation. One-fifth of the whole of Scotland was given over to deer forests, he said, and on the fringes of those grounds, pheasants were fed while peasants starved. He had heard of a secret memorandum issued by the labour ministry to the Juvenile Employment Committees in Scotland pointing out that they were desirous of emigrating 500 boys of 14 to 17 years of age from the country every month. It was a diabolical scheme, he said, and it was a shame seeking to take those children away from their parents.

Neil Maclean declared there was no need to send men away from the country, and for half the sum spent on emigration they could settle people on the land. The people desired to go on the land. He pointed out that the secretary of Scotland had thousands more applicants from ex-servicemen to settle on the land in Scotland than he could find land for.

When someone interjected that the land was all developed, Maclean disagreed. There were miles and miles of land that had been taken away from development and turned into game reserves, he said. Members again interjected, and asked where? In Perthshire, Sutherlandshire, Ross-shire and Inverness-shire, he replied.

Continuing, he said if they wished the country to become merely a pleasure-ground for those that could afford to buy land, that was all very fine from their point of view, but the men who had been born in this country, had fought for this country had been cheated and robbed. They were now told there was no room for them in this country and were given £150 to leave it. A system of empire settlement started on that basis was absurd.[16]

~

The accumulated frustrations of the Clydesiders were released in scenes of wild celebration and confrontation on the floor of the House of Commons on 10 and 11 April. The spark was a snap division called by the opposition after the government's dismissive response to concerns raised about the drop in pay being experienced by ex-servicemen who moved from temporary to permanent positions in the civil service. On the procedural question that the Speaker leave the Chair on going into committee on the Civil Service Estimates, the government was defeated by seven votes.[17]

The following day saw 'grave disorder' in the House. The government attempted to proceed with normal business as though nothing had happened, but by a prolonged shouted chorus of 'sit down' Labour members prevented this. The Speaker announced the House would adjourn for an hour. The *Times* described what happened next.

> An amazing scene followed. The Labour members surged up to the Ministerial bench. Mr Robert Murray, a diminutive member of the Labour Party, rushed up to Mr Ormsby-Gore [Conservative MP for Stafford] and exclaimed, in excited fashion, 'Take that grin off your face.' A Ministerialist sitting behind, thinking that this was an attempt to assault Mr Ormsby-Gore, flicked Mr Murray with an order paper. The Labour member aimed a blow which caught Mr Walter Guinness [Conservative member for Bury St Edmunds] on the nose. A scuffle then took place in front of the mace and the Chancellor of the Exchequer [Stanley Baldwin] and Mr Ramsay MacDonald hastened to separate their followers.
>
> The fiery Mr Buchanan came tearing across the floor, and inquired, 'Who was it that hit you, Bob?' Mr Murray pointed in the direction of the Speaker's Chair and Mr Buchanan dashed out in pursuit, followed by Mr Murray, but they were intercepted. Meantime there was a mix-up on the floor and Mr Robertson shouted: 'You dirty cowards; if you want to assault us, do it outside.' A number of younger Ministerialists, some of them members of the government, were having angry words with a number of Labour men, including Mr Neil Maclean and Mr Jack Jones, and one of the former was heard to say: 'If you want a free fight outside, we'll take you on.'[18]

The House was cleared and when members returned after an hour, tempers had cooled but it was clear there would be no further business that night. The Speaker announced that the House would adjourn.

The next day, the government agreed to set up a parliamentary select committee to look into the issue of the ex-servicemen's pay. Emmanuel Shinwell [Labour MP for Linlithgow] put the government on notice. Unless the matter was dealt with in the spirit manifested by the House, he said, there would be a repetition of the incidents of the past two days. However anxious he was to conform to the rules, he would use every weapon in his power to compel the government to do justice to the ex-servicemen.[19]

At the May Day demonstration on Glasgow Green a few weeks later, James Maxton declared that nobody got anything done in the country unless they were prepared to make a noise and fight for their desire. Labour members had been criticised for making rows in the House of Commons, but he thought the mistake they had made was in having rows too seldom, and not being noisy enough when rows started. But after all, he said, progress of the working-class movement would not be gained by rows in parliament: it would depend upon the people themselves refusing to accept injustice or a policy of starvation in a land of peace and plenty.[20]

As threatened, Maxton would make a much louder noise in the summer.

65

UPROAR IN THE HOUSE

On the afternoon of Wednesday 27 June, the House of Commons went into Committee of Supply on the Scottish Estimates. In the absence of the Speaker, the deputy chairman,[1] Captain Fitzroy was in the Chair. The *Glasgow Herald* observed:

> The placidity of these occasions has in the past been regarded by the English members as synonymous in dullness, and they have consistently occupied themselves elsewhere. Glasgow Labour altered this estimate tonight, and the great body of members found themselves sharing in a succession of whirling and passionate scenes which culminated in the suspension of the services of the House of four of the Clyde leaders.[2]

The Parliamentary Under-Secretary of Health for Scotland, Captain Walter Elliot, Unionist MP for Lanark, opened the debate by giving a review of the activities of the Board of Health in Scotland. He covered the outlay of outdoor relief by parish councils to the unemployed, public health statistics, the effect of the withdrawal of the grant for maternity and child welfare, and government expenditure on housing.

James Maxton rose in response and said that after reading the annual report of the Scottish Board of Health, he felt justified in in bringing against the board, the government that decided its policy and the members of the House who supported that policy, a very serious charge of grave negligence with reference to the public welfare.[3]

At a time when the infant death-rate was at a higher point than it had been for many years, the Board of Health withdrew the supply of milk sanctioned under child welfare schemes, he said. At the same time, the board notified local authorities that it could no longer approve of the provision of hospital accommodation for children suffering from whooping cough or measles. The children consequently were condemned to live in the one-roomed and room and kitchen houses, which were the breeding ground for disease. He quoted a sentence from the board's report: 'We have continued to carry out a policy of rigorous economy because we must save money.'

At that point, Sir Frederick Banbury, Conservative MP for the City of London, a stockbroker and the former chairman of the Great Northern Railway, shouted 'Hear, hear!'

The crass and unfeeling interjection was too much for Maxton, whose wife Sissie had died in 1921, shortly after giving birth to their son. He responded:

> I only saw one case and that made a mark on me which I shall never lose. I saw a mother struggling with the last ounce of her energy to save an infant life, and in saving it she lost her own. I am not interested in the statistics of this – I am only interested in the tens of thousands of fathers and mothers tonight watching over the cots of little babies, wondering whether they are going to live or die. If I could strike the public conscience to see that this is absolutely wrong and unjustifiable in a Christian nation, I should think I had rendered some service to my country.[4]

He turned to face Banbury. 'Does he mean to tell me that the withdrawal of milk from a baby gives it a better chance at life? ... In the interests of economy they condemned hundreds of children to death and I call it murder. I call the men who initiated the policy murderers. They have blood on their hands – the blood of infants. In order to save money they were prepared to destroy children. In the interests of economy, they were to be put in the front of the firing line.'[5]

Banbury rose on a point of order, but before he could address the Chair, Maxton said, 'I am not going to give way to him. You,' he said, addressing Banbury, 'are the very worst in the whole House.'

Banbury asked if was in order for a hon. member to call other hon. members 'murderers'? The deputy chairman said, 'I do not think it is in order.'

Maxton refused to withdraw, and doubled down. 'It is the only word that applies, and I apply it to all who supported the initiation of this policy, and I apply it particularly to the right hon. member for the City of London, who when an economy was mentioned, called out "Hear, hear".'

Maxton was asked to withdraw the remark several times, but refused on every occasion. Ramsay MacDonald tried to defuse the situation, without success. Then up stood John Wheatley.

The hon. Member for Bridgeton (Mr Maxton) quoted figures to prove that with the knowledge that every ordinary member of the House possesses of the effect of starvation on human life, the government and its supporters in the interest of economy and money saving had withheld sustenance from the children. He said that was murder and that the people who supported it were murderers. I repeat the statement and I will not withdraw it. I say the right hon baronet, the member for the City of London sitting on that bench is one of the murderers.[6]

Further attempts to get Maxton and Wheatley to withdraw proved fruitless, and the Speaker, John Henry Whitley, was sent for. The two recalcitrants were named and a motion of suspension was carried by 256 votes to 70. Immediately after the announcement of the figures, the Speaker asked them to withdraw. They at once rose, bowed to the Chair and amid cheers from the Labour Party, left the House.[7]

The Speaker left the Chair which was taken by the chairman, James Hope, and the House was returning to Committee of Supply, when Campbell Stephen, the Labour member for Camlachie, rose and announced 'I want to repeat the statement that was made.' Amid calls of 'Order', he continued, 'It is all very well for those accused of murdering these Scottish children to go into the lobby and vote for the suspension of those that made the charge.' Cue uproar.

Stephen refused to withdraw. He was named, a second motion of suspension was carried by 276 votes to 60, and Stephen left the House. This time there were no cheers.

Amidst a great din, Jack Jones (Labour, Silverton) rose, but the chairman ignored him and put the motion for the vote on the Scottish Estimates. Neil Maclean (Labour, Govan) and George Buchanan (Labour, Gorbals) both rose and wanted to debate the suspension of their colleagues. The chairman pointed out that the Scottish Board of Health was the subject of debate.

Emmanuel Shinwell (Labour, Linlithgow) said he wanted to resume the discussion at the point it left off. He wanted to remind the committee that the reason for the interruption was largely down to the demeanour and action of Sir Frederick Banbury. Although expressions were used by his quarter of the House that were sometimes held to be unseemly, they were largely due to the inspiration of the hon. and right hon. gentlemen opposite.

Sir George Hamilton (Conservative, Altrincham) shouted 'Jew!'

The interjection caused pandemonium, with Labour members Buchanan,

Jack Jones, George Lansbury and Joseph Westwood rising simultaneously and shouting with accusing fingers at Hamilton and Banbury.

The House was in a 'welter of confusion'. When it had calmed down somewhat, Shinwell went on with his speech, saying he regarded the observation as unparliamentary, but was not at all affected by it.

George Buchanan shouted across the chamber, 'Stand up, you dirty dog!' The chairman said the remark was very much to be deprecated. Pointing at Hamilton, Buchanan asked, 'Why don't you suspend him?' The chairman said the remark had not reached his ears. Buchanan said, 'There he stands a white livered cur', then addressed the chairman. 'A chairman should not differentiate between one side and the other. That is partisanship. That is not entitled to respect. That is only worthy of contempt.'

The chairman called for order, but Buchanan was not for stopping. 'I am not going to be ordered by you,' he said. 'You are no chairman that takes sides. You are not impartial. You are a disgrace (loud cries of 'Order'). I am not afraid of anyone and I am not going to sit down.'

The Speaker was again called for, and a motion for suspension was carried by 286 votes to 58. Buchanan quietly bowed to the Speaker and left the chamber, to cheers from his friends on the Labour benches.

The chairman resumed the Chair and to calls for Hamilton to withdraw his remark said the expression did not reach his ear, but if it was as suggested, it was to be deprecated. Hamilton apologised and withdrew. Shinwell accepted the apology and resumed his speech on the estimates.

At the conclusion of the debate Captain Elliot returned to the suspension of the Labour members. 'He said they recognised the close interest that Mr Maxton took in these subjects, stimulated by personal circumstances which were within the knowledge of many members of the House. This, no doubt, accounted for the bitterness of feeling which might be pardoned by many members (Hear, hear.) They all recognised Mr Maxton as one of the most sincere and most sympathetic, and in many ways one of the finest characters in the House.'[8]

~

The Labour Party conference was meeting in London on the day after the suspensions, and Ramsay MacDonald announced that the Parliamentary Labour Party would discuss the matter the following week. James Maxton, who was sitting in the balcony, rose to speak, but was not recognised by the chairman. Amid cries of 'Maxton, Maxton', most of the conference demanded order in support of the chairman, whereupon Maxton shouted, 'Surely Mr Chairman you are going to show a colleague a little fair play.' The matter went to a card vote in favour of moving to the next item of business, but the chairman allowed Maxton to make a personal statement. Maxton said his intention had not been to cause controversy, but to associate himself with the statement of his party leader. They had acted, as they thought, in the best interests of the party and the working class, but on any question of discipline, they were prepared to accept the decision of the parliamentary party.[9]

When the party met on 3 July, a conciliatory speech from Ramsay MacDonald led into a full and frank discussion about how to handle scenes of disorder such as had occurred the previous week. No resolution was adopted, instead 'a general understanding was reached with cordial unanimity'. No discussion took place on the policy to be adopted by the four suspended members; it being considered this was a question for them in consultation with the party leader. A resolution was adopted however on the issue that had led to their suspension.

> That the Labour members of Parliament, assembled in Caxton Hall, direct the attention of the government and the country to the fearful infant mortality in our land, and urge upon them the necessity of re-establishing child welfare work on at least the 1920 standard.[10]

The gang of four was back in Glasgow for two large demonstrations on the following weekend. Hosted by the Independent Labour Party, the events at the City Hall and the Olympia Theatre, Bridgeton, both passed a resolution:

> That this meeting endorses the protest made by Messrs. Maxton, Wheatley, Stephen and Buchanan against the murderous policy of the government regarding child welfare and social reform, considers that their suspension is a violation of representative government and calls upon the House of Commons to grant them unconditional reinstatement.[11]

'Was it not perfectly clear,' said Wheatley, 'that the excessive slaughter of Scottish infants was due to the inferior housing conditions and the great poverty of the Scottish working class, and that these were removable causes? The causes would not be removed while the people patiently tolerated them, and their action in Parliament was dictated solely by a desire to arouse the public to a sense of their responsibility and power. We are not going to be disturbed by the fears of timid friends, or the criticisms of interested foes. Our public duty is to make Scotland a land in which it is safe to be born.'

Maxton's comment that not one of the four had any intention of withdrawing drew prolonged applause. 'If they had been inclined to waver in that frame of mind the very foolish and very cheap threat that had been put forward by some of the Tory members of the House that their pays should be stopped – (laughter) – would have hardened them very much in refusing to make any apology,' he said.[12]

The campaign had an immediate practical impact. The Glasgow Health Board demanded a 100 per cent increase in its grant and the local authority offered to contribute the same amount.[13]

~

Both Ramsay MacDonald and Stanley Baldwin, who had become prime minister in May when Bonar Law resigned due to ill-health, were keen to have the suspensions of the Glasgow MPs withdrawn before the summer recess, to avoid a campaign that might become 'undignified'. Neil Maclean, now a Labour whip, told Wheatley that MacDonald would move the withdrawal of the suspensions after Question Time on 31 July.[14]

Wheatley drafted a letter to the Speaker on behalf of the four suspended members announcing their intention to demand admittance to the House at 4 pm on 31 July. 'We have been suspended for a period of over four weeks,' the letter said, 'and our constituencies have during that period been unrepresented in the House of Commons.'[15]

On 31 July, the prime minister moved that the suspensions be lifted, Ramsay MacDonald concurred and, despite dissention from Sir Frederick Banbury and some of his colleagues, the motion was carried on the voices.

Have tipped off the press, the four members took a taxi down to the House towards the end of Question Time, and demanded entry to New Palace Yard. 'To the delight of the press and a small crowd, the policeman on duty courteously refused. Maxton got out and began to address to inspector in measured constitutional terms, but was, as expected, interrupted by members running out from Westminster Hall shouting that the suspension had been withdrawn, and to the maximum publicity, the four swept in past Big Ben and into the Chamber.'[16]

66

RECONCILIATION

At the end of June 1923, John Maclean went to Dublin to visit James Larkin, who had returned to Ireland after a decade in the United States. He was accompanied by Peter Marshall and James Hamilton, who paid all the expenses in appreciation of Maclean's campaign to get him reinstated at the Govan Cross picture theatre.

In 1907, Larkin had led the dockers in the Belfast dock strike and invited Maclean to come over and speak to the strikers. It was Maclean's first direct experience of a big strike and it had a profound impact on him. Ripley and McHugh wrote: 'Maclean found the situation electrifying and full of implications for his conception of the process of social transformation. He spoke before enthusiastic mass meeting of a size he could have hardly encountered before.'[1]

Maclean wrote to his daughters on his return from Dublin, telling them that as well as meeting James again, he had met Larkin's brothers Jack and Peter. James had been in prison in the US for two years; Jack had also been in prison there; and Peter had been in prison in Australia for four years for opposing conscription. 'So we were all a fine company of pirates, weren't we?' he joshed.

On a more serious note, he wrote, 'Jim Larkin is the greatest man in Ireland and is out for an Irish Workers' Republic, as I am out for a Scottish Workers' Republic. Remember his name, and remember what I say ...'[2]

Agnes, Jean and Nan were planning to come to Glasgow for a holiday in early August and on 24 July, Maclean wrote and insisted that his daughters stay at home with him. While Nan had few recollections of the holiday, apart from the fact her father was so shabby that she was ashamed to walk down the street with him, it marked a late upturn in his personal life.

When John saw Agnes on 4 August for the first time in many years he was shocked by her appearance. Not only was life in the backwaters of the

Borders stultifying, but during the previous winter she had been very ill with pleurisy and was still down in health and spirits.

Maclean wrote to James Clunie on 22 August telling him that his children had come on holiday and stayed with him, but he couldn't give them the time he desired because he was campaigning for the council by-election in Townhead. On top of that had come the late stages of his sister Margaret who died on 17 August. 'I haven't had the chance to do anything right,' he lamented.[3]

There was no solace in the result of the by-election on 21 August either. He came a distant third, with 891 votes, behind the Moderate (3532) and 'Pink' Labour (2239) candidates.

He wrote to Agnes on 28 August.

When at [Maclean's sister] Lizzie's I tried to study your face and I felt that it was that of a broken person. Had your separation from home at Bonchester improved your appearance and spirits I would have been content to leave things alone, but your appearance has left me far from comfortable, to put it mildly.

When you were here I was afraid to ask you to stay as I had no sure source of income to guarantee a passable existence.

I have revolved the matter several times over, and have come to the conclusion now to leave it to you to definitely decide on your course of action, whether you'll stay at B [Bonchester] or return home.

So far as my activities are concerned, they must go on even more intensely than before, as my livelihood is now completely dependent on my public efforts. As you know perfectly well, the authorities will preclude me from any position at all.

Again I'm going to make an effort for re-instatement, but the prospects aren't at all rosy as the Authority is hiding behind the surplus of teachers ...

Above everything else I feel sure you are longing to be here, and that satisfies me that I am doing the right thing in penning this letter ... No one more than me would wish to see you shake off the depressing load and become the genial soul you were long ago.[4]

Agnes immediately replied.

This is a real red letter day, and a turning point surely in our lives! I have been waiting for such a letter to come for some time now, so I much have had the presentiment that you had a longing for me to be back home. Am I right? I take it that you would not have asked me unless your trust in me is firm once more. I have been through hell these last four years because you lost faith in me. It has been very hard.

I never realized how sweet home was till I lost it or how comforting (I can't get another word) hubby was till I lost him. Need I say more!! I don't know what Rose will feel about it as she has been very good & spent a lot of money getting a comfortable home together.

As you say, the finance will be a difficulty. I am afraid for that part of it, but have faith that you will fall in for a position suited to your ability.[5]

~

Maclean's dispute with the Scottish Labour College had continued through the summer. JCP Millar convened a meeting in Edinburgh to which Maclean was not invited as he was no longer a tutor at the college. 'How far CPGB tactics are at work I don't know exactly at present, but the action of Millar confirms my attack on him,' Maclean told Clunie.[6]

On 19 June, Maclean attended a meeting of the Glasgow District Council of the SLC convened to consider the formation of classes during the coming winter session. He told Clunie, 'Woods in Glasgow will be unable to do anything this winter ... When winter comes I'll see that the college work runs on a scale in Glasgow never known before. Meantime, I'll let the fools have their "fool" swing.' He warned Clunie not to be a tool of Millar, 'who appears to me to have let his ambition outrun the best interests of the College movement'.[7]

On 7 July, he told Clunie:

Each week we are starting new [SWRP] branches here, and by the time classes are reopened I fancy we'll have the classes, who ever may control the machinery. Then a very severe struggle will start for control. Nothing was done by the committee here outside of Joe Maxwell's classes and these were on English and Public Speaking.[8]

He followed up to Clunie on 22 August:

The convenor of the classes committee, Sydney Walker, wrote me asking the dates for classes. I replied offering Sundays and four week nights. Then I got a reply from Woods drawing my attention to clause 2 and 10 of the Constitution re: object and control of classes. There will be trouble and I'm preparing to run my classes independently until Glasgow gets right again. There appears to be some kind of "United Front" as you suggest, but it can only have the committee and we'll have the classes. Thus the C.P.

[Communist Party] have "captured" the unemployed movement, but now there is nothing but committees.⁹

And at the end of his letter of 4 September, he noted the preparations being made for the return of Agnes and his family.

> The Labour men and the C.P. are jumping because the united "affront" has been burst by us. The fight, as expected, is becoming ever bitterer ...
> My W. Regent St. meeting ever grows. Now at least 3000 pack up the street. It is a great sight and is most encouraging, tho' money is absolutely scarce.
> After a public statement re: Woods and myself and the Glasgow District of the SLC, I think I'll have peace over the winter. I'm giving 4 nights and a Sunday afternoon every week. An imposing schedule (on paper) will soon be advertised in "Forward", but I know you'll be able to estimate it at its proper worth.
> As my house has for a week been in turmoil thro' a thorough clean-up (the first for years) I'm not in fit form to write or even read, so you must excuse my seeming carelessness once again. With me it's from one damned thing into another without cessation!¹⁰

~

Agnes had to go to Glasgow towards the end of September to look after her two small nieces whose mother was ill, so she was able to spend some time with her husband. Back in the Borders, she wrote saying how very sorry she had been to leave Glasgow. John replied: 'My dearest Agnes. Yes, last weekend was the best I've had for four years at least & naturally I'd wish it every weekend till the end of time.'¹¹

Agnes wrote on 4 October:

> My dearest Johnnie. Looking forward to weekends won't satisfy me although it is a lot to keep one going on with. I long to be with you all the time. I just feel it can't be too soon – we are missing precious time. I am buoying myself with the thought that by Xmas you will be able to keep us. Yes, Lizzie is far from well. A good rest and a tonic might work wonders with her. A week in Rothesay would be fine and would do you a world of good also. Dear me – you surely are having a rest this week. I'm glad the open air meetings are over.¹²

On 5 October, Maclean wrote a long letter to Clunie.

So far as the SLC work in Glasgow is concerned, I'm at loggerheads with the Committee over their "constitution", one that is tying them up rather than fostering education. I've had to attack them twice at W. Regent St, and I think that will do good. Publicity I find my only safeguard against the opposition parties.

I gave four nights a week and not one class has been started yet. There's business ability for you! ... Had I left my Sunday class to the Committee, it too would have had a belated start. Happily I got the Ardgowan Picture House and have pushed the advertisement of the class. In the past I used to issue 10,000 leaflets announcing the class. This time the Committee has issued nothing meantime. Fortunately the manager at the Ardgowan has advertised in [a] leaflet ... and on the screen this week. He caters for Kinning Park and Kingston so a wide area is thus tapped. Latterly I've been getting about 3000 at W. Regent St, the biggest crowds ever held Sunday after Sunday in Glasgow, and I've pushed the class as well at the Monument [at Glasgow Green] every Sunday afternoon.

The Committee wish the course to be 12 lectures for 2s. 6d., but I'm insisting on at least 20. If the Committee doesn't agree, then I'll run the class independently and save all the petty interference of incompetents. No attempt to put the 'hems' on me will succeed and no freezing out process either.

The SWRP, I expect will have at least a dozen candidates up in November, and we are using all our speakers as candidates, so as to put on the utmost pressure. ...

The situation in Germany where all the Propertied Parties are joining against the Pink Soc. Dems. will help us tremendously from now right on to the election. I expect a rapid landslide our way sooner or later, if our men have the grit to hold on as have done this summer.

But no matter what is now done, capitalism has lost its balance and is staggering and plunging to its well-merited doom. The capitalist reactionaries for the moment are swinging politically into power, but the next swing will be more decided to the 'Left' (red) and then may rapidly evolve a situation calling us into power.

The size of my Sunday night audience is largely due to the fair interpretation of evolving events in general and in detail. As things are going, a growing number of Glasgow people are quite alive; and should a crisis arise I feel sure the people will come to me for guidance. That is one tremendous advantage of the continuity of meetings and concentration of efforts on Glasgow.[13]

On 14 October John wrote to Agnes, and for the only time in his correspondence, expressed a depression of spirits.

... the wretched weather, a worse throat and an empty pocket just about make one sink into one's self and cut entirely with the rest of the world. This bright though sharp Sunday morning however revives one's spirits most wonderfully. Tom has just come for my dirty clothes which he religiously comes for to take to Lizzie's.

It was so unlike him that Agnes replied immediately.

Your letter arrived this morning, but what a gloomy one and so hopeless. I want to sit down and have a right good cry, but there's no time for that. I want so very much to be beside you, but how can I take the girls from here meantime? Surely you are getting less money than ever this last month or so. It is no paying concern Johnnie and you can't afford to give of your health and strength for nothing. Your health appears to me to be going down or you would not be feeling like that. I was in that condition last November and I could not get my spirits up at all. A strong tonic from the doctor made me feel quite different. Do look after yourself Johnnie. For if anything happened to you now, after that little glimmer of hope you have given me, I would go down through myself & what about Jean and Nan. We must live & help to give them a good start to life. If your throat is so bad, you will have to give up speaking & take a holiday in the meantime off that. Now Johnnie I am scribbling this when I should be getting the dinner ready, will have to rush it. I am not on with you standing as a candidate in your present condition. Again, it is wasting your health when it should be given to your wife and bairns. No one would be better pleased that me to help for the common good, but you can't help [original emphasis] effectively when the home is not right. A man must have some standing and be comfortable to do any good. My thoughts are with you all the time. Do get someone that has no bad throat to stand in your place. Your time will come again. Warmest love and best wishes and plenty of kisses from one who loves you best, your sweetheart, Agnes.[14]

Two days later, on Wednesday 17 October, she wrote again.

I was in such a desperate hurry that I hardly know now what I did say (in my letter). I just felt heartbroken all Monday. However I am a bit brighter again but will be back again if I don't get a letter from you this week. Write often Johnnie. Your letters to me are all private and it will help each other to have little confidences. Never mind having no money to send, we are getting along all right meantime. Letters breathing of confidence and trust is what I stand most in need of.[15]

John replied the following day, in a more upbeat tone.

There is no fear of depression, except that of depression of income. The situation here is so dependent on that in Germany & the continent generally, where things are rapidly moving from bad to worse, that I am apprehensive of a winter severer than any that has gone by yet. Your idea of taking in two lodgers, helpful though it might be, is not likely to solve the problem of an assured income. Where I've to get work of a suitable character, when so many competent men in every branch of industry are idle is just the puzzle I can't solve. That being so, on I go with the work fiercer than ever before. On that I decided long ago and I'm not going back now. We are putting forward 12 candidates for the Town Council in November and we'll keep the fight right on after.[16]

67

THE FINAL COUNTDOWN

On 28 October, Maclean wrote to James Clunie, apologising for the irregularity of his correspondence, but saying 'the task of running twelve candidates, talk and all the rest of it', precluded writing unless absolutely necessary. The nominations for the council election were made on 26 October and the following day, the *Glasgow Herald* noted that most of the contests would be three-cornered, largely because of the incursion of John Maclean and his supporters, standing as nominees of the Scottish Workers' Republican Party. 'This development is not regarded with favour by the Labour Party', the paper wrote, 'for which it may have serious effects in areas in which electors may be evenly divided. It is obvious that while votes obtained by Mr Maclean's group may not be numerous, they will be cast by voters who, in the absence of the Communist candidate, would probably vote for the official Labour nominee.'[1]

Maclean told Clunie that the Glasgow district of the SLC was advertising for a tutor and he and Peter Marshall would both apply, although he was sure neither of them would get it.

He then gave an account of a large demonstration on unemployment, which had broken up in disarray the previous Wednesday. The meeting in Glasgow's City Hall had been organised by the Trades and Labour Council and had advertised Robert Smillie and George Lansbury as speakers. In Maclean's letter he referred to the 'Poplar Battle', which had seen police attack a gathering of unemployed in the working class borough in the East End of London.

The Poplar Board of Guardians, which administered relief to the unemployed, was dominated by Labour and Communist representatives. Despite this, in September 1923, and with winter approaching, it had deducted the 1s. 2d. coal allowance. On 26 September a deputation from the Unemployed Workers' Organisation pleaded with the board to restore the coal allowance and increase the scale of relief to single men and women.

The guardians of the board refused both requests and the board told the deputation it was contemplating a reduction in the scale of relief to lower the burden on ratepayers by £85,000.

There were some two hundred unemployed people inside the building and when informed of the board's position, they locked the main doors of the building and told the guardians they must remain for the night unless they reversed their decision. The action was relayed to a crowd estimated at two to three thousand who had gathered outside the board's offices and 'The Red Flag' was sung.

This was not an unprecedented action – guardians had been locked in many times before, in Poplar and in other boroughs. But what happened this time was unprecedented. The guardians called in the police who cleared a space outside the doors then broke in and forcibly ejected the unemployed, beating them lustily with their truncheons. Many suffered head injuries and had to seek hospital treatment.

Sylvia Pankhurst wrote an account of the incident in the *Workers' Dreadnought*. In it she pilloried the actions of the most prominent guardian, Labour MP George Lansbury. 'Men rushed to George Lansbury, crying "George, can't you stop it?" Mr Lansbury spurned them: "They have asked for it and now they will get it. It will be a lesson to them," he answered.'

Pankhurst made the point that 'the result of working class representatives taking part in the administration of capitalist machinery is that the working class representatives become responsible for maintaining capitalist law and order and for enforcing the regulations of the capitalist system itself.'[2]

For Maclean, the incident was a telling illustration of the difference between the Pinks and the Reds; and the SWRP prepared a leaflet based on Pankhurst's article which they distributed at the Trades and Labour Council demonstration. The leaflet was titled 'George Lansbury and Robert Smillie to the rescue'. In it, Maclean criticised Lansbury for his role at Poplar and Smillie for resigning from the miners' federation in the lead up to the owners' lock-out in 1921. He told Clunie:

> The police, present outside in large numbers, prevented our announced counter-demonstration, so I asked our folks to go inside. Smillie got a hearing. Trouble began when John Robertson, M.P., rose to speak, but when Hannington (C.P. and Sect. Unemployed Conv.) rose to take Lansbury's place (absent) and to explain away the Poplar incident, the row got so hot that the

meeting had to be abandoned. Our comrade, Ball, who made for the platform was hustled out by the stewards. All the stewards were C.P. men. So there you have it – the C.P. acting as scavengers for the 'Pinks'. We are having ours on Friday and yesterday I had a wire from Sylvie Pankhurst that she's coming up on Friday. Whatever happens we'll score in the long run.[3]

The *Glasgow Herald* noted that when John Robertson got up to speak there was some interruption at the back of the hall. 'When the speaker observed that there was a movement in Glasgow to divide the workers, the disturbing element grew more noisy. The interrupters refused to desist, and numerous calls were heard, amid the din, for John Maclean.'[4]

~

The municipal election address penned by Maclean and used by all the SWRP candidates for the 6 November election painted a bleak picture.

> Today the wage-earning class is either partly or wholly idle and living on a starvation insurance or a parish allowance, or fully employed at wages well below the 1913 level. Rotten food, under supplies of food, insufficient clothing, overcrowding in sunless slums, loss of household goods to pawnbrokers, loss and reduction of pensions, worry of debts and the constant fear of eviction form the fate of a growing mass of workers.
>
> Capitalism is smashing itself to death in competition, strife and bloodshed. In its path to destruction hundreds of millions of helpless people and being crushed by a growing poverty.
>
> The hope of humanity and the path to progress lies in the revolt of the wage-earners against the propertied class, and the seizure of the land and the means of production from the propertied class. ...
>
> Until developments are ripe for a great mass movement, our party considers it right and proper to take part in the everyday struggle of our class for a sufficient allowance of food, clothing, shelter, education and leisure, and in the defence of members of our class unjustly treated.[5]

On 28 October, Maclean wrote to Agnes.

> My many and distracting activities are making me again neglect the house. I don't seem to have any object in keeping it tidy at all, so it's drifting back once more. The sight of it makes me feel like sitting down and reading, reading, reading and let everything go to the devil. However after the election I may have more time to devote to matters domestic.[6]

Agnes replied on 1 November.

> Funny you into all that excitement once again after complaining of a sore throat & empty pockets – they will be emptier still at the end of it & your throat – what about it now? I hope you are not suffering with it. Are you having Sylvia Pankhurst tomorrow night? Is she still carrying on the Dreadnought? I have not heard of her for years. The last time I heard of her, her health was very poor. I don't understand you folks, lining up against Lansbury. He seems to me to have given the unemployed as much as possible under the circumstances, but of course I never hear the extreme side nowadays. I hope there will be no election for a long time, that is from my point of view, every one for themselves. I want to get settled in my own home & have no disturbing influences for a long time. I have had more than my share.[7]

That same day, the Glasgow Education Committee refused an application by John Maclean for reinstatement as a teacher.[8]

~

On 25 October 1923, out of a clear blue sky, Prime Minister Stanley Baldwin told the National Unionist Association Conference in Plymouth that his proposed solution to the unemployment crisis was to abandon Britain's long standing commitment to free trade and to introduce tariffs on imports. As Bonar Law had explicitly ruled out trade protection in the 1922 election, it soon become obvious that Baldwin would have to go to the polls for a mandate to reverse the government's policy.

On 4 November, John sent some money to Agnes, and told her that he was going to contest the coming general election.

> I won't keep you waiting in suspense for so long this time as I have something to send more important than words, viz, £4. The fact that I have so far been impotent to help has made me inclined to stop writing, for the pain of inability to help made writing anything but easy or spontaneous. Sylvia came on Friday and after tea at the Ca' Dora [in Union St] she arrived in the City Hall all right, but naturally tired. The City Hall was filled and if it had been free for the unemployed we could have filled it three times over.
>
> The ILP are using every filth against me in the campaign and are persistently spreading he lie that I am in the pay of the Moderates! However they are getting more than they ever bargained for and the drift of the people's minds is our way. Now that the ILP has formed a united from with the govt to drive me out I am all the more determined to go on, and as a

matter of fact I have already announced that I'll contest the Gorbals, let the General Election come when it may. As I've to see Sylvia around I've no time to myself. I'm off to a meeting.⁹

Agnes replied on 7 November.

You deserve an extra hug for sending the £4. I was on my last pound and had ordered new combinations for Nan. All the same I hope you are managing to pay your way. Is there no danger of you getting some furniture sold if you don't pay your rates? I see you have very poor results from the election. You fill me with dismay at the thought of you contesting the Gorbals. It is just throwing yourself away & money that is needed to keep your family. I am up against it here – the loneliness and depressing atmosphere is more than I can stand. Last winter I said I would never come through another such, however I keep sticking it for the sake of the children, but I am at the end of my tether. I have constant headaches – my head is just like to burst. My mind is made up it must end or it will finish me. I have decided to come home at Xmas & if you can't manage to get a job, then I intend to strike out for myself & go in for nursing or something that will give me some independence & will be a bit cheerier. We will need to arrange about the children in some way. What about the reinstatement? What a god send if you got back! Do you think there is the ghost of a chance? What about your poor throat after the busy time you have given it?¹⁰

The results of the November election were indeed disappointing for Maclean and his colleagues. In Kinning Park, Maclean himself trailed a distant third behind the successful Moderate candidate (4527 votes) and the Labour runner-up (3440). He got only 623 votes, which was 7.25 per cent of the total. Of the rest, the best of the meagre offerings were in the south side wards of Govan (where Peter Marshall got 4.4 per cent of the vote); Hutchesontown (where John Ball got 4.3 per cent); and Gorbals (where Norman McNeill got 4.2 per cent). Elsewhere, in Calton, Thomas Hitman, who was serving 15 months in Barlinnie Prison for 'speaking for the unemployed', got 3.3 per cent; in Kingston, Colin Maclean got 2 per cent and in Cowcaddens, Frank Shevelin got 1.3 per cent. In each of the northern and eastern wards of Anderston, Maryhill, Mile End, Townhead and Woodside, the SWRP candidate got less than 1 per cent.¹¹

~

After three weeks of shilly-shallying, on 13 November Stanley Baldwin announced he had advised the King to dissolve parliament, and a general election would be held on 6 December.

John wrote to Agnes the following day.

> Yesterday I received a letter from the secretary of the SLC saying I was on the short list of 6 for a Glasgow appointment. However they are jambing me by inserting a clause to the effect that the tutor must take no active part in politics. That condition I'm refusing to accept, so the fight in that quarter will now really begin. My only hope of economic security (of a kind) at present is from the masses, so I must ever keep in the fight. I am therefore standing again in the Gorbals. The press suggest the election will be Weds 5 or Thurs 6 Dec. Now any chance I have of holding my own against the deluge of ILP lies against me at the Nov election e.g., that I was in the pay of the Moderates, your severance from me, is through your immediate return home and appearing in public with me. If you cannot come I'll be blackened worse than ever & will be economically doomed. If that is so, I have made up my mind for the worst – that we will never come together again.
>
> If I go down I must go down with my flag at the mast-top. Nothing on earth will now shift me from that. Now there's the tragedy for you, as clearly and as bluntly as I can put it.
>
> If it's your duty to be here, as I maintain it now is, I content it is your duty to stand shoulder to shoulder with me in the hardest and dirtiest battle of my life. If we have to go under we had better go down fighting together than fighting one another. Realising this is the greatest crisis in our lives I cannot find words to say more.
>
> If you come I'd prefer you to come at once and walk right in.
>
> Whatever course we follow, remember that you are the only woman I love and can now love.
>
> Tell Nan & Jean, I don't at present feel in the mood to write them, as I would so keenly desire to do.
>
> Your loving husband, Johnnie.[12]

Agnes' letter to John on the same day crossed in the mail.

> Well John Maclean, it will just be the limit if you refuse the chance of a tutorship. <u>It will be very wrong of you</u> [original emphasis] and that's that. You have been burning the candle at both ends for too long and it would just be a god send if you had no time to take an active part in politics for a year or so at least. Think what it would mean for us – for my sake <u>don't</u> refuse

it. I am to be considered as well as you. You know what you have made me come through and it's got to stop – as I said in my last letter, I am at the end of my tether & it's up to you to save me. You are the only person to help me. It is your duty to stand by me and leave the election alone for this time. Let your friends know that your wife's health will not stand the excitement of an election. That will not damn you, but the very opposite. I will come back to you this weekend Johnnie, but Jean and Nan will follow on later, if we can get the wherewith all to feed them. Fancy, coming home at long last. I will try to be with the train arriving Queen St about 5 p.m. It is a big hurry at Edin to catch that one but I may manage it. This has come very sudden. I am saying this on paper but have no preparation made etc., but all the same I am coming home on Frid. You will be at the station. I am not writing anyone else. You can tell Lizzie, only she may be away nursing Grandpa Mason, if he is still living. Fondest love till then, your own, Agnes.

Thursday morning: Am realizing this morning that Frid. will be too big a rush for me, so will come at the same time on Sat. afternoon. A fearful snowstorm today. They are all away to school – am wondering how they will get back. Hope it will be off by Sat. yours Agnes.'[13]

Agnes arrived back to find John in an alarming condition. According to Nan Milton, his health was completely ruined by malnutrition and constant political activity. 'Although suffering from severe sinus trouble and a chronic sore throat', she wrote, 'he was outside every night speaking, often in a dense November fog. Accustomed as he had been all his life to health and fitness, he seemed quite unable to realise his own weakness.'[14]

The Reverend William Fulton, the chaplain from Barlinnie Prison, recalled seeing Maclean around this time. 'The last time I saw him was one Sunday evening as he addressed a big open-air gathering in Govan. I was on my way home from a Communion service and was wearing a silk hat. It may have been the hat that attracted his attention, or my standing beside a Police Inspector known to both if us. In any event, he saw and named me as a good friend in Barlinnie. When he left the rostrum, we exchanged greetings. He wasn't well looking and the Inspector and I both counselled him to go home and go to bed.'[15]

Maclean penned his general election address for Gorbals on 23 November. He pooh-poohed Baldwin's protection policy as a solution to unemployment, saying all it would do would pull the empire more closely together for a bigger and bloodier war than the last.

For the wage-earning class there is but one alternative to a capitalist war for markets. The root of all the trouble in society at present is the inevitable robbery of the workers by the propertied class, simply because it is the propertied class. To end that robbery would be to end the social troubles of modern society. The way to end that robbery is the transfer of the land and the means of production, and ownership is Communism. The transfer is a Social Revolution, not the bloodshed that may or may not accompany the transfer.

Russia could not produce the world revolution. Neither can we in the Gorbals, in Scotland, in Great Britain. Before England is ready, the next war will be on us. I therefore consider that Scotland's wisest policy is to declare for a Republic in Scotland, so that the youth of Scotland will not have to die for England's market.

I accordingly stand out as a Scottish Republican candidate, feeling sure that if Scotland had to elect a Parliament to sit in Glasgow, it would vote for a working-class Parliament.

Such a Parliament would have to use the might of the workers to force the land and the means of production out of the grasp of the brutal few who control them., and place them at the full disposal of the community. The Social Revolution is possible sooner in Scotland than in England.

My policy of a Workers' Republic in Scotland debars me from going to John Bull's London Parliament. Last year I told you I would not go as I could get nothing there. So you sent George Buchanan to get your rents back. Buchanan and his friends have spent a fruitless year and have returned home empty handed. So, after all, I was right. Had the Labour men stayed in Glasgow and started a Scottish Parliament, as did the genuine Irish in Dublin in 1918, England would have sat up and made concessions to Scotland, just to keep her ramshackle Empire intact to bluff other countries.

Neither free trade or protection is of use to the workers. Taxation of land or capital, including the capital levy [a Labour policy], is of no use to the workers. No housing or other social reform is really possible while industry is paralysed and the earnings of the workers are ever shrinking. The only possible hope of the working class is community ownership of the means of production. The increasing poverty and misery in Gorbals ought to convince the most conservative of workers that all the 'Woolworth' pottering of the petty politicians of all the 'practical' parties (the Labour Party included) has brought no improvement into the life of the citizens of the Gorbals. Your only course now is to back me up for the complete change in the ownership of the world. Every vote cast against me is one cast for world war and the further starvation of the world's workers.

Every vote cast for me is for world peace and eternal economic security for the human family.[16]

~

Maclean's last meeting was at the Rex Cinema on Rutherglen Road on Sunday 25 November. He was coughing so violently he had to be taken home. The next day he contracted a severe chill which developed into double pneumonia.

The deadline for candidates to lodge their election deposit was Monday 26 November. Maclean's long term friend Tom Anderson later recalled: 'Two days before the nomination day I received from him [Maclean] £25 in an envelope marked "Comrade Tom Anderson", which I had given him as part of the £150 deposit. Comrade John's wife brought it to me and I knew something serious was wrong.'[17]

On Tuesday the *Daily Record* reported, 'There was to have been a Communist-Republican candidate for the Gorbals Division, but at the County Buildings yesterday Mr John Maclean did not roll up with his deposit of £150.'[18]

Almost before Agnes and his friends fully realised the seriousness of his condition, he died on the morning of Friday 30 November. It was St Andrew's Day.[19]

68

TRIBUTES

The funeral took place on Monday 3 December 1923. On a dry but chilly day, on which the temperature reached just 5 degrees Celsius, a crowd estimated at 10,000 attended. It was claimed to be the biggest funeral Glasgow had ever seen. The whole thing was organised by Tom Anderson, founder of the socialist Sunday schools in Glasgow before the war, and in truth it was more like one of John Maclean's political rallies than a religious service.

Led by the Clyde Workers' Silver Band, a crowd estimated at between three and five thousand marched from the Eglinton Toll to Maclean's house at 42 Auldhouse Road, Newlands. At the house, Anderson gave a short service and Labour MPs James Maxton and George Buchanan were among the pall bearers as Maclean's coffin was transferred to the waiting hearse.

The funeral procession, now doubled in size, made its way the mile and a half to Eastwood New Cemetery to the strains of Handel's 'Dead March' from *Saul*. At the graveside, Anderson and the Reverend Richard Lee, from Ross Street Unitarian Street Church, conducted a secular service. The small cemetery was full to bursting and there was certainly nothing religious in the music, as the crowd sang 'A Rebel Song', 'The Red Flag', and 'The Internationale'.[1] As well as Maxton and Buchanan, among the mourners were fellow Labour MPs Campbell Stephen, Thomas Henderson and John Muir.[2]

The tributes and messages of condolence came: from friends, former friends, and even from foes.

There was a telegram from Helen Crawfurd. 'My deepest sympathy to you and yours. His big honest selfless fight is over. Broken on the wheel but fearless and honest to the end. The world is poorer today.'[3]

In an editorial for the *Workers' Dreadnought*, Sylvia Pankhurst wrote:

> He was a fighter: that is the first thought that comes to mind when one hears of John Maclean's death. One is surprised to learn he was only 44 years of age

for he had been long in the forefront of the struggle. His hair was white and his rugged face deeply lined. He seemed a much older man; but hardships, particularly hardships in childhood, age one swiftly.

Again, one thinks, as one recalls him, What a fighter! 'Wild man' some called him in Scotland. Never daunted, he would not trim his words to escape imprisonment, even though an army of detectives were around him. He expected persecution: he met it without flinching. Never apologizing, never explaining away his words; always ready to repeat them with emphasis.

He had gathered round him latterly a big movement in Glasgow. When we saw him a month ago he was holding great meetings and seemed stronger and more confident than ever. Yet he lived the bare lonely life of an ascetic. Parted from his wife and children by the financial difficulties which followed his dismissal from his school post on account of his political activities, he lived quite alone, doing his own cooking and housework; a greater hardship this, for the strenuous agitator who is speaking continuously in all weathers, than the inexperienced can realize. He was talking enthusiastically of the nourishing properties of pease brose, which in English is plain pease flour porridge, when we last saw him, declaring that pease brose was one of his daily meals. His tones bespoke his cheerful frugality, which was only too near to want.

His imprisonments, his hunger strikes, and that ugly thing, force feeding, have undermined what must have been originally a very strong constitution.[4]

George Lansbury wrote in the *Daily Herald*:

I wish to put on record my very high appreciation of the life and work of John Maclean. It is true that on many matters we were not agreed; he was much more a born fighter in the sense of hard slogging than I could ever be: he saw evil and his whole being was ablaze with wrath.

He was impatient because all around him he saw little children wasting away and perishing because of a brutal callous system which man had built up. His wrath took one form. The wrath of other men and women equally true and brave as he took other forms; yet all of us can respect the honesty, courage and sincerity with which he pursued his way through life. We who survive him, and who during his lifetime found ourselves strongly opposed to his methods, must now we are on the threshold of success, make up our minds that this is our testing time. ...

In his home he treated me, although I was years his senior, with a genial tolerance when we spoke of morals and religion because for him there was but one expression of true worth and that [was] the economic emancipation of the workers.

People outside of Glasgow and the West of Scotland wonder how it is that part of our Island has become permeated with Socialism. There are many causes which have conspired to produce the Scottish Labour Party in the House of Commons. Nobody who knows the facts will deny that the educational work of John Maclean has played a great part in building up our movement.

We whom he fought against because of our methods can only stand by with bowed heads [and] pay our tribute of praise to one who gave himself to the service of others.

Ten thousand people followed him to his grave; many tens of thousands influenced by his teachings in class and at street corners will carry on the good tidings which he taught – that the common people of the world shall possess the world.

To Mrs Maclean and his family, we can only send our tribute of respect and love. She has shared his trials and difficulties, and has been a true helpmate to him in all his work. One consolation is hers: that however much many of us found ourselves apart from him, disagreeing with his methods and expressions, not one of us would have said or thought evil of him, even when his wrath was directed against ourselves. We know him as she knew him, as one whose sincerity of purpose and devotion to the cause was always beyond doubt. [5]

In the *Workers' Weekly*, the official newspaper of the Communist Party of Great Britain, the executive committee of the CPGB paid its respects.

It is with the deepest regret that we learn of the death of John Maclean. The whole working class movement has lost in him one of its most fearless and undaunted champions. Always on the alert and ready to hurl defiance in the very teeth of Capitalism, yet none was more warmhearted and sympathetic to the struggles of the workers. We wish to place on record our appreciation of his work for the movement, and extend our heart-felt sympathy to those who directly and personally feel this bereavement.[6]

In the same edition, the CPGB's first chairman, Arthur MacManus, who had been elected to the executive committee of the Comintern in September, said:

The unique place of esteem and honour in the revolutionary working class movement of this country attained by John Maclean is the result of a long martyrdom. The medical certificates, I understand, record 'Death from double pneumonia'. Bah! He was the victim of a calculated political murder. Maybe the perpetrators will sleep a little more soundly now that their vile work has reached its consummation? We who knew and respected him, aye, and fully understood him, are stricken with the tragedy of it all. A chill of desolation envelops us. We pay our more or less impotent tribute to his memory, and turn once again to our task at least a little more strengthened in our efforts to erect the only fitting tombstone to one such as he – A Liberated World Working Class.[7]

Even Willie Gallacher, who Maclean had fallen out with so bitterly at the end of 1920, got in on the act, with a tribute published in the January 1924 *Communist International*, the English edition of the journal of the Executive Committee of the Communist International.

In the midst of an election campaign, I read the announcement in the press, 'Death of John Maclean'. I could scarcely credit the evidence of my eyesight. Surely it couldn't be true! Just a week or so before, I had left Glasgow for Dundee, and at that time Maclean was holding meetings all over Glasgow. But then, that was the real make of the man. His body may be broken, his physical strength might fail, but the revolutionary spirit that inspired him kept him going no matter how great the obstacles were that opposed him.

During the past two years, his rigid revolutionary integrity brought him into bitter opposition with the official labour movement, and as a result many smug, self-satisfied successful parliamentary representatives are inclined to refer to him with a sneer, more or less hidden in their voice, but I, who was through all the fighting on the Clyde, fighting that has made it possible for many of these men to score their electoral victories, know that no man played a bigger part in making Glasgow and its surroundings Red than John Maclean. It is so easy for small men to step into the limelight and make fervent protestations of abiding devotion to the workers' cause, when the workers' cause is popular and offers splendid opportunities for political advancement: it is so easy to fulminate against the evils of capitalism to the accompaniment of enthusiastic plaudits from assemblies of workers, but it is also easy, and oh! so convenient, to forget that the chains that bound these workers to the policy of their masters had to be smashed, and that the smashing wasn't easy. It was not a popular task: it was a task that meant calumny, abuse and imprisonment, and all these Maclean faced, with a dauntless courage and a never failing belief in the workers to whom he carried his message of revolutionary deliverance.

With his death there passes one of the greatest fighters the movement in this country has known. But he left the movement a heritage that is worthy of the devotion he gave to the cause. Hundreds of young men, scattered throughout the country, in the colonies and America, heard the message from Maclean, were inspired by Maclean and now continue the work that death and death alone could force him to lay aside.[8]

It was all bit much for Guy Aldred, a leading figure in the Glasgow Anarchist Group, who had been in Barlinnie Prison with Maclean in 1921 and 1922. In a chapter of his booklet on Maclean titled 'By the Graveside', Aldred declared himself 'wearied and dissatisfied with the tributes paid in death, that were the dead to rise, would be withdrawn and replaced by gibes and sneers'.

> I know not whether these tributes be sincerities or hypocrisies. But methinks, 'twould have been better to have uttered them while the warrior still fought, whilst the battle oppressed him, and when a mead of praise and some slight suggestion of help would have comforted. My conscience could not praise in death the man whom I had attacked and outcasted in life.
>
> Beside the grave I have no tongue for eloquence, no gift of speech. I would bury the dead in silent meditation and keep the memory of their heroism green in my heart, and borrow their courage to maintain my spirit. I have not the words with which to point the moral of the dream that is rounded by two eternal sleeps. I only know that John Maclean was a brave and tireless fighter, uncorrupted by hopes of reward, loved, and hated too, because he served the outraged and oppressed. ...
>
> John Maclean sleeps. His soul goes marching on. Wherever Socialism calls its hosts to battle, wherever the rebel falls before reaction, the memory of John Maclean will stir the heart of man, sobering yet enhancing success, comforting and sustaining in defeat. The man of whom so much can be said in death lived the short day of man not in vain. Rest, brave chief, rest! We are the braver for your struggle, and must battle on to achieve the glory of your ideal, until, one day, the great silence calls us too, and the kindly fates bestow their gift of everlasting peace.[9]

69

AFTERMATH

Maclean biographer Gerard Cairns said that between Willie Gallacher's obituary to Maclean in January 1924 and the publication of *Revolt on the Clyde* in 1936, John Maclean was a non-person in political terms. Maclean's autonomous Scottish socialism didn't sit with a unified British communist party taking its direction from Moscow; nor with the prevalent socialist orthodoxy of electing a British Labour government. Neither did his politics chime with the Scottish National Party, formed in 1934, whose vision of independence was home rule with dominion status.[1]

In 1948, on the twenty-fifth anniversary of his death, a John Maclean Memorial Meeting was held at St Andrew's Hall in Glasgow. The poet Hugh MacDiarmid, who had felt like a lone voice championing the Maclean line, recalled that when the event was first mooted there were doubts as to the response. 'Maclean had died way back in 1923, the younger people knew nothing of him, [and] no book had been published doing justice to his lifework ...'[2] But the tremendous response showed that Maclean had not been forgotten. The event was notable for the first public performance of Hamish Henderson's 'The John Maclean March'.

In 1973, on the fiftieth anniversary of his death, a cairn was unveiled to his memory in Pollokshaws and two important biographies were published, one by his daughter Nan Milton and another, with an introduction by MacDiarmid, by John Broom. MacDiarmid praised Broom's book as a 'clear and concise narrative [that has] brought John Maclean back to the Clyde'.[3]

But in Nan Milton's opinion, a third book released that year contained the very heart of the legend. Published by the John Maclean Society, *Homage to John Maclean* was a collection of songs and poems spanning the previous 55 years, and included works by MacDiarmid, Hamish Henderson, Edwin Morgan, and the great Gaelic poet Somhairle MhacGill-Eain (Sorley MacLean) In the foreword Owen Dudley Edwards wrote: 'The work as a totality has everything to tell us about the impact of Maclean on the survival of Scottish culture as well as of Scottish socialism. Maclean in terms of political statistics failed: in terms of ideas and art he triumphed.[14]

Hamish Henderson's songs widened the circle of awareness. Maclean was acknowledged in 'The Freedom Come-All-Ye' (1960), Scotland's alternative national anthem. The song was subsequently adopted by the Scottish CND (Campaign for Nuclear Disarmament) peace marchers and the anti-Polaris campaign in the 1960s. But even more influential was 'The John Maclean March', recorded by The Clutha (1971), The Laggan (1972) and Dick Gaughan (1972). Which is where I came in.

~

The 21st century resurgence in Scottish nationalism, leading to the electoral successes of the Scottish National Party and the burgeoning pro-independence movement have sparked a revived interest in John Maclean's late career advocacy of a Scottish republic.

However, Maclean's vision of a Scottish socialist republic might stick in the craw of many a well-off SNP supporter. The Scottish Socialist Party, a left-wing microparty, is the true inheritor of his vision and does its best to keep the fight going.

These are very different times in the United Kingdom. In Maclean's day, Britain led the world in trade, finance and shipping, and had strong bases in manufacturing and mining. As I write this, coal is gone, steel is on life support and the once mighty shipbuilding industry on the Clyde is down to two yards; the former Yarrow yard at Scotstoun, and Fairfield's at Govan, both operated by BAE Systems. The industrial working class army whose power Maclean sought to harness in the cause of social revolution is now gone.

What has not changed is the tendency of democratic governments to supress dissent, protest and freedom of speech. John Maclean's anti-war and political activities led to him being dismissed and then blackballed from his teaching career. For his public speeches he was persecuted mercilessly under the Defence of the Realm Regulations and the Emergency Powers Act. The prison terms he served for sedition not only disrupted his educational and political initiatives, but strongly contributed to the physical and mental ill-health that resulted in his early death.

There is a war going on in Western democracies at present – a war on protest. In the UK, the Public Order Act introduced in 2023 introduced measures that significantly increased the power of the police to respond to protests and put restrictions in place for those taking part in them. Amnesty International says the right of peaceful assembly is coming under severe attack as states across Europe increasingly stigmatise, criminalise and crack down on peaceful protests. In Australia most states have introduced laws that target environmental protests amid the global climate crisis.

The biggest threat to civil rights is unsurprisingly in the home of global capitalism, the United States of America. The International Center for Not-for-profit Law reports that at the time of writing (May 2025), three hundred and forty-seven Bills have been introduced by state and federal lawmakers since January 2017 that would limit the right to protest. Fifty-one of these have been enacted. The Bills are usually introduced in response to prominent protest movements, including movements for racial justice, campaigns against new oil and gas pipelines, demonstrations on college campuses and protests in support of better working conditions for teachers.[5] According to the *Guardian*, the number of anti-protest Bills – especially those targeting those speaking out on the US-backed war in Gaza and the climate crisis – have spiked since the second inauguration of President Donald Trump.[6]

~

So, who was John Maclean?

George Barnes, Maclean's opponent in Gorbals at the 1918 general election said of him, 'He is a stocky little man of about forty with a "bee in his bonnet".'[7]

That's probably not inaccurate, but I do prefer the assessment of the Reverend William Fulton. Fulton was chaplain at Barlinnie Prison, Glasgow when Maclean served the last of his five terms of imprisonment there.

> Summing up, I do not hesitate to pronounce John Maclean as one of the finest men I have ever met. Stockily built, quiet and reserved in bearing, straight-forward in speech, well-informed in an infinite variety of subjects, earnest and sincere. ... Even while in prison the fire within burned fiercely ... indeed it burned him up and burned him out in the end, for if ever any man merited the name of martyr to the causes he espoused so passionately, it was John Maclean.[8]

ACKNOWLEDGEMENTS

My thanks to Ian R. Mitchell and my cousin Roddy Robertson for their interest, support and comments on the manuscript. Particular thanks to Ian for the walking and driving tours of John Maclean's Glasgow and to Roddy for the eye-opening visit to Peterhead Prison.

My thanks to staff at the National Library of Scotland, Glasgow's Mitchell Library, the University of Glasgow archives, and the State Library of New South Wales. My thanks also to the National Library of Australia for providing access to the *Times* digital archive, to Google News for providing access to archived editions of the *Glasgow Herald*, and to the British Newspaper Archive for providing access to other newspapers.

My grateful appreciation to Christine Donnelly, Gavin Oakes, Anne Parbury, Calum Robertson, and Collette Snowden for their perceptive and useful comments on drafts of the book.

Special shout-out to Madeleine Davis for her heroic effort in compiling the index.

Luke Harris at Working Type Studio has done an absolutely splendid job with the book's layout and design, not to mention the terrific cover – thank you, Luke.

And finally huge thanks to Fred and Duncan at Resistance Books for their willingness to take the project on and see it through to publication.

ABBREVIATIONS

ASE	Amalgamated Society of Engineers
BSP	British Socialist Party
CI	Communist International
CLC	Central Labour College
CLP	Communist Labour Party
CP (BTSI)	Communist Party (British Section of the Third International)
CP/CPGB	Communist Party of Great Britain
CWC	Clyde Workers' Committee
EC	Executive Committee
ECCI	Executive Committee of the Communist International
ILP	Independent Labour Party
IRA	Irish Republican Army
MFGB	Miners' Federation of Great Britain
MRC	Military Revolutionary Committee
NAC	National Administrative Council
NEC	National Executive Committee
OS	Old Style calendar, which was 13 days behind the Gregorian or New Style calendar.
NUR	National Union of Railwaymen
PRIB	People's Russian Information Bureau
RIC	Royal Irish Constabulary
RSDLP	Russian Social Democratic Labour Party
SDF	Social Democratic Federation
SDP	Social Democratic Party
SLC	Scottish Labour College

SLP	Socialist Labour Party
SWRP	Scottish Workers' Republican Party
SWSS	South Wales Socialist Society
TUC	Trades Union Congress
WSF	Workers' Socialist Federation.

BIBLIOGRAPHY

OFFICIAL RECORDS

Dáil Éireann, vol. 1, 21 January 1919, 'Message to the free nations of the world'.
Govan Parish School Board Minutes, 1915; Lambhill Street School log, 1915; and Lorne Street School log, 1915; in the Mitchell Library, Glasgow.
Great Britain, *Coal industry commission 1919*, 3 vols, HMSO, London.
Great Britain. Ministry of Munitions 2009, *Official history of the Ministry of Munitions, vol. 1, Industrial mobilisation 1914-15; vol. IV, The supply and control of labour 1915-1916*, and *vol. V, Wages and welfare*, Naval & Military Press Ltd, London.

COLLECTIONS OF LETTERS, ARTICLES AND SPEECHES

Maclean, J 1978, *In the rapids of revolution: essays, articles and letters 1902-23*, ed. Nan Milton, Allison & Busby London.
Maclean, J 2014, *Essential writings & speeches*, ed. Will Jonson, Createspace Independent Publishing Platform.
Papers of John Maclean, Clydeside agitator, 1909-1923, National Library of Scotland, Edinburgh.
Papers of William Douglas Weir, University of Glasgow Archives.

CONTEMPORARY AND PARTICIPANT ACCOUNTS AND MATERIALS

Aldred, GA 1940, *John Maclean*, Bakunin Press, Glasgow.
Barnes, GN 1918, 'Imprisonment of John Maclean', 26 November, The National Archives of the UK, CAB 23/70/82.
Barnes, GN 1924, *From workshop to War Cabinet*, Herbert Jenkins, London.
Beaverbrook, Max Aitken, Baron 1928, *Politicians and the war 1914-1916*, Thornton Butterworth, London.
Beaverbrook, Max Aitken, Baron 1956, *Men and power 1917-1918*, Hutchinson, London.
Bell, T 1941, *Pioneering days*, Lawrence & Wishart, London.
Bell, T 1944, *John Maclean: a fighter for freedom*, Communist Party, Scottish Committee, Glasgow.
Beveridge, W 1953, *Power and influence*, Hodder & Stoughton, London.
Blatchford, R (as Numquad) 1893, *Merrie England*, Clarion, London.
Bridges Adams, M 1916, 'The sentence on John Maclean', *Cotton Factory Times*, 21 April.
Bridges Adams, M 1916, 'The approach of the iron heel', *Cotton Factory Times*, 28 April.

Bridges Adams, M 1916, 'The ground we are losing', *Cotton Factory Times*, 12 May.
Bridges Adams, M 1916, 'The release of Maclean', *Cotton Factory Times*, 30 June.
Buchanan, G 1923, *My mission to Russia*, Cassell, London.
Chicherin, G 1916, 'The Scottish labour movement and the reaction in England', *Nashe Slovo* (May-June, in five parts), translated by Maria Artamanova.
Clunie, J 1958, *The voice of labour: the autobiography of a house painter*, A Romanes, Dunfermline, Scotland.
Clyde Workers Committee, 1915, 'To All Clyde Workers', leaflet, October.
Clyde Workers Committee, 1916, 'A call to all workers', *Worker*, no. 4, 29 January.
Council of Action for Peace and Reconstruction (Great Britain), 1920, *Report of the Special Conference on Labour and the Russian-Polish War*.
Davidson, N 2001, 'Marx and Engels on the Scottish Highlands', *Science & Society*, vol. 65, no. 3.
Diack, W 1919, 'Scottish and Irish Labour Colleges', *The Scottish Review*, vol. 42 issue 96.
Gallacher, W 1916, 'Prepare for action', *Worker*, January.
Gallacher, W 1924, 'John Maclean', *Communist International*, No.30, January.
Gallacher, W 1947, *The rolling of the thunder*, Lawrence & Wishart, London.
Gallacher, W 1966, *The last memoirs of William Gallacher*, Lawrence & Wishart, London.
Gallacher, W 2017, *Revolt on the Clyde*, 5th edn, Lawrence & Wishart, London.
Gleason, A 1920, *What the workers want: a study of British Labour*, Allen & Unwin, London.
Gould, G 1921, *The lesson of Black Friday*, The Labour Publishing Company and George Allen & Unwin, London.
Henderson, A 1917, 'British mission to Russia, June and July 1917', The National Archives of the UK, CAB 24/4/2.
Joint Strike Committee, Glasgow 1919, *Manifesto*, January.
Kellogg, PU & Gleason, A 1919, *British Labor and the war*, Boni and Liveright, New York.
Keynes, JM 1920, *Economic consequences of the peace*, Macmillan, London.
Kirkwood, D 1915, 'Rent Strikes: Serious Situation', *Forward*, 9 October.
Kirkwood, D 1935, *My life in revolt*, George G. Harrap & Co, London.
Labour and Russia Council of Action, 1920, *Manifesto*.
Labour and Russia Council of Action, 1920, *Report of the Council of Action, August to October 1920*.
Lansbury, G 1923, 'The heart of a revolutionary', *Daily Herald*, 15 December.
Lansbury, G 1931, *My life*, Constable, London.
The Left Wing Group of the ILP, 1920, *Moscow's reply to the ILP*, Glasgow.
Lenin, VI 1965, *Collected works*, Progress Publishers, Moscow.
McBride A 1915, 'The Rent Fight: Past and Present', Glasgow Labour Party Housing Association pamphlet.
Macdougall, JD 1915, 'Appeal to the Clyde Munition Workers', *Vanguard*, October.
Macdougall, JD, 1915, 'The Threat of Conscription', *Vanguard*, November.
Macdougall, JD 1927, 'The Scottish coalminer', in *The nineteenth century and after*, no. 102.
Maclean, J 1915, 'The conscription menace', *Vanguard*, December.

Maclean, J 1917, 'Letter on first release from prison', *Call*, 19 July.
Maclean, J 1917, 'Lead from Lanarkshire: miners' historic protest against profiteers', *Call*, 9 August.
Maclean, J 1917, 'A Glasgow appeal to Lancashire: movement on behalf of interned Russians', *Cotton Factory Times*, 9 November.
Maclean, J 1917, 'Russian Political Refugees Defence Committee', *Call*, 29 November.
Maclean, J 1918, 'The release of John Maclean – special message to 'The Call'', *Call*, 12 December.
Maclean, J 1919, 'Now's the day and now's the hour', *Call*, 23 Jan.
Maclean, J 1919, 'Life in prison', *Red Dawn*, vol. 1, no. 1, March.
Maclean, J 1919, 'The coal situation', *Call*, 6 March.
Maclean, J 1919, 'The miners next move', *Call*, 23 October.
Maclean, J 1920, 'The Vanguard resurrected', *Vanguard*, May.
Maclean, J 1920, *The Irish tragedy: Scotland's disgrace ...*, pamphlet.
Maclean, J 1920, 'The battle of Motherwell', *Vanguard*, August.
Maclean, J 1920, *All hail, the Scottish Communist Republic!* pamphlet.
Maclean, J 1920, 'The Highland land seizures', *Vanguard*, September.
Maclean, J 1920, *Russia's appeal to British workers: preface by John Maclean*, Executive Committee of the Communist International, Glasgow.
Maclean, J 1920, 'The Irish tragedy: up Scottish revolutionists', *Vanguard*, November.
Maclean, J 1920, 'The unemployed', *Vanguard*, November.
Maclean, J 1920, 'A Scottish Communist Party', *Vanguard*, December.
Maclean, J 1921, 'Open letter to Lenin', *Socialist*, 30 January.
McShane, H 1977, 'Remembering John Maclean', John Maclean Society.
McShane, H & Smith, J 1978, *No mean fighter*, Pluto Press, London.
Malone, CJL 1920, *The Russian republic*, Harcourt, Brace & Howe, New York.
Montefiore, D 1925, *From a Victorian to a modern*, E Archer, London.
Munro, R 1918, 'Revolutionary agitation in Glasgow and Clydeside with special reference to the cases of John Maclean and others', The National Archives of the UK, 7 March, CAB 24/44/38 Annex I.
National Administrative Council of the ILP, 1920, *Moscow's reply to the ILP*, London.
Pankhurst, ES 1919, 'The new war', *Communist International*, June.
Pankhurst, ES 1923, 'Obituary to John Maclean', *Workers' Dreadnought*, 8 December.
Pankhurst, ES 1987, *The home front*, The Cresset Library, London.
Petroff, P 1915, 'International Socialism', *Vanguard*, no. 2, October.
Petroff, P 1915, 'The breakdown of the International', *Vanguard*, no. 3, November.
Petroff, P 1915, 'Rebuilding the International', *Vanguard*, no. 4. December,
Petroff, P 1916, 'Peter Petroff replies', *Justice* 27 January.
Petroff, P (n. d.), 'Kentish Town BSP'.
Petroff, P (n. d.), *In and out of the swamp*, Peter Petroff Papers, International Institute of Social History, Amsterdam.

Quelch, T & McLaine, WM 1920, 'Report as to the Communist Movement in Britain', *Communist International*, June-July.

Ransome, A 1998, 'The Third International', *Russia in 1919*, Project Gutenberg, Salt Lake City, USA.

Reed, J 1960, *Ten days that shook the world*, The Modern Library, New York.

Rothstein, T 1919, 'The meaning of Social Revolution', *Call*, 9 Jan.

Rothstein, T 1919, 'Our martyred dead', *Call*, 30 Jan.

Rothstein, T 1919, 'What is our position?', *Call*, 17 April,

Russell, B 1971, *The autobiography of Bertrand Russell: vol. 2: 1914 – 1944*, Allen & Unwin, London.

Russian Anti-Intervention Committee, 1918, 'Resolution in support of the Soviet Republic of the Russian workers'.

Soviet of the People's Commissars, 1918, *To the toiling masses of France, Britain, America, Italy and Japan*, 1 August.

Smith, F 1917, 'The Stockholm Conference. Memorandum by the Attorney-General with a covering note by Sir Edward Carson', 6 August, The National Archives of the UK, War Cabinet, CAB 24/22/24.

Trotsky, L 1930, *My life*, Charles Schribner's Sons, New York.

Trotsky, L 1932, *The history of the Russian Revolution*, Simon & Schuster, New York.

US Department of Labor, Bureau of Labor Statistics, 1917, *Industrial unrest in Great Britain*, no. 237, October.

Unofficial Reform Committee, 1991, *The miners' next step*, Germinal and Phoenix Press, Swansea, Wales.

Wheatley, J 1915, 'Eviction of a soldier's wife and family at Shettleston', *Forward*, 12 June.

Wilson, W 2006, *Woodrow Wilson: essential writings and speeches of the scholar-president*, NYU Press, New York.

LATER WORKS

Aris, R 1993, *Continuity and Change: The role of trade unions in state industrial relations policy in Britain 1910-1921*, PhD thesis, University of Warwick.

Arnot, RP 1953, *The miners: years of struggle*, Routledge, London.

Bain, G 1983, *John Maclean: his life and work 1918-1923*, John Maclean Society.

Beevor, A 2022, *Russia: revolution and civil war 1917-1921*, Weidenfeld & Nicolson, London.

Bell, H 2018, *John Maclean: hero of Red Clydeside*, Pluto Press, London.

Booth, J 2019, 'Hands off Russia', Workers' Liberty, 15 April.

Broom, J 1973, *John Maclean*, Macdonald Publishers, Loanhead, Scotland.

Brotherstone, T 1969, 'The suppression of the *Forward*', *Scottish Labour History Society Journal*, 1.

Brotherstone, T 1988, 'John Maclean and the Russian Revolution' *Scottish Labour History Society Journal*, 23.

Cairns, G 1990, 'John Maclean, socialism and the Scottish question', *Scottish Labour History Society Journal*, 4.

Cairns, G 2017, *The red and the green: a portrait of John Maclean*, Calton Books, Glasgow.

Cairns, G 2021, *No language! No nation!* Rymour Books, Perth, Scotland.

Campbell, A 1989, 'From independent collier to militant miner; Scottish miners 1874-1929', *Scottish Labour History Society Journal*, 24.

Castells, M 1983, 'The industrial city and the working class: the Glasgow rent strike of 1915', in *The city and the grassroots*, Edward Arnold, London.

Challinor, R, 1977, *The origins of British Bolshevism*, Croom Helm, London.

Cliff, T 1986, 'The Tragedy of AJ Cook', *International Socialism*, 2:31, Spring.

Cliff, T & Gluckstein, D 1986, *Marxism and trade union struggle: the general strike of 1926*, Bookmarks, London and Chicago.

Cliff, T & Gluckstein, D 1988, *The Labour Party – a Marxist history*, Bookmarks, London, 1988.

Cole, GDH 1948, *A history of the Labour Party from 1914*, Routledge and Kegan Paul, London.

Cole, M 1952, *Beatrice Webb's diaries 1912-1924*, Longmans, London.

Cowan, T 2011, *Labour of love: the story of Robert Smillie*, Neil Wilson Publishing, Glasgow.

Craig, M 2011, *When the Clyde ran red*, Birlinn, Edinburgh.

Crooke, S 2009, 'The socialism of John Maclean', Alliance for Workers' Liberty Scotland.

Crowley, DW 1956, 'The Crofters' Party - 1885 to 1892: The first British independent common people's political party', *Scottish Historical Review*, Vol. 35.

Coyle, S 2016, 'The fire of revolt: from Clydeside to Dublin's GPO', *Saothar*, vol. 41.

Coyle, S 2023, 'From red and green Clydeside to Liberty Hall', *Scottish Labour History*, 58.

Dalton, I 2017, 'June 1917: when workers in Britain first tried to form soviets', Socialist Party, 31 May.

Davidson, N 2001, 'Marx and Engels on the Scottish Highlands', *Science & Society*, vol. 65, no. 3.

Davidson, R 1974, 'War-time labour policy 1914-1916: a reappraisal', *Scottish Labour History Society Journal*, 8.

Davies, N 1971, 'Lloyd George and Poland, 1919-20', *Journal of Contemporary History*, vol. 6, no. 3.

Debo, RK 1966, 'The making of a Bolshevik: Georgii Chicherin in England 1914-1918', *Slavic Review*, Vol 25, No 4, December.

Dudden, AP and von Laue, TH 1955, 'The RSDLP and Joseph Fels: a study in intercultural contact', *The American Historical Review*, vol. 61, no. 1, October.

Ellis, PB and Mac a' Ghobhainn, S 2016, *The radical rising: the Scottish insurrection of 1820*, Birlinn, Edinburgh.

Engelstein, L 2019, *Russia in flames: war, revolution, civil war 1914-1921*, Oxford University Press.

Englander, D 1979, *Landlord and tenant in urban Britain: the politics of housing reform, 1838-1924*, PhD thesis, University of Warwick.

Figes, O 2017, *A people's tragedy: the Russian Revolution*, The Bodley Head, London.

Floud, R, Wachter, K & Gregory, A 1990, 'Regional and occupational differentials in British heights', in *Height, health and history: nutritional status in the United Kingdom, 1750–1980*, Cambridge University Press.

Foster, J 1988, 'Scotland and the Russian Revolution', *Scottish Labour History Society Journal*, 23.

Gill, P 2012, 'National coal strike'.

Girod, G 2011, '"We were carrying on a strike when we should have been making a revolution": the rise of Marxist leaders in Glasgow during WWI, *Voces Nova*, Chapman University Historical Review Vol 3, No 1.

Gourley, D (n.d.), 'The Buckingham Palace plot 1916', *Journal of Liberal History*.

Grant, R 1984, *British radicals and socialists and their attitudes to Russia, c1890-1917*, PhD thesis, University of Glasgow.

Griffin P 2015, *The spatial politics of Red Clydeside: historical labour geographies and radical connections*, PhD thesis, University of Glasgow.

Hallas, D 1973, 'The first shop stewards' movement', *International Socialism*, no. 65, December.

Harrison, S 2003, *Sylvia Pankhurst: a crusading life*, Aurum Press, London.

Harvie, CT. 2016, *No gods and precious few heroes: Scotland 1914-2015*, 4th edn, Edinburgh University Press.

Haslam, J 1983, *Soviet foreign policy, 1930–33: the impact of the depression*, St. Martin's Press, New York.

Heath, S 2013, 'The historical context of rent control in the private rented sector', Social Policy Section, House of Commons Library, London.

Henderson, H 2004, *Alias Macalias: writings on songs, folk and literature*, Polygon, Edinburgh.

Henderson, P 1973, *William Morris*, Pelican, London.

Hinton, J 1973, *The first shop stewards' movement*, Allen & Unwin, London.

Hobsbawm, E 1975, *The age of capital (1848-1875)*, Weidenfeld & Nicolson, London.

Houston, RA & Knox, WWJ (eds) 2001, *The new Penguin history of Scotland*, Penguin, London.

Howell, D 1986, *A lost left: three studies in socialism and nationalism*, Manchester University Press.

Hunter, J 2014, *On the other side of sorrow: nature and people in the Scottish Highlands*, Birlinn, Edinburgh.

Independent Labour Party, 1920, *The ILP and the 3rd International*.

Ives, M 2017, *Reform, revolution and direct action amongst British miners*, Haymarket Books, Chicago.

Jenkins, R 2002, *Churchill*, Pan, London.

Johnston, I 2014, *A shipyard at war: unseen photographs from John Brown's, Clydebank 1914-1918*, Seaforth Publishing, Barnsley, England.

Johnston, T 1974, *The history of the working classes in Scotland*, 4th edn, EP Publishing, Wakefield, England.

Johnstone, A 2012, 'The crofters' wars', *Socialist Courier*.

Jones, K 2020, 'The Peterhead harbour of refuge railway', *The Railway Magazine*, 30 Nov.

Kendall, W, 1969, *The revolutionary movement in Britain 1900-21*, Weidenfeld & Nicolson, London.

Kendall, W 1979, 'John Maclean and the Communist International', *John Maclean Centenary Essays*, John Maclean Society.

Kendall, W 1979, 'Comintern: sixty years after: reflections on the anniversary', *Survey*, Vol 24, No 1, Winter.

Kendall, W 2001, 'The Communist Party of Great Britain', *Revolutionary History*, Vol 8, No. 1.

Kenefick, W 2007, *Red Scotland, the rise and fall of the radical left 1872-1932*, Edinburgh University Press.

Law, TS & Berwick, T (eds) 1979, *Homage to John Maclean*, Edinburgh University Student Publications Board.

MacAskill, K 2019, *Glasgow 1919*, Biteback Publishing, London.

McCormick, MP 2020, *Arthur Henderson and the 1917 Stockholm conference: a reappraisal*, PhD thesis, University of Birmingham.

MacGill-Eain, S 2011, *An Cuilithionn 1939 and unpublished poems*, Association for Scottish Literary Studies, Glasgow.

McHugh, J 2000, 'Peter Petroff: The view from the Home Office', *Scottish Labour History*, 35.

McHugh, J & Ripley, BJ 1985, 'Russian political internees in First World War Britain: the cases of George Chicherin and Peter Petroff', *The Historical Journal*, 28, 3.

McHugh, J & Ripley, BJ 1983, John Maclean, the Scottish Workers' Republican Party and Scottish Nationalism', *Scottish Labour History Society Journal*, 18.

McKay, J 1996, 'Red Clydeside after 75 years: a reply to Ian McLean', *Scottish Labour History Society Journal*, 31.

Mackinnon, J 1921, *The social and industrial history of Scotland*, Longmans, London.

Marr, A 1992, *The battle for Scotland*, Penguin, London.

Marriott, JAR 1948, *Modern England: 1885-1945*, Methuen, London.

Martin, J 2010, *Making Socialists*, Manchester University Press.

Martin, JF 1982, *The government and control of the British coal industry 1914-18*, PhD thesis, Loughborough University.

McLean, IS 1972, *The labour movement in Clydeside politics, 1914-1922*, PhD thesis, University of Oxford.

Meynell, H 1960, 'The Stockholm Conference of 1917', *International Review of Social History*, vol. 5.

Middlemas, R 1965, *The Clydesiders*, Hutchinson, London.

Miéville, C 2017, *October*, Verso, London.

Miller, JW 1939, 'Foreign government and politics: emergency legislation in Great Britain', *American Political Science Review*, vol. 33, no. 6, December.

Milton, N 1973, *John Maclean*, Pluto Press, London.

Mitchell, IR 2013, *A Glasgow mosaic*, Luath Press, Edinburgh.

Mitchell, IR 2014, *Walking through Glasgow's industrial past*, Luath Press, Edinburgh.

Moore, J 2015, *Glasgow: mapping the city*, Birlinn, Edinburgh.

Moorhouse, B, Wilson, M & Chamberlain, C 1972, 'Rent strikes - direct action and the working class', *Socialist Register 1972*, vol 9.

Morgan, K 2013, 'In and out of the swamp: the unpublished biography of Peter Petroff', *Scottish Labour History*, 48.

Morgan, KO 1992, *Labour people: Hardie to Kinnock*, Oxford University Press.

Morris, RJ 1983, 'Skilled workers and the politics of the Red Clyde', *Scottish Labour History Society Journal*, No 18.

Murray, A 2022, 'Unionism, nationalism, cosmopolitanism: Ruraidh Erskine of Marr at the *fin de siècle*', *Studies in Scottish Literature*, vol. 48, iss. 1

Neill, AS 1986, *A dominie's log*, Hogarth Press, London.

Pitt, B 1987, 'Syndicalism in South Wales: the origins of "The Miners' Next Step"'.

Pitt, B 1995, 'The real John Maclean', *Workers Liberty*.

Pitt, R 1996, *John Maclean and the CPGB*, 2nd edn.

Pittock, M 2022, *Scotland: the global history, 1603 to the present*, Yale University Press, New Haven, USA.

Pye, D 1995, *Fellowship is life: the National Clarion Cycling Club 1895-1995*, Clarion, Bolton.

Ransom, BC 1975, *James Connolly and the Scottish Left 1890-1916*, PhD thesis, University of Edinburgh.

Rappaport, H (n.d.), 'Lenin in London' Helen Rappaport Footnotes.

Reader, WJ 1968, *The architect of air power*, Collins, London.

Renshaw, P 1971, 'Black Friday, 1921', *History Today*, vol. 21, iss. 6, June.

Ripley, BJ & McHugh, J 1989, *John Maclean*, Manchester University Press.

Romero, PW 1987, *E. Sylvia Pankhurst: portrait of a rebel*, Yale University Press, New Haven and London.

Rubin, GR 1984, *The enforcement of the Munitions of War Acts 1915-17*, PhD thesis, University of Warwick.

Senn, AE 1972, 'The Politics of Golos and Nashe Slovo', *International Review of Social History*, 17(2).

Service, R 2009, *Trotsky: a biography*, Macmillan, London.

Sherry, D 2014, *Empire and revolution: a socialist history of the First World War*, Bookmarks, London.

Sherry, D 2014, *John Maclean: Red Clydesider*, Bookmarks, London.

Showalter, DE & Royde-Smith, JG 2024, 'The end of the German war', *Encyclopedia Britannica*.

Simkin, J (n.d.), 'Denis Hird'.

Simon, B 1965, *Education & the Labour movement 1870-1920*, Lawrence & Wishart, London.

Smount, TC 1986, *A century of the Scottish people 1830-1950*, Collins, London.

Smyth, JJ 2003, 'Resisting Labour: Unionists, Liberals and Moderates in Glasgow between the wars', *The Historical Journal*, 46, 2, pp. 375-401.

Steven, 2013, 'The Brotherhood Church'.

Taylor, AJP 1965, *English history 1914-1945*, Oxford University Press.

Taylor, AJP 1963, *The First World War: an illustrated history*, Hamish Hamilton, London.

Taylor, S 2022, 'The history of Peterhead's harbour refuge built by inmates from "Scotland's toughest jail"', *AberdeenLive*.

Thatcher, ID 1992, 'John Maclean: Soviet versions', *History*, vol. 77, no. 251 (October).

Thatcher, ID 1999, 'Representations of Scotland in *Nashe Slovo* during World War One: a brief note', *The Scottish Historical Review*, vol. 78, no. 206, Part 2.

The Irish War (n.d.), 'The Irish War of Independence'.

Tolly, K 1969, 'Our Russian War of 1918–1919', *US Naval Institute*, vol. 95/2/792.

Townshend, C 2005, *Easter 1916: the Irish rebellion*, Penguin, London.

Treble, JH 1978, 'The market for unskilled labour in Glasgow, 1891-1914', in MacDougall, I (ed), *Essays in Scottish Labour History*, John Donald, Edinburgh.

Tuchman, B 1980, *August 1914*, Papermac, London.

US Department of State (n.d.), 'America enters the war; Wilson's plan for peace'.

Wecter, D 1972, *The hero in America: a chronicle of hero-worship*, Scribner, New York.

Wheeler-Bennett, JW 1939, *Brest-Litovsk: the forgotten peace*, Macmillan & Co., London.

Wightman, A 2015, *The poor had no lawyers: who owns Scotland (and how they got it)*, 3rd edn, Birlinn, Edinburgh.

Wilkins, K 2019, *Daring and defiant: Helen Crawfurd (1877-1954) Scottish suffragette and international communist*, PhD thesis, Central European University, Budapest.

Williams, JE 1962, *The Derbyshire miners*, Allen & Unwin, London.

Winter, JM 1972, 'Arthur Henderson, the Russian revolution, and the reconstruction of the Labour Party', *Historical Journal*, xv.

Witt, P 2013, 'Connections across the North Channel: Ruaraidh Erskine and Irish influence in Scottish discontent, 1906-1920'. *The Irish Story*.

Woodhouse, M 1966, 'Syndicalism, communism and the trade unions in Britain 1910-26', *Marxist*, vol. 4 no. 3.

Wright, D 2017, *Churchill's secret war with Lenin: British and Commonwealth military intervention in the Russian Civil War, 1918-20*, Helion, Solihull, England.

Wrigley, C 1990, *Arthur Henderson*, GPC, Cardiff.

Wrigley, C 2015, 'Labour, Labour movements, trade unions and strikes (Great Britain and Ireland)', *International Encyclopedia of the First World War*, Berlin.

Yamanouchi, A 1989, 'Internationalised Bolshevism - the Bolsheviks and the International 1914-17', *Acta Slavica Iaponica*, 7.

Young, JD 1976, 'Land, Labour and homerule', *Journal of the Scottish Labour Party*, vol. 1, Spring.

Young, JD 1988, *John Maclean: educator of the working class*, Clydeside Press, Glasgow.

Young, JD 1992, *John Maclean, Clydeside Socialist*, Clydeside Press, Glasgow.

ENDNOTES

1. Making socialists

1. Milton, N 1973, *John Maclean*, Pluto Press, London, p. 16.
2. Milton, N 1973, p. 17.
3. Burnett, J 1923, 'Passing of John Maclean', *Daily Standard*, Brisbane, 11 December, p. 8.
4. Bell, T 1944, *John Maclean: a fighter for freedom*, Communist Party, Scottish Committee, Glasgow, p. 8.
5. Blatchford, R (as Numquad) 1893, *Merrie England*, Clarion, London, p. 12.
6. Groom, T (n. d.), cited in Bullock, I, 'The Origins of the Clarion', viewed 22 April 2024, <https://clarioncc.org/about-the-national-clarion/history/>
7. McShane, H & Smith, J 1978, *No mean fighter*, Pluto Press, London, p. 30.
8. Bell, T 1944, p. 7.
9. Henderson, P 1973, *William Morris*, Pelican, London, p. 286.
10. Henderson, P 1973, p. 286.
11. Bell, T 1944, p. 8.
12. McShane, H & Smith, J 1978, p. 54.
13. Unofficial Reform Committee, 1991, *The miners' next step*, Germinal & Phoenix Press, Swansea, p. 28, (originally published 1919), viewed 2 November 2024, <https://www.thesparrowsnest.org.uk/collections/public_archive/1698.pdf>
14. Gill, P 2012, 'National coal strike', viewed 15 November 2023, <https://web.archive.org/web/20120920172933/http://dspace.dial.pipex.com/town/parade/abj76/PG/pieces/lawrence/national_coal_strike.shtml>
15. Macdougall, JD 1927, 'The Scottish coalminer', in *The nineteenth century and after*, no. 102, pp. 762-81.

2. Second city of the Empire

1. Hobsbawm, E 1975, *The age of capital (1848-1875)*, Weidenfeld & Nicolson, London, p. 55.
2. Foster, J 2001, 'The Twentieth Century, 1914-1979' in *The new Penguin history of Scotland*, eds Houston, RA & Knox, WWJ, Penguin, London, p. 417.
3. Foster, J 2001, p. 417.
4. Foster, J 2001, p. 420.
5. Johnston, T 1974, *The history of the working classes in Scotland*, 4th edn, EP Publishing Ltd, Wakefield, UK, p. 290.
6. Johnston, T 1974, p. 294.
7. Johnston, T 1974, p. 294.
8. Johnston, T 1974, p. 295.
9. Johnston, T 1974, p. 317.
10. Johnston, T 1974, p. 321.
11. Mackinnon, J 1921, *The social and industrial history of Scotland*, Longmans, London, p. 162.
12. Challinor, R, 1977, *The origins of British Bolshevism*, Croom Helm, London, p. 11.
13. The Second International was an organisation of socialist and labour parties, formed on 14 July 1889.
14. Johnston, T 1974, p. 383.
15. Johnston, T 1974, p. 387.

3. Lord Kitchener wants you

1. Tuchman, B 1980, *August 1914*, Papermac, London, p. 193.
2. Floud, R, Wachter, K, Gregory A 1990, 'Regional and occupational differentials in British heights', in *Height, health and history: nutritional status in the United Kingdom, 1750–1980*, Cambridge University Press, pp. 196-224.
3. Taylor, AJP 1965, *English history 1914-1945*, Oxford University Press, p. 21.
4. Great Britain. Ministry of Munitions 2009, *Official history of the Ministry of Munitions, vol. IV, The supply & control of labour 1915-1916*, Naval & Military Press Ltd, London, pt. II, p. 36.
5. McShane, H & Smith, J 1978, p. 66.
6. Milton, N 1973, p. 82.
7. Great Britain. Ministry of Munitions 2009, vol. IV, pt. II, p. 37.
8. Morris, RJ 1983, 'Skilled workers and the politics of the Red Clyde', *Scottish Labour History Society Journal*, No 18, pp 6-17.
9. McLean, IS 1972, *The labour movement in Clydeside politics, 1914-1922*, PhD thesis, University of Oxford, p. 15.

10. Treble, J H 1978, 'The market for unskilled labour in Glasgow, 1891-1914', in MacDougall, I (ed), *Essays in Scottish labour history*, John Donald Publishers, Edinburgh, pp. 115-142.
11. Reader, W J 1968, *The architect of air power*, Collins, London, ch. 2.
12. Bell, T 1941, *Pioneering days*, Lawrence & Wishart, London, p. 107.
13. Weir, W 1914, letter to Percy Fawcett, Thos Firth & Sons, Sheffield, 13 October, in Papers of William Douglas Weir, University of Glasgow archives.
14. Weir, W 1914, letter to Kenneth Brown, 13 October, in Papers of William Douglas Weir.
15. Weir, W 1914, letter to Rear Admiral GG Goodwin, Admiralty, 13 October, in Papers of William Douglas Weir.
16. Reader, W J 1968, ch. 2.
17. Weir, W 1914, letter to Allan Coats, The TCN Company, Harrison, New Jersey, 23 December, in Papers of William Douglas Weir.
18. McShane, H & Smith, J 1978, p. 73.
19. 'Our most urgent need', *Times*, 1 March 1915, p. 9.
20. Weir, W 1915, letter to Lord Northcliffe, *Times*, London, 18 March, in Papers of William Douglas Weir.

4. Munitions of war

1. Beaverbrook, Max Aitken, Baron 1928, *Politicians and the war 1914-1916*, Thornton Butterworth, London, p. 63.
2. Reproduced in *Forward*, 1 January 1916 and 24 April 1916.
3. Beaverbrook, 1928, p. 90.
4. 'Need for shells', *Times*, 14 May 1915, p. 8.
5. Beaverbrook, 1928, p. 94.
6. The Conservative Party adopted the name 'Unionist' to embrace the Liberal Unionists, who in 1886 had broken with the Liberal Party on the issue of Irish Home Rule. The governments of Lord Salisbury and Arthur Balfour in the period 1895-1905 were given the name of 'Unionist'. The Liberal Unionist and Conservatives formally merged as the Conservative and Unionist Party in 1912. The description of the merged party as 'Unionist' faded after the creation of the Irish Free State in December 1922. I have used Unionist as the description for Conservative and Unionist Party, as that was the style at the time. Although the Scottish Unionist Party that formed in 1912 was an independent party, it effectively acted as the Conservative Party in Scotland and its MPs took the Conservative whip at Westminster.
7. Beaverbrook, 1928, p. 112.
8. Weir, W 1915, letter to J Paterson, Secy, Glasgow and West of Scotland Armaments Committee, 14 May, Papers of William Douglas Weir.
9. Weir, W 1915, letter to Commander Emden, HMS Achilles, 13 May, Papers of William Douglas Weir.
10. 'War work on the Clyde', *Glasgow Herald*, 21 May 1915, p. 10.
11. Weir, W 1915, letter to Andrew Bonar Law, 20 May, Papers of William Douglas Weir.
12. Weir, W 1915, letter to JW Gullard, Government Whip, Westminster, 20 May, Papers of William Douglas Weir.
13. Marriott, JAR 1948, *Modern England: 1885-1945*, Methuen, London, p. 376.
14. Weir, W 1915, letter to Lloyd George, Ministry of Munitions, 2 July, Papers of William Douglas Weir.
15. 'London correspondence', *Glasgow Herald*, 31 July 1915, p. 7.
16. Great Britain. Ministry of Munitions 2009, vol. IV, pt. II, p. 60.
17. Great Britain. Ministry of Munitions 2009, vol. IV, pt. I, p. 36.
18. As president of the Board of Education, the Rt Hon Arthur Henderson was the first member of the Labour Party to become a member of the Cabinet, in the coalition government of Herbert Asquith.
19. Macdougall, JD 1915, 'Appeal to the Clyde Munition Workers', *Vanguard*, October, viewed 14 December 2023 <https://www.marxists.org/history/international/social-democracy/vanguard/1915/clyde-munitions.htm>
20. Great Britain. Ministry of Munitions 2009, vol. IV, pt. II, p. 54.
21. Gallacher, W 2017, *Revolt on the Clyde*, 5th edn, Lawrence & Wishart, London, p. 62.
22. Gallacher, W 2017, p. 62.
23. Great Britain. Ministry of Munitions 2009, vol. IV, pt. II, p. 60.
24. Clyde Workers Committee, 1915, 'To All Clyde Workers', leaflet, October, viewed 12 December 2023 <https://www.marxists.org/archive/gallacher/1915/clyde-committee.htm>

5. 'We are not paying increased rent'

1. In Scotland a factor (or property manager) is a person or firm charged with superintending or managing properties and estates – sometimes where the owner

2. McShane, H & Smith, J 1978, p. 74.
3. Castells, M 1983, 'The industrial city and the working class: the Glasgow rent strike of 1915', in *The city and the grassroots*, Edward Arnold, London, p. 28.
4. McBride A 1915, 'The Rent Fight: Past and Present', Glasgow Labour Party Housing Association pamphlet, in Red Clydeside, Glasgow Digital Library, viewed 21 April 2024, <http://gdl.cdlr.strath.ac.uk/redclyde/redcly208a.html>
5. McBride, A 1915.
6. Englander, D 1979, 'Landlord and Tenant in Urban Britain: The Politics of Housing Reform, 1838-1924', PhD thesis, University of Warwick, p. 349.
7. Englander, D 1979, p. 351.
8. Wheatley, J 1915, 'Eviction of a Soldier's Wife and Family at Shettleston', *Forward*, 12 June, viewed 2 November 2024, <https://www.scran.ac.uk/ID 000-000-505-710-C>
9. 'Resisting eviction', *Glasgow Herald*, 11 June 1915, p. 10.
10. Englander, D 1979, p. 355.

6. 'A scandalous act of tyranny and a gross injustice'

1. Maclean, J 1915, 'Govan School Board scandal', 15 June, in John Maclean Papers, National Library of Scotland, Edinburgh.
2. Govan Parish School Board Minutes, 1915, in the Mitchell Library, Glasgow.
3. Maclean, J 1915, 'Govan School Board scandal'.
4. Lambhill Street School log, 1915, in the Mitchell Library, Glasgow.
5. Maclean, J 1915, 'The Fight for Freedom in Glasgow', *Vanguard*, October, p. 5.
6. Govan Parish School Board Minutes, 1915.
7. Broom, J 1973, *John Maclean*, Macdonald Publishers, Loanhead, Scotland, p. 60.
8. Broom, J 1973, p. 60.

7. Fighting the Prussians of Partick

1. 'Glasgow rent strike', *Daily Record*, 29 September 1915, p. 3, viewed 22 April 2024, <https://www.newspapers.com/article/daily-record-daily-record-29-sep-1915/100697930/>
2. Gallacher, W 2017, p. 61.
3. Bell, T 1941, p. 98.
4. Kirkwood, D 1915, 'Rent Strikes: Serious Situation', *Forward*, 9 October, p. 1, viewed 2 November 2024, <https://www.scran.ac.uk/ID 000-000-505-716-C>
5. 'Rents in Glasgow', *Glasgow Herald*, 8 October 1915, p. 8.
6. Englander, D 1979, p. 360.
7. The lord advocate was the chief legal adviser of the British Government and the Crown on Scottish legal matters, both civil and criminal.
8. Englander, D 1979, p. 360.
9. Under Scots law, an arrestment of wages allows a creditor to recover money owed by forcing an employer to deduct it from a person's wages.
10. Englander, D 1979, p. 368.

8. 'A person who holds advanced political views'

1. 'Defence of the Realm Act: John Maclean fined £5', *Forward*, 20 November 1915, p. 3, viewed 14 December 2023, <http://gdl.cdlr.strath.ac.uk/redclyde/redcly199a.html> and 'John Maclean's Trial', *Vanguard*, December 1915, pp. 1-2, viewed 13 December 2023, <https://www.marxists.org/history/international/social-democracy/vanguard/1915/macleans-trial.htm>

9. A question of school discipline

1. 'Teacher dismissed: protest by Govan crowd', *Glasgow Herald*, 17 November 1915, p. 10.
2. Milton, N 1973, p. 101.
3. Govan Parish School Minutes, 1915.
4. 'Teacher dismissed: protest by Govan crowd'.
5. Milton, N 1973, p. 102.
6. 'Govan School Board', *Glasgow Herald*, 22 December 1915, p. 8.

10. A great victory for the rent strikers

1. Englander, D 1979, p. 369.
2. Gallacher, W 2017, p. 57.
3. Milton, N 1973, p. 103.
4. Milton, N 1973, p. 103.
5. 'The rent strike', *Glasgow Herald*, 18 November 1915, p. 10.
6. 'Rent victories', *Vanguard*, December 1915, p. 4, viewed 25 April 2024, <https://www.marxists.org/history/international/social-democracy/vanguard/1915/rent-victories.htm>
7. Milton, N 1973, p. 104.

11. Peter Petroff

1. Ripley, BJ & McHugh, J 1989, *John Maclean*, Manchester University Press, p. 68.

2. Kendall, W, 1969, *The revolutionary movement in Britain 1900-21*, Weidenfeld & Nicolson, London, p. 78.
3. Kendall, W 1969, p. 81.
4. Dudden, AP and von Laue, TH 1955, 'The RSDLP and Joseph Fels: A Study in Intercultural Contact', *The American Historical Review*, vol. 61, no. 1, October, p. 23.
5. Dudden, AP & von Laue, TH 1955, p. 28.
6. Morgan, K 2013, 'In and out of the swamp: the unpublished biography of Peter Petroff', *Scottish Labour History*, 48, p. 29.
7. Morgan, K 2013, p. 34.
8. Petroff, P (n. d.) 'Kentish Town BSP', viewed 4 July 2024, <https://www.marxists.org/archive/petroff/memoirs/kentish-town.htm>
9. Martin, J 2010, *Making Socialists*, Manchester University Press, p. 192.
10. Pankhurst, ES 1987, *The home front*, The Cresset Library, London, p. 301.
11. Petroff, P (n. d.), *In and out of the swamp*, Peter Petroff Papers, International Institute of Social History, Amsterdam, ch. 13, p. 2.
12. Petroff, P (n. d.), *In and out of the swamp*, ch. 13, p. 10.
13. Ripley, BJ & McHugh, J 1989, p. 87.
14. McShane, H & Smith, J 1978, p. 77.
15. Gallacher, W 2017, p. 58.
16. McShane, H & Smith, J 1978, p. 78.
17. Petroff, P (n. d.), *In and out of the swamp*, ch. 13, p. 12.
18. Gallacher, W 2017, p. 60.
19. Petroff, P (n. d.), *In and out of the swamp*, ch. 13, p. 21.
20. France, Russia and the United Kingdom of Great Britain and Ireland.
21. Challinor, R, 1977, p. 163.
22. Petroff, P 1915, 'International Socialism', *Vanguard*, no. 2, October, p. 7, viewed 25 April 2024, <https://www.marxists.org/history/international/social-democracy/vanguard/1915/international.htm>
23. Petroff, P 1915, 'The Breakdown of the International', *Vanguard*, no. 3, November, pp. 1-2, viewed 25 April 2024, <https://www.marxists.org/archive/petroff/1915/breakdown-international.htm>
24. Challinor, R 1977, p. 164.
25. Petroff, P 1915, 'Rebuilding the International', *Vanguard*, no. 4. December, pp. 5-6, viewed 25 April 2024, <https://www.marxists.org/archive/petroff/1915/rebuild-international.htm>
26. 'What and Who is Peter Petroff?', *Justice*, 23 December 1915, viewed 2 November 2024, <https://www.marxists.org/archive/hyndman/1915/12/who-is-petroff.htm>
27. Maclean, J 1915, 'Concerning P. Petroff' (letter), *Justice*, 30 December, p. 7, <https://www.marxists.org/archive/maclean/1915/12/concerning-petroff.htm>
28. Petroff, P 1916, 'Peter Petroff Replies', *Justice* 27 January, p. 7, viewed 2 November 2024, <https://www.marxists.org/archive/petroff/1916/reply-by-petroff.htm>

12. Conscription

1. Great Britain. Ministry of Munitions 2009, vol. IV, pt. III, p. 8
2. Great Britain. Ministry of Munitions 2009, vol. IV, pt. I, p. 1.
3. Great Britain. Ministry of Munitions 2009, vol. IV, pt. III, p. 32.
4. Great Britain. Ministry of Munitions 2009, vol. IV, pt. III, p. 33.
5. Great Britain. Ministry of Munitions 2009, vol. IV, pt. III, p. 35.
6. During 1915, the Russian Empire suffered heavy defeats and losses of vast territories, including the entire Kingdom of Poland, part of the Baltic states, and some Russian provinces.
7. Great Britain. Ministry of Munitions 2009, vol. IV, pt. III, p. 37.
8. Great Britain. Ministry of Munitions 2009, vol. IV, pt. III, p. 40.
9. Maclean, J 1915, 'The Conscription Menace', *Vanguard*, December, p. 5, viewed 25 April 2024, <https://www.marxists.org/archive/maclean/1915/12/conscription-menace.htm>
10. Macdougall, J, 1915, 'The Threat of Conscription', *Vanguard*, November, p. 6, viewed 25 April 2024, <https://www.marxists.org/history/international/social-democracy/vanguard/1915/threat-conscription.htm>
11. The Herald League was founded to popularise and raise funds for the socialist newspaper the *Daily Herald*. It developed into a political network which many syndicalists and trade unionists joined.
12. Petroff, P (n. d.), *In and out of the swamp*, ch. 13, p. 18.
13. Lansbury, G 1931, *My life*, Constable, London, p. 95.

14	Petroff, P (n. d.), *In and out of the swamp*, ch. 13, p. 19.	**14.**	**Suppression of Forward and the Vanguard**
15	Pankhurst, ES 1987, p. 264.	1	Brotherstone, T 1969, 'The Suppression of the *Forward*', *Scottish Labour History Society Journal*, no. 1, pp. 5-23.
16	Petroff, P (n. d.), *In and out of the swamp*, ch. 13, p. 20.		
17	Pankhurst, ES 1987, p. 263.	2	Great Britain. Ministry of Munitions 2009, vol. IV, pt. IV, p.111.
18	Pankhurst, ES 1987, p. 281.		
19	Pankhurst, ES 1987, p. 281.	3	Brotherstone, T 1969.
20	'Glasgow street meetings', *Glasgow Herald*, 22 December 1915, p. 8.	4	Brotherstone, T 1969.
		5	Hansard HC Deb 04 January 1916 vol. 77 cc801-5.
21	Broom, J 1973, p. 71.		
22	Great Britain. Ministry of Munitions 2009, vol. IV, pt. III, p. 56.	6	Hansard HC Deb 10 January 1916, vol. 77 cc1394-420.
13.	**Lloyd George comes to Glasgow**	7	The Press Association, founded by provincial newspapers on a co-operative basis in 1868, is the oldest and largest news agency operating exclusively in Britain. It supplies news to all the London daily and Sunday newspapers, provincial papers, and trade journals and other periodicals, viewed 8 March 2024, <https://www.britannica.com/topic/news-agency#ref203537>
1	Great Britain. Ministry of Munitions 2009, vol. IV, pt. II, p. 81.		
2	Hansard HC Deb 04 January 1916 vol. 77 cc877-81.		
3	Hansard HC Deb 20 December 1915 vol. 77 cc95-165.		
4	McLean, IS 1972, p. 79.		
5	Great Britain. Ministry of Munitions 2009, vol. IV, pt. IV, p. 102.		
6	Great Britain. Ministry of Munitions 2009, vol. IV, pt. IV, p. 102.	8	Great Britain. Ministry of Munitions 2009, vol. IV, pt. IV, p. 111.
7	Gallacher, W 2017, p. 71.	9	Brotherstone, T 1969.
8	William Sharp, district secretary, United Society of Boilermakers and Iron and Steel Shipbuilders; William Lorimer, assistant general secretary, Associated Blacksmiths and Iron Workers' Society and secretary of the committee of trade unions that had made the arrangements for the meetings; Sam Bunton, secretary of the Glasgow District Committee of the Amalgamated Society of Engineers.	10	Hansard HC Deb 10 January 1916 vol. 77 cc1394-420.
		11	Beveridge, W 1953, *Power and influence*, Hodder & Stoughton, London, p. 133.
		12	Regulation 42: If any person attempts to cause mutiny, sedition or disaffection among any of His Majesty's Forces or among the civilian population, or to impede, delay or restrict the production, repair or transport of war material or any other work necessary for the successful prosecution of the war, he shall be guilty of an offence against these Regulations.
9	Gallacher, W 2017, p. 72.		
10	Gallacher, W 2017, p. 73.		
11	Gallacher, W 2017, p. 78.		
12	Great Britain. Ministry of Munitions 2009, vol. IV, pt. IV, p. 103.	13	Brotherstone, T 1969.
13	Great Britain. Ministry of Munitions 2009, vol. IV, pt. IV, p. 104.	14	Beveridge, W 1953, p. 133.
		15.	**Defence of the Realm**
14	Gallacher, W 2017, p. 79.	1	Syndicalism is an economic philosophy that promotes the control of the economy by labour unions. Although syndicalism advocates the control of production units by the workers it does not, as is the case for socialism, advocate the central control of the economy.
15	Gallacher, W 2017, p. 81.		
16	Petroff, P (n. d.), *In and out of the swamp*, ch. 13, p. 24.		
17	McLean, IS 1972, p. 73.		
18	Great Britain. Ministry of Munitions 2009, vol. IV, pt. IV, app. XIX, p. 176.		
19	Petroff, P (n. d.), *In and out of the swamp*, ch. 13, p. 26.	2	McLean, IS, 1972, pp. 114-115.
		3	Ripley, BJ & McHugh, J 1989, p. 92, note 46.
20	Great Britain. Ministry of Munitions 2009, vol. IV, pt. IV, app. XIX, p. 180.	4	Milton, N 1973, p. 117.
		5	Hansard HC Deb 17 February 1916, vol. 80, cc222-3.
		6	Great Britain. Ministry of Munitions 2009, vol. IV, pt. IV, p. 125.

16. The Scottish Labour College

1. Maclean, J 1915, 'Concerning P. Petroff'.
2. Pitt, B 1987, 'Syndicalism in South Wales', viewed 1 April 2024, <www.whatnextjournal.org.uk/Pages/History/Nextstep.html>
3. Simkin, J, 'Denis Hird', viewed 1 April 2024, <https://spartacus-educational.com/Dennis_Hird.htm>
4. Milton, N 1973, p. 42.
5. Maclean, J 1915, 'A Labour College for Scotland', *Forward*, 25 December.
6. 'Proposed Labour College', *Glasgow Herald*, 14 February 1916, p. 10.
7. 'Proposed Scottish Labour College', *Scotsman*, 14 February 1916.

17. Dilution on the Clyde

1. 'Ministry of Munitions', *Glasgow Herald*, 30 December 1915, p. 6.
2. McLean, IS 1972, p. 93.
3. McLean, IS 1972, p. 94.
4. Ministry of Munitions, 1916, 'Summary of Dilution Programme as based (with modifications) on Mr Weir's memorandum', 20 January, viewed 10 March 2024, <https://www.scran.ac.uk/000-000-505-596-C>
5. McLean, IS 1972, p. 94.
6. Great Britain. Ministry of Munitions 2009, vol. IV, pt. IV, p. 115.
7. Great Britain. Ministry of Munitions 2009, vol. IV, pt. IV, p. 117.
8. Great Britain. Ministry of Munitions 2009, vol. IV, pt. IV, pp. 119-123.
9. Gallacher, W 2017, p. 85.
10. McShane, H & Smith J, 1978, p. 80.
11. Gallacher, W 2017, p. 86,
12. Kirkwood, D 1935, *My life in revolt*, George G. Harrap & Co, London, p. 125.
13. Kirkwood, D 1935, p. 126.
14. Great Britain. Ministry of Munitions 2009, vol. IV, pt. IV, p. 129.
15. McLean, IS 1972, p. 121.
16. Great Britain. Ministry of Munitions 2009, vol. IV, pt. IV, p. 131.
17. Weir W, 1916, letter to JAN Barlow, Private Secretary to Dr. Addison MP, 28 March, viewed 4 March 2024, <https://www.scran.ac.uk/000-000-505-584-C>
18. Great Britain. Ministry of Munitions 2009, vol. IV, pt. IV, p. 132.
19. 'Banished!', *Forward* report, 1 April 1916, p. 1, viewed 25 April 2024, <https://www.scran.ac.uk/000-000-505-723-R>
20. McShane, H & Smith J, 1978, p. 81.
21. 'Indictment papers sent to James Maxton and James McDougall for their 1916 trial for sedition', in James Maxton Papers, Glasgow City Archives, viewed 7 March 2024, <https://www.scran.ac.uk/000-000-596-464-C>
22. Weir W, 1916, letter to JT Davies, Ministry of Munitions, 27 March, viewed 4 March 2024, <https://www.scran.ac.uk/000-000-505-581-C>
23. Great Britain. Ministry of Munitions 2009, vol. IV, pt. IV, p. 132.
24. 'Strikes on the Clyde', *Glasgow Herald*, 29 March 1916, p. 6.
25. 'Statement by Workers' Committee', *Glasgow Herald*, 30 March 1916, p. 5.
26. Gallacher, W 2017, p. 87.
27. Gallacher, W 2017, p. 89.
28. 'The Clyde Strikes', *Glasgow Herald*, 31 March 1916, p. 7.
29. 'The Clyde Strikes'.
30. Gallacher, W 2017, p. 91.
31. A British federation of small craft unions.
32. 'The Government's Responsibility', *Glasgow Herald*, 1 April 1916, p. 4.
33. Gallacher, W 2017, p. 91.

18. German gold, and German alarm clocks

1. 'Spreading sedition', *Glasgow Herald*, 14 April 1916, pp. 7-8.
2. In Scottish law, court hearings are known as diets.
3. Milton, N 1973, p. 122.
4. Milton, N 1973, p. 122.
5. Fletcher, ZA 2022, 'When a WWI German Zeppelin tried to bomb Edinburgh Castle - and missed', 16 September, viewed 27 April 2024, <https://www.historynet.com/ww1-edinburgh-castle-zeppelin-attack/>
6. The Lord Justice General was the most senior judge in Scotland. They were the head of the judiciary, and the presiding judge of the College of Justice, the Court of Session, and the High Court of Justiciary.
7. Alexander Ure was the Liberal MP for Linlithgowshire from 1895 to 1913, and held the position of lord advocate from 1909 to 1913. On leaving parliament in 1913, Ure was appointed to the bench as Lord Strathclyde.
8. Advocates in Scotland (sometimes known as counsel) perform similar roles as barristers in England and Wales.
9. The description of court proceedings is taken from: 'Clyde disaffection', *Glasgow Herald*, 12 April 1916, pp. 7-8; 'Seditious speeches', *Glasgow Herald*, 13 April 1916, p. 8; 'Alleged seditious speeches', *Scotsman*, 12 April 1916; 'Glasgow teacher's seditious

speeches', *Scotsman*, 13 April 1916; and 'The sedition trials', *Forward*, 22 April 1916, viewed 2 November 2024, <https://www.scran.ac.uk/000-000-505-726-C>

10 Regulation 42 of the *Defence of the Realm Regulations*, which made incitement to strike an offence.

11 'Spreading sedition', *Glasgow Herald*, 14 April 1916, p. 8.

19. The Worker trial

1   Description of court proceedings taken from: 'Spreading sedition', *Glasgow Herald*, 14 April 1916, pp. 7-8; 'Sedition trial', *Glasgow Herald*, 15 April 1916, p. 8; and 'A seditious article', *Scotsman*, 14 April 1916.

2   'Should the Workers Arm? A Desperate Situation', *Worker*, no. 4, 29 January 1916, p. 5, viewed 2 November 2024, <https://marxists.architexturez.net/history/international/social-democracy/worker/1916/n4-workers-arm.htm>

3   Gallacher, W 2017, p. 94.

4   Gallacher, W 2017, p. 94.

5   'Clyde agitators', *Glasgow Herald*, 12 May 1916, p. 7.

6   Gallacher, W 2017, p. 94.

7   'Promoters of disaffection', *Glasgow Herald*, 15 April 1916, p. 6.

20. Peterhead

1   'Scottish shipwrecks', Scottish shipwrecks, viewed 8 May 2024, <https://www.scottishshipwrecks.com/scottish-shipwrecks/>

2   Jones, K 2020, 'The Peterhead Harbour of Refuge Railway', *The Railway Magazine*, 30 Nov.

3   Milton, N 1973, p. 126.

4   Bridges Adams, M 1916, 'The ground we are losing', *Cotton Factory Times*, 12 May, p. 4.

5   'Peterhead Prison railway', Railscot, viewed 8 May 2024, <https://www.railscot.co.uk/companies/P/Peterhead_Prison_Railway/>

6   Taylor, S 2022, 'The history of Peterhead's Harbour Refuge built by inmates from "Scotland's toughest jail"', *AberdeenLive*, viewed 8 May, 2014, <https://www.aberdeenlive.news/news/history/history-peterheads-harbour-refuge-built-7222653>

7   Maclean, J 1919, 'Life in Prison', *Red Dawn*, vol. 1, no. 1, March.

8   Bridges Adams, M 1916, 'The sentence on John Maclean', *Cotton Factory Times*, 21 April, p. 5.

9   Bridges Adams, M 1916, 'The approach of the iron heel', *Cotton Factory Times*, 28 April, p. 4.

10 'Rivals in socialism', *Glasgow Herald*, 25 April 1916, p. 3.

11 'Compulsory service: trade unionist views', *Glasgow Herald*, 1 May 1916, p. 9.

12 Milton, N 1973, p. 132.

13 Bridges Adams, M 1916, 'The release of Maclean', *Cotton Factory Times*, 30 June, p. 4.

14 Ripley, BJ & McHugh, J 1989, p. 98.

15 Hansard HC Deb 16 August 1916 vol. 85 cc1886-7W.

21. European superstar

1   Senn, AE 1972, 'The Politics of Golos and Nashe Slovo', *International Review of Social History*, 17(2), pp. 675–704, doi:10.1017/S0020859000006829.

2   Service, R 2009, *Trotsky: a biography*, Macmillan, London, p. 138.

3   Thatcher, ID 1999, 'Representations of Scotland in Nashe Slovo during World War One: A Brief Note', *The Scottish Historical Review*, vol. 78, no. 206, Part 2, pp. 243-252.

4   Martin, J 2010, p. 66.

5   Grant, R 1984, *British radicals and socialists and their attitudes to Russia, c1890-1917*, PhD thesis, University of Glasgow, p. 238.

6   Chicherin, G 1916, 'The Scottish labour movement and the reaction in England', *Nashe Slovo* (May-June, in five parts), translated by Maria Artamanova, viewed 14 March 2024, <https://www.scotland-russia.llc.ed.ac.uk/the-scottish-labour-movement-nashe-slovo-1916/>

7   Thatcher, ID 1999, p. 248.

8   Grant, R 1984, p. 238.

9   Chicherin, G 1916.

10 Chicherin, G 1916.

11 Chicherin, G 1916.

12 Chicherin, G 1916.

13 Thatcher, ID 1999, p. 250.

14 Thatcher, ID 1992, 'John Maclean: Soviet Versions', *History*, vol. 77, no. 251 (October), pp. 421-429.

15 Lenin, VI 1965, *Collected works*, vol. 23, Progress Publishers, Moscow, p. 210, viewed 2 November 2024, <https://www.marxists.org/archive/lenin/works/cw/pdf/lenin-cw-vol-23.pdf>

22. I shall be released

1   Maclean, J 1919, 'Life in Prison'.

2   Broom, J 1973, p. 89.

3   Gallacher, W 2017, p. 105.

4. Hansard HC Deb 21 February 1917 vol. 90 c1332.
5. Hansard HC Deb 21 February 1917 vol. 90 c1356-W.
6. Taylor, AJP 1965, p.61.
7. Gourley, D 'The Buckingham Palace plot 1916', *Journal of Liberal History*, viewed 23 May 2024, <https://liberalhistory.org.uk/history/the-buckingham-palace-plot-1916/>
8. Taylor, AJP 1965, p.88.
9. In 1917, Russia still used the Julian or Old Style calendar, which was 13 days behind the Gregorian or New Style calendar. Russia adopted the New Style calendar on 24 January 1918. Dates used here are New Style with Old Style dates in brackets (OS).
10. Miéville, C 2017, *October*, Verso, London, p. 59
11. 'Independent Labour Party: effects of Russian revolution', *Glasgow Herald*, 9 April 1917, p. 7.
12. Milton, N 1973, p. 137.
13. Broom, J 1973, p. 90.
14. Broom, J 1973, p. 90.
15. Grant, R 1984, p. 312.
16. The Council of Workers and Soldiers Delegates, 1917, 'What happened at Leeds', London, 3 June, viewed 24 May 2024, <https://www.marxists.org/history/international/social-democracy/1917/leeds.htm>
17. The Council of Workers and Soldiers Delegates 1917, 'What happened at Leeds'.
18. The Council of Workers and Soldiers Delegates.
19. The Council of Workers and Soldiers Delegates.
20. The Council of Workers and Soldiers Delegates.
21. Hinton, J 1973, *The first shop stewards' movement*, Allen & Unwin, London, p. 239.
22. The Council of Workers and Soldiers Delegates.
23. Hinton, J 1973, p. 239.
24. Dalton, I 2017, 'June 1917: when workers in Britain first tried to form soviets', Socialist Party, 31 May, <https://www.socialistparty.org.uk/articles/25581/31-05-2017/june-1917-when-workers-in-britain-first-tried-to-form-soviets/>
25. Taylor, AJP 1965, p. 89.
26. Broom, J 1973, p. 90.
27. Ripley, BJ & McHugh, J 1989, p. 101.
28. Hansard HC Deb 19 June 1917 vol. 94 c1632W.
29. Hansard HC Deb 25 June 1917 vol. 95 c20.
30. Gallacher, W 2017, p.116.
31. Gallacher, W 2017, p.117.

23. A quiet life

1. Ripley, BJ & McHugh, J 1989, p. 103.
2. Gallacher, W 2017, p. 117.
3. Milton, N 1973, p. 141.
4. Milton, N 1973, p. 141.
5. Gallacher, W 2017, p. 118.
6. Maclean, J 1917, 'Letter on first release from prison', *Call*, 19 July, p. 4, viewed 7 June 2024, <https://www.marxists.org/archive/maclean/works/1917-prison.htm>
7. Work of National Importance was one of the many alternatives to military service that conscientious objectors were made to take up after securing exemption from conscription. It took the form of regular employment, but its mechanisms and rules ensured that it was also a punishment.
8. Macdougall, J 1927, p. 766.
9. Macdougall, J 1927, p. 767.
10. Ives, M 2017, *Reform, revolution and direct action amongst British miners*, Haymarket Books, Chicago, p. 90.
11. Maclean, J 1917, 'Lead from Lanarkshire: miners' historic protest against profiteers', *Call*, 9 August, p. 3, accessed 7 July 2024, <https://www.marxists.org/archive/maclean/works/1917-lead.htm>
12. Steven, 2013, 'The Brotherhood Church', viewed 8 June 2024, <https://libcom.org/library/16-brotherhood-church#footnote16_xjg0nct>
13. Challinor, R 1977, p. 183.
14. Steven, 2013.
15. Russell, B 1971, *The autobiography of Bertrand Russell: vol. 2: 1914–1944*, Allen & Unwin, London, pp. 31-32.
16. Milton, N 1973, p.
17. 'Workers' and soldiers' council: riotous meetings', *Glasgow Herald*, 30 July 1917, p. 6.
18. 'Workers' and soldiers' councils: riotous meetings'.
19. The National Archives of the UK, War Cabinet, 8 August 1917, CAB 23/3/55.
20. 'Workers' and soldiers' council: Glasgow meeting prohibited', *Glasgow Herald*, 10 August 1917, p. 4.
21. Gallacher W, 2017, p.119.
22. McShane, H & Smith J, 1978, p. 94.
23. Grant, R 1984, p. 257.
24. Debo, RK 1966, 'The Making of a Bolshevik: Georgii Chicherin in England

1914-1918', *Slavic Review*, Vol 25, No 4, December, p. 657.
25 Grant, R 1984, p. 307.
26 Debo, RK 1966, p. 658.
27 Debo, RK 1966, p. 659.
28 Bridges Adams, M 1917, *Cotton Factory Times*, 26 October.
29 Grant, R 1984, p. 259.
30 Ripley BJ & McHugh, J, 1989, p. 104.

24. Give peace a chance
1 Miéville, C 2017, p. 114.
2 Miéville, C 2017, p. 117.
3 Miéville, C 2017, p. 118.
4 Miéville, C 2017, p. 130.
5 Meynell, H 1960, 'The Stockholm Conference of 1917', *International Review of Social History*, vol. 5, p. 12.
6 Meynell, H 1960, p. 8.
7 Lenin, 1917, 'Speech on the Proposal to Call an International Socialist Conference 25 April (8 May)', at The Seventh (April) All-Russia Conference of the RSDLP(B.), viewed 18 July 2024, <https://www.marxists.org/archive/lenin/works/1917/7thconf/25.htm#v24zz99h-247-GUESS>
8 McCormick, MP 2020, *Arthur Henderson and the 1917 Stockholm conference: a reappraisal*, PhD thesis, University of Birmingham, p. 107.
9 The National Archives of the UK, War Cabinet, 21 May 1917, CAB 23/2/59.

25. Arthur Henderson goes to Russia
1 McCormick, MP 2020, p. 119.
2 Meynell, H 1960, p. 18.
3 McCormick, MP 2020, p. 119.
4 McCormick, MP 2020, p. 119.
5 McCormick, MP 2020, p. 119.
6 McCormick, MP 2020, p. 115.
7 Miéville, C 2017, p. 152.
8 Miéville, C 2017, p. 156.
9 Miéville, C 2017, p. 163.
10 Miéville, C 2017, p. 163.
11 Henderson, A 1917, 'British mission to Russia, June and July 1917', The National Archives of the UK, CAB 24/4/2.
12 Henderson, A 1917.
13 'The preparation for a people's peace', *Glasgow Herald*, 14 July 1917, p. 6.
14 'Mr Henderson's views on Stockholm', *Times*, 24 July 1917, p. 5.
15 Meynell, H 1960, p. 19.
16 Miéville, C 2017, p. 174.
17 Miéville, C 2017, p. 180.
18 Miéville, C 2017, p. 196.

26. How Stockholm begat the modern British Labour Party
1 McCormick, MP 2020, p. 148.
2 The National Archives of the UK, War Cabinet, 1 August 1917, CAB 23/3/50.
3 'Parliament: Labourists and the Stockholm conference', *Glasgow Herald*, 3 August 1917, p. 7.
4 Smith, F 1917, 'The Stockholm Conference. Memorandum by the Attorney-General with a covering note by Sir Edward Carson', 6 August, The National Archives of the UK, War Cabinet, CAB 24/22/24.
5 The National Archives of the UK, War Cabinet, 8 August 1917, CAB 23/3/55.
6 Winter, JM 1972, p. 768.
7 Kellogg, PU & Gleason, A 1919, *British Labor and the War*, Boni & Liveright, New York, p. 95.
8 Meynell, H 1960, p. 213.
9 Meynell, H 1960, p. 216.
10 'BSP's peace terms', *Daily Telegraph*, 27 August 1917, p. 6.
11 'Peace fiasco', *Daily Telegraph*, 30 August 1917, p. 5.
12 Meynell, H 1960, pp. 218-219.
13 Taylor, AJP 1965, p. 90.

27. Russia turns red
1 Miéville, C 2017, p. 238.
2 Miéville, C 2017, p. 246.
3 Miéville, C 2017, p. 253.
4 Trotsky, L 1932, *The history of the Russian Revolution*, vol. 3, ch. 41 'The Military-Revolutionary Committee', (translated by Max Eastman), viewed 2 August 2024, <https://www.marxists.org/archive/trotsky/1930/hrr/ch41.htm>
5 Trotsky, L 1932, ch. 41.
6 Figes, O 2017, *A people's tragedy: the Russian Revolution*, The Bodley Head, London, p. 480.
7 Figes, O 2017, p. 480.
8 Figes, O 2017, p. 481.
9 Trotsky, L 1932, ch. 44, 'The Conquest of the Capital', viewed 2 August 2024, <https://www.marxists.org/archive/trotsky/1930/hrr/ch44.htm>
10 Figes, O 2017, p. 484.
11 Trotsky, L 1932, ch. 44.
12 Lenin, V 1965, *Collected works*, vol. 26, Progress Publishers, Moscow, p. 236, viewed 3 November 2024, <https://www.marxists.org/archive/lenin/works/cw/pdf/lenin-cw-vol-26.pdf>
13 Figes, O 2017, p. 486.
14 Figes, O 2017, p. 486.

15 Trotsky, L 1932, ch. 47, 'The Congress of the Soviet Dictatorship', viewed 2 August 2024, <https://www.marxists.org/archive/trotsky/1930/hrr/ch47.htm>
16 Trotsky, L 1932, ch. 47.
17 Trotsky, L 1932, ch. 47.
18 Reed, J 1960, *Ten days that shook the world*, The Modern Library, New York, p. 172.
19 Lenin, V 1917, 'Decree on Peace', Second All-Russia Congress of Soviets of Workers' and Soldiers' Deputies, 9 November (26 October OS), viewed 11 August 2024, <https://www.marxists.org/archive/lenin/works/1917/oct/25-26/26b.htm>

28. Consolidating Bolshevik power
1 Figes, O 2027, p. 501.
2 Figes, O 2017, p. 503.
3 Figes, O 2017, p. 504.
4 Figes, O 2017, p. 506.
5 Figes, O 2017, pp. 509-510.
6 Lenin, V 1972, 'Theses on the Constituent Assembly', *Collected works*, Progress Publishers, Moscow, Volume 26, pp. 379-383 (originally published 8 January 1918 (26 December 1917 OS), in *Prava* no. 213), viewed on 19 August 2024, <https://www.marxists.org/archive/lenin/works/1917/dec/11a.htm>
7 Figes, O 2017, pp. 513.

29. The release of Chicherin and Petroff
1 Broom, J 1973, p 95.
2 Maclean, J 1917, 'A Glasgow appeal to Lancashire: movement on behalf of interned Russians', *Cotton Factory Times*, 9 November, p. 4.
3 Maclean, J 1917, 'A Glasgow appeal to Lancashire: movement on behalf of interned Russians'.
4 Maclean, J 1917, 'A Glasgow appeal to Lancashire: movement on behalf of interned Russians'.
5 Petroff, P 1917, letter to Irma Petroff, letter 166, 30 November, viewed 13 August 2024, <https://www.marxists.org/archive/petroff/1918/letters.htm>
6 'Russia silent', *Glasgow Herald*, 16 November 1917, p. 7.
7 Milton, N 1973, p. 152.
8 *Cotton Factory Times*, 30 November 1917, p. 2.
9 Buchanan, G 1923, *My mission to Russia*, Cassell, London, p. 227.
10 The National Archives of the UK, War Cabinet, 10 December 1917, CAB 23/4/69.
11 Debo, R K 1966, p. 662.

30. The shop stewards' movement returns
1 US Department of Labor, Bureau of Labor Statistics, 1917, *Industrial unrest in Great Britain*, no. 237, October, viewed 23 August 2024, <https://fraser.stlouisfed.org/files/docs/publications/bls/bls_0237_1917.pdf>
2 Bell, T 1941, p. 125.
3 Kendall, W 1969, p. 158.
4 Gallacher, W 2017, p. 115.
5 Gallacher, W 2017, p. 125.
6 Gallacher, W 2017, p. 126.
7 Hinton, J 1973, p. 251.
8 Great Britain. Ministry of Munitions 2009, *Official history of the Ministry of Munitions, vol. V, Wages and welfare*, Naval & Military Press Ltd, London, pt. 1, pp. 181-182.
9 Great Britain. Ministry of Munitions 2009, *Official history of the Ministry of Munitions*, vol. V, pt. 1, p. 192.
10 Hinton, J 1973, p. 254.

31. Brest-Litovsk: the armistice
1 'Russia's lapse', *Glasgow Herald*, 3 December 1917, p. 8.
2 Distracted Russia', *Times*, 29 November 1917, p. 8.
3 Wheeler-Bennett, J W 1939, *Brest-Litovsk: the forgotten peace*, Macmillan & Co., London, p. 89.
4 Wheeler-Bennett, J W 1939, p. 89.
5 Wheeler-Bennett, J W 1939, p. 92.
6 Wheeler-Bennett, J W 1939, p. 92.
7 Wheeler-Bennett, J W 1939, p. 78.
8 Wheeler-Bennett, J W 1939, p. 125.
9 Wheeler-Bennett, J W 1939, p. 137.
10 US Department of State, 'America Enters the War; Wilson's Plan for Peace', viewed 3 October 2024, <https://history.state.gov/departmenthistory/short-history/war>
11 'President Wilson on peace', *Glasgow Herald*, 9 January 1918, p. 7.
12 'The world's peace', *Times*, 9 January 1918, p. 7.
13 Wilson, W 2006, *Woodrow Wilson: essential writings and speeches of the scholar-president*, NYU Press, New York, p. 35.
14 Wheeler-Bennett, J W 1939, p. 147.
15 Wecter, D 1972, *The hero in America: a chronicle of hero-worship*, Scribner, New York, p. 402.

32. Man power
1 Taylor, A J P 1963, *The First World War: an illustrated history*, Hamish Hamilton, London, p. 146.

2   Cole, GDH 1948, *A history of the Labour Party from 1914*, Routledge and Kegan Paul, London, p. 39.
3   'Allied terms of peace', *Glasgow Herald*, 7 January 1918, p. 7.
4   'Allied terms of peace'.
5   Bell, T 1941, p. 303.
6   Hinton, J 1973, p. 238.
7   Bell, T 1941, p. 304.
8   Hinton, J 1973, p. 256.
9   Gallacher, W 2017, p. 129.
10 Hansard HC Deb 14 January 1918 vol. 101 cc58-134.
11 Hansard HC Deb 14 January 1918 vol. 101 cc58-134.
12 'Sir Auckland Geddes in Liverpool', *Glasgow Herald* 28 January 1918, p. 6.
13 Gallacher, W 2017, 131.
14 Gallacher, W 2017, 132.
15 'Man-Power: Glasgow workers and the Bill', *Glasgow Herald*, 29 January 1918, p. 4.
16 Hinton, J 1973, p. 260.
17 Gallacher, 2017, p. 133.
18 'Man-Power: Glasgow workers and the Bill'.
19 Editorial, *Glasgow Herald*, 29 January 1918, p. 4.
20 Hinton, J 1973, p. 264.
21 The National Archives of the UK, War Cabinet, 5 February 1918, CAB 23/5/31.
22 The *Herald*, 9 February 1918.
23 Hinton, J 1973, p. 263.
24 Hinton, J 1973, p. 263.
25 'Man-Power: Clyde workers' revised resolution', *Glasgow Herald*, 31 January 1918, p. 4.
26 Hinton, J 1973, p. 264.
27 Hinton, J 1973, p. 265.
28 'Premier and miners', *Glasgow Herald*, 23 March 1918, p. 4.
29 'Man-Power': Engineers threaten trouble', *Glasgow Herald*, 25 March 1918, p. 9.

33. Soviet consul

1   Haslam, J 1983, *Soviet Foreign Policy, 1930–33: The Impact of the Depression*, St. Martin's Press, New York, p. 11.
2   McHugh, J & Ripley, BJ 1985, 'Russian political internees in First World War Britain: the cases of George Chicherin and Peter Petroff', *The Historical Journal*, 28, 3, pp. 727-738.
3   'BSP raided', *Call*, 24 January 1918, p. 1, viewed 3 November 2024, <https://www.marx-memorial-library.org.uk/project/socialist-opposition-ww1/call-no-94-24-january-1918>
4   'Russian ambassador and Bolsheviks', *Glasgow Herald*, 23 January 1918, p. 5.
5   Buchanan, G 1923, p. 256.
6   Broom, J 1973, p.97.
7   Trotsky, L 1930, *My life*, Charles Schribner's Sons, New York, ch. 30, viewed 15 September 2024, <https://www.marxists.org/archive/trotsky/1930/mylife/ch30.htm>
8   Ripley, BJ & McHugh, J 1989, p. 105.
9   'A Bolshevik consul for Glasgow', *Glasgow Herald*, 30 January 1918, p. 8.
10 'Bolshevists against German terms', *Glasgow Herald*, 26 January 1918, p. 5.
11 Bell, T 1941, p. 152.
12 Gallacher, W 2017, p. 126.
13 Munro, R 1918, 'Revolutionary agitation in Glasgow and Clydeside with special reference to the cases of John Maclean and others', The National Archives of the UK, 7 March, CAB 24/44/38 Annex I.
14 Munro, R 1918.
15 The National Archives of the UK, War Cabinet, 12 March 1918, CAB 23/5/56.
16 Litvinov, M 1973, *Scottish Marxist*, no. 5, November 1973, p. 12-13 (original written in 1918).
17 Milton, N 1973, p. 157.
18 Gallacher, W 2017, p. 127.
19 'An industrial volcano', *Glasgow Herald*, 15 January 1918, p. 6.
20 'Glasgow Labourists and Mr Barnes', *Glasgow Herald*, 17 January 1918, p. 5.
21 'Labour Party and government: Bitter speeches at the conference', *Glasgow Herald*, 25 January 1918, p, 5.
22 Milton, N 1973, p. 159.
23 Kendall, W 1969, p. 176.
24 Kendall, W 1969, p. 179.
25 Kendall, W 1969, p. 180.
26 Kendall, W 1969, p. 179.
27 'The BSP conference', *Call*, 4 April 1918, p. 2.

34. Brest-Litovsk: the treaty

1   Wheeler-Bennett, JW 1939, p. 152.
2   Wheeler-Bennett, JW 1939, p. 156.
3   Wheeler-Bennett, JW 1939, p. 157.
4   Wheeler-Bennett, JW 1939, p. 157.
5   Wheeler-Bennett, JW 1939, p. 162.
6   Wheeler-Bennett, JW 1939, p. 165.
7   Wheeler-Bennett, JW 1939, p. 173.
8   Wheeler-Bennett, JW 1939, p. 175.
9   Wheeler-Bennett, JW 1939, p. 185.
10 Figes, O 2017, p. 544, Wheeler-Bennett, JW 1939, p. 193.
11 Wheeler-Bennett, JW 1939, p. 196.
12 Wheeler-Bennett, JW 1939, pp. 196-197.
13 Wheeler-Bennett, JW 1939, p. 211.

14	Wheeler-Bennett, J W 1939, p. 219.		britannica.com/event/World-War-I/The-end-of-the-German-war>
15	Wheeler-Bennett, J W 1939, p. 220.	21	Taylor, AJP 1963, p. 183.
16	Figes, O 2017, pp. 544-545.	22	Taylor, AJP 1963, p. 184.
17	Figes, O 2017, p. 548.	23	Showalter, DE & Royde-Smith, JG 2024.

35. Accuser of capitalism.

1. 'John Maclean's trial and sentence', *Call*, 16 May 1918, p. 5, viewed 3 November 2024, <https://www.marx-memorial-library.org.uk/project/socialist-opposition-ww1/call-no-110-16-may-1918>
2. 'Sedition trial in Edinburgh: Bolshevist Consul sent to penal servitude', *Scotsman*, 10 May 1918.
3. Milton, N 1973, p. 168.
4. Milton, N 1973, p. 169.
5. 'Sedition trial in Edinburgh: Bolshevist Consul sent to penal servitude'.
6. 'Sedition charge: Glasgow socialist sentenced', *Glasgow Herald*, 10 May 1918, p. 6.
7. Maclean, J 1918, 'Speech from the dock', viewed 24 October 2024, <https://www.marxists.org/archive/maclean/works/1918-dock.htm>
8. Broom, J 1973, p. 105.

36. Peterhead again

1. Editorial, *Scotsman*, 10 May 1918.
2. 'A savage sentence', *Call*, 16 May 1918, p. 1.
3. Lenin, VI 1965, *Collected works*, vol. 27, Progress Publishers, Moscow, pp. 457-491.
4. Milton, N 1973, p. 176.
5. 'Socialists' conflict with police in Glasgow', *Glasgow Herald*, 8 July 1918, p. 6.
6. Milton, N 1973, p. 176.
7. Cole, GDH 1948, p. 58.
8. 'The Labour Conference: withdrawal from party truce', *Times*, 27 June 1918, p. 7.
9. 'The Labour Conference: withdrawal from party truce'.
10. Gallacher, W 2017, p. 146.
11. 'Discharged soldiers and Mr Barnes', *Aberdeen Journal*, 20 August 1918, p. 3.
12. 'Mr Barnes MP in Blackfriars', *Glasgow Herald*, 20 August 1918, p. 4.
13. 'Discharged soldiers and Mr Barnes'.
14. Maclean, J 1918, 'Speech from the dock'.
15. Broom, J 1973, p. 111.
16. Maclean, J 1919, 'Life in prison', *Red Dawn*, Vol 1, No 1, March 1919, pp. 8-9.
17. Taylor, AJP 1963, p. 172.
18. Taylor, AJP 1963, p. 180.
19. Taylor, AJP 1963, p. 182.
20. Showalter, DE & Royde-Smith, JG 2024, 'The end of the German war', *Encyclopedia Britannica*, 19 Oct. 2024, accessed 22 October 2024, <https://www.
21. Taylor, AJP 1963, p. 183.
22. Taylor, AJP 1963, p. 184.
23. Showalter, DE & Royde-Smith, JG 2024.
24. 'Labour Party: No support for coalition', *Glasgow Herald*, 15 November 1918, p. 5.
25. Hansard HC Deb 14 November 1918 vol. 110 cc2914-3022.
26. Gallacher, W 2017, pp. 150-151.
27. Broom, J 1973, p. 115.
28. 'Bolshevist candidate: Mr Barnes' fight at Glasgow', *Times*, 28 November, 1918, p. 8.

37. Thanksgiving

1. 'King George leaves for Paris', *Glasgow Herald*, 28 November 1918, p. 5.
2. Lenin, VI 1965, *Collected works*, Vol 28, July 1918-March 1919, Progress Publishers, Moscow 1965, p. 126, viewed 3 November 2024, <https://www.marxists.org/archive/lenin/works/cw/pdf/lenin-cw-vol-28.pdf>
3. Barnes, GN 1918, 'Imprisonment of John Maclean', 26 November, The National Archives of the UK, CAB 23/70/82.
4. Maclean, J 1918, letter to Agnes Maclean, 16 November [letter], in Papers of John Maclean, Clydeside agitator, 1909-1923, National Library of Scotland, Edinburgh.
5. The National Archives of the UK, War Cabinet, 28 November 1918, CAB 23/42/10.
6. 'Dundee: Mr Churchill's peace terms', *Glasgow Herald*, 28 November 1918, p. 6.
7. 'The Lord Advocate and the case of John Maclean', *Glasgow Herald*, 29 November 1918, p. 6.

38. The khaki election

1. McShane, H & Smith, J 1978, p. 99.
2. Montefiore, D 1918, 'Impressions of the reception of John Maclean', *Call*, 12 December, p. 6, viewed 3 November 2024, <https://www.marxists.org/archive/montefiore/1918/12/12.htm>
3. Gallacher, W 2017, p. 151.
4. Montefiore, D 1918, 'Impressions of the reception of John Maclean'.
5. Gallacher, W 2017, p. 151.
6. Milton, N 1973, p. 181.
7. 'Mr John Maclean's arrival in Glasgow', *Glasgow Herald*, 4 December 1918, p. 9.
8. 'The fight in Gorbals', *Glasgow Herald*, 5 December 1918, p. 8.
9. 'The fight in Gorbals'.
10. Montefiore, D 1925, *From a Victorian to a modern*, E Archer, London, viewed 31 October 2024, <https://www.

marxists.org/archive/montefiore/1925/autobiography/15.htm>
11 Maclean, J 1918, 'The Release of John Maclean – Special Message to 'The Call'', *Call*, 12 December, p. 6, viewed 3 November 2024, <https://www.marxists.org/archive/maclean/works/1917-release.htm>
12 'Mr John Maclean reappears', *Glasgow Herald*, 14 December 1918, p. 7.
13 Gallacher, W 1966, *The last memoirs of William Gallacher*, Lawrence & Wishart, London, p. 117.
14 Bell, T 1944, p. 87.
15 'Mr John Maclean reappears'.
16 'ILP at Huddersfield', *Glasgow Herald*, 22 April 1919, p. 6.
17 'Mr Ramsay Macdonald and Labour poll', *Glasgow Herald*, 6 January 1919, p. 9.
18 Keynes, JM 1920, *Economic consequences of the peace*, ch. 5, Macmillan, London, p. 127.
19 'The election', *Times*, 9 December 1918, p. 9.
20 Keynes, JM 1920, p. 133.

39. Back to the miners
1 Gallacher, W 1966, p. 119.
2 Maclean, J 1919, 'Now's the Day and Now's the Hour', *Call*, 23 Jan.
3 Maclean, J 1919, 'Now's the Day and Now's the Hour'.
4 McShane, H & Smith J, 1978, p. 101.
5 Ives, M 2017, p. 75.
6 'ILP conference: Scottish resolutions for national meeting', *Glasgow Herald*, 6 January 1919, p. 9.
7 Cliff, T & Gluckstein, D 1986, *Marxism and trade union struggle: the general strike of 1926*, Bookmarks: London & Chicago, viewed 31 October 2024, <https://www.marxists.org/archive/cliff/works/1986/tradeunion/ch06.htm>
8 Ives, M 2017, p. 97.

40. The 40-hour strike
1 '40 hours week: call for a general strike', *Glasgow Herald*, 20 January 1919, p. 6.
2 '40 hours week: call for a general strike'.
3 'Nationalisation: mines, railways and ships', *Glasgow Herald*, 17 January 1919, p. 10.
4 'Visit of John Maclean', *Motherwell Times*, 31 January 1919.
5 Ives, M 2017, p. 100.
6 McShane, H & Smith J, 1978, p. 104.
7 'Shorter work strike', *Glasgow Herald*, 28 January 1919, pp. 5-6.
8 'Attitude of miners', *Glasgow Herald*, 28 January 1919, p. 6.
9 Ives, M 2017, p. 105.
10 The National Archives of the UK, War Cabinet, 31 January 1919, CAB 23/9/10.

41. The battle of George Square
1 'Arrests at Bellshill', *Glasgow Herald*, 1 February 1919, p. 6.
2 Gallacher, W 2017, pp. 160-162.
3 'Glasgow street fighting', *Glasgow Herald*, 1 February 1919, p. 5.
4 Gallacher, W 2017, p. 162.
5 Gallacher, W 2017, p. 163.
6 Gallacher, W 2017, p. 163.
7 'Glasgow street fighting'.
8 McShane, H & Smith J, 1978, p. 107.

42. The miners mobilise
1 'Labour unrest: a national conference', *Glasgow Herald*, 18 February 1919, p. 6.
2 'The Triple Alliance', *Glasgow Herald* 26 February 1919, p. 7.
3 Bevan, A 1952, *In place of fear*, William Heinemann, London, p. 20.
4 'Hold together', *Glasgow Herald*, 28 February 1919, p. 7.
5 Cowan, T 2011, *Labour of love: the story of Robert Smillie*, Neil Wilson Publishing, Glasgow, p. 274.
6 Maclean, J 1919, 'The Coal Situation', *Call*, 6 March, p. 1, viewed 1 November 2024, <https://www.marxists.org/archive/maclean/works/1919-coal-situation.htm>

43. Hands off Russia
1 Tolly, K 1969, 'Our Russian War of 1918–1919', US Naval Institute, vol. 95/2/792, viewed 9 November 2024, <https://www.usni.org/magazines/proceedings/1969/february/our-russian-war-1918-1919>
2 Hansard HC Deb 05 August 1918 vol 109 cc904-6.
3 Soviet of the People's Commissars, 1918, *To the toiling masses of France, Britain, America, Italy and Japan*, 1 August, viewed 11 November 2014, <https://www.marxists.org/history/ussr/government/foreign-relations/1917-1918/1918/August/1.htm>
4 Russian Anti-Intervention Committee, 1918, 'Resolution in support of the Soviet Republic of the Russian workers', Warwick digital collections, viewed 9 November 2024, <https://cdm21047.contentdm.oclc.org/digital/collection/russian/id/946>
5 'Whirling words', *Glasgow Herald*, 10 February 1919, p. 10.
6 Milton, N 1973, p. 192.

7. Beevor, A 2022, *Russia: revolution and civil war 1917-1921*, Weidenfeld & Nicolson, London, p. 279.
8. Jenkins, R 2002, *Churchill*, Pan, London, p. 350.
9. Beevor, A 2022, p. 280.

44. The Coal Commission

1. Cowan, T 2011, p. 275.
2. Arnot, RP 1953, *The miners: years of struggle*, Routledge, London, p. 189.
3. Arnot, RP 1953, p. 200.
4. Cole, M 1952, *Beatrice Webb's diaries 1912-1924*, Longmans, London, p. 152.
5. Gleason, A 1920, *What the workers want: a study of British Labour*, Allen & Unwin, London, p. 48.
6. Ives, M 2017, p. 203.
7. Ives, M 2017, p. 204.
8. Great Britain, Coal industry commission 1919, 'Reports and minutes of evidence on the first stage of the inquiry', p. viii, viewed 1 November 2024, <https://archive.org/details/reportsminutesof00greauoft>
9. 'Coal Commission reports', *Glasgow Herald*, 21 March 1919, p. 7.
10. Ives, M 2017, p. 205.
11. 'A miner's ballot', *Glasgow Herald*, 27 March 1919, p. 7.
12. Ives, M 2017, p. 206.
13. Ives, M 2017, p. 179.
14. Ives, M 2017, p. 191.
15. Williams, JE 1962, *The Derbyshire miners*, Allen & Unwin, London, p. 618
16. Macdougall, JD 1927, p. 774.
17. Ives, M 2017, p. 192.
18. Maclean, J 1978, 'Onward, ever onward', *In the rapids of revolution*, p. 153 (originally published in the *Worker*, 12 April 1919).
19. Arnot, RP 1953, p. 202.

45. The Third International

1. Wikipedia, 'International Workingmen's Association', viewed 1 November, 2024, <https://en.wikipedia.org/wiki/International_Workingmen%27s_Association>
2. Trotsky, L, 1973, 'Invitation to the First World Congress', in *The first five years of the Communist International* Vol 1, New Park, London, (original published 24 January 1919), viewed 1 November 2024, <https://www.marxists.org/archive/trotsky/1924/ffyci-1/app04.htm>
3. Ransome, A 1998, 'The Third International', *Russia in 1919*, Project Gutenberg, Salt Lake City, USA, (original published 1919), viewed 1 November 2024, <https://www.marxists.org/history/archive/ransome/works/1919-russia/ch27.htm>
4. Stevenson, G 2010, 'Joe Fineberg', viewed 1 November 2024, <https://grahamstevenson.me.uk/2010/06/20/fineberg-joe/>
5. Trotsky, L 1973, 'Manifesto of the Communist International to the Workers of the World', in *The First Five Years of the Communist International*, Vol 1, New Park, London, (originally published 1919), viewed 1 November 2024, <https://www.marxists.org/archive/trotsky/1924/ffyci-1/ch01.htm>
6. Bell, T 1941, p. 177.

46. Soviets in Britain?

1. 'British Bolsheviks', *Glasgow Herald*, 17 April 1919, p. 9.
2. Rothstein, T 1919, 'What is our position?', *Call*, 17 April, p. 4, (as John Bryan), viewed 11 November 2024, <https://www.marxists.org/archive/rothstein/1919/04/17.htm>
3. Milton, N 1973, p. 201.
4. Milton, N 1973, p. 201.
5. 'British Socialists', *Glasgow Herald*, 21 April 1919, p. 8.
6. 'British Socialists', *Glasgow Herald*, 21 April 1919, p. 8.
7. 'Easter meetings: BSP and the Glasgow rioters', *Glasgow Herald*, 22 April 1919, p. 6.
8. 'Easter meetings: BSP and the Glasgow rioters', *Glasgow Herald*, 22 April 1919, p. 6.
9. Milton, N 1973, p. 203.
10. Ives, M 2017, p. 207.
11. Milton, N 1973, p. 208.

47. Nationalisation

1. Cowan, T 2011, p. 290.
2. Ives, M 2017, p. 226.
3. Ives, M 2017, p. 227.
4. Hansard HC Deb 09 July 1919 vol 117 cc1817-22.
5. Ives, M 2017, p. 254.
6. Macdougall, J 1927, p. 744.
7. Ives, M 2017, p. 261-262.
8. Ives, M 2017, p. 266.
9. Ives, M 2017, p. 218.
10. Ives, M 2017, p. 285.
11. Ives, M 2017, p. 222.
12. The National Archives of the UK, War Cabinet, 19 July 1919, CAB 23/15/21.
13. Hansard HC Deb 21 July 1919 vol 118 cc916-8.
14. 'Danger to the mines', *Times*, 22 July 1919, p. 13.

15	'The Government and the Miners', *Times*, 22 July 1919, p. 13.	7	Hansard HC Deb 16 April 1919 vol 114 cc2942-4.
16	Hansard HC DEB 23 July 1919 vol 118 c1360.	8	The National Archives of the UK, War Cabinet, 11 June 1919, CAB 23/15/15.
17	Ives, M 2017, p. 295.		
18	Ives, M 2017, p. 294.	9	Beevor, A 2022, p. 314.
19	Ives, M 2017, p. 313.	10	Beevor, A 2022, p. 309.
20	Arnot, RP 1953, p. 212.	11	Beevor, A 2022, p. 292.
21	Cowan, T 2017, p. 293.	12	Beevor, A 2022, pp. 299-300.

48.   The moment passes

1	'Miners reject coal scheme', *Times*, 3 September 1919, p. 11.	13	The National Archives of the UK, War Cabinet, 27 June 1919, CAB 23/15/18.
2	Cowan, T 2011, p. 297.	14	The National Archives of the UK, War Cabinet, 4 July 1919, CAB 23/15/19.
3	'Miners' decision', *Times*, 4 September 1919, p. 14.	15	Hansard HC Deb 05 August 1919 vol 119 cc143-4
4	'Triple Alliance decision', *Times*, 5 September 1919, p. 10.	16	Hansard HC Deb 05 August 1919 vol 119 cc144-5
5	'Direct action condemned', *Times*, 9 September 1919, p. 10.	17	'British aid to Russia', *Times*, 15 August 1919, p. 12.
6	'Direct action', *Times*, 10 September 1919, p. 10.	18	Wright, D 2017, *Churchill's secret war with Lenin: British and Commonwealth military intervention in the Russian Civil War, 1918-20*, Helion, Solihull, pp. 178–179.
7	'State mines demanded', *Times*, 11 September 1919, p. 10.		
8	'Trades Union Congress', *Times*, 11 September 1919, p. 12.	19	Beevor, A 2022, p. 365-66.
9	'Trades Union Congress', *Times*, 12 September 1919, p. 12.	20	Trotsky, L 1930, ch. 35.
10	'Trades Union Congress', *Times*, 12 September 1919, p. 12.	21	'The Guildhall banquet', *Times*, 10 November 1919, p. 9.
11	'Trades Union Congress', *Times*, 12 September 1919, p. 12.	22	Hansard HC Deb 17 November 1919 vol 121 cc681-772.

50.   Break-ups

12	'Trades Union Congress', *Times*, 13 September 1919, p. 12.	1	Milton, N 1973, p. 196.
13	'Direct action', *Times*, 15 September 1919, p. 14.	2	Milton, N 1973, p. 267.
		3	Kendall, W 1969, p. 202.
14	'No national mines', *Times*, 11 October 1919, p. 6.	4	Kendall, W 1969, p. 203.
		5	Kendall, W 1969, p. 204.
15	'ca'-canny - the policy of deliberately limiting output at work. Originally Scots, in the sense 'proceed warily'): from *ca'* (variant of call (verb)) and *canny* (shrewd).	6	'Our Bolshevists', *Times*, 11 November 1919, p. 16.
		7	'Our Bolshevists', *Times*, 11 November 1919, p. 16.
		8	'Hands off Russia', *Times*, 1 December 1919, p. 11.
16	Maclean, J 1978, 'The miners' next move', *In the rapids of revolution*, p. 156 (originally published in the *Call*, 23 October 1919).	9	Broom, J 1973, p.127.
		10	'Glasgow Socialists and Bolshevism', *Glasgow Herald*, 1 December 1919, p. 8.
17	'Trades Union Congress', *Times*, 10 December 1919, p. 8.	11	Malone, CJL 1920, *The Russian republic*, Harcourt, Brace & Howe, New York, p. 34.
18	Cowan, T 2011, p. 300.	12	Maclean, J 1919, 'The miners next move', *Call*, 23 October, viewed 19 December 2024, <https://www.marxists.org/archive/maclean/works/1919-miners.htm>

49.   Britain's war against Russia

1	Jenkins, R 2002, p. 351,		
2	Beevor, A 2022, p. 270.		
3	Beevor, A 2022, p. 283.	13	Ripley, BJ & McHugh, J 1989, p. 124.
4	The National Archives of the UK, War Cabinet, 4 March 1919, CAB 23/15/6.	14	McShane, H & Smith, J 1978, p. 112.
		15	'Our Bolshevists', *Times*, 1 March 1920, p. 16.
5	Hansard HC Deb 16 April 1919 vol 114 cc2939-41.	16	Maclean, J 1978, 'A Scottish Communist Party', *In the rapids of revolution*, p. 224
6	Hansard HC Deb 16 April 1919 vol 114 cc2941-2.		

17 Kendall, W 1969, p. 179.
18 Milton, N 1973, p. 228.
19 McShane, H & Smith, J 1978, p. 111.
20 Milton, N 1973, p. 228.
21 Pitt, B 1995, 'The real John Maclean', *Workers Liberty*, viewed 30 December 2024, <https://www.workersliberty.org/story/2010-06-13/real-john-maclean>
22 Milton, N 1973, p. 228.
23 McShane, H & Smith, J 1978, p. 112.
24 Maclean, J 1978, 'A Scottish Communist Party'.
25 Milton, N 1973, p. 219.
26 Milton, N 1973, p. 228.
27 Ripley, BJ & McHugh, J 1989, p. 136.
28 Bell, T 1944, pp. 152-153.
29 'No mean fighter: the Harry McShane interviews', University of Warwick, accessed 16 March 2025, <warwick.ac.uk/services/library/mrc/archives_online/speakingarchives/mcshane>

51. Alba and Erin

1 'May Day', *Glasgow Herald*, 3 May 1920, p. 9.
2 Milton, N 1973, p. 231.
3 Maclean, J 1920, 'The Vanguard resurrected', *Vanguard*, May, viewed 24 December 2014, <https://www.marxists.org/archive/maclean/works/1920-tvr.htm>
4 McShane, H & Smith, J 1978, p. 113.
5 Milton, N 1973, p. 233.
6 'History of unemployment', Scottish Unemployed Workers' Network, viewed 5 January 2025, <https://scottishunemployedworkers.net/history-of-unemployment/>
7 McShane, H & Smith, J 1978, p. 115.
8 Milton, N 1973, p. 234.
9 Milton, N 1973, p. 234.
10 Milton, N 1973, p. 235.
11 'A Labour causerie', *Glasgow Herald*, 5 June 1920, p. 4.
12 Maclean, J 1920, 'The Irish tragedy: Scotland's disgrace …', viewed 4 January 2025, <https://www.marxists.org/archive/maclean/works/1920-tit.htm>
13 Dáil Éireann, vol. 1, 21 January 1919, 'Message to the free nations of the world', viewed 3 January 2025, <https://web.archive.org/web/20070319033113/http://historical-debates.oireachtas.ie/D/DT/D.F.O.191901210013.html>
14 The Irish War, 'The Irish War of Independence', viewed 3 January 2025, <https://www.theirishwar.com/history/irish-war-of-independence/>
15 The Irish War, 'The Irish War of Independence'.
16 The Irish War, 'The Irish War of Independence'.
17 McShane, H & Smith, J 1978, p. 117.
18 McShane, H & Smith, J 1978, p. 117.
19 Maclean, J 1920, 'The Battle of Motherwell', *Vanguard*, August, pp. 7-8.
20 Maclean, J 1920, 'The Battle of Motherwell'.
21 Maclean J, 1915, 'The conscription menace' *In the rapids of revolution*, pp. 87-88 (originally published in *Vanguard*, December 1915).

52. The Comintern lays down the law

1 Milton, N 1973, p. 242.
2 Kendall, W 1969, p. 270.
3 Kendall, W 1969, p. 270.
4 Kendall, W 1969, p. 271.
5 The Left Wing Group of the ILP, 1920, *Moscow's reply to the ILP*, Glasgow, p. 9, viewed 18 January 2025, <https://wdc.contentdm.oclc.org/digital/collection/russian/id/5636/>
6 The Left Wing Group of the ILP, 1920, *Moscow's reply to the ILP*, Glasgow, pp. 10-11.
7 The Left Wing Group of the ILP, 1920, *Moscow's reply to the ILP*, Glasgow, p. 14.
8 Independent Labour Party, 1920, *The ILP and the 3rd International*, pp. 5-6.
9 The Left Wing Group of the ILP, 1920, *Moscow's reply to the ILP*, Glasgow, p. 1.
10 Milton, N 1973, p. 242.
11 Kendall, W 1969, p. 287.
12 Kendall, W 1969, p. 287.
13 Milton, N 1973, p. 241.
14 Kendall, W 1969, p. 287.
15 Gallacher, W 1947, *The rolling of the thunder*, Lawrence & Wishart, London, p. 7.
16 Wilkins, K 2019, *Daring and defiant: Helen Crawfurd (1877-1954) Scottish suffragette and international communist*, PhD thesis, Central European University, Budapest, p. 111-114.
17 Wilkins, K 2019, p. 116.
18 Bell, T 1944, pp. 107-108.
19 Lenin, V 1920, *"Left-Wing" Communism: an infantile disorder*, viewed 22 January 2025 <https://www.marxists.org/archive/lenin/works/1920/lwc/index.htm>
20 Lenin, V 1920, '"Left-Wing" Communism in Great Britain', viewed 23 January 2025, <https://www.marxists.org/archive/lenin/works/1920/lwc/ch09.htm>

(originally published in *Vanguard*, December 1920).

21. Lenin, V 1920, '"Left-Wing" Communism in Great Britain'.
22. *Minutes of the Second Congress of the Communist International*, 1920, Thirteenth session, 6 August, Moscow, viewed 23 January 2025, <https://www.marxists.org/history/international/comintern/2nd-congress/ch13.htm>
23. *Minutes of the Second Congress of the Communist International*, 1920, Thirteenth session, 6 August.
24. Kendall, W 1969, p. 228.
25. Kendall, W 1969. p. 216.
26. Kendall, W 1969. p. 233.
27. Gallacher, W 2017, p. 175.

53. The communism of the clans

1. Broom, J 1973, pp. 117-118.
2. 'Chronicles of the Quarters', *The Scottish Review*, vol. 42 issue 96, p. 448, viewed 30 December 2024, <https://archive.org/details/sim_scottish-review_winter-1919_42_96/page/448/mode/2up>
3. Witt, P 2013, 'Connections across the North Channel: Ruaraidh Erskine and Irish influence in Scottish discontent, 1906-1920'. *The Irish Story*, viewed 19 December 2014, <https://www.theirishstory.com/2013/04/17/connections-across-the-north-channel-ruaraidh-erskine-and-irish-influence-in-scottish-discontent-1906-1920/#.Vg6cO1MQGKJ>
4. Crowley, DW 1956, 'The Crofters' Party - 1885 to 1892: The first British independent common people's political party', *Scottish Historical Review*, vol. 35, viewed 8 January 2015, <http://www.caledonia.org.uk/land/documents/Crofters%27%20Party.pdf>
5. Cairns, G 2021, *No language! No nation!* Rymour Books, Perth, Scotland, p. 55.
6. Cairns, G 2021, p. 55.
7. Diack, W 1919, 'Scottish and Irish Labour Colleges', *The Scottish Review*, vol. 42 issue 96, p. 385, viewed 30 December 2024, <https://archive.org/details/sim_scottish-review_winter-1919_42_96/page/380/mode/2up>
8. Diack, W 1919, p. 390.
9. Cairns, G 2017, *The red and the green – a portrait of John Maclean*, Calton Books, Glasgow, p. 112.
10. Cairns, G 2017, p. 113.
11. Cairns, G 2021, p. 60.
12. Cairns, G 2017, p. 105.
13. 'Land League and Highland Raiders', *Aberdeen Journal*, 31 July 1920, p. 6.
14. 'The Rt. Hon. 1st Viscount Leverhulme - His Tenure and Legacy (1918-1923)', Stornoway Facilities - Isle of Lewis, Outer Hebrides, Scotland, viewed 2 February 2025, <https://stornowayfacilities.weebly.com/lord-leverhulmes-tenure-and-legacy-1918-1923.html>
15. 'Land seizures and the trade unions', *Glasgow Herald*, 9 August 1920, p. 5.
16. 'House rents strike', *Glasgow Herald*, 9 August 1920, p. 8.
17. McShane, H & Smith, J 1978, p. 118.
18. Maclean, J 1920, *All hail, the Scottish Communist Republic!* pamphlet, viewed 9 January 2025, <https://www.marxists.org/archive/maclean/works/1922-swr.htm>
19. Davidson, N 2001, 'Marx and Engels on the Scottish Highlands', *Science & Society*, vol. 65, no. 3, pp. 286-326.
20. 'The Lewis raids', *Glasgow Herald*, 23 August 1920, p. 8.
21. 'The Lewis raids', *Glasgow Herald*, 23 August 1920, p. 8.
22. 'The Lewis raids', *Glasgow Herald*, 23 August 1920, p. 8.
23. 'The Lewis raids', *Glasgow Herald*, 23 August 1920, p. 8.
24. Maclean, J 1920, 'The Highland land seizures', *Vanguard*, September, pp. 2-3, viewed 2 February 2025, <https://www.marxists.org/archive/maclean/works/1920-highland.htm>
25. 'The Lewis raids', *Glasgow Herald*, 23 August 1920, p. 8.
26. A letter to the Pope from Scottish barons dated 6 April 1320, that asserted Scotland's status as an independent, sovereign state and defended Scotland's right to use military action when unjustly attacked.

54. Poland

1. Labour and Russia Council of Action, 1920, *Report of the Council of Action, August to October 1920*, p. 1, Warwick Digital Collections, viewed 24 January 2025, <https://cdm21047.contentdm.oclc.org/digital/collection/russian/id/852>
2. 'Arms for Poland stopped', *Times*, 14 May 1920, p. 10.
3. Labour and Russia Council of Action, 1920, *Manifesto*, Warwick Digital Collections, viewed 1 February 2025, <https://cdm21047.contentdm.oclc.org/digital/collection/russian/id/3727>

4   Council of Action for Peace and Reconstruction (Great Britain), 1920, *Report of the Special Conference on Labour and the Russian-Polish War*, p. 16, Warwick Digital Collections, viewed 1 February 2025, <https://cdm21047.contentdm.oclc.org/digital/collection/russian/id/594>
5   Engelstein, L 2019, *Russia in flames: war, revolution, civil war 1914-1921*, Oxford University Press, p. 492.
6   Engelstein, L 2019, p. 494.
7   Engelstein, L 2019, p. 493.
8   Davies, N 1971, 'Lloyd George and Poland, 1919-20', *Journal of Contemporary History*, vol. 6, no. 3, p. 141, viewed 30 January 2025, <https://www.jstor.org/stable/259884>
9   Engelstein, L 2019, p. 496.
10 Engelstein, L 2019, p. 497.
11 Engelstein, L 2019, p. 498.
12 'Poland and her friends', *Times*, 4 August 1920, p. 11.
13 'Poland and her friends', *Times*, 4 August 1920.
14 Engelstein, L 2019, pp. 505-509.
15 Labour and Russia Council of Action, 1920, *Report of the Council of Action, August to October 1920*, p. 8.
16 Maclean, J 1920, *Russia's appeal to British workers/ preface by John Maclean*, Executive Committee of the Communist International, Glasgow, Warwick Digital Collections, viewed 24 January 2025, <https://wdc.contentdm.oclc.org/digital/collection/russian/id/1737>
17 'British Soviets: Organising the Communist Party', *Times*, 31 August 1920, p. 10.

55. A Scottish Communist Party

1   'Communist Unity Convention Delegates', viewed 24 January 2025, <https://www.marxists.org/history/international/comintern/sections/britain/subject/unity_convention/delegates.htm>
2   Kendall, W 1969, p. 259.
3   Gallacher, W 2017, p. 175.
4   McShane, H & Smith, J 1978, p. 119.
5   Kendall, W 1969, p. 260.
6   McShane, H & Smith, J 1978, p. 119.
7   Milton, N 1973, p. 255 (from 'The Irish Tragedy: up Scottish revolutionists', originally published in *Vanguard*, November 1920, pp. 5-6).
8   Kendall, W 1969, p. 261
9   Milton, N 1978, p. 224-225 (from 'A Scottish Communist Party', originally published in *Vanguard*, December 1920, p. 7).
10 Gallacher, W 1966, *The last memoirs of William Gallacher*, Lawrence & Wishart, London, p. 163.
11 Gallacher, W 1966, p. 164.
12 Gallacher, W 1966, p. 164.
13 The description of the meeting is taken from, 'Socialist hatred, Leaders kill Fusion, Angry Scenes, Maclean and Gallacher Duel', *Daily Record and Mail*, 27 December 1920; Gallacher, W 1966, pp. 165;
14 McShane, H & Smith, J 1978, p. 124.
15 Milton, N 1973, p. 257.
16 Maclean, J 1921, 'Open letter to Lenin', *Socialist*, 30 January, viewed 10 February 2025, <https://www.marxists.org/archive/maclean/works/1921-oll.htm>
17 Maclean, J 1921, 'Open letter to Lenin'.
18 Maclean, J 1921, 'Open letter to Lenin'.
19 Maclean, J 1921, 'Open letter to Lenin'.
20 Figes, O, 'Bolshevism in retreat', viewed 25 April 2025, <http://www.orlandofiges.info/section7_TheRussianCivilWar/BolshevisminRetreat.php>

56. The unemployed

1   Foster, J 2001, p. 425.
2   Foster, J 2001, p. 427.
3   Foster, J 2001, p. 428.
4   Taylor, AJP 1965, p. 145.
5   Foster, J 2001, p. 428.
6   Maclean, J 1920, 'The Unemployed', *Vanguard*, November, viewed 11 February 2025, <https://www.marxists.org/archive/maclean/works/1920-tun.htm>
7   Taylor, AJP 1965, p. 148, and Scottish Unemployed Workers' Network, 'History of unemployment', viewed 5 January 2025, <https://scottishunemployedworkers.net/history-of-unemployment/>
8   McShane, H & Smith, J 1978, p. 121.
9   Challinor, R, 1977, p. 264.
10 McShane, H & Smith, J 1978, p. 121.
11 Challinor, R, 1977, p. 265.

57. Decontrol

1   Arnot, RP 1953, p. 233.
2   Arnot, RP 1953, pp. 233-234.
3   Arnot, RP 1953, p. 236.
4   'Miners' strike threat', *Times*, 9 July 1920, p. 16.
5   Arnot, RP 1953, p. 239.
6   Arnot, RP 1953, p. 245.
7   Arnot, RP 1953, p. 251.
8   Arnot, RP 1953, pp. 253-254
9   Arnot, RP 1953, pp. 254-255.

10	Arnot, RP 1953, pp. 255-256.
11	Arnot, RP 1953, p. 259.
12	Arnot, RP 1953, p. 260.
13	Arnot, RP 1953, p. 262.
14	Arnot, RP 1953, p. 264.
15	Arnot, RP 1953, pp. 271-274.
16	The National Archives of the UK, Cabinet, 28 January 1921, CAB 23/24/5.
17	The National Archives of the UK, 'Position of the coal industry', Cabinet, 28 January 1921, CAB 24/118/92.
18	'Government and coal profits', Times, 3 February 1921, p. 12.
19	Cowan, T 2011, p. 320.
20	'Wage offers mean distress', Times, 4 April 1921, p. 15.
21	Renshaw, P 1971, 'Black Friday, 1921', History Today, vol. 21, iss. 6, June, viewed 18 February 2025, <https://www.historytoday.com/archive/black-friday-1921>

58. Black Friday

1	'Four days to think', Times, 9 April 1921, p. 8.
2	'The government denounced', Times, 12 April 1921, p. 10.
3	'The government denounced', Times, 12 April 1921.
4	'Conference break', Times, 13 April 1921, p. 10.
5	'New Alliance challenge', Times, 14 April 1921, p. 10.
6	'Labour rally to miners', Times, 15 April 1921, p. 10.
7	'What Mr Hodges said', Times, 16 April 1921, p. 8.
8	'What Mr Hodges said', Times, 16 April 1921.
9	'Commons to rescue', Times, 15 April 1921, p. 10.
10	Renshaw, P 1971.
11	'No Alliance strike', Times, 16 April 1921, p. 8.
12	No Alliance strike', Times, 16 April 1921.
13	Gould, G 1921, The lesson of Black Friday, The Labour Publishing Company and George Allen & Unwin, London, p. 14, viewed 15 February, 2025, <https://collections.swansea.ac.uk/s/black-friday-and-the-1921-lockout/page/blackfriday#?c=0&m=0&s=0&cv=0>

59. A state of emergency

1	The National Archives of the UK, Cabinet, 6 July 1920, CAB 24/108/78.
2	The National Archives of the UK, Cabinet, 4 August 1920, CAB 23/22/7.
3	'New emergency powers', Times, 5 April 1921, p. 10.
4	Miller, JW 1939, p. 1077.
5	Hansard HC Deb 06 April 1921 vol 140 cc297-372.
6	Hansard HC Deb 06 April 1921 vol 140 cc297-372.
7	'Sylvia Pankhurst charged', Times, 21 October 1920, p. 7; 'Sentence on Sylvia Pankhurst'. Times, 29 October 1920, p. 4; 'Sylvia Pankhurst's appeal', Times, 6 January 1921, p. 7.
8	'Our Bolsheviks: wild talk in Albert Hall', Times, 8 November 1920, p. 14.
9	'Mr Malone's appeal dismissed', Times, 18 January 1921, p. 12.
10	'Clyde Labour leader', Daily Record, 12 February 1921, p. 1; Gallacher, W 1978, pp. 176-178.
11	Ripley, BJ & McHugh, J 1989, p. 146.
12	'Scottish red leaders', Daily Record, 11 April 1921, p. 2.
13	'Scottish mine riots', Times, 6 April 1921, p. 10.
14	'More rioting in Scotland', Times, 7 April 1921, p. 10.
15	Milton, N 1973, p. 268.
16	'Three months for John Maclean and Alex Ross', Glasgow Herald, 18 May 1921, p. 10.
17	Milton, N 1973, pp. 268-269.
18	Hansard HC Deb 03 June 1921 vol 142 cc1403-4W.
19	Hansard HC Deb 02 June 1921 vol 142 cc1277-337.
20	'Fight for freedom of speech', Daily Herald, 3 June 1921, p. 1.
21	Milton, N 1973, p. 269.
22	Milton, N 1973, pp. 269-270.

60. More porridge

1	'Communists in prison', Daily Herald, 3 August 1921, p. 6; and 'Out of gaol's mouth', Daily Herald, 17 August 1921, p. 6.
2	Milton, N 1973, p. 270.
3	'A misguided man', Glasgow Herald, 27 October 1921, p. 11.
4	'Cardiff trades congress', Glasgow Herald, 6 September 1921, p. 7.
5	'Cardiff trades congress', Glasgow Herald, 6 September 1921, p. 7; Enemies of labour', Times, 6 September 1921, p. 8; 'Shirking workers', Daily Telegraph, 6 September, 1921, p. 9; 'Labour "Premier's" speech', Guardian, 6 September, 1921, p. 4.
6	McShane, H & Smith, J 1978, p. 132.
7	'John McLean [sic] arrested', Glasgow Herald, 21 September 1921, p. 7.

8 'John Maclean charged', *Daily Herald*, 22 September 1921, p. 5.
9 McShane H, & Smith J, 1978, p. 134.
10 'Sedition charge', *Daily Herald*, 24 September 1921, p. 2.
11 'Help! Help!! Help!!!', *Daily Herald*, 29 September 1921, p. 6.
12 'Maclean seriously ill', *Daily Herald*, 3 October 1921, p. 5; 'John Maclean, *Daily Herald*, 5 October 1921, p. 2; and 'John Maclean', *Daily Herald*, 11 October 1921, p. 5.
13 Description of the trial taken from 'John Maclean on trial', *Daily Herald*, 26 October 1921, p. 2; 'John Maclean sentenced', *Daily Record*, 26 October 1921, p. 9; and 'Seditious speeches', *Glasgow Herald*, 26 October 1921, p.12.
14 Description of the trial taken from 'Four months for Ross', *Daily Record*, 27 October 1921, p. 5; and 'A misguided man', *Glasgow Herald*, 27 October 1921, p.11.
15 McShane, H & Smith, J 1978, p. 134.
16 'Government of Glasgow', *Glasgow Herald*, 2 November 1921, p. 10.
17 Broom, J 1973, pp. 142-143.
18 'Begin at home', *Daily Herald*, 3 November 1921, p. 4.
19 'Release all the prisoners', *Daily Herald*, 28 December 1921, p. 1.

61. The Tramp Trust dissolve

1 McShane, H & Smith, J 1978, p. 135.
2 Milton, N 1973, p.273.
3 Broom, J 1973, pp. 144-145.
4 McNabb, J 1922, letter to Agnes Maclean, 26 August [letter], in John Maclean Papers, National Library of Scotland, Edinburgh.
5 Broom, J 1973, p. 145.
6 Broom, J 1973, pp. 145-146.
7 'bonny fechter'– fearless fighter (Scots).
8 Broom, J 1973, pp. 147-148. Though still living in Hawick, Agnes Maclean returned to Auldhouse Road periodically to make sure the house was in order while John was in prison.
9 McShane, H & Smith, J 1978, p. 136.
10 McShane, H & Smith, J 1978, p. 139.
11 McShane, H & Smith, J 1978, p. 140.

62. The Clydesiders triumphant

1 'Kinning Park Ward', *Glasgow Herald*, 2 November 1922, p. 3.
2 Milton, N 1973, p. 278.
3 Ripley, BJ & McHugh, J 1989, p. 150.
4 Clunie, J 1958, *The voice of labour: the autobiography of a house painter*, A Romanes, Dunfermline, Scotland, letter from John Maclean to James Clunie, 24 November 1922 [letter], pp. 87-88.
5 Downes, J 1973, 'Reminiscences of John Maclean', *Scottish Marxist*, no. 5, November, pp. 26-27.
6 Broom, J 1973, p. 150.
7 Broom, J 1973, p. 151.
8 Milton, N 1973, p. 280.
9 'Gorbals: four-part discord', *Glasgow Herald*, 9 November 1922, p. 11.
10 Middlemas, R 1965, *The Clydesiders*, Hutchinson, London, pp. 110-111.
11 'Street scenes', *Glasgow Herald*, 16 November 1922, p. 7.
12 'Street scenes', *Glasgow Herald*, 16 November 1922.
13 'Street scenes', *Glasgow Herald*, 16 November 1922.
14 'Glasgow's poll', *Glasgow Herald*, 16 November 1922, p. 7.
15 Bell, T 1944, pp. 151-152.
16 Taylor, AJP 1965, p.198.
17 Middlemas, R 1965, pp. 111-112.
18 'Glasgow Labour M.P.'s', *Glasgow Herald*, 20 November 1922, p. 11.
19 'ILP rejoicings', *Glasgow Herald*, 20 November 1922, pp. 11-12.
20 Milton, N 1973, p. 282; and 'Send-off scenes', *Glasgow Herald*, 20 November 1922, p. 12.
21 'Send-off scenes', *Glasgow Herald*, 20 November 1922, p. 12.

63. Oot and aboot

1 Clunie, J 1958, letter from John Maclean to James Clunie, 24 November 1922 [letter].
2 Clunie, J 1958, letter from John Maclean to James Clunie, 24 November 1922 [letter].
3 Clunie, J 1958, letter from John Maclean to James Clunie, 24 November 1922 [letter].
4 Clunie, J 1958, letter from John Maclean to James Clunie, 24 November 1922 [letter].
5 Milton, N 1973, p. 283.
6 'Association football', *Glasgow Herald*, 26 December 1922, p. 12.
7 'Scottish Labour College: series of lectures', *Wishaw Press*, 29 December 1922, p. 1.
8 Ripley, BJ & McHugh, J 1989, p. 151.
9 Milton, N 1973, p. 284.
10 'Glasgow unemployed', *Daily Record*, 8 January 1923, p. 2.
11 Milton, N 1973, p. 286.
12 Broom, J 1973, p. 156.
13 Clunie, J 1958, letter from John Maclean to James Clunie, 20 April 1923 [letter], p. 90.
14 Broom, J 1973, pp. 156-157.
15 Smyth, JJ 2003, 'Resisting Labour: Unionists, Liberals and Moderates in

Glasgow between the wars', *The Historical Journal*, 46, 2, pp. 375-401.
16 Clunie, J 1958, letter from John Maclean to James Clunie, 23 May 1923 [letter], p. 91.
17 Clunie, J 1958, letter from John Maclean to James Clunie, 4 June 1923 [letter], p. 92.
18 Clunie, J 1958, letter from John Maclean to James Clunie, 4 June 1923 [letter], p. 92.
19 Clunie, J 1958, letter from John Maclean to James Clunie, 4 June 1923 [letter], pp. 92-93.

64. *The Clydesiders in London*
1 Middlemas, R 1965, p. 127.
2 'The Clyde black squad', *Times*, 18 December 1922, p. 12.
3 Heath, S 2013, 'The historical context of rent control in the private rented sector', Social Policy Section, House of Commons Library, viewed 25 March 2025, <https://researchbriefings.files.parliament.uk/documents/SN06760/snsp-06747.pdf>
4 'Clyde rent strike', *Times*, 29 December 1922, p. 8.
5 Moorhouse, B, Wilson, M & Chamberlain, C 1972, 'Rent strikes - direct action and the working class', *Socialist Register 1972*, vol 9, pp. 133-156, viewed 25 March 2025, <https://socialistregister.com/index.php/srv/article/view/5309>
6 'Clyde rent strike', *Times*, 29 December 1922.
7 'House of Commons', *Times*, 23 February 1923, p. 6.
8 Hansard HC Deb 8 May 1923, vol. 163 cc2199-200.
9 Hansard HC Deb 8 May 1923, vol. 163 cc2200-222.
10 Hansard HC Deb 8 May 1923, vol. 163 cc2264-265.
11 Hansard HC Deb 8 May 1923, vol. 163 cc2288-290.
12 'Unemployment', *Glasgow Herald*, 2 March 1923, p. 11.
13 'Glasgow's school children', *Glasgow Herald*, 17 March 1923, p. 4.
14 'Seditious teaching bill', *Glasgow Herald*, 28 March 1923, p. 14
15 'Empire migration', *Times*, 20 March 1923, p. 9.
16 'No need for emigration', *Glasgow Herald*, 28 March 1923, p. 14.
17 'Government defeat', *Times*, 11 April 1923, p. 12.
18 'Uproar in the Commons', *Times*, 12 April 1923, p. 12.
19 'Parliament: the government defeat', *Times*, 13 April 1923, p. 7.
20 'May Day', *Glasgow Herald*, 2 May 1923, p. 11.

65. *Uproar in the House*
1 The Chairman of Ways and Means and the Deputy Chairman of Ways and Means were the Deputy Speakers of the House of Commons.
2 'Uproar in Commons', *Glasgow Herald*, 28 June 1923, p. 7.
3 'Disorderly scene', *Times*, 28 June 1923, p. 8+.
4 Middlemas, R 1965, p. 128, quoting Hansard HC Deb 27 June 1923 vol. 165 c2379 et seq.
5 'Mr Maxton's outburst', *Glasgow Herald*, 28 June 1923, p. 7.
6 'Disorderly scene', *Times*, 28 June 1923.
7 'The Speaker sent for', *Times*, 28 June 1923, p. 8+.
8 'Sir G Hamilton's apology', *Times*, 28 June 1923, p. 8+.
9 'Labour Party and disarmament,' *Times*, 29 June 1923, p. 16.
10 'Labour MPs and parliamentary "scenes"', *Glasgow Herald*, 4 July 1923, p. 9.
11 'No apology', *Glasgow Herald*, 9 July 1923, p. 10.
12 'No apology', *Glasgow Herald*, 9 July 1923.
13 Middlemas, R 1965, p. 130.
14 Middlemas, R 1965, p. 131.
15 'Problems for Mr Baldwin', *Times*, 30 July 1923, p. 10.
16 Middlemas, R 1965, p. 131.

66. *Reconciliation*
1 Ripley, BJ & McHugh, J 1989, p. 30.
2 Milton, N 1973, p. 290.
3 Clunie, J 1958, letter from John Maclean to James Clunie, 22 August 1923 [letter], pp. 97-98.
4 Maclean, J 1923, letter to Agnes Maclean, 28 August [letter], in Papers of John Maclean, NLS.
5 Maclean, A 1923, letter to John Maclean, 29 August [letter], in Papers of John Maclean, NLS.
6 Clunie, J 1958, letter from John Maclean to James Clunie, 13 June 1923 [letter], pp. 93-94.
7 Clunie, J 1958, letter from John Maclean to James Clunie, 13 June 1923 [letter].
8 Clunie, J 1958, letter from John Maclean to James Clunie, 23 July 1923 [letter], p. 96.
9 Clunie, J 1958, letter from John Maclean to James Clunie, 22 August 1923 [letter], pp. 97-98.

10. Clunie, J 1958, letter from John Maclean to James Clunie, 4 September 1923 [letter], pp. 98-99.
11. Maclean, J 1923, letter to Agnes Maclean, 30 September [letter], in Papers of John Maclean, NLS.
12. Maclean, A 1923, letter to John Maclean, 4 October [letter], in Papers of John Maclean, NLS.
13. Clunie, J 1958, letter from John Maclean to James Clunie, 5 October 1923 [letter], pp. 99-100.
14. Maclean, A 1923, letter to John Maclean, 15 October [letter], in Papers of John Maclean, NLS.
15. Maclean, A 1923, letter to John Maclean, 17 October [letter], in Papers of John Maclean, NLS.
16. Maclean, J 1923, letter to Agnes Maclean, 18 October [letter], in Papers of John Maclean, NLS.

67. *The final countdown*

1. 'Municipal elections', *Glasgow Herald*, 27 October 1923, p. 5.
2. 'Big stick in Poplar, By Sylvia Pankhurst, 1923', *Communist Left* 3, December 1990, viewed 29 March 2025, <https://intcp.org/en/texts/13131/big-stick-in-poplar-by-syborough in the lvia-pankhurst-1923/>
3. Clunie, J 1958, letter from John Maclean to James Clunie, 28 October 1923 [letter], p. 101.
4. 'Glasgow Labourists', *Glasgow Herald*, 25 October 1923, p. 10.
5. Maclean, J 1978, pp. 244-245.
6. Maclean, J 1923, letter to Agnes Maclean, 28 October [letter], in Papers of John Maclean, NLS.
7. Maclean, A 1923, letter to John Maclean, 1 November [letter], in Papers of John Maclean, NLS.
8. 'With the workers', *Daily Herald*, 2 November 1923, p. 6.
9. Maclean, J 1923, letter to Agnes Maclean, 4 November [letter], in Papers of John Maclean, NLS.
10. Maclean, A 1923, letter to John Maclean, 7 November [letter], in Papers of John Maclean, NLS.
11. 'Civic government', *Glasgow Herald*, 7 November 1923, p. 11-12.
12. Maclean, J 1923, letter to Agnes Maclean, 14 November [letter], in Papers of John Maclean, NLS.
13. Maclean, A 1923, letter to John Maclean, 14 November [letter], in Papers of John Maclean, NLS.
14. Milton, N 1973, p. 303.
15. Broom, J 1973, p. 148.
16. Maclean, J 1978, pp. 246-248.
17. Cairns, G 2017, p. 178.
18. 'Glasgow's choice', *Daily Record*, 27 November 1923, p. 10.
19. Broom, J 1973, p. 170.

68. *Tributes*

1. Cairns, G 2017,
2. 'Funeral of John Maclean', *Glasgow Herald*, 4 December 1923, p. 7.
3. In Papers of John Maclean, NLS.
4. Pankhurst, ES 1923, 'Obituary to John Maclean', *Workers' Dreadnought*, 8 December.
5. Lansbury, G 1923, 'The heart of a revolutionary', *Daily Herald*, 15 December.
6. Pitt, R 1996, *John Maclean and the CPGB*, 2nd edn, app 5, quoting *Workers Weekly*, 7 December 1923, viewed 1 April 2025, <https://www.whatnextjournal.org.uk/Pages/Pamph/Maclean.html#App5>
7. Pitt, R 1996, *John Maclean and the CPGB*, 2nd edn, app 5.
8. Gallacher, W 1924, 'John Maclean', *Communist International*, No.30, January, pp. 45-48, viewed 1 April 2025, <https://www.marxists.org/archive/gallacher/1924/ci/maclean.htm>
9. Aldred, GA 1940, *John Maclean*, Bakunin Press, Glasgow, pp. 49-50.

69. *Aftermath*

1. Cairns, G 2017, pp. 186-187.
2. Broom, J 1973, p. 12.
3. Broom, J 1973, p. 13.
4. Edwards, OD 1979, 'Foreword', *Homage to John Maclean*, eds Law, TS & Berwick, T, Edinburgh University Student Publications Board.
5. 'US protest law tracker', International Center for Not-for Profit Law, viewed 29 April 2025, <https://www.icnl.org/usprotestlawtracker/>
6. Lakhani, N 2025, 'US intensifies crackdown on peaceful protest under Trump', *Guardian*, 10 April.
7. Barnes, GN 1924, *From workshop to War Cabinet*, Herbert Jenkins, London, p.203.
8. Broom, J 1973, p. 148.

INDEX

A

Ablett, Noah, 13, 112, 113, 171, 434; Plebs League *See* Plebs League

Acts of Parliament (UK): *Redistribution of Seats Act 1885*, 10; *Third Reform Act 1884*, 10, 19; *Coal Mines (Minimum Wage) Act 1912*, 13, 14; Factory Acts, 19; Truck Acts (1831-1896), 22; *Increase of Rent and Mortgage Interest (War Restrictions) Act 1915*, 63, 374; *National Registration Act 1915*, 78; *Alien Restriction Act*, 110; *Trade Disputes Act*, 116, 121; *Increase of Rent and Mortgage Interest (Restrictions) Act 1920*, 177, 484; *Crofting Holdings (Scotland) Act 1885*, 405; *National Insurance Act 1911*, 429; *Poor Law (Scotland) Act 1845*, 429–30, 487–89; *Coal Mines Control Agreement (Confirmation) Act 1918*, 433; *Coal Mines (Emergency) Act 1920*, 433, 437; *Emergency Powers Act 1920*, 445, 522; *Poor Law Emergency Provisions (Scotland) Act 1921*, 487–88; *Empire Settlement Act 1922*, 490; *Public Order Act 2023*, 523; *Defence of the Realm Act 1914 See* Defence of the Realm Act 1914 (DORA); *Military Service Act 1916 See* Military Service Act (1916); *Munitions of War Act 1915 See* Munitions of War Act 1915

Adair (Admiral), 91

Addison, Dr Christopher, 103; dilution agreements, 124, 125, 126

Adler, Friedrich, 24, 244

Admiralty, 28, 34, 78, 151, 221, 369 *See also* First Lord of the Admiralty

Aisne, Battle of, 23, 167

Albion Motor Works, 60; strike (1916), 111; dilution agreement, 119, 125–26; dilution strike, 123, 128

Aldred, Guy, 520

Alexander, HW, 375

Alexander, Neil, 318, 320–22

Alien Restriction Act, 110

All-Russian Congress of Soviets (First), 190

All-Russian Congress of Soviets (Second): election of Bolshevik-dominated executive committee, 210; executive bypassed by Sovnarkom, 215

All-Russian Congress of Soviets (Third): Declaration of the Rights of the Working People, 217; John Maclean, honorary vice-president, 244

All-Russian Executive Committee of Soviets: endorsement of Directorate, 204

Allen, Clifford, 394

Allied intervention in Russia: Czechoslovakia, 264, 284, 367–68; Canada, 284, 330, 368; Japan, 284, 369, 377; America, 329, 331, 368; Italy, 330, 368; Lenin and Trotsky, 330; aims, 332; Baltic Sea, 364, 365; Caucasus, 364; North Russia, 364, 366–67, 371; Siberia, 364, 368–69; Ukraine and Crimea, 365; Romania, 368; Britain *See* British intervention in Russia

Allied Labour and Socialist Conference, 232

Amalgamated Society of Carpenters and Joiners, 58, 236

Amalgamated Society of Engineers (ASE): tuppence an hour strike, 26; influence of socialists, 27; lock-out, 27; Maclean-Fulton dispute, 47, 58; support for Maclean, 47, 58; James Brownlie (secretary), 93, 223; Lloyd George meeting, 115, 116, 117; meeting with employers, 116; Sam Bunton (district secretary), 116; Lang's, Johnstone strike, 117; Parkhead Forge strike (1916), 120–23; Glasgow District Committee, 128; Munitions of War Bill 1917 strike, 222–23; Man Power Bill, 231–32, 235, 239–41; George Barnes, 248; Clyde Workers' Committee, 304; 40-hour strike (1919), 307, 311; districts, 307; district secretary *See* Hopkins, Harry; secretary *See* Mann, Tom

  dilution, 120; strikes, 117, 121, 123–24, 128; deportation orders and protests, 122, 127–28, 172

Amalgamated Society of Toolmakers, 26

America, 523; Civil War (1860s), 15; Stockholm peace conference, 186, 192; World War I, 213, 228, 229, 265–66; intervention in Russia, 329, 331, 368 *See also* Wilson, Woodrow

Ammon, Charles, 169–70

'An Cuilithionn' (poem, 1939), 1

Anderson, Tom, 9, 302, 515; Maclean's funeral, 516

Anderson, William (Labour MP), 89, 104, 170, 172, 179

arbitration, 31, 32, 36, 125, 224, 434

armistice: Russia and Central Powers, 227; Allies and Austria-Hungary, 283; Allies and Germany, 283; Allies and Turkey, 283; Brest-Litovsk *See* Brest-Litovsk treaty

Arras, Battle of, 167

ASE *See* Amalgamated Society of Engineers (ASE)

Asquith, Herbert, 197; Prime Minister, 16, 31, 32, 33, 34, 61, 62, 78, 79, 87, 89, 166; Military Service Bill 1916, 86–87, 135; dilution (skilled labour), 116; resignation, 166; 1918 general election, 284; Polish-Soviet war, 415; 1922 general election, 472

Associated Ironmoulders' Union, 58

Aurora (Russian battle cruiser), 208–9, 210

Australasia: Scottish investment in, 16

Australia: representation on Imperial War Cabinet, 284; release of Maclean, 287–88; White Australia policy, 490–91; opposition to conscription, 500; crackdown on protests and dissent, 523

Austria-Hungary: war aims, 232; food shortages, 253, strikes and soviets, 256-257; armistice, 283; Emperor Karl I, 283 *See also* Brest Litovsk treaty

Axelrod, Pavel, 66

B

Baldwin, Stanley: Prime Minister, 499, 510, 512
Balfour, Arthur, 221, 288–89, 329; First Lord of the Admiralty, 79; opposition to conscription, 79–80; release of Maclean, 288
Balfour (Lord), 39
Balfour-Macassey Commission, 88
Balkan States, 74, 188
Banbury, Sir Frederick (Conservative MP), 495–99
Barbour, Mary, 42
Barnes, George (Labour MP), 110, 200, 248–49, 273–74, 279, 294, 296-97, 299, 523; release of Maclean, 285–89; 1918 general election, 300–301
Barr & Stroud: strike (1916), 111; dilution agreement, 119, 125–26
Barrow-in-Furness, 68, 165, 316
'Battle of George Square', 316–23; trial, 348
Beardmore, Sir William, 91, 111, 119, 120, 427
Beardmore's (company), 38, 57 109, 117, 124, 135; Dalmuir factory, 28, 60, 223, 303; Dalmuir strikes (1916), 111, 121, 123, 125, 128; East Hope shell factory strike (1917), 224–25; Parkhead Forge See Parkhead Forge
Beaverbrook (Lord), 33
Begg, Rev. Dr, 17
Belfast, 391 427; 44-hour week strike, 312, 316
Belgium, 158, 186, 232, 285, 296; Labour Party, 24; Inter-Allied Socialist Conference (1917), 200
Bell, Tom, 9, 11, 28, 50, 172, 224
Bell, Walter: *Worker* trial (1916) See *Worker* trial (1916)
Bevan, Aneurin (Nye), 325
Beveridge, William, 107, 108
Bevin, Ernest, 435, 444
Bills (UK Parliament): Munitions of War Bill 1915, 34–35; Increase Of Rent And Mortgage Interest (War Restrictions) Bill, 63; National Registration Bill, 78; Military Service Bill, 86, 133, 135; Munitions of War (Amendment) Bill, 88–89, 223; Munitions of War Bill 1917, 222–23; Man Power Bill, 232, 234–41, 245, 264, 266–67; Scottish Education Bill, 278; Coal Industry Commission Bill, 325; Police Bill, 354; Ministry of Mines Bill, 433; Coal Mines (Decontrol) Bill, 438; Emergency Powers Bill, 445; Rent Restrictions Bill, 484–87; Consolidated Fund Bill, 490; Seditious And Blasphemous Teaching To Children Bill, 490
Black Friday, 444
Blatchford, Robert, 8, 24, 162; *Merrie England* (essays), 7; *Clarion* See Clarion (socialist newspaper)
Board of Health (Scotland), 17, 494, 496
Bolshevik Military Organisation, 190, 193
Bolshevik Party/Bolsheviks: origin of name, 66; attitude to first provisional government, 184; opposition to second provisional government, 185, 194; Stockholm peace conference, 186–87, 192–93; opposition to defencism, 190; triumph among Petrograd proletariat, 191; insurrection deemed premature, 193; supporters called on to disperse, 194; control of Committee for Struggle against the Counterrevolution, 203; de facto leadership assumed by Trotsky, 204; control of Petrograd infrastructure, 208; order for insurrection, 208; on executive committee of Congress of Soviets, 210; leaders in hiding or in jail, 212; consolidation of power, 214; dissolution of constituent assembly, 217; leader See Lenin, Vladimir Ilyich; MRC See Military Revolutionary Committee (MRC)
Bonar Law, Andrew (Unionist Party), 196, 427; director Clydesdale Bank, 16; partner steel broking business, 16; British War Cabinet, 33, 166; letter from William Weir, 34; invitation to form government, 166; war aims, 197; Stockholm peace conference, 198, 200; loss of seat in 1906 election, 248; 1918 general election, 277, 284, 300; splinter of coalition government, 284; release of Maclean, 288–89; 40-hour strike (1919), 311–15, 317; adoption of Sankey report, 337; coal output, 352; coal price, 352; Chancellor of the Exchequer, 427; miners' claim, 434; party leader/ Prime Minister, 468; 1922 general election, 471; resignation as Prime Minister, 499; trade protection policy, 510
Borden, Sir Robert, 288
Borgbjerg, Frederik, 187
Branting, Hjalmar, 192
Bremner, Joseph, 134
Brest-Litovsk treaty, 226–30, 232, 234, 243, 250, 252–259; Allied governments, 226–27, 230, 265; armistice negotiations, 226–27; Trotsky, 227, 252–59; Joffe, 227–28, 252; Czernin, 228, 252, 257; Hoffmann, 228, 253–55, 258; Kuhlmann, von, 228, 252–54, 257–58; Lenin, 252, 255–56, 259; Ukraine, 254–55, 257–58, 259; Courland, 259; Estonia, 259, 413; Finland, 259; Lithuania, 259; Poland, 259
Bridges, RA, 124
Bridges Adams, Mary, 152, 153, 154–55, 158–59, 182
Britain See Great Britain
British Army (WWI), 55, 80–81, 349; British Expeditionary Force, 23, 81; casualties, 23; divisions, reserves, Territorials, 23; enlistment campaign, 24; conscription See conscription; recruitment See Derby scheme; *Military Service Act 1916*; Military Service Bill 1916
British intervention in Russia, 364–73; North Russia, 329–31, 367–68, 371–72; aims, 330; Transcaspian region, 331; Baltic Sea, 364–65, 370–71; Estonia, 365; Russian mutinies, 367–68; Caspian Sea, 368; Siberia, 368; Labour view of Russia policy, 369–70; state of war, 370–71; Caucasus, 371; cost, 371; withdrawal of support for Whites, 373
British Seafarer's Union, 134, 307
British Socialist Party (BSP), 24, 29, 41, 54, 82 98 182; Pollokshaws Branch, 58, 379; annual conferences, 64, 68, 153, 168, 249, 345, 374, 379–80; Glasgow District Committee, 64, 154; social patriots, 64, 74, 159, 172, 181, 344; views on WWI, 64; anti-war meeting, 71–72; *Vanguard* articles, 74–75; Executive

Committee, 75, 76; St Andrew's Halls meeting, 98, 100–102; provision for Maclean family, 131; response to Maclean DORA trial (1916), 153–54; petition for Maclean's release (1916), 154–55; Kentish Town Branch, 158; and internationalists, 159; Russian revolution (February 1917), 168; statement of war aims, 201; seizure of literature, 242–43; affiliation to Labour Party, 249–50, 348; 1918 general election, 300; Third International, 343, 346–47, 375; British communist party, 345, 347, 376, 379; 399–402; revolutionary identity, 346; Second International, 375; Tradeston Branch, 380–81, 387; Scotland, 382; Maclean's dissatisfaction with, 386; *Call See Call* (BSP journal); co-operative movement *See* co-operative movement; secretary *See* Inkpin, Albert; *Justice See Justice* (journal, SDF later BSP); Leeds Conference *See* Leeds Conference (1917)

British War Cabinet, 4, 33, 166, 180, 188, 191, 202, 220, 221 224, 231, 239, 246, 247, 248, 273, 279, 311, 317, 355, 365, 366, 367, 369-70; Stockholm peace treaty, 196–200; representation by imperial ministers, 284 *See also* Imperial War Cabinet

Brotherhood Church (London), 67; riot, 178–79, 182; workers' and soldiers' councils mtg, 178–79

BSP *See* British Socialist Party (BSP)

Buchanan, Sir George, 188, 221, 243–44

Buchanan, George (Labour MP), 469–71, 486, 489, 492, 496–98, 514; Maclean's funeral, 516

Building Trades and Electricians, 307

Bulgaria, 74, 227, 276

Bunton, Sam, 94, 95, 116, 178

Burnett, James, 6–7

Burns, Robert, 15, 18

Burton, John Hill, 151

Butcher, Sir John (Conservative MP), 490

C

Call (BSP journal), 173, 175, 177, 242, 385; articles by Maclean, 175–76, 177–78; articles by Chicherin, 182

Calton Jail: Macdougall, 152; Maclean, 152, 260

Campbell, JR, 430

Campbell, Allan (Chief Detective-Inspector), 143

Canada: Allied intervention in Russia, 284, 330, 368; representation on Imperial War Cabinet, 284; release of Maclean, 288

Cant, Ernie, 380–81

Capital (Marx), 7, 10, 406, 463

capitalist industrialism (Britain), 20; Truck Stores, 21–22; Truck Acts (1831-1896), 22

Carson, Sir Edward (Lord), 392, 461; against Irish Home Rule, 290–91; British War Cabinet *See* British War Cabinet

Cassells, John, 54, 55, 154

Cateau, Battle of, 23

Cathcart engineering works *See* G & J Weir (engineering company)

Cave, (Lord): release of Maclean, 287

Cecil, Robert (Lord), 188

Celtic communism, 407, 411

Central Labour College (CLC) (Oxford, later London), 113, 158, 251, 349, 478

Central Munitions Supply Committee, 37

Central Powers, 73, 182, 184, 186, 189, 213, 228, 229, 252, 253–58, 342; separate peace with Russia, 221; Supreme Command, 254, 258, 275–76; treaty with Ukraine, 254, 257, 258; Brest-Litovsk *See* Brest-Litovsk treaty

Chernov, Viktor, 193, 194

Chicherin, Georgy, 76, 158–62, 218–19, 242, 244, 258–59; Russian Political Prisoners and Exiles Relief Committee, 158–59; articles in *Nashe Slovo*, 159–62; arrest and jail, 182; articles in *Call*, 182; Foreign Minister, 258; Maclean, 182–83; Malone, 378; Polish-Soviet war, 415

child labour, 19

Christian Socialists, 12, 19; Sunday schools, 9

Churchill, Winston: First Lord of the Admiralty, 33, 34, 79; Minister of Munitions, 224; pro-war resolutions, 239; 1918 general election, 290; 40-hour strike (1919), 312–15; Prinkipo peace conference, 333; war against Russia, 333; strikes, 341; Russia policy, 366; North Russia, 367; 1922 general election, 472, 474

CI *See* Communist International

Cinderella Clubs, 8

Civic Press, 104, 111

Clarion Clubs, 21

Clarion Cycle Clubs, 8

Clarion Scouts, 8, 9, 83

Clarion (socialist newspaper), 7, 8

Clarion Youth Houses, 8

Clark, Tommy, 96, 109, 172, 223; deportation order, 172

CLC *See* Central Labour College (CLC) (Oxford, later London)

Clemenceau, Georges: Prinkipo peace conference, 333

CLP *See* Communist Labour Party (CLP)

Clunie, James, 430, 463–64, 476–78, 480–82, 501–3, 507–8

Clyde, James Avon: Lord Advocate, 246, 261–63, 290, 314; 1918 general election, 290; 40-hour strike (1919), 314

Clyde District Defence Committee, 270

Clyde District Shop Stewards Committee: working hours, 306

Clyde Workers' Committee (CWC), 58, 76, 84, 85, 91, 93, 95–96, 103, 107, 109, 111, 160; establishment, 40; expulsion of Petroff and Macdougall from meetings, 71–72; Lloyd George visit to Glasgow, 93-102; dilution (skilled labour), 96–97, 109, 116, 118–19, 121, 124–25, 126; reconstituted, 1917, 224; Man Power Bill, 236–38; alternative to official unions, 304; 30-hour week, 305; Chairman *See* Gallacher, Willie; members *See* Clark, Tommy; Kirkwood, David; MacManus, Arthur; Messer, James; Muir, John (Johnny); *Worker See Worker* (CWC newspaper)

Clydebank, 3, 4, 38, 60, 281, 387

Clydesider MPs, 473, 483; disorder in the House, 491–92, 494–99; suspensions, 495–99

co-operative movement, 24, 57, 70, 84, 114, 169, 201, 272, 362, 479; Maclean's involvement, 21, 22; Kinning Park Co-operative Guild, 42
coal: government control, 308–9, 326–27, 436–39; profits, 335–36, 432–33, 436–39, 441; price, 352, 432–33, 436–37; output, 352–54, 358, 434–38
Coal Commission *See* Coal Industry Commission
coal crisis (1921): lock-out of miners, 439; naval and military reserves, 440–41; negotiations, 440–41, 443; Triple Alliance strike threat, 440–44; Scottish disturbances, 449–50
Coal Industry Commission, 386, 434–35; Act to establish and powers, 325; Bill, 325; hearings, 335; membership, 335; nationalisation, 337, 351–57; first reports, 337–41; second reports, 351
coal miners, 40, 63; *The Miners Next Step* (pamphlet), 13, 113
strikes: nationwide (1912), 13, 14; Rhondda (1911), 13; Bowhill (1916), 73; Blantyre (1917), 177; Lanarkshire (1917), 177–78; Lanarkshire (1919), 310; Derbyshire (1919), 339; Sheffield (1919), 339; South Wales (1919), 339; Staffordshire (1919), 339; Lancashire (1919), 353; Sankey Award (1919), 353; Yorkshire (1919), 353–54, 356; Datum Line (1920), 436, 445; nationwide (1921), 439–44
Coal Mines (Decontrol) Bill, 438
Coal Mines (Minimum Wage) Act 1912, 13, 14
collective bargaining, 19
Comintern, manifesto, 344; British communist party, 375; questions from ILP and response, 394–97; Second World Congress, 397–402; 'Twenty-one points', affiliation conditions, 401; *See also* Third International: Maclean *See* Maclean, John (Comintern)
Committee for Struggle against the Counterrevolution *See* Petrograd Soviet
Commonweal (journal), 8
Commonwealth League, 409
Communist International (CI), 519
Communist International (journal), 519–20
Communist Labour Party (CLP), 419, 420, 429–30
Communist Party (British Section of the Third International), 401–2
Communist Party of Great Britain (CPGB), 9, 65, 66, 297, 380, 381, 400, 401, 407, 417, 418, 421, 422, 424, 479, 481, 502; Communist Unity conventions, 401, 418, 423; formation, 401, 423–24, 426; affiliation to Labour Party, 401–2, 418, 420; unemployed movement, 430, 466, 476, 502–3, 508–9; arrests of officials, 450; Harry McShane, 465–66; 1922 general election, 472; Scottish Labour College, 478; Kingston by-election, 481; Clydesider MPs, 483; tribute to Maclean, 518–19
Communist Party *See* Communist Party of Great Britain (CPGB)
Communist Sunday schools, 490
Communist Unity conventions, 401, 418, 423
Connelly, Thomas, 139
Connolly, James, 12, 24, 339, 404

conscientious objection, conscientious objectors, 175-176, 278, 287, 387; demonstration, 122–23
conscription, 78–87; *National Registration Act 1915*, 78; protection of skilled workers, 78; War Service badges/certificates, 78; overview, 78–87; opposition to, 79–80, 81–83, 85–86, 161; public protest, 82–84, 85–86; Derby scheme, 85, 86–87; Military Service Bill 1916, 86–87, 135; Maclean *See* Maclean, John (DORA trial, 1916) *See also Military Service Act 1916;*
Conservative Party, 490, 492, 495, 496
Consolidated Fund Bill, 490
Cook, AJ, 13, 434
Cook, Sir J, 287
Cossacks, 193, 194
Council of Action (Labour Party/TUC), 412–13, 416
Council of People's Commissars *See* Sovnarkom
Courland, 228, 254; Brest-Litovsk treaty, 259 *See also* Latvia
Coventry Ordnance Works, strikes (1916), 111, 123
CPGB *See* Communist Party of Great Britain (CPGB)
'craft conservatism', 26–27
Crawfurd, Helen, 42, 61, 220; Scottish Labour College, 114; Russia visit, 398, 402; municipal elections, 461; tribute to Maclean, 516
Crimea, 329, 416; Allied intervention in Russia, 365
crofters: Highland Land League, 404–5, 407, 409; 'Battle of the Braes', 405; Isle of Lewis, 407–10; land raids, Hebrides, 407–10; Lord Leverhulme, 408–10
Crossgates, Fife, 261–62
Curzon, George (Lord), 112–13, 287, 369, 397, 398, 414, 415; release of Maclean, 287
Curzon Line, 414–15
CWC *See* Clyde Workers' Committee (CWC)
Czechoslovakia: Allied intervention in Russia, 264, 284, 367–68
Czechoslovakian republic, 283
Czernin (Count), 228, 252, 257

D

Dalmuir, 60, 111, 128; Beardmore's factory *See* Beardmore's (company)
Dalrymple, James, 317
Dan (Fyodor), 158
Darkest Russia (supplement), 68
Das Kapital (Marx) *See Capital* (Marx)
de Leon, Daniel, 14, 85
de Valera, Eamon, 288–89
Debs, Eugene, 349, 377, 462
'Declaration of the Rights of the Working People', 217
Defence of the Realm Act 1914 (DORA), 89, 123, 173–74, 260, 267, 269, 270, 285, 314, 445; Maclean's trials *See* Maclean, John (DORA trial,1915); Maclean, John (DORA trial,1916); *Worker* trial (1916) *See Worker* trial (1916)
Defence of the Realm Regulations, 106, 165, 181, 242, 246, 247, 260, 443, 445, 448–49, 522; Regulation 42, 89, 108 110, 448, 449; seizure of *Forward* Jan 1916 issue, 104, 105, 106,

561

108; Regulation 27, 105, 107, 110, 446, 447; Regulation 51, 111; Regulation 14, 121; Maclean *See* Maclean, John (DORA trial, 1915); Maclean, John (DORA trial, 1916); *Worker* trial (1916) *See Worker* trial (1916)
Democratic Federation *See* Social Democratic Federation (SDF)
Denikin (General), 364, 371–72, 414
Denistoun, 51
Denmark: Social Democratic Party, 187
deportation: ASE, 122, 127–28, 172; dilution (skilled labour), 122, 123, 125, 126, 127–28, 154, 161, 172; *Forward* (journal), 122; Kirkwood, 122, 172; MacManus, 122, 172; Messer, 122, 172; MacDonald, 125; Clark, 172
Derby (Lord), 86
Derby scheme, 85, 86–87
Dickenson, Arthur, 335
dilution (skilled labour), 115–28; trade unions, 31, 32, 35, 36–38, 40; engineers/engineering, 36–38; munitions production (WWI), 36–38, 78, 90–93; shop stewards, 37, 91; Lloyd George, 90–93, 116; CWC position, 96–97, 109, 116, 118–19; Weir's dilution scheme, 115–16, 121–22, 123–24; Dilution Commission, 116–18, 119, 120, 121, 122, 124; strikes, 117, 120–28; women's wages, 117; ASE dilution agreement, 118–19, 125–26; Gallacher, 118–19, 125–26; deportation orders and protests, 122, 123, 125, 126, 127–28, 154, 161, 172; MacDonald, 125; Parkhead Forge *See* Parkhead Forge
District Trades Councils, 19
Dollan, Pat J, 114, 470; opposition to conscription, 85–86; 'Hands off Russia' campaign, 377
DORA *See Defence of the Realm Act 1914* (DORA)
Downes, James, 468–69
Duffes (Mr): Maclean DORA trial (1916), 132, 139; *Worker* trial (1916), 143, 144; Maxton/Macdougall/Smith DORA trial (1916), 149–50
Duncan, Charles (Labour MP), 165
Duncan Stewart & Co, 123
Dunlop, Thomas, 34
Dutt, Ranjani Palme, 483, 489;

E

East End, Glasgow, 489; rent increases/evictions, 43, 50–51
East End, London, 68, 507
Easter Rising/Uprising, Ireland (1916), 12, 404
Eastwood New Cemetery, 3, 516
Ebert, Friedrich, 283
Ebury, George, 348
Elliot, Walter (Unionist MP), 494, 497
Emergency Powers Act 1920, 445, 522
Emergency Powers Bill, 445
Emergency Powers Regulations, 445–48, 451–52
emigration, solution to unemployment, 490–91
Engineering Employers' Federation, 26
engineers/engineering, 15, 20, 30, 34, 36–37, 39, 40, 176, 178, 217, 221, 223, 224, 231, 303, 304, 312, 428; Amalgamated Society of Toolmakers, 26; Engineering Employers' Federation, 26; Steam Engine Makers'

Society, 26; lock-out (1897-98), 27; technical/organisational change, 27; introduction of Taylorism, 28; munitions production (WWI), 31–32; dilution (skilled labour), 36–38; Amalgamated Society of Engineers *See* Amalgamated Society of Engineers (ASE); G & J Weir *See* G & J Weir (engineering company)
Erskine of Marr, Ruaraidh, 403–7, 411; *Guth na Bliadhna* (journal), 403; *Scottish Review* (journal), 403, 406
Estonia, 228, 259, 268, 364–65, 378, 413, 414; Operation Albion, 204; Brest-Litovsk treaty, 259, 413; Red Army, 365
Ewart, Sir Spencer, 103, 247

F

Fabian Society, 20, 169, 200, 272
Factory Acts, 19
Fairchild, EC, 249–50; Leeds conference (1917), 169; 'Hands off Russia' campaign, 333; BSP revolutionary position, 347; resignation from BSP, 375; Maclean, 379
Fairfield's shipyards, 38–39, 57, 60, 63, 522; unfair dismissal dispute, 38–39
Federation of Engineering and Shipbuilding Trades, 91, 93, 127, 234, 236, 240
Federation of Engineers and Shipyard Workers, 91, 93
Fels, Joseph, 66
Ferguson, Robert Munro, See Novar (Lord)
Fineberg, Joseph, 178, 344
Finland: independence, 214, 413; loss by Russia, 259; civil war, 364
First Dáil (Irish Parliament), 390, 391
First International, 342, 344–45; establishment (1864), 341
First Lord of the Admiralty (UK): Churchill, Winston, 33, 79; Geddes, Sir Eric, 288, 301; Balfour, Arthur, 79
First Machine Gun Regiment (Petrograd), 193
First Sea Lord (Fisher), 33, 34
First World War *See* World War I
Fisher, 'Jackie' (Admiral, Lord), 33, 34
Foch (Marshal), 275–77
food: allowance (poorhouses), 18; unemployed unable to afford, 456–60; provision to school children, 488-90
food, prison, 152–53, 451, 457, 463, 465; Maclean's drugging claims, 164, 274, 298
food distribution, 222, 233, 264, 428–29, 446, 450; co-operative movement, 21–22, 417
food prices: Britain, 25, 127, 142, 222, 487; non-European producers, 428
food production: co-operative movement, 21–22; government department, 167, 178
food rationing: Russia, 167; Britain, 177, 233
food shortages: Britain, 164, 166–67, 246, 265–66, 354, 356, 509; Austria-Hungary, 253; Russia, 426
food supplies: to Britain, 79; from Ukraine, 253–54; to White Russians, 271, 369; to Europe, 285
Forbes (Detective-Inspector), 143

Ford, John, 261–62
Foreign Office, 182, 242, 397
40-hour strike (1919), 306–15, 316; 'Call to Arms to the Workers', 307; Lanarkshire miners, 310; Belfast, 316; Edinburgh, 316; 'Battle of George Square', 316–23
Forward (journal), 43, 54, 55, 99; suppression of, 103–8, 111, 161; article by Maclean, 113; deportation orders, 122; assistance to Gallacher, Muir and Bell W families, 131; editor *See* Johnston, Tom
Foster, Sir George, 284, 288
foundry workers, moulders, 224, 332
France: Napoleonic wars, 15; French Socialist Party, 74; restoration of occupied territory, 168, 197, 232–233; Stockholm peace conference, 186–87, 189, 192, 196–97, 200–201; Treaty of London, 1914, 226; war aims, 238; Allied intervention in Russia, 329–30, 365, 368
Fraser, MP (Mr): Maclean DORA trial (1916); *Worker* trial (1916), 143
Free Church Training College, 6
Free Speech Committee, 70, 82; DORA trial (Maclean, 1915), 48, 54; 'The Town Council Scandal', 83
freedom of speech, 55, 169–70, 253, 264, 267, 446, 452–53, 457, 462, 490, 522–23
French, Sir John (Lord), 32–33, 81
Fulton, Hugh *See* Maclean-Fulton dispute
Fulton, Reverend William, 464–65, 513, 523

G

G & J Weir (engineering company), 27–28, 34, 58, 98, 117, 122, 135, 136, 386; Cathcart works, 27, 60, 93, 111, 123, 133; introduction of Taylorism, 28; munitions production, 28–29; 'Responsibility and Duty' (pamphlet), 28–29; strike (1915), 29; visit of Lloyd George, 93; strike (1916), 111, 123–24
Gaelic language, 404, 405, 407, 521
Gallacher, Jean, 302, 320–22
Gallacher, Willie: rent strike, 60–61; attitude to the war, 71; *Revolt on the Clyde* (1936), 72, 93–94, 97, 521; free speech/no conscription trial, 85; Pankhurst description of, 85; *Worker* trial (1916) *See Worker* trial (1916)
 Comintern: Second World Congress, 397, 400, 402; '"Left-Wing" Communism in Great Britain', 399; interview with Lenin, 402
 CPGB: '"Left-Wing" Communism in Great Britain', 399; affiliation to Labour Party, 400, 402, 418; one British Communist party, 402, 418–19; *Worker* group, 429–30; 1922 general election, 472
 CWC: Fairfield's strike, 28–39; Clyde Labour Withholding Committee, 29; introductory leaflet, 40; Kirkwood, 50; Petroff, 71–72; dilution (skilled) labour, 72, 93–102, 118–19, 125–28, 304; Lloyd George (Glasgow), 93–98, 174; possible deportee, 109; meeting with Addison, 125–27; chairman of reconstituted CWC, 224, 296; support for foundry workers' strike, 224; Man Power Bill, 236–38, 246; *Worker*, arrest and trial *See Worker* trial (1916)
 40-hour strike (1919): 'Battle of George Square', 317–18, 320–22; trial, 348; welcome back meeting, 349
 Maclean, and: economics class, 12; criticism by Maclean, 71, 419–25, 469, 471; call for Maclean's release (1917), 165; welcome back for Maclean, 175; Maclean's campaigns (1917-18), 245; Maclean's election campaign (1918), 273, 279, 292–93, 296–98; Rothesay holiday, 302; criticism of Maclean, 421–23; tribute to Maclean, 519–20
 shop stewards' movement: National Administrative Council, 223; arrest and trial, 448, 449
 workers' and soldiers' councils: Leeds Conference, 171–72; Glasgow, 181
 workplaces: Albion Motor Works, 60, 119, 125; Beardmore's, Dalmuir, 223
Gallipoli, Battle of, 51, 78
Gardner, James, 224
Gardner (Mr), 61, 62
Gaughan, Dick, 3, 4; *No More Forever* (record), 3; 'The John Maclean March' (song), 3–5, 521
Geddes, Alex, 418
Geddes, Sir Auckland, 234, 237–38, 246, 264, 352, 354–55, 427
Geddes, Sir Eric, 427; release of Maclean, 288; 1918 general election, 301; 40-hour strike (1919), 312–15
Gellrich, Irma *See* Petroff, Irma
George, David Lloyd *See* Lloyd George, David
George V, King: Paris visit, 283
German High Command, 254, 258; Headquarters East (Brest-Litovsk), 226
Germany: Social Democratic Party, 24, 186, 283; German Democratic Party, 74; Spartacists, 186, 327; peace proposals, 196; soviets, 256–57; German republic, 283; WWI *See* World War I
Gladstone, William, 10, 27, 317
Glasgow Anarchist Group, 520
Glasgow and West of Scotland Armaments Committee, 34
Glasgow Central Socialist Sunday School, 9
Glasgow District Committee (BSP), 64; launch of *Vanguard See Vanguard*
Glasgow Gorbals (UK Parliamentary constituency), 249; Barnes, 249, 273–74, 279, 286, 296, 299–300; Maclean, 249, 273, 279, 292–300, 467–77, 510–15; 1918 general election, 273, 279, 292–300; 1922 general election, 467–75; Buchanan, 469–71; 1923 general election, 510–15
Glasgow Green, 5, 122, 127, 149, 168, 224, 271–72, 322, 349, 385, 408, 428, 454, 459, 478, 493; speeches by John Maclean, 111, 133, 349, 504
Glasgow Health Board, 499
Glasgow Labour Party Housing Association, 408
Glasgow Labour Party Housing Committee, 41, 42, 43

Glasgow Sheriff Court, 54, 61
Glasgow Town Council, 44, 52, 82-83, 172, 321, 428, 458, 468, 482, 506
Glasgow Trades and Labour Council, 475; 481; working hours, 306–7; 'Hands off Russia' campaign, 377; unemployment meeting, 507, 508
Glasgow Trades Council, 41, 54, 114, 134, 164, 182, 249; president *See* Shanks, George; chairman *See* Shinwell, Emmanuel
Glasgow Women's Housing Association, 41, 42
Glass, H, 124
Glee Clubs, 8
Golos (newspaper), 157
Goodbye to All That (Graves), 81
Gorky, Maxim, 184
Gosling, Harry, 434–35, 454
Govan, 35, 42–44, 53, 61, 63, 71, 83, 218, 456–57, 475, 511, 513, 522
Govan and District United Trades Council *See* Govan Trades Council
Govan Cross Picture Palace, 480–81, 500
Govan Labour Representation Committee, 59
Govan Parish Council, 430, 456
Govan Parish School Board *See* Govan School Board
Govan School Board, 45–46, 48, 57, 58, 61, 63, 82, 109, 135, 373; Maclean application, 374
Govan Trades Council, 38, 47, 54, 58, 59, 82–83
Govanhill Socialist Sunday School, 58
Graves, Robert, 81
Great Britain: WWI aims, 200–201, 232, 236, 239, 265–66; Treaty of London, 1914, 226; peace celebrations, 354; post-war boom, 387, 427–28, 429, 438; post-industrial economy, 522; army *See* British Army (WWI); intervention in Russia *See* British intervention in Russia
Great War *See* World War I
Greece, 51, 200, 276
Greenock District Committee, 26
Groom, Tom, 8
Gullard, John, 34
Guth na Bliadhna (journal), 403

H

Haggerty, James, 122
Haig, Douglas (General), 81, 231
Halliday, Thomas, 139
Hamilton, James, 480, 500
Hamilton, Sir George (Conservative MP), 496–97
'Hands off Russia' campaign, 331, 353, 364, 381; Pankhurst, 332; Maclean, 332–33, 377–79, 381; Fairchild, 333; Lansbury, 333; Dollan, 377; Glasgow Trades and Labour Council, 377; Malone, 378–79; Polish-Soviet war, 412
Harbour of Refuge (National), 151, 152
Hardie, George (Labour MP), 471
Hartshorn, Vernon, 354, 433–34; nationalisation of mines, 357–58
heavy industry (Scotland), 15–17 387; iron and steel, 15, 16, 176, 305; engineering *See* engineers/engineering *See also* Parkhead Forge: shipbuilding *See* shipbuilding

Henderson, Arthur: chairman of the Parliamentary Labour Party, 37, 91, 202; Lloyd George visit to Glasgow, 37, 91–102; opposition to conscription, 80; Kirkwood, 93; *Munitions Act of War Act 1915*, 93; appeal to Glasgow union delegates, 94; meeting with CWC, 98–102; Stockholm peace conference, 188, 191–93, 196–200; in Petrograd, 188–90, 191; return from Stockholm, 196; resignation from War Cabinet, 200; changes to Labour Party initiated, 202; Labour Party constitution, 202, 272; partnership with Ramsay MacDonald, 202; secretary of the Labour Party, 219, 278; Chicherin, 221; 1918 general election, 272–73; Comintern opinion of, 395
Henderson, Hamish: 'The John Maclean March' (song), 3–5, 281, 521, 522; 'The Freedom Come-All-Ye', 522
Henderson, Thomas (Labour MP), 471, 474; Maclean's funeral, 516
Herald League, 82, 155
High Court of Justiciary, 77, 110, 131, 132, 141, 260, 348; Lord Justice General *See* Strathclyde (Lord)
Highland Clearances, 10, 404, 405
Highland Land League, 404–5, 407, 409
Hindenburg, Paul von (Field Marshal), 275–77
Hird, Denis, 113
Hitman, Thomas, 482, 511
Hobsbawm, Eric, 15
Hodges, Frank, 437, 438, 442–443; Coal Industry Commission hearings, 335; direct action, 361
Hodgson, JF, 376
Hoffmann, Max (Major-General), 228, 253–55, 258
Hogge, James (Liberal MP), 110
Höglund (Zeth), 162, 163
Home Office, 34, 70, 247, 445
Hood, Andrew, 53
Hopkins, Harry, 38, 47, 57, 58, 85, 168, 311; opposition to conscription, 85–86; Maclean release committee, 168; 40-hour strike (1919), 311
Horne, Sir Robert, 437, 446; miners' claim, 324
House Letting Act *See* Increase of Rent and Mortgage Interest (War Restrictions) Act 1915
Hughes, Billy, 287–88
Hungarian republic, 283
hunger strike, 4, 273–74, 450, 456, 457, 461
Hunter (Lord), 53
Huysmans, Camille, 186, 192, 193, 250–51
Hyndman, Henry, 8, 10, 12, 21, 24, 64, 75, 153, 162, 163, 380, 385; resignation as chairman of BSP, 21 *See also Justice* (journal, SDF later BSP)

I

ILP *See* Independent Labour Party (ILP)
Imperial War Cabinet, 283-289, 290
Increase of Rent and Mortgage Interest (War Restrictions) Act 1915, 63, 374
Increase Of Rent And Mortgage Interest (War Restrictions) Bill, 63
Independent Labour Party (ILP), 8, 12, 21, 29, 47, 50, 54, 57, 58, 82, 113, 161, 162, 374, 386–87,

394, 418, 424, 498, 510, 512; establishment (1893), 20; Glasgow Women's Housing Association, 41, 42; anti-war meeting, 71–72; February 1917 Russian revolution, 168; statement of war aims, 201; 1918 general election, 300; working hours, 304; Allied intervention in Russia, 331; Left Wing, 394, 396, 402; National Administrative Council, 394; questions to Comintern and response, 394–97; 1922 general election, 470–75; Leeds Conference *See* Leeds Conference (1917); chairman Scottish ILP *See* Maxton, James; John Wheatley *See* Wheatley, John
Industrial Revolution, 15
Industrial Workers of the World, 14, 307, 342, 343
Inkpin, Albert, 155, 380, 450
Inter-Allied Socialist Conference (1917), 200–201, 232
International Socialist Bureau (ISB), 73, 75, 76, 242, 250; Stockholm peace conference, 168, 186–87; United Socialist Council, 168–69
International Socialist Conference (1912), 24, 250
internationalist/internationalism, 4, 9, 64, 71, 157, 158, 161; BSP, 159 *See also* Zimmerwald movement
IRA *See* Irish Republican Army (IRA)
Irish Home Rule, 10, 291, 390, 391
Irish Parliament *See* First Dáil
Irish Republican Army (IRA), 391
Irish Trades Union Congress, 332
Irish War of Independence, 390–92; Black and Tans, 392
Ironside (General), 367
ISB *See* International Socialist Bureau (ISB)
Iskra (newspaper), 65–66
Italy: Italian Socialist Party, 74; Stockholm peace conference, 186, 192, 200; restoration of occupied territory, 188; war aims, 238; Macedonian Front, 1918, 276; Allied intervention in Russia, 330, 368; fascists, 427

J

J Lang & Sons, Johnstone, 36–37, 117
Janin, Pierre (General), 368
Japan: forthcoming war with America, 268; intervention in Russia, 284, 369, 377; spread of class war to, 377
Jaurès, Jean, 24
Jeff, Andrew, 42
Jeff, Mary, 42
Joffe, Adolf, 227–28, 252
John Brown (company): strike (1916), 111
Johnston, Tom, 17–18, 19, 21, 22, 106, 108, 175, 404, 472; editor of *Forward See Forward* (journal)
Johnstone, Jimmy, 292
Justice (journal, SDF later BSP), 24, 75, 76, 112, 153, 159, 407; control by Hyndman, 7–8, 21, 64, 74, 385; articles by Maclean, 22, 41, 76, 112; RSDLP congress (1907), 66; articles by Petroff, 68, 76; criticism of Petroff, 75–76

K

Kadet Party (Russia), 215
Kamenev, Lev, 253

Karl I, Emperor (Austria-Hungary), 283
Keir Hardie, James, 19–20, 474, 474
Kennedy, G, 124
Kerensky, Alexander: Minister for War, 185; sending of war aims urged, 185; Henderson meeting, 189; defencism policy approved, 190; appointment of Kornilov as commander-in-chief, 195; Prime Minister, 195; creation of Directorate, 203; formation of third provisional government, 204; deteriorating position, 206; assault on Bolsheviks ordered, 207; MRC ordered to be liquidated, 207; Cossacks called on to save government, 208; departure from Winter Palace, 209; at British Labour Party conference, 1918, 273
Keynes, John Maynard, 300–301
King, Joseph (Liberal MP), 173, 330
Kinning Park Co-operative Guild, 42
Kirkwood, David, 50–51, 52, 109, 118, 220, 223, 279, 404, 472, 487; Pankhurst description of, 84–85; Lloyd George visit to Glasgow, 91–93, 96, 97, 100, 120; dilution (skilled labour), 118, 119–20, 124; *My Life of Revolt*, 119; deportation order, 122, 172; 'Battle of George Square', 318, 320, 322
Kitchener (Lord), 23, 24, 31, 32, 78, 166
Kolchack (Admiral), 364, 367, 369, 371
Kornilov (General), 195, 203
Krupskaya, Nadezhda, 65, 398
Kuhlmann, Richard von (Baron), 228, 252–54, 257–58

L

'La Marseillaise' (song), 24
'labour aristocracy', 26–27
Labour Party (Britain), 20, 24, 37, 41, 186, 188, 196, 200–202, 250, 394, 416, 514; Parliamentary Labour Party, 37, 91, 248, 442, 444, 472, 497; Stockholm peace conference, 186, 199–200; National Executive Committee, 196, 273, 279, 442, 444; international socialist policy, 201; statement of war aims, 201; *Labour and the New Social Order*, 202, 272; new platform and expanded membership, 202; new constitution (1918), 272; end of electoral truce, 272–73; decision to leave coalition, 278; resolution on release of Maclean (1918), 278; 1918 general election, 284, 299–300; 1922 general election, 472
Labour Representation Committee, 20, 59, 249 *See also* Labour Party (Britain)
Labour Withholding Committee (Clyde), 29, 38, 40, 144–45
Laird, Mary Burns, 42
Lamb, John: 40-hour strike (1919), 314; 'Battle of George Square', 317
Lambhill Street School, 45, 47, 49
Lanarkshire miners, 13–14, 63, 73, 176–78, 218, 246–48, 305, 309–11, 316, 332, 339, 374, 387, 417, 449–50, 453, 478
Lanarkshire Miners' Reform Committee (LMRC), 177–78, 353; Maclean meeting, 309; 40-hour strike (1919), 310
Lanarkshire Miners' Union: strike 1917, 177–78

Lang's, Johnstone *See* J Lang & Sons, Johnstone
Langside Halls, 47, 48, 49, 54, 55, 64
Lansbury, George, 507–8, 510; opposition to conscription, 82, 83; clemency for Maclean, 154–55, 168, 173; 'Hands off Russia' campaign, 333; tribute to Maclean, 517–18
Larkin, Jim, 377
Latvia, 66, 214, 259, 365, 413–14; independence, 214; Riga, 254–55, 257; Red Army, 365 *See also* Courland
Lawson, William, 236–37
Lee, HW, 24
Lee, Rev. Richard, 516
Lee (Sheriff), 54, 55, 56, 61, 62, 465
Leeds Conference (1917), 168–72; February 1917 Russian revolution, 169; war aims/peace policy (Russia), 169; civil liberties, 169–70; establishment of district councils *See* workers' and soldiers' councils (Britain)
Left Social Revolutionaries: join Sovnarkom, 216; agree with Bolsheviks to dissolve constituent assembly, 217 *See also* Social Revolutionaries
"*Left-Wing*" *Communism: an infantile disorder* (Lenin), 399
Leinster (Irish ship), 276–77
Lenin, Vladimir Ilyich, 5, 24, 181; *What is to be done?* (pamphlet), 65; in London, 65–66; differences with Martov on RSDLP, 66, 67; Trotsky, 157; praise for Maclean, 162–63; reaction to February 1917 Russian revolution, 167; return to Russia, 167, 184; opposition to peace conference, 187, 192–93; attitude to war, 191; rumour of being a German spy, 194; in hiding, 195, 204; call for Bolsheviks to take power, 204–6; taking of Winter Palace, 208; proclamation announcing Soviet government, 212; 'The decree on peace', 212; 'Declaration of the Rights of the Working People', 217; praised by Maclean, 220, 403, 465; separate peace with Central Powers, 221; Third All-Russian Congress of Soviets, 244; Brest-Litovsk treaty, 252, 255–56, 259; British and American imperialism, 284; Allied intervention in Russia, 330; invitation to first congress of Third International, 343; Estonia, 365; ILP questions, 394; Helen Crawfurd, 398; "*Left-Wing*" *Communism: an infantile disorder*, 399; British communist party, 399–400, 402, 419–20; Gallacher, 402, 419–20, 425; Soviet-led governments in border states, 413; Polish-Soviet war, 415; Maclean's disagreement on British communist party, 419–20, 423–25; invitation to Maclean, 420–21; Maclean's 'Open letter to Lenin', 423–26; peasant wars and strikes, 426
Leverhulme (Lord), 408–10
Lewis, Isle of, 407–10
Liberal government (1915), fall of, 33, 34
Liberal Party, 9–10, 33, 167, 284, 301, 405; 1918 general election, 301
Liberty (journal), 407
Liebknecht, Karl, 5, 24, 129, 162, 163, 244, 302, 345, 395; Third International, 345
Lithgow, James, 427

Lithuania, 214, 228, 254–55, 365, 413–14; independence, 214; Brest-Litovsk treaty, 259; Red Army, 365
Litvinov, Maxim, 66, 242, 243, 244, 245, 247, 248, 270, 378; plenipotentiary in Britain, 242, 243, 244; at Labour conference, 1919, 243–44; *charge d'affairs* in Britain, 245, 247, 248, 270
Livonia, 228
Lloyd George, David, 37–38, 39, 52, 62, 89–91, 104, 133, 160, 172; munitions supply, 31, 33–34, 35; Cabinet shell committee, 32; Minister of Munitions, 33; dilution (skilled labour), 90–93, 116, 121, 125–26, 127; visit to Newcastle, 91, 93; Glasgow visit, 91–102, 120, 144, 161, 172; meeting with CWC, 95-98; suppression of *Forward*, 103, 104, 106, 107–8; meeting with ASE, 115, 116, 117; Minister of War, 166; 1922 general election, 472; War Cabinet *See* British War Cabinet; conscription *See* conscription
  Prime Minister: appointment as, 166–67; freedom of the city (Glasgow), 172, 174; release of Maclean, 174, 286–89; Allied war conference, 196; Stockholm peace conference, 197–98; war aims, 232; 1918 general election, 284, 298, 300–301; miners' claims, 324, 435–36, 443; Triple Alliance, 326; war against Russia, 333; nationalisation of mines, 357, 362; Russia policy, 366, 373; Polish-Soviet war, 414–16; Proclamation mobilising reserves, 440; Unionist dissatisfaction, 467–68; resignation as Prime Minister, 468
lock-outs, 19, 22, 27, 439, 440, 444, 445, 449, 453, 508; engineers (1897-98), 27; Treasury Agreement (WWI), 31–32, 35, 223; WWI regulations *See Munitions of War Act 1915*; Munitions of War Bill 1915
Long, Walter, 288–89
Loos, Battle of, 80–81
Lord Advocate (Scotland): Munro, Robert, 52, 104, 110, 111, 132, 143, 165; Clyde, James Avon, 246, 261, 290, 314
Lorne Street School, 47, 49, 60–61
Luch (newspaper), 68
Ludendorff, Erich (General), 275–77
Luxemburg, Rosa, 24, 66, 302, 344, 345, 395
Lvov, Prince, 195

M

Macassey, Lynden, 39
MacDiarmid, Hugh, 521
MacDonald, Angus (Highland Land League), 404, 409
MacDonald, James Ramsay (Labour MP): RSDLP 1907 congress, 67; dilution agreements and deportations, 125; Gallacher, 125; Leeds Conference, 169, 172; Glasgow workers' and soldiers' council, 180–81; workers' and soldiers' councils, 181; discussion between British, French and Russian socialists, 197; German peace proposals, 197; partnership with Arthur Henderson, 202; war aims, 232; Maclean's appointment as Soviet consul, 245;

request to transfer Maclean, 274; 1918 general election, 300; Sankey report, 349; Comintern opinion of, 395; Maclean opinion of, 424; 1922 general election, 471; Rents Restriction Bill, 485; disorder in the House, 492; Maxton, 495; suspension of Clyde MPs, 497–99

Macdougall, James, 338, 352, 419, 449, 453; classes for miners, 13, 218; miners' strike (1912, UK), 14; Bath St meetings, 25, 54–55; Labour Withholding Committee, 38; Maclean's 1915 trial, 54–55; rent strike, 61; expelled from CWC meetings, 71–72; Peter Petroff at CWC meeting, 71–72; defence of Maclean, 81, 82; opposition to conscription, 81–82; government campaign against Maclean, 82; Scottish Labour College, 114, 453; conscientious objection, 123, 176; arrests, 123, 456; sedition trial, 149–50; prison sentences, 149, 152, 457; release demanded by BSP, 154; coverage of trial in *Nashe Slovo*, 161; release from prison, 165; miners' reform movement, 176, 339, 353, 386; work of national importance, 176; speeches on man power, 246; 1918 general election, 300; Lancashire Miners' Reform Committee, 353; Tramp Trust Unlimited, 387, 449, 465; Scottish Communist Party, 418–19, 421–23; Tramp Trust meetings for Lanarkshire miners, 449; Lanarkshire coalfields *See* Lanarkshire Miners' Reform Committee; sedition trial *See* Maxton/Macdougall/Smith DORA trial (1916)

Macfarlane, James (Moderate), 467

Macgregor, Tom, 480

Mackenzie, Alastair, 316–17, 320

MacLaine, William, 349

Maclean, Agnes (wife), 22, 110, 131, 453, 464–65; marriage to Maclean, 12; Maclean in prison, 152, 154, 155, 164, 274–75; Hastings holiday, 175; Rothesay holiday, 302; Maclean's political activity, 374–75; separation from Maclean, 375; reconciliation with Maclean, 500–506, 509–13, 515

Maclean, Anne (mother), 5, 6, 21

Maclean, Daniel (brother), 5, 6

Maclean, Daniel (father), 5, 6, 21

Maclean, Elizabeth (Lizzie, sister), 5, 131, 375, 501, 503, 513

Maclean, Jean (daughter), 22, 131, 175, 375, 477, 500, 505, 513

Maclean, John: opposition to WWI, 4, 24–25, 64–65, 71; birth (1879), 5; descriptions of, 6–7, 12–13, 84, 382, 464, 523; joins SDF, 11, 12; co-operative movement, 21, 22; rental increases/evictions, 44, 49, 61, 62; partnership with Petroff, 64, 68, 70–71, 425; opposition to conscription, 82–83, 85–86; socialist hero, 162–63; Hastings holiday, 175–76; workers' and soldiers' councils, 178, 180; Chicherin, 182–83; Inter-Allied Socialist Conference (1917), 201; Third All-Russian Congress of Soviets, 244; 1918 election campaign, 294–99; Rothesay holiday, 302; Coal Industry Commission, 327; 'Hands off Russia' campaign, 332–33, 377–79, 381; Sankey report, 340; Third International, 343; BSP revolutionary position, 347; May Day meetings 1919, 348; Dublin, 349, 374; second anniversary of Russian Revolution, 376; Malone, 378–79; BSP, 379, 380; Rothstein, 381; *Socialist*, 423, 431, 449, 451, 476; witness for McShane, 454; Pankhurst, 509, 510; death and tributes, 515, 516–20; biographies, 521; *Homage to John Maclean*, songs and poems, 521; journal articles *See Call* (BSP journal); *Forward* (journal); *Justice* (journal, SDF later BSP); *Socialist (journal); Vanguard* (journal); Free Speech Committee *See* Free Speech Committee; Gallacher *See* Gallacher, Willie (Maclean); Agnes Maclean *See* Maclean, Agnes (wife) dispute with Fulton *See* Maclean-Fulton dispute

anniversaries: 25th, Memorial meeting, 521; 50th, cairn in Pollokshaws, 521

Bath St meetings, 25, 71, 110, 218, 220, 386; DORA trial (1915) *See* Maclean, John (DORA trial, 1915)

career: Strathbungo School (asst master), 6; University of Glasgow MA, 6–7; lecturer in economics (SDF), 12–13, 84, 113, 159–60, 176, 263, 305, 349, 477; Lambhill Street School, 45; applications for teaching position, 476, 501, 510

Comintern: Scottish ILP, 394; passport, 397–98; Second World Congress, 397–98; 'Open letter to Lenin', 423–26

DORA trial, 1915, 110–11, 161; Langside Halls meeting, 47–49, 54–55, 64; Free Speech Committee, 48, 54; Bath St meetings, 48–49, 54–55, 57, 71; conviction and sentence, 56, 58, 63, 139

DORA trial, 1916, 4, 109–11, 131–39, 150, 161, 173–74; charge, 132–33; witnesses, 134; cross-examination, 135–37; summation, 138–39; conviction and sentence, 139; 'Red Flag' disturbance, 139–40; protests at sentence, 154–55; prison *See* Calton Jail; Peterhead Prison

economics classes/lectures, 64, 84, 113, 159-160, 176, 218, 245, 263, 349, 305, 387, 477–78

education: Free Church Training College, 6; Polmadie School, 6; Queen's Park School, 6; University of Glasgow, 6–7

election addresses: 1918 general election, Glasgow Gorbals, 296–97; Kinning Park, 1921, 456; 1922 general election, Glasgow Gorbals, 469; Glasgow 30th Ward, 1923, 479; Kinning Park, 1923, 509; 1923 general election, Glasgow Gorbals, 513–15

funeral, 516–20; Eastwood New Cemetery, 3, 516; Buchanan, 516; Crawfurd, 516; Henderson, 516; Lee (Rev), 516; Maxton, 516; Muir, 516; Stephen, 516; Tom Anderson, 516; Pankhurst, 516–17; Lansbury, 517–18; MacManus, 518–19; *Workers' Weekly*, 518–19; *Communist International*, 519–20; Gallacher, 519–20; Aldred, 520 general elections: Labour candidate, Glasgow Gorbals, 248–49, 273, 279; 1918, 273, 279, 292–300; 1922, 467–72, 475, 477; 1923, 510, 512–15

Ireland: *The Irish tragedy: Scotland's disgrace* (pamphlet), 388, 390, 392; 'The Battle for Motherwell', in *Vanguard*, 392–93; Belfast visit (1907), 500; Dublin visit, 500; Larkin, 500

miners: South Wales, 13, 160, 287, 332, 339, 348, 362, 455; Fife, 13–14, 73, 160, 246–47, 260–62, 305, 332, 374; Lanarkshire, 13–14, 63, 160, 177, 246–48, 260, 305, 309, 332, 339, 374, 449; Durham, 251, 349, 374; miners reform movement, 303–5, 309, 327, 362, 386; Lothians, 305, 349; Lancashire, 309, 339, 353

municipal elections, 456, 506, 507, 509; Kinning Park, 456, 458, 460–61, 467–68, 511; Glasgow 30th Ward, 1923, 479; Kingston, 481; Townhead, 501

pamphlets: *The Irish tragedy: Scotland's disgrace*, 388, 390, 392; *All hail, the Scottish Communist Republic!*, 409; *Russia's appeal to the British workers*, 416

prison: hunger strikes, 4, 274, 452, 456, 457–58, 461; Duke Street Prison, 63, 174, 260, 457; 'To John Maclean Tortured in a Capitalist Prison' (poem, Montefiore), 129; Calton Jail, 152, 260; Peterhead Prison (1916-17), 152-53; campaign for release, 154-56, 165–66, 168, 170, 172–74, 270–75, 278–79, 285–87, 461–62; claims of drugged food, 164, 274, 298; Peterhead Prison (1918), 274–75; Barlinnie Prison, 451–54, 456–66, 477–78, 513, 520, 523;

Russian Political Refugees Defence Committee: Shammes, 218–19; Chicherin, 218–21; Petroff, 219–21

Scottish Communist Party: Scottish Communist Republic, 416–17; Communist Council of Action, 417; in opposition to CPGB, 418; discussions on formation, 418–20; intervention of Willie Gallacher, 419–23; Scottish Workers' Republic, 469, 477–79, 500

Scottish Labour College, 245, 349, 374, 469, 476, 478, 502, 503, 504; resuscitation of SLC committee, 218; tutor, 248, 453, 502, 507, 512

Scottish Workers' Republic, 469, 477, 479, 500

Scottish Workers' Republican Party, 479–80, 502, 504, 507–9, 511, 514

Scottishness: Erskine of Marr, 403–4, 406–7, 411; Scottish socialist, 407; Declaration of Arbroath anniversary, 411

Socialist Labour Party, 386, 417, 418, 421, 423, 430, 431, 460, 476

Soviet consul, 4, 279, 285, 309, 377, 425; appointment, 244–45, 270–71; government reaction, 246–48, 271; consulate, 247–48; role and activities, 248, 265, 270–71; Shammes, 248

Tramp Trust: Fighting Program, 386–87; 'The Battle for Motherwell', in *Vanguard*, 392–93; miners' meeting, Blantyre, 449

trial for obstruction, 1915, 85–86

trial for sedition, Airdrie 1921, 450–51

trial for sedition, Glasgow 1921: arrest, 456; trial, 457–59; conviction and sentence, 459; protests, 461–62

trial under DORA, 1916: arrest and indictment, 110–11, 131; trial, 132–38; conviction and sentence, 138–39; protests, 153

trial under DORA, 1918: arrest, 251; charges, 260; trial, 261–69; speech from the dock, 263–68; conviction and sentence, 268–69; protests, 270–75, 278–79

unemployed movement: Fighting Program, 386–87; letter to Lenin, 426; Glasgow Town Council, 428–29; Communist Party, 429–30, 466, 476, 479, 502–3, 508–9; parish councils, 430–31, 456; Trades Union Congress, Cardiff, 454–55; Scottish Workers' Republican Party, 479; Govan Cross Picture Palace, 480–81

Maclean, Margaret (sister), 5, 501

Maclean, Nan (daughter), 22, 175, 131, 375, 477, 500, 505, 511, 513; biography of Maclean (as Nan Milton), 4, 58, 113, 132, 220, 271–72, 374, 380–81, 513, 521

Maclean, Neil (Labour MP), 292, 404, 452, 471, 474, 491–92, 496, 499; 1918 general election, 300; 'Battle of George Square', 318, 320; 'Hands off Russia' campaign, 332

Maclean, Sir Donald, 371

MacLean, Sorley, 521; 'An Cuilithionn' (poem, 1939), 1

Maclean-Fulton dispute: Lambhill Street School suspension, 45, 47, 49; Govan Parish School Board, 45–46, 48, 57, 58, 61, 63, 82, 109, 135, 373; Maclean Defence Committee, 47; Maclean's transfer to Lorne Street School, 47, 49, 60–61; Maclean's arrest, 47–48; support for Maclean, 57–58; Maclean's dismissal as teacher, 57–59, 61, 112, 135, 161

MacManus, Arthur, 109, 122, 172, 220, 222–23, 237–238, 246, 401; opposition to conscription, 85–86; Lloyd George visit to Glasgow, 96, 97; deportation order, 122, 172; tribute to Maclean, 518–19

MacNamara, Thomas (Conservative MP), 490-91

MacRobert (Mr), 132, 135, 137

Mainwaring, Will, 13

Malone, Cecil L'Estrange, 425, 448–49; British Socialist Party, 378; 'Hands off Russia' campaign, 378–79

Man Power Bill, 232–41, 246, 264, 266–67

Manchester Guardian, 7, 184

Mann, Tom, 8, 463, 464; secretary (ASE), 376

Mannerheim (General), 364

Markiewicz, Constance, 348

Marshall, Peter, 387, 465, 478, 500, 507, 511
Martov, Julius, 65, 66, 67, 157, 158, 186, 210, 211; differences with Lenin on RSDLP, 66, 67; return to Russia, 186; proposal of united democratic government, 210–11; walk out from Congress of Soviets, 211
Marx, Eleanor, 10
Marx, Karl, 7, 10, 85; *Das Kapital*, 7, 10, 406, 463
Marxism/Marxist, 4, 11, 159, 160, 182, 380
Mavor & Coulson, 123
Max, Prince (of Baden), 276–77
Maxton, James, 290; Maclean's economics class, 12; free speech trial, 85; opposition to conscription, 85–86; chairman of Scottish ILP, 114; protest about arrest of Maclean, 114; Scottish Labour College, 114; conscientious objector, 123; sedition trial, 149-150; prison sentence, 149; release demanded by BSP, 154; coverage of trial in *Nashe Slovo*, 161; release from prison, 165; Russian Political Refugees Defence Committee, 220; Glasgow meeting on Man Power Bill, 238; 1918 general election, 292; Maclean's release from Peterhead Prison, 292; Erskine of Marr's National Committee, 404; support for Maclean in prison, 465; 1922 general election, 471, 474–75; description by *Times*, 483; child welfare and social reform, 489, 494–99; disorder in the House, 493; suspension from the House, 496–99; Maclean's funeral, 516; sedition trial *See* Maxton/Macdougall/Smith DORA trial (1916)
Maxton/Macdougall/Smith DORA trial (1916), 123, 149–50, 161; sentences, 149; BSP protest at sentences, 154
May Day, 9, 169, 348–49, 381, 382, 385, 493; Glasgow 1917, 168; Glasgow 1920, 385–86
McArthur, Archie, 9
McBain, Jock, 224, 322
McBride, Andrew, 41, 42, 44, 52, 61
McClure, James, 114
McGill, Willie, 82, 154–55
McGimpsey (Chief Detective-Inspector), 134–35
McLennan (Detective-Inspector), 134
McNabb, James, 464
McPhater, Dugald (Superintendent), 143
McShane, Harry, 8, 123; Scottish socialist movement, 8; Maclean's economics class, 12–13; Bath St meetings, 25; workshop committees, 29; rent increases, 41; Gallacher, 71; workers' and soldiers' councils, 181; Maclean's release from Peterhead Prison, 292; working hours during the war, 303; 40-hour strike (1919), 310; 'Battle of George Square', 323; BSP 'Hands off Russia' policy, 379; Tradeston branch break with BSP, 380; Maclean's departure from BSP, 381–82; *Vanguard*, 386; Tramp Trust, 386–87, 392, 465–66; *All hail, the Scottish Communist Republic!*, 408–9; Scottish Communist Party, 418–19, 423; unemployed movement, 428, 430–31, 476; Maclean's Airdrie trial, 451; support for Maclean in prison, 453, 460, 463, 465–66; arrested, 454, 465; municipal election campaigns, 456, 460, 481; witness for Maclean and Ross, 458–59; joined Communist Party, 466; eviction protest, 481
Meachan's, 60, 128
Meek, William, 139
Mehmet IV, Sultan (Ottoman Empire), 283
Menshevik-Internationals, 210
Mensheviks: origin of name, 66; support coalition government, 194; discuss socialist coalition, 204; on presidium of Petrograd Soviet, 204; call for new committee of struggle, 205; decline seats on executive committee of Congress of Soviets, 210; denounce assault on Winter Palace, 211; walk out from Congress of Soviets, 211; leader *See* Martov, Julius
Merrie England (essays), 7
Messer, James, 29, 40, 71, 96, 109, 122, 223, 224; deportation order, 122, 172
MFGB *See* Miners' Federation of Great Britain (MFGB)
MhacGill-Eain, Somhairle *See* MacLean, Sorley
Military Revolutionary Committee (MRC): creation by Petrograd Soviet, 204; control by Bolsheviks, 206; control of Petrograd garrison, 206; troops at Peter and Paul fortress switch allegiance to, 207; surrender of Winter Palace, 210; troops on Northern Front announce solidarity with, 212; as government, 215
Military Service Act 1916, 87, 133, 147, 148, 161, 234; demands for repeal, 122–23, 124, 135
Military Service Bill 1916, 86–87, 135
Military Services Tribunals, 122
Millar, JCP, 478, 502
Milner (Lord): release of Maclean, 287
Milton, Nan *See* Maclean, Nan (daughter)
Milyukov, Pavel, 184, 185, 190
Miners' Charter (MFGB version), 308
Miners' Charter (original version), 303, 305, 338, 339
Miners' Federation of Great Britain (MFGB), 13, 32, 169, 239; men for military service, 240–41; piece rates, 303, 352, 356; size, 303; miners' reform movements, 304; *Miners' Charter* (MFGB version), 308; Triple Alliance, 308–9, 341; miners' claim, 324; nationalisation of the mines, 324, 357–59, 362; working hours, 324; strike ballot, 325; Coal Industry Commission, 327; ballot on government offer, 338; acceptance of government offer, 341; coal output, 352–54, 358, 434–36, 438; coal price, 432; wages, 432, 434, 436–39, 441–44, 450; strike ballot, 433; Datum Line strike, 436, 445; lock-out, 439; coal crisis (1921), 439–44; negotiations with owners and government, 440–41, 443; labour movement support, 442, 444; Black Friday, 444; president *See* Smillie, Robert
miners' reform movement, 304, 309, 327, 386
Miners' Reform Movement (South Wales), 176, 303
Mining Association of Great Britain, 351
Minister of Munitions *See* Churchill, Winston; Lloyd George, David
Minister of War (Britain) *See* Kitchener (Lord); Lloyd George, David

Ministry of Mines Bill, 433
Ministry of Munitions, 35–36, 37, 88, 90, 99, 106, 109, 111; drain of skilled workers, 78; dilution program, 115–16, 121, 125–26
Mitchell, Tom, 421, 450, 463
Moderates (Glasgow), 460, 467, 480–81, 501, 510–12
Money, Sir Leo: Coal Industry Commission hearings, 335
Mons, Battle of, 23
Montagu, Edwin: release of Maclean, 288
Montefiore, Dora: 'To John Maclean Tortured in a Capitalist Prison' (poem), 129; Leeds Conference (1917), 169; Maclean's 1918 election campaign, 292, 293, 295
Morris, William, 9, 10
Morrison, William, 285
moulders, See foundry workers
MRC See Military Revolutionary Committee (MRC)
Muir, John (Johnny), 71–72, 96–98, 102, 109, 119, 471; dilution agreement, 125–26, 127; release from prison, 165; Maclean's funeral, 516; *Worker* trial (1916) See *Worker* trial (1916)
Muirhead, Roland, 410
municipal elections: Kingston, 456, 460–61, 481, 511; Kinning Park, 456, 458, 460–61, 467–68, 511; Glasgow, 458, 467, 479–82, 506, 507, 509; Townhead, 501, 511
Municipal Employees Association, 307
Munitions Board, 60, 62
Munitions of War Act 1915, 32, 35–36, 37, 38, 39, 40, 63, 88, 89–90, 92–93, 100, 120, 124, 133, 142, 147, 148, 160–61, 222; Amendment Bill, 88–89
Munitions of War Bill 1915, 34–35
Munitions of War Bill 1917, 222–23
munitions production (WWI): G & J Weir, 28–29; engineers/engineering, 31–32; Cabinet shell committee, 32; Munitions of War Bill 1915, 34–35; controlled establishments, 36, 37, 88, 116; influx of workers, 41; Munitions Workers Recruiting, 91; Munitions of War Bill 1917, 222–23; war bonus, 12 and a half per cent (1917), 224–25, 246, 249; Minister of Munitions See Churchill, Winston; Lloyd George, David; dilution (skilled labour) See dilution (skilled labour); *Munitions of War Act 1915* See *Munitions of War Act 1915*
Munitions Tribunal, 38
Munitions Workers Recruiting, 91
Munro, Robert: Lord Advocate, 52, 104, 110, 111; Maclean DORA trial (1915), 132, 135, 136, 137, 138; *Worker* trial (1916), 143, 144, 145, 146; release of Maclean, 165–66; Secretary for Scotland, 173–74, 247, 278, 279, 289, 313, 410; 40-hour strike (1919), 312–15
Muranov (Matvei), 162
Murmansk Soviet, 329
Murphy, JT, 400, 402
Murray (Lord), 91, 95–96
Murray, Robert (Labour MP), 492
My Life of Revolt (Kirkwood), 119

N

Napoleonic wars, 15
Nasha Zarya (newspaper), 68
Nashe Slovo (newspaper), 157–62, 186; articles on British socialism, 158; articles by Chicherin, 159–62
National Industrial Conference, 325
National Liberals, 472
National Registration Act 1915, 78
National Registration Bill, 78
National Transport Workers' Federation, 171, 308 See also Transport Workers' Federation
National Unemployed Workers' Movement, 454
National Union of Railwaymen (NUR), 113, 326, 360, 413; Glasgow and West of Scotland District Council, 58; Triple Alliance, 308, 433, 440, 444; hours and wages claims, 325, 354
National Union of Scottish Mine Workers, 311
Neuve Chapelle, Battle of, 32–33
Newbold, John Walton, 394, 402, 472
Nicholas II, Tsar: abdication, 167; execution, 284
Nicholson, Daniel, 50, 53, 61
No More Forever (record), 3; 'The John Maclean March', 3–5, 521
North British Diesel Works, 120–21
Northcliffe (Lord), 29, 33
Norway, 74, 196, 221, 398
Novar (Lord), 488–90
NUR See National Union of Railwaymen (NUR)

O

Original Secessionist Church, 6
O'Shannon, Cathal, 333
Ormsby-Gore, Mr (Conservative MP), 492
Our Word See Nashe Slovo (newspaper)
Outhwaite, Robert (Liberal MP), 104
Owen, Robert, 153
Oxford University, 112

P

Pankhurst, Sylvia, 24, 68, 171, 509-10; opposition to conscription, 82; descriptions of Maclean, Kirkwood, Gallacher, 84–85; People's Russia Information Bureau, 331; 'Hands off Russia' campaign, 332; Comintern visitor, 375–76; at Comintern Second Congress, 398, 400, 402; British communist party, 399–402; arrest, 448; Poplar Board of Guardians, 508; Maclean, 509, 510; tribute to Maclean, 516–17
Paris Peace Conference (1919-20), 300, 324, 403, 413
parish councils (Scotland), 429–30, 487–89, 494
Parkhead, 15, 50; rent increases/evictions, 50–52, 60
Parkhead Forge: Lloyd George visit, 91–93; dilution (skilled workers), 118, 119–20, 122, 124–25, 128; dilution strike (1916), 120–21, 125 See also Beardmore's (company); Kirkwood, David
Parliamentary Labour Party See Labour Party (Britain)
Partick: rent increases/evictions, 42, 44, 50–53
Partick Tenants' Defence Association, 53

Passchendaele (Third Battle of Ypres), 231
Paterson, J, 109–10
Paton (Mr): Maclean DORA trial (1916), 143, 144, 146, 148
Paul, William, 339
Peace, Graham, 409–10
peace resolution (German Reichstag, 1917), 197, 254
peace treaties: Ukraine-Central Powers, 254, 257, 258; Allies-Germany (Versailles), 278, 300, 354; Allies-Turkey, 445; Anglo-Irish, 462; Brest-Litovsk *See* Brest-Litovsk treaty
People's Russia Information Bureau (PRIB), 331
Peter and Paul Fortress, 210, 211; switches allegiance to Military Revolutionary Committee, 207
Peterhead Prison, 151; Maclean *See* Maclean, John, prison
Petliura, Simon, 414–15
Petroff, Irma, 64, 68, 70, 182, 219; arrest and internment, 161, 176, 182
Petroff, Peter, 64–77, 83, 84, 109, 160; partnership with Maclean, 64, 68, 70–71; articles in journals/newspapers, 68, 74, 75; member of SDP (later BSP), 68, 70; expelled from CWC meetings, 71–72; arrest at Bowhill, 73, 76–77; St Andrew's Halls meeting, 98, 100–102; arrest and internment, 110, 158, 161, 176, 182; agitation for release, 218–21; return to Russia, 221, 242
Petrograd garrison: mutiny, 167, 204
Petrograd Soviet: formation, 167; war aims/peace policy, 167–68; peace manifesto, 184–85; support of second provisional government, 185; Stockholm peace conference, 186–87, 189, 192; proposed peace conference, 187, 189; demonstration in support of peace, 190; urged to take power, 193–94; no action against Bolsheviks, 194–95; Committee for Struggle against the Counterrevolution, 203; in favour of working class government, 203; Bolshevik majority on presidium, 204; Military Revolutionary Committee, 204, 207; resolution not to work with third provisional government, 204; Workers' and Soldiers' Deputies *See* Workers' and Soldiers' Deputies (Petrograd Soviet)
Petrovsky (Grigory), 162
Pichon, Stephen, 228
Pilsudski, Józef, 413–16
Plebs League, 112, 114, 251, 331, 478; Rhondda, 113; Ruskin Hall strike (1909), 113; Scottish Labour College, 349 *See also* Unofficial Reform Committee
Plekhanov, Georgy, 66, 158, 163
Poland, 228, 230, 255, 259; Brest-Litovsk treaty, 259; Polish independence, 413–14; Polish Republic (Second), 413–15; Polish-Soviet war *See* Polish-Soviet war
Police Bill, 354
Polish-Soviet war: British military supplies, 412; 'Hands off Russia' campaign, 412; *SS Jolly George* (cargo ship), 412; Council of Action (Labour Party and TUC), 412–13; Lloyd George, 414–16; Asquith, 415; Chichern, 415; Polish-Ukrainian agreement, 415
Pollokshaws Branch (BSP), 58, 379
Pollokshaws Co-operative Society, 21
Polmadie School, 6
Poole (Major General), 331
Poor Law (Scotland) Act 1845, 429–30, 487–88
Poplar Board of Guardians, 507–8
Poplar incident, 507–8
Portugal, 200–201
Postal Clerks Union, 169
Pringle, William (Liberal MP): suppression of *Forward*, 104, 105–6; dilution (skilled labour), 124, 125–26
Prison Commission (Scotland), 151
Public Order Act 2023, 523

Q

Quadruple Alliance, 227
Queen's Park (football team), 477
Queen's Park Police station, 48
Queen's Park School, 6
Quelch, Tom, 171–72, 397

R

Rada (parliament of the Ukrainian People's Republic), 254, 257, 258
Radicals, 9, 10
Raeburn, Sir William (Unionist MP), 451
Ransome, Arthur, 344
Reading (Lord), 288
Red Army, 284; North Russia, 329, 331; Crimea, 365; Estonia, 365; Latvia, 365; Lithuania, 365; Ukraine, 365, 372; Urals, 367; Petrograd, 372; Siberia, 372; Tula, 378; Polish-Soviet war, 415–16
'Red Flag, The' (anthem), 56, 57, 100, 132, 139, 236, 238, 271, 278, 311, 475, 508, 516
Red Guards, 203
Redistribution of Seats Act 1885, 10
Reid, William, 62
rent controls, 483–87
rent increases/evictions: Partick, 42, 44, 50–53; South Govan, 42–44; East End, 43, 50–51; McHugh family, 43; Parkhead, 50–52; Cathcart, 51, 60; Denistoun, 51; Small Debts Court, 52, 53, 60; Dalmuir, 60; demonstrations, 60, 61; Hydepark, 60; Tenants' Defence Committee, 62; *Increase of Rent and Mortgage Interest (War Restrictions) Act 1915*, 63; strikes *See* strikes
Rent Restriction Act *See* Increase of Rent and Mortgage Interest (War Restrictions) Act 1915
Rents Restriction Bill, 484–87
Revolt on the Clyde (1936, Gallacher), 521
revolutionary defencism, 167, 190
Rhondda (Wales): strike (1911), 13; Plebs League, 113
RIC *See* Royal Irish Constabulary (RIC)
Richmond Park, 44
Robertson, John (Labour MP), 404, 472, 485, 488–89, 492, 508–509; Coal Industry Commission hearings, 336
Robertson, Matthew, 139

Robertson, Sir William: 40-hour strike (1919), 313
Roch, Walter (Liberal MP), 89
Romania: restoration of occupied territory, 233; Allied intervention in Russia, 368
Ross, Sandy, 387, 421, 449–52, 454, 456, 458, 459, 460, 462, 465
Rosslyn Mitchell, Edward, 471
Rothstein, Theodore, 158, 242, 346–47, 378, 380, 381; and SDF, 65, 66; influence on BSP, 159, 380; BSP revolutionary identity, 346; Russia's official agent, 346; Malone, 378
Royal Irish Constabulary (RIC), 391, 392
Royal Navy, 21, 197, 305, 356, 368, 378
RSDLP *See* Russian Social Democratic Labour Party (RSDLP)
Rurik (Russian flagship), 68
Ruskin Hall (later College, Oxford), 112; student strike (1909), 113; Plebs League *See* Plebs League
Russell, Bertrand, 172, 179–80
Russian Anti-Intervention Committee, 331
Russian civil war, 283, 302, 333, 364, 366–69, 372–72, 414
Russian Constituent Assembly: voting results, 215; closure, 255
Russian émigrés, 65, 68, 157 *See also* Chicherin, Georgy; Litvinov, Maxim; Petroff, Peter; Rothstein, Theodore; Shammes, Louis
Russian peace treaties: Estonia, 414; Latvia, 414; Brest-Litovsk *See* Brest-Litovsk treaty
Russian Political Prisoners and Exiles Relief Committee, 158–59
Russian Political Refugees Defence Committee, 182, 218–20
Russian provisional government (First): formation, 167; war aims/peace policy, 169, 171
Russian provisional government (Second), 195; formation, 185; resignation, 203
Russian provisional government (Third): formation, 204; seeks advice about moving from Petrograd, 204; loses effective military control of Petrograd, 207; ministers arrested at Winter Palace, 211
Russian revolution (1905), 65, 158
Russian revolution (February 1917), 66, 166–72, 182, 184–85, 193–95, 201
Russian revolution (October 1917), 163, 206–13
Russian Social Democratic Labour Party (RSDLP), 65, 66, 67, 76, 158, 178; congress (1903), 66; congress (1907), 66–67, 158 *See also* Bolshevik Party/Bolsheviks; Mensheviks

S

Salisbury Committee, 484 *See also* rent controls
Sankey, Justice John: Coal Industry Commission, 327, 335–37; Chairman's report, 337–41
Sankey Award, 352–53, 355
Sankey Commission, *See* Coal Industry Commission
Scott, Alexander MacCallum (Liberal MP), 124, 125
Scottish Board of Health *See* Board of Health (Scotland)

Scottish Co-operative Wholesale Society, 180
Scottish Communist Party, 417–23, 477
Scottish Education Bill, 278
Scottish Engineering Employers' Association, 26
Scottish Federation of Tenants Associations, 41
Scottish Home Rule, 474
Scottish Home Rule Association, 403–4, 410
Scottish Horse and Motor Men's Union, 307
Scottish independence, 403–5, 407, 409–10, 431, 474, 521–22
Scottish Labour College (SLC), 112–14; Crawfurd, 114; Macdougall, 114, 453; Maxton, 114; provisional committee, 114; Smillie, 114; conferences, 248, 387; constitution, 248, 478, 502–3; curriculum, 248, 406; Plebs League, 349; annual meetings, 387–88, 453; raid, 450; Clunie, 463; CPGB, 478 *See also* Central Labour College (CLC) (Oxford, later London): Maclean *See* Maclean, John, Scottish Labour College
Scottish Labour Party, 20, 518 *See also* Independent Labour Party (ILP)
Scottish Land and Labour League, 10
Scottish Law Courts Record, 32
Scottish National Party, 521–22
Scottish Office, 155, 314, 317, 488, 489, 490
Scottish Poor Law *See* Poor Law (Scotland) Act 1845
Scottish Review (journal), 403, 406
Scottish Socialist Party, 522
Scottish Trades Union Congress (STUC), 154; 40-hour strike (1919), 306–7; Parliamentary Committee, 307
Scottish Union of Dock Labourers, 307
Scottish Workers' Committee(s), 392, 418
Scottish Workers' Republic, 469, 477, 479, 500
Scottish Workers' Republican Party (SWRP), 479–80, 502, 504, 507–9, 511
SDF *See* Social Democratic Federation (SDF)
SDP *See* Social Democratic Party (SDP)
Second International, 163, 202, 342, 343, 344, 345, 347, 394, 395; Congress (1912), 21; factions, 73; collapse, 342, 344–45
secret treaties, 226, 230
Secretary for Scotland: Thomas McKinnon Wood, 39, 52, 53, 110; Harold Tennant, 155–56; Robert Munro, 173, 180–81, 247, 278, 279, 289, 313, 410; Lord Novar, 488–90
sedition: Maxton/Macdougall/Smith DORA trial (1916), 123, 149–50; Maclean (trial, Airdrie 1921), 450–51; Maclean (DORA trial, 1916) *See* Maclean, John (DORA trial, 1916); Maclean (trial, Glasgow 1921) *See* Maclean, John (trial for sedition, Glasgow 1921); *Worker* trial (1916) *See Worker* trial (1916)
Seditious And Blasphemous Teaching To Children Bill, 490
Serbia, 51, 232
Shackleton, David, 313, 369
Shammes, Louis, 182, 218–19, 247–48
Shanks, George, 114
Sharp (William), 178
Shaw, Fred, 171
Shaw, Tom, 360–61
Sherwood-Kelly, John (Lieutenant Colonel), 371-72

Shettleston, 43, 44, 471
Shields, Sam, 122
Shinwell, Emmanuel, 134, 348, 472, 492-93, 496, 497; opposition to conscription, 85–86; working hours, 307; 40-hour strike (1919), 311; 'Battle of George Square', 318, 320, 348
shipbuilding, 15, 16, 17, 27, 40, 178, 303, 312, 427, 428, 522; Yarrow's, 60, 522; Barrow-in-Furness, 68, 165, 316; Fairfield's *See* Fairfield's shipyards
shop stewards, 29, 57, 94, 119, 123, 292, 304; role, 28; dilution (skilled labour), 37, 91, 93, 115, 116 *See also* Kirkwood, David; Smith, Jack
Shop Stewards Committee (Clyde), 307
shop stewards' movement, 30, 172, 222–25, 233–34, 239–40, 343, 349, 400, 402; National Administrative Council, 223 *See also* Gallacher, Willie (shop stewards' movement)
Shortt, Edward, 445; miners' claim, 324
Siberia: Allied intervention in, 364, 366–69; Red Army, 372
Sims, George, 113
Sinn Féin, 289, 390, 462
skilled labour dilution *See* dilution (skilled labour)
SLC *See* Scottish Labour College (SLC)
SLP *See* Socialist Labour Party (SLP)
Smillie, Robert, 177, 178, 272, 386, 404, 433–34, 437–38, 454, 474–75, 507, 508; Scottish Labour College, 114; Leeds Conference (1917), 169; miners' claim, 324; Lloyd George on Triple Alliance, 326; Coal Industry Commission, 327; hearings, 335–38; nationalisation of mines, 357–58, 362–63; Trades Union Congress, 359; direct action, 360–61
Smith, Herbert: Coal Industry Commission hearings, 335
Smith, Jack, 93; sedition trial *See* Maxton/Macdougall/Smith DORA trial (1916)
Smith, Jennie, 46–47
Smith, Sir Hubert Llewellyn, 109
Smuts, Jan, 288–89
Snowden, Ethel, 171, 178, 179
Snowden, Philip (Labour MP), 7, 172, 300, 348, 395, 424; remission/release for Maclean, 155, 165; Leeds conference (1917), 169; 1918 general election, 300; Sankey report, 349
Social Democratic Federation (SDF), 7, 10, 11–12, 20, 21, 66, 67, 68, 379, 425; departure of Scottish wing, 12; Glasgow Branch, 12; Theodore Rothstein, 65, 66; *Iskra* (newspaper), 66; *Justice See Justice* (journal, SDF later BSP); Maclean economics classes *See* Maclean, John (career); renamed as SDP *See* Social Democratic Party (SDP)
Social Democratic Party (Denmark), 187
Social Democratic Party (Germany), 186, 283
Social Democratic Party (SDP), 379; BSP, merger with, 21; Peter Petroff, 65, 68; Kentish Town Branch, 68
Social Democratic Party (Sweden), 192
social patriots, 64, 74, 159, 172, 181, 344
Social Revolutionaries: support second provisional government, 194, 211; discuss socialist coalition, 204; on Military Revolutionary Committee, 206; on executive committee of Congress of Soviets, 210; walk out of Congress of Soviets, 211 *see also* Left Social Revolutionaries
Socialist (journal), 450, 451, 463; articles by Maclean, 423, 431, 449, 476
Socialist Labour Party (SLP), 9, 14, 50, 71–72, 248, 286, 342, 345, 347, 418, 430, 450, 476; formation, 12; shop stewards, 29; Free Speech Committee, 54; Russian Anti-Intervention Committee, 331; 'Hands off Russia', 332; Third International, 343; discussion about British communist party, 347, 376, 399, 401–2; Maclean's opinion of, 386; Communist Council of Action, 417; Scottish Communist Party, 418, 421–23; Maclean-Gallacher feud, 421–23; proposed general strike about unemployment, 430; Maclean's relationship with, 431, 460, 476; *Socialist* (journal), 431
Socialist Labour Press, 143, 146, 476
Socialist League, 8, 10; *Commonweal* (journal), 8
South Africa: Daniel Maclean, 5; Scottish investment in, 16; Inter-Allied Socialist Conference (1917), 200; representation on Imperial War Cabinet, 284; release of Maclean, 288–89
South Govan, 42, 51
South Govan Tenants Committee, 43
South Govan Women's Housing Association, 42
South Side Socialist Sunday School, 9, 58
South Wales Miners' Federation, 13 113; Sankey report, 339
South Wales Miners' Reform Movement: *Miners' Charter,* 303
South Wales Socialist Society, 332, 338, 376, 399, 401; Sankey report, 338–39
Soviet Executive, 256; demands constituent assembly subordinate itself to soviets, 217
Soviet fleet, 364, 368
Soviet Ukrainian Republic, 257
Sovnarkom (Council of People's Commissars): assumes executive authority, 215; overshadows work of Soviet executive, 215; undermines result of election for constituent assembly, 216
Spartacist League (Germany), 343
SS Jolly George (cargo ship), 412
Stalin, Josef, 66; editor of Bolshevik newspaper, 204
Steam Engine Makers' Society, 26
Stephen, Campbell (Labour MP), 471, 490, 496, 498; Maclean's funeral, 516
Stevenson, James V, 316–18
Stewart, George, 262
Stewart, James, 52, 83, 469, 471, 489
Stewart, James Watson (Lord Provost), 311, 316–17, 320
Stewart, Robert, 57, 58, 450
Stockholm peace conference (1917), 168, 186–88, 196–202; International Socialist Bureau, 168, 186–87; America, 186, 192, 200; Italy, 186, 192, 200; Denmark, 186–87; France, 186–87, 192, 200; Germany, 186–87; Petrograd Soviet, 186–87, 189, 192; Dutch-Scandinavian

Committee, 186–88; Great Britain, 186–88, 192, 198–200; discussion between British, French and Russian socialists, 196–97 *See also* Henderson, Arthur

Strathclyde (Lord), 261, 268–69; Maclean's DORA trial (1916), 132, 138–39, 140; *Worker* trial (1916), 141, 147–49; Maxton/Macdougall/Smith DORA trial (1916), 149

strikes, 19, 22; Rhondda strike (1911), 13; non-union labour, against, 26, 29; tuppence an hour strike (1915), 26–29, 38, 93, 145, 160; Treasury Agreement (WWI), 31–32; Fairfield's (1915), 38–39; rent strikes, 42–44, 50, 51–53, 60–63, 136, 161, 398, 465, 483; Albion Motor Works (1916), 111, 123, 128; Barr & Stroud (1916), 111; Beardmore's, Dalmuir (1916), 111, 121, 125; Coventry Ordnance Works (1916), 111, 123; Plebs League (1909), 113; ASE dilution strikes (1916), 117, 120–23, 128; Lang's, Johnstone (1916), 117, 144; North British Diesel Works (1916), 120; Beardmore's, Parkhead Forge (1916), 120–21, 125; Duncan Stewart and Co.(1916), 123; Mavor & Coulson (1916), 123; Weir's, Cathcart (1916), 123; Russia (1917), 167; Russian civil service (1917), 214; Munitions of War Bill (1917), 222–23; foundry workers, Scotland (1917), 224; Beardmore's, East Hope (1917), 224–25; Germany and Austria (1918), 256–57; bakers (1919), 354; police (1919), 354, 356; Russia (1921), 426; railwaymen (1919), 441, 445; Belfast dockers (1907), 500; coal miners *See* coal miners' strikes; 40-hour strike (1919) *See* 40-hour strike (1919); WWI regulations *See* Munitions of War Act 1915; Munitions of War Bill 1915

STUC *See* Scottish Trades Union Congress (STUC)

Sunday schools (socialist), 9, 70, 515; Christian Socialist, 9; Glasgow Central Socialist, 9; South Side Socialist, 9, 59; Govanhill Socialist, 58 *See also* Communist Sunday schools

Supreme Allied War Conference: Prinkipo peace conference, 333

Supreme Command (Central Powers), 254, 258, 275–76

Sweden: Social Democratic Party (Sweden), 192

Switzerland, 74, 157, 184

SWRP *See* Scottish Workers' Republican Party (SWRP)

T

tariffs, solution to unemployment, 510, 513–14

Tawney, Richard, 335

TCN Company (New Jersey), 29

Tennant, Harold, 155–56

Tennant family, 16

Tereshchenko, Mikhail, 190

textile industry (Scotland), 15

'The decree on peace': see, Lenin, Vladimir

'The Internationale' (anthem), 24, 516

'The John Maclean March' (song), 3–5, 281, 521, 522

The Miners Next Step (pamphlet), 13, 113

'The Red Flag' (anthem) *See* 'Red Flag, The' (anthem)

The Spark See Iskra (newspaper)

Third International, 162, 163, 193, 342–45, 346, 347, 375, 394, 396, 419, 420; invitation, 342–43; first congress, 344; manifesto, 344; British Section, 401, 402, 423 *See also* Comintern

Third Reform Act 1884, 10, 19

Thomas, Albert, 188, 189

Thomas, JH, 340, 413, 434, 435, 440, 441, 443, 444, 454, 455; National Industrial Conference, 326; direct action, 360; British intervention in Russia, 361

Thompson, Sir Basil, 178–79

Thorne, Sir Robert: 434, 40-hour strike (1919), 311–15

Tillett, Ben, 434

'To John Maclean Tortured in a Capitalist Prison' (poem, Montefiore), 129

Tory party, 33

Town Council Labour Group (Glasgow), 41

Trade Disputes Act, 116, 121

trade unions, 12, 19, 20, 31, 39, 90, 94, 112, 114, 115, 153, 155, 299, 375, 386; dilution (skilled labour), 31, 32, 35, 36–38, 40; Treasury Agreement (WWI), 31–32; shipbuilding, 38–39; engineering, 39; Govan, 43; French, 74; Leeds Conference, 169; Man Power Bill, 235, 236; 40-hour week, 306, 307; Council of Action, 412–13, 416, 417; arbitration *See* arbitration *See also* Clyde Workers Committee: WWI regulations *See Munitions of War Act 1915;* Munitions of War Bill 1915; shop stewards *See* shop stewards

Trades and Labour Council *See* Glasgow Trades and Labour Council

Trades Union Congress (TUC), 24, 25, 201, 232, 358, 359, 369, 412, 432, 454, 455; British intervention in Russia, 359, 361; nationalisation of the mines, 359, 363, 432; Parliamentary Committee, 359, 361–62, 442, 444; direct action, 359–60; unemployed, 454–55 *See also* Irish Trades Union Congress; Scottish Trades Union Congress

Tramp Trust Unlimited: formation, 387; Marshall, 387, 465; Ross, 387, 421, 449–52, 454, 456, 458–60, 462, 465; Irish War of Independence, 392; Motherwell meeting, 392–93; Scottish Communist Party, 418-19; miners' meetings, Lanarkshire, 449; Govan, 456; agitation on behalf of the unemployed, 457-58; dissolution, 465–66, 476

Transport Workers' Federation, 433–35, 440–44; Triple Alliance, 308; hours and wages claims, 325, 354; Harry Gosling, 434–35, 454; Ernest Bevin, 435, 444 *See also* National Transport Workers' Federation

Treasury Agreement (WWI), 31–32, 35, 223

Treaty of London (1914), 226

Triple Alliance: revival, 306; National Union of Railwaymen, 308, 433, 440, 444; Transport Workers' Federation, 308; Miners' Federation of Great Britain, 308–9, 341; no individual settlements, 325; Lloyd George, 326; aims,

326–27; ballot on military intervention, 355, 359; miners' claim, 433–34, 440; 'paper alliance', 435, 444; coal crisis, 1921, 440–44; strike threats, 440–44; Black Friday, 444

Trotsky, Leon, 24, 66, 74; Paris, 157; return to Russia, 185; failure of 1917 Russian offensive, 191; rescue of Chernov from mob, 194; member of Petrograd Soviet presidium, 204; release from prison, 204; mutiny of Petrograd garrison, 205; accusation of government counter-revolutionary coup, 207–8; declaration that provisional government no longer exists, 210; justification of insurrection, 211; praised by Maclean, 220, 266, 403; release of Chicherin and Petroff, 220–21; armistice with Germany, 226–27; invitation to Allies re armistice, 226–27; Brest-Litovsk, 227, 252–59; call for peace, 234; relations with Britain, 243–44; return of Chicherin, 244; Third All-Russian Congress of Soviets, 244; Maxim Litvinov, 245; description of, 252; Allied intervention in Russia, 329–31; invitation to first congress of Third International, 343; defence of Petrograd, 372; Malone, 378; Polish-Soviet war, 415–16

Truck Acts (1831-1896), 22
Truck Stores, 21–22
Tsereteli, Irakli, 189, 191, 192
TUC See Trades Union Congress (TUC)
Twentieth Century Press, 66
27th (Plantation) Ward Committee, 58

U

Ukraine: independence, 214, 413; food supplies, 253; treaty with Central Powers, 254, 257, 258; Brest-Litovsk treaty, 254–55, 257–58, 259; military victories of Bolsheviks, 1918, 257; French zone of influence, 329, 365; Allied intervention in Russia, 365; Red Army, 365, 372; Polish-Soviet war, 414, 415
Ukrainian People's Republic, 254, 257, 258
unemployed, 11, 41, 294, 303, 307–8, 386, 426, 428–31, 454–57, 464, 490, 494, 508, 510
unemployed movement: McShane, 428, 460, 466; deputation to Glasgow Town Council, 428–29; Communist Party, 429–30, 466, 476, 479, 502–3, 508–9; *Poor Law (Scotland) Act 1845*, 429–30, 487–88; parish councils, 430–31, 456; National Unemployed Workers' Movement, 454; Trades Union Congress, Cardiff, 454–55; municipal council elections, 456, 467–68; Scottish Workers' Republican Party, 479; Govan Cross Picture Palace, 480–81
Unemployed Workers' Organisation, 507–8
unemployment, 386–87, 428–30, 444, 456, 468, 470, 479, 487–90, 507, 510, 513
unemployment insurance, 429
unemployment relief, 488–89, 494
Unionist Party, 33, 34, 113, 166, 248, 277, 285, 290, 467–68, 510; 1922 general election, 472; leader See Bonar Law, Andrew (Unionist Party)

unions See trade unions
United Socialist Council, 168
United Society of Boilermakers, 178
United States See America
University of Glasgow, 6–7
Unofficial Reform Committee, 339; *The Miners Next Step* (pamphlet), 13, 113

V

Vandervelde, Emile, 188, 189, 192; International Socialist Bureau, 73, 75–76
Vanguard (journal), 38, 54, 64-65, 71, 159; publisher/editor/articles by Maclean, 47-48, 63, 81, 104, 107, 110, 129, 385–86, 419, 420, 428-29; launch of, 65; articles by Petroff, 74, 75; suppression of, 104, 107–8, 111, 161; revived, 385–86; discontinued, 431, 476
Versailles peace treaty, 278, 300, 354

W

W Beardmore See Beardmore's (company)
Wainwright, Robert, 122
Wallace, Rev. James, 57
Wallhead, Dick (ILP chairman): Russia visit, 394
War Aims Committee, 239
War Cabinet See British War Cabinet
War Office, 34, 44, 78, 79, 111, 121, 315, 370
War Policy Committee, 79
Wardle, George, 196
Warwick (Lady), 333
Watson, Billy, 376
Watt, Henry (Liberal MP), 173–74
Webb, Sidney, 200, 202, 232, 272; Coal Industry Commission hearings, 335
Wedgwood, Josiah (Colonel), 446–48
Weir, Duncan (Chief Detective-Inspector), 143
Weir, George, 27
Weir, James, 27
Weir, William, 27–30, 81, 91, 93, 427; 'Responsibility and Duty' (pamphlet), 28–29; munitions production, 34–35; dilution scheme, 115–16, 121–22, 123–24 See also G & J Weir (engineering company)
Wellington (Duke of), 24
Western Front (WWI), 23, 31, 32, 78, 79, 81, 167, 188, 213, 227, 231, 251, 275, 276, 277, 284; Ypres, 23, 33, 231; Somme, 166, 167; Arras, 167; Hindenburg Line, 167
Westwood, Joseph (Labour MP), 491, 497
What is to be done? (pamphlet), 65
Wheatley, John, 41, 43, 50, 144, 470; Labour MP for Shettleston, 471, 484, 485-86, 495–96, 498-99
Whigs, 10
White, Jack (Captain, Irish Citizen Army), 155, 408, 449
White Finns, 329, 364
Whitehead, James (Bailie), 95, 321
Whitehouse, John Howard (Liberal MP), 278
Whites/White armies, 284, 332, 414, 416; support from foreign troops, 284, 353; Caucasus, 364, 368, 372; Northern Corps, Northwestern Army, 364, 370–72; Siberia, 364, 367; British support, 366, 371–73

Wilhelm II (Kaiser), 277; abdication, 283; prosecution for war crimes, 285
Williams, Robert, 171, 360
Willis, Fred, 376
Wilson, Sir HH, 284
Wilson, Woodrow, 265-66, 364, 403; 'Fourteen Points', war aims, 229–30, 276–77; Prinkipo peace conference, 333
Winter Palace (Petrograd): bombardment begins, 210; troop morale collapses, 210; Bolshevik troops enter, 211
Wolf, Lucien, 68
Women's International League, 114
Women's Labour League, 41–42
Wood, Thomas McKinnon, 39, 52, 53, 110
Worker (CWC journal), 114, 131; suppression of, 111, 161; editor *See* Muir, John; trial *See* Worker trial (1916)
Worker (newspaper), 418, 461
Worker group, 418, 429–30
Worker trial (1916), 141–49; Gallacher, Muir, Bell, W, 111, 114, 118, 131, 141–49, 150, 154, 158, 161, 165; charge, 141–43; witnesses, 143–46; summation, 146–48; verdict and sentence, 147–49; BSP protest at sentences, 154; *Nashe Slovo* article, 158
workers' and soldiers' councils (Britain), 170–72; pacifists v revolutionaries, 171–72; Brotherhood Church riot, 178–79, 182; meetings, 178–81
Workers' and Soldiers' Deputies (Petrograd Soviet), 167, 169, 172, 181, 208, 209; Council, 171, 187
Workers' Dreadnought (journal), 399, 448, 508, 510, 516-17
Workers' Socialist Federation, 375; discussion about British communist party, 345, 399–402
Workers' Union, 165
Workers' Weekly (CPGB newspaper), 518–19
working class (Scotland): living conditions, 17–18, 176; housing accommodation *See* rent increases/evictions; adult education *See* Scottish Labour College
World War I, 4, 8, 16, 23–24, 27, 40, 51, 74, 75, 157, 158, 229, 291, 342, 344, 353, 374, 378, 382, 388, 392, 408, 429; Maclean's opposition to, 4, 24–25, 64–65, 71; lack of munitions, 31–34, 79; Serbia, 51, 232; Eastern Front, 79, 184, 187, 226, 230, 257; Zeppelin raid, 132; Hindenburg Line, 167; Operation Albion, 204; America, 213, 228; Macedonian Front, 276; armistice *See* armistice; Brest Litovsk *See* Brest-Litovsk treaty; British Army *See* British Army (WWI) *See also* British intervention in Russia: conscientious objection *See* conscientious objection; munitions production *See* munitions production (WWI); peace treaties *See* peace treaties; Western Front *See* Western Front (WWI); aims *See* World War I (aims); battles *See* World War I (battles)
    World War I (aims): Russia, 167, 169, 171, 184–85; Allies, 175, 189–90, 201; Britain, 200–201, 232, 236, 239, 265–66; America, 229, 265–66; Austria-Hungary, 232; Germany, 232, 254; Labour Party and the Trades Union Congress, 232
World War I (battles): Aisne, 23, 167; Cateau, 23; Mons, 23; Ypres, 23, 33, 231; Neuve Chapelle, 32–33; Gallipoli, 51, 78; Loos, 80–81; Somme, 166, 167; Arras, 167; Passchendaele, 231
Wyndham Childs: 40-hour strike (1919), 313

Y

Yorkshire Miners' Association, 353–56
Ypres, Battle of, 23, 33, 231
Yudenich, Nikolai (General), 364, 370

Z

Zimmerwald movement, 74–75, 163, 193
Zinoviev, Grigory, 66, 162, 168

ABOUT THE AUTHOR

Donald Robertson was born in Kinlochleven, the 'electric village' in the Scottish Highlands, and grew up in the steel towns of Corby, England; and Whyalla, South Australia. After graduating from the University of Adelaide, he co-founded and published the Australian music and arts magazine *Roadrunner* (1978-83), and was the first editor of *Countdown* magazine (1983-86). He has written for the *Australian Financial Review*, the *Sydney Morning Herald*, the *Age* (Melbourne), the *Advertiser* (Adelaide), the *West Australian*, and *Rolling Stone*. His previous books include *Roll over Beethoven: contemporary music education for secondary schools* (Fairfax 1987), *Rock around the clock: careers in the Australian music industry* (Ausmusic 1992), *The big beat: rock music in Australia 1978-83* (Roadrunnertwice 2019) and *No Fixed Address: the story of Australia's trailblazing Aboriginal rock 'n' reggae band* (Hybrid Publishers 2023). A selection of his writing can be found at roadrunnertwice.com.au. (Photo: Janice Robertson.)

ABOUT THE PUBLISHERS

Resistance Books is a radical publisher of internationalist, ecosocialist, and feminist books in London. Resistance Books publishes books in collaboration with the International Institute for Research and Education (https://iire.org/), and the Fourth International (https://fourth.international). For further information, including a full list of titles available and how to order them, go to the website.

info@resistancebooks.org  www.resistancebooks.org

www.ingramcontent.com/pod-product-compliance
Lightning Source LLC
Chambersburg PA
CBHW052043280426
43661CB00085B/112